Seventh Edition

Research Methods in Psychology

John J. Shaughnessy
Hope College

Eugene B. Zechmeister
Loyola University of Chicago

Jeanne S. Zechmeister

Boston   Burr Ridge, IL   Dubuque, IA   Madison, WI   New York   San Francisco   St. Louis
Bangkok   Bogotá   Caracas   Kuala Lumpur   Lisbon   London   Madrid   Mexico City
Milan   Montreal   New Delhi   Santiago   Seoul   Singapore   Sydney   Taipei   Toronto

The McGraw-Hill Companies

Higher Education

RESEARCH METHODS IN PSYCHOLOGY
Published by McGraw-Hill, a business unit of The McGraw-Hill Companies, Inc., 1221 Avenue of the Americas, New York, NY, 10020. Copyright © 2006, 2003, 2000, 1997, 1994, 1990 by The McGraw-Hill Companies, Inc. All rights reserved. Previous edition © 1985 by Alfred A. Knopf, Inc. All rights reserved. No part of this publication may be reproduced or distributed in any form or by any means, or stored in a database or retrieval system, without the prior written consent of The McGraw-Hill Companies, Inc., including, but not limited to, in any network or other electronic storage or transmission, or broadcast for distance learning.
Some ancillaries, including electronic and print components, may not be available to customers outside the United States.

This book is printed on acid-free paper.

1 2 3 4 5 6 7 8 9 0 DOC/DOC 0 9 8 7 6 5

ISBN 0-07-298622-0

Editor in Chief: *Emily Barrosse*
Publisher: *Stephen Rutter*
Senior Sponsoring Editor: *John T. Wannemacher*
Marketing Manager: *Melissa Caughlin*
Developmental Editor: *Kirsten Stoller*
Managing Editor: *Jean Dal Porto*
Project Manager: *Catherine R. Iammartino*
Manuscript Editor: *Terri Schiesl*

Art Director: *Jeanne Schreiber*
Lead Designer: *Gino Cieslik*
Cover Designer: *Jenny El-Shammy*
Art Editor: *Katherine McNab*
Photo Research Coordinator: *Nora Agbayani*
Senior Print Supplements Producer: *Louis Swaim*
Media Project Manager: *Alexander Rohrs*
Production Supervisor: *Jason I. Huls*
Senior Media Producer: *Stephanie George*
Composition: *10/12 Palatino by Interactive Composition Corporation*
Printing: *Black and PMS 2945, 45 # New Era Matte, R. R. Donnelly and Sons Inc./Crawfordsville, IN.*

Credits: The credits section for this book begins on page 561 and is considered an extension of the copyright page.

Library of Congress Cataloging-in-Publication Data

Shaughnessy, John J., 1947-
    Research methods in psychology / John J. Shaughnessy, Eugene B. Zechmeister, Jeanne
S. Zechmeister.—7th ed.
        p. cm.
    Includes bibliographical references and indexes.
    ISBN 0-07-298622-0 (alk. paper)
    1. Psychology—Research—Methodology—Textbooks. 2. Psychology,
Experimental—Textbooks. I. Zechmeister, Eugene B., 1944- II. Zechmeister, Jeanne S.
III. Title.
BF76.5.S46 2006
150'.72—dc22

                                                                2004063231

The Internet addresses listed in the text were accurate at the time of publication. The inclusion of a website does not indicate an endorsement by the authors of McGraw-Hill, and McGraw-Hill does not guarantee the accuracy of the information presented at these sites.

www.mhhe.com

Brief Contents

Contents

About the Authors

JOHN J. SHAUGHNESSY is Professor of Psychology at Hope College, a relatively small, select, undergraduate liberal arts college in Holland, Michigan. After completing the B.S. degree at Loyola University of Chicago in 1969, he received the Ph.D. in 1972 from Northwestern University. He is a Fellow of the American Psychological Society whose recent research has focused on practical aspects of memory. He is coauthor, with Benton J. Underwood, of *Experimentation in Psychology* (Wiley, 1975). Students selected him as the Hope Outstanding Professor Educator in 1992, and he serves as a mentor in the College's Faculty Development Program.

EUGENE B. ZECHMEISTER is Professor Emeritus of Psychology at Loyola University of Chicago, a large metropolitan university where he taught both undergraduate and graduate courses since 1970. Professor Zechmeister completed his B.A. degree in 1966 at the University of New Mexico. He later received both the M.S. (1968) and Ph.D. (1970) from Northwestern University. A specialist in the field of human cognition, and experimental methodology, Professor Zechmeister has co-authored books on human memory, critical thinking, statistics and research methods. *Data Analysis and Interpretation in the Behavioral Sciences,* written with E. J. Posavac, was recently published by Wadsworth (2003). He has been a Fellow both of the American Psychological Association (Divisions 1, 2, and 3) and the American Psychological Society. In 1994 he was awarded the Loyola University Sujack Award for Teaching Excellence in the College of Arts and Sciences.

JEANNE S. ZECHMEISTER was a member of the Psychology faculty at Loyola University of Chicago from 1990 to 2002. Professor Zechmeister completed her B.A. at University of Wisconsin-Madison (1983) and her M.S. (1988) and Ph.D. (1990) in Clinical Psychology at Northwestern University. She taught undergraduate and graduate courses in research methodology, and her research focused on psychological processes associated with forgiveness. Her effectiveness as a teacher is evidenced by her many years of high teacher ratings and by her being identified consistently each year by graduating seniors as one of their best teachers at Loyola. Dr. Zechmeister now writes professionally in Santa Fe, New Mexico.

To Paula
(J.J.S.)

To the Memory of Ruth O'Keane,
James O'Keane,
Kathleen O'Keane Zechmeister,
and My Mother
(E.B.Z.)

To the Memory of
my Father, Harold W. Sumi
(J.S.Z.)

Preface

For over two decades we have been writing this research methods textbook hoping that we could capture for students the excitement of psychological inquiry, and convey an understanding the methods used to conduct research. Our greatest satisfaction from writing this textbook and teaching research methods has been seeing students who enter the course feeling mild trepidations, leave not only feeling competent and confident but also excited about their understanding of the research process.

Changes in this, the 7th edition, are the result of both student comments and comments (often lengthy) made by psychology instructors who reviewed the previous edition. We are grateful to both the students and the instructors. Pleasing everyone is never possible, but we hope that the changes incorporated into this newest edition have made for an even better introduction to research methods in psychology. For those who are new to this textbook, let us first review our basic organization and approach. Those who have used the previous edition may want to go directly to "Changes in This Edition" to see what is new.

ORGANIZATION AND APPROACH

Our approach is based on our years of teaching experience. As instructors of research methods, we recognize that most students in our classes will be consumers of research and not producers of research. Students who choose to take on either role will benefit from developing critical thinking skills. We believe that we can best help our students think critically by taking a problem-solving approach to the study of research methods. Researchers begin with a good question and then select a research method that can best help them answer their question. The sometimes painstaking task of gathering evidence is only the beginning of the research process. Analyzing and interpreting the evidence are equally important in making claims about psychological processes. Researchers (and students) must analyze the strengths and weaknesses of the method they have chosen in order to be able to evaluate critically the nature of the evidence they have obtained.

Another feature that we continue from our last edition is the website designed for our book. There are interactive exercises and quizzes for students to test their knowledge of text material, as well as links to other important psychology websites. Instructors will find the instructor's manual and lecture/discussion aids helpful. Both students and instructors may easily contact the authors via this site. Please come see us at *www.mhhe.com/shaughnessy7*.

Finally, we believe that research methods are best taught in the context of published psychological research. Thus, we continue to use the rich psychology literature to provide examples of ways in which researchers actually use the methods we discuss. It is always fun for us to update the research examples, while continuing to include important "classic" findings and studies that have proved effective in helping students learn research methods. We believe that one way to motivate students to join us on this exciting path of pursuing knowledge is to show the "payoff" that psychological research provides.

CHANGES IN THIS EDITION

We continue to use bullet points within the chapters and Review Questions at the end of chapters to help students see clearly the points we think are most important for them to learn. And we continue to rely on the Challenge Questions at the end of chapters to help students learn to apply the principles they have learned. Building on the model of the Challenge Questions, we have embedded Stretching Exercises in most chapters to allow students to apply research principles while they are learning about the principles. An extensive review of statistics remains at the end of the book (Chapters 12 and 13), and we continue to introduce these issues briefly in the appropriate places in the text. We believe our approach provides important flexibility that allows instructors to decide when and how they will cover statistics in a research methods course. In this edition we have tried to make the connection even clearer for students. We have introduced a new pedagogical aid identified as "Stat Tips" We welcome feedback from instructors about how well this new feature works for them. We, of course, appreciate that methods and statistics are closely linked, and we have tried to emphasize that to students in the text and as part of the new "Stat Tips" feature. We hope that our approach will prove effective for both students and instructors.

The following are major changes in this edition:

- We have thoroughly revised the first chapter to make it more engaging and challenging for students. We begin the book with a new section, "The Science of Psychology," which we hope serves two purposes: to emphasize the importance of the scientific method and to generate enthusiasm for psychological research by highlighting key findings from research on media violence. We also are pleased to describe the Nobel Prize-winning (2002) research of Daniel Kahneman. Chapter 1 concludes with a table that illustrates the steps of the research process and provides students with an informal outline for the text. As has been our approach for each edition of the text, students learn that a *multimethod approach* to answering questions will best advance the science of psychology and that one goal of the text is to "fill their toolbox" with strategies for conducting research. Finally, we have strengthened the first chapter by adding bullet points, key concepts, and review and challenge questions.

  Chapter 2 is little changed from the previous edition in its attempt to describe the important aspects of the scientific method. Here, and throughout the text, we've tried to eliminate nuances that prove confusing to students (e.g., including individual differences variables in the introduction of independent variables). Reviewers also suggested new names for the last two goals of our four goals of research, which we have adopted: *Description, Prediction, Explanation,* and *Application.*

- In an effort to help students better understand important concepts, we have identified "key concepts" in the chapter where a concept is first introduced (with a few exceptions). This has meant that some concepts are now identified as key concepts in different chapters (typically earlier) than in the previous edition. A margin icon and boldfaced font will help students to locate these key concepts in the text, and all key concepts are listed at the end of each chapter. The following concepts have been added to the list of key concepts in this edition: *applied and basic research, Cohen's d, comparison of two means, construct, ethnocentrism, novelty effects,* and *null hypothesis significance testing (NHST).*

- One of the most exciting advances in research methodology that has occurred over the past few years is the increase in Internet-based research. Researchers now post experiments on websites and attract literally thousands of participants. However, this cutting-edge methodology raises important ethical issues. We discuss both the use of the Internet in research and the ethical issues it raises in several chapters, but especially in Chapter 3 (ethics) and Chapter 5 (survey research).

- The title of Chapter 10 has been changed to "Single-Case Designs and Small-*n* Research" to better reflect the research conducted in that field. The content, however, remains largely the same.

- As mentioned previously, to help students see the link between methodology and statistical techniques more clearly, we have included in most chapters one or more "Stat Tips" that draw students' attention to questions of statistical analysis. In some cases we answer these questions for students; in other instances we refer them to material in Chapters 12 and 13. We hope that these tips will reinforce students' learning of the important links between gathering data and analyzing data.

- Also related to our treatment of statistics is a change made in the recommendations for "follow-up" analyses when more than two levels of an independent variable are involved. We focus students on comparisons of "two means" and have dropped our emphasis on analytical comparisons based on determining coefficients for the planned comparisons. In conducting "follow-up" analyses, we continue to emphasize the critical importance of confidence intervals in the interpretation of the patterns of obtained means. As several observers have pointed out (e.g., Fidler, Thomason, Cumming, Finch, & Leeman, 2004; Gigerenzer, Krauss, & Vitouch, 2004), despite recommendations from many experts to reduce their reliance on null hypothesis significance testing, researchers continue to rely primarily on this traditional approach. We want students to know that there are many tools in their statistical toolbox, not just one.

WORDS OF THANKS

The cumulative contributions of many people to the 7th edition of our textbook are impossible to acknowledge adequately. Most recently we wish to thank the following reviewers, as well as offer our regrets if we were not able to incorporate all of their suggested changes:

Stephen Burgess
Southerwestern Oklahoma State University
Laura Carlson
University of Notre Dame
Lindsey L. Cohen
West Virginia University
Philip T. Dunwoody
Mercer University
Samuel Hill
The Sage Colleges
Rolf Holtz
University of Florida
Christine Elizabeth Hughes
University of North Carolina at Wilmington
H. Durell Johnson
Pennsylvania State University—Worthington Scranton

Elizabeth C. Lanthier
Northern Virginia Community College
Corrinne Lim
Purdue University
Richard E. Mattson
State University of New York at Binghamton
Mark O'Dekirk
Meredith College
Steven L. Schandler
Chapman University
Jerry I. Shaw
California State University—Northridge
John Shelley-Tremblay
University of South Alabama
Michael Young
Southern Illinois University

We wish also to thank our colleagues at Loyola University of Chicago, Emil Posavac and Patricia Rupert, for their continued support of our textbook and the many fine suggestions for its improvement.

The editorial and production staff at McGraw-Hill once again earn our praises for facilitating the publication of yet another edition. We want to acknowledge especially the support we have been given by Melissa Caughlin and John Wannemacher. Others at McGraw-Hill to whom we are indebted include Kirsten Stoller, Developmental Editor; Cathy Iammartino, Project Manager; Gino Cieslik, Designer; Nora Agbayani, Photo Research Coordinator; Jason Huls, Production Supervisor; and Katherine McNab, Art Editor.

John J. Shaughnessy
Eugene B. Zechmeister
Jeanne S. Zechmeister

PART ONE

General Issues

CHAPTER ONE

Introduction

CHAPTER OUTLINE

THE SCIENCE OF PSYCHOLOGY

- Psychologists develop theories and conduct psychological research to answer questions about behavior and mental processes; these answers can impact individuals and society.
- The scientific method, a means to gain knowledge, refers to the ways in which questions are asked and the logic and methods used to gain answers.
- Two important characteristics of the scientific method are an empirical approach and a skeptical attitude.

It seems safe to assume that you've been exposed to many research findings in psychology, both in media presentations and in your psychology course work. If you are like the authors of your textbook, you are very curious about the mind and behavior. You like to think about people's (and animals') behavior. You wonder about people—why they act the way they do, how they became the people they are, and how they will continue to grow and change. And you may wonder about your own behavior and how your mind works. These thoughts and reflections set you apart from other people—not everyone is curious about the mind, and not everyone considers the reasons for behavior. But if you are curious, if you do wonder why people and animals behave the way they do, you have already taken the first step in the intriguing, exciting, and, yes, sometimes challenging, journey into research methods in psychology.

Many students enter the field of psychology because of their interest in improving people's lives. But what methods and interventions are helpful to people? For example, students with a career goal that involves conducting psychotherapy must learn to identify patterns of behavior that are maladaptive and to distinguish psychological interventions that are helpful from those that are not. Psychologists gain understanding and insight into the means for improving people's lives by developing theories and conducting psychological research to answer their questions about behavior.

Let us consider one very important research question among the many investigated by psychologists: What is the effect of violence in the media? Researchers have investigated aspects of this question for more than five decades in hundreds of research studies. A review of research on this topic appeared in *Psychological Science in the Public Interest* (Anderson et al., 2003), a psychology journal dedicated to publishing reports of behavioral research on important issues of public interest. Other recent topics in this journal include early psychological intervention for posttraumatic stress (McNally, Bryant, & Ehlers, 2003); the role of high self-esteem on performance, success, happiness, and health (Baumeister, Campbell, Krueger, & Vohs, 2003); and the treatment and prevention of depression (Hollon, Thase, & Markowitz, 2002). Although these topics differ, the critical and common feature of research reported in this and other high-caliber psychology journals is the reliance on sound research design and methods to answer questions about behavior.

After decades of research, what do psychologists say about the behavioral, emotional, and social effects of media violence? Anderson et al. (2003) reported several key findings in their review of research that investigated violence in television, films, video games, the Internet, and music:

—Exposure to media violence causes an increase in the likelihood of aggressive and violent thoughts, emotions, and behavior in short- and long-term contexts.

—The effects of violence in the media are consistent across a variety of research studies and methods, types of media, and samples of people.

—Recent long-term studies link frequent childhood exposure to media violence with adult aggression, including physical assaults and spouse abuse.

—Research evidence supports psychologists' theories that media violence "activates" (primes) people's aggressive cognitions and physiological arousal, facilitates people's learning of aggressive behaviors through observation, and desensitizes people to violence.

—Factors that influence the likelihood of aggression in response to media violence include characteristics of viewers (e.g., age and extent to which they identify with aggressive characters), social environments (e.g., parental monitoring of media violence), and media content (e.g., realism of violent depictions and consequences of violence).

—*No one* is immune to the effects of media violence.

A number of studies reveal that children and youth spend an inordinate amount of time as media consumers, possibly second only to sleeping (Lyle & Hoffman, 1972). Thus, an implication of the research findings listed is that one way to lessen the devastating impact of aggression and violence in our society is to decrease exposure to media violence. Indeed, psychological research played an important role in the development of the V-chip (the "V" stands for "Violence") on televisions so that parents can block violent content (Anderson et al., 2003).

More research questions remain. One important question concerns the distinction between *passive* observation of violence (e.g., television depictions) and the *active* engagement with violent media that occurs with video and Internet games (Figure 1.1). Is it possible that the effects of media violence are even stronger when viewers are actively engaged with violence while playing video games? This might be the case if active involvement reinforces aggressive tendencies to a greater degree than does passive observation. Other research questions concern the steps needed to decrease the impact of violence in our society and the role that limiting violence in the media should play in a free society. Perhaps these questions will some day be *your* research questions, or perhaps you are interested in exploring the causes of drug addiction or the roots of prejudice. Literally thousands of important research questions remain. As you continue your study of research in psychology, one day you may contribute to psychologists' efforts to improve our human condition!

Key Concept

Psychologists seek to answer questions about behavior, thoughts, and feelings by using the scientific method. The **scientific method** is an abstract concept that refers to the ways in which questions are asked and the logic and methods

FIGURE 1.1   Does the effect of violent media differ for (a) passive television viewing versus (b) active video game performance?

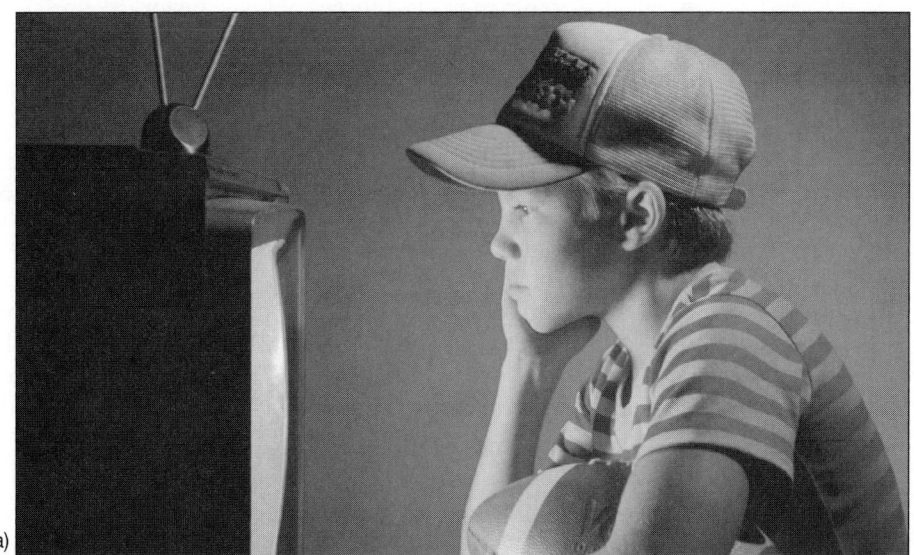

(a)

(b)

used to gain answers. Two important characteristics of the scientific method are the reliance on an empirical approach and the skeptical attitude scientists adopt toward explanations of behavior and mental processes. We will discuss these two characteristics as part of our introduction to psychological research in this chapter, and in Chapter 2 we will describe additional characteristics of the scientific method.

Science in Context

- Science occurs in at least three contexts: historical, social-cultural, and moral contexts.

Although the concept of the scientific method may be abstract, the practice of psychological science is very much a concrete human activity that affects us on several levels. Psychologists can have an impact at the level of the individual (e.g., therapeutic intervention for aggression), the family (e.g., parental control over their children's media use), and society (e.g., efforts to decrease violent programming on television networks). *To be effective, however, psychologists must build upon a foundation of carefully designed and executed research.*

Human activities are influenced heavily by the context in which they occur, and scientific activity is no exception. We can suggest that at least three contexts play a critical role in influencing science: historical context, social-cultural context, and moral context. We will briefly describe each of these in turn.

Historical Context

- An empirical approach, which relies on direct observation and experimentation for answering questions, was cited for developing the science of psychology.
- The computer revolution has been a key factor in the shift from behaviorism to cognitive psychology as the dominant theme in psychological inquiry.

We don't really know exactly when psychology first became an independent discipline. Psychology emerged gradually, with roots in the thinking of Aristotle (Keller, 1937), in the writings of later philosophers such as Descartes and Locke, and later, in the work of early 19th-century physiologists and physicists. The official beginning of psychology is often marked as occurring in 1879 when Wilhelm Wundt established a formal psychology laboratory in Leipzig, Germany.

One of the decisions that faced early psychologists at the end of the 19th century concerned whether psychology should more closely affiliate with the physical sciences or remain a subdiscipline of philosophy (Sokal, 1992). With the development of psychophysical methods (especially Gustav Theodor Fechner) and reaction time methods for understanding nervous system transmission (in particular, Hermann von Helmholtz), psychologists believed they could eventually measure thought itself (Coon, 1992). With these powerful methods of observation, psychology was on the way to becoming a quantifiable, laboratory-based science. Scientific psychologists hoped that their study of the mind would achieve equal prominence with the more established sciences of physics, chemistry, and astronomy (Coon, 1992).

One of the roadblocks to the emerging science of psychology was the public's strong interest in spiritualism and psychic phenomena at the turn of the 20th century (Coon, 1992). The general public viewed these topics of "the mind" to be within the province of psychology and sought scientific answers to their questions about mysticism, clairvoyance, telepathy, and communication with the dead. However, many psychologists wished to divorce the young science from these pseudoscientific topics. To establish psychology as a science, psychologists embraced empiricism as the means to advance understanding about human behavior. The **empirical approach** emphasizes direct observation and experimentation as a way of answering questions. It is perhaps the most important characteristic of the scientific method. Using this approach, psychologists focused on behaviors and experiences that could be observed directly.

Key Concept

Although psychology continues to emphasize the empirical approach, psychology has changed significantly since its beginnings. Early psychologists were primarily interested in questions of sensation and perception—for instance, visual illusions and imagery. In the early 20th century, psychology in the United States was heavily influenced by a behaviorist approach introduced by John B. Watson. Psychological theories focused on learning, and psychologists relied mostly on experiments with animals to test their theories. For behaviorism, the "mind" was a "black box" representing activity between a stimulus and a response. Behaviorism was the dominant perspective in psychology well into the middle of the 20th century. Nevertheless, by the time Ulric Neisser's book, *Cognitive Psychology,* was published in 1967, psychology had turned again to an interest in mental processes. Cognitive psychologists also returned to the reaction time experiments that were used in the early psychology laboratories to investigate the nature of cognitive processes. The cognitive perspective is still dominant in psychology, and cognition recently has been a major topic within the field of neuroscience as investigators study the biology of the mind. There is great potential for the development of scientific psychology in the early 21st century.

A significant factor in the rise to prominence of cognitive psychology was the computer revolution (Robins, Gosling, & Craik, 1999). With the advent of computers, behaviorism's "black box" was represented using a computer metaphor. Psychologists spoke of information processing, storage, and retrieval between input (stimulus) and output (response). Just as the computer provided a useful metaphor for understanding cognitive processes, the continued development of readily available, powerful computers has proved to be exceptionally useful in broadening the scope and precision of measuring cognitive processes. Today in psychology laboratories throughout the United States and the world, computer technology is replacing paper-and-pencil measures of people's thoughts, feelings, and behaviors. Similarly, continued improvements in the technology of brain imaging (e.g., functional Magnetic Resonance Imaging) will advance neuroscience as an important discipline within the fields of psychology and biology.

These broad trends in the historical development of psychology, from behaviorism to cognitive neuroscience, represent the "bigger picture" of what happened in psychology in the 20th century. A closer look, however, reveals the myriad topics investigated in the science of psychology. Psychologists today do research in such general areas as clinical, social, organizational, counseling, physiological, cognitive, educational, developmental, and health psychology.

Investigations in all of these areas help us to understand the complexity of behavior and mental processes.

Science in general—and psychology in particular—has changed because of the brilliant ideas of exceptional individuals. The ideas of Galileo, Darwin, and Einstein not only changed the way scientists viewed their disciplines, but their

---

BOX 1.1

PSYCHOLOGY AND THE NOBEL PRIZE

Each year, the Royal Swedish Academy of Sciences awards the distinguished Nobel Prize for researchers' work in a variety of fields. In October 2002, Daniel Kahneman, Ph.D., became the first psychologist to win this award. He was recognized for his research on intuitive judgment, human reasoning, and decision making in conditions of uncertainty. His research, conducted with his long-term collaborator, Amos Tversky (1937–1996), was honored because of its influential role in economic theories (Kahneman, 2003). Kahneman shared the Nobel Economics Prize with economist Vernon Smith, who was cited for his work in developing laboratory experiments (an important topic in this text) in economics.

Although trained in fields other than psychology, several scientists have been awarded the Nobel Prize for research directly related to the behavioral sciences (Chernoff, 2002; Pickren, 2003), for example:

- **1904,** Physiology or Medicine: Ivan Pavlov won the Nobel Prize for his research on digestion, which subsequently influenced his work on classical conditioning.
- **1961,** Physiology or Medicine: A physicist, Georg von Békésy, won the Nobel Prize for his work on psychoacoustics—the perception of sound.
- **1973,** Physiology or Medicine: Three ethologists, Karl von Frisch, Konrad Lorenz, and Nikolaas Tinbergen, were honored with the first Nobel Prize awarded for purely behavioral research (Pickren, 2003). Ethology is a branch of biology in which researchers observe behavior of organisms in relation to their natural environment (see Chapter 4).
- **1978,** Economics: Herbert A. Simon was awarded the Nobel Prize for his groundbreaking research on organizational decision making (MacCoun, 2002; Pickren, 2003). Kahneman, referring to his 2002 Nobel Prize, cited Simon's research as instrumental for his own research.

- **1981,** Physiology or Medicine: The Nobel Prize was awarded to Roger W. Sperry, a zoologist who demonstrated the distinct roles of the two brain hemispheres using the "split-brain" procedure.

The achievements of these scientists and many others testify to the breadth and importance of behavioral research in the sciences. Although there is not a "Nobel Prize for Psychology" (a distinction shared by the field of Mathematics), the work of scientists in a variety of areas is recognized as contributing to our understanding of behavior.

ideas also changed the way people understand themselves and their world. Similarly, many exceptional individuals have influenced the progress of psychology (Haggbloom et al., 2002), including Nobel Prize winners (see Box 1.1). Early in American psychology, William James (1842–1910) wrote the first introductory textbook, *The Principles of Psychology,* and gained insight into mental processes using his technique of introspection. As the prominence of behaviorism grew, B. F. Skinner (1904–1995) expanded our understanding of responses to reinforcement through the experimental analysis of behavior. Along with Skinner, Sigmund Freud (1856–1939) is often one of the most recognized figures in psychology, but the ideas and methods of the two could not be more different! Freud's theories on personality, mental disorders, and the unconscious dramatically shifted attention from behavior to mental processes through his method of free association. Many other individuals greatly influenced thinking within specific areas of psychology, such as developmental, clinical, social, and cognitive psychology. We sincerely hope you will be able to learn more about these influential psychologists, both from the past and the present, in the areas most of interest to you.

Science also changes less dramatically, in ways that result from the cumulative efforts of many individuals. One way to describe these more gradual changes is by describing the growth of the profession of psychology. The American Psychological Association (APA) was formed in 1892. The APA had only a few dozen members in that first year; in 1992, when the APA celebrated its 100th birthday, there were approximately 70,000 members. Promotion of psychological research is a concern of the APA as well as the American Psychological Society (APS). APS was formed in 1988 to emphasize scientific issues in psychology. APA and APS both sponsor annual conventions, which psychologists attend to learn about the most recent developments in their fields. Each organization also publishes scientific journals in order to communicate the latest research findings to its members and to society in general.

FIGURE 1.2　Many influential people helped to develop the field of psychology, including (a) William James, (b) B. F. Skinner, and (c) Sigmund Freud.

(a)　　　　　　　　　　(b)　　　　　　　　　　(c)

You can become part of psychology's history in the making. Both APA and APS encourage student affiliation, which provides educational and research opportunities for both undergraduate and graduate psychology students. Information about joining APA and APS as a regular member or as a student affiliate can be obtained by consulting their Internet websites:

(APA) http://www.apa.org
(APS) http://www.psychologicalscience.org

Both the APA and APS websites provide news about important recent psychological research findings, information about psychology publications (including relatively low-cost student subscription rates for major psychology journals), and links to many psychology organizations. Take a look!

Social and Cultural Context

- The social and cultural context influences researchers' choice of topics, society's acceptance of findings, and the locations in which research takes place.
- Ethnocentrism occurs when people's views of another culture are biased by the framework or lens of their own culture.

Science is influenced not only by its historical context but also by the prevailing social and cultural context. This prevailing context is sometimes referred to as the *zeitgeist*—the spirit of the times. Psychological research and its application exist in a reciprocal relationship with society: research has an effect on and is affected by society. The social and cultural context can influence what researchers choose to study, the resources available to support their research, and society's acceptance of their findings. For example, researchers have developed new research programs because of an increasing emphasis on women's issues (and because of increasing numbers of women doing research). Topics in this emerging area include the "glass ceiling" that impedes women's advancement in organizations, the interplay between work and family for dual-career couples, and the effects of the availability of quality child care on productivity in the workforce and on children's development. Social and cultural attitudes can affect not only what researchers study but how they choose to do their research. Society's attitude toward bilingualism, for instance, can affect whether researchers emphasize *problems* that arise for children in bilingual education or the *benefits* that children gain from bilingual education.

Social and cultural values can affect how people react to reported findings from psychological research. For example, reports of research on controversial topics such as sexual orientation, recovered memories of childhood sexual abuse, and televised violence receive more media attention because of the public's interest in these issues. At times, this greater interest engenders public debate about the interpretation of the findings and the implications of the findings for social policy. Public reaction can be extreme, as illustrated by the response to an article on child sexual abuse published in *Psychological Bulletin* (Rind, Tromovitch, &

Bauserman, 1998). In their review and analysis of 59 studies of the effects of child sexual abuse (CSA), Rind et al. concluded that "CSA does not cause intense harm on a pervasive basis regardless of gender in the college population" (p. 46). After their research was promoted by pedophilia advocacy sites on the Web, "Dr. Laura" (talk show host, Laura Schlessinger) characterized the article as endorsing adult sex with children (*not* the investigators' intention) and criticized the American Psychological Association for publishing the study in its prestigious journal, *Psychological Bulletin* (Ondersma et al., 2001). In 1999, the U.S. House of Representatives responded to negative media attention by passing unanimously a resolution of censure of the research reported in this article. Also, scientific debate over the controversial findings continues, with criticisms and rebuttals appearing in *Psychological Bulletin* (Dallam et al., 2001; Ondersma et al., 2001; Rind, Tromovitch, & Bauserman, 2001), other journals, and books. Such public criticisms of research findings, even findings based on solid, empirical science, appear to be a growing trend. Legal, administrative, and political attacks arise from those who oppose research findings because of strongly held personal beliefs or financial interests (Loftus, 2003). These attacks can have the unfortunate consequence of impeding legitimate scientific inquiry and debate.

Psychologists' sensitivity to societal concerns, such as child sexual abuse, is one reason why psychology has not developed strictly as a laboratory science. Although laboratory investigation remains at the heart of psychological inquiry, psychologists and other behavioral scientists do research in schools, clinics, businesses, hospitals, and other nonlaboratory settings, including the Internet. In fact, the Internet is becoming a useful and popular research tool for psychological scientists (e.g., Birnbaum, 2000). According to U.S. Census data, by the year 2000, 54 million U.S. households (51%) had one or more computers. In 44 million households (42%) there was at least one person who used the Internet at home (Newburger, 2001). These data obviously underestimate the number of U.S. Internet users since numbers refer to households and not individual users, and they do not consider online access through business or educational settings. Importantly, these figures also do not take into account the use of the Internet in countries other than the United States. Estimates of the number of worldwide Internet users by the year 2005 range from 300 million to 600 million. Suffice it to say, it did not take behavioral scientists very long to recognize the potential of an amazingly large and diverse "participant pool" for their research (see, for example, Birnbaum, 2000; Gosling, Vazire, Srivastava, & John, 2004; Skitka & Sargis, 2005). Aided by the development of the Internet in the 1990s and associated hypertext markup languages (HTML), psychologists soon began to carry out online research (e.g., Musch & Reips, 2000). The Web allows practically any type of psychological research that uses computers as equipment and humans as participants (Krantz & Dalal, 2000). One way that researchers recruit participants for their studies is to post research opportunities on various research-based websites. For example, APS maintains a Web page that allows Internet users to participate in psychological research. Check out Internet research opportunities at http://psych.hanover.edu/APS/exponnet.html. We will have much more to say about research on the Internet as we introduce you to particular research methods in psychology. Of particular importance are ethical issues raised by this form of research (see Chapter 3).

If we acknowledge that science is affected by social and cultural values, a question still remains as to whose culture is having—and whose culture should have—an influence. A potential problem occurs when we attempt to understand the behavior of individuals in a *different* culture through the framework or views of our *own* culture (Figure 1.3). This potential source of bias is called **ethnocentrism.** As an example of ethnocentrism, let's consider the controversy concerning theories of moral development. In his six-stage theory of moral development, Kohlberg (1981, 1984) identified the highest stage of moral development (postconventional development) as one in which individuals make moral

Key Concept

FIGURE 1.3   By removing our cultural lenses, we gain new ideas for research topics that investigate (a) strengths in aging, (b) abilities rather than disabilities, and (c) nurturing fathers and career mothers.

(a)

(b)

(c)

decisions based on their self-defined ethical principles and their recognition of individual rights. Research evidence suggests that Kohlberg's theory provides a good description of moral development for American and European males— cultures emphasizing individualism. In contrast, people who live in cultures that emphasize collectivism, such as communal societies in China or Papua, New Guinea, do not fit Kohlberg's description. Collectivist cultures value the well-being of the community over that of the individual. We would be demonstrating ethnocentrism if we were to use Kohlberg's theory to declare that individuals from such collectivist cultures were less morally developed. We would be interpreting their behavior through an inappropriate cultural lens, namely, individualism. Cross-cultural research is one way to help us avoid studying only one dominant culture and to remind us that we need to be careful to use cultural lenses beyond our own in our research.

Moral Context

- The moral context of research demands that researchers maintain the highest standards of ethical behavior.
- The APA's code of ethics guides research and helps researchers to evaluate ethical dilemmas such as the risks and benefits associated with deception and the use of animals in research.

Science is a search for truth. Individual scientists and the collective enterprise of science need to ensure that the moral context in which scientific activity takes place meets the highest of standards. Fraud, lies, and misrepresentations should play no part in a scientific investigation. But science is also a human endeavor, and frequently much more is at stake than truth. Both scientists and the institutions that hire them compete for rewards in a game with jobs, money, and reputations on the line. The number of scientific publications authored by a university faculty member, for instance, is usually a major factor influencing decisions regarding professional advancement through promotion and tenure. Under these circumstances, there are unfortunate, but seemingly inevitable, cases of scientific misconduct.

A variety of activities constitute violations of scientific integrity. They include fabrication of data, plagiarism, selective reporting of research findings, failure to acknowledge individuals who made significant contributions to the research, misuse of research funds, and unethical treatment of humans or animals (see Adler, 1991). Some transgressions are easier to detect than others. Out-and-out fabrication of data, for instance, can be revealed when, in the normal course of science, independent researchers are not able to reproduce (replicate) results, or when logical inconsistencies appear in published reports. However, more subtle transgressions, such as reporting only data that meet expectations or misleading reports of results, are difficult to detect. The dividing line between intentional misconduct and simply bad science is not always clear.

To educate researchers about the proper conduct of science, and to help guide them around the many ethical pitfalls that are present, most scientific organizations have adopted formal codes of ethics. In Chapter 3 we will introduce you to the APA ethical principles governing research with humans and animals. As you will see, ethical dilemmas often arise. Consider research by Heath and Davidson (1988) who asked groups of university women to help prepare a new rape-prevention pamphlet. In fact, the researchers did not intend to produce a rape-prevention pamphlet. As part of the "pamphlet development," however, they asked women to read rape situations that were presented as controllable or as uncontrollable to investigate whether the participants perceived themselves to be vulnerable to rape. The results of their research indicated that women who read about rape situations that were presented as uncontrollable reported more anxiety and greater intentions to take precautionary steps to prevent rape. The researchers learned, however, that these intentions are not always followed by actual changes in cautious behavior because some women may view their attempts to avoid rape as futile. This research raises an important question: Under what conditions should researchers be allowed to deceive research participants? Does the benefit of the information gained about women's perceptions of their vulnerability to rape outweigh the risk associated with deception?

Deception is just one of the many ethical issues that researchers must confront. As yet another illustration of ethical concerns, consider that animal subjects sometimes are used to help understand human psychopathology. This may mean exposing animal subjects to stressful and even painful conditions, and sometimes killing the animals for postmortem examinations. Under what conditions should psychological research with animal subjects be permitted? The list of ethical questions raised by psychological research is a lengthy one. Thus, it is of the utmost importance that you become familiar with the APA ethical principles and their application at an early stage in your research career, and that you participate (as research participant, assistant, or principal investigator) only in research that meets the highest standards of scientific integrity. Our hope is that your study of research methods will allow you to do good research and to discern what research is good to do.

THINKING LIKE A RESEARCHER

- To "think like a researcher" is to be skeptical regarding claims about the causes of behavior and mental processes, even those that are made on the basis of "published" scientific findings.
- The strongest evidence for a claim about behavior comes from converging evidence across many studies, although scientists recognize that claims are always probabilistic.
- A research hypothesis is a tentative explanation for a phenomenon; it is often stated in the form of a prediction together with an explanation for the predicted outcome.
- A multimethod approach, one that searches for answers using various research methodologies and measures, is psychology's best hope for understanding behavior and the mind.

One important step a student of psychology must make is to learn to think like a researcher. More than anything else, scientists are skeptical. A skeptical attitude regarding claims about the causes of behavior and mental processes is another important characteristic of the scientific method in psychology. Not only do scientists want to "see it before believing it," but they are likely to want to see it again and again, perhaps under conditions of their own choosing. Researchers strive to draw conclusions based on empirical evidence rather than their subjective judgment. The strongest scientific evidence is converging evidence obtained across different studies examining the same research question. Behavioral scientists are skeptical because they recognize that behavior is complex and often many factors interact to cause a psychological phenomenon. Discovering these factors is often a difficult task. The explanations proposed are sometimes premature because not all factors that may account for a phenomenon have been considered or even noticed. Behavioral scientists also recognize that science is a human endeavor. People make mistakes. Human inference is not always to be trusted. Therefore scientists tend to be skeptical about "new discoveries" and extraordinary claims, even those that are from "published" research studies.

The skepticism of scientists leads them to be more cautious than many people without scientific training. Many people are apparently all too ready to accept explanations that are based on insufficient or inadequate evidence. This is illustrated by the widespread belief in the occult. Rather than approaching the claims about paranormal events cautiously, many people accept these claims uncritically. According to public opinion surveys, a large majority of Americans believe in ESP (extrasensory perception), and some people are convinced that beings from outer space have visited earth. About two in five Americans believe horoscopes are credible, and as many as 12 million adults report changing their behavior after reading astrology reports (Miller, 1986). Such beliefs are held despite minimal and often negative evidence for the validity of horoscopes.

Scientists do not, of course, automatically assume that unconventional interpretations of unexplained phenomena could not possibly be true. They simply insist on being allowed to test all claims and to reject those that are inherently untestable. Scientific skepticism is a gullible public's defense against charlatans and others who would sell them ineffective medicines and cures, impossible schemes to get rich, and supernatural explanations for natural phenomena. At the same time, however, it is important to remember that trust plays as large a role as skepticism in the life of a scientist. Scientists need to trust their instruments, their participants, their colleagues' reports of research, and their own professional judgment in carrying out their research.

We've described that to think like a researcher you need to be skeptical about evidence and claims. You already know something about evidence and claims if you've read any book detailing a crime and trial, or watched any number of popular movie or television legal dramas. Detectives, lawyers, and others in the legal profession collect evidence from a variety of sources and seek converging evidence in order to make claims about people's behavior. A small amount of evidence may be enough to *suspect* someone of a crime, but converging evidence from many sources is needed to *convict* the person.

Psychological scientists work in much the same way—they collect evidence in order to make claims about behavior and psychological processes. Consider these statements and decide what kinds of evidence you think are implied by each statement.

1 In a *survey* of U.S. adults, 96% of married people reported they had been faithful to their spouse during the past year.

2 Research has shown that whether a teen begins to smoke is more *related* to whether the teen's friends smoke than to whether the teen's parents smoke.

3 Experimental research demonstrates that writing about emotional experiences associated with beginning college (compared with writing about superficial events) *causes* college students to have better health and academic outcomes.

4 Over many *replications* (repetitions) of the same false-memory experiment, researchers consistently found that about three-fourths of the time participants falsely remembered that certain words were presented when, in fact, the words were never presented in the experiment.

You likely noticed that these four statements cover a range of research topics in psychology, from marital fidelity to the formation of false memories. The measures (e.g., surveys, smoking, health and academic outcomes, false memories) that researchers use to gather evidence vary because of the specific area of psychology they are investigating. As you considered the four research statements, you may have noticed that they also varied in terms of the extent and quality of the evidence. Just as legal professionals must have different types of evidence to suspect *versus* convict a person of a crime, researchers must have different types of evidence to *describe* behavior *versus* state they've identified factors that *cause* a behavior to occur.

As you proceed in your study of research methods, you will find that there are important—and different—scientific principles that apply to reporting a survey statistic or behavioral observation, identifying a relationship between factors (or "variables"), and stating there is a causal link between variables. The main emphasis of this text will be to detail the different research methods that result in different types of evidence and conclusions. The strongest scientific evidence is akin to the converging evidence needed in a trial to obtain a conviction. For instance, when the same procedure is used to induce false memories in several experiments with different participants and equivalent results are obtained, our confidence in the conclusion that people can form false memories is increased. Even when researchers have strong evidence for their conclusions from replications of an experiment, they are in a similar situation as juries that have found a person guilty beyond a reasonable doubt. Researchers and juries both seek the truth, but their conclusions are ultimately probabilistic. Certainty is often beyond the grasp of both jurors and scientists.

While you were considering the evidence described in the four research statements, you may have found yourself reacting to the findings. Perhaps you were encouraged by the high rate of reported marital fidelity, or perhaps you found it hard to believe that marital fidelity could be so high. If so, you are already beginning to think like a researcher. Like detectives, researchers follow hunches and leads as they seek evidence in support of the theories they are testing. However, jurors and researchers also develop preconceptions and initial impressions that can result in biased judgments as they evaluate the evidence. But, legal decisions and research conclusions are ultimately supposed to be based on the evidence and not on our subjective judgments. Researchers use the scientific method to constrain their subjective judgment and to draw appropriate conclusions based on the evidence.

STRETCHING EXERCISE

Consider the type of evidence that is demonstrated in each of the four research statements in the left column. Match each statement to the type of evidence listed in the right column. Which research statements do you find convincing, and why? Citations to the original articles are included so you can read more about the research studies.

Research Statement

1 Mimicking the behavior and posture of participants in a study caused the participants subsequently to be more helpful, compared to participants who were not mimicked.
2 A review of research indicated that several types of treatments have been shown to be effective in treating depression, including medication, interpersonal psychotherapy, and cognitive behavior therapy.
3 Based on analysis of traffic fatalities between 1996 and 2000, an estimated 353 additional fatalities occurred in the 3 months following September 11, 2001, perhaps because people avoided air travel.
4 Adolescent girls in grades 7 and 8 who perceived a strong pressure to be thin were more likely to be dissatisfied with their body when questioned one year later.

Type of Evidence

a Converging findings across studies
b Observation of events
c Cause-and-effect relationship
d Relationship between two variables

References:
1 van Baaren, R. B., Holland, R. W., Kawakami, K., & van Knippenberg, A. (2004). Mimicry and prosocial behavior. *Psychological Science, 15,* 71–74.
2 Hollon, S. D., Thase, M. E., & Markowitz, J. C. (2002). Treatment and prevention of depression. *Psychological Science in the Public Interest, 3,* 39–77.
3 Gigerenzer, G. (2004). Dread risk, September 11, and fatal traffic accidents. *Psychological Science, 15,* 286–287.
4 Stice, E., & Whitenton, K. (2002). Risk factors for body dissatisfaction in adolescent girls: A longitudinal investigation. *Developmental Psychology, 38,* 669–678.

By learning to think like a researcher you can develop two important sets of skills. The first skill will enable you to be a more effective consumer of scientific findings so that you can make more informed personal and professional decisions. The second skill will enable you to learn how to do research so that you can contribute to the science of psychology. We will be fleshing out these two aspects of the scientific method throughout the text, but we will briefly outline them in this chapter. We will first describe an illustration of why it is important to think like a researcher when evaluating research claims made in the media. We will then describe how researchers get started when they want to gather evidence using the scientific method.

Evaluating Research Findings Reported in the Media

Researchers in psychology report their findings in professional journals that are available in printed and electronic form. Most people who encounter psychological research findings, however, do so by learning about research findings in the media—on the Internet, in newspapers and magazines, and on radio and TV. Much of this research is worthwhile. Psychological research can help people in a variety of areas, such as helping people to learn ways to communicate with a relative with Alzheimer's, to avoid arguments, or to learn how to forgive. Two serious problems can arise, however, when research is reported in the media. The first problem is that the research reported in the media is not always good research. A critical reader needs to sort out the good research from the bad— what are solid findings and which have not yet been confirmed. We must also decide which findings are worth applying in our lives and which require a wait-and-see attitude. It is fair to say that much of the research is not very good given all the different media in which psychological research is reported. So we have good reason to question the research we read or hear about in the media.

A second problem that can arise when scientific research is reported in the media is that "something can be lost in the translation." Media reports are typically summaries of the original research, and critical aspects of the method, results, or interpretation of the research may be missing in the media summary. The more you learn about the scientific method, the better your questions will be for discerning the quality of research reported in the media and for determining the critical information that is lacking in the media report. For now, we can give you a taste of the types of questions you will want to ask by looking at an example of research reported in the media.

A few years ago there was a widely publicized phenomenon called the "Mozart effect." Headlines such as "Classical Music Good for Babies' Brains" were common at the time. These headlines caught people's attention, especially the attention of new parents. Media reports indicated that parents were playing classical music to infants in the hope of raising their children's intelligence. One million new mothers were given a free CD called "Smart Symphonies" along with free infant formula. Clearly the distributors and many new parents were persuaded that the Mozart effect was real.

The idea that listening to music might raise the intelligence scores of new-borns is an intriguing idea. When you encounter intriguing ideas in the media such as this one, a good first step is to *go to the original source in which the research was reported.* In this case the original article was reported in a respectable journal, *Nature.* Rauscher, Shaw, and Ky (1993) described an experiment in which a single group of college students listened to a 10-minute Mozart piece, sat in silence for 10 minutes, or listened to relaxation instructions for 10 minutes before taking a spatial reasoning test. Performance on the test was better after listening to Mozart than in the other two conditions, but the effect disappeared after an additional 10- to 15-minute period.

The findings reported in the original source may be judged as solid, but the extrapolations of these findings are very shaky. A million women were being encouraged to play "smart symphonies" for their infants on the basis of an effect demonstrated on a very specific type of reasoning test with college students and the effect lasted 15 minutes at the most! Although some studies with children were done, the ambiguous results of all the research studies indicate that something had been lost in the "translation" (by the media) from the original research reports to the widespread application of the Mozart effect. People who are skeptical enough to ask questions when they hear or read reports of research in the media and knowledgeable enough to read research in the original sources are less likely to be misinformed. Your job is to be skeptical; our job is to provide the knowledge in this text to allow you to read critically original sources that report research findings.

Getting Started Doing Research

As you begin learning about how researchers in psychology gather evidence, we will pass along advice from several expert researchers about one of the most fundamental aspects of research—getting started. We will organize this section around three questions that researchers ask themselves as they begin a research project:

—What should I study?
—How do I develop a hypothesis to test in my research?
—Is my research question a good one?

There are many decisions that must be made before beginning to do research in psychology. The first one, of course, is what topic to study. Many students approach the field of psychology with interests in psychopathology and issues associated with mental health. Others are intrigued with the puzzles surrounding human cognition, such as memory, problem solving, and decision making. Still others are interested in problems of developmental and social psychology. Psychology provides a smorgasbord of research possibilities to explore, as is illustrated by the literally hundreds of scientific journals that publish the results of psychological research. You can quickly find information about the many research areas within psychology by reviewing the contents of a standard introductory psychology textbook. More specific information can be found, of course, in the many classes offered by the psychology department of your college or university, such as abnormal psychology, cognitive psychology, and social psychology.

Students often develop their initial research topics through interactions with their psychology instructors. Many professors conduct research and are eager to involve students on research teams. You may only need to ask. Psychology departments also offer many other resources to help students develop research ideas. One opportunity is in the form of "colloquia." A colloquium (plural: colloquia) is a formal research presentation in which researchers, sometimes from other universities, present their theories and research findings to faculty and students in the department. Watch for announcements of upcoming colloquia in your psychology department.

Key Concept

The next decision is a bit harder. As researchers get started, they seek to identify their research hypothesis. A **hypothesis** (plural: hypotheses) is a tentative explanation for a phenomenon. Often a hypothesis is stated in the form of a prediction for some outcome, along with an explanation for the prediction. We proposed a research hypothesis earlier when we suggested that the effects (e.g., increased aggression) of violent media may be stronger for video games than for passive television viewing because players are actively engaged in the aggressive actions, thus increasing their aggressive tendencies. (An alternative hypothesis might suggest that the effects of video games might be *less* because game players have the opportunity to release the aggressive impulses that passive television viewers do not.)

McGuire (1997) identified 49 simple rules ("heuristics") for generating a hypothesis to be tested scientifically. We cannot review all 49 suggestions here, but we can give you some insight into McGuire's thinking by listing some of these heuristics. He suggests, for example, that we might generate a hypothesis for a research study by:

—thinking about deviations (oddities, exceptions) from a general trend or principle;
—imagining how we would behave in a task or if faced with a specific problem;
—considering similar problems whose solution is known;
—making sustained, deliberate observations of a person or phenomenon (e.g., performing a "case study");
—generating counterexamples for an obvious conclusion about behavior;
—borrowing ideas or theories from other disciplines.

No matter how or where you begin to develop a hypothesis for your research, at some point you will need to explore the published literature of psychological research. There are several reasons why you must search the psychology literature before beginning to do research. One obvious reason is that the answer to your research question may already be there. Someone else may have entertained the same question and provided an answer, or at least a partial one. It is very likely that you will discover research findings that are related to your research question. Although you may be disappointed to find your research question has been explored, consider that finding other people who have done research on the same or similar idea affirms the importance of your idea. Doing research without a careful examination of what is already known may be interesting or fun (it certainly may be easy); perhaps you could call it a "hobby," but we can't call it science. *Science is a cumulative enterprise—current research builds on previous research.*

Once you have identified a body of literature related to your research idea, your reading may lead you to discover inconsistencies or contradictions in the published research. You may also find that the research findings are limited in terms of the nature of the participants studied or the circumstances under which the research was done, or that there is a psychological theory in need of testing. Having made such a discovery, you have found a solid research lead, a path to follow.

When reading the psychological literature and thinking about possible research questions, you might also consider how the results of psychological studies are applied to societal problems. As you learn how to do research in psychology, you may consider ways this knowledge can be used to generate research investigations that will make humankind just a little better off.

Searching the psychological literature is not the tedious task that it once was; computer-aided literature searches, including use of the Internet, have made identifying psychological research a relatively easy, even exciting task. In Chapter 14 of this book, we outline how to search the psychology literature, including ways to use computer databases for your search.

Finally, as Sternberg (1997) points out, choosing a question to investigate should not be taken lightly. Some questions are simply not worth asking because their answers offer no hope of advancing the science of psychology. The questions are, in a word, meaningless, or at best, trivial. Sternberg (1997) suggests that students new to the field of psychological research consider several questions before deciding they have a good research question:

—Why might this question be scientifically important?
—What is the scope of this question?
—What are the likely outcomes if I carry out this research project?
—To what extent will psychological science be advanced by knowing the answer to this question?
—Why would anyone be interested in the results obtained by asking this question?

As you begin the research process, finding answers to these questions may require guidance from research advisors and others who have successfully conducted their own research. We also hope that your ability to answer these questions will be enhanced as you learn more about theory and research in psychology, and as you read about the many examples of interesting and meaningful psychological research that we describe in this book.

Of course, identifying a research question doesn't necessarily tell you how to do the research. What is it exactly that you want to know? Answering this question will mean that you must make other decisions that we will address throughout this text. As a researcher, you will ask yourself questions such as, "Should I do a qualitative or quantitative research study? What is the nature of the variables I wish to investigate? How do I find reliable and valid measures of behavior? What is the research method best suited to my research question? What kinds of statistical analyses will be needed? Do the methods I choose meet accepted moral and ethical standards? These and other steps associated with the scientific process are illustrated in Table 1.1. Don't be concerned if the terms

TABLE 1.1   STEPS OF THE RESEARCH PROCESS

Step	How?	Chapter
Develop a research question.	• Be aware of ethnocentrism.	1
	• Gain personal experiences doing research.	1
	• Read psychological literature.	1, 14
Generate a research hypothesis.	• Read psychological theories on your topic.	1, 2
	• Consider personal experience, think of exceptions, and notice inconsistencies in previous research.	1
Form operational definitions.	• Look to previous research to see how others have defined the same or similar constructs.	2
	• Identify the variables you will examine.	2
Choose a research design.	• Identify a sample of participants.	4, 5
	• Decide whether your research question seeks to describe, allow prediction, or identify causal relationships.	2
	➤ Choose observational and correlational designs for description and prediction.	4, 5, 6
	➤ Choose an experimental design for a causal research question.	7, 8, 9
	➤ Choose a single-case design when seeking to understand and treat a small group or one individual.	10
	➤ Choose a quasi-experimental design for a causal research question in settings where experimental control is less feasible.	11
Evaluate the ethics of your research.	• Identify the potential risks and benefits of the research and the ways in which participants' welfare will be protected.	3
	• Submit a proposal to an ethics review committee.	3
	• Seek permission from those in authority.	3, 11
Collect and analyze data; form conclusions.	• Get to know the data.	12
	• Summarize the data.	12
	• Confirm what the data reveal.	13
Report research results.	• Present the findings at a psychology conference.	14
	• Submit a written report of the study to a psychology journal.	14

in these questions and in Table 1.1 are unfamiliar. As you proceed through this text on research methods in psychology, you will learn about these steps of the research process. Table 1.1 will be a useful guide when you begin conducting your own research.

Key Concept }

This text introduces you to the ways in which psychologists use the scientific method. As you know, psychology is a discipline with many areas of study and many questions. No single research methodology can answer all the questions psychologists have about behavior and mental processes. Thus, the best approach to answering our questions is the **multimethod approach**—that is, searching for an answer using various research methodologies and measures of behavior. The goal of this book is to help you to fill a "toolbox" with strategies for conducting research. As you will learn throughout this text, any one method or measure of behavior may be flawed or incomplete in its ability to answer research questions fully. When researchers use multiple methods, the flaws associated with any particular method are surmounted by other methods that "fill in the gaps." Thus, an important advantage of the multimethod approach is that researchers obtain a more complete understanding of behavior and mental processes. It is our hope that with these tools—the research methods described in this text—you will be on the path toward answering your own questions in the field of psychology.

SUMMARY

Psychologists seek to understand behavior and mental processes by developing theories and conducting psychological research. Psychological studies can have an important impact on individuals and society; one example is research demonstrating the negative impact of violence in the media. Researchers use the scientific method, which emphasizes an empirical approach to understanding behavior; this approach relies on direct observation and experimentation to answer questions. Scientific practice occurs in historical, social-cultural, and moral contexts. Historically, the computer revolution was instrumental in the shift in emphasis from behaviorism to cognitive psychology. Many psychologists, past and present, have helped to develop the diverse field of psychology.

The social-cultural context influences psychological research in terms of what researchers choose to study and society's acceptance of their findings. Culture also influences research when ethnocentrism occurs. In this bias people attempt to understand the behavior of individuals who live in a different culture through the framework or views of their own culture. The moral context demands that researchers maintain the highest standards of ethical behavior. Clear violations of scientific integrity include fabrication of data, plagiarism, selective reporting of research findings, failure to acknowledge individuals who made significant contributions to the research, misuse of research funds, and unethical treatment of humans or animals. The APA's code of ethics guides research and helps researchers to evaluate ethical dilemmas such as the risks and benefits associated with deception and the use of animals in research.

Researchers must be skeptical regarding claims about behavior and mental processes. The strongest evidence for a claim comes from converging evidence across many studies, although scientists recognize that all research findings are probabilistic rather than definitive. Two problems arise with media reports of research: the research may not meet high standards, and media reports are typically summaries of the original research. An important first step in evaluating media reports is to go to the original publication to learn more about the methods and procedures of the research.

The first step in beginning research is to generate a research question. Students gain research ideas from their textbooks and courses, and through interactions with instructors. The next step is to develop a research hypothesis. A research hypothesis is a tentative explanation for the phenomenon to be tested, and it is often stated in the form of a prediction together with an explanation for the predicted outcome. Although research hypotheses are developed in many ways, an essential part of this step is to review psychological research literature related to the topic. Finally, it is important to evaluate whether answers to a research question will meaningfully contribute to psychologists' understanding of behavior and mental processes.

A multimethod approach employs various research methodologies and measures to answer research questions and to gain a more complete understanding of behavior. Scientists recognize that any one method or measure of behavior is flawed or incomplete; multiple methods allow researchers to "fill in the gaps" left by any particular method. The aim of this textbook is to introduce you to the variety of research methods used by psychologists to answer their questions.

KEY CONCEPTS

scientific method	hypothesis
empirical approach	multimethod approach
ethnocentrism	

REVIEW QUESTIONS

1 Describe two important characteristics of the scientific method.
2 Why did early psychologists choose the empirical approach as the favored method for psychological investigations?
3 Identify two ways in which the computer was critical to the development of psychology in the 20th century.
4 Provide an example of (1) how social and cultural factors may influence psychologists' choice of research topics and (2) how social-cultural factors may influence society's acceptance of research findings.
5 Describe how ethnocentrism can be a problem in research and suggest one way in which researchers can prevent this bias.
6 What does it mean that research is conducted in a "moral context"?
7 Describe two ethical dilemmas that psychologists may face when conducting research.

8 Explain why researchers are skeptical about research findings, and explain how their attitude likely differs from that of the general public.

9 Identify the type of evidence that researchers look for when they seek to make a strong claim about behavior or psychological processes.

10 Identify two reasons you would give another person as to why they should critically evaluate the results of the research reported in the news media (e.g., television, magazines).

11 What are the three initial steps researchers take as they begin a research project?

12 Identify two reasons for why it is important to search the psychological literature when beginning research.

13 Describe the multimethod approach to research and identify its main advantage.

CHALLENGE QUESTIONS

1 Consider the hypothesis that playing violent video games causes people to be more aggressive compared to watching passive violence on television.

  A How might you test this hypothesis? That is, what might you do to compare the two different experiences of exposure to violence?

  B How would you determine whether people acted in an aggressive manner after exposure to violence?

  C What additional factors would you have to consider to make sure that *exposure to violence* was the important factor, and not some other factor?

2 In your courses you have learned a variety of approaches to gaining knowledge about people. For example, in reading literature, we learn about people through the eyes of the author and the characters he or she has developed. How is this approach to gaining knowledge different from that used by researchers in psychology? What are the advantages and disadvantages of each approach?

3 Across the history of research in psychology, we have witnessed a change in emphases from sensation-perception to behaviorism and then to cognitive psychology. Within the different areas or subdisciplines of psychology (e.g., clinical, developmental, neuroscience, social), the number of research topics has increased tremendously.

  A What area(s) within psychology is of most interest to you, and why?

  B At your library, page through three or four current issues of journals within your area of interest (e.g., *Developmental Psychology, Journal of Consulting and Clinical Psychology, Journal of Personality and Social Psychology*). (Ask your instructor or librarian for names of additional journals.) What topics did the researchers investigate? Can you observe any trends in the topics or in the kind of research that is being conducted? Describe your findings.

4 Identify how ethnocentrism might play a role in the type of research the following groups choose to pursue by providing a sample research question that would likely be of interest for each group.

  A men vs. women

  B ethnic majority vs. ethnic minority

  C political conservative vs. political liberal

  D age 18–25 vs. 35–45 vs. 55–65 vs. 75–85

Answer to Stretching Exercise

1c, 2a, 3b, 4d

The most convincing research evidence is found in statement #2 because it describes a review of treatment studies involving medication, interpersonal psychotherapy, and cognitive behavior therapy. Converging evidence across studies—in this case, concerning the treatment of depression—allows us to be most confident about the findings. The second-most convincing evidence occurs when a cause-and-effect relationship is identified (we will discuss this more in

Chapter 2 and later chapters). The first statement describes a finding that *if (and only if)* participants' behavior is mimicked, *then* they will be more helpful. That is, mimicking causes people to be more helpful. The next level of convincing evidence occurs when a relationship is demonstrated between two variables, as in statement #4. In this statement, the two variables are (a) the extent to which adolescent girls perceive a pressure to be thin and (2) the degree to which they are dissatisfied with their body. Note that describing this relationship doesn't allow one to say that perceiving a pressure to be thin *causes* girls to be dissatisfied. It's also possible, for example, that being dissatisfied with their body causes girls to perceive a pressure to be thin (i.e., just the reverse). Finally, the last, or lowest, level of convincing evidence comprises an observation of an event. In statement #3, an observation is made that traffic fatalities appeared to increase in October–December, 2001. We can't say why fatalities increased, but we can *guess* that the increase may be due to people's reactions to the events of September 11, 2001.

Answer to Challenge Question 1

A One way to test this hypothesis would be to have two groups of participants. One group would play violent video games, and a second group would watch violence on television. A second way to test the hypothesis would be to use the same group of participants and expose them to both types of violence at different points in time.

B To determine whether people behaved more aggressively following exposure to video games or television, you would need some measure of aggressive behavior. A potentially limitless number of measures exists, perhaps limited only by the ingenuity of the researcher. A good first step is to use measures that other investigators have used; that way, you can compare the results of your study with previous results. Measures of aggression include asking people to indicate how they would respond to hypothetical situations involving anger, or observing how they respond to experimenters (or others) following exposure to violence. In the latter case, the researcher would need a checklist or some other method for recording participants' violent (or nonviolent) behavior. Keep in mind that aggression can be defined in a number of ways, including physical behaviors, verbal behaviors, and even thoughts (but note the difficulty in measuring the latter).

C It would be important to make sure that the two groups—television *vs.* video game—are similar in every way *except* for television or video game exposure. For example, suppose your research had two groups of participants: one group watched television and the other group played video games. Suppose, also, that your results indicated that participants who played video games were more aggressive than participants who watched television on your aggression measure.

One problem would occur if the video game participants were naturally more aggressive to begin with compared to the television participants. It would be impossible to know whether exposure to violence in your research or their natural differences in aggressiveness accounted for the observed difference in aggressiveness in your experiment. You would want to make sure, therefore, that the participants in each group are similar before the exposure to violence. Later in this text you will learn how to make the groups similar.

You would also want to make sure that other aspects of the participants' experiences are similar. For example, you would ensure that the length of time exposed to violence in each group is similar. In addition, you would try to make sure that the degree of violence in the television program is similar to the degree of violence in the video game. It would also be important that participants' experiences do not differ for a number of additional factors, such as whether other people are present and the time of day. In order to demonstrate that video game playing causes more (or less) aggression than television viewing, the most important point is that the only factor that should differ between the groups is the type of exposure.

CHAPTER TWO

The Scientific Method

CHAPTER OUTLINE

Scientific and Everyday Approaches to Knowledge

- The scientific method is empirical and requires systematic, controlled observation.
- Scientists gain the greatest control when they conduct an experiment; in an experiment, researchers manipulate independent variables to determine their effect on behavior.
- Dependent variables are measures of behavior used to assess the effects of independent variables.
- Scientific reporting is unbiased and objective; clear communication of constructs occurs when operational definitions are used.
- Scientific instruments are accurate and precise; physical and psychological measurement should be valid and reliable.
- A hypothesis is a tentative explanation for a phenomenon; testable hypotheses have clearly defined concepts (operational definitions), are not circular, and refer to concepts that can be observed.

For over 100 years the scientific method has been the basis for investigation in the discipline of psychology. The scientific method does not require a particular type of equipment, nor is it associated with a particular procedure or technique. As first described in Chapter 1, the scientific method refers to the ways in which scientists ask questions and the logic and methods used to gain answers. There are many fruitful approaches to gaining knowledge about ourselves and our world, such as philosophy, theology, literature, art, and other disciplines. The scientific method is distinguishable from the other approaches, but all of them share the same goal—seeking the truth. One of the best ways to understand the scientific method as a means of seeking truth is to distinguish it from our "everyday" ways of knowing. Just as a telescope and a microscope extend our everyday abilities to see, the scientific method extends our everyday ways of knowing.

Several major differences between scientific and our everyday ways of knowing are outlined in Table 2.1. Collectively, the characteristics listed under

TABLE 2.1   CHARACTERISTICS OF SCIENTIFIC AND NONSCIENTIFIC (EVERYDAY) APPROACHES TO KNOWLEDGE*

	Nonscientific (everyday)	Scientific
General approach:	Intuitive	Empirical
Attitude:	Uncritical, accepting	Critical, skeptical
Observation:	Casual, uncontrolled	Systematic, controlled
Reporting:	Biased, subjective	Unbiased, objective
Concepts:	Ambiguous, with surplus meanings	Clear definitions, operational specificity
Instruments:	Inaccurate, imprecise	Accurate, precise
Measurement:	Not valid or reliable	Valid and reliable
Hypotheses:	Untestable	Testable

*Based in part on distinctions suggested by Marx (1963).

"Scientific" define the scientific method. The distinctions made in Table 2.1 highlight differences between the ways of thinking that characterize a scientist's approach to knowledge and the informal and casual approach that often characterizes our everyday thinking. These distinctions are briefly summarized in the following pages.

General Approach

We described in Chapter 1 that in order to think like a researcher you must be skeptical. Psychological scientists are cautious about accepting claims about behavior and mental processes, and they critically evaluate the evidence before accepting any claims. In our everyday ways of thinking, however, we often accept evidence and claims with little or no evaluation of the evidence. In general, we make many of our everyday judgments intuitively. This usually means that we act on the basis of what "feels right" or what "seems reasonable." Intuition is not based on a formal decision process. The many everyday inferences and conclusions we reach intuitively are the product of insight and of what we quickly perceive as true based on our personal experiences. Although intuition can be valuable when we have little other information, intuition is not always correct. Consider, for example, what intuition might suggest regarding ratings of video games, movies, and television programs for violent and sexual content. Intuition might suggest that ratings are effective tools for preventing exposure to violent content. In fact, just the opposite may take place! Research indicates that these ratings can entice adolescent viewers to watch the violent and sexy programs—what Bushman and Cantor (2003) called a "forbidden-fruit effect." Thus, rather than limiting exposure to violent and sexual content, ratings may instead *increase* exposure because "ratings may serve as a convenient way to find such content" (p. 138).

Our intuition about what is true does not always agree with what is actually true because we fail to recognize that our perceptions may be distorted by cognitive biases, or because we neglect to weigh available evidence appropriately (Kahneman & Tversky, 1973; Tversky & Kahneman, 1974). Daniel Kahneman won the Nobel Prize in 2002 for his research on how cognitive biases influence people's economic choices. One type of cognitive bias, called illusory correlation, is our tendency to perceive a relationship between events when none exists. Susskind (2003) showed that children are susceptible to this bias when they make judgments about men's and women's behaviors. Children in 2nd grade and 4th grade were shown many pictures of men and women performing stereotypical (e.g., a woman knitting), counterstereotypical (e.g., a man knitting), and neutral behaviors (e.g., a woman or a man reading a book). The children's task was to estimate how frequently they saw each picture. The results indicated that children overestimated the number of times they saw pictures displaying stereotypical behavior. By responding in this way, the children showed that they were susceptible to an illusory correlation. That is, their expectations that men and women behave in stereotypical ways led the children to believe that these types of pictures were displayed more often than they were. One possible basis for the illusory correlation bias is that we are more likely to notice events that are consistent with our beliefs than events that violate our beliefs.

The scientific approach to knowledge is empirical rather than intuitive. An empirical approach emphasizes direct observation and experimentation as a way of answering questions. This does not mean that intuition plays no role in science. Any scientist can probably recount tales of obtaining empirical results that intuition had suggested would emerge. On the other hand, the same scientist is also likely to have come up with just as many findings that were counterintuitive. Research at first may be guided by the scientist's intuitive hunches as to what direction to take. Eventually, however, the scientist strives to be guided by the empirical evidence that direct observation and experimentation provide.

Observation

We can learn a great deal about behavior by simply observing the actions of others. However, everyday observations are not always made carefully or systematically. Most people do not attempt to control or eliminate factors that might influence the events they are observing. As a result, we often make incorrect conclusions based on our casual observations. Consider, for instance, the classic case of Clever Hans. Hans was a horse who was said by his owner, a German mathematics teacher, to have amazing talents. Hans could count, do simple addition and subtraction (even involving fractions), read German, answer simple questions ("What is the lady holding in her hands?"), and give the date, and tell time (Watson, 1914/1967). Hans answered questions by tapping with his forefoot or by pointing with his nose at different alternatives shown to him. His owner considered Hans to be truly intelligent and denied using any tricks to guide his horse's behavior. And, in fact, Clever Hans was clever even when the questioner was someone other than his owner.

Newspapers carried accounts of Hans' performances, and hundreds of people came to view this amazing horse (Figure 2.1). In 1904 a scientific commission was established with the goal of discovering the basis for Hans' abilities. Much to his owner's dismay, the scientists observed that Hans was not clever in two situations. First, Hans did not know the answers to questions if the questioner also did not know the answers. Second, Hans was not very clever if he could not see his questioner. What did the scientists observe? They discovered that Hans was responding to the questioner's subtle movements. A slight bending forward by the questioner would start Hans tapping, and any movement upward or backward would cause Hans to stop tapping. The commission demonstrated that questioners were unintentionally cuing Hans as he tapped his forefoot or pointed. Thus, it seems that Hans was a better observer than many of the people who observed him!

Key Concept }

This famous account of Clever Hans illustrates the fact that scientific observation (unlike casual observation) is systematic and controlled. Indeed, it has been suggested that **control** is the essential ingredient of science, distinguishing it from nonscientific procedures (Boring, 1954; Marx, 1963). In the case of Clever

FIGURE 2.1   Top: Clever Hans performing before onlookers. Bottom: Hans being tested under more controlled conditions when Hans could not see the questioner.

Hans, investigators exercised control by manipulating, one at a time, conditions such as whether the questioner knew the answer to the questions asked and whether Hans could see the questioner (see Figure 2.1). By using controlled observation, scientists gain a clearer picture of the factors that produce a phenomenon. The careful and systematic observation of Clever Hans is one example of the control used by scientists to gain understanding about behavior.

Key Concepts   }

Scientists gain the greatest control when they conduct an experiment. In an **experiment**, scientists manipulate one or more factors and observe the effects of this manipulation on behavior. The factors that the researcher controls or manipulates in order to determine their effect on behavior are called the **independent variables.**[1] In the simplest of studies, the independent variable has two levels. These two levels often represent the presence and the absence of some treatment, respectively. The condition in which the treatment is present is commonly called the experimental condition; the condition in which the treatment is absent is called the control condition. For example, if we wanted to study the effect of drinking alcohol on the ability to process complex information quickly and accurately, the independent variable would be the presence or absence of alcohol in a drink. Participants in the experimental condition would receive alcohol, while participants in the control condition would receive the same drink without alcohol. After manipulating this independent variable, the researcher might ask participants to play a complicated video game to see whether they are able to process complex information.

Key Concept   }

The measures of behavior that are used to assess the effect (if any) of the independent variables are called **dependent variables.** In our example of a study that investigates the effects of alcohol on processing complex information, the researcher might measure the number of errors made by control and experimental participants when playing the difficult video game. The number of errors, then, would be the dependent variable.

Scientists seek to determine whether any differences in their observations of the dependent variable are caused by the different conditions of the independent variable. In our example, this would mean that a difference in errors when playing the video game is caused by the different independent variable conditions—whether alcohol is present or absent. To form this clear conclusion, however, scientists must use proper control techniques. The story of Clever Hans was used to show how scientists use careful, controlled observation to eliminate alternative explanations for a phenomenon (e.g., that Clever Hans was, in fact, clever). Each chapter of this book will emphasize how researchers use control techniques to study behavior and the mind.

Reporting

Suppose you ask someone to tell you about a class you missed. You probably want an accurate report of what happened in class. Or perhaps you missed a party at which two of your friends had a heated argument, and you want to hear from someone what happened. As you might imagine, personal biases and subjective impressions often enter into everyday reports that we receive. When

---

[1] Sometimes the levels of the independent variable are *selected* by a researcher rather than manipulated. An *individual differences variable* is a characteristic or trait that varies across individuals; for example, sex of the participants (male, female) is an individual differences variable. When researchers investigate whether behavior differs according to participants' sex, they select men and women and examine this factor as an individual differences variable. As we will see in Chapter 7, there are important differences between manipulated and selected independent variables.

STRETCHING EXERCISE

In this exercise you are to respond to the questions that appear after this brief description of a research report.

A research report appeared with an eye-catching title, "If the Television Program Bleeds, Memory for the Advertisement Recedes" (Bushman & Phillips, 2001). The researchers stated that more than half of television programs are violent and that hundreds of research studies have shown that viewing TV violence causes an increase in violent behavior. Finally, they noted that advertisers continue to sponsor violent programs.

The researchers focused their study on an analysis of 12 experiments that tested the effects of the type of TV program on people's memory for the commercial messages that were shown during the program. In a typical experiment, the same ads were presented to participants who either watched a violent or a nonviolent TV show. Participants' memory for the names of the brands advertised and the details in the commercial message was measured using recall and recognition tests. The major finding was that memory for the commercial was poorer when it had been presented in a violent TV show than in a nonviolent TV show. The authors explained these results by saying that violent programs make people angry and that anger interferes with memory. The authors also suggested that their findings indicated "that sponsoring violent programs might not be a profitable venture for advertisers" (p. 43).

1 Identify the independent variable (including its levels) and the dependent variable in this study.
2 The researchers concluded that violent programming decreases memory for the commercial. Can you think of an alternative interpretation for these findings based on the idea that nonviolent programming *enhances* memory for the commercial?

---

you ask others to describe an event, you are likely to receive details of the event (not always correct) along with their personal impressions. You may also find that the details reported to you are not the ones that you would have reported. We often report events in terms of our own interests and attitudes. Obviously, these interests and attitudes do not always coincide with those of others. The next time you take a class examination, poll several classmates on their impressions of the test. Their reports are likely to vary dramatically, depending on such factors as how well prepared they were, what they concentrated on when they studied, and their expectations about what the instructor was going to emphasize on the test.

When scientists report their findings, they seek to separate what they have observed from what they conclude or infer on the basis of these observations. For example, consider the photograph in Figure 2.2. How would you describe to someone what you see there? One way to describe this scene is to say that two people are running along a path with another person running in front of them. You might also describe this scene as three people racing each other. If you use this second description, you are reporting an inference drawn from what you have seen and not just reporting what you have observed. The description of three people running would be preferred in a scientific report.

This distinction between description and inference in reporting can be carried to extremes. For example, describing what is shown in Figure 2.2 as running could be considered an inference, the actual observation being that three people are moving their legs up and down and forward in rapid, long

FIGURE 2.2   How would you describe this scene?

strides. Such a literal description also would not be appropriate. The point is that, in scientific reporting, observers must guard against a tendency to draw inferences too quickly. Further, events should be described in sufficient detail without including trivial and unnecessary minutiae. Proper methods for making observations and reporting them will be discussed in Chapter 4.

Scientific reporting seeks to be *unbiased* and *objective*. One accepted check on whether a report is unbiased is whether it can be verified by more than one independent observer. A measure of interobserver agreement, for example, is usually found in observational studies. Unfortunately, many biases are subtle and not always detected even in scientific reporting. Consider the fact that there is a species of fish in which the eggs are incubated in the mouth of the male parent until they hatch. The first scientist to observe the eggs disappear into their father's mouth could certainly be forgiven for assuming, momentarily, that he was eating them. That's simply what we expect organisms to do with their mouths! But the careful observer waits, watches for unexpected results, and takes nothing for granted.

Concepts

We use the term *concepts* to refer to things (both living and inanimate), to events (things in action), and to relationships among things or events, as well as to their characteristics (Marx, 1963). "Dog" is a concept, as is "barking," and so is "obedience." Concepts are the symbols by which we ordinarily communicate. Clear, unambiguous communication of ideas requires that we use concepts that are clearly defined.

In everyday conversation we often get by without having to worry too much about how we define a concept. Many words, for instance, are commonly used and apparently understood even though neither party in the conversation knows exactly what the words mean. That is, people frequently communicate with one another without being fully aware of what they are talking about! This may sound ridiculous but, to illustrate our point, try the following.

Ask a few people whether they believe that intelligence is mostly inherited or mostly learned. You might try arguing a point of view opposite to theirs just for the fun of it. After discussing the roots of intelligence, ask them what they mean by "intelligence." You will probably find that most people have a difficult time defining this concept, even after debating its origins. Yet people are frequently willing to debate an important point regarding intelligence, and even take a definite stand on the issue, without being able to say exactly what "intelligence" is. When someone does provide a definition, it is unlikely to be exactly the same as that given by another person. That is, "intelligence" means one thing to one person and something else to another. Clearly, in order to attempt to answer the question of whether intelligence is mainly inherited or mainly learned, we need to have an exact definition that all parties involved can accept.

The study of "concepts" is so important in psychological science that researchers refer to concepts by a special name: constructs. A **construct** is a concept or idea; examples of psychological constructs include intelligence, depression, aggression, and memory. One way in which a scientist gives meaning to a construct is by defining it operationally. An **operational definition** explains a concept solely in terms of the observable procedures used to produce and measure it. Intelligence, for instance, can be defined operationally by using a paper-and-pencil test emphasizing understanding of logical relationships, short-term memory, and familiarity with the meaning of words. Some may not like this operational definition of intelligence, but once a particular test has been identified, there can at least be no argument about what intelligence means *according to this definition*. Operational definitions facilitate communication, at least among those who know how and why they are used.

Although exact meaning is conveyed via operational definitions, this approach to communication has not escaped criticism. One problem has been alluded to already. That is, if we don't like one operational definition of intelligence, there is nothing to prevent us from giving intelligence another operational definition. Does this mean that there are as many kinds of intelligence as there are operational definitions? Each time a new set of questions is added to a paper-and-pencil test of intelligence, do we have a new definition of intelligence? The answer, unfortunately, is that we don't really know. To determine whether a different procedure yields a new definition of intelligence, we would have to seek additional evidence. For example, do people who score high on one test also score high on the second test? If they do, the new test may be measuring the same construct as the old one.

Key Concepts

FIGURE 2.3   If balancing a ball on your nose is an operational definition of intelligence, would seals be considered more intelligent than humans?

Another criticism of using operational definitions is that the definitions are not always meaningful. For example, defining intelligence in terms of how long one can balance a ball on one's nose is an operational definition that most people would not find very meaningful. How do we decide whether a construct has been meaningfully defined? Once again, the solution is to appeal to other forms of evidence. How does performance on a balancing task compare to performance on other tasks that are commonly accepted as measures of intelligence? We must also be willing to apply common sense to the situation. Do people usually consider balancing a ball evidence of intelligence? Scientists are generally aware of the limitations of operational definitions; however, a major strength of using operational definitions is that they help to clarify communication among scientists about their constructs. This strength is assumed to outweigh the limitations.

Instruments

You depend on instruments to measure events more than you probably realize. The speedometer in the car, the clock in the bedroom, and the thermometer used to measure body temperature are all instruments that we would find difficult to do without. And you can appreciate the problems that arise if one of these instruments is inaccurate. *Accuracy* refers to the difference between what an instrument says is true and what is known to be true. A clock that is

FIGURE 2.4   Scientific-instruments used in psychology have increased dramatically in their precision and accuracy.

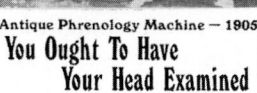

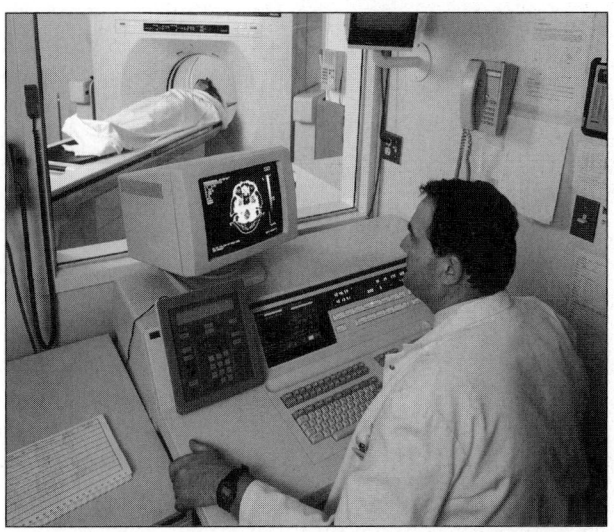

consistently 5 minutes slow is not very accurate. Inaccurate clocks can make us late, inaccurate speedometers can earn us traffic tickets, and inaccurate thermometers can lead us to believe that we are not ill when we are. The accuracy of an instrument is determined by *calibrating* it, or checking it with another instrument known to be true. The accuracy of speedometers can be checked using a combination of observations of roadside distance markers and measuring the elapsed time using an accurate watch.

Measurements can be made at varying levels of *precision*. A measure of time in tenths of a second is not as precise as one that is in hundredths of a second. One instrument that yields imprecise measures is the gas gauge in most cars. Although reasonably accurate, gas gauges do not give very precise readings. Most of us have wished at one time or another that the gas gauge would permit us to determine whether we had that extra half gallon of gas that would get us to the next service station.

We also need instruments to measure behavior. Wilhelm Wundt established a formal psychology laboratory in 1879, an event that marks the official beginning of scientific psychology. Wundt used a reaction-time apparatus to measure the time required for cognitive processing. You can be assured that the precision, and even the accuracy, of instruments of this kind have improved significantly in the last 100 years. Today, electronic counters provide precise measures of reaction time in milliseconds (thousandths of a second). Many other instruments are employed in contemporary psychology. To perform a psychophysiology experiment (e.g., when assessing a person's arousal level) requires instruments that give accurate measures of such internal states as heart rate and blood pressure. Tests of anxiety sometimes employ instruments to measure galvanic skin response (GSR).

Other behavioral instruments are of the paper-and-pencil variety. Questionnaires and tests are popular instruments used by psychologists to measure behavior. So, too, are the rating scales used by human observers. For instance, rating aggression in children on a 7-point scale ranging from not at all aggressive (1) to very aggressive (7) can yield relatively accurate (although perhaps not too precise) measures of aggression. It is the responsibility of the behavioral scientist to use instruments that are as accurate and as precise as possible.

Measurement

In order to investigate events and phenomena, scientists use instruments to obtain measurements. Measurements provide the record of the careful and controlled observations that characterize the scientific method. One type of scientific measurement, *physical measurement*, involves dimensions for which there is an agreed-upon standard and an instrument for doing the measuring. For example, length is a dimension that can be scaled with physical measurement, and there are agreed-upon standards for units of length (e.g., inches, meters). Similarly, units of weight and time represent physical measurement.

Although researchers in psychology use physical measurement, most of the dimensions measured in psychological research do not involve physical measurement. Rulers do not exist for measuring psychological constructs such as beauty, aggression, or intelligence. For these dimensions we must use a second type of measurement—*psychological measurement*. In a sense, the human observer is the instrument for psychological measurement. More specifically, agreement among a number of observers provides the basis for psychological measurement. If several independent observers agree that a certain action warrants a rating of 3 on a 7-point rating scale of aggression, we can say that we have a psychological measurement of the aggressiveness of the action.

Key Concept

Just as it is important that instruments be accurate and as precise as possible, it is important that measurement be both valid and reliable. In general, **validity** refers to the "truthfulness" of a measure. A valid measure of a construct is one that measures what it claims to measure. We discussed this aspect of measurement when we mentioned possible operational definitions of intelligence. Intelligence, it was suggested, could be defined in terms of performance on a task requiring one to balance a ball on one's nose. According to the principle of "operationalism," this is a perfectly permissible operational definition. However, most of us would question whether such a balancing act is really a measure of intelligence. In other words, we would question whether this is a valid measure of intelligence. Can intelligence actually be measured by how long we can keep a ball balanced on our nose? As we indicated earlier, evidence bearing on the validity of this definition would have to come from other sources. The validity of a measure is supported to the extent that people do as well on it as they do on independent measures that are presumed to measure the same construct. For example, if time spent balancing a ball is a valid measure of intelligence, then a person who does well on the balancing task should also do well on measures such as size of vocabulary, reasoning ability, and other accepted measures of intelligence.

Key Concept } The **reliability** of a measurement is indicated by its consistency. Several different kinds of reliability can be distinguished. When we speak of instrument reliability, we are discussing whether an instrument works consistently. The car that sometimes starts and sometimes doesn't when we engage the ignition is not very reliable. Observations made by two or more independent observers are said to be reliable if they show agreement—that is, if the observations are consistent from one observer to another. When several psychologists asked college students to rate the "happiness" of medal winners at the 1992 Summer Olympics in Barcelona, Spain, they found that rater agreement was very high (Medvec, Madey, & Gilovich, 1995). They also found, somewhat counterintuitively, that bronze (third place) medal winners were perceived as happier than silver (second place) medal winners, a finding that was explained by a theory of counterfactual thinking. Apparently, people are happier just making it (to the medal stand) than they are just missing it (i.e., missing a gold medal).

The validity and reliability of measurements are central issues in psychological research. You will encounter various ways in which researchers determine reliability and validity as we introduce you to different research methods.

Hypotheses

A hypothesis is a tentative explanation for something. Hypotheses frequently attempt to answer the questions "How?" and "Why?" At one level, a hypothesis may simply suggest how particular variables are related. For example, in our popular culture we frequently associate white or brightness with "good" and black or darkness with "bad" (Meier, Robinson, & Clore, 2004). In the movie *Star Wars*, for instance, Luke Skywalker and Princess Leia were dressed in white and Darth Vader was completely in black. Across many religions (e.g., Buddhism, Christianity, Hinduism, Islam, Zoroastrianism) an association exists between light and God or goodness, and between darkness and Satan or evil. Whether something is considered good or bad is referred to as an *affective* judgment. On the other hand, our experience of brightness (and darkness) is a sensory perception. In their research, Meier and his colleagues hypothesized that the association between affective judgments and sensory perceptions of brightness is automatic—that is, people automatically judge brighter objects as good and darker objects as bad.

To test their hypothesis, Meier and his associates (2004) asked participants in a series of experiments to judge whether 100 words presented on a computer screen were *negative* or *positive*. Fifty of the words were previously rated as reflecting positive affect (e.g., *candy, love, pretty, sleep*), and 50 of the words represented negative affect (e.g., *bitter, cancer, devil, rude*). The researchers manipulated whether the words were presented in a bright font or a dark font. Their results indicated that when the affect and the brightness of the word conflicted (e.g., *love* presented in a dark font), participants took longer and made more errors when judging whether the word was positive or negative, compared to when the words "matched" the associated brightness (e.g., *love* presented in a bright font).

At a more theoretical level, a hypothesis may offer a reason (the "why") for the way that particular variables are related. For example, Meier and his colleagues (2004) considered theories that suggest the human brain has developed in a way that makes conceptual thinking, such as affective judgments, automatically tied to physical perception (e.g., Barsalou, 1999; Lakoff & Johnson, 1999). Based on these theories, the researchers suggested that people cannot judge the affect of a word (or any other object) without first automatically considering its physical features, such as brightness. In their experiment, when the brightness conflicted with the correct affective judgment, additional processing (i.e., time, thought) was required for people to override their automatic association and to make the correct judgment about whether the word was negative or positive.

Nearly everyone has proposed hypotheses to explain some human behavior at one time or another. Why do people commit apparently senseless acts of violence? What causes people to start smoking cigarettes? Why are some students academically more successful than others? One characteristic that distinguishes casual, everyday hypotheses from scientific hypotheses is *testability*. If a hypothesis cannot be tested, it is not useful to science (Marx, 1963). Three types of hypotheses fail to pass the "testability test." A hypothesis is not testable when its constructs are not adequately defined, when the hypothesis is circular, and when the hypothesis appeals to ideas not recognized by science.

Hypotheses are not testable if the concepts to which they refer are not adequately defined. Consider a hypothesis saying that a would-be assassin shot a U.S. president or other prominent figure because he was mentally disturbed. This hypothesis would not be testable unless a definition of "mentally disturbed" can be agreed upon. Unfortunately, psychologists and psychiatrists cannot always agree on what terms such as "mentally disturbed" mean because an accepted operational definition is often not available for these concepts. In addition to facilitating clarity in communication, operational definitions also offer a means of evaluating whether our hypotheses contain scientifically acceptable concepts.

Hypotheses are also untestable if they are circular. A circular hypothesis occurs when an event itself is used as the explanation of the event (Kimble, 1989, p. 495). As an illustration, consider the statement that an "eight-year-old boy is distractable in school and having trouble reading because he has an attention deficit disorder." An attention deficit disorder is defined by the inability to pay attention. Thus, the statement simply says that the boy doesn't pay attention because he doesn't pay attention—that's a circular hypothesis.

A hypothesis also may be untestable if it appeals to ideas or forces that are not recognized by science. Science deals with the observable, the demonstrable, the empirical. To suggest that people who commit horrendous acts of violence are under orders from the Devil is not testable because it invokes a principle (the Devil) that is not in the province of science. Such hypotheses might be of value to philosophers or theologians but not to the scientist.

GOALS OF THE SCIENTIFIC METHOD

- The scientific method is intended to meet four goals: description, prediction, explanation, and application.

In the first part of this chapter we examined the ways in which our everyday ways of thinking differ from the scientific method. In general, the scientific method is characterized by an empirical approach, systematic and controlled observation, unbiased and objective reporting, clear operational definitions of constructs, accurate and precise instruments, valid and reliable measures, and testable hypotheses. In this next section, we examine goals of the scientific method. Psychologists use the scientific method to meet four research goals: description, prediction, explanation, and application.

Description

- Psychologists seek to describe events and relationships between variables; most often, researchers use the nomothetic approach and quantitative analysis.

Description refers to the procedures researchers use to define, classify, catalogue, or categorize events and their relationships. Clinical research, for instance, provides practitioners with criteria for classifying mental disorders. Many of these are found in the American Psychiatric Association's *Diagnostic and Statistical Manual of Mental Disorders* (4th ed., Text Revision, 2000), also known as DSM-IV-TR (see Fig. 2.5). Consider, as one example, the criteria used to define the disorder labeled dissociative fugue (formerly psychogenic fugue).

Diagnostic Criteria for Dissociative Fugue

A The predominant disturbance is sudden, unexpected travel away from home or one's customary place of work, with inability to recall one's past.

B Confusion about personal identity or assumption of a new identity (partial or complete).

C The disturbance does not occur exclusively during the course of Dissociative Identity Disorder and is not due to the direct physiological effects of a substance (e.g., a drug of abuse, medication) or a general medical condition (e.g., temporal lobe epilepsy).

D The symptoms cause clinically significant stress or impairment in social, occupational, or other important areas of functioning. (DSM-IV-TR, 2000, p. 526)

The diagnostic criteria used to define dissociative fugue provide an operational definition for this disorder. Like many other unusual mental disorders, dissociative fugues are relatively rare; thus, we typically learn about these kinds of disorders based on individual descriptions of people exhibiting them. These descriptions are called "case studies." Researchers also seek to provide clinicians with descriptions of the prevalence of a mental disorder as well as the relationship between the presence of various symptoms and other variables

FIGURE 2.5   Mental disorders are usually classified according to criteria found in the American Psychiatric Association's *Diagnostic and Statistical Manual of Mental Disorders.*

such as gender and age. According to the DSM-IV-TR (2000), for instance, dissociative fugue is seen primarily in adults, and although it is relatively rare, it is more frequent "during times of extremely stressful events such as wartime or natural disaster" (p. 524).

Science in general and psychology in particular develop descriptions of phenomena using the *nomothetic approach*. Using the nomothetic approach, psychologists try to establish broad generalizations and general laws that apply to a diverse population. To accomplish this goal, psychological studies most often involve large numbers of participants. Researchers seek to describe the "average," or typical, performance of a group. This average may or may not describe the performance of any one individual in the group.

For example, Levine (1990) described the "pace of life" in various cultures and countries of the world by noting the accuracy of outdoor bank clocks and by timing the walking speed of pedestrians over a distance of 100 feet. The results of this study are shown in Figure 2.6. The citizens of Japan exhibited, overall, the fastest pace of life with U.S. citizens second. The citizens of Indonesia were the slowest. Not all citizens of Japan or the United States, however, are on the fast track. In fact, Levine (1990) and his colleagues found wide differences in the pace of life among various cities within the United States depending on the region of the country. Cities in the Northeast (e.g., Boston, New York) had a faster tempo than did cities on the West Coast (e.g., Sacramento, Los Angeles).

FIGURE 2.6 Measures of accuracy of a country's bank clocks, pedestrian walking speed, and the speed of postal clerks performing a routine task served to describe the pace of life in a country. In the graph a longer bar represents greater accuracy of clocks or greater speed of walking and performing a task. (From Levine, 1990).

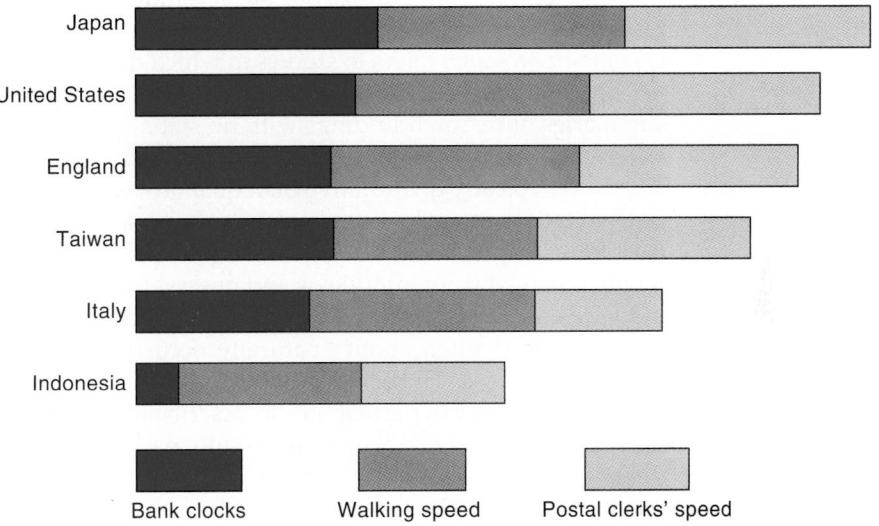

Of course, there will be individual variations within cities as well. Not all citizens of Los Angeles are going to be slow-paced, nor are all New Yorkers going to be fast-paced. Nevertheless, the Japanese move *in general* at a faster pace than do Indonesians, and Americans on the West Coast exhibit, *on the average,* a slower pace of life than do residents of the Northeast.

Researchers who use the nomothetic approach appreciate that there are important differences among individuals; they seek, however, to emphasize the similarities rather than the differences. For example, a person's individuality is not threatened by our knowledge that that person's heart, like the hearts of other human beings, is located in the upper left chest cavity. Similarly, we do not deny a person's individuality when we state that that person's behavior is influenced by patterns of reinforcement (e.g., rewards, punishments). Researchers merely seek to describe what organisms are like in general on the basis of the average performance of a group of different organisms.

Some psychologists, notably Gordon Allport (1961), argue that the nomothetic approach is inadequate—unique individuals cannot be described by an average value. Researchers who use the *idiographic approach* study the individual rather than groups. These researchers believe that although individuals behave in ways that conform to general laws or principles, the uniqueness of individuals must also be described. A major form of idiographic research is the case study method, which we will describe in Chapter 10.

Depending on their research question, researchers decide whether to describe groups of individuals or one individual's behavior. Although many researchers do mainly one or the other kind of research, others may do both. A clinical psychologist, for instance, may decide to pursue mainly idiographic investigations of a few clients in therapy but consider nomothetic issues when doing research with groups of college students. Another decision that the researcher must make is whether to do quantitative or qualitative research. *Quantitative research* refers to studies in which the findings are mainly the product of statistical summary and analysis. *Qualitative research* produces verbal summaries of research findings with no statistical summaries or analysis. Just as psychological research is more frequently nomothetic than idiographic, it is also more typically quantitative than qualitative.

Qualitative research is used extensively by sociologists and anthropologists (see, for example, Seale, 1999). The data of qualitative research are most commonly obtained from interviews and observations and can be used to describe individuals, groups, and social movements (Strauss & Corbin, 1990). Qualitative research is often about "naturally occurring, ordinary events in natural settings" (Miles & Huberman, 1994, p. 10). Central to qualitative research is that investigators ask participants to describe their experiences in ways that are meaningful to *them,* rather than asking participants to use categories and dimensions established by theorists and previous research (Kidd, 2002). This qualitative approach was used by Kidd and Kral (2002) to gain insight into the experiences of 29 Toronto street youth (ages 17–24). A focus of the interviews concerned experiences with suicide. The majority (76%) of those interviewed reported a history of attempted suicide, and analysis of their narratives revealed that suicidal experiences were linked especially to feelings of isolation, rejection/betrayal, low self-worth, and prostitution. Importantly, the researchers reported that their analyses revealed several topics associated with suicidal experiences not identified in previous research involving street youth. Namely, "loss of control, assault during prostituted sex, drug abuse as a 'slow suicide,' and breakups in intimate relationships" were related to these youths' suicidal experiences (p. 411). Other examples of qualitative research are found in Chapter 4 when we discuss narrative records of observed behavior; case studies described in Chapter 10 also are a form of qualitative research.

Prediction

- Correlational relationships allow psychologists to predict behavior or events, but do not allow psychologists to infer what causes these relationships.

Description of events and their relationships often provides a basis for *prediction*, the second goal of the scientific method. There are important questions in psychology that call for predictions. For example: Does the early loss of a parent make a child especially vulnerable to depression? Are children who are overly aggressive likely to have emotional problems as adults? Do stressful life events lead to increased physical illness? Research findings suggest an affirmative answer to all of these questions. This information not only adds valuable knowledge to the discipline of psychology but is also helpful in both the treatment and the prevention of emotional disorders.

An important occupation of many psychologists is the prediction of later performance (e.g., on the job, in school, or in specific vocations) on the basis of earlier performance on various standardized tests. For instance, scores on the Graduate Record Examination (GRE), as well as undergraduate grade point average (GPA), can be used to predict how well a student will do in graduate school. Sternberg and Williams (1997) did find that GRE scores predicted fairly well the first-year grades of graduate students at their institution. They also found, however, that the GRE was not predictive of other, important performance criteria such as advisors' ratings of a student's creativity, ability to teach, and ability to do research. Not surprisingly, these researchers have sparked a debate by questioning the predictive validity (i.e., accuracy of prediction) of the GRE, which is widely regarded as a predictor of students' later professional development (see, for example, "Comment" section of *American Psychologist*, 1998, 53, 566–577).

Key Concept }
When scores on one variable can be used to predict scores on a second variable, we say that the two variables are correlated. A **correlation** exists when two different measures of the same people, events, or things vary together—that is, when particular scores on one variable tend to be associated with particular scores on another variable. When this occurs, the scores are said to "covary." For example, stress and illness are known to be correlated; the more stressful life events people experience, the more likely they are to experience physical illnesses.

Consider a measure with which you likely have had some experience, namely, teacher/course evaluations in classes you have taken. College students are commonly asked to evaluate their instructors and the course material toward the end of a course. By the time a course is over, you probably have formed many impressions of a teacher (e.g., whether the instructor is supportive, enthusiastic, likeable). After all, you have just spent as many as 12 or 14 weeks (perhaps more than 30 hours) in this instructor's classroom. Ambady and Rosenthal (1993) asked how well teacher evaluations by students not enrolled in the class would correlate with end-of-the-semester evaluations made by students in the class. They showed video clips (without sound) of teachers to a group of female undergraduates. But, and here is the interesting part, they showed the video clips for only 30 seconds, 10 seconds, or just 6 seconds (across several studies). The researchers found that teacher evaluations based on these "thin slices of nonverbal behavior" correlated well with end-of-the-semester teacher evaluations made by students who were enrolled in the class. That is, more positive course evaluations of teachers were associated with higher ratings for their videotaped behavior; similarly, more negative course evaluations were associated with lower ratings of videotaped behavior. These results indicate that people (in this case, teachers) reveal much about themselves when their nonverbal behavior is seen only briefly, and also that we (as observers) can make relatively accurate judgments of affective behavior quite quickly.

Ambady and Rosenthal's findings, of course, do not mean that all the information in teaching evaluations can be captured by this method as they focused only on judgments of affective behavior (e.g., likeableness).

It is important to point out that successful prediction doesn't always depend on knowing *why* a relationship exists between two variables. Consider the report that the Chinese rely on observing animal behavior to help them predict earthquakes. Certain animals apparently behave in an unusual manner just before an earthquake. The dog that barks and runs in circles and the snake seen fleeing its hole, therefore, may be reliable predictors of earthquakes. If so, they could be used to warn people of forthcoming disasters. We might even imagine that in areas where earthquakes are likely, residents would be asked to keep certain animals under observation (as miners once kept canaries) to warn them of conditions of which they are as yet unaware. This would not require that we understand *why* certain animals behave strangely before an earthquake, or even why earthquakes occur.

Interestingly, Levine (1990) showed that measures of the pace of a city can be used to predict death rates from heart disease. However, we can only speculate about why these measures are related. One possible explanation for this correlation suggested by the researchers is that people living in time-urgent environments engage in unhealthy behaviors, for example, cigarette smoking and poor eating habits, which increase their risk of heart disease (Levine, 1990). Ambady and Rosenthal (1993) proposed an explanation for their correlation between teacher evaluations by students not in the class and by students enrolled in the class. They suggested that people are "attuned" to quickly picking up information about a person's affect because this information is important (adaptive) in real-life decision making. Without additional information, however, the proposed explanations for these two phenomena are speculative.

Explanation

- Psychologists understand the cause of a phenomenon when the three conditions for causal inference are met: covariation, time-order relationship, and elimination of plausible alternative causes.
- The experimental method, in which researchers manipulate independent variables to determine their effect on dependent variables, establishes time-order and allows a clearer determination of covariation.
- Plausible alternative causes for a relationship are eliminated if there are no confoundings in a study.
- Researchers seek to generalize a study's findings to describe different populations, settings, and conditions.

Although description and prediction are important goals in science, they are only the first steps in our ability to explain and understand a phenomenon. Explanation is the third goal of the scientific method. We understand and can explain a phenomenon when we can identify its causes. Researchers typically conduct *experiments* to identify the causes of a phenomenon. Experimental research differs from descriptive and predictive (correlational) research because of the high degree of control scientists seek in experiments. Recall that when researchers control a situation, they manipulate independent variables one at a time to determine their effect on the dependent variable—the phenomenon of interest. By conducting controlled experiments, psychologists infer what causes a phenomenon; they make a causal inference. Because experiments are very important to psychologists' efforts to form causal inferences, we have dedicated Chapters 7, 8, and 9 to a detailed discussion of the experimental method.

Key Concept

Scientists set three important conditions for making a **causal inference:** *covariation of events, a time-order relationship,* and *the elimination of plausible alternative causes.* A simple illustration will help you to understand these three conditions. Suppose you hit your head on a door and experience a headache; presumably you would *infer* that hitting your head *caused* the headache. The first condition for causal inference is covariation of events. If one event is the cause of another, the two events must vary together; that is, when one changes, the other must also change. In our illustration, the event of changing your head position from upright to hitting against the door must covary with experience of no headache to the experience of a headache.

The second condition for a causal inference is a *time-order relationship* (also known as contingency). The presumed cause (hitting your head) must occur before the presumed effect (headache). If the headache began before you hit your head, you wouldn't infer that hitting your head caused the headache. In other words, the headache was contingent on you hitting your head first. Finally, causal explanations are accepted only when other possible causes of the effect have been ruled out—when *plausible alternative causes have been eliminated.* In our illustration, this means that to make the causal inference that hitting your head caused the headache, you would have to consider and rule out other possible causes of your headache (such as reading a difficult textbook).

Unfortunately, people have a tendency to conclude that all three conditions for a causal inference have been met when really only the first condition is satisfied. For example, it has been suggested that parents who are stern disciplinarians and who use physical punishment are more likely to have aggressive children than are parents who are less stern and use other forms of discipline. Parental discipline and children's aggressiveness obviously covary. Moreover, the fact that parents are typically assumed to influence how their children behave might lead us to think that the time-order condition has been met— parents use physical discipline and children's aggressiveness results. It is also the case, however, that infants vary in how active and aggressive they are and that the infant's behavior has a strong influence on the parents' responses in trying to exercise control. In other words, some children may be naturally aggressive and require stern discipline rather than stern discipline producing aggressive children. Therefore, the direction of the causal relationship may be opposite to what we thought at first.

It is important to recognize, however, that the causes of events cannot be identified unless covariation has been demonstrated. The first objective of the scientific method, description, can be met by describing events under a single set of circumstances. The goal of understanding, however, requires more than this. For example, suppose a teacher wished to demonstrate that so-called "active learning strategies" (e.g., debates, group presentations) help students learn. She could teach students using this approach and then describe the performance of the students who received instruction in this particular way. But, at this point, what would she know? Perhaps another group of students taught using a different approach might learn the same amount. Before the teacher could claim that active learning stategies *caused* the performance she observed, she would have to compare this method with some other reasonable approach. That is, she would look for a difference in learning between the group using active learning strategies and a group not using this method. Such a finding would show that teaching strategy and performance covary. When a controlled experiment is done, a bonus comes along when the independent and dependent variables covary. The time-order condition for a causal inference is met because the researcher manipulates the independent variable (e.g., teaching method) and *subsequently* measures the changes in the dependent variable (e.g., a measure of student learning).

By far the most challenging condition researchers must meet in order to make a causal inference is eliminating other plausible alternative causes. Consider a study in which the effect of two different teaching approaches (active and passive) is assessed. Suppose the researcher assigns students to teaching conditions by having all men in one group and all women in the other. If this were done, any difference between the two groups could be due either to the teaching method *or* to the gender of the students. Thus, the researcher would not be able to determine whether the difference in performance between the two groups was due to the independent variable (active or passive learning) or to the alternative explanation of students' gender. Said more formally, the independent variable of teaching method would be "confounded" with the independent variable of gender. **Confounding** occurs when two potentially effective independent variables are allowed to covary simultaneously. When research is confounded, it is impossible to determine what variable is responsible for any obtained difference in performance.

Key Concept

Researchers seek to explain the causes of phenomena by conducting experiments. However, even when a carefully controlled experiment allows the researcher to form a causal inference, additional questions remain. One important question concerns the extent to which the findings of the experiment apply only to the people who participated in the experiment. Researchers often seek to generalize their findings to describe people who did not participate in the experiment.

Most of the participants in psychology research are introductory psychology students in colleges and universities. Are psychologists developing principles that apply only to college freshmen and sophomores? Similarly, laboratory research is often conducted under more controlled conditions than are found in natural settings. Thus, an important task of the scientist is to determine whether laboratory findings generalize to the "real world." Some people automatically assume that laboratory research is useless or irrelevant to real-world concerns. However, as we explore research methods throughout this text, we will see that these views about the relationship between laboratory science and the "real world" are not helpful or satisfying. Instead, psychologists recognize the importance of both: Findings from laboratory experiments help to explain phenomena, and this knowledge is applied to real-world problems in research and interventions.

Application

- In applied research, psychologists apply their knowledge and research methods to improve people's lives; psychologists conduct basic research to gain knowledge about behavior and mental processes and to test theories.

The fourth goal of research in psychology is application. Although psychologists are interested in describing, predicting, and explaining behavior and mental processes, this knowledge doesn't exist in a vacuum. Instead, this knowledge exists in a world in which people suffer from mental disorders, are victims of violence and aggression, and in which stereotypes and prejudices impact how people live and function in society (to name but a few problems we face). The list of problems in our world may at times seem endless, but this shouldn't discourage us. The breadth of psychologists' research questions and findings provide many ways for researchers to help address important aspects of our lives and to create change in individuals' lives. We are likely to discover even more avenues for creating positive change as psychologists in the 21st century focus on "positive psychology"—the ways we can maximize our growth and potential (Seligman & Csikszentmihalyi, 2000).

Key Concept

Research on creating change is often called "applied research." In **applied research,** psychologists conduct research in order to change people's lives for the better. For people suffering from mental disorders, this change may occur through research on therapeutic techniques. However, applied psychologists are involved with many different types of interventions, including those aimed at improving the lives of students in schools, employees at work, and individuals in the community. On the other hand, researchers who conduct **basic research** seek primarily to understand behavior and mental processes. People often describe basic research as "seeking knowledge for its own sake." Basic research is typically carried out in a laboratory setting with the goal of testing a theory about a phenomenon.

Key Concept

SCIENTIFIC THEORY CONSTRUCTION AND TESTING

- Theories are proposed explanations for the causes of phenomena, and they vary in scope and level of explanation.
- A scientific theory is a logically organized set of propositions that defines events, describes relationships among events, and explains the occurrence of events.

- Successful scientific theories organize empirical knowledge, guide research by offering testable hypotheses, and survive rigorous testing.
- Researchers evaluate theories by judging the theory's internal consistency, observing whether hypothesized outcomes occur when the theory is tested, and noting whether the theory makes precise predictions based on parsimonious explanations.

Theories are "ideas" about how nature works. Psychologists propose theories about the nature of behavior and mental processes, as well as about the reasons people and animals behave and think the way they do. A psychological theory can be developed on different levels; for example, the theory can either be developed on a physiological or on a symbolic level (see Anderson, 1990; Simon, 1992). A physiologically-based theory of schizophrenia would propose biological causes such as specific genetic carriers. A theory developed on a symbolic level would more likely propose psychological causes such as patterns of emotional conflict or stress. It would also be possible for a theory of schizophrenia to include both biological and psychological causes. The propositions contained in theories may be expressed as verbal statements, as mathematical equations, or as computer programs.

Theories often differ in their scope—the range of phenomena they seek to explain. Some theories attempt to explain specific phenomena. For example, Brown and Kulik's (1977) theory attempted to explain the phenomenon of "flashbulb memory." A flashbulb memory refers to the finding that we remember very specific personal circumstances surrounding particularly surprising and emotional events in our lives, such as the horrific events of September 11, 2001. Other theories have much broader scope as they try to describe and explain more complex phenomena such as love (Sternberg, 1986) or human cognition (Anderson, 1990; 1993; Anderson & Milson, 1989). In general, the greater the scope of a theory, the more complex it is likely to be. Most theories in contemporary psychology tend to be relatively modest in scope, attempting to account only for a limited range of phenomena.

Scientists develop theories from a mixture of intuition, personal observation, and discovered knowledge (known facts and ideas). The famous philosopher of science, Karl Popper (1976, pp. 268–269), suggested that truly creative theories spring from a combination of "intense interest in a problem (and thus a readiness to try again and again)" and "critical imagination." Critical imagination is the ability to think critically, but there is more. Critical imagination also means traveling beyond what others have said are the boundaries of thinking about a problem—commonly referred to as thinking "outside the box." Assuming we have the necessary burning desire to pursue a problem, one fruitful path to follow in constructing a scientific theory is to examine critically what is known about the problem and to look for flaws or unseen sources of error in our existing knowledge. The approach is similar to the one we described earlier for coming up with a hypothesis when getting started on research (McGuire, 1997).

Key Concept }

Although theories differ in their level of explanation and scope, amid these differences there are commonalities that define all theories. We can offer the following formal definition of a scientific **theory:** *a logically organized set of propositions (claims, statements, assertions) that serves to define events (concepts), describe relationships among these events, and explain the occurrence of these events.* For example, a theory of flashbulb memory needs to state exactly what a flashbulb memory is, including a description of how a flashbulb memory differs from typical memories. The theory would also need to include descriptions of relationships such as the relationship between degree of emotional involvement and amount remembered. Finally, the theory would also have to explain why in some cases a person's so-called flashbulb memory is clearly wrong, even though the individual expresses high confidence in the (inaccurate) memory (see Neisser & Harsch, 1992). Such was the case in Talarico and Rubin's (2003) findings for students' memories of the September 11, 2001, terrorist attacks; despite a decrease in the accuracy of their memories over time, participants maintained confidence in their very vivid memories.

The major functions of a theory are to *organize* empirical knowledge and to *guide* research (Marx, 1963). Even in relatively specific areas like the study of flashbulb memories, there are many studies that have been done. As the scope of a theory increases to issues like love or human cognition, the body of related knowledge also grows larger. Scientific theories provide an invaluable service by presenting a logical organization of the individual findings and identifying the important relationships among the findings. In addition to providing a logical organization for a set of research findings, scientific theories guide research by suggesting testable hypotheses.

Theories frequently require that we propose intervening processes to account for observed behavior (Underwood & Shaughnessy 1975). These intervening processes provide a link between the independent variables researchers manipulate and the dependent variables they subsequently measure. Because these processes "go between" the independent and dependent variables, they are called *intervening variables*. You probably are familiar with what we mean by an intervening variable if you think about your computer use. As you press keys on the keyboard or click the "mouse," you see (and hear) various outcomes on the monitor, printer, and from the speakers. Yet it isn't your keystrokes and mouse clicks that *directly* cause these outcomes; the intervening variable is the "invisible" software that serves as a connection between your keystrokes and the outcome on your monitor.

Intervening variables are like computer software. Corresponding to the connection between keystrokes and what you see on your monitor, intervening variables connect independent and dependent variables. Another familiar example from psychology is the construct of "thirst." For example, a researcher might manipulate the number of hours participants are deprived of liquid and after the specified time measure the amount of liquid consumed. Between the deprivation time and the time participants are allowed to drink liquid, we may say that the participants are "thirsty"—the psychological experience of needing to replenish body fluids. Thirst, like computer software, is a construct that allows theorists to connect variables such as "number of hours deprived of liquid" (the independent variable) and the amount of liquid consumed (the dependent variable). Just as was true for computer software, thirst serves as an invisible connection. That is, thirst is a construct that we infer based on observations of what people do when they've been deprived of liquids for a period of time. *Intervening variables such as thirst not only link independent and dependent variables; intervening variables also are used to explain why the variables are connected.* Thus, intervening variables play an important role when researchers use theories to explain their findings.

Intervening variables and theories are useful because they allow researchers to identify relationships among seemingly dissimilar variables. Other independent variables likely influence "thirst." Consider, for example, a different independent variable: amount of salt consumed. On the surface, these two independent variables—number of hours deprived of liquid and amount of salt consumed—are very dissimilar. However, both influence subsequent consumption of liquid and can be explained by the intervening variable of thirst. Other independent variables related to liquid consumption include amount of exercise and temperature; the more exercise or the higher the temperature, the more people are "thirsty" and the more liquid they consume. Although these examples emphasize independent variables, it's important to note that dependent variables also play a role in theory development. Thus, rather than measuring "liquid consumption" as the dependent variable, inventive researchers may measure other effects related to the psychological experience of thirst. For example, when deprived of liquid, individuals may go to greater efforts to obtain liquid or may even drink liquids that taste bitter. Thus, effort to obtain liquids or the amount of bitterness in the liquid could be measured as dependent variables.

Intervening variables are critical to theory development in psychology. In our example, the apparently dissimilar variables of liquid deprivation, salt consumption, exercise, temperature, liquid consumption, effort to obtain liquid, and taste of liquids can be united in one theory that relies on the intervening variable of "thirst." Other examples of intervening variables—and theories—abound in psychology. The intervening variable of "depression," for example, connects the factors theorized to cause depression (e.g., neurological factors, exposure to trauma) and the various symptoms (e.g., sadness, hopelessness, sleep and appetite disturbance). Similarly, "memory" as an intervening variable is used to explain the relationship between the amount (or quality) of time spent studying and later performance on a test. As you will learn in your study of psychology, intervening variables provide the key that unlocks the complex relationships among variables.

How we evaluate and test scientific theories is one of the most difficult issues in psychology and philosophy (e.g., Meehl, 1978, 1990a, 1990b; Popper, 1959). Kimble (1989) has suggested a simple and straightforward approach. He says, "The best theory is the one that survives the fires of logical and empirical testing"

(p. 498). Scientists first evaluate a theory by considering whether it is logical. That is, they determine whether the theory makes sense and whether its propositions are free of contradictions. The logical consistency of theories is tested through the lens of the critical eye of the scientific community. Ideas about the exact definition of flashbulb memories, for example, have been debated at length in the psychology literature (e.g., Cohen, McCloskey, & Wible, 1990; Pillemer, 1990; Winograd & Neisser, 1992).

The second "fire" that Kimble (1989) recommends for evaluating theories is to subject hypotheses derived from a theory to empirical tests. Successful tests of a hypothesis serve to increase the acceptability of a theory; unsuccessful tests serve to decrease the theory's acceptability. The best theory, in this view, is the one that passes these tests successfully. But there are serious obstacles to testing hypotheses and, as a consequence, confirming or disconfirming scientific theories. For example, a theory, especially a complex one, may produce many specific testable hypotheses. A theory is not likely to fail on the basis of a single test (e.g., Lakatos, 1978). Moreover, theories may include propositions and concepts that have not been adequately defined or suggest intervening processes that are related to behavior and to each other in complex and even mysterious ways. Such theories may have a long life, but their value to science is questionable (Meehl, 1978). Ultimately, it is the judgment of the scientific community that determines whether any test of a theory is definitive.

In general, theories that provide *precision of prediction* are likely to be much more useful (Meehl, 1990a). For example, a theory that predicts that children will typically demonstrate abstract reasoning by age 12 is more precise (and testable) in its predictions than a theory that predicts the development of abstract reasoning by ages 12 to 20. When constructing and evaluating a theory, scientists also place a premium on parsimony (Marx, 1963). The *rule of parsimony* is followed when the simplest of alternative explanations is accepted. Scientists prefer theories that provide the simplest explanations for phenomena. As part of a study in 1932 of productive thinking, Erika Fromm sent letters to 100 leading scientists and philosophers asking them about the cognitive "process that occurred when [he] had [his] most productive thought" (Fromm, 1998, p. 1195). Albert Einstein's response included a concise illustration of the rule of parsimony when he described the nature of thinking that led to his theory of relativity:

> It was always the search for a logically simple meaning of empirically established relationships, propelled by the conviction that there existed a simple logical meaning. (Fromm, 1998)

In summary, a good scientific theory is one that is able to pass the most rigorous tests. Somewhat counterintuitively, rigorous testing will be more informative when researchers do tests that seek to *falsify* a theory's propositions than when they do tests that seek to confirm them (Shadish, Cook, & Campbell, 2002). Although tests that confirm a particular theory's propositions do provide support for the specific theory that is being tested, confirmation logically does not rule out other, alternative theories of the same phenomenon. Tests of falsification are the best way to prune a theory of its dead branches. Constructing and evaluating scientific theories is at the core of the scientific enterprise and is absolutely essential for the healthy growth of the science of psychology.

SUMMARY

As an approach to knowledge, the scientific method is characterized by a reliance on empirical procedures, rather than relying only on intuition, and by an attempt to control the investigation of those factors believed responsible for a phenomenon. Scientists gain the greatest control when they conduct an experiment. In an experiment, those factors that are systematically manipulated in an attempt to determine their effect on behavior are called independent variables. The measures of behavior used to assess the effect (if any) of the independent variables are called dependent variables.

Scientists seek to report results in an unbiased and objective manner. This goal is enhanced by giving operational definitions to concepts. Psychological researchers refer to concepts as "constructs." Scientists also use instruments that are as accurate and precise as possible. Phenomena are quantified with both physical and psychological measurement. Scientists seek measures that have both validity and reliability. Hypotheses are tentative explanations of events. To be useful to the scientist, however, hypotheses must be testable. Hypotheses that lack adequate definition, that are circular, or that appeal to ideas or forces outside the province of science are not testable. Hypotheses are often derived from theories.

The goals of the scientific method are description, prediction, explanation, and application. Both quantitative and qualitative research are used to describe behavior. Observation is the principal basis of scientific description. When two measures correlate, we can predict the value of one measure by knowing the value of the other. Understanding and explanation are achieved when the causes of a phenomenon are discovered. This requires that evidence be provided for co-variation of events, that a time-order relationship exists, and that alternative causes be eliminated. When two potentially effective variables covary such that the independent effect of each variable on behavior cannot be determined, we say that our research is confounded. Even when a carefully controlled experiment allows the researcher to form a causal inference, additional questions remain concerning the extent to which the findings may generalize to describe other people and settings. In applied research, psychologists strive to apply their knowledge and research methods to improve people's lives. Basic research is conducted to gain knowledge about behavior and mental processes and to test theories.

Scientific theory construction and testing are at the core of the scientific approach to psychology. A theory is defined as a logically organized set of propositions that serves to define events, describe relationships among these events, and explain the occurrence of the events. Theories have the important functions of organizing empirical knowledge and guiding research by offering testable hypotheses. Intervening variables are critical to theory development in psychology because these constructs allow researchers to explain the relationships between independent and dependent variables.

KEY CONCEPTS

control
experiment
independent variable
dependent variable
construct
operational definition
validity

reliability
correlation
causal inference
confounding
applied research
basic research
theory

REVIEW QUESTIONS

1 For each of the following characteristics, distinguish between the scientific approach and everyday approaches to knowledge: general approach, observation, reporting, concepts, instruments, measurement, and hypotheses.

2 Differentiate between an independent variable and a dependent variable, and provide an example of each that could be used in an experiment.

3 What is the major advantage of using operational definitions in psychology? In what two ways has the use of operational definitions been criticized?

4 Distinguish between the accuracy and the precision of a measuring instrument.

5 What is the difference between the validity of a measure and the reliability of a measure?

6 What three characteristics are used to describe testable hypotheses?

7 Identify the four goals of the scientific method and briefly describe what each goal is intended to accomplish.

8 Distinguish between the nomothetic approach and the idiographic approach in terms of who is studied and the nature of the generalizations that are sought.

9 What is the value of knowing that two variables are correlated (i.e., what does this allow researchers to do)?

10 Give an example from a research study described in the text that illustrates each of the three conditions for a causal inference. [You may use the same example for more than one condition.]

11 What is the difference between basic and applied research?

12 What is an intervening variable? Propose a psychological construct that could serve as an intervening variable between "insult" (present/absent) and "aggressive responses." Explain how these variables might be related by proposing a hypothesis that includes your intervening variable.

13 Describe the roles of logical consistency and empirical testing in evaluating a scientific theory.

14 Explain why rigorous tests of a theory that seek to falsify a theory's propositions can be more informative than tests that seek to confirm a theory's propositions.

CHALLENGE QUESTIONS

1 In each of the following descriptions of research studies, you are to identify the independent variable(s). You should also be able to identify at least one dependent variable in each study.

A A psychologist was interested in the effect of food deprivation on motor activity. She assigned each of 60 rats to one of four conditions differing in the length of time for which the animals were deprived of food: 0 hours, 8 hours, 16 hours, 24 hours. She then measured the amount of time the animals spent in the activity wheel in their cages.

B A physical education instructor was interested in specifying the changes in motor coordination that occur as children gain experience with large playground equipment (e.g., slides, swings, climbing walls). For a span of 8 weeks, preschool children were assigned to 4, 6, or 8 hours per week for time allowed on the equipment. She then tested their motor coordination by asking them to skip, jump, and stand on one foot.

C A developmental psychologist was interested in the amount of verbal behavior very young children displayed depending on who else was present. The children in the study were 3 years old. These children were observed in a laboratory setting for a 30-minute period. Half of the children were assigned to a condition in which an adult was present with the child during the session. The other half of the children were assigned to a condition in which another young child was present during the session with the child being observed. The psychologist measured the number, duration, and complexity of the verbal utterances of each observed child.

2 A physiological psychologist developed a drug that she thought would revolutionize the world of horse racing. She named the drug Speedo, and it was her contention that this drug would lead horses to run much faster than they do now. (For the sake of this hypothetical problem, we are ignoring the fact that it is illegal to give drugs to racehorses.) She selected two groups of horses and gave one of the groups injections of Speedo once a week for 4 weeks. Because Speedo was known to have some negative effects on the horses' digestive systems, those horses given the Speedo had to be placed on a special high-protein diet. Those horses not given the Speedo were maintained on their regular diet. After the 4-week period, all the horses were timed in a 2-mile race and the mean (average) times for the horses given Speedo were significantly faster than the mean times for those not given Speedo. The psychologist concluded that her drug was effective.

A Identify the independent variable of interest (and its levels) and a potentially relevant independent variable with which the primary independent variable is confounded. Explain clearly how the confounding occurred.

B State exactly what conclusion can be supported on the basis of the evidence presented.

C Finally, suggest ways in which the study could be done so that you could make a clear conclusion about the effectiveness of the drug Speedo.

3 The *New York Times* reported the results of a 2-year, $1.5 million study by researchers at Carnegie Mellon University funded by the National Science Foundation and major technology companies. There were 169 participants in the study drawn from the Pittsburgh area. The researchers examined the relationship between Internet use and psychological well-being. A director of the study stated that the study did not involve testing extreme amounts of Internet use. The participants were normal adults and their families. On average, for those who used the Internet the most, psychological well-being was worse. For example, one hour a week of Internet use led to slight increases on a depression scale and on a loneliness scale and a reported decline in personal interaction with family members. The researchers concluded that Internet use appears to cause a decline in psychological well-being. They suggested that users of the Internet were building shallow relationships that led to an overall decline in feelings of connection to other people.

A The researchers claim that use of the Internet leads to a decline in people's well-being. What evidence is present in this summary of the report to meet the conditions necessary for drawing this causal inference and what evidence is lacking?

B What sources beyond this question would you want to check before reaching a conclusion about the findings reported here? [You might begin with the *New York Times* piece, "The Lonely Net," August 30, 1998 and the *Washington Post* piece, "Net Depression Study Criticized," September 7, 1998.]

C What effect would there be on your evaluation of this study given that it was funded in part by major technology companies?

4 A study was done to determine whether taking notes in a developmental psychology course affected

students' test performance. Students recorded their notes over the entire semester in a 125-page study guide. The study guide included questions on course content covered both in the textbook and in class lectures. Students' notes were measured using three dimensions: completeness, length, and accuracy. Results of the study indicated that students with more accurate notes performed better on essay and multiple-choice tests in the course than did students with less accurate notes. Based on these findings, the researchers suggested that instructors should use instructional techniques such as pausing for brief periods during the lecture and asking questions to clarify information. The researchers argued that these techniques could facilitate the accuracy of the notes students take in class, and that accurate note taking could contribute significantly to students' overall success in college courses.

A What evidence is present in this report to meet the conditions for a causal inference between accuracy of students' notes and their test performance? What evidence is lacking? (Be sure to identify clearly the three conditions for a causal inference.)

B Identify a goal of the scientific method that could be met on the basis of findings of this study.

Answer to Stretching Exercise

1   The independent variable in this study is the type of the TV program in which the commercial is presented. The levels of the independent variable are: violent TV program and nonviolent TV program. The dependent variable is the participants' memory for the content of the commercial as measured by recall and recognition memory tests.

2   When an independent variable is manipulated at two levels, there are always two possible interpretations when the dependent variable differs between the two levels. Either one of the conditions resulted in better performance or the other condition led to poorer performance. (If two people differ in height, it is equally true that one is taller and the other is shorter.) In this case the researchers interpreted their findings by saying that violent TV programs *decreased* memory for the commercials. There is no way with only two levels (violent and nonviolent TV programs) to refute the alternative interpretation that nonviolent TV programs *increased* memory for the commercials. One way to distinguish these two interpretations is to manipulate the independent variable of interest using three levels. In this case, we could vary the independent variable of the nature of the TV program at three levels: positive, neutral, and violent. The interpretation that violent programs decrease memory would be supported if memory for the commercial did not differ for the positive and neutral programs but was worse for the violent programs. On the other hand, the interpretation that nonviolent (positive) programs increased memory would be supported if memory for the commercial for the violent and neutral programs did not differ but memory was better for the positive programs. Other patterns of findings could occur when this independent variable is manipulated at three levels. The most important idea to take away from this exercise is that how we manipulate an independent variable has a strong influence on how we can interpret our findings.

Answer to Challenge Question 1

A Independent Variable (IV): hours of food deprivation with four levels; Dependent Variable (DV): time (e.g. in minutes) animals spent in activity wheel

B IV: time on playground equipment with three levels: 4, 6, or 8 hours per week; DV: scores on test of motor coordination

C IV: additional person present with two levels (present, absent); DV: number, duration, and complexity of child's verbal utterances

CHAPTER THREE

Ethical Issues in the Conduct of Psychological Research

CHAPTER OUTLINE

INTRODUCTION

Good science requires good scientists. Scientists' professional competence and integrity are essential for ensuring high quality science. Maintaining the integrity of the scientific process is a shared responsibility of individual scientists and the community of scientists (as represented by professional organizations such as APA and APS). Each individual scientist has an ethical responsibility to seek knowledge and to strive to improve the quality of life. Diener and Crandall (1978) identify several specific responsibilities that follow from this general mandate. Scientists should:

—carry out research in a competent manner;
—report results accurately;
—manage research resources honestly;
—fairly acknowledge, in scientific communications, the individuals who have contributed their ideas or their time and effort;
—consider the consequences to society of any research endeavor;
—speak out publicly on societal concerns related to a scientist's knowledge and expertise.

In striving to meet these obligations, individual scientists face challenging and, at times, ambiguous ethical issues and questions. To guide individual psychologists in making ethical decisions, the American Psychological Association (APA) has formulated an Ethics Code that "provides a common set of principles and standards upon which psychologists build their professional and scientific work" (American Psychological Association, 2002, p. 1062). These values are summarized in five General Principles: Beneficence and Non-maleficence; Fidelity and Responsibility; Integrity; Justice; and Respect for People's Rights and Dignity. Based on these five general principles, the APA Ethics Code sets forth standards for ethical behavior for psychologists who do research or therapy or who teach or serve as administrators (see American Psychological Association, 2002). The Ethics Code deals with such diverse issues as sexual harassment, fees for psychological services, providing advice to the public in the media, test construction, and classroom teaching.

As stated in the Preamble to the Ethics Code, psychologists are expected to make "a personal commitment and lifelong effort to act ethically; to encourage ethical behavior by students, supervisees, employees, and colleagues; and to consult with others concerning ethical problems" (American Psychological Association, 2002, p. 1062). It is also important for all students of psychology to make every effort to live up to these stated ideals and standards of behavior. You can familiarize yourself with the Ethics Code by going to the APA website [http://www.apa.org/ethics].

Many of the ethical standards in the APA Ethics Code deal directly with psychological research (see especially Standards 8.01 to 8.15 of the Code), including the treatment of both humans and animals in psychological research. As with most ethical codes, the standards tend to be general in nature and require specific definition in particular contexts. More than one ethical standard can apply to a specific research situation, and at times the standards may even appear to contradict one another. For instance, ethical research requires that human participants be protected from physical injury. Research that involves drugs or other invasive treatments, however, may place participants at risk of physical harm. The welfare of animal subjects should be protected, but certain kinds of research may involve inflicting pain or other suffering on an animal. Solving these ethical dilemmas is not always easy and requires a deliberate, conscientious problem-solving approach to ethical decision making.

The Internet has changed the way many scientists do research, and psychologists are no exception. Researchers from around the world, for example, often collaborate on scientific projects and can now quickly and easily exchange ideas and findings with one another via the Internet. Vast quantities of archival information are accessible though government-sponsored Internet sites (e.g., U.S. Census Bureau). In the last decades of the 20th century, researchers began to collect data from human participants via the World Wide Web. There is the potential to include *millions* of people in one study! Types of psychological research on the Internet include simple observation (e.g., recording "behavior" in chat rooms), surveys (questionnaires, including personality tests), and experiments involving manipulated variables.

Although the Internet offers many opportunities for the behavioral scientist, it also raises many ethical concerns. Major issues arise due to the absence of the researcher in an online research setting, the difficulty of obtaining adequate informed consent and providing debriefing, and concerns about protecting participant confidentiality (see especially Kraut et al., 2004, and Nosek, Banaji, & Greenwald, 2002, for reviews of these problems and some suggested solutions). We discuss some of these ethical issues in the present chapter and also continue this discussion in later chapters when we describe specific research methods.

Ethical decisions are best made after consultation with others, including one's peers but especially those who are more experienced or knowledgeable in a particular area. In fact, review of a research plan by people not involved in the research is legally required in some situations. In the remaining sections of this chapter, we identify those standards from the Ethics Code that deal specifically with psychological research. We also offer a brief commentary on some aspects of these standards and present several hypothetical research scenarios that raise ethical questions. By putting yourself in the position of having to make judgments about the ethical issues raised in these research proposals, you will begin to learn to grapple with the challenges that arise in applying particular ethical standards and with the difficulties of ethical decision making in general. We urge you to discuss these proposals with peers, professors, and others who have had prior experience doing psychological research.

ETHICAL ISSUES TO CONSIDER BEFORE BEGINNING RESEARCH

- Prior to conducting any study, the proposed research must be reviewed to determine if it meets ethical standards.

Researchers must begin to consider ethical issues before they begin a research project. Ethical problems can be avoided only by planning carefully and consulting with appropriate individuals and groups *prior to doing the research.* The failure to conduct research in an ethical manner undermines the entire scientific process, impedes the advancement of knowledge, and erodes the public's respect for scientific and academic communities. It can also lead to significant legal and financial penalties for individuals and institutions. The following ethical standards from the APA Ethics Code (American Psychological Association, 2002, pp. 1069–1071) describe the most important issues that researchers must address as they begin to do psychological research.

APA Ethical Standards

8.01 Institutional Approval   When institutional approval is required, psychologists provide accurate information about their research proposals and obtain approval prior to conducting the research. They conduct the research in accordance with the approved research protocol.

Commentary

- Institutional Review Boards (IRBs) review psychological research to protect the rights and welfare of human participants.
- Institutional Animal Care and Use Committees (IACUCs) review research conducted with animals to ensure that animals are treated humanely.

The National Research Act, signed into law in 1974, resulted in the creation of the National Commission for the Protection of Human Subjects of Biomedical and Behavioral Research. This act requires that institutions that seek research funds from specific federal agencies must establish committees to review research sponsored by the institution. Colleges and universities have established these committees that are referred to as *Institutional Review Boards (IRBs).* You can review the federal regulations for IRBs at the website [http://www.hhs.gov/ohrp]. The IRB review is done so the institution can ensure that researchers protect participants from harm and safeguard participants' rights. Federal regulations impose very specific requirements on the membership and duties of IRBs (see *Federal Register,* June 18, 1991). For example, an IRB must be composed of at least five members with varying backgrounds and fields of expertise. Both scientists and nonscientists must be represented, and there must be at least one IRB member who is not affiliated with the institution. Responsible members of the community, such as members of the clergy, lawyers, and nurses, are often asked to serve on these committees.

FIGURE 3.1   Many ethical questions are raised when research is performed with humans.

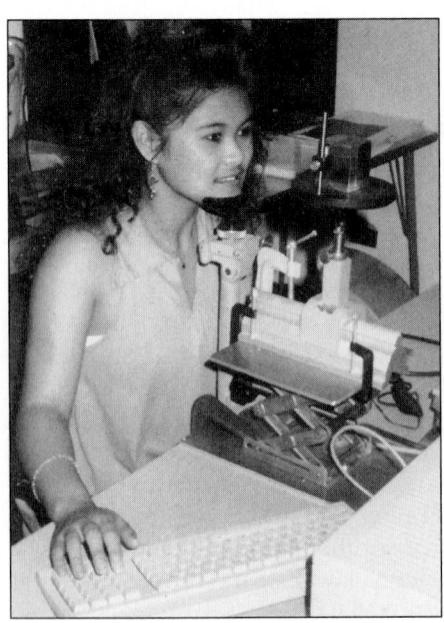
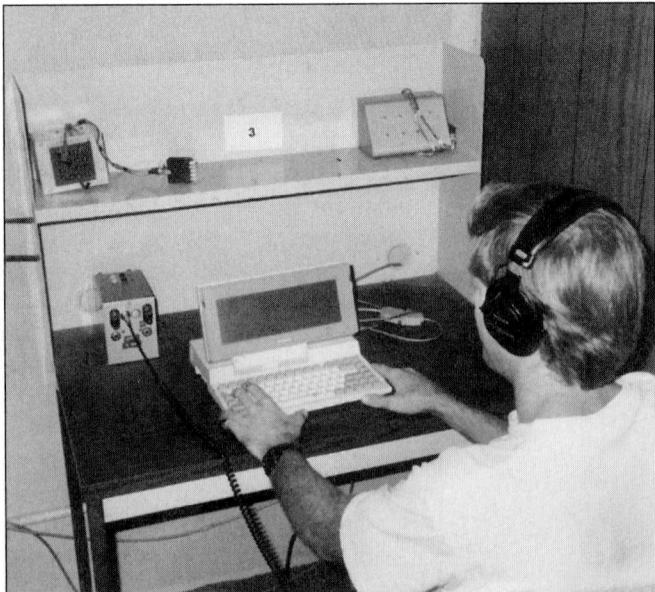

FIGURE 3.2   Following World War II, the Nuremberg War Crimes Court charged German doctors with crimes against humanity, which included performing medical experiments on human beings without their consent. The Court's verdict in these cases led to the development of the Nuremberg Code, which set rules for permissible experimentation with human beings.

A psychology student seeking to do research with human participants is likely to submit a research proposal to a department committee charged with reviewing research conducted in the psychology department. Depending on the association of this departmental committee with an IRB, research falling into various well-defined categories is either reviewed at the departmental level or referred to the IRB for review. The IRB has the authority to approve, disapprove, or require modifications of the research plan prior to their approval of the research. The IRB also has the ethical responsibility to make sure that their review of the research proposals is fair by considering the perspectives of the institution, the researcher, and the research participants (Chastain & Landrum, 1999).

In 1985, the Department of Agriculture, as well as the Public Health Service, formulated new guidelines for the care of laboratory animals (Holden, 1987). As a result, institutions doing research with animal subjects are now required to have an Institutional Animal Care and Use Committee (IACUC). These committees must include, minimally, a scientist, a veterinarian, and at least one person not affiliated with the institution. Review of animal research by IACUCs extends to more than simply overseeing the research procedures. Federal regulations governing the conduct of animal research extend to specifications of animal living quarters and the proper training of personnel who work directly with the animals (Holden, 1987).

Nearly every college and university require that all research conducted at the institution be reviewed at some stage by an independent committee. Violation of federal regulations regarding the review of research involving humans or animals can bring a halt to research at an institution, spell the loss of federal funds, and result in substantial fines (Holden, 1987). Given the complex nature of federal regulations and the policies of most institutions requiring review of research with humans and animals, *any individual who wants to do research should inquire of the proper authorities, prior to starting research, about the appropriate procedure for institutional review.* Helpful advice is available for students planning to submit a research proposal to an IRB (McCallum, 2001) or to an IACUC (LeBlanc, 2001).

THE RISK/BENEFIT RATIO

- A subjective evaluation of the risks and benefits of a research project is used to determine whether the research should be conducted.

In addition to checking if appropriate ethical principles are being followed, an IRB considers the *risk/benefit ratio* for a study. Society and individuals benefit from research when new knowledge is gained and when treatments are identified that improve people's lives. There are also potential costs when research is *not* done. We miss the opportunity to gain knowledge and, ultimately, we lose the opportunity to improve the human condition. Research can also be costly to individual participants. For example, research participants risk injury when exposed to potentially harmful circumstances. The principal investigator must, of course, be the first one to consider these potential costs and benefits. An IRB is made up of knowledgeable individuals who do not have a personal interest in the research. As such, an IRB is in a better position to determine the risk/benefit ratio and, ultimately, to decide whether to approve the proposed research.

Key Concept }

The **risk/benefit ratio** asks the question, *Is it worth it?* There are no mathematical answers to the risk/benefit ratio. Instead, when deciding whether to approve a research proposal, members of an IRB strive to reach consensus on a subjective evaluation of the risks and benefits both to individual participants and to society. When the risks outweigh the potential benefits, then the IRB does not approve the research; when the benefits outweigh the risks, the IRB approves the research. Many factors affect a decision regarding the proper balance of risks and benefits of a research activity. The most basic are the nature of the risk and the magnitude of the probable benefit to the participant as well as the potential scientific and social value of the research (Fisher & Fryberg, 1994). We can tolerate greater risk when we foresee clear and immediate benefits to individuals or when we judge that the research has obvious scientific and social value. For instance, a research project investigating a new treatment for psychotic behavior may entail risk for the participants. If the proposed treatment has a good chance of having a beneficial effect, however, then the possible benefits to both the individuals and society could outweigh the risk involved in the study.

In determining the risk/benefit ratio, researchers also consider whether valid and interpretable results will be produced. Rosenthal (1994b) makes a strong case for considering the quality of the research as a factor in the ethical review of proposed research. "Everything else being equal, research that is of a higher scientific quality is more ethically defensible" (p. 127). More specifically, "If because of the poor quality of the science no good can come of a research study, how are we to justify the use of participants' time, attention, and effort and the money, space, supplies, and other resources that have been expended on the research project?" (Rosenthal, 1994b, p. 128). Thus, *an investigator is obliged to seek to do research that meets the highest standards of scientific excellence.*

When there is potential risk, a researcher must make sure there are no alternative, low-risk procedures that could be substituted. The researcher must also be sure that previous research has not already successfully addressed the research question being asked. Without careful prior review of the psychological literature, a researcher might carry out research that has already been done, thus exposing individuals to needless risk.

Determining Risk

- Potential risks in psychological research include risk of physical injury, social injury, and mental or emotional stress.
- Risks must be evaluated in terms of potential participants' everyday activities, their physical and mental health, and capabilities.

Determining whether research participants are "at risk" illustrates the difficulties involved in ethical decision making. Life itself is a risky affair. Commuting to work or school, crossing streets, and riding on elevators are all activities that have an element of risk. Simply showing up for a psychology experiment has some degree of risk. To say that human participants in psychological research can never face any risks would bring all research to a halt. Decisions about what constitutes risk must take into consideration those risks that are part of everyday life.

We must also consider the characteristics of the participants when we determine risk. Certain activities might pose a serious risk for some individuals but not for others. Running up a flight of stairs may increase the risk of a heart attack for an elderly person, but the same task would probably not be risky for most young adults. Similarly, individuals who are exceptionally depressed or anxious might show more severe reactions to certain psychological tasks than would other people. Thus, when considering risk, researchers must consider the specific populations or individuals who are likely to participate in the study.

We often think of risk in terms of the possibility of physical injury. Frequently, however, participants in social science research risk social or psychological injury. The potential for social risk exists when information gained about individuals through their participation in psychological research is revealed to others. If someone found out that an individual completed a questionnaire inquiring about deviant sexual practices, there is the potential for a social risk for that individual, such as embarrassment. Personal information collected during psychological research may include facts about intelligence, personality traits, and political, social, or religious beliefs. A research participant probably does not want this personal information revealed to teachers, employers, or peers. If researchers do not protect the confidentiality of participants' responses, the social risk for these participants may increase. It has been suggested that the greatest risk to participants in Internet-based research is the possible disclosure of identifiable personal information outside the research situation (Kraut et al., 2004). Other researchers suggest that although the Internet affords a "perception of anonymity" (Nosek, et al., 2002, p. 165), in some circumstances that perception is false, and investigators must consider ways to protect confidentiality in data transmission, data storage, and post-study interactions with participants.

Some psychological research may pose psychological risk if participants in the study experience serious mental or emotional stress. Imagine the stress a participant may experience when smoke enters the room in which she is waiting. The smoke may be entering the room so the researcher can simulate an emergency. Until the true nature of the smoke is revealed, participants may experience considerable distress. In addition, simply participating in a psychology experiment is anxiety-provoking for some individuals. After learning a list of nonsense syllables, a student participant once said that he was sure the researcher now knew a great deal about him! The student assumed the psychologist was interested in learning about his personality by examining the word associations he used when learning the list. In reality, this person was participating in a simple memory experiment designed to measure forgetting. *A researcher is obligated to protect participants from emotional or mental stress, including, when possible, stress that might arise due to participants' misconceptions about the psychological task.*

Minimal Risk

- A study is described as involving "minimal risk" when the procedures or activities in the study are similar to those experienced by participants in their everyday life.

Key Concept   }

A distinction is sometimes made between a participant "at risk" and one who is "at minimal risk." **Minimal risk** means that the harm or discomfort participants may experience in the research *is not greater than* what they might experience in their daily lives or during routine physical or psychological tests. As an example of minimal risk, consider the fact that many psychology laboratory studies involve lengthy paper-and-pencil tests intended to assess various mental abilities. Participants may be asked to complete the tests quickly and may receive specific feedback about their performance. Although there is likely to be stress in this situation, the risk of psychological injury is likely no greater than that of being a student. Therefore, such studies would involve only minimal risk for college students. When the possibility of injury is judged to be more than minimal, individuals are considered to be *at risk*. When a study places participants at risk, the researcher has more serious obligations to protect their welfare.

Dealing with Risk

- Whether "at risk" or "at minimal risk," research participants must be protected. More safeguards are needed as risks become greater.
- To protect participants from social risks, information they provide should be anonymous, or if that is not possible, the confidentiality of their information should be maintained.

Even if the potential risk is small, researchers should try to minimize risk and protect participants. For instance, the level of stress that some participants experience can be reduced simply by stating at the beginning of a memory experiment that the tasks are not intended to measure intelligence or personality. In situations where the possibility of harm is judged to be significantly greater than that occurring in daily life, the researcher's obligation to protect participants increases correspondingly. For example, when participants are exposed to the possibility of serious emotional stress in a psychology experiment, an IRB could require that a clinical psychologist be available to counsel individuals about their experience in the study. As you can imagine, online research poses difficult ethical dilemmas in this regard. Participants can experience emotional distress in the context of an Internet study just as they do in a laboratory-based study. Thus, in some research situations, online participants might be at risk, and a risk/benefit evaluation must be made by an IRB. However, because the researcher is absent from the research situation, "the special concern is that researchers may have a diminished ability to monitor subjects in online research and remediate any harm caused by the research" (Kraut et al., 2004, p. 112). One approach might be to obtain preliminary data with the goal of identifying those who might be at risk and excluding them from the actual study. It may be the case, however, that studies with high risk may not be ethically performed on the Internet (Kraut et al., 2004).

No research activity involving more than minimal risk to participants should be carried out unless alternative methods of data collection with lower risk have been explored. In some cases, descriptive approaches involving observation or questionnaires should be used instead of experimental treatments. Researchers can also take advantage of naturally occurring "treatments" that do not involve experimentally inducing stress. For example, Anderson (1976) interviewed owner-managers of small businesses that had been damaged by hurricane floods. He found that there was an optimum level of stress that led to effective problem-solving and coping behaviors by the participants. Above or below this optimum stress level, problem-solving performance decreased. A similar relationship has been demonstrated in a number of experimental laboratory tasks using experimenter-induced stress.

In order to protect research participants from social injury, data collection should keep participants' responses anonymous by asking participants not to use their names or any identifying information. When this is not possible, researchers should keep participants' responses confidential by removing any identifying information from their records of their responses during the research. When the researcher must test people on more than one occasion or otherwise

STRETCHING EXERCISE

For each of the following research situations, you are to decide whether "minimal risk" is present (i.e., risk not greater than that of everyday life) or if participants are "at risk." If you decide that participants are "at risk," you might think of what recommendations you would make to the researcher to safeguard the participants by reducing the risk. As you do so, you will undoubtedly begin to anticipate some of the ethical issues yet to be discussed in this chapter.

1 College students are asked to complete an adjective checklist describing their current mood. The researcher is seeking to identify students who are depressed so that they can be included in a study examining cognitive deficits associated with depression.

2 Elderly adults in a nursing home are given a battery of achievement tests in the dayroom at their home. A psychologist seeks to determine if there is a decline in mental functioning with advancing age.

3 Students in a psychology research methods class see another student enter their classroom in the middle of the class period, speak loudly and angrily with the instructor, and then leave. As part of a study of eyewitness testimony, the students are then asked to describe the intruder.

4 A researcher recruits students from introductory psychology classes to participate in a study of the effects of alcohol on cognitive functioning. The experiment requires that some students drink 2 ounces of alcohol (mixed with orange juice) before performing a computer game.

track specific individuals, numbers can be randomly assigned to participants at the beginning of a study. Only these numbers need appear on participants' response sheets. If the information supplied by participants is particularly sensitive, a coding scheme may be useful to minimize social risk. One procedure is to assign code numbers to participants. Names are then linked with the code numbers on a master list and access to this list is restricted by keeping it under lock and key. Online researchers need to be particularly sensitive to the possibility of electronic eavesdropping or hacking of stored data and must take appropriate precautions (see Kraut et al., 2004).

Making sure participants' responses are anonymous or confidential can also benefit the researcher if this leads participants to be more honest and open when responding (Blanck, Bellack, Rosnow, Rotheram-Borus, & Schooler, 1992). Participants will be less likely to lie or withhold information if they do not worry about who will have access to their responses.

Informed Consent

- Researchers and participants enter into a social contract, often using an informed consent procedure.
- Researchers are ethically obligated to describe the research procedures clearly, identify any potential risks that might influence individuals' willingness to participate, and answer any questions participants have about the research.
- Research participants are ethically obligated to behave appropriately during the research by not lying, cheating, or engaging in other fraudulent behavior.

FIGURE 3.3   The U.S. Public Health Service between 1932 and 1972 examined the course of untreated
syphilis in poor African American men from Macon County, Alabama, who had not given
informed consent. They were unaware they had syphilis and their disease was left untreated.

Successful psychological research depends on the willingness of students,
patients, clients, and other members of the community to take part in a scientific
investigation. In some research, participants are given money or other compensation for their time and effort. Often, people simply volunteer to participate in
research with no compensation. In either case, the researcher and the participant enter into a social contract. As part of this contract, *a researcher has an ethical
responsibility to make clear to the participant what the research entails, including any
possible risk to the participant, and to respect the dignity and rights of the individual
during the research experience.* Researchers must make every effort to ensure that
they obtain the *informed consent* of participants to take part in the research.

The research participants who consent to participate in research also have
ethical responsibilities to behave in an appropriate manner. For example,
participants should pay attention to instructions and perform tasks in the manner
requested by the researcher. Taylor and Shepperd (1996) describe a study that illustrates the possible consequences when participants do not behave responsibly.
In the study, participants were briefly left alone by an experimenter who admon-
ished them not to discuss the experiment among themselves. Once they were

alone, however, the participants talked about the experiment and obtained information from each other that in effect negated the value of the research. Moreover, when the experimenter later asked the participants about what they knew of the procedures and goals of the study, none revealed that they had gained important knowledge about the study during their illicit conversation. This example illustrates the broader principle that *lying, cheating, or other fraudulent behavior by research participants violates the scientific integrity of the research situation.*

APA Ethical Standards

3.10 Informed Consent

(a) When psychologists conduct research or provide assessment, therapy, counseling, or consulting services in person or via electronic transmission or other forms of communication, they obtain the informed consent of the individual or individuals using language that is reasonably understandable to that person or persons except when conducting such activities without consent as mandated or prescribed by law or governmental regulation or as otherwise provided in this Ethics Code. The content of informed consent will vary depending on many circumstances; however, informed consent ordinarily requires that the person (1) has the capacity to consent, (2) has been provided information concerning participation in the activity that reasonably might affect his or her willingness to participate including limits of confidentiality and monetary or other costs or reimbursements, (3) is aware of the voluntary nature of participation and has freely and without undue influence expressed consent, and (4) has had the opportunity to ask questions and receive answers regarding the activities. (See also Standards 8.02, Informed Consent to Research; 9.03, Informed Consent in Assessments; and 10.01, Informed Consent to Therapy.)

(b) For persons who are legally incapable of giving informed consent, psychologists nevertheless (1) provide an appropriate explanation, (2) seek the individual's assent, (3) consider such persons' preferences and best interests, and (4) obtain appropriate permission from a legally authorized person, if such substitute consent is permitted or required by law. When consent by a legally authorized person is not permitted or required by law, psychologists take reasonable steps to protect the individual's rights and welfare.

(c) When psychological services are court ordered or otherwise mandated, psychologists inform the individual of the nature of the anticipated services, including whether the services are court ordered or mandated and any limits of confidentiality, before proceeding.

(d) Psychologists appropriately document written or oral consent, permission, and assent. (See also Standards 8.02, Informed Consent to Research; 9.03, Informed Consent in Assessments; and 10.01, Informed Consent to Therapy.)

8.02 Informed Consent to Research

(a) When obtaining informed consent as required in Standard 3.10, Informed Consent, psychologists inform participants about (1) the purpose of the research, expected duration, and procedures; (2) their right to decline to participate and to withdraw from the research once participation has begun; (3) the foreseeable consequences of declining or withdrawing; (4) reasonably foreseeable factors that may be expected to influence their willingness to participate such as potential risks, discomfort, or adverse effects; (5) any prospective research benefits; (6) limits of confidentiality; (7) incentives for participation; and (8) whom to contact for questions about the research and research participants' rights. They provide opportunity for the prospective participants to ask questions and receive answers. (See also Standards 8.03, Informed Consent for Recording Voices and Images in Research; 8.05, Dispensing with Informed Consent for Research; and 8.07, Deception in Research.)

   (b) Psychologists conducting intervention research involving the use of experimental treatments clarify to participants at the outset of the research (1) the experimental nature of the treatment; (2) the services that will or will not be available in the control group(s) if appropriate; (3) the means by which assignment to treatment and control groups will be made; (4) available treatment alternatives if an individual does not wish to participate in the research or wishes to withdraw once a study has begun; and (5) compensation for or monetary costs of participating including, if appropriate, whether reimbursement from the participant or a third-party will be sought. (See also Standard 8.02a, Informed Consent to Research.)

8.03 Informed Consent for Recording Voice and Images in Research

Psychologists obtain informed consent from research participants prior to recording their voice or image for data collection unless (1) the research consists solely of naturalistic observation in public places and it is not anticipated that the recording will be used in a manner that would cause personal identification or harm or (2) the research design includes deception and consent is obtained during debriefing. (See also Standard 8.07, Deception in Research.)

8.04 Client/Patient, Student, and Subordinate Research Participants

   (a) When psychologists conduct research with clients/patients, students, or subordinates as participants, psychologists take steps to protect the prospective participants from adverse consequences of declining or withdrawing from participation.

   (b) When research participation is a course requirement or opportunity for extra credit, the prospective participant is given the choice of equitable alternative activities.

8.05 Dispensing with Informed Consent for Research

Psychologists may dispense with informed consent only (1) where research would not reasonably be assumed to create distress or harm and involves (a) the study of normal educational practices, curricula, or classroom management methods conducted in educational settings; (b) only anonymous questionnaires, naturalistic observation, or archival research for which disclosure of responses would not place participants at risk of criminal or civil liability or damage their financial standing, employability, or reputation, and confidentiality is protected; or (c) the study of factors related to job or organization effectiveness conducted in organizational settings for which there is not risk to participants' employability, and confidentiality is protected or (2) where otherwise permitted by law or federal or institutional regulations.

8.06 Offering Inducements for Research Participants

(a) Psychologists make reasonable efforts to avoid offering excessive or inappropriate financial or other inducements for research participation, when such inducements are likely to coerce participation.

(b) When offering professional services as an inducement for research participation, psychologists clarify the nature of the services, as well as the risks, obligations, and limitations. (See also Standard 6.05, Barter with Clients/Patients.)

4.01 Maintaining Confidentiality Psychologists have a primary obligation and take reasonable precautions to protect confidential information obtained through or stored in any medium, recognizing that the extent and limits of confidentiality may be regulated by law or established by institutional rules or professional or scientific relationship. (See also Standard 2.05, Delegation of Work to Others.)

Commentary

- Potential research participants must be made aware of all aspects of the study that may influence their willingness to participate.
- Research participants must be allowed to withdraw their consent at any time without penalties.
- Individuals must not be pressured to participate in research.
- Informed consent must be obtained from legal guardians for individuals unable to provide consent (e.g., children, mentally impaired individuals); assent to participate should be obtained from individuals unable to provide informed consent.
- Researchers should consult with knowledgeable others, including an IRB, when deciding whether to dispense with informed consent, such as when research is conducted in public settings. These settings require special attention to protecting individuals' privacy.
- Privacy refers to the rights of individuals to decide how information about them is to be communicated to others.

Key Concept

A substantial portion of the Ethics Code dealing with research is devoted to issues related to informed consent. This is appropriate because informed consent is an essential component of the social contract between the researcher and the participant. **Informed consent** is a person's explicitly expressed willingness to participate in a research project based on a clear understanding of the nature

FIGURE 3.4 The issue of informed consent is especially important when children participate in research.

of the research, of the consequences of not participating, and of all factors that might be expected to influence that person's willingness to participate. Ethical research practice requires that research participants be fully informed about foreseeable factors that could influence their willingness to participate and they should know what they are consenting to do in the research project. Participants should also know that they are free to withdraw their consent at any time without penalty or prejudice. Researchers must also make reasonable efforts to respond to any questions the participants have about the research. In this way individuals can make an informed decision about their participation. Participants' consent must be given freely, without undue inducement or pressure. Researchers should always obtain informed consent. *Written informed consent is absolutely essential when participants are exposed to more than minimal risk.*

True informed consent cannot be obtained from certain individuals, such as the mentally impaired or emotionally disturbed, young children, and those who have limited ability to understand the nature of research and the possible risks. Whenever possible, "assent" should always be obtained from the participants themselves. In these cases, however, formal informed consent must be obtained from the participants' parents or legal guardians. Ethical guidelines like those involved with obtaining informed consent also raise methodological issues (see Adair, Dushenko, & Lindsay, 1985). For example, in one study the children of parents who did not provide parental consent for a research project were found to be academically less successful and less popular with their peers than were children of parents who did provide consent (Frame & Strauss, 1987). Studies like this one raise questions about whether findings obtained when studying children whose parents gave consent would also apply to children whose parents did not give parental consent. What is not in question, however, is that doing ethical research takes precedence over these possible methodological concerns.

Once again, online research poses particular ethical problems in this area. Consider that in most cases online participants typically click a button on their computer screen to indicate that they have read and understood the consent statement. But does this constitute a legally binding "signature" of the research participant? How does a researcher know if participants are really of legal age or that they fully understood the informed consent statement? One suggestion for determining whether participants have understood the informed consent statement is to administer short quizzes about its content; procedures to distinguish children from adults might include requiring information that is generally only available to adults (Kraut et al., 2004).

Consider the dilemma faced by a graduate student who was seeking to interview adolescents receiving services from a family planning clinic (Landers, 1988). Parental permission was not required for the teens to attend the clinic. Obtaining permission of parents before conducting research with minors is standard ethical practice and also is mandated by federal laws. Thus, if the investigator asked the parents for permission for their children to participate in the study, she would be revealing to the parents the teens' use of the clinic's services. The graduate student correctly sought advice from members of APA's Committee for the Protection of Human Participants in Research to help her make a decision regarding proper ethical procedures in this difficult case. The student used the expert advice to formulate the procedures that she proposed to use as part of her dissertation research. Whenever ethical dilemmas arise, it is wise to seek advice from knowledgeable professionals, but the *final responsibility for conducting ethical research always rests with the investigator.*

It is not always easy to decide what constitutes undue inducement or pressure to participate. Paying college students $9 an hour to take part in a psychology experiment would not generally be considered improper coercion. Recruiting very poor or disadvantaged persons from the streets with a $9 offer may be more coercive and less acceptable (Kelman, 1972). Prisoners may believe that any refusal on their part to participate in a psychology experiment will be viewed by the authorities as evidence of uncooperativeness and will therefore make it more difficult for them to be paroled. When college students are asked to fulfill a class requirement by serving as participants in psychology experiments (an experience that presumably has some educational value), an alternative method of earning class credit must be made available to those who do not wish to participate in psychological research. The time and effort required for these alternative options should be equivalent to that required for research participation. Alternative assignments that are used frequently include reading and summarizing journal articles describing research, making informal field observations of behavior, attending presentations of research findings by graduate students or faculty, and doing volunteer community service (see Kimmel, 1996).

IRBs require investigators to document that the proper informed consent procedure has been followed for any research involving human participants. In previous editions of this book we provided a sample consent form for use in minimal-risk research when deception is not involved. However, it is important to recognize that, as guidelines from the federal Office for Human Research Protections state, "informed consent is a process, not just a form." One IRB chairperson told us that she tells investigators to imagine they are sitting down with the person and explaining the project. Therefore, in this edition we provide some tips on the process of obtaining proper informed consent (see Box 3.1) and omit a sample form that may imply that "one form fits all." Proper consent procedures and written documentation will vary somewhat across situations and populations. Members of an IRB are a good source for advice on how to obtain and document informed consent in a way that meets ethical guidelines and protects the rights of the participants.

In some situations researchers are not required to obtain informed consent. The clearest example is when researchers are observing individuals' behavior in public places without any intervention. For instance, an investigator might want to gather evidence about race relations on a college campus by observing the frequency of mixed-race versus unmixed-race groups walking across campus. The investigator would not need to obtain students' permission before making the observations. Informed consent would be required, however, if the identity of specific individuals was going to be recorded.

Deciding when behavior is public or private is not always clear-cut. Diener and Crandall (1978) identify three major dimensions that researchers can consider to help them decide what information is private: the sensitivity of the information, the setting, and the method of dissemination of the information. Clearly, some kinds of information are more sensitive than others. Individuals interviewed about their sexual practices, religious beliefs, or criminal activities are likely to be more concerned about how the information will be used than those interviewed about who they believe will win the World Series.

The setting also plays a role in deciding whether behavior is public or private. Some behaviors, such as attending a concert, can reasonably be considered public. In public settings people give up a certain degree of privacy. Some behaviors that occur in public settings, however, are not easily classified as public or private. When you drive in your car, use a public bathroom, or enjoy a family picnic in the park, are these behaviors public or private? Is communication in an Internet "chatroom" public or private? Decisions about ethical practice in these situations depend on the sensitivity of the data being gathered and the ways in which the information will be used.

BOX 3.1

TIPS ON OBTAINING INFORMED CONSENT

A proper informed consent should clearly indicate the purpose or research question, the identity and affiliation of the researcher, procedures to be followed, risks/benefits associated with participation, compensation (if any), costs to the participants (if any), alternatives to research participation, procedures for maintaining confidentiality, that participation is voluntary and withdrawal can be made at any time without penalty, information about contacts if there are problems or questions, signatures of researcher(s) and participant, and the date of the research experience. Additional requirements will sometimes be added by the IRB depending on the situation. The federal Office for Human Research Protections (OHRP) has published "tips" to aid researchers in this process. Our adaptation of the OHRP tips follows. The complete text of the OHRP tips, as well as links to important related federal documents, can be obtained from: http://www.hhs.gov/ohrp/humansubjects/guidance/ictips.htm

- Avoid scientific jargon or technical terms; the informed consent document should be written in language clearly understandable to the participant.
- Avoid use of the first person (e.g., "I understand that . . ." or "I agree to . . ."), as this can be interpreted as suggestive and incorrectly used as a substitute for sufficient factual information. Phrasing such as, "If you agree to participate, you will be asked to do the following," would be preferred. "Think of the document primarily as a teaching tool and not as a legal instrument."
- Describe the overall experience that will be encountered in a way that identifies the nature of the experience (e.g., how it is experimental), as well as reasonably foreseeable harms, discomfort, inconveniences, and risks.
- Describe the benefits to the participants for their participation. If the benefits simply are helping society or science in general, that should be stated.
- Describe any alternatives to participation. If a college student "participant pool" is being tapped, then alternative ways to learn about psychological research must be explained.
- Participants must be told how personally identifiable information will be held in confidence. In situations where highly sensitive information is collected, an IRB may require additional safeguards such as a Certificate of Confidentiality.
- If research-related injury is possible in research that is more than minimal risk, then an explanation must be given regarding voluntary compensation and treatment.
- Legal rights of participants must not be waived.
- A "contact person" who is knowledgeable about the research must be identified so that participants who have post-research questions may have them answered. Questions may arise in any of the following three areas, *and these areas must be explicitly stated and addressed in the consent process and documentation:* the research experience, rights of the participants, and research-related injuries. At times this may involve more than one contact person, for example, referring the participant to the IRB or an institutional representative.
- A statement of voluntary participation must be included, which emphasizes the participant's right to withdraw from the research at any time without penalty.

When information is disseminated in terms of group averages or proportions, it is unlikely to reflect on specific individuals. In other situations, code systems can be used to protect participants' confidentiality. *Disseminating sensitive information about individuals or groups without their permission is a serious breach of ethics.* When potentially sensitive information about individuals has been collected without their knowledge (e.g., by a concealed observer), researchers can contact the individuals after the observations have been made and ask whether they can use the information. The researcher would not be able to use the information from participants who decline to give their permission. The most difficult decisions regarding privacy involve situations in which there is an obvious ethical problem on one dimension but not on the other two, or situations in which there is a slight problem on all three dimensions. For instance, the behavior of individuals in the darkened setting of a movie theater would appear to have the potential of yielding sensitive information about the individual, but the setting could be reasonably classified as public.

Key Concept }

Privacy refers to the rights of individuals to decide how information about them is to be communicated to others. The APA Ethics Code clearly states that "psychologists have a primary obligation and take reasonable precautions to protect confidential information obtained" from research participants (American Psychological Association, 2002, p. 1066). Whenever possible, the manner in which information about participants will be kept confidential should be explained to participants in psychological research so they may judge for themselves whether the safeguards taken to ensure their confidentiality are reasonable. Implementing the principle of informed consent requires that the investigator seeks to balance the need to investigate human behavior on the one hand with the rights of human participants on the other.

FIGURE 3.5   Deciding what is public or what is private behavior is not always easy.

STRETCHING EXERCISE

The APA Code of Ethics states that psychologists may dispense with informed consent when research involves naturalistic observation (see Standard 8.05). As we have just seen, however, deciding when naturalistic observation is being done in a "public" setting is not always easy. Consider the following research scenarios and decide whether you think informed consent of participants should be required before the researcher begins the research. It may be that you will want more information from the researcher. If so, what additional information would you want before deciding whether informed consent is needed in the situation? You will see that requiring informed consent can have a dramatic effect on a research situation. Requiring informed consent, for example, can make it difficult for a researcher to record behavior under "natural" conditions. Such are the dilemmas of ethical decision making.

1 In a study of drinking behavior of college students, an undergraduate working for a faculty member attends a fraternity party and records the amount drunk by other students at the party.

2 As part of a study of the gay community, a gay researcher joins a gay baseball team with the goal of recording behaviors of participants in the context of team competition during the season. All the games are played in a city recreation league with the general public as spectators.

3 Public bathroom behavior (e.g., flushing, hand washing, littering, writing graffiti, etc.) of men and women is observed by male and female researchers concealed in the stalls of the respective restrooms.

4 A graduate student wants to investigate cheating behaviors of college students. He conceals himself in a projection booth in an auditorium where exams are administered to students in very large classes. From his vantage point he can see the movements of most students with the aid of binoculars. He records head movements, switching papers, passing notes, and other suspicious exam-taking behaviors.

DECEPTION IN PSYCHOLOGICAL RESEARCH

- Deception in psychological research occurs when researchers withhold information or intentionally misinform participants about the research. By its nature, deception violates the ethical principle of informed consent, yet it is considered a necessary research strategy in certain areas of psychology.

Key Concept }

The most controversial ethical issue related to research is deception. Some people argue that research participants should *never* be deceived because ethical practice requires that the relationship between experimenter and participant be open and honest. To some, deception is morally repugnant; it is no different from lying. **Deception** can occur either through *omission*, the withholding of information, or *commission*, intentionally misinforming participants about an aspect of the research. Either kind of deception contradicts the principle of informed consent. Despite the increased attention given to deception in research over the last several decades, the use of deception in psychological research has not declined and remains a popular research strategy (Sharpe, Adair, & Roese, 1992). Skitka and Sargis (2005) surveyed social psychologists who used the Internet as a data collection tool and found that 27 percent of the reported studies involved deception of Internet participants.

FIGURE 3.6 In the 1960s, participants in Stanley Milgram's experiments were not told that the purpose of the research was to observe people's obedience to authority and many followed instructions of the researcher to give severe electric shock to another human being.

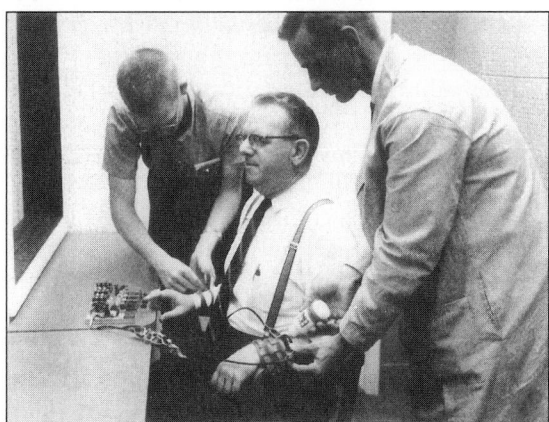

APA Ethical Standards

8.07 Deception in Research

(a) Psychologists do not conduct a study involving deception unless they have determined that the use of deceptive techniques is justified by the study's significant prospective scientific, educational, or applied value and that effective nondeceptive alternative procedures are not feasible.

(b) Psychologists do not deceive prospective participants about research that is reasonably expected to cause physical pain or severe emotional distress.

(c) Psychologists explain any deception that is an integral feature of the design and conduct of an experiment to participants as early as is feasible, preferably at the conclusion of their participation, but no later than at the conclusion of the data collection, and permit participants to withdraw their data. (See also Standard 8.08, Debriefing.)

Commentary

- Deception is a necessary research strategy in some psychological research.
- Deceiving individuals in order to get them to participate in the research is always unethical.
- Researchers must carefully weigh the costs of deception against the potential benefits of the research when considering the use of deception.
- Researchers are ethically obligated to explain to participants their use of deception as soon as is feasible.

It is impossible to carry out certain kinds of research without withholding information from participants about some aspects of the research. In other situations, it is necessary to misinform participants in order to have them adopt certain attitudes or behaviors. For example, Kassin and Kiechel (1996) investigated factors affecting whether people will falsely confess to having done something that they did not do. Their goal was to understand what would lead criminal suspects to falsely confess to a crime. In their experiment, the participants' task was to type letters that were being read aloud. They were told not to hit the "Alt" key while typing because this would crash the computer. The computer was rigged to crash after a brief time and the experimenter accused the participant of hitting the "Alt" key. Even though none of the participants had hit the "Alt" key, nearly 70% of the participants signed a written confession that they had done so. If the participants had known in advance that the procedures were trying to elicit their false confessions, they probably would not have confessed. The disclosure required for informed consent would have made it impossible to study the likelihood that people would make a false confession. Although deception is sometimes justified to make it possible to investigate important research questions, deceiving participants for the purpose of getting them to participate in research that involves more than minimal risk is always unethical. As stated in the Ethics Code, "*Psychologists do not deceive prospective participants about research that is reasonably expected to cause physical pain or severe emotional distress*" (Standard 8.07b).

A goal of research is to observe people's normal behavior. A basic assumption underlying the use of deception is that sometimes it is necessary to conceal the true nature of an experiment so that participants will behave as they normally would or so they will act according to the instructions provided by the experimenter. A problem occurs, however, with frequent and casual use of deception (Kelman, 1967). If people believe that researchers often mislead participants, they may expect to be deceived when participating in a psychology experiment. Participants' suspicions about the research may prevent them from behaving as they normally would (see Box 3.2). This is exactly the opposite of what the researchers hope to achieve. Interestingly, Epley and Huff (1998) directly compared reactions of participants who were told or not told in a debriefing following the experiment that they had been deceived. Those who were told of the deception were subsequently more suspicious about future psychological research than were participants who were unaware of the deception. As the frequency of online research increases, it is important that researchers give particular attention to the use of deception, not only because of the potential for increasing the distrust of researchers by society's members, but also because deception has the potential to "poison" a vehicle (i.e., the Internet) that people use for social support and connecting with others (Skitka & Sargis, 2005).

Kelman (1972) suggests that, *before using deception, a researcher must give very serious consideration to (1) the importance of the study to our scientific knowledge, (2) the availability of alternative, deception-free methods, and (3) the "noxiousness" of*

BOX 3.2

TO DECEIVE OR NOT TO DECEIVE: THAT'S A TOUGH QUESTION

Researchers continue to use deceptive practices in psychological research (e.g., Sieber, Iannuzzo, & Rodriguez, 1995). The debate in the scientific community concerning the use of deception also has not abated (see, for example, Bröder, 1998; Fisher & Fryberg, 1994; Ortmann & Hertwig, 1997). It is a complex issue, with those taking part in the debate sometimes at odds over the definition of deception (see Ortmann & Hertwig, 1998). Fisher and Fryberg (1994) summarized the debate as follows: "Ethical arguments have focused on whether deceptive research practices are justified on the basis of their potential societal benefit or violate moral principles of beneficence and respect for individuals and the fiduciary obligations of psychologists to research participants" (p. 417). This is quite a mouthful; so let us see if we can break it down.

A moral principle of "beneficence" refers to the idea that research activities should be beneficent (bring benefits) for individuals and society. If deception is shown to harm individuals or society, then the beneficence of the research can be questioned. The moral principle of "respect for individuals" is just that: People should be treated as persons and not "objects" for study, for example. This principle would suggest that people have a right to make their own judgments about the procedures and purpose of the research in which they are participating (Fisher & Fryberg, 1994). "Fiduciary obligations of psychologists" refer to the responsibilities of individuals who are given trust over others, even if only temporarily. In the case of psychological research, the researcher is considered to have responsibility for the welfare of participants during the study and for the consequences of their participation.

These ideas and principles can perhaps be illustrated through the arguments of Baumrind (1985), who argues persuasively that "the use of intentional deception in the research setting is unethical, imprudent, and unwarranted scientifically" (p. 165). Specifically, she argues that the costs to the participants, to the profession, and to society of the use of deception are too great to warrant its continued use. Although these arguments are lengthy and complex, let us attempt a brief summary. First, according to Baumrind, deception exacts a cost to participants because it undermines the participants' trust in their own judgment and in a "fiduciary" (someone who is holding something in trust for another person). When research participants find they have been duped or tricked, Baumrind believes this may lead the participants to question what they have learned about themselves and to lead them to distrust individuals (e.g., social scientists) whom they might have previously trusted to provide valid information and advice. A cost to the profession is exacted because participants (and society at large) soon come to realize that psychologists are "tricksters" and not to be believed when giving instructions about research participation. If participants tend to suspect psychologists of lying, then one may question whether deception will work as it is intended by the researcher, a point raised earlier by Kelman (1972). Baumrind also argues that the use of deception reveals psychologists are willing to lie, which seemingly contradicts their supposed dedication to seeking truth. Finally, there is harm done to society because deception undermines people's trust in experts and makes them suspicious in general about all contrived events.

Of course, these are not the views of all psychologists (see Christensen, 1988; Kimmel, 1998). Milgram (1977), for instance, suggested that deceptive practices of psychologists are really a kind of "technical illusion" and should be permitted in the interests of scientific inquiry. After all, illusions are sometimes created in real-life situations in order to make people believe something. When listening to a radio program, people are not generally bothered by the fact that the thunder they hear or the sound of a horse galloping are merely technical illusions created by a sound effects specialist. Milgram argues that technical illusions should be permitted in the case of scientific inquiry. We

(Contd.)

deceive children into believing in Santa Claus. Why cannot scientists create illusions in order to help them understand human behavior?

Just as illusions are often created in real-life situations, in other situations, Milgram points out, there can be a suspension of a general moral principle. If we learn of a crime, we are ethically bound to report it to the authorities. On the other hand, a lawyer who is given information by a client must consider this information privileged even if it reveals that the client is guilty. Physicians perform very personal examinations of our bodies. Although it is morally permissible in a physician's office, the same type of behavior would not be condoned outside the office. Milgram argues that, in the interest of science, psychologists should occasionally be allowed to suspend the moral principle of truthfulness and honesty.

Those who defend deception point to studies showing that participants on the average do not appear to react negatively to being deceived (e.g., Christensen, 1988; Epley & Huff, 1998; Kimmel, 1996). Although people's "suspiciousness" about psychological research may increase, the overall effects seem to be small (see Kimmel, 1998). Nevertheless, the bottom line according to those who argue for the continued use of deception is well summarized by Kimmel (1998): "An absolute rule prohibiting the use of deception in all psychological research would have the egregious consequence of preventing researchers from carrying out a wide range of important studies" (p. 805). No one in the scientific community suggests that deceptive practices be taken lightly; however, for many scientists the use of deception is less noxious (to use Kelman's term) than doing without the knowledge gained by such studies.

What do you think about whether deception should be used in psychological research?

the deception. This last consideration refers to the degree of deception involved and to the possibility of injury to the participants. In Kelman's (p. 997) view: "Only if a study is very important and no alternative methods are available can anything more than the mildest form of deception be justified." *When deception is used, the researcher must inform participants in a debriefing after the experiment of the reasons for the deception, discuss any misconceptions they may have, and remove any harmful effects of the deception.* One goal of debriefing is to educate the participant about why the deception was necessary. Participants in the Kassin and Kiechel (1996) experiment on false confessions learned about the reasons for the use of deception in a debriefing. The participants reported that they found the study meaningful and that they thought their own contribution to the research was valuable.

DEBRIEFING

- Researchers are ethically obligated to seek ways to benefit participants even after the research is completed. One of the best ways to accomplish this goal is by providing participants with a thorough debriefing.

Over the years, many researchers have fallen into the trap of viewing human participants in their research chiefly as means to an end. The researchers see participants as if they were "objects" from which researchers can obtain data in order to meet their own research goals. Researchers sometimes have considered that their responsibility to participants ends when the final data are collected. A handshake or "thank you" was frequently all that marked the end of the research session. Participants likely left with unanswered questions about the research situation and with only the vaguest idea of their role in the study. It is important when planning and conducting research to consider how the experience may affect the research participant *after* the research is completed, and to seek ways in which the participant can benefit from participation. These concerns follow directly from two of the moral principles identified in the Ethics Code, beneficence and respect for people's rights and dignity.

APA Ethical Standards

8.08 Debriefing

(a) Psychologists provide a prompt opportunity for participants to obtain appropriate information about the nature, results, and conclusions of the research, and they take reasonable steps to correct any misconceptions that participants may have of which the psychologists are aware.

(b) If scientific or humane values justify delaying or withholding this information, psychologists take reasonable measures to reduce the risk of harm.

(c) When psychologists become aware that research procedures have harmed a participant, they take reasonable steps to minimize the harm.

Commentary

- Debriefing benefits both participants and researchers.
- Debriefing informs participants about the nature of the research, their role in the study, and educates them about the research process. The overriding goal of debriefing is to have individuals feel good about their participation.
- Debriefing allows researchers to learn how participants viewed the procedures, allows potential insights into the nature of the research findings, and provides ideas for future research.

Key Concept }

Earlier we discussed that protecting the confidentiality of participants' responses benefits both the participants (safeguarding them from social injury) and the researcher (e.g., by increasing the likelihood that participants will respond honestly). Similarly, **debriefing** participants at the end of a research session benefits both participants and the researcher (Blanck et al., 1992). When deception has been used in research, *debriefing is necessary to explain to participants the need for deception, to address any misconceptions participants may have about their participation, and to remove any harmful effects resulting from the deception. Debriefing also has the important goals of educating participants about the research (rationale, method, results) and of leaving them with positive feelings about their participation.* Researchers should provide opportunities for participants to

FIGURE 3.7   An informative debriefing is critical in ensuring that research participants have a good experience.

learn more about their particular contribution to the research study and to feel more personally involved in the scientific process. For example, researchers can e-mail a report summarizing the study's findings to the participants when the study is completed. Following an online study, a researcher may post debriefing material at a website and even update these materials as new results come in (see Kraut et al., 2004).

Debriefing provides an opportunity for participants to learn more about research in general. For instance, participants can learn that their individual performance in a study is not a direct measure of their abilities. How well they perform on a memory test, for instance, is affected by how good a memory they have, but their performance is also affected by factors such as what the researcher asks them to remember and how they are tested. Because the educational value of participation in psychological research is used to justify the use of large numbers of volunteers from introductory psychology classes, researchers testing college students have an important obligation to ensure that research participation is an educational experience for students. Classroom instructors have sometimes built on the educational foundation of the debriefing and asked their students to reflect on their research experience by writing brief reports describing details about the study's purpose, the techniques used, and the significance of the research to understanding behavior. An evaluation of one such procedure showed that students who wrote reports were more satisfied with their research experience and they gained a greater overall educational benefit from it than did students who did not write reports (Richardson, Pegalis, & Britton, 1992).

Debriefing helps researchers learn how participants viewed the procedures in the study. A researcher may want to find out whether participants perceived a particular experimental procedure in the way the investigator intended (Blanck et al., 1992). For example, a study of how people respond to failure may include tasks that are impossible to complete. If participants don't judge their performance as a failure, however, the researcher's hypothesis cannot be tested. Debriefing allows the investigator to find out whether participants perceived that they had failed at the tasks or whether they perceived that they had no chance to succeed.

When trying to learn participants' perceptions of the study, researchers shouldn't press them too hard. Research participants generally want to help with the scientific process. The participants may know that in psychological research information may be withheld from them. They may even fear that they will "ruin" the research if they reveal that they really did know important details about the study (e.g., the tasks really were impossible). To avoid this possible problem, debriefing should be informal and indirect. This is often best accomplished by using general questions in an open-ended format (e.g., What do you think this study was about? or What did you think about your experience in this research?). The researcher can then follow up with more specific questions about the research procedures. As much as possible, these specific questions should not cue the participant about what responses are expected (Orne, 1962).

Debriefing also benefits researchers because it can provide "leads for future research and help identify problems in their current protocols" (Blanck et al., 1992, p. 962). Debriefing, in other words, can provide clues to the reasons for participants' performance, which may help researchers interpret the results of the study. What researchers learn in debriefings can also provide them with ideas for future research. Finally, participants sometimes detect errors in experimental materials—for instance, missing information or ambiguous instructions—and they can report these to the researcher during the debriefing. As we said, *debriefing is good for both the participant and the researcher.* Because a researcher is absent in an online research setting, an appropriate debriefing process may be difficult, and this aspect of Internet research adds to the list of ethical dilemmas posed by this kind of research (Kraut et al., 2004). The fact that online participants can easily withdraw from the study at any time is particularly troublesome in this regard. One suggestion is to program the experiment in such a way that a debriefing page is presented automatically if a participant prematurely closes the window (Nosek et al., 2002).

Researchers' responsibilities to educate people about their research are not limited to effective debriefing of participants. The goal of science to create change and improve the human condition entails an obligation for scientists to speak out on issues related to their research. Meeting this responsibility presents ethical challenges for scientists. Psychologists do research on important issues of social concern such as discrimination, violent behavior, and childhood sexual abuse.

Issues of concern to society are often controversial issues that can be fiercely contested by people with differing political views. Individual researchers who present their research findings in the media risk criticism and even hostile reactions from people who strongly disagree with their conclusions. The American Psychological Society (APS) is making an effort to inform society about how psychological research can contribute constructively to issues of social concern. APS forms study groups made up of experts in an area of research related to an important social issue. The conclusions and recommendations formulated by these study groups are then published in the journal, *Psychological Science in the Public Interest*. Issues addressed in this way include the impact of class size on student achievement and the psychological science of making diagnostic decisions in areas such as predicting violence and diagnosing cancer.

RESEARCH WITH ANIMALS

Each year millions of animals are tested in laboratory investigations aimed at answering a wide range of important questions. New drugs are tested on animals before they are used with humans. Substances introduced into the environment are first given to animals to test their effects. Animals are exposed to diseases in order that investigators may observe symptoms and test various possible cures. New surgical procedures—especially those involving the brain—are often first tried on animals. Many animals are also studied in behavioral research, for example, by ethologists and experimental psychologists. For instance, animal models of the relationship between stress and diabetes have helped researchers to understand psychosomatic factors involved in diabetes (Surwit & Williams, 1996). These investigations yield much information that contributes to human welfare (Miller, 1985). In the process, however, many animals are subjected to pain and discomfort, stress and sickness, and death. Although rodents, particularly rats and mice, are the largest group of laboratory animals, researchers use a wide variety of species in their investigations, including monkeys, fish, dogs, and cats. Specific animals are frequently chosen because they provide good models for human responses. For example, psychologists interested in hearing sometimes use chinchillas as subjects because their auditory processes are very similar to those of humans.

APA Ethical Standards

8.09 Humane Care and Use of Animals in Research

(a) Psychologists acquire, care for, use, and dispose of animals in compliance with current federal, state, and local laws and regulations, and with professional standards.

(b) Psychologists trained in research methods and experienced in the care of laboratory animals supervise all procedures involving animals and are responsible for ensuring appropriate consideration of their comfort, health, and humane treatment.

FIGURE 3.8   Ethical guidelines for the use of animals in research address how animals may be treated before, during, and after they are tested.

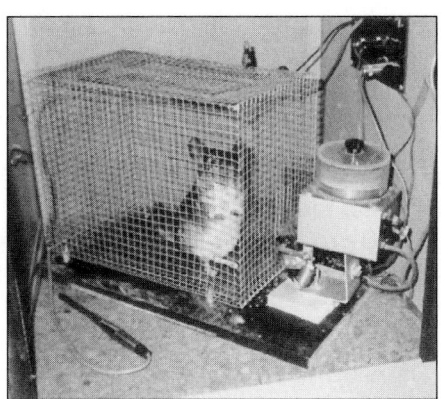 

(c) Psychologists ensure that all individuals under their supervision who are using animals have received instruction in research methods and in the care, maintenance, and handling of the species being used, to the extent appropriate to their role. (See also Standard 2.05, Delegation of Work to Others.)

(d) Psychologists make reasonable efforts to minimize the discomfort, infection, illness, and pain of animal subjects.

(e) Psychologists use a procedure subjecting animals to pain, stress, or privation only when an alternative procedure is unavailable and the goal is justified by its prospective scientific, educational, or applied value.

(f) Psychologists perform surgical procedures under appropriate anesthesia and follow techniques to avoid infection and minimize pain during and after surgery.

(g) When it is appropriate that the animal's life be terminated, psychologists proceed rapidly, with an effort to minimize pain, and in accordance with accepted procedures.

Commentary

- Animals are used in research to gain knowledge that will benefit humans, for example, by helping to cure diseases.
- Researchers are ethically obligated to acquire, care for, use, and dispose of animals in compliance with current federal, state, and local laws and regulations, and with professional standards.
- The use of animals in research involves complex issues and is the subject of debate.

The use of animals as laboratory subjects has often been taken for granted. In fact, the biblical reference to humans' "dominion" over all lesser creatures is sometimes invoked to justify the use of animals as laboratory subjects (Johnson, 1990). More often, however, research with animal subjects is justified by the need to gain knowledge *without putting humans in jeopardy*. Most cures, drugs, vaccines, or therapies have been developed through experimentation on animals (Rosenfeld, 1981). Maestripieri and Carroll (1998) also point out that investigation of naturally occurring infant maltreatment in monkeys can inform scientists about child abuse and neglect.

Many questions, however, have been raised about the role of animal subjects in laboratory research (Novak, 1991; Shapiro, 1998; Ulrich, 1991). These questions include the most basic one, whether animals should be used at all in scientific investigations, as well as important questions about the care and protection of animal subjects. Clearly, according to the APA Ethics Code, *the researcher who uses animal subjects in an investigation has an ethical obligation to acquire, care for, use, and dispose of animals in compliance with federal, state, and local laws and regulations, and with professional standards.* Research with animals is a highly regulated enterprise with the overriding goal of protecting the welfare of research animals. Only individuals qualified to do research and to manage and care for the particular species should be allowed to work with the animals. When researchers expose animals to pain or discomfort, they must justify their procedures with any potential scientific, educational, or applied goals. As we noted earlier, animal review boards (IACUCs) are now in place at research facilities receiving funds from the Public Health Service. These committees determine the adequacy of the procedures for controlling pain, carrying out euthanasia, housing animals, and training personnel. IACUCs also determine whether experimental designs are sufficient to gain important new information and whether the use of an animal model is appropriate or whether nonanimal models could be used (Holden, 1987).

Partly in response to concerns expressed by members of animal rights groups during the 1980s, investigators must satisfy many federal, state, and local requirements, including inspection of animal facilities by veterinarians from the U.S. Department of Agriculture (see National Research Council, 1996). These regulations are often welcomed by members of the scientific community, and many animal researchers belong to groups that seek to protect laboratory animals. The APA has developed a list of specific guidelines to be followed when animal subjects are used in psychological research. These guidelines are at www.apa.org/science/anguide.html.

As with any ethically sensitive issue, however, compromises must be made with regard to the use of animals in research. For example, until alternatives to animal research can be found, the need to conduct research using animal subjects in order to battle human disease and suffering must be balanced against the need to protect the welfare of animals in laboratory research (Goodall, 1987). As APA's former chief executive officer, Raymond Fowler, pointed out, it is also important that the use of animal subjects not be restricted when the application of the research is not immediately apparent (Fowler, 1992). "The charges that animal research is of no value because it cannot always be linked to potential applications is a charge that can be made against all basic research." Such an indictment "threatens the intellectual and scientific foundation" of all psychology, including both "scientists and practitioners" (p. 2).

Although few scientists disagree that restrictions are necessary to prevent needless suffering in animals, most want to avoid a quagmire of bureaucratic restrictions and high costs that will undermine research. Feeney (1987) suggests that severe restrictions and high costs, as well as the negative publicity (and occasional emotional demonstrations) directed toward individuals and institutions by extremists within the animal activist groups, may deter young scientists from entering the field of animal research. If this were to occur, the (presently) incurably ill or permanently paralyzed could possibly be deprived of the hope that can come through scientific research. Clearly, the issues surrounding the debate over the relevance of animal research to the human condition are many and complex (see Box 3.3). Ulrich (1992) said it well—the discussion of these issues must be approached with "wisdom and balance" (p. 386).

BOX 3.3

MORAL STATUS OF HUMANS AND NONHUMAN ANIMALS?

Ethical decision making often pits opposing philosophical positions against one another. This is clearly seen in the debate over the use of animals in research. At the center of this debate is the question of the "moral status" of humans and nonhuman animals. As the Australian philosopher Peter Singer (1990, p. 9) points out, two generally accepted moral principles are:

1 All humans are equal in moral status.
2 All humans are of superior moral status to nonhuman animals.

Thus, Singer continues, "On the basis of these principles, it is commonly held that we should put human welfare ahead of the suffering of nonhuman animals; this assumption is reflected in our treatment of animals in many areas, including farming, hunting, experimentation, and entertainment" (p. 9).

Singer, however, does not agree with these commonly held views. He argues that "there is no rational ethical justification for always putting human suffering ahead of that of nonhuman animals" (p. 9). Unless we appeal to religious viewpoints (which Singer rejects as a basis for making decisions in a pluralistic society), there is, according to Singer, no special moral status to "being human." This position has roots in the philosophical tradition known as utilitarianism, which began with the writings of David Hume (1711–1776) and Jeremy Bentham (1748–1832), as well as John Stuart Mill (1806–1873) (Rachels, 1986). Basically, this viewpoint holds that whenever we have choices between alternative actions we should choose the one that has the best overall consequences (produces the most "happiness") for everyone involved. What matters in this view is whether the individual in question is capable of experiencing happiness/unhappiness, pleasure/pain; whether the individual is human or nonhuman is not relevant (Rachels, 1986).

What do you think about the moral status of humans and animals and its relation to psychological research?

REVIEW QUESTIONS

1 Explain why researchers submit research proposals to Institutional Review Boards (IRBs) or Institutional Animal Care and Use Committees (IACUCs) before beginning a research project and briefly describe the functions of these committees in the research process.

2 Explain how the risk/benefit ratio is used in making ethical decisions. Briefly describe the characteristics of a research project that are used to assess its potential benefit.

3 Explain why research cannot be risk free and describe the standard that researchers use to determine whether research participants are "at risk." Describe briefly how characteristics of the participants in the research can affect the assessment of risk.

4 Differentiate among the three possible types of risk that can be present in psychological research: physical, psychological, social. How do researchers typically safeguard against the possibility of social risk?

5 What are three important ethical issues raised by online research?

6 What information does the researcher have an ethical obligation to make clear to the participant in order to ensure the participant's informed consent? Under what conditions does the APA Ethics Code indicate that informed consent may not be necessary?

7 What three dimensions do Diener and Crandall (1978) recommend that researchers consider when they attempt to decide whether information is public or private?

8 Explain why deception may sometimes be necessary in psychological research. Describe briefly the questions researchers should ask before using deception and describe the conditions under which it is always unethical to deceive participants.

9 In what ways can debriefing benefit the participant? In what ways can debriefing benefit the researcher?

10 What ethical obligations are specified in the APA Ethics Code for researchers who use animals in their research?

11 What two conditions are required by the APA Ethics Code before animals may be subjected to stress or pain?

12 Explain how researchers decide when an individual can be credited as an author of a published scientific report.

13 Describe the procedures an author must follow to avoid plagiarism when citing information from an original source or from a secondary source.

CHALLENGE QUESTIONS

Note: Unlike in other chapters, no answers to the Challenge Questions or Stretching Exercises are provided in this chapter. To resolve ethical dilemmas, you must be able to apply the appropriate ethical standards and to reach an agreement regarding the proposed research after discussion with others whose backgrounds and knowledge differ from your own. You will therefore have to consider points of view different from your own.

We urge you to approach these problems as part of a group discussion of these important issues.

The first two challenge questions for this chapter include a hypothetical research proposal involving a rationale and method similar to that of actual published research. To answer these questions, you will need to be familiar with the APA ethical principles and other material on ethical decision making presented in this chapter, including the recommended steps for decision making that were outlined at the end of this chapter. As you will see, your task is to decide whether specific ethical standards have been violated and to make recommendations regarding the proposed research, including the most basic recommendation of whether the investigator should be allowed to proceed.

1 IRB Proposal

Instructions   Assume you are a member of an Institutional Review Board (IRB). Besides yourself, the committee includes a clinical psychologist, a social psychologist, a social worker, a philosopher, a Protestant minister, a history professor, and a respected business executive in the community. The following is a summary of a research proposal that has been submitted to the IRB for review. You are asked to consider what questions you might want to ask the investigator and whether you would approve carrying out the study at your institution in its present form, whether modification should be made before approval, or whether the proposal should not be approved. (An actual research proposal submitted to an IRB would include more details than we present here.)

Rationale   Psychological conformity occurs when people accept the opinions or judgments of others in the absence of significant reasons to do so or in the face of evidence to the contrary. Previous research has investigated the conditions under which conformity is likely to occur and has shown, for example, that conformity increases when people anticipate unpleasant events (e.g., shock) and when the pressure to conform comes from individuals with whom the individuals identify. The proposed research examines psychological conformity in the context of discussions about alcohol consumption among teenage students. The goal of the research is to identify factors that contribute to students' willingness to attend social events where alcohol is served to minors and to allow obviously intoxicated persons to drive an automobile. This research seeks to investigate conformity in a natural setting and in circumstances where unpleasant events (e.g., legal penalties, school suspension, injury, or even death) can be avoided by not conforming to peer pressure.

Method   The research will involve 36 high school students between the ages of 16 and 18 who have volunteered to participate in a research project investigating "beliefs and attitudes of today's high school students." Participants will be assigned to four-person discussion groups. Each person in the group will be given the same 20 questions to answer; however, they will be asked to discuss each question with members of the group before writing down their answers. Four of the 20 questions deal with alcohol consumption by teenagers and with possible actions that might be taken to reduce teenage drinking and driving. One member of the group will be appointed discussion leader by the principal investigator. Unknown to the participants, they will be assigned randomly to three different groups. In each group, there will be either 0, 1, or 2 students who are actually working for the principal investigator. Each of these "confederates" has received prior instructions from the investigator regarding what to say during the group discussion of the critical questions about teenage drinking. (The use of confederates in psychological research is discussed in Chapter 4.) Specifically, confederates have been asked to follow a script which presents the argument that the majority of people who reach the legal driving age (16), and all individuals who are old enough (18) to vote in national elections and serve in the armed forces, are old enough to make their own decisions about drinking alcohol; moreover, because it is up to each individual to make this decision, other individuals do not have the right to intervene if someone under the legal age chooses to drink alcohol. Each of the confederates "admits" to drinking alcohol on at least two previous occasions. Thus, the experimental manipulation involves either 0, 1, or 2 persons in the four-person groups suggesting they do not believe students have a responsibility to avoid situations where alcohol is served to minors or to intervene when someone chooses to drink and drive. The effect of this argument on the written answers given by the actual participants in this experiment will be evaluated. Moreover, audiotapes of the sessions will be made without participants' knowledge, and the contents of these audiotapes will be analyzed. Following the experiment, the nature of the deception and the reasons for making audiotapes of the discussions will be explained to the participants.

2 IACUC Proposal

Instructions   Assume you are a member of an Institutional Animal Care and Use Committee (IACUC). Besides yourself, the committee includes a veterinarian, a biologist, a philosopher, and a

(Contd.)

respected business executive in the community. The following is a summary of a research proposal that has been submitted to the IACUC for review. You are asked to consider what questions you might want to ask the investigator and whether you would approve carrying out this study at your institution in its present form, whether modification should be made before approval, or whether the proposal should not be approved. (An actual research proposal submitted to an IACUC would include more details than we present here.)

Rationale   The investigators seek to investigate the role of subcortical structures in the limbic system in moderating emotion and aggression. This proposal is based on previous research from this laboratory which has shown a significant relationship between damage in various subcortical brain areas of monkey subjects and changes in eating, aggression, and other social behaviors (e.g., courtship). The areas under investigation are those that sometimes have been excised in psychosurgery with humans when attempting to control hyperaggressive and assaultive behaviors. Moreover, the particular subcortical area that is the focus of the present proposal has been hypothesized to be involved in controlling certain sexual activities that are sometimes the subject of psychological treatment (e.g., hypersexuality). Previous studies have been unable to pinpoint the exact areas thought to be involved in controlling certain behaviors; the proposed research seeks to improve on this knowledge.

Method   Two groups of rhesus monkeys will be the subjects. One group ($N = 4$) will be a control group. These animals will undergo a sham operation, which involves anesthetizing the animals and drilling a hole in the skull. These animals then will be tested and evaluated in the same manner as the experimental animals. The experimental group will undergo an operation to lesion a small part of a subcortical structure known as the amygdala. Two of the animals will have lesions in one site; the remaining two will receive lesions in another site of this structure. After recovery, all animals will be tested on a variety of tasks measuring their food preferences, social behaviors with same and opposite-sex monkeys (normals), and emotional responsiveness (e.g., reactions to a novel fear stimulus: an experimenter in a clown face). The animals will be housed in a modern animal laboratory; the operations will be performed and recovery monitored by a licensed veterinarian. After testing, the experimental animals will be sacrificed and the brains prepared for histological examination.

(Histology is necessary to confirm the locus and extent of lesions.) The control animals will not be killed; they will be returned to the colony for use in future experiments.

3 Research done by Stanley Milgram on compliance has led to a great deal of discussion about the ethical issues surrounding the use of deception in psychological research (see Box 3.2). Compliance involves the likelihood that a person will follow instructions given by an authority figure. For Part A of this question you are to read a summary describing the basic procedure Milgram used in his experiments. Then you are to treat this summary as if it were a research proposal submitted to an IRB of which you are a member. For the second part of the question you are to consider the additional information in Part B about Milgram's research on compliance using this paradigm. Then you are to explain why you would or would not change the decision you made based on your review in Part A.

A Two people come to a psychology laboratory supposedly to participate in a learning experiment. They are told that the study was concerned with the effects of punishment on learning. The individuals drew slips of paper to determine who would be the "teacher" and who would be the "learner." One person was actually an accomplice of the principal investigator, and the drawing was rigged so that the real participant in the experiment was always given the role of teacher. The participant watched as the learner was taken to an adjacent room and strapped into a chair and an electrode was attached to the wrist. The participant then heard the experimenter say that the learner would receive an electric shock for every error made while learning a list of word pairs. The teacher was then taken to the laboratory room, which housed an impressive-looking shock generator with 30 lever switches. Each switch was labeled with a voltage designation (ranging from 15 to 450 volts), and next to the switches were verbal labels describing the amount of shock, for example, "Slight Shock," "Strong Shock," "Danger, Severe Shock." Two switches after the last verbal description were simply marked XXX. The teacher was given a sample shock and told to administer the electric shock to the learner whenever the learner made a mistake. The learner's responses were communicated via a set of four switches that lit up a number on the top of the shock generator. The teacher was also told to move one lever higher on the shock generator after each wrong response. As the experiment progressed, the learner offered various protests to the shock. These complaints could be heard through the walls of the room and included shouts to the effect that the shocks were becoming painful, and, later, that the learner wanted the experimenter to end the procedure. When the teacher moved the switch at 180 volts, the learner yelled, "I can't stand it any more" and at the 270 volts gave an agonizing scream. At 300 volts the learner yelled, "I will not give any more answers" but continued to scream. After the switch corresponding to 330 volts was pressed, the learner was not heard from anymore. The learner was not actually shocked, and the major dependent variable was the maximum shock that the participant would give in response to the "orders" of the experimenter. All participants were debriefed after the experiment and, at times, the researcher talked with a participant for some length of time. All participants also received a follow-up questionnaire. Before conducting the experiment Milgram described his planned procedure to 37 psychiatrists; none predicted that participants would administer the most shock.

B Milgram conducted more than a dozen experiments using this procedure (see Milgram, 1974). In an experiment when the teacher could hear the screams of the learner but not actually see the learner, approximately 60% of the participants gave the learner the maximum shock. The major justification for continuing this line of research after such an unexpected finding was that no participants were apparently seriously injured by the experiment and that an overwhelming majority (84%) said they were glad to have been in the experiment. Many participants (74%) responded to the follow-up questionnaire saying that they had gained something of personal value from the experience. In subsequent experiments Milgram found that the likelihood of participants complying was affected by situational factors. For example, participants were less likely to comply when the learner was in the room with the teacher and participants were

least likely to administer the highest shock when the teacher could choose the level of voltage. One interpretation of the original finding is that people will readily comply—they behave like proverbial sheep. A different view of people's willingness to comply is evidenced by the findings of the entire series of experiments. Milgram demonstrated that people are sensitive to many aspects of the situation in which they are asked to comply. A question remains. Does the benefit of what we have learned about people's tendencies to comply based on Milgrim's findings warrant the risks that his paradigm entails? More generally, how can IRBs best estimate the potential benefits of proposed research when it is impossible for them to use the outcome of the research in their assessment of its potential benefits?

4 Consider the following scenario presented by Fine and Kurdek (1993) as part of their discussion of the issue of determining authorship of a publication.

An undergraduate student asked a psychology faculty member to supervise an honors thesis. The student proposed a topic, the faculty member primarily developed the research methodology, the student collected and entered the data, the faculty member conducted the statistical analyses, and the student used part of the analyses for the thesis. The student wrote the thesis under very close supervision by the faculty member. After the honors thesis was completed, the faculty member decided that data from the entire project were sufficiently interesting to warrant publication as a unit. Because the student did not have the skills necessary to write the entire study for a scientific journal, the faculty member did so. The student's thesis contained approximately one-third of the material presented in the article.

A Explain what factors of the situation you would consider to determine if the student should be an author of any publication resulting from this work or if the student's work should be acknowledged in a footnote to the article.

B If you decide that the student should be an author, explain whether you think the student should be first author or the second author of the article.

PART TWO

Descriptive Methods

CHAPTER FOUR

Observation

CHAPTER OUTLINE

OVERVIEW

All of us observe behavior every day. Failing to be observant while walking or driving can be life threatening. When traveling in another country, we can avoid embarrassment by observing how people behave in that culture. We can learn a lot by observing people's behavior when they are in line at the grocery store, riding on a bus, or sitting in a classroom. Scientists, too, rely on their observations to learn a lot about behavior. However, our everyday observations and those of a scientist differ in many ways. When we observe casually we may not be aware of factors that bias our observations, and we rarely keep formal records of our observations. Instead, we rely on our memory of events even though our own experience (and the observations of psychologists) confirms that our memory is not perfect! *Scientific observation, on the other hand, is made under precisely defined conditions, in a systematic and objective manner, and with careful record keeping.*

Systematic observation is an important tool not only of psychologists but of anthropologists, sociologists, and ethologists. In this chapter we will focus on observation in natural settings, but you should remember that the principles of good observation apply equally well in natural settings and in the laboratory.

The primary goal of observational methods is to describe behavior. Scientists strive to describe behavior *fully* and as *accurately* as possible. Researchers face serious challenges in reaching this goal. Clearly, it is impossible for researchers to observe *all* of a person's behavior. Scientists rely on observing *samples* of people's behavior, but they must decide whether their samples represent people's *usual* behavior. In this chapter we'll describe how scientists select samples of behavior.

Researchers face a second challenge in trying to describe behavior fully: Behavior frequently changes depending on the context in which the behavior occurs. Consider your own behavior in this regard. Do you behave the same at home as in school, or at a party compared to in a classroom? Does your observation of others lead you to conclude that context is important? Have you not observed that children sometimes change their behavior when they are with one or the other of their parents? Social psychologists, for example, have long been aware that behavior sometimes is affected simply by the presence of another person. The effect may be one of social facilitation (i.e., improved performance) or social inhibition, as when performance is impaired by the presence of another (see, for example, Bond & Titus, 1983). Complete descriptions of behavior require that observations be made across many different situations and at different times.

Observation provides a rich source of hypotheses about behavior and so observation can also be a first step in discovering why we behave the way we do. For example, Kagan, Reznick, and Snidman (1988) observed the reactions of a group of 2- and 3-year-old children in the presence of an unfamiliar person or object. The researchers identified those children who were consistently shy, quiet, and timid and those who were consistently sociable, talkative, and affectively spontaneous. When the same children were observed at 7 years of age, a majority of the children in each group exhibited similar behaviors. Based on these observations the researchers developed a hypothesis relating shyness in childhood to extreme social anxiety in adulthood. They argued that both were the result of temperamental differences present at birth. In a similar vein, Caspi and his colleagues (1997) found that observations made at age 3 could be used to successfully predict health-risk behaviors (e.g., abusing alcohol) of young adults. These findings support the hypothesis that temperamental differences observed early in childhood are linked to distinct adult behavior patterns.

In this chapter you will see that the scientist-observer is not always passively recording behavior as it occurs. We'll take a look at reasons why scientists intervene to create special situations for their observations. We will also introduce you to methods for recording and for analyzing observational data. Finally, we will describe important challenges that can make it difficult to interpret the results of studies using observation.

SAMPLING BEHAVIOR

- When a complete record of behavior cannot be obtained, researchers seek to obtain a representative sample of behavior.
- The extent to which observations may be generalized (external validity) depends on how behavior is sampled.

Before conducting an observational study, researchers must make a number of important decisions about when and where observations will be made. In most observational studies the investigator cannot observe all behavior. Only certain behaviors occurring at particular times, in specific settings, and under particular conditions can be observed. In other words, behavior must be *sampled*. This sample is used to *represent* the larger population of all possible behaviors. By choosing times, settings, and conditions for their observations that are representative of a population, researchers can *generalize* their findings to that population. The sampling of times, situations, and conditions strongly influences the most important dimension of sampling—who the participants will be. Results can be generalized only to participants, times, settings, and conditions *similar* to those in the study in which the observations were made. The key feature of *representative samples* is that they are "like" the larger population of participants, times, settings, and conditions from which they are drawn. For example, observations made of classroom behavior at the beginning of a school year may not yield results that are typical of behavior seen at the end of the school year.

Key Concept

External validity refers to the extent to which the results of a research study can be generalized to different populations, settings, and conditions. Recall that validity concerns "truthfulness." When we seek to establish the external validity of a study, we examine the extent to which a study's findings may be used to describe people, settings, and conditions beyond those used in the study. In this section we will describe how time sampling and situation sampling are used to enhance the external validity of observational findings.

Time Sampling

- Time sampling refers to researchers choosing time intervals for making observations either systematically or randomly.
- When researchers are interested in events that happen infrequently, they rely on event sampling to sample behavior.

Key Concept }

Researchers typically use a combination of time sampling and situation sampling to identify representative samples. In **time sampling,** researchers seek representative samples by choosing various time intervals for their observations. Intervals may be selected systematically (e.g., observing the first day of each week), randomly, or both.

Consider how time sampling could be used to observe children's classroom behavior. Researchers in this study want to observe the children for a total of two hours each day. If the researchers restricted their observations to certain times of the day (say, mornings only), they would not be able to generalize their findings to the rest of the school day. One approach to obtaining a representative sample is to schedule observation periods *systematically* throughout the school day. Observations might be made during four 30-minute periods beginning every two hours. The first observation period could begin at 9 A.M., the second at 11 A.M., and so forth. Another possibility would be to schedule 10-minute observation periods every half hour during the school day. A *random* time-sampling technique could be used in the same situation by distributing four 30-minute periods (or a dozen 10-minute periods) randomly over the course of the day. A different random schedule would be determined each day on which observations are made. Times would vary from day to day but, over the long run, behavior would be sampled equally from all times of the school day. Electronic devices provide a major advantage in carrying out time sampling using randomization. Electronic pagers can be programmed to signal participants on a random time schedule (normal sleeping times are excluded). For example, in their study of middle-class youth, Larson and others (Larson, Richards, Moneta, Holmbeck, & Duckett, 1996) obtained self-reports on adolescents' experiences at "16,477 random moments" in their lives.

Systematic and random time-sampling procedures are often combined, as when observation intervals are scheduled systematically but observations within an interval are made at random times. For example, having scheduled four 30-minute observation periods at the same time each day (e.g., 9 A.M., 11 A.M., etc.), an observer might then decide to observe only during 20-second intervals that are randomly distributed within each 30-minute period. Whatever time-sampling procedure is used, the observer must carefully consider both the advantages and limitations of the schedule in terms of its potential to yield a representative sample of behavior.

Time sampling is not an effective method of sampling behavior when the event of interest occurs infrequently. Researchers who use time sampling for infrequent events may miss the event entirely. Or, if the event lasts a long time, time sampling may lead the researcher to miss an important portion of the event, such as its beginning or end. Event sampling is a more effective and efficient sampling method for infrequent events. In *event sampling* the observer records each event that meets a predetermined definition. For example, researchers interested in observing children's reactions to special events in school, such as a holiday play, would use event sampling. The special event defines when the observations are to be made. Researchers would certainly not want to use time sampling in this situation in the hope that a special event might occur during one of their randomly selected observation periods.

Event sampling also is useful in situations other than for observing formally scheduled events like a school play. Researchers are often interested in events that occur unpredictably, such as natural or technical disasters. Whenever possible, observers try to be present at those times when an event of interest occurs or is likely to occur. For example, in a study of children's "rough-and-tumble" play, an observer positioned herself in the corner of a playground to observe members of a nursery school class (Smith & Lewis, 1985). Due to the relatively low frequency of this behavior, event sampling was the method of choice in this study. The researcher made observations whenever rough play began and continued to observe until the given episode of rough play ended. Although event sampling is an efficient method for observing unpredictable events, the use of event sampling can easily introduce biases into the behavioral record. For instance, event sampling could lead an observer to sample at the times that are most "convenient" or only when an event is certain to occur. The resulting sample of behavior at these times may not be representative of the same behavior at other times. In most situations, an observer is likely to achieve a representative sample of behavior only when some form of time sampling is used.

Situation Sampling

- Situation sampling involves studying behavior in different locations and under different circumstances and conditions.
- Situation sampling enhances the external validity of findings.
- Within situations, subject sampling may be used to observe some people in the setting.

Key Concept }

Researchers can significantly increase the external validity of observational findings by using situation sampling. **Situation sampling** involves observing behavior in as many different locations and under as many different circumstances and conditions as possible. By sampling different situations, researchers reduce the chance that their results will be peculiar to a certain set of circumstances or conditions. Animals do not behave the same way in zoos as they do in the wild. Children do not always behave the same way with one parent as they do with the other parent. By sampling different situations, a researcher can also increase the diversity of the subject sample and hence achieve greater generality than could be claimed if only particular types of individuals were observed.

As part of a naturalistic observation of beer drinking among college students, investigators purposely sampled behavior in various settings where beer was served, including five town bars and a student center (see Geller, Russ, & Altomari, 1986). In a different study, LaFrance and Mayo (1976) investigated racial differences in eye contact, and sampled many different situations. Pairs of individuals were observed in college cafeterias, business-district fast-food outlets, hospital and airport waiting rooms, and restaurants. By using situation sampling, the investigators were able to include in their sample people who differed in age, socioeconomic class, sex, and race. Their observations of cultural differences in eye contact have considerably greater external validity than if they had studied only certain types of participants in only a specific situation.

In most situations researchers observe the behavior of all the individuals who are present at the time and place they selected to sample. If, for instance, researchers wished to observe how well students can concentrate while studying in the library in the morning and in the evening, they would observe all students in the library at the designated times. There are situations, however, when there may be more going on than can be effectively observed. For example, if researchers observed students' food selections in the dining hall during peak hours, they would not be able to observe all the students. In this case, and in others like it, the researcher would use *subject sampling* to determine which students to observe. Similar to the procedures for time sampling, the researcher could either select students systematically (every tenth student) or select students randomly. In what is likely by now a familiar refrain, the goal of subject sampling is to obtain a representative sample of students eating at the dining hall.

CLASSIFICATION OF OBSERVATIONAL METHODS

- Observational methods can be classified as "observation with intervention" or "observation without intervention."
- Methods for recording behavior can be classified in terms of how much of behavior is recorded.

Observational methods can be classified on two dimensions (Willems, 1969). The first important distinction is between observation with intervention and observation without intervention. The second dimension involves the methods of recording behavior. Observation studies can be distinguished in terms of whether all (or nearly all) of the behavior is recorded or whether only particular units of behavior are recorded. In some situations researchers seek a comprehensive description of behavior. They accomplish this by recording behavior using film, tapes, or lengthy verbal descriptions. More often, researchers record specific units of behavior that are related to the goals of a particular study. For example, Chambers and Ascione (1987) observed children while they played either an aggressive video game or a video game with prosocial content. Children who played the aggressive game were later observed to put less money in a donation box and were less likely to help sharpen pencils than children who played the prosocial game. Thus, in this study, the researchers recorded specific responses related to the children's prosocial behavior.

We will discuss observational methods first in terms of the extent of observer intervention and then in terms of methods for recording behavior.

OBSERVATION WITHOUT INTERVENTION

- The goals of naturalistic observation are to describe behavior as it normally occurs and to examine relationships among variables.
- Naturalistic observation helps to establish the external validity of laboratory findings.
- When ethical and moral considerations prevent experimental control, naturalistic observation is an important research strategy.

Key Concept

Observation of behavior in a natural setting, *without* any attempt by the observer to intervene, is frequently called **naturalistic observation.** An observer using this method of observation acts as a passive recorder of what occurs. The events occur naturally and are not manipulated or controlled by the observer. Although it is not easy to define a natural setting precisely (see Bickman, 1976), we can consider a natural setting one in which behavior ordinarily occurs and that has not been arranged specifically for the purpose of observing behavior. Observing people in a psychology laboratory would not, for instance, be considered naturalistic observation. The laboratory situation has been created specifically to study behavior. In that sense, the laboratory is an artificial rather than a natural setting. In fact, observation in natural settings serves, among other functions, as a way of establishing the external validity of laboratory findings— bringing the lab into the "real world." Observation of behavior in Internet discussion groups and chat rooms is yet another way that researchers have sought to describe behavior as it normally occurs. This recent form of "naturalistic" observation, however, raises serious ethical issues which we discussed in Chapter 3 and will discuss later in this chapter (see also Kraut et al., 2004).

The major goals of observation in natural settings are to describe behavior as it ordinarily occurs and to investigate the relationship among variables that are present. Hartup (1974), for instance, chose naturalistic observation to investigate the frequency and types of aggression exhibited by preschoolers in a St. Paul, Minnesota, children's center. He distinguished hostile aggression (person-oriented) from instrumental aggression (aimed at the retrieval of an object, territory, or privilege). Although he observed boys to be more aggressive overall than girls, his observations provided no evidence that the types of aggression differed between the sexes. Thus Hartup was able to conclude that, with respect to hostile aggression, there was no evidence that boys and girls were "wired" differently.

Hartup's study of children's aggression illustrates why a researcher may choose to use naturalistic observation rather than to manipulate experimental conditions related to behavior. There are certain aspects of human behavior that moral or ethical considerations prevent us from controlling. For example,

FIGURE 4.1 Animal researchers such as Jane Goodall frequently rely on naturalistic observation to obtain information about the behavior of their subjects.

researchers are interested in the relationship between early childhood isolation and later emotional and psychological development. However, we would object strenuously if they tried to take children from their parents in order to raise them in isolation. Alternative methods of data collection must be considered if this problem is to be investigated. For example, the effect of early isolation on later development has been studied through experimentation on animal subjects (Harlow & Harlow, 1966); descriptions of so-called feral children raised outside of human culture, presumably by animals (Candland, 1993); case studies of children subjected to unusual conditions of isolation by their parents (Curtiss, 1977); and systematic observation of institutionalized children (Spitz, 1965). Moral and ethical sanctions also apply to investigating the nature of children's aggression. We would not want to see children intentionally harassed and picked on simply to record their reactions. However, as anyone knows who has observed children, there is plenty of naturally occurring aggression. Hartup's study shows how naturalistic observation can be a useful method of gaining knowledge about children's aggression within moral and ethical constraints.

Psychologists are not the only researchers who observe behavior in natural settings. Observation is a fundamental method in ethology. Although related to psychology, *ethology* is generally considered a branch of biology (Eibl-Eibesfeldt, 1975). Ethologists study the behavior of organisms in relation to their natural environment. They adopt a comparative approach to understanding behavior and often seek to explain behavior in one animal species on the basis of innate patterns of behavior observed in species lower on the evolutionary scale. Speculations about the role of innate mechanisms in determining human behavior are not uncommon among ethologists. The focus of an ethological investigation is often the development of an *ethogram*. This is a complete catalog of all the behavior patterns of an organism, including information on frequency, duration, and context of occurrence for each behavior. In addition, an ethological perspective has proven important for the understanding of both normal and abnormal human behavior. An interesting example is the ethological analysis of psychiatric problems based on comprehensive descriptions of facial behavior of schizophrenic patients (see Pitman et al., 1987).

OBSERVATION WITH INTERVENTION

- Most psychological research uses observation with intervention.
- The three methods of observation with intervention are participant observation, structured observation, and the field experiment.

Let's face it. Scientists like to "tamper" with nature. They like to intervene in order to observe the effects and perhaps to test a theory. Intervention rather than nonintervention characterizes most psychological research. Although the types of intervention employed by psychologists are too numerous and diverse to classify, their reasons for intervening are generally one or more of the following:

1 To precipitate or cause an event that occurs infrequently in nature or that normally occurs under conditions that make it difficult to observe.

2 To investigate the limits of an organism's response by varying systematically the qualities of a stimulus event.

3 To gain access to a situation or event that is generally not open to scientific observation.

4 To arrange conditions so that important antecedent events are controlled and consequent behaviors can be readily observed.

5 To establish a comparison by manipulating one or more independent variables to determine their effect on behavior.

There are three important methods of observation that researchers use when they choose to intervene in natural settings: participant observation, structured observation, and the field experiment. The nature and degree of intervention varies across these three methods. We will consider each method in turn.

Participant Observation

- Undisguised participant observation is often used to understand the culture and behavior of groups of individuals.
- Disguised participant observation is often used when researchers believe individuals would change their behavior if they knew it was being recorded.

- Participant observation allows researchers to observe behaviors and situations that are not usually open to scientific observation.
- Participant observers may sometimes lose their objectivity or may unduly influence the individuals whose behavior they are recording.

Key Concept }

In **participant observation,** observers play a dual role. They observe people's behavior and they participate actively in the situation they are observing. In *undisguised* participant observation, individuals who are being observed know that the observer is present for the purpose of collecting information about their behavior. This method is used frequently by anthropologists who seek to understand the culture and behavior of groups by living and working with members of the group.

In *disguised* participant observation, those who are being observed do not know that they are being observed. As you might imagine, people do not always behave in the way they ordinarily would when they know their behavior is being recorded. Politicians, for instance, often make different statements when speaking to the press, depending on whether their comments are "for" or "off" the record. Our own behavior is likely to be affected by knowing that we are being watched. Because of this possibility, researchers may decide to disguise their role as observers if they believe that people being observed will not act as they ordinarily would if they know their activities are being recorded. Disguised participant observation raises ethical issues (e.g., privacy and informed consent) which must be addressed prior to implementing the study. We have considered these ethical issues in Chapter 3 and we will discuss them further later in this chapter.

Rosenhan (1973) used disguised participant observation to investigate psychiatric diagnosis and hospitalization. Eight individuals (including psychologists, a pediatrician, and a housewife) misrepresented their names, occupations, and symptoms and sought admission to twelve different mental hospitals. Each complained of the same general symptom: that he or she was hearing voices. Most of the pseudopatients were diagnosed with schizophrenia.

Immediately after being hospitalized, the researchers stopped complaining of any symptoms and refrained from acting abnormally (except, for a while, their continued anxiety about being "caught"). In addition to observing patient-staff interactions, the observers were interested in how long it took for a "sane" person to be released from the hospital. The researchers were hospitalized from 7 to 52 days, and when they were discharged, their schizophrenia was said to be "in remission." Apparently, once the pseudopatients were labeled schizophrenic, they were stuck with that label no matter what the nature of their subsequent behavior. There are, however, reasons to challenge this specific conclusion and other aspects of Rosenhan's (1973) study (see Box 4.1).

Participant observation allows an observer to gain access to a situation that is not usually open to scientific observation. For example, a researcher analyzing hate crimes against African Americans entered various "White racist Internet chat rooms" while posing as a "curious neophyte" (Glaser, Dixit, & Green, 2002).

BOX 4.1

THINKING CRITICALLY ABOUT "ON BEING SANE IN INSANE PLACES"

In his article, "On Being Sane in Insane Places," Rosenhan (1973) questioned the nature of psychiatric diagnosis and hospitalization. How could normal people be labeled as schizophrenic, one of the most severe mental illnesses we know? Why didn't the hospital staff recognize the pseudopatients were faking their symptoms? After days or weeks of hospitalization, why didn't the staff recognize that the pseudopatients were "sane," not insane?

These are important questions. After Rosenhan's research article was published in *Science* magazine, many psychologists and psychiatrists met and wrote articles in response to Rosenhan's questions (e.g., Spitzer, 1976; Weiner, 1975). Presented below are just a few of the criticisms of Rosenhan's research.

—We cannot criticize the staff for making a wrong diagnosis: a diagnosis based on faked symptoms will, of course, be wrong.
—The pseudopatients had more than one symptom; they were anxious (about being "caught"), reported they were distressed and sought hospitalization. Is it "normal" to seek admission into a mental hospital?
—Did the pseudopatients really behave normally once in the hospital? Perhaps normal behavior would be to say something like, "Hey, I only pretended to be insane to see if I could be hospitalized, but really, I lied, and now I want to go home."
—Schizophrenics' behavior is not always psychotic; "true" schizophrenics often behave "normally." Thus, it's not surprising that the staff took many days to determine that the pseudopatients no longer experienced symptoms.

—A diagnosis of "in remission" was quite rare, and reflects staff members' recognition that a pseudopatient was no longer experiencing symptoms. However, research on schizophrenia demonstrates that once a person shows signs of schizophrenia, he or she is more likely than others to experience these symptoms again. Therefore, the diagnosis of "in remission" guides mental health professionals as they try to understand a person's subsequent behavior.
—"Sane" and "insane" are legal terms, not psychiatric. The legal decision of whether someone is insane requires a judgment about whether a person knows right from wrong, which is irrelevant to this study.

As you can see, Rosenhan's research was controversial. Most professionals now believe that this study does not help us to understand psychiatric diagnosis. However, several important long-term benefits of Rosenhan's research have emerged:

—Mental health professionals are more likely to postpone a diagnosis until more information is gathered about a patient's symptoms; this is called "diagnosis deferred."
—Mental health professionals are more aware of how their theoretical and personal biases may influence interpretations of patients' behaviors, and guard against biased judgments.
—Rosenhan's research illustrated the depersonalization and powerlessness experienced by many patients in mental health settings. His research influenced the mental health field to examine its practices and improve conditions for patients.

Such venues, of course, where violence is sometimes advocated, would normally not be open to scientific investigation. A participant observer may also be in a position to have the same experiences as the people under study. This experience may provide important insights and understanding of individuals or groups. The pseudopatients in the Rosenhan study, for instance, felt what it was like to be labeled schizophrenic and not to know how long it would be before they could return to society. An important contribution of Rosenhan's (1973) study was its illustration of the dehumanization that occurs in institutional settings. Similarly, in the fall of 1959, John Howard Griffin set out to investigate "what it was like to be a Negro in a land where we keep the Negro down." Griffin, a White man, darkened his skin using medication and stain in order to pass himself off as Black. For more than a month he traveled (walking, hitchhiking, riding buses) through Mississippi, Alabama, and Georgia. He described his experiences as a participant observer in his book *Black Like Me* (1960), which was an important precursor of the civil rights movement of the 1960s.

A participant observer's role in a situation can pose serious problems in carrying out a successful study. Observers may, for instance, lose the objectivity required for valid observations if they identify with the individuals under study. Changes in a participant observer are sometimes dramatic and are not easily anticipated. Witness the experiences of a criminologist who used undisguised participant observation to study police officers at work. Kirkham (1975) went through police academy training like any recruit and became a uniformed patrol officer assigned to a high-crime area in a city of about half a million. His immersion in the daily activities of an officer on the beat led to marked changes in his attitudes and personality. As Kirkham himself noted:

> As the weeks and months of my new career as a slum policeman went by, I slowly but inexorably began to become indistinguishable in attitudes and behavior from the policemen with whom I worked. . . . According to the accounts of my family, colleagues and friends, I began to increasingly display attitudinal and behavioral elements that were entirely foreign to my previous personality—punitiveness, pervasive cynicism and mistrust of others, chronic irritability and free-floating hostility, racism, a diffuse personal anxiety over the menace of crime and criminals that seemed at times to border on the obsessive. A former opponent of capital punishment, I became its vociferous advocate in cases involving felony murder, kidnapping and the homicide of police officers—even though as a criminologist I continued to recognize its ineffectiveness as a deterrent to crime (p. 19).

Participant observers must be aware of the threat to objective reporting that arises due to their involvement in the situation they are studying. This threat necessarily increases as degree of involvement increases.

Another potential problem with observer involvement is the effect the observer can have on the behavior of those being studied. It is more than likely that the participant observer will have to interact with people, make decisions, initiate activities, assume responsibilities, and otherwise act like everyone else in that situation. Whenever observers intervene in a natural setting, they must ask to what degree participants and events are affected by their intervention. Is what is being observed the same as it would have been if the observer had never appeared? It is difficult to generalize results to other situations if intervention produces behavior that is specific to the conditions and events created by the observer.

The extent of a participant observer's influence on the behavior under observation is not easily assessed. Several factors must be considered, such as whether participation is disguised or undisguised, the size of the group entered, and the role of the observer in the group. The disguised participant observation in the

Rosenhan study appears to have been successful. Rosenhan and his associates seem not to have significantly affected the natural environment of the hospital unit by assuming the role of patients. However, some of the patients—though none of the staff—apparently detected the sanity of the pseudopatients, suggesting to the observers that they were there to check up on the hospital.

When the group under observation is small or the activities of the participant observer are prominent, the observer is more likely to have a significant effect on participants' behavior. This problem confronted several social psychologists who infiltrated a group of people who claimed to be in contact with beings from outer space (Festinger, Riecken, & Schachter, 1956). A leader of the group said he had received a message from the aliens predicting a cataclysmic flood on a specific date. The flood was to stretch from the Arctic Circle to the Gulf of Mexico. Because of the attitudes of members of the group toward "nonbelievers," the researchers were forced to make up bizarre stories in order to gain access to the group. This tactic worked too well. One of the observers was even thought to be a spaceman bringing a message. The researchers had inadvertently reinforced the group's beliefs and influenced in an undetermined way the course of events that followed. By the way, the flood never occurred, but at least some of the group members came to use this disconfirmation as a means of strengthening their initial belief. They began to seek new members by arguing that their faith had prevented the prophesied flood.

Thus, although participant observation may permit an observer to gain access to situations not usually open to scientific investigation, the observer using this technique must seek ways to deal with the possible loss of objectivity and the potential effects that a participant observer may have on the behavior under study.

Structured Observation

- Structured observations are set up to record behaviors that may be difficult to observe using naturalistic observation.
- Structured observations are often used by clinical and developmental psychologists.
- Problems in interpreting structured observations can occur when the same observation procedures are not followed across observations or observers, or when important variables are not controlled.

Key Concept }

There are a variety of observational methods using intervention that are not easily categorized. These procedures differ from naturalistic observation because researchers intervene to exert some control over the events they are observing. The degree of intervention and control over events is less, however, than that seen in field experiments (which we describe briefly in the next section and in more detail in Chapter 7). We have labeled these procedures **structured observation.** Often the observer intervenes in order to cause an event to occur or to "set up" a situation so that events can be more easily recorded than they would be without intervention. In other cases the observer may create quite elaborate procedures to investigate a particular behavior more fully.

Simons and Levin (1998) used structured observation to study a phenomenon called change blindness. Change blindness occurs when people fail to notice changes in their environment. With so much going on around us, it is impossible for us to notice every little change. Simons and Levin demonstrated, however, that people often fail to notice changes even when they are paying attention. In their study the researchers used *confederates,* that is, individuals in the research situation who are instructed to behave in a certain way in order to create a situation for observing behavior. One confederate approached a pedestrian walking across campus and asked for directions. About 15 seconds into the conversation two other confederates rudely passed between them carrying a door. As the door passed, the original confederate and one of the confederates carrying the door changed places. This structured observation created a changed environment with the new confederate now conversing with the pedestrian (see Figure 4.2). The new confederate typically made eye contact

FIGURE 4.2   Frames from a video of a subject from Experiment 1. Frames *a–c* show the sequence of the switch. Frame *d* shows the two experimenters side by side.

with the pedestrian, and differed from the original confederate in height, voice, and clothing. Only about half of the pedestrians noticed the switch; half of the pedestrians were blind to the change.

Structured observations may occur in a natural setting as in the Simons and Levin (1998) study or in a laboratory setting. Clinical psychologists often use structured observations when making behavioral assessments of parent-child interactions (see, for example, Hughes & Haynes, 1978). Animal researchers also frequently structure an observational situation to create events that would normally be difficult to observe in natural settings. An interesting example in this regard comes from a series of studies investigating differences in the cognitive capacity of apes and humans. (Was Darwin right? Is it just a matter of degree?) One type of structured observation involves assessing the gaze-following behavior of chimpanzees (see Povinelli & Bering, 2002). A human caretaker makes eye contact with the chimpanzee and then looks above the chimpanzee. Observations reveal that chimpanzees do indeed follow the caretaker's gaze (i.e., looking above); however, controversy exists as to what this behavior really means. Do apes "understand" the mental state of the human caretaker (i.e., that the person has seen something)?

Developmental psychologists also frequently use structured observations. Jean Piaget (1896–1980) is perhaps most notable for his use of these methods. In many of Piaget's studies, a child is first given a problem to solve and then given several variations of the problem to test the limits of the child's understanding. The observer acquaints the child with the nature of the problem and then asks questions to probe the child's reasoning processes. These structured observations have provided a wealth of information regarding children's cognition and are the basis for Piaget's "stage theory" of intellectual development. Piaget-type tasks are also frequently used by animal researchers to investigate aspects of animal cognition. In one such study, orangutans outperformed squirrel monkeys on a classic test of object permanence, the ability to represent cognitively the existence of an unperceived (e.g., unseen) object (de Blois, Novak, & Bond, 1998.)

Structured observation represents a compromise between the passive nonintervention of naturalistic observation and the systematic manipulation of independent variables and precise control that characterize laboratory experiments. The advantage of such a compromise is that it permits observations to be made under conditions that are more natural than the more artificial conditions imposed in a laboratory. Nevertheless, there may be a price to pay. The failure to follow similar procedures each time an observation is made may make it difficult for other observers to obtain the same results when investigating the same problem. Uncontrolled, and perhaps unknown, variables may play an important part in producing the behavior under observation. For example, observers who use structured observations like those used by Piaget do not always follow the same procedure from one observation to another. This inconsistency in procedure across observations is a potential problem with these techniques (see Brainerd, 1978).

FIGURE 4.3   Jean Piaget (1896–1980) used structured observation to investigate children's cognitive development.

Field Experiments

- In a field experiment, researchers manipulate one or more independent variables in a natural setting to determine the effect on behavior.

Key Concept }

When an observer manipulates one or more independent variables in a natural setting in order to determine their effect on behavior, the procedure is called a **field experiment.** We mention field experiments in this chapter because they represent the most extreme form of intervention in observational methods. The essential difference between field experiments and other observational methods is that researchers exert more control in field experiments. In a field experiment, researchers typically manipulate an independent variable to create two or more conditions and they measure the effect of the independent variable on behavior. Field experiments are frequently used in social psychology (Bickman, 1976). For example, confederates have posed as robbers when bystander reaction to a crime has been investigated (Latané & Darley, 1970) and as individuals cutting into a waiting line in order to study the reactions of those already in line (Milgram, Liberty, Toledo, & Wackenhut, 1986). Our discussion of experimental methods will continue in Chapter 7.

STRETCHING EXERCISE

In this exercise we ask you to respond to the questions that follow this brief description of an observational study.

Students in a research methods class did an observational study to investigate whether students' ability to concentrate while studying was affected by where they studied. Specifically, the research methods students observed students in two locations on campus, the library and a lounge in the student union. The research methods students made their observations while appearing to be studying in locations in the library or the lounge from which they could observe the other students who were present. They observed only students sitting alone in each location who had study materials such as a textbook or a notebook open in front of them. The observers recorded the amount of time during a 5-minute observation period that the student was studying as indicated by either looking at the materials or writing. The observers made sure that they recorded each student they observed only once during the observation period. The student observers expected to find that students would be able to concentrate better in the library than in the student union.

There were five student observers who observed a total of 60 students in the library and 50 students in the lounge from 9 to 11 P.M. on the same Monday evening. The student observers found that the mean time that students in the library spent studying was 4.4 of the 5.0 minutes.

The corresponding mean time for the students in the student union was 4.5 of the 5.0 minutes. The student observers were surprised by two aspects of their findings. They were surprised to find that students studied for nearly 90% of the 5-minute study interval. They were even more surprised that, contrary to their prediction, the study times did not differ for the two locations.

1 Identify what type of observational method the students used in their study and explain what characteristics of their study you used to make your identification.
2 How well do you think that the operational definition of concentration that the students used for their dependent variable "captured" students' concentration? How could their operational definition of the dependent variable have contributed to both the high overall level of study time they observed and the lack of a difference between the two locations? What would you recommend to improve the operational definition of concentration in this study?
3 Why would the time-sampling plan in a study of this type be especially important? How could the time-sampling plan used in this study be improved to increase external validity?
4 Consider for the sake of this question that students can concentrate better in the library than in the student union. How could the nature of the material that the students were studying in the two locations have led to the finding that there was no difference between the observed concentration by students in the library and in the student union?

Recording Behavior

- The goals of the observational research determine whether researchers seek a comprehensive description of behavior or a description of only selected behaviors.
- How the results of a study are ultimately summarized, analyzed, and reported depends on how behavioral observations are initially recorded.

Observational methods differ in the degree of observer intervention. The passive nonintervention of naturalistic observation anchors one end of the intervention dimension, and the active manipulation of independent variables that characterizes field experiments anchors the other end. Observational methods also differ in the manner in which behavior is recorded. A particularly important feature is the degree to which behavior is abstracted from the situation in which it is observed (see Willems, 1969, for a thorough discussion of this aspect of observational methods). Sometimes researchers seek a *comprehensive* description of behavior and the situation in which it occurs. More often they focus on only certain behaviors or events. Whether all behavior in a setting or only *selected* aspects are observed depends on the purpose of the study and the researchers' goals. Decisions regarding how behavior is recorded also depend on whether the investigator is doing qualitative or quantitative research. The results of a qualitative study are presented chiefly in the form of verbal description and logical argument. Reports of quantitative research mainly emphasize statistical description and analysis of data to support a study's conclusions. *The most important point to remember is that how you choose to record behavior determines how the results of your study are eventually measured, summarized, analyzed, and reported.*

Qualitative Records of Behavior

- Narrative records in the form of written descriptions of behavior, audiotapes, and videotapes are comprehensive records of observed behavior.
- Researchers classify and organize data from narrative records to test their hypotheses about behavior.
- Narrative records should be made during or soon after behavior is observed, and observers must be carefully trained to record behavior according to established criteria.

Key Concept }

When researchers seek a comprehensive record of behavior, they often use narrative records. **Narrative records** provide a more or less faithful reproduction of behavior as it originally occurred. To create a narrative record, an observer can write descriptions of behavior or use audiotape recordings, videotapes, and films. Ethologists are interested in every detail of a behavioral event, so they often use motion picture film to record behavior (Eibl-Eibesfeldt, 1975). For example, ethologists studied the function of the "eyebrow flash" in social interactions by filming 67 hours of individuals in naturally occurring social situations (Grammer, Schiefenhoevel, Schleidt, Lorenz, & Eibl-Eibesfeldt, 1988). Across three different cultures, they found that the eyebrow flash, usually accompanied by a smile, was a universal social signal (e.g., a sign of saying "yes").

Once narrative records are created, researchers can study, classify, and organize the records. Particular hypotheses or expectations about the behaviors under observation can be tested by examining the data. Narrative records differ from other forms of recording and measuring behavior because the classification of behaviors is done *after* the observations are made. Thus, researchers must make sure that the narrative records capture the information that will be needed to evaluate the hypotheses they are testing in the study.

Hartup (1974) obtained narrative records as part of his naturalistic study of children's aggression. He investigated a number of different aspects of children's aggression, including the relationship between particular kinds of events that preceded aggressive behavior and the nature of the aggressive episodes that followed these precipitating events. Consider this sample narrative record from Hartup's study (p. 339):

> Marian [a 7-year-old] . . . is complaining to all that David [who is also present] had squirted her on the pants she has to wear tonight. She says, "I'm gonna do it to him to see how he likes it." She fills a can with water and David runs to the teacher and tells of her threat. The teacher takes the can from Marian. Marian attacks David and pulls his hair very hard. He cries and swings at Marian as the teacher tries to restrain him; then she takes him upstairs . . . . Later, Marian and Elaine go upstairs and into the room where David is seated with a teacher. He throws a book at Marian. The teacher asks Marian to leave. Marian kicks David, then leaves. David cries and screams, "Get out of here, they're just gonna tease me."

Hartup (1974) instructed his observers to use precise language in describing behavior and to avoid making inferences about the intentions, motives, or feelings of the participants. Note that we are not told why David might want to throw a book at Marian or how Marian feels about being attacked. Hartup believed that certain antecedent behaviors were related to specific types of aggression. By strictly excluding any inferences or impressions of the observers, individuals coding the narrative would not be influenced by what the observer inferred was going on. Thus, the content of the narrative records could be classified and coded in a more objective manner.

Not all narrative records are as focused as those obtained by Hartup, nor do narrative records always avoid inferences and impressions of the observer. Narrative records are also not always meant to be comprehensive descriptions of behavior. For example, *field notes* include only the observer's running descriptions of the participants, events, settings, and behaviors. Field notes are used by journalists, social workers, anthropologists, ethologists, and others. They do not always contain an exact record of everything that occurred. Events and behaviors that especially interest the observer are recorded and are likely to be interpreted in terms of the observer's specialized knowledge or expertise. For example, an ethologist might record how the behavior of one species appears to parallel that of another. Field notes tend to be highly personalized (Brandt, 1972), but they are probably used more frequently than any other kind of narrative record. Their usefulness as scientific records depends on the accuracy and precision of their content. Accuracy and precision depend critically on the training of the observer and the extent to which the observations that are recorded can be verified by independent observers and through other means of investigation.

Practical, as well as methodological, considerations dictate the manner in which narrative records are made. *As a general rule, records should be made during or as soon as possible after behavior is observed.* The passage of time blurs details and makes it harder to reproduce the original sequence of actions. Adjang (1986) used a portable cassette recorder to make narrative records of his spoken observations of the teasing behavior of young chimpanzees; however, he then transcribed these spoken reports onto paper "as soon as possible" (p. 139). This rule is sometimes not easy to follow when observations are made in natural settings. An ethologist who is trying to record the behavior of animals in the wild is sometimes hampered by bad weather, animal migration, dwindling daylight, and so forth. Notes may have to be made quickly—even while the observer is quite literally on the run. At other times observers may have to wait until they return to camp to make written records of behavior.

Decisions regarding what should be included in a narrative record must be made prior to observing behavior. We have seen, for example, that verbal narratives may differ in terms of the degree of observer inference that is appropriate or the completeness of the behavioral record. Thus, these aspects of a narrative record, as well as others, must be decided upon prior to beginning a study (see, for example, Brandt, 1972). Once the content of narrative records is decided, observers must be trained to record behavior according to the criteria that have been set up. Practice observations may have to be conducted and records critiqued by more than one investigator before "real" data are collected.

Quantitative Measures of Behavior

- Researchers often obtain quantitative measures such as frequency or duration of occurrence when they seek to describe specific behaviors or events.
- Quantitative measures of behavior use one of the four levels of measurement scales: nominal, ordinal, interval, and ratio.
- Rating scales, often used to measure psychological dimensions, are frequently treated as if they are interval scales even though they usually represent ordinal measurement.
- Electronic recording devices may be used in natural settings to record behavior, and pagers sometimes are used to signal participants to report their behavior (e.g., on a questionnaire).

Often researchers are interested only in certain behaviors or specific aspects of individuals and settings. They may have specific hypotheses about the behaviors they expect and clear definitions of the behaviors they are investigating. For example, assume you want to do a naturalistic observation study investigating reactions to individuals with obvious physical disabilities by those who do not have such disabilities. In order to conduct your study, it would be necessary to define what constitutes a "reaction" to a physically disabled individual. Are you interested, for example, in helping behaviors, approach/avoidance behaviors, eye contact, length of conversation, or in some other behavioral reaction? As you consider what behaviors you will use to define people's "reactions," you will also have to decide how you will measure these behaviors. Assume, for instance, that you have decided to measure people's reactions by observing eye contact between individuals who do not have obvious physical disabilities and those who do. You would still need to decide exactly how you should measure eye contact. Should you simply measure whether a passerby does or does not make eye contact, or do you want to measure the duration of any eye contact? Of course, you may wish to use more than one measure, a research strategy that is recommended whenever it is feasible. The decisions you make will depend on the particular hypotheses or goals of your study. In making your decisions, you should take advantage of information you can gain by examining previous published studies that have used the same or similar behavioral measures. Thompson (1982), for example, has measured reactions to physically disabled individuals and found that the reactions frequently can be classified as unfavorable. We will now describe four general ways in which behavioral measures can be defined.

Measurement Scales   Quantitative measures of behavior differ depending upon the scale of measurement that you decide to use. Thus, it is important for you to be familiar with the types of measurement scales used in behavioral re-

Key Concept }

search. **Measurement scales** represent different levels at which behaviors can be quantified and the different measurement scales influence how data are subsequently analyzed. There are four measurement scales that apply to both physical and psychological measurement: nominal, ordinal, interval, and ratio. The characteristics of each measurement scale are described in Table 4.1 and a more detailed description of measurement scales is provided in Box 4.2. You will need to keep these four measurement scales in mind as you select statistical procedures for analyzing the results of the research you will be doing. In this section we will describe how the measurement scales can be used in observational research.

A *checklist* is often used to record nominal scale measures. The observer could record on a checklist, for example, whether individuals make eye contact with a physically disabled person, whether children in a classroom are talking or are quiet, whether people use seat belts or do not use seat belts. Characteristics of participants—such as age, race, and sex—are also frequently recorded using a checklist, as are features of the setting—such as time of day, location, and whether other people are present. Researchers are often interested in observing behavior as a function of participant and context variables. Do males use seat

TABLE 4.1   CHARACTERISTICS OF MEASUREMENT SCALES

Type of scale	Operations	Objective
Nominal	Equal/not equal	Sort stimuli into discrete categories
Ordinal	Greater than/less than	Rank-order stimuli on a single dimension
Interval	Addition/multiplication/ subtraction/division	Specify the distance between stimuli on a given dimension
Ratio	Addition/multiplication/ subtraction/division/ formation of ratios of values	Specify the distance between stimuli on a given dimension and express ratios of scale values

BOX 4.2

MEASUREMENT "ON THE LEVEL"

The lowest level of measurement is called a *nominal scale;* it involves categorizing an event into one of a number of discrete categories. For instance, we could measure the color of people's eyes by classifying them as "brown-eyed" or "blue-eyed." When studying people's reactions to individuals with obvious physical disabilities, a researcher might use a nominal scale by measuring whether participants make eye contact or do not make eye contact with someone who has an obvious physical disability.

Summarizing and analyzing data measured on a nominal scale is limited. The only arithmetic operations that we can perform on nominal data involve the relationships "equal" and "not equal." A common way of summarizing nominal data is to report frequency in the form of proportion or percent of instances in each of the several categories.

The second level of measurement is called an ordinal scale. An *ordinal scale* involves ordering or ranking events to be measured. Ordinal scales add the arithmetic relationships "greater than" and "less than" to the measurement process. The outcome of a race is a familiar ordinal scale. When we know that an Olympic distance runner won a silver medal, we do not know whether she finished second in a photo finish or trailed 200 meters behind the gold medal winner.

The third level of measurement is called an interval scale. An *interval scale* involves specifying how far apart two events are on a given dimension. On an ordinal scale, the difference between an event ranked first and one ranked third does not necessarily equal the distance between those events ranked third and fifth. For example, the difference between the finishing times of the first- and third-place runners may not be the same as the difference in times between the third- and fifth-place runners. On an interval scale, however, differences of the same numerical size in scale values are equal. For example, the difference between 50 and 70 correct answers on an aptitude test is equal to the difference between 70 and 90 correct answers. What is missing from an interval scale is a meaningful zero point. For instance, if someone's score was zero on a verbal aptitude test, he or she would not necessarily have absolutely zero verbal ability (after all, the person presumably had enough verbal ability to take the test). Importantly, the standard arithmetic operations of addition, multiplication, subtraction, and division can be performed on data that are measured on an interval scale. Whenever possible, therefore, psychologists try to measure psychological dimensions using interval scales.

The fourth level of measurement is called a ratio scale. A *ratio scale* has all the properties of an interval scale, but a ratio scale also has an absolute zero point. In terms of arithmetic operations, a zero point makes the ratio of scale values meaningful. For example, temperature as expressed on the Celsius scale represents an interval scale of measurement. A reading of 0 degrees Celsius does not really mean absolutely no temperature. Therefore it is not meaningful to say that 100 degrees Celsius is twice as hot as 50 degrees, or that 20 degrees is three times colder than 60 degrees. On the other hand, the Kelvin scale of temperature does have an absolute zero, and the ratio of scale values can be meaningfully calculated. Physical scales measuring time, weight, and distance can usually be treated as ratio scales.

belts more than females? Are people who drive inexpensive automobiles more likely to carpool than people who drive expensive automobiles? These questions can be answered by observing the presence or absence of certain behaviors (seat-belt use or carpooling) for different categories of participants and settings (male and female, expensive and inexpensive automobiles).

Tassinary and Hansen (1998) used an ordinal scale to measure male and female undergraduate students' reactions to line drawings of female figures. The figures varied on physical dimensions such as height, weight, and hip size. The undergraduates rank ordered sets of figures in terms of attractiveness and fecundity (i.e., capability of bearing children). According to evolutionary psychology theory, female attractiveness is defined on the basis of cues simultaneously signaling both physical attractiveness and reproductive potential. One specific prediction based on evolutionary psychology theory is that the waist-to-hip ratio should be an invariant perceptual cue for *both* attractiveness and fecundity. Contrary to this expectation, the results of this study showed that relative hip size and weight were positively related to the rankings of fecundity and negatively related to physical attractiveness.

In order to quantify behavior in an observational study, observers sometimes make ratings of behaviors and events. Observers usually make ratings on the basis of their subjective judgments about the degree or quantity of some trait or condition (see Brandt, 1972). For example, Dickie (1987) asked observers to rate parent-infant interactions in the context of a study designed to assess the effects of a parent training program. Her observers visited the home and rated both the mother and the father while the parents interacted with their infant child. During most of the observation period, the observers sat in the room with the infant and asked the parents to "act as normal as possible—just as if we [the observers] weren't here." She also used structured observations involving assigned play with each parent. Parent-infant interactions were rated on 13 different dimensions, including degree of verbal, physical, and emotional interaction. For each dimension a continuum was defined that represented different degrees of this variable rated on a 7-point scale. A rating of 1 represented the absence or very little of the characteristic and larger numbers represented increasingly more of the trait.

Table 4.2 outlines one of the dimensions used by the observers in this study: warmth and affection directed toward the child. Note that precise verbal descriptions are given with the four odd-numbered scale values to help observers define different degrees of this trait. The even-numbered values (2, 4, 6) are used by observers to rate events that they judge fall between the more clearly defined values. The investigators found that parents who had taken part in a program aimed at developing competency in dealing with an infant were rated higher than were untrained parents on many of the variables.

At first glance, a rating scale such as that used by Dickie would appear to represent an interval scale of measurement. There is no true zero, and the intervals seem to be equal. And, in fact, many researchers treat such rating systems as if they represent interval scales of measurement. Closer examination, however, reveals that most of the rating scales used by observers to evaluate people or events on a psychological dimension really yield only ordinal information. For a rating system to be truly an interval level of measurement, a rating of 2, for instance, would have to be the same distance from a rating of 3 as a rating of 4 is from 5 or a rating of 6 is from 7. It is highly unlikely that human observers

TABLE 4.2 EXAMPLE OF RATING SCALE USED TO MEASURE A PARENT'S WARMTH AND AFFECTION TOWARD AN INFANT CHILD*

Scale value	Description
1	There is an absence of warmth, affection, and pleasure. Excessive hostility, coldness, distance, and isolation from the child are predominant. Relationship is on an attacking level.
2	
3	There is occasional warmth and pleasure in interaction. Parent shows little evidence of pride in the child, or pride is shown in relation to deviant or bizarre behavior by the child. Parent's manner of relating is contrived, intellectual, not genuine.
4	
5	There is moderate pleasure and warmth in the interaction. Parent shows pleasure in some areas but not in others.
6	
7	Warmth and pleasure are characteristic of the interaction with the child. There is evidence of pleasure and pride in the child. Pleasure response is appropriate to the child's behavior.

*From materials provided by Jane Dickie.

can make subjective judgments of traits such as warmth, pleasure, aggressiveness, or anxiety, in a manner that yields precise interval distances between ratings. However, most researchers assume an interval level of measurement when they use rating scales. Deciding what measurement scale applies for any given measure of behavior is not always easy. If you are in doubt, you should seek advice from knowledgeable experts so that you can make appropriate decisions about the statistical description and analysis of your data.

LaFrance and Mayo (1976) provide an example of ratio measurement in their study of racial differences in the amount of eye contact between individuals of the same race engaged in conversation. Pairs of Black individuals and pairs of White individuals were observed in natural settings. The amount of time each member of the pair spent looking into the face of the other member was recorded. Duration of eye contact represents a ratio level of measurement because units of time (e.g., seconds) have equal intervals and "zero" is a meaningul value (i.e., no eye contact). The researchers found that Blacks gazed less at another person while listening to conversation than did Whites. LaFrance and Mayo suggest that subtle differences in eye contact may be a source of social misunderstandings. White speakers may feel that lack of eye contact by a Black listener indicates untrustworthiness or lack of interest when it may reflect cultural differences between the races.

Another important measure of behavior is *frequency* of occurrence. Checklists can be used to measure the frequency of particular behaviors in the same individual or group of individuals by making repeated observations of the same individual or group over a period of time. The presence or absence of specific behaviors is noted at the time of each observation. In these situations, frequency of responding can be assumed to represent a ratio level of measurement. That is, if "units" of some behavior (e.g., occasions when a child leaves a classroom seat) are being counted, then zero represents an absence of that specific behavior. Ratios of scale values would be meaningful as long as, for instance, an individual with 20 units had twice as many units as someone with 10. McKinney, Mason, Perkerson, and Clifford (1975), for instance, used the Schedule for Classroom Activity Norms (SCAN), which is a checklist that divides classroom behavior into 27 discrete categories. At repeated intervals of time, an observer records what each child in the classroom is doing. Many observations of the same child show which categories of behavior are most frequent for that child. Using the SCAN checklist, researchers found that combining information obtained from observing the children's behavior with information obtained from IQ tests yielded a more accurate prediction of school achievement than could be obtained by using either observation or IQ information alone.

Electronic Recording and Tracking   Behavior is sometimes measured by using electronic recording and tracking devices. For example, as part of a study investigating the relationship between cognitive coping strategies and blood pressure among college students, participants were outfitted with an ambulatory blood pressure monitor (Dolan, Sherwood, & Light, 1992). College students wore the electronic recording device during two "typical" school days, one of which, however, included an exam. Participants also completed a questionnaire assessing coping strategies and kept detailed logs of their daily activities. The researchers compared blood pressure readings for different times of the day and as a function of coping style. Students classified as exhibiting "high self-focused coping" (that is, who showed tendencies "to keep to themselves and/or blame themselves in stressful situations," p. 233), had higher blood pressure responses during and after an exam than did those who were classified as low in self-focused coping strategies. The use of electronic recording in research is likely to grow with advancements in the technology of Personal Digital Assistants (PDAs).

Researchers also have used an innovative procedure known as the Experience Sampling Method (ESM). They supply participants with electronic pagers, usually for a week at a time. Participants are asked to report on their activities when signaled by the pagers (e.g., Csikszentimihalyi & Larson, 1987; Larson, 1989). In one study of adolescent interactions with their families, 220 middle- and working-class youth provided reports at two periods in their lives, grades 5 to 8 and grades 9 to 12 (Larson et al., 1996). When randomly "beeped," the adolescents used a checklist to indicate whom they were with, responded on 7-point scales regarding their emotional state and perceptions of the people they were with, and answered open-ended questions about their activities. As might be expected, the data revealed a sharp decline in the time adolescents spend with family members across grades 5 to 12. What was a surprising finding, however, was that amount of adolescent-family conflict was not related to changes in family time, something not seen in other primates where conflict frequently leads to disengagement from the family group. The researchers argued that for human adolescents "the negative experience with family is as likely to be a stimulus for continued interaction—like one might see in an embattled, enmeshed family—as it is to be a stimulus for physical withdrawal" (p. 752). The ESM procedure also has been used to study the emotional states of chronic mental patients (e.g., Delespaul, 1995).

Park, Armeli, and Tennen (2004) used an "Internet daily diary methodology" to obtain measures of stress and coping by University of Connecticut undergraduates. A total of 190 students participated by logging into a secure Internet website on each of 28 days. (E-mail reminders were sent each day.) Participants recorded information about the day's most stressful event. They then rated the event for how controllable they thought it was and answered questions about their mood and strategies of coping. Positive moods were linked more with problem-focused coping strategies than avoidance strategies, especially when stressors were viewed as controllable.

Both ESM and daily diary methods rely on participants' self-reports of mood and activities, and not on direct observation of their behavior. As such, it is important that techniques be devised to detect biases in data collection (e.g., possible omission or misrepresentation of personal activities by participants) (see Larson, 1989, for a discussion of possible biases using the ESM method). These problems can be weighed against the time and labor costs sometimes required to obtain a comprehensive description of behavior through direct observation (e.g., Barker, Wright, Schoggen, & Barker, 1978).

ANALYSIS OF OBSERVATIONAL DATA

Data Reduction

- Observational data are summarized through the process of data reduction.
- Researchers quantify the data in narrative records by coding behaviors according to specified criteria, for example, by categorizing behaviors.
- Data are summarized using descriptive measures such as frequency counts, means, and standard deviations.

Analysis of Narrative Records   Narrative records can provide a wealth of information about behavior in natural settings. Once collected, how do researchers summarize all this information? Data reduction is often an important step in analyzing the content of narrative records. **Data reduction** is the process of abstracting and summarizing behavioral data. Using *qualitative data analysis*, researchers seek to provide a *verbal* summary of their observations and to develop a theory that explains behavior in the narrative records. In qualitative analysis, data reduction occurs when researchers verbally summarize information, identify themes, categorize information, group various pieces of information, and record their own observations about the narrative records.

Data reduction often involves the process of **coding,** the identification of units of behavior or particular events according to specific criteria. For instance,

Key Concept

Key Concept

Hartup's (1974) 10-week observation of children's aggression yielded information about 758 units of aggression. As part of an ethological study of preschool children, McGrew (1972) identified 115 different behavior patterns. He developed coding schemes to classify patterns of behavior according to the body part involved, ranging from facial expressions such as bared teeth, grin face, and pucker face, to locomotion behaviors such as gallop, crawl, run, skip, and step. Coders used the coding schemes to classify these behavioral patterns while they watched videotape recordings of the observations that showed children attending nursery school.

Coding is often based on units of behavior or events that are related to the goals of the study. For instance, Hartup used nine categories to code the nature of aggressive episodes. Data reduction using coding allows researchers to determine relationships between specific types of behavior and the events that are the antecedents of these behaviors. For example, McGrew (1972) found that children exhibit a "pout face" after losing a fight over a toy. This ethologist-observer noted that young chimpanzees show a similar expression when seeking reunion with their mother. Just after being frustrated (and often just prior to weeping), children exhibited a "pucker face." Interestingly, there seems to be no record of a pucker face in nonhuman primates.

Descriptive Measures   Descriptive measures are used to summarize observational data when quantitative data analysis is used. When events are classified into mutually exclusive categories (nominal scale), the most common descriptive measure is relative frequency. A ratio of the frequency with which various behaviors occur over the total frequency of events observed is a relative frequency measure. Relative frequency measures are expressed as either a proportion or a percentage. For example, Jenni and Jenni (1976) observed students on six college campuses. They reported that 82% of female college students carried their books by wrapping one or both arms around the books (with the short edges resting on their hip or in front of their body). Only 3% of male students used this particular book-carrying method!

Different—and more informative—descriptive statistics are reported when behavior is recorded on at least an interval scale of measurement. One or more measures of central tendency are used when observations are recorded using interval-scale ratings or when ratio-scale measures of time (duration, latency) are used. The most common measure of central tendency is the *arithmetic mean,* or *average.* The mean describes the "typical" score in a group of scores and provides a useful measure to summarize the performance of a group. For a more complete description of group performance, researchers also report measures of variability or dispersion of scores around the mean. The *standard deviation* approximates the average distance of a score from the mean.

Now may be a good time to review measures of central tendency and variability, as well as general guidelines for systematically analyzing data sets. The first few pages of Chapter 12 are devoted to these issues.

TABLE 4.3 MEANS AND STANDARD DEVIATIONS DESCRIBING THE TIME (IN SECONDS) THAT LISTEN-
ERS SPENT LOOKING INTO THE FACE OF A SPEAKER PER
1-MINUTE OBSERVATION UNIT*

Group	Mean	Standard deviation
Black conversants		
Male pairs	19.3	6.9
Female pairs	28.4	10.2
Male-female pairs	24.9	11.6
White conversants		
Male pairs	35.8	8.6
Female pairs	39.9	10.7
Male-female pairs	29.9	11.2

*From LaFrance and Mayo (1976).

LaFrance and Mayo (1976) reported means and standard deviations in their study of eye contact between same-race pairs of Black and White people in conversation. The number of seconds that each listener in a pair spent looking into the speaker's face was recorded. Table 4.3 gives the means and standard deviations summarizing the results of this study. The means in Table 4.3 show that White listeners spent more time looking into the faces of White speakers than Black listeners spent looking into the faces of Black speakers. This finding was obtained for both same-sex pairs and mixed-sex pairs. The standard deviations indicate that male pairs showed less variability than either female pairs or mixed-sex pairs. Measures of central tendency and variability provide a remarkably efficient and effective summary of the large numbers of observations that were made in this study.

Observer Reliability

- Interobserver reliability refers to the extent to which independent observers agree in their observations.
- Interobserver reliability is increased by providing clear definitions about behaviors and events to be recorded, by training observers, and by providing feedback about discrepancies.
- High interobserver reliability increases researchers' confidence that observations about behavior are accurate (valid).
- Interobserver reliability is assessed by calculating percentage agreement or correlations, depending on how the behaviors were measured and recorded.

Another important aspect of analyzing observational data is assessing the reliability of the observations. Unless the observations are reliable, they are unlikely to tell us anything meaningful about behavior. One way researchers assess the reliability of an observer is to ask, "Would another observer viewing the same events obtain the same results?"

Key Concept }

Interobserver Reliability   The degree to which two independent observers agree is referred to as **interobserver reliability.** When observers disagree we become uncertain about what is being measured and what behaviors and events actually occurred. Low interobserver reliability is likely to result when the event to be recorded is not clearly defined. Imagine Hartup (1974) asking his observers to record aggressive episodes among children without giving them an exact definition of aggression. What exactly is aggression? Some observers might decide to define aggression as one child's physical attack on another; other observers might include verbal assaults in their definition of aggression. What is a playful push and what is an angry shove? Without a clear definition of behavior or of the events to be recorded, observers do not always agree—and hence show low interobserver reliability. In addition to providing precise verbal definitions, giving concrete examples of a phenomenon generally helps increase reliability among observers. Showing observers photographs or videotapes of aggressive and nonaggressive episodes would be a good way to improve their ability to classify aggressive behaviors reliably. Observer reliability is also generally increased by training observers and giving them practice doing the observations. It is especially helpful during the training and practice to give the observers specific feedback regarding any discrepancies between their observations and those of other observers (Judd, Smith, & Kidder, 1991).

The observations of a highly reliable observer are not necessarily accurate observations. Consider two observers who reliably agree about what they saw but who are both "in error" to the same degree. Neither observer is providing an accurate record of behavior. For example, both might be influenced in a similar way by what they expect the outcome of the observational study to be. Instances are occasionally reported in the media of several observers claiming to see the same thing (for instance, an unidentified flying object, or UFO), only to have the event or object turn out to be something other than what observers claimed it to be (for instance, a weather balloon). Nevertheless, when two independent observers agree, we are generally more inclined to believe that their observations are accurate and valid than when data are based on the observations of a single observer. In order for observers to be independent, each must be unaware of what the other has recorded. The chance of both observers being influenced to the same degree by outcome expectancies, fatigue, or boredom is generally so small that we can be confident that what was reported actually occurred. Of course, the more independent observers agree, the more confident we become.

Measures of Reliability   The way in which interobserver reliability is assessed depends on how behavior is measured. When events are classified according to mutually exclusive categories (nominal scale), observer reliability is generally assessed using a percentage agreement measure. A formula for calculating percentage agreement between observers is:

$$\frac{\text{Number of times two observers agree}}{\text{Number of opportunities to agree}} \times 100$$

Hartup (1974) reported measures of reliability using percentage agreement that ranged from 83% to 94% for judges who coded narrative records according to type of aggression and nature of antecedent events. Although there is no hard-and-fast percentage of agreement that defines low interobserver reliability, researchers generally report estimates of reliability that exceed 85% in the published literature, suggesting that agreement much lower than that is unacceptable.

In many observational studies data are collected by several observers who observe at different times. Under these circumstances, researchers use only a sample of the observations to measure reliability. For example, two observers might be asked to record behavior according to a time-sampling procedure such that there is only a subset of times during which both observers are present. Amount of agreement for the times when both observers were present can be used to indicate the degree of reliability for the study as a whole.

When observational data represent at least an interval scale, such as when time is the variable being measured, observer reliability can be assessed using a Pearson Product-Moment Correlation Coefficient r. For example, LaFrance and Mayo (1976) obtained measures of reliability when observers recorded how much of the time a listener gazed into the speaker's face during a conversation. Observer reliability in their study was good; they found an average correlation of .92 between pairs of observers who recorded time engaged in eye contact.

Key Concept

Stat Tip

A *correlation* exists when two different measures of the same people, events, or things vary together—that is, when scores on one variable covary with scores on another variable. A **correlation coefficient** is a quantitative index of the degree of this covariation. As noted above, when interval or ratio data are collected a Pearson correlation coefficient, r, may be used to obtain a measure of interobserver reliability. This measure tells us how well ratings of two observers agree.

The correlation coefficient indicates the *direction* and *strength* of the correlation. Direction can be either positive or negative. A positive correlation indicates that as the values for one measure increase, the values of the other measure also increase. (Measures of smoking and lung cancer are positively correlated.) A negative correlation indicates that as the value of one measure increases, the value of the other measure decreases. (Time spent watching television and scores on academic tests are negatively correlated.) Clearly, when assessing interobserver reliability we are looking for positive correlations. The strength of a correlation refers to the degree of covariation present (or, as is sometimes said, the strength of the predictive relationship), since correlation is the basis for making predictions about behavior and events. (This aspect of correlation is discussed more fully in Chapters 5 and 12.)

Correlation coefficients range in size from −1.00 (a perfect negative relationship) to 1.00 (a perfect positive relationship). A value of 0.0 indicates there is no relationship between the two variables (and hence no basis for making predictions). The closer a correlation coefficient is to 1.0 or –1.0, the stronger the relationship between the two variables. Note that the sign of the correlation signifies only its direction; a correlation coefficient of –.46 indicates a stronger relationship than one that is .20. We suggest that measures of interobserver reliability that exceed .85 indicate good agreement between observers (but the greater the better!). As you have seen, LaFrance and Mayo (1976) reported average interobserver correlations of .92, showing very good agreement between their observers.

In Chapter 12 we discuss correlations more fully, including how relationships between two variables can be described graphically using scatterplots, how Pearson Product-Moment Correlation Coefficients are computed, and how these correlations are best interpreted. If you want to become more familiar with the topic of correlation, refer to the material on correlation in Chapter 12.

THINKING CRITICALLY ABOUT OBSERVATIONAL RESEARCH

Influence of the Observer

- If individuals change their behavior when they know they are being observed ("reactivity"), their behavior may no longer be representative of their normal behavior.
- Research participants may respond to demand characteristics in the research situation to guide their behavior.
- Methods to control reactivity include unobtrusive (nonreactive) measurement, adaptation (habituation, desensitization), and indirect observations of behavior.
- Researchers must consider ethical issues when attempting to control reactivity.

Conducting a good observational study involves choosing how to sample behavior and events to observe, choosing the appropriate observational method, and choosing how to record and analyze observational data. Now that you know the basics of observational methods, you also need to know about potential problems that can occur. The first problem occurs because people often change their behavior when they know they are being observed. A second problem occurs when observers' biases influence what behavior they chose to record. We'll consider each of these problems in turn.

Key Concept

Reactivity   The presence of an observer can lead people to change their behavior because they know they are being observed. When the observer influences the behavior being observed, the problem of **reactivity** is present. When individuals "react" to the presence of an observer, their behavior may not be representative of behavior when an observer is not present. Underwood and

Shaughnessy (1975) relate how a student, as part of a class assignment, set out to observe whether drivers came to a complete stop at an intersection with a stop sign. The observer located himself on the street corner with clipboard in hand. He soon noticed that all the cars were stopping at the stop sign. He then realized that his presence was influencing the drivers' behavior. When he concealed himself near the intersection, he found that drivers' behavior changed and he was able to gather data to test his hypothesis.

Research participants can respond in very subtle ways when they are aware that their behavior is being observed. For instance, participants are sometimes apprehensive and more than a little anxious about participating in psychological research. Measures of arousal, such as heart rate and galvanic skin response (GSR), may show changes simply as a function of an observer's presence. Wearing an electronic beeper that signals when to record behavioral activities and mood also can be expected to affect participants' behavior (e.g., Larson, 1989).

Key Concept

Research participants often react to the presence of an observer by trying to behave in ways they think the researcher wants them to behave. Knowing they are part of a scientific investigation, individuals usually want to cooperate and be "good" participants. Research participants often try to guess what behaviors are expected, and they may use cues and other information to guide their behavior (Orne, 1962). These cues in the research situation are called **demand characteristics.** Orne suggests that individuals generally ask themselves the question, "What am I supposed to be doing here?" To answer this question, participants pay attention to cues present in the setting, the research procedure itself, and implicit cues given by the researcher. As participants try to guess what is expected, they may change their behaviors accordingly. Participants' responses to the demand characteristics of a research situation pose a threat to the external validity of psychological research. Our ability to generalize the research findings (external validity) is threatened when research participants behave in a manner that is not representative of their behavior outside the psychological research setting. Interpretation of the study's findings is potentially threatened because participants may unintentionally make a research variable look more effective than it actually is or even nullify the effects of an otherwise significant variable. The problem of demand characteristics can be reduced by limiting individuals' knowledge about their role in a study or about the hypothesis being tested in the study. The researcher's goal in keeping participants unaware of important details regarding the study is to obtain more representative behavior. This methodological "solution" to the problem of demand characteristics does raise ethical concerns about important issues such as informed consent.

Controlling Reactivity   There are several approaches that researchers use to control the problem of reactivity. Researchers can eliminate reactivity by making sure that research participants do not detect the presence of the observer. Measures of behavior when participants do not know they are being observed are referred to as *unobtrusive (nonreactive) measures.* Obtaining unobtrusive measures may involve concealing the observer or hiding mechanical recording devices such as tape recorders and videotape cameras. LaFrance and Mayo (1976) observed people in conversation without their knowledge. Observations were made in a variety of natural settings, such as restaurants and waiting rooms, so we can imagine that observers had to keep their stopwatches and data sheets hidden behind menus and potted plants in order to obtain unobtrusive measures of behavior. Yet another approach is for researchers to use disguised participant observation and to adopt a role in the situation other than that of observer. You may remember this procedure was used by social psychologists studying the behavior of individuals who claimed to be in contact with aliens from outer space (Festinger et al., 1956). When researchers use unobtrusive measures, they assume that participants act as they ordinarily would because the participants do not know that an observer is present. In Chapter 6 we describe research methods that use unobtrusive measures.

Another approach researchers use to deal with reactivity is to adapt participants to the presence of an observer. Researchers make a reasonable assumption that as participants get used to an observer being present, they will come to behave normally in that person's presence. Adaptation can be accomplished through either habituation or desensitization. In a *habituation* procedure, observers simply introduce themselves into a situation on many different occasions until the participants cease to react to their presence. In order to film a documentary entitled "An American Family," which was shown on public television in the early 1970s, observers (with their cameras) literally moved into a California home and recorded the activities of a family over a 7-month period. Although it is impossible to tell how much of their behavior was influenced by the observers' presence, the events that unfolded and remarks made by family members gave evidence of a habituation process having taken place. During filming, the family broke up, the mother asking the father to move out of the house. When interviewed later about having the divorce announced to millions of television viewers, the father admitted that they could have asked the camera crew to get out but that, by this time, "we had gotten used to it" (*Newsweek,* 1973, p. 49).

Desensitization as a means of dealing with reactivity is similar to the desensitization used in the behavioral treatment of phobias. In a therapy situation, an individual with a specific fear (say, an irrational fear of spiders) is first exposed to the feared stimulus at a very low intensity. The patient may be asked to think of things that are related to spiders, such as dusty rooms and cobwebs. At the same time the therapist helps the patient practice relaxation. Gradually the intensity of the stimulus is increased until the patient can tolerate the actual stimulus itself.

Desensitization is often used by ethologists to adapt animal subjects to the presence of an observer. Prior to a violent death in the land of her beloved subjects, Fossey (1981, 1983) conducted fascinating observational studies of the mountain gorilla in Africa. Over a period of time she moved closer and closer to the gorillas so that they would get used to her presence. She found that by imitating their movements—for instance, by munching the foliage they ate and by scratching herself—she could put the gorillas at ease. Eventually she was able to sit among the gorillas and observe them as they touched her and explored the research equipment she was using.

FIGURE 4.4 Unobtrusive (nonreactive) measures of people's behavior can be obtained by searching their trash for physical traces, but ethical issues regarding privacy must be considered.

Finally, nonreactive measures of behavior can be obtained by observing behavior indirectly (see Webb, Campbell, Schwartz, Sechrest, & Grove, 1981). This may involve examining physical traces left behind or examining archival information, which are records kept by society about individuals and events. One researcher investigated the drinking behavior of people living in a town that was officially "dry" by counting empty liquor bottles in their trash cans (see Figure 4.4). Another researcher used the records kept by a library to assess the effect on a community of the introduction of television. Withdrawals of fiction titles dropped, but the demand for nonfiction was not affected (see Webb et al., 1981). Physical traces and archival data are important unobtrusive measures that can be valuable sources of information about behavior. As noted, these methods will be introduced in greater detail in Chapter 6.

Ethical Issues Whenever researchers try to control for reactivity by observing individuals without their knowledge, important ethical issues arise. For instance, observing people without their consent can represent a serious invasion of privacy. Deciding what constitutes an invasion of privacy is not always easy (as we discussed in Chapter 3), and must include a consideration of the sensitivity of the information, the setting where observation takes place, and the method of dissemination of the information obtained (e.g., Deiner & Crandall, 1978).

As we have seen, recent behavioral studies using the Internet introduce new ethical dilemmas. When researchers entered Internet chat rooms as disguised participant observers to find out what makes racists advocate racial violence (Glaser et al., 2002), the information they obtained could be seen as gathering incriminating evidence without the respondents' knowledge, not unlike a "sting" operation. The dilemma, of course, is that if informed consent were obtained it is very unlikely that respondents would cooperate. In this case the IRB approved the research by agreeing with the researchers that the chat room constituted a "public forum," that these topics were common to that forum, and that the researchers had instituted sufficient safeguards to protect the respondents' identities (e.g., by carefully separating names, typically the pseudonyms commonly used by individuals in this chat room, from the responses). On the other hand, there are instances in which people have felt that their privacy was violated when they learned that researchers observed their online discussions without their knowledge (see Skitka & Sargis, 2005). Behavioral research using the Internet is just beginning, and both researchers and IRB members are in a learning phase. Creative problem solving will be required by both groups if these ethical dilemmas are to be resolved (see Kraut et al., 2004).

When individuals are involved in situations that are deliberately arranged by an investigator, as might happen in a structured observation or in a field experiment, ethical problems associated with placing participants at risk may arise. Consider, for instance, a study designed to investigate how college students' attitudes toward racial harassment are affected by hearing other students either condone or condemn racism (Blanchard, Crandall, Brigham, & Vaughn, 1994). More than 200 White undergraduate women attending various universities were "naive participants." The women were approached by a White interviewer as they walked across campus and were invited to answer a short series of questions about "how their college should respond to acts of racism" (p. 994). A female confederate, posing as a student, approached the interviewer so that she arrived at the same time as the naive participant. The interviewers asked both "students" the same five questions; however, the interviewer always questioned the confederate student first. At this point, the confederate responded by either condemning or condoning racists' acts. Of interest was the effect of these statements on the naive participants' responses to the same questions. The results were clear: Hearing another student condemn racism produced more condemning responses relative to a no-influence control group, and hearing another student condone racism produced more condoning reactions to racism than hearing no one else express an opinion. Thus, as the authors suggest, the findings "imply that a few outspoken people can influence the normative climate of interracial social settings in either direction" (p. 997).

Were the naive participants "at risk?" If you think the participants were at risk, what degree of risk was present? Did the goals of the study, and the knowledge potentially obtained, outweigh the risks involved in the study? Although participants were "debriefed immediately" in this study, is that sufficient to address any concerns that the naive students might have about how they behaved when confronted with racist opinions, or even to restore confidence in a science that seeks knowledge through deception? Attempting to provide answers to these kinds of questions highlights the difficulty of ethical decision making. (In responding to these ethical questions it may be helpful to refer to the recommended steps in the process of ethical decision making that are outlined at the end of Chapter 3.)

Observer Bias

- Observer bias occurs when researchers' biases determine which behaviors they choose to observe and when observers' expectations about behavior lead to systematic errors in identifying and recording behavior.
- Expectancy effects can occur when observers are aware of hypotheses for the outcome of the study or the outcome of previous studies.
- The first step in controlling observer bias is to recognize that it may be present.
- Observer bias may be reduced by keeping observers unaware ("blind") of the goals and hypotheses of the study.

Key Concept }

Earlier in this chapter we described a study in which Rosenhan (1973) and his colleagues observed the interaction between staff members and patients in mental hospitals, and they found a serious bias on the part of the staff. Once patients were labeled schizophrenic, their behavior was interpreted solely in light of this label. Staff members interpreted behaviors that might have been considered normal when performed by sane individuals as evidence of the patients' insanity. For instance, the researchers later learned that note taking by the participant observers, which was done openly, had been cited by members of the staff as an example of the pseudopatients' pathological state. Thus, the staff tended to interpret patients' behavior in terms of the label that had been given them. This example clearly illustrates the potential danger of **observer bias,** the systematic errors in observation that result from an observer's expectations.

Expectancy Effects In many scientific studies the observer has some expectations about what behavior should be like in a particular situation or following a specific psychological treatment. This expectancy may be created by knowledge of the results of past investigations or perhaps by the observer's own hypothesis about behavior in this situation. Expectancies can be a source of observer bias—*expectancy effects*—if they lead to systematic errors in observation (Rosenthal, 1966, 1976).

Cordaro and Ison (1963) designed a study to document expectancy effects. The study required college student observers to record the number of head turns and body contractions made by two groups of flatworms. The observers were led to expect different rates of turning and contracting in the two groups. The worms in the groups were, however, essentially identical.

What differed was the observers' expectations about what they would see. Results showed that the observers reported twice as many head turns and three times as many body contractions when a high rate of movement was expected than when a low rate was expected. Apparently, the students interpreted the actions of the worms differently depending on what they expected to observe.

Other Biases An observer's expectancies regarding the outcome of a study may not be the only source of observer bias. You might think that using automated equipment such as movie cameras would eliminate observer bias. Although automation reduces the opportunity for observer bias, it does not necessarily eliminate it. Consider the fact that, in order to record behavior on film, the observer must determine the angle, location, and time of filming. To the extent that these aspects of the study are influenced by personal biases of the observer, such decisions can introduce systematic errors into the results. Altmann (1974) describes an observational study of animal behavior in which the observers biased the results by taking a midday break whenever the animals were inactive. Observations of the animals during this period of inactivity were conspicuously absent from the observational records. Furthermore, using automated equipment generally only postpones the process of classification and interpretation, and it is perfectly possible for the effects of observer bias to be introduced when narrative records are coded and analyzed.

Controlling Observer Bias Observer bias cannot be eliminated, but it can be reduced in several ways. As we mentioned, the use of automatic recording equipment can help, although the potential for bias is still present. *Probably the most important factor in dealing with observer bias is the awareness that it might be present.* That is, an observer who knows about this bias will be more likely to take steps to reduce its effect.

Observer bias also can be reduced by limiting the information provided to observers. When Hartup (1974) analyzed the results of his observational study of children's aggression, the individuals who performed the analysis were not permitted to see all the narrative records. When the nature of the aggressive act was classified, the antecedent events were blacked out; and when antecedent events were coded, the nature of the aggressive act was blacked out. Therefore, in making their classifications, the coders could not be influenced by information related to the event that they were coding. In a manner of speaking, the coders were "blind" to certain aspects of the study. Observers are *blind* when they do not know why the observations are being made or the goals of a study. In addition, when LaFrance and Mayo (1976) investigated eye contact between individuals conversing in natural settings, their observers did not know that possible differences along racial lines were being probed. Using blind observers greatly reduces the possibility of introducing systematic errors due to observer expectancies.

SUMMARY

Researchers can rarely observe all behavior that occurs. Consequently, researchers must use some form of behavior sampling such as time and situation sampling. An important goal of sampling is to achieve a representative sample of behavior. Observational methods can be classified on two dimensions: the degree of observer intervention and the manner in which behavior is recorded. Observation in a natural setting without observer intervention is called naturalistic observation. Observation with intervention can take the form of participant observation, structured observation (frequently used by developmental psychologists) and field experiments (often used by social psychologists). In an observational study, behavior can be recorded either with a comprehensive description of behavior or by recording only certain predefined units of behavior. Narrative records are used to provide comprehensive descriptions of behavior and checklists are typically used when researchers are interested in whether a specific behavior has occurred (and under what conditions). Frequency, duration, and ratings of behaviors are common dependent variables in observational studies.

How quantitative data are described and analyzed depends on the scale of measurement used. The four measurement scales used by psychologists are nominal, ordinal, interval, and ratio. When narrative records are made, some type of coding system is generally used as one step in the process of data reduction. Measures of frequency and duration, as well as ratings, are typically summarized using descriptive statistics such as the mean and standard deviation. It is essential to provide measures of observer reliability when reporting the results of an observational study. Depending on the level of measurement that has been used, either a percentage agreement measure or a correlation coefficient can be used to assess reliability.

Possible problems due to reactivity or observer bias must be controlled in any observational study. Finally, researchers must address ethical issues prior to beginning a research study. Ethical issues are especially salient when an observational study involves a form of deception such as disguised participant observation or the use of unidentified confederates. Internet research raises new ethical dilemmas that need to be addressed both by researchers and IRB members.

KEY CONCEPTS

external validity	measurement scale
time sampling	data reduction
situation sampling	coding
naturalistic observation	interobserver reliability
participant observation	correlation coefficient
structured observation	reactivity
field experiment	demand characteristics
narrative records	observer bias

REVIEW QUESTIONS

1 Identify three characteristics of scientific observation that distinguish it from our everyday observation.

2 Explain why researchers use sampling in observational studies, and describe what the proper use of sampling is intended to accomplish.

3 Explain how the degree of intervention and the method of recording behavior can be used to classify observational methods.

4 Describe a research situation in which naturalistic observation can be useful when ethical considerations prevent researchers from controlling aspects of human behavior.

5 Identify three factors in participant observation that researchers need to consider to determine the extent of the observer's influence on the behavior being observed.

6 Structured observation represents a compromise between naturalistic observation and laboratory experiments. What are the primary advantage and potential cost of this compromise?

7 Give an example using each of the four measurement scales of how a researcher could measure eye contact between pairs of people in conversation with each other.

8 What are the most common descriptive measures (a) when events are measured on a nominal scale and (b) when behavior is recorded on at least an interval scale?

9 Describe the effects of each of the following factors on interobserver reliability: definition of the event being observed, training, practice with feedback.

10 What two types of information do you gain by knowing the sign and the numerical value of a correlation coefficient?

11 Identify the measurement scales that require a correlation coefficient to assess interobserver reliability, and explain what a negative correlation would indicate in this situation.

12 Explain whether high interobserver reliability ensures that the observations are accurate and valid.

13 Explain why participants' reactions to demand characteristics can be a threat to the external validity of psychological research and to the interpretation of a study's findings.

14 Explain how the ethical issues of privacy and risk can arise when researchers use unobtrusive measures such as concealing the presence of an observer.

15 Describe two ways in which observer bias (expectancy effects) can occur in psychological research.

16 What is the best procedure to reduce observer bias?

CHALLENGE QUESTIONS

1 Students in a developmental psychology lab course conducted an observational study of parent-infant interactions in the home. When they first entered the home on each of the 4 days they observed a given family, they greeted both the parents and the infant (and any other children at home). They instructed the family to follow its daily routine and they asked a series of questions about the activities of that day to determine whether it was a "normal" day or whether anything unusual had happened. The students tried to make the family feel comfortable, but they also tried to minimize their interactions with the family and with each other. For any given 2-hour observation period there were always two student observers present in the home, and the two observers recorded their notes independently of each other.

Each of six pairs of students was randomly assigned to observe two of the 12 families who volunteered to serve in the study. The same pair of observers always observed a given family for the entire 8 hours of observation for that family. The observers used rating scales to record behaviors on a number of different dimensions, such as mutual warmth and affection of the parent-infant interaction.

A Cite two specific procedures used by the students to ensure the reliability of their findings.

B Cite one possible threat to the external validity of the findings of this study; once again, cite a specific example from the description provided.

C Cite one specific aspect of their procedure that indicated that the students were sensitive to the possibility that their measurements might be reactive. What other methods might they have used to deal with this problem of reactivity?

2 An observational study was done to assess the effects of environmental influences on drinking by college students in a university-sponsored pub. Eighty-two students over the age of 21 were observed. The observers used a checklist to record whether the participant was male or female and whether the participant was with one other person or was in a group of two or more other people. Each observation session was always from 3 P.M. to 1 A.M., and observations were made Monday through Saturday. The observations were made over a 3-month period. Two observers were always present during any observation session. Each participant was observed for up to 1 hour from the time he or she ordered the first beer. The data were summarized in terms of the number of beers drunk per hour. The results showed that men drank more and men drank faster than did women. Men drank faster when with other men, and women also drank faster with men present. Both men and women drank more in groups than when with one other person. These results do indicate that the environment within which drinking occurs plays an important role in the nature and extent of that drinking.

A Identify the observational method being used in this study, and explain why you decided on the observational method you chose.

B Identify the independent and dependent variables in this study, and describe the operational definition of each level of the independent variable.

C How could the researchers control for reactivity in this study? What ethical concerns might arise from their approach?

D Identify one aspect of the procedures in this study that would likely *increase* the reliability of the observations.

E Identify one aspect of the procedures in this study that would likely *limit* the external validity of the findings of this study.

3 A friend of yours is absolutely convinced that he has a positive influence on the friendliness of conversations in which he is a participant. He has reached this conclusion on the basis of his everyday observations. You convince him that a systematic study is needed to confirm his hypothesis. Your friend (still smiling) carefully develops an operational definition of the friendliness of a conversation and records a rating for each of the next 50 conversations in which he is a participant. His results show that 75% of these conversations are rated "very friendly," 20% are rated "friendly," and 5% are rated "neutral." Your friend returns to you—now convinced beyond a shadow of a doubt that he has a positive effect on the friendliness of a conversation. Although your friend won't be pleased with you, explain to him why his study is seriously flawed as a basis for confirming his hypothesis. In your critique of your friend's study be sure to address the following issues related to the study:

A Explain what comparison set of observations he needs before he can begin to make a claim that he has a positive influence on the friendliness of conversations. Explain how this comparison set of observations could even lead to the conclusion that your friend has a negative effect on the friendliness of conversations.

B Explain why your friend should not be the one to select the conversations to observe nor the one who records how friendly the conversations were.

C Does your critique of your friend's study allow you to conclude that your friend does not have a positive effect on conversations in which he is a participant? Why or why not?

4 Four students were doing internships at the Social Science Research Institute of their university. The research institute had a contract to do a series of studies on traffic safety for the downtown development agency of a small city near the university. The internship students were assigned to carry out one of the studies. Specifically, they were to do a study to determine how likely it was that cars actually came to a stop at intersections with stop signs with pedestrian crosswalks in the downtown area. You are to respond to the following questions

(Contd.)

that the students are considering in planning their study.

A The students want to distinguish the extent to which the cars stop beyond a "yes" or "no" classification. How could the students develop an operational definition for the cars stopping that would include cars that came to a full stop, a rolling stop, and not stopping at all?

B What steps could the students take before beginning to collect data for the actual study to increase the interobserver reliability of their observations?

C The students are interested in determining the likelihood that cars will stop when pedestrian

traffic downtown is light and when it is heavy. What time-sampling plan could the students use to make this determination?

D The students are especially interested in determining the likelihood of cars stopping at the stop sign independent of whether other cars have stopped. How would the students need to sample the cars they observed in order to study the independent stopping of cars? What information could the students record that would allow them to include all cars in their sample and still determine the likelihood of cars stopping independently?

Answer to Stretching Exercise

1. The students used naturalistic observation in this study. They did not intervene in the situations they were observing and nonintervention is a defining characteristic of naturalistic observation. The study was also done in natural settings, the library and the student union.

2. The students' choice to use a 5-minute observation period may have limited their ability to measure students' concentration effectively. The 5-minute observation period (especially if the observers began timing the 5-minute interval when the student was looking at the material or writing) may have been too short to "show" changes in concentration. If the 5-minute interval was too short to show changes in concentration, then it is unlikely that differences in concentration would have been observed between the two locations. One possible way to improve the operational definition would be to lengthen the observation interval to 20 or 30 minutes.

3. Students' ability to concentrate may vary across days of the week and times of the day. The students chose to observe on a Monday evening from 9 to 11 P.M. because they thought they would be observing at a "prime" study time for students. The time-sampling plan could be improved to increase external validity by making observations at different times of the day, on different days of the week, and across the weeks of the semester.

4. If we assume that students can concentrate better in the library than in the student union, then we need to find some way to explain why study times were the same in this study across the two locations. One possibility is that students chose to study different material in the two locations. If students in the student union were studying "easier" material, then they could have concentrated as well as students who were studying harder material in the library. One of the challenges in doing naturalistic observation is that the researcher cannot control factors that possibly could influence the outcome of the observations (because of the nonintervention that characterizes naturalistic observation).

Answer to Challenge Question 1

A The students' procedures that enhanced reliability were as follows: observing each family for 8 hours, using two independent observers, and using checklists to provide operational definitions.

B One possible threat to the external validity of the findings was that the 12 families volunteered for the study and such families may differ from typical families.

C The students' efforts to minimize interactions with the family and with each other suggested that they were sensitive to the problem of reactivity. Two other methods they might have used are habituation and desensitization.

CHAPTER FIVE

Survey Research

CHAPTER OUTLINE

OVERVIEW

What are your favorite foods? How much sleep do you get? What type of car do you drive? Do you use the library on campus? Are you satisfied with your life at this point? At some time you have probably been asked questions like these as part of a survey. Psychologists, sociologists, political scientists, market researchers, magazine editors, and others use surveys to gain information about people's thoughts and feelings. The results of a survey are often used to *describe* people's opinions, attitudes, and preferences. For example, the results of pre-election polls describe potential voters' preferences for the candidates or their opinions about election issues. Survey researchers also use the results of surveys to make *predictions* about people's behavior. For example, a market researcher may try to predict which households are likely to use a new product, or a psychologist may design a questionnaire to identify people at risk for suicide. **Correlational research** provides a basis for making predictions. Relationships among naturally occurring variables are assessed with the goal of identifying *predictive relationships*. As we discussed in Chapter 4, a *correlation coefficient* is a quantitative index of the direction and magnitude of a predictive relationship. We will discuss correlational research in the context of survey methodology later in this chapter.

Key Concept }

Surveys typically are conducted with samples of people. In this chapter we first introduce the basic logic and techniques of sampling—the process of selecting a subset of a population to represent the population as a whole. You will then learn about the advantages and disadvantages of various survey-research methods and survey-research designs. The primary instrument of survey research is the questionnaire and so we describe the basics of constructing a good questionnaire. We also discuss an important question that needs to be addressed in survey research, "Do people really do what they say they do?" We conclude the chapter by critically examining a broader question, "Just what can we conclude about causality when a correlation exists between two variables?"

USES OF SURVEYS

- Survey research is used to assess people's thoughts, opinions, and feelings.
- Surveys can be specific and limited in scope or more global in their goals.
- The best way to determine whether results of a survey are biased is to examine the survey procedures and analyses.

We discussed in Chapter 4 how psychologists use observational methods to infer what people must have been thinking or feeling to have behaved in a certain way. Survey research is designed to deal more directly with the nature of people's thoughts, opinions, and feelings. On the surface, survey research is deceptively simple. If you want to know what people are thinking, ask them! Similarly, if you want to know what people are doing, observe them! As we have seen, however, when we hope to infer general principles of behavior, our observations must be more sophisticated than our everyday, casual observations. So, too, survey research requires more than simply asking people questions.

Social scientists, such as political scientists, psychologists, and sociologists, use surveys in their research for a variety of reasons, both theoretical and applied. Surveys also are used to meet the more pragmatic needs of the media, political candidates, public health officials, professional organizations, and advertising and marketing directors. In other words, the scope and purpose of surveys can be limited and specific, or they can be more global. For example, the Practice Directorate of APA conducted a survey with a limited and specific purpose (Peterson, 1995). The Practice Directorate is a branch of APA that focuses primarily on the concerns of clinical psychologists. Their national survey of 1,087 adults was designed to understand better what the public thinks psychologists do, what kind of education psychologists have, and in what settings psychologists practice. The survey produced many observations—including that 46% of respondents reported having seen a mental health professional or that someone in their family had, and 80% said that psychologists usually work in private practice. In fact, although more than half of psychologists do work in the mental health field, fewer than half of those work in private practice. Clearly, the public's estimate of 80% is high. Results from this survey were useful to the Directorate in focusing their public education strategies.

Myers and Diener (1995), on the other hand, conducted a survey with a more global scope, examining people's personal sense of well-being. They reported the results of a survey sampling people from 24 countries representing every continent but Antarctica. One of the research questions was whether people in wealthy countries have a greater sense of well-being than those in not-so-wealthy countries. Is being "well-off" associated with greater "well-being"? The survey results showed that national wealth, as measured by gross national product per capita, is positively correlated with well-being (.67). But this relationship is not simple because national wealth is also correlated with other variables that are themselves highly correlated with well-being, such as number of continuous years of democracy (.85). Myers and Diener (1995) is just one illustration of how surveys can be used to address complex issues of global concern.

One of the ways that surveys can be used deserves mention because it raises ethical concerns. An ethical dilemma arises when sponsors of survey research have vested interests in how the results turn out. Crossen (1994) highlighted this by stating, ". . . more and more of the information we use to buy, elect, advise, acquit, and heal has been created not to expand our knowledge but to sell a product or advance a cause" (p. 14). Crossen cites examples such as a national survey sponsored by the zinc industry showing that 62% of respondents wanted to keep the penny (which is zinc based), and a survey sponsored by a manufacturer of cellular phones showing that 70% of respondents (all of whom used cellular phones) agreed that people who use cellular telephones are more successful in business.

Is it reasonable to conclude that survey results are biased anytime the outcome of the survey is favorable for the sponsoring agency? Answers to ethical questions are rarely simple and the answer to this one certainly is not. High-quality and ethical research can be done when the sponsor has an interest in the outcome. Knowing the sponsor of the research is important when evaluating survey results, but is not sufficient for judging whether the study is biased. It is much more important to know whether a biased sample has been used, or whether the wording of questions has been slanted, or whether the data have been selectively analyzed or reported. Any of these aspects of survey research can bias the results, and unethical researchers can use these techniques to make the results "turn out right." The best protection against unethical researchers and poor-quality research is to examine carefully the procedures and analyses used in the survey research.

CHARACTERISTICS OF SURVEYS

- Survey research involves selecting a sample (or samples) and using a predetermined set of questions.

Though they differ in how they are used, all surveys share common characteristics that make properly conducted surveys an excellent method for describing people's attitudes and opinions. First, surveys generally involve sampling, which is a characteristic of nearly all behavioral research. This concept was introduced in our discussion of time and situation sampling in observational research in Chapter 4. We will discuss sampling as it is used in survey research in the next section of this chapter. Surveys also are characterized by their use of a set of predetermined questions for all respondents. Oral or written responses to these questions constitute the principal data obtained in a survey. By using the same phrasing and ordering of questions, it is possible to summarize the views of all respondents succinctly.

When a *representative sample* of people is asked the same set of questions, we can describe the attitudes of the population from which the sample was drawn. Furthermore, when the same questions are used, we can compare the attitudes of different populations or look for changes in attitudes over time. Plous (1998), for example, studied changes in attitudes over time in two surveys of animal rights activists. The first survey was done in 1990 at a national march in Washington, DC, and the second was done at a similar event in 1996. The results of the two surveys revealed that the priorities of people in the animal rights movement had changed during this time. Specifically, in 1990 a majority of activists viewed animal research as the most important issue facing the movement; in 1996, animal agriculture was viewed as the most important issue. These findings illustrate how survey research can be used to study changes in people's attitudes by presenting the same questions to samples selected at different times.

SAMPLING IN SURVEY RESEARCH

- Careful selection of a survey sample allows researchers to generalize findings from the sample to the population.

Assume you've decided your research question is best answered using a survey, and you've determined the population of interest for your survey. The next step is to decide who to interview. This involves selecting a sample of respondents to represent the population. The power and efficiency of sampling are aptly summarized by survey researcher Angus Campbell (1981, p. 17):

> The method of choice for portraying all the variety of a large heterogeneous population is clearly that of the sample survey. Ever since statisticians and social scientists learned how to draw a sample from a large universe in such a way that every member of the universe has an equal chance of being chosen, it has been possible to describe the national population accurately by obtaining information from a few thousand carefully selected individuals.

Whether we are describing a national population or a much smaller one (e.g., the students of one university), the procedures for obtaining a representative sample are the same. We explain in this section how to make that careful selection of individuals which Campbell describes.

Basic Terms of Sampling

- The identification and selection of elements that will make up the sample is at the heart of all sampling techniques; the sample is chosen from the sampling frame, or list of all members of the population of interest.
- Researchers are not interested simply in the responses of those surveyed; instead, they seek to describe the larger population from which the sample was drawn.
- The ability to generalize from a sample to the population depends critically on the representativeness of the sample.
- A biased sample is one in which the characteristics of the sample are systematically different from the characteristics of the population.
- Selection bias occurs when the procedures used to select a sample result in the overrepresentation or underrepresentation of some segment(s) of the population.

Key Concept

As we begin to talk about sampling techniques, we need to be clear about the definitions of four terms: *population, sampling frame, sample,* and *element*. The relationships among the four critical sampling terms are summarized in Figure 5.1. A **population** is the set of all cases of interest. For example, if you are interested in the attitudes of students on your campus toward computer services, your population is all students on your campus. Contacting everyone in a large population is often practically impossible. Therefore, researchers usually select a subset of the population to represent the population as a whole.

We need to develop a specific list of the members of the population in order to select a subset of that population. This specific list is called a *sampling frame* and is, in a sense, an operational definition of the population of interest. In a survey of students' attitudes toward computer services, the sampling frame might be a list obtained from the registrar's office of all currently enrolled students. The extent to which the sampling frame truly reflects the population of interest determines the adequacy of the sample we ultimately select. The list

FIGURE 5.1   Illustration of relationships among four basic terms in sampling.

provided by the registrar should provide a good sampling frame, but some students might be excluded, such as students who registered late.

The subset of the population actually drawn from the sampling frame is called the **sample.** We might select 100 students from the registrar's list to serve as the sample for our computer survey. How closely the attitudes of this sample of students will represent all students' attitudes depends critically on how the sample is selected. Each member of the population is called an *element*. The identification and selection of elements that will make up the sample are at the heart of all sampling techniques.

It is important to emphasize at this point that samples are of little or no interest in themselves. A new computer facility is not going to be built for the sole use of the 100 students surveyed. Similarly, the social psychologist is not interested solely in the racial attitudes of the 50 people he surveyed, nor is the marketing director interested only in the preferences of the 200 consumers she surveyed. *Populations, not samples, are of primary interest.* The "power" of samples to describe the larger population is based on the assumption that survey responses in a sample are applicable to the population from which the sample was drawn.

Key Concept

> *Key Concept*

The ability to generalize from a sample to the population depends critically on the **representativeness** of the sample. Clearly, individuals in a population differ in many ways, and populations differ from each other. For example, one population might be 40% male and 60% female, whereas in another population the distribution might be 75% female and 25% male. *A sample is representative of the population to the extent that it exhibits the same distribution of characteristics as the population.* If a representative sample of 200 adults has 80 men and 120 women, which of the above-mentioned populations does it represent? You can use the illustrations in Box 5.1 to gain additional practice in identifying representative samples.

The major threat to representativeness is bias. A *biased sample* is one in which the distribution of characteristics in the sample is systematically different from the target population. A sample of 100 adults that included 80 women and 20 men would likely be biased if the population was 60% female and 40% male. In this case, women would be overrepresented and men would be underrepresented in the sample. There are two sources of bias: selection bias and response

---

BOX 5.1

IDENTIFYING REPRESENTATIVE SAMPLES

Presented on the left side are descriptions of four populations. Find the sample on the right side that represents each population.

Populations	Samples
1 60% women, 40% men 90% ages 18–22, 10% age >22 70% freshman/sophomore, 30% junior/senior	**A** 132 women, 44 men 114 ages 18–22, 62 age >22 141 freshman/sophomore, 35 junior/senior
2 80% women, 20% men 60% ages 18–22, 40% age >22 70% freshman/sophomore, 30% junior/senior	**B** 244 women, 61 men 183 ages 18–22, 122 age >22 213 freshman/sophomore, 92 junior/senior
3 75% women, 25% men 65% ages 18–22, 35% age >22 80% freshman/sophomore, 20% junior/senior	**C** 48 women, 12 men 54 ages 18–22, 6 age >22 42 freshman/sophomore, 18 junior/senior
4 80% women, 20% men 90% ages 18–22, 10% age >22 70% freshman/sophomore, 30% junior/senior	**D** 150 women, 100 men 225 ages 18–22, 25 age >22 175 freshman/sophomore, 75 junior/senior

Answers

1. D   2. B   3. A   4. C

From Zechmeister, Zechmeister & Shaughnessy, *Essentials of Research Methods in Psychology*, McGraw-Hill, 2001, p. 124.

Key Concept

bias. **Selection bias** occurs when the procedures used to select the sample result in the overrepresentation of some segment of the population or, conversely, in the exclusion or underrepresentation of a significant segment. We will describe response bias in the next section, "Survey Methods."

Charles Madigan, a senior writer for the *Chicago Tribune,* documented a selection bias in samples surveyed for the 1994 national election. He identified the selection bias by comparing the demographic characteristics of the voters interviewed in exit polls to characteristics of the population drawn from U.S. census data. Note that the U.S. census data, representing the entire population, include voters and nonvoters, whereas the exit-poll sample comprises voters only. Madigan determined that the exit-poll sample differed in systematic ways from the U.S. population in terms of age, race, education, income, and the proportion of working women. These differences indicate that the sample was not representative of the population due to a selection bias. Although the voter poll may accurately reflect the interests and attitudes of those people who voted, their votes and survey responses may not be used to characterize the attitudes of the population (which includes people who did not vote). Clearly, politicians cannot assume a "mandate" based on a biased sample of individuals who voted.

A more general lesson can be learned from the exit poll example. Namely, what constitutes a representative sample depends on the population of interest. For example, if a university wants to know student drivers' opinions about on-campus parking, then the target population is college students who bring cars to campus (not college students in general). An unbiased sample would, in this case, be one that is representative of the population of students who have cars on campus.

Approaches to Sampling

- Two approaches to selecting a survey sample are nonprobability sampling and probability sampling.
- Nonprobability sampling (such as convenience sampling) does not guarantee that every element in the population has an equal chance of being included in the sample.
- Probability sampling (simple random sampling and stratified random sampling) allows researchers to estimate the likelihood that their findings for the sample differ from those for the population.
- In simple random sampling each element of the population has an equal chance of being included in the sample; in stratified random sampling, the population is divided into subpopulations (strata), and random samples are drawn from the strata.
- Probability sampling is the method of choice for obtaining a representative sample.

Key Concept

There are two basic approaches to sampling—nonprobability sampling and probability sampling. In **nonprobability sampling** we have no guarantee that each element has some chance of being included and no way to estimate the probability of each element's being included in the sample. In the computer survey we described earlier, if a researcher interviewed the first 30 students who entered the library, she would be using nonprobability sampling. Clearly, not all students would be equally likely to be at the library at that particular time, and some students would have essentially no chance of being included in the sample.

Key Concept }

By contrast, if the researcher were to select 30 students randomly from the registrar's list of enrolled students, she would be using probability sampling. In **probability sampling** all registered students (elements) have an equal chance of being included in the sample. We can describe this researcher's approach as probability sampling because her sampling procedure (i.e., random selection from a predetermined list) allows all students to have an equal chance of being selected for the survey. Probability sampling is preferred because it allows researchers to estimate the likelihood that their sample findings differ from the findings they would have obtained by studying the whole population. *Probability sampling is far superior to nonprobability sampling in ensuring that selected samples represent the population.* Thus, the researcher who selects 30 students randomly from the registrar's list of students is more likely to have a representative sample than the researcher who bases her survey results on the first 30 students who show up at the library.

Nonprobability Sampling The most common form of nonprobability sampling is convenience sampling. *Convenience sampling* involves selecting respondents primarily on the basis of their availability and willingness to respond. Newspapers often interview "the person on the street" and publish their comments. Their comments may make interesting reading, but their opinions are not likely to represent those of the wider community. This lack of representativeness arises because convenience sampling is nonprobability sampling and we can't be sure that every person in the community had a chance to be included in the sample. Convenience sampling also is involved when people respond to surveys in magazines because the magazine has to be available (and purchased), and people must be willing to send in their responses. The "participant pool" that is tapped by many psychologists at colleges and universities is a convenience sample typically comprised of students registered for the introductory psychology course.

Crossen (1994) describes the drawbacks of another variation of convenience sampling, call-in surveys. Call-in surveys are used by TV and radio shows to poll the views of their audience. Those who happen to be "tuned in" and who are willing to call (and sometimes to pay the charge for calling a 900 number) make up the sample for these call-in surveys. Thus, we need to remember that people who make calls in response to a call-in request differ from the general population not only because they are part of the particular show's audience, but because they are motivated enough to make a call. Similarly, online computer users who respond to a "pop up" survey question displayed on their home page will differ from those who choose not to respond (or do not have access to computers).

A prime-time TV news show once conducted a call-in survey with a question concerning the preferred location for the United Nations (Crossen, 1994). It turns out that another survey research study involving about 500 randomly selected respondents also asked the same question. The question was whether the United Nations (UN) headquarters should remain in the United States. Of the 186,000 callers who responded, a solid majority (67%) wanted the UN *out of the United States*. Of the 500 respondents to the survey research study (a random sample of individuals), a clear majority (72%) wanted the UN *to stay in the United States*. How could these two surveys yield such different—even opposite—results? Should we put more confidence in the results of the call-in survey because of the massive sample size? Absolutely not! A large convenience sample is just as likely to be an unrepresentative sample as is any other convenience sample. As a general rule, *you should consider that convenience sampling will result in a biased sample unless you have strong evidence confirming the representativeness of the sample.*

Probability Sampling   The distinguishing characteristic of probability sampling is that the researcher can specify, for each element of the population, the probability that it will be included in the sample. Two common types of probability sampling are simple random sampling and stratified random sampling. Simple random sampling is the basic technique of probability sampling. The most common definition of **simple random sampling** is that every element has an equal chance of being included in the sample. The procedures for simple random sampling are outlined in Box 5.2.

Key Concept

One critical decision that must be made in selecting a random sample is how large it should be. For now, we will simply note that the size of a random sample needed to represent a population depends on the homogeneity (variability) of the population. For example, college students in Ivy League schools represent a more homogeneous population than college students in *all* U.S. colleges in terms of their academic abilities. At one extreme, the most homogeneous population would be one in which all members of the population are identical. A sample of one element would be representative of this population regardless of the size of the population. At the other extreme, the most heterogeneous population would be one in which each member was completely different from all other members on all characteristics. No sample, regardless of its size, could be representative of this population. Every individual would have to be included to describe such a heterogeneous population. Fortunately, the populations with which survey researchers work typically fall somewhere between these two extremes. Thus the representativeness of samples, like the joy of eating a piece of chocolate cake, increases with increasing size—up to a point.

Key Concept

The representativeness of a sample can often be increased by using stratified random sampling. In **stratified random sampling,** the population is divided into subpopulations called strata (singular, stratum) and random samples are drawn from each of these strata. There are two general ways to determine how many elements should be drawn from each stratum. One way (illustrated in the last

BOX 5.2

SAMPLES OF RANDOM SAMPLES

The following names represent a scaled-down version of a sampling frame obtained from the registrar's office of a small college campus. Procedures for drawing both a simple random sample and a stratified random sample from this list are described below.

Adamski	F	Jr
Alderink	F	Sr
Baxter	M	Sr
Bowen	F	Sr
Broder	M	So
Brown	M	Jr
Bufford	M	So
Campbell	F	Fr
Carnahan	F	So
Cowan	F	Fr
Cushman	M	Sr
Dawes	M	Jr
Dennis	M	Sr
Douglas	F	Fr
Dunne	M	So
Fahey	M	Fr
Fedder	M	Fr
Foley	F	So
Grossman	F	Jr
Harris	F	Jr
Hedlund	F	So
Johnson	F	Fr
Klaaren	F	Jr
Ludwig	M	Fr
Nadeau	F	Sr
Nowaczyk	M	Jr
O'Keane	F	Sr
Osgood	M	So
Owens	F	So
Penzien	M	Jr
Powers	M	Sr
Ryan	M	Fr
Sawyer	M	Jr
Shaw	M	Sr
Sonders	F	Sr
Suffolk	F	So
Taylor	F	Fr
Thompson	M	Fr
Watterson	F	Jr
Zimmerman	M	So

Drawing a simple random sample:

Step 1. Number each element in the sampling frame: Adamski would be number 1, Harris number 20, and Zimmerman number 40.

Step 2. Decide on the sample size you want to use. This is just an illustration, so we will use a sample size of 5.

Step 3. Choose a starting point in the Table of Random Numbers in the Appendix (Table A.1) (a finger stab with your eyes closed works just fine—our stab came down at column 8, row 22 at the entry 26384). Because our sampling frame ranges only from 1 to 40, we had decided *prior* to entering the table to use the left two numbers in each set of five and to go across the table from left to right. We could just as easily have decided to go up, down, or from right to left. We could also have used the middle two or the last two digits of each set of five, but one should make these decisions before entering the table.

Step 4. Identify the numbers to be included in your sampling by moving across the table. We got the numbers 26, 06, 21, 15, and 32. Notice that numbers over 40 are ignored. The same would be true if we had come across a repetition of a number we had already selected.

Step 5. List the names corresponding to the selected numbers. In our case the sample will include Nowaczyk, Brown, Hedlund, Dunne, and Ryan.

An even easier system, called *systematic sampling,* can be used to obtain a random sample. In this procedure you divide the sample size you want into the size of the sampling frame to obtain the value *k*. Then you select every *k*th element after choosing the first one randomly. In our example we want a sample size of 5 from a sampling frame of 40, so *k* would be 8. Thus we would choose one of the first eight people randomly and then take every eighth person thereafter. If Alderink were chosen from among the first 8, the remaining members of the sample would be Cowan, Foley, Nowaczyk, and Shaw. Note: This

(Contd.)

system should *not* be used if the sampling frame has a periodic organization—if, for example, you had a list of dormitory residents arranged by room and every tenth pair listed occupied a corner room. You can readily see that, in such a list, if your sampling interval was 10 you could end up with all people from corner rooms or no people from corner rooms.

Freshmen	Sophomores
1 Campbell	1 Broder
2 Cowan	2 Bufford
3 Douglas	3 Carnahan
4 Fahey	4 Dunne
5 Fedder	5 Foley
6 Johnson	6 Hedlund
7 Ludwig	7 Osgood
8 Ryan	8 Owens
9 Taylor	9 Suffolk
10 Thompson	10 Zimmerman

Juniors	Seniors
1 Adamski	1 Alderink
2 Brown	2 Baxter
3 Dawes	3 Bowen
4 Grossman	4 Cushman
5 Harris	5 Dennis
6 Klaaren	6 Nadeau
7 Nowaczyk	7 O'Keane
8 Penzien	8 Powers
9 Sawyer	9 Shaw
10 Watterson	10 Sonders

Drawing a stratified random sample:

Step 1. Arrange the sampling frame in strata. For our example we will stratify by class standing, so our sampling frame now looks like this:

In our example the strata are equal in size, but this need not be the case.

Step 2. Number each element within each stratum, as has been done in the foregoing list.

Step 3. Decide on the overall sample size you want to use. For our example we will draw a sample of 8.

Step 4. Draw an equal-sized sample from each stratum such that you obtain the desired overall sample size. For our example this would mean drawing 2 from each stratum.

Step 5. Follow the steps for drawing a random sample and repeat for each stratum. We used the previously determined starting point (column 8, line 22) in the Table of Random Numbers (Table A.1), but this time we used the last digit in each set of five. The numbers identified for each stratum were: Freshmen (4 and 1), Sophomores (6 and 4), Juniors (7 and 9), and Seniors (2 and 9).

Step 6. List the names corresponding to the selected numbers. Our stratified random sample would include Fahey, Campbell, Hedlund, Dunne, Nowaczyk, Sawyer, Baxter, and Shaw.

example of Box 5.2) is to draw equal-sized samples from each stratum. The second way is to draw elements for the sample on a proportional basis. Consider a population of undergraduate students made up of 30% freshmen, 30% sophomores, 20% juniors, and 20% seniors (class years are the strata). A stratified random sample of 200 students drawn from this population would include 60 freshmen, 60 sophomores, 40 juniors, and 40 seniors. In contrast, drawing equal-sized samples from each stratum would result in 50 students for each class year. *Only the stratified sample on a proportional basis would be representative.*

In addition to its potential for increasing the representativeness of samples, stratified random sampling is useful when you want to describe specific portions of the population. For example, a simple random sample of 100 students would be sufficient to survey students' attitudes on a campus of 2,000 students.

STRETCHING EXERCISE

Two student researchers have been asked to do a survey to determine the attitudes of students toward fraternities and sororities on campus. There are 3,200 students in the school. About 25% of the students belong to the Greek organizations and 75% do not. The two student researchers disagree about what sampling plan is best for the study. One researcher thinks they should draw a stratified random sample of 200 students: 100 from among those students who belong to Greek organizations and 100 from among the independent students. The second researcher thinks they should draw one simple random sample of 100 students from the campus as a whole.

1 Comment critically on these two sampling plans in terms of their representativeness and the likelihood that they would measure reliably the views of students who belong to Greek organizations.

2 Develop your own sampling plan if you decide that neither of the ones proposed so far is optimal.

Suppose, however, your sample included only 2 of the 40 chemistry majors on campus, and you wish to describe the views of students according to different majors. Although this accurately reflects the proportion of chemistry majors in the campus population, it would be risky to use the views of only 2 chemistry students to represent all 40 chemistry majors (2 is too few). In this case (and more generally when a stratum is small in number), you could sample more chemistry majors to describe their views better. We can't say precisely how many to sample because, as we learned earlier, the sample size needed to represent a population depends on the heterogeneity of the population.

SURVEY METHODS

- Four methods for obtaining survey data are mail surveys, personal interviews, telephone interviews, and Internet surveys.

Selecting the sample is only one of several important decisions to make when doing survey research. You also need to decide how you will obtain information from the respondents. There are four general methods: mail surveys, personal interviews, telephone interviews, and Internet surveys. As is often true when doing research, there is no one best survey method for all circumstances. Each survey method has its own advantages and disadvantages. The challenge you face is to select the method that best fits the research question you are investigating.

Mail Surveys

- Although mail surveys are quick and convenient, they may have the problem of response bias when individuals fail to complete and return the survey.
- Due to response bias, the final sample for a mail survey may not represent the population.

Mail surveys are used to distribute self-administered questionnaires that respondents fill out on their own. One advantage of mail surveys is that they usually can be completed relatively quickly. Because they are self-administered, mail surveys also avoid the problems due to interviewer bias (to be defined in the next section). Among the four survey methods, mail surveys are the best for dealing with highly personal or embarrassing topics, especially when anonymity of respondents is preserved.

Unfortunately, there are many disadvantages to mail surveys. Some of these disadvantages are less serious than others. For instance, because respondents will not be able to ask questions, the questionnaire used in the survey must be completely self-explanatory. A second less serious disadvantage is that the researcher has little control over the order in which the respondent answers the questions. The order of questions may affect how respondents answer certain questions. A serious problem with mail surveys, however, is response bias.

Key Concept

Response bias is a threat to the representativeness of a sample because not all respondents complete the survey. There are many reasons why this occurs. For example, respondents with literacy problems, low educational background, or vision problems may not complete the survey; therefore, people with these characteristics may not be represented well in the final sample of respondents. Often, people included in a sample are too busy or not interested enough in the study to return a completed questionnaire. Low response rate (i.e., failure to complete and return the survey) is the major factor leading to response bias in mail surveys.

Low response rates necessarily produce smaller samples than the researcher intended. Generally, however, the size of the sample is not the most serious concern. The problem is that low response rates typically suggest response bias. Because of response bias, a carefully selected probability sample may become a nonprobability sample—a convenience sample in which individuals' availability and willingness determine whether they complete the survey. For example, for a survey concerning introductory psychology courses, Zechmeister and Zechmeister (2000) used *Peterson's Guide to Four-Year Colleges 1998* to randomly select 250 universities and colleges in the United States and then sent surveys to their psychology departments. The response rate was 56%—surveys were returned from 140 psychology departments.

Unless the return rate is 100%, the potential for response bias exists regardless of how carefully the initial sample was selected. The researcher must demonstrate the absence of response bias. That is, the researcher needs to show that the sample of respondents who returned the survey is representative of the population, and that no segment of the population is overrepresented or underrepresented. For example, Zechmeister and Zechmeister were able to demonstrate that colleges for which a survey was returned were not different from colleges for which a survey was not returned by using information published in *Peterson's Guide to Four-Year Colleges 1998.*

The typical return rate for mail surveys is only around 30%. There are things you can do, however, to increase the return rate.

Return rates generally will be higher when:

—the questionnaire has a "personal touch" (e.g., respondents are addressed by name and not simply "resident" or "student");
—responding requires minimal effort from the respondent;
—the topic of the survey is of intrinsic interest to the respondent; and
—the respondent identifies in some way with the organization or researcher sponsoring the survey.

Personal Interviews

- Although costly, personal interviews allow researchers to gain more control over how the survey is administered.
- Interviewer bias occurs when survey responses are recorded inaccurately or when interviewers guide individuals' responses.

When personal interviews are used to collect survey data, respondents are usually contacted in their homes or in a shopping mall, and trained interviewers administer the questionnaire. The personal interview allows greater flexibility in asking questions than does the mail survey. In a personal interview the respondent can obtain clarification when questions are unclear and the trained interviewer can follow up incomplete or ambiguous answers to open-ended questions. The interviewer controls the order of questions and can ensure that all respondents complete the questions in the same order. Traditionally, the response rate to personal interviews has been higher than for mail surveys.

The advantages of using personal interviews are impressive, but there are also a few disadvantages. Increasing fear of urban crime and an increasing number of households with no one home during the day have reduced the attractiveness of using personal interviews in the home. A significant disadvantage of conducting personal interviews is the cost. The use of trained interviewers is expensive in terms of both money and time. Perhaps the most critical disadvantage of personal interviews involves the potential for interviewer bias. The interviewer should be a neutral medium through which questions and an-

Key Concept }

swers are transmitted. **Interviewer bias** occurs when the interviewer records only selected portions of the respondents' answers or tries to adjust the wording of a question to "fit" the respondent. For example, suppose a respondent in a survey about television states, "The biggest problem with TV shows is too much violence." Interviewer bias would occur if the interviewer writes down "problem with TV is violence" instead of the respondent's full response. In a follow-up question, interview bias also would occur if the interviewer asked, "By violence do you mean murders, muggings, and rapes?" A more neutral probe would allow the respondent to describe what he or she means by asking, "Could you elaborate on what you mean by violence?"

The best protection against interviewer bias is to employ highly motivated, well-paid interviewers who are trained to follow question wording exactly, to record responses accurately, and to use follow-up questions judiciously.

Interviewers should also be given a detailed list of instructions about how difficult or confusing situations are to be handled. Finally, interviewers should be closely supervised by the director of the survey project. The decision to use personal interviews is not one survey researchers take lightly. Such a procedure was used by Golombok et al. (2003) in a study of children with lesbian parents. Samples of both lesbian and heterosexual parents (and their children) were obtained from a birth registry in Avon, England. Trained researchers visited the families at home and used a standardized interview procedure supplemented by individuals' responses to standardized questionnaires. The interview lasted from $1^1/_2$ to 2 hours and was tape recorded. Ratings were made of parents' behavior (e.g., "expressed warmth") on the basis of responses to interviewers' questions, and interviewers met regularly to discuss rating procedures in order to reduce rater discrepancy. Children (approximately 7 years of age) were also interviewed and were administered short personality questionnaires that were read aloud to them by the interviewers. Inter-rater reliability was calculated for ratings obtained from randomly sampled interviews and ranged from .73 to 1.00 across variables of the study (see Chapter 4). Among other findings, the researchers reported that "boys and girls in lesbian-mother families did not differ in gender-typed behavior from their counterparts from heterosexual homes," a finding that "contradicts the view that heterosexual parents are essential for children's acquisition of gender-typed behavior" (p. 31). Because research in this sensitive area is just beginning, it remains to be seen whether future research studies, perhaps with larger and more diverse samples, will support these findings.

Computer technology makes it possible to use a hybrid of a self-administered survey and a personal interview. A person can listen to computer-recorded questions read by an interviewer and then respond to the questions on the computer. With this technology each respondent literally hears the questions read by the same interviewer in the same way thereby reducing the risk of interviewer bias. This technology also allows respondents to answer very personal questions in relative privacy (Rasinski, Willis, Baldwin, Yeh, & Lee, 1999).

Telephone Interviews

- Despite some disadvantages, telephone interviews are used frequently for brief surveys.

The prohibitive cost of personal interviews and difficulties supervising interviewers have led survey researchers to turn to telephone or Internet surveys. Phone interviewing met with considerable criticism when it was first used because of serious limitations on the sampling frame of potential respondents. Many people had unlisted numbers, and the poor and those in rural areas were less likely to have a phone. By 2000, however, more than 97% of all U.S. households had telephones (U.S. Census Bureau, 2000), and households with unlisted numbers could be reached using random-digit dialing. The random-digit dialing technique permits researchers to contact efficiently a generally representative

FIGURE 5.2   Random-digit dialing allows researchers efficient access to a generally representative sample of telephone owners for brief surveys.

sample of U.S. telephone owners. Telephone interviewing also provides better access to dangerous neighborhoods, locked buildings, and respondents available only during evening hours (have you ever been asked to complete a telephone survey during dinner?). Interviews can be completed more quickly when contacts are made by phone, and interviewers can be better supervised when all interviews are conducted from one location (Figure 5.2).

The telephone survey, like the other survey methods, is not without its drawbacks. A possible selection bias exists when respondents are limited to those who have telephones and the problem of interviewer bias remains. There is a limit to how long respondents are willing to stay on the phone, and individuals may respond differently when talking to a "faceless voice." The proliferation of cell phones also adds an unknown effect, given that cell phone users are frequently "on the go" or in business settings when they answer their phone. This cultural change may result in lower response rates from telephone surveys. In addition, one may assume that individuals from higher socioeconomic groups are more likely to have multiple phone numbers and hence might be overrepresented in a survey based on random-digit dialing. Hippler and Schwarz (1987) suggest that people take less time to form judgments during phone interviews and they may have difficulty remembering the response options offered by the interviewer. Moreover, extensive use of phone solicitation for selling products and requesting contributions has led many people to be less willing to be interviewed. Options that allow for screening calls and voice mail have made it easier for people to avoid unwanted calls. And many people who are working two jobs are rarely at home to answer the phone. In spite of these limitations and perhaps others you can think of, telephone interviews are frequently used for brief surveys.

Internet Surveys

- The Internet offers several advantages for survey research because it is an efficient, low-cost method for obtaining survey responses from large, potentially diverse and underrepresented samples.
- Disadvantages associated with Internet survey research include the potential for response and selection biases, and lack of control over the research environment.

Surveys were among the earliest Internet-based behavioral studies. Participants complete a questionnaire online and click on a "submit" button to have their responses recorded. Depending on the sophistication of the software, there is the potential for literally millions of responses to be automatically recorded and summarized as they are processed by the receiving server. Programs also exist to permit manipulation of variables and the random assignment of participants to experimental conditions. (See, for example, Fraley, 2004, for a "beginner's guide" to HTML-based psychological research on the Internet, and Kraut et al., 2004, for useful Internet resources.)

Numerous advantages of using the Internet for survey research immediately come to mind. At the top of the list are efficiency and cost (e.g., see Buchanan, 2000; Skitka & Sargis, 2005). Thousands, if not millions, of participants who vary in age, ethnicity, and even nationality can be contacted through a few keystrokes on a computer. Time and labor are dramatically reduced relative to mail or telephone surveys, let alone personal interviews. Online questionnaires are paperless, thus saving natural resources and copying costs. Participants may respond when it is convenient and do so without leaving the comfort of their home, office, dorm room, or other Internet site.

In addition to reaching large and potentially diverse samples, Skitka and Sargis (2005) suggest that the Internet also has the potential for accessing groups that typically are underrepresented in psychological research. The prevalence on the Web of chat rooms, special interest groups, and support groups provides an "in" for a researcher seeking specific samples of participants, whether it be pet owners, members of hate groups, cancer survivors, victims of various crimes, or any of a multitude of respondent types that may not be as easily reached by more traditional survey methods. Because the Internet is truly a worldwide source of participants, it also opens up new possibilities for cross-cultural research (e.g., Gosling et al., 2004).

Internet-based surveys are also not without their disadvantages. At the top of this list is the potential for sample biases (Birnbaum, 2001; Kraut et al., 2004;

Schmidt, 1997). Both response and selection biases are likely to be present. Response bias can occur due to nonresponding just as it does for other survey methods. In fact, response rates typically are lower for online surveys than for comparable mail or telephone surveys (see Kraut et al., 2004; Skitka & Sargis, 2005). As we have seen, individuals who respond to a survey are going to differ on important characteristics from those who do not respond. Selection bias is present because respondents are a convenience sample comprised of individuals who have Internet access. Higher-income households in the United States are more likely to have Internet access, and those households with children are more likely to have access than those without children. White and Asian householders are nearly twice as likely to have Internet access than those householders who are Black or Hispanic (Newburger, 2001). However, *the pool of Internet users in the United States is no more or less representative of the U.S. population than is the participant pool of college freshmen and sophomores who are recruited for many psychology studies.*

Selection biases can be exaggerated due to the method of soliciting participants. Researchers can obtain samples of respondents by posting research notices on websites that promote research opportunities (e.g., the website associated with APS identified in Chapter 1) or by simply creating a Web page with the survey (e.g., *personality survey*) and wait for users to locate it ("hits") via Internet search engines (Krantz & Dalal, 2000). More active strategies include sending notices of the research project to individuals or groups likely to respond because of their interest in the survey topic. As Skitka and Sargis (2005) emphasize, however, not only are Internet users not representative of the general population, but also members of special interest groups are not necessarily representative of their specific groups (e.g., victims of sexual abuse). At present there is no way to generate a random sample of Internet users (Kraut et al., 2004).

Lack of control over the research environment is also a major disadvantage of Internet surveys (Birnbaum, 2000; Kraut et al., 2004). As we mentioned in Chapter 3, this lack of control raises serious ethical issues related to informed consent and protecting individuals from harm as a consequence of their participation (e.g., emotional distress over survey questions). Because the researcher is not present there is no easy way to determine if respondents understand clearly the instructions, are answering conscientiously and not frivolously or even maliciously, or creating multiple submissions (e.g., Kraut et al., 2004). Respondents may participate alone or in groups, under distracting conditions, without the knowledge of the researcher (Skitka & Sargis, 2005). One Internet researcher worried that respondents to survey questions about probability and risk were using calculators even though instructions requested them not to (Birnbaum, 2000).

It seems safe to say that the advantages of Internet surveys will overcome many of the disadvantages. As technology improves and IRB committees devise acceptable methods for protecting human participants, survey research on the Internet will continue to grow.

SURVEY-RESEARCH DESIGNS

- The three types of survey design are the cross-sectional design, successive independent samples design, and the longitudinal design.

One of the most important decisions survey researchers must make is the choice of a research design. A survey-research design is the overall plan or structure used to conduct the entire study. There are three general types of survey-research designs: the cross-sectional design, the successive independent samples design, and the longitudinal design. There is no all-purpose survey-research design. Researchers choose a design based on the goals of the study.

Cross-Sectional Design

- In the cross-sectional design one or more samples are drawn from the population(s) at one point in time.
- Cross-sectional designs allow researchers to describe the characteristics of a population or the differences between two or more populations, and correlational findings from cross-sectional designs allow researchers to make predictions.

Key Concept }

The cross-sectional design is one of the most commonly used survey-research designs. In a **cross-sectional design,** one or more samples are drawn from the population *at one time.* The focus in a cross-sectional design is description—describing the characteristics of a population or the differences among two or more populations at a particular point in time. For example, Goodman and her colleagues (1997) used a cross-sectional design in their nationwide study of mental disorders in 9- to 17-year-olds. The purpose of their study was to determine if youths who receive outpatient mental health services for their disorder differ in systematic ways from the larger population of children and adolescents with mental disorders. They questioned whether previous research findings observed for samples of youths who receive treatment ("clinical samples") may be generalized to describe youth who do not obtain treatment. They were especially interested in this question because only a small proportion of children and adolescents with mental disorders receive treatment.

To answer this question they examined data collected in a study sponsored by the National Institute of Mental Health (NIMH) on mental disorders in children and adolescents. A community-based sample of parent-youth pairs from Connecticut, Georgia, New York, and Puerto Rico completed surveys and were interviewed in their homes. A total of 1,285 parent-youth pairs participated. (Thus, you can see that even cross-sectional designs are not necessarily simple or quick.) Goodman et al. made many observations to describe differences between youths with mental disorders who received outpatient mental health services and youths with mental disorders who did not receive treatment.

Of their sample, 747 (58%) of the youths had no mental disorder (within the past 6 months); however 25 (3%) of these had received mental health services. A total of 535 (42%) were diagnosed with some type of mental disorder; of these, only 69 (13%) received outpatient mental health services. How did the 69 children and adolescents with mental disorders who received treatment differ from the 466 who did not? Goodman et al. looked at a number of variables, and found that the youths who received mental health services were more likely to be identified as non-Hispanic White relative to other ethnic groups, and were less likely to be prepubertal girls. They were also judged to be more impaired, less competent, and more likely to have two or more disorders. Their parents differed too. Parents of youths who received treatment were more educated but were less satisfied with their family life, did not monitor their children, and were more likely to use mental health services themselves. Based on these data, Goodman et al. concluded that research samples of youths who receive treatment are not representative of all youths who have a mental disorder.

Cross-sectional designs are ideally suited for the descriptive and predictive goals of survey research. Surveys are also used to assess changes in attitudes or behaviors over time and to determine the effect of some naturally occurring event, such as the passage of a law to raise the drinking age. For these purposes the cross-sectional design is not the method of choice. Rather, research designs are needed that systematically sample respondents over time. Two such designs are discussed in the next two sections.

Successive Independent Samples Design

- In the successive independent samples design, different samples of respondents from the population complete the survey over a time period.
- The successive independent samples design allows researchers to study changes in a population over time.
- The successive independent samples design does not allow researchers to infer how individual respondents have changed over time.
- A problem with the successive independent samples design occurs when the samples drawn from the population are not comparable—that is, not equally representative of the population.

Key Concept

In the **successive independent samples design,** a series of cross-sectional surveys are conducted over time (successively). The samples are independent because a *different* sample of respondents completes the survey at each point in time. There are two key ingredients: (1) the same set of questions should be asked of each sample of respondents, and (2) the different samples should be drawn from the same population. If these two conditions are met, researchers can legitimately compare survey responses over time. This design is most appropriate when the major goal of the study is to describe changes in the attitudes or behaviors within a population over time. For example, public opinion researchers frequently ask independent samples of Americans the extent to which they approve of the U.S. president (referred to as the president "approval ratings"). Changes in approval ratings over time are used to characterize Americans' opinions of the president's actions.

As another example, consider a study that you may have been part of, one that has been conducted every year since 1966. Each year some 350,000 full-time freshmen from a nationally representative sample of approximately 700 colleges and universities are surveyed (Sax et al., 2003). This research project represents the largest and longest empirical study of higher education in the United States, with over 1,500 universities and over 10 million students participating during the 38-plus years of the study. Students are asked approximately 40 questions covering a number of topics, and although some changes have occurred in the questions over the decades, many questions have been asked each year, making this an excellent example of a successive independent samples design.

What can be said about changes in students' values and goals during this time period? Sax et al. (2003) reported the results for the portion of the survey in which students are asked to rate the importance of different values. Two values were of particular interest: "the importance of developing a meaningful philosophy of life" and "the importance of being very well off financially" (pp. 6–7). Figure 5.3 displays the results for the percentage of students who endorsed these values as "very important" or "essential." In the late 1960s over 80% of students indicated that developing a meaningful philosophy of life was very important or essential—in fact, this was the top value endorsed by students. In contrast, being well-off financially was very important or essential to less than 45% of the students, and ranked fifth or sixth among students' values during the late 1960s.

FIGURE 5.3   Contrasting trends in values for college freshmen from 1966–2003.
Source: Figure 7 (p. 7), Sax et al. (2003).

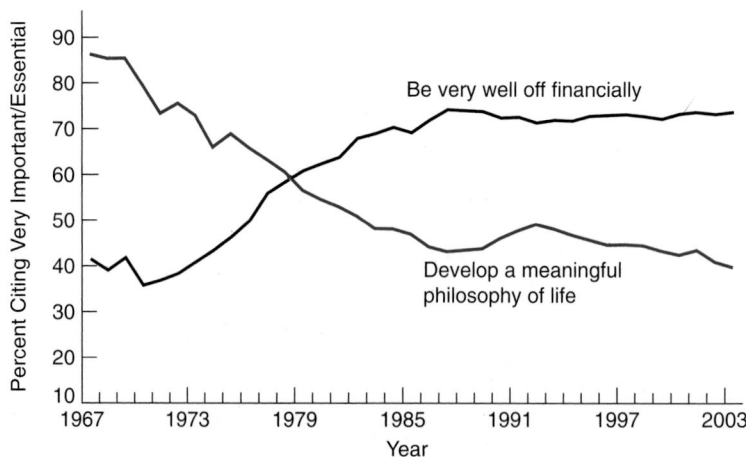

In 2003, the position of these values was reversed, with 73.8% of students endorsing being well-off financially as very important or essential. In 2003, developing a meaningful philosophy of life dropped to its lowest value in the survey history, with 39.3% of students endorsing this as very important or essential. As can be seen in Figure 5.3, these contrasting trends in values began to shift in the early 1970s, crossed in 1977, and were completely reversed by the late 1980s. Since then they have remained relatively unchanged. Sax et al. (2003) emphasize that the recent contrasting values "reflect the continuing tension between extrinsic and intrinsic values within this generation of college students" (p. 7). Interestingly, these researchers also reported that 2003 was a record year for "volunteerism," with 83.1% of the college freshmen indicating that they participated in volunteer work their last year of high school, and a record number reported that there is a "very good chance" they will participate in volunteer work or community service work during their college years.

The successive independent samples design has limitations. Consider hypothetical results from a successive independent samples design. Suppose you hear it reported that in 1974 35% of college students surveyed said they don't trust the U.S. government, 25% reported that they had mixed feelings, and 40% reported that they did trust the U.S. government. Then you hear reported that in 2004 results to the same survey question showed that 50% of students say they don't trust the government, 20% say they have mixed feelings, and 30% do have trust. How can we interpret these results? To account for the 50:20:30 split in 2004, can one conclude, for example, that 5% of the 1974 "mixed feelings" group and 10% of the 1974 "do trust" group have changed their minds and now don't trust the government? No! And perhaps you can see why.

What we must remember is that the students surveyed in 1974 (in our hypothetical survey) were not the same students surveyed in 2004. The extent to which specific individuals change their views over time can be determined only by testing the same individuals on both occasions. We cannot determine in the successive independent samples design who has changed their views or by how much. It would be just as easy to suggest an entirely different numbers scenario to account for the 2004 results (and just as unwise without additional evidence). You may have considered a similar problem of interpretation when examining the results of the Sax et al. (2003) survey presented in Figure 5.3. What accounts for the changes in students' attitudes observed from 1966 to 2003? We can't say on the basis of these data. The purpose of the successive independent samples design is to describe changes over time in the distribution of *population* characteristics, not to describe changes in *individual* respondents. Accordingly, the successive independent samples design is not very helpful in ferreting out reasons for observed changes like those shown in Figure 5.3. (As you will soon see, another survey design, the longitudinal design, is more appropriate in these situations.)

A second potential limitation of the successive independent samples design arises when the successive samples are not representative of the same population. Imagine that in our hypothetical survey of students' attitude toward the

U.S. government, the sample comprised students from small rural colleges in 1974 and students from large urban universities in 2004. The comparisons of students' attitudes toward the government over this time period would be meaningless. That is, we wouldn't be able to state that the student population had become less trusting over time because it's possible that the degree of trust differs for rural and urban students, which could also account for the difference between 1974 and 2004 results. The rural and urban samples illustrate the problem of *noncomparable successive samples*. Changes in the population across time can be described accurately only when the successive independent samples represent the same population. Thus, it is important to assure that the successive independent samples are comparable. Although sophisticated statistical procedures exist to help unravel the problems associated with noncomparable successive samples, the best solution is to avoid the problem by carefully selecting successive samples that represent *the same* population.

Longitudinal Design

- In the longitudinal design, the same respondents are surveyed over time in order to examine changes in individual respondents.
- Because of the correlational nature of survey data, it is difficult to identify the causes of individuals' changes over time.
- As people drop out of the study over time (attrition), the final sample may no longer be comparable to the original sample or represent the population.

Key Concept The distinguishing characteristic of the **longitudinal design** is that the same sample of respondents is surveyed more than once. For example, in a study of depressed mothers, researchers interviewed the same women during pregnancy, at 3 months postpartum, and when their child was 1, 4, and 11 years of age (Hay, Pawlby, Angold, Harold, & Sharp, 2003). The researchers found a link between the mothers' postnatal depression and children's violent behavior at age 11.

The longitudinal design has two important advantages. First, the investigator can determine the direction and extent of change for individual respondents. Also, because changes in each individual's responses are assessed, it's easier to investigate reasons for attitude or behavior changes. Second, the longitudinal design is the best survey design when a researcher wishes to assess the effect of some naturally occurring event. For example, by measuring people's attitudes before and after a national election, the researcher can assess the effect of this event.

Heatherton, Mahamedi, Striepe, Field, and Keel (1997) used the longitudinal design to investigate changes in attitudes and behaviors related to eating during the transition from college to early adulthood. Although much is known about eating disorders in adolescents and college students, Heatherton and his colleagues were interested in learning how disordered eating may progress over time as individuals settle down, marry, establish careers, begin families, and importantly, gain a stronger sense of identity. These researchers hypothesized that as individuals change their roles and life goals during their twenties, their emphasis on physical appearance may decrease, which would decrease the prevalence of eating problems. To test their hypothesis, they randomly selected a sample of 800 women and 400 men from a private northeastern college in 1982 to complete a survey about eating and dieting. Their response rate was 78% ($N = 625$) for women and 69% ($N = 276$) for men. In 1992, they contacted these same individuals (with the help of the alumni office) and gave them the same survey again about their eating attitudes and behaviors. The distinguishing characteristic of the longitudinal design is the fact that the *same* individuals were surveyed in each phase of the study.

As you may imagine, longitudinal designs involve a massive effort. The potential power of such an effort, however, is that researchers can examine changes within individuals over time. In Heatherton et al.'s (1997) study, results indicated different changes in eating and weight gain for women and men.

FIGURE 5.4   Survey research such as that of Heatherton et al. (1997) is aimed at discovering how women are affected by eating disorders as they grow older.

Survey responses suggested that during the decade since college, women's eating disorder symptoms, chronic dieting, and body dissatisfaction decreased. However, despite these decreases, women's dissatisfaction with their body and their desire to lose weight remained high. Men, in contrast, rarely had problems with eating and weight during college. Ten years later, however, they had experienced weight gain (an average of almost 12 pounds, compared to women's average gain of 4 pounds). Men also reported increased dieting and symptoms of disordered eating on the 1992 survey, although this was still low relative to women.

Heatherton et al. (1997) made some interesting observations that are relevant to our understanding of longitudinal surveys. They proposed that decreases in women's eating problems reflect their maturation during their twenties, changes in their roles, and being away from the college campus (and the pressures to be thin that occur on college campuses). It's possible, however, that other processes may account for changes within the individuals in the sample. Using a successive independent samples design in which separate samples of college students were surveyed in 1982 and 1992, Heatherton, Nichols, Mahamedi, and Keel (1995) noted that eating-disordered symptoms and body dissatisfaction also were lower for the college students in the 1992 sample relative to the 1982 sample. These findings suggest that decreases in eating-disordered attitudes and behaviors may reflect changes at a societal level over the ten-year period (e.g., due to increasing information about eating disorders in the media). One potential problem with longitudinal survey designs is that it is difficult to pinpoint the exact causes for individuals' changes over time.[1]

Another potential problem with longitudinal designs is that it can be difficult to obtain a sample of respondents who will agree to participate over time in a longitudinal study. Even when the respondents do agree to participate, there can be further problems. You might think the longitudinal design solves the problem of noncomparable samples because the same people participate over and over (so of course the sample represents the same population each time). Unfortunately, the samples over time in a longitudinal design are identical *only if* all members of the original sample participate throughout the study. This is unlikely. For example, in the Heatherton et al. (1997) study, of the 901 participants in the original 1982 sample, only 724 (80%) returned a useable survey in 1992.

Unless all the respondents in the original sample complete all phases of a longitudinal design, there is a possible problem due to *attrition*. Attrition is probably the most serious disadvantage of the longitudinal design because as samples decrease over time, they are less likely to represent the original population from which the sample was drawn. It is usually possible, however, to

---

[1]Heatherton et al. (1997) noted that because the decreases in problem eating were larger among individuals in the longitudinal survey than in the successive independent sample survey, maturational processes within individuals likely were operating to decrease problem eating over time, in addition to societal changes.

determine whether the final sample is comparable to the original sample in a longitudinal design. The characteristics of nonrespondents in the follow-up phase(s) are known because they participated in the original sample. Therefore, researchers can look at participants' original responses to see how these nonresponding individuals may differ from those who continued their participation.

The advantages of the longitudinal design, such as determining changes for individual respondents, arise because the same individuals are surveyed more than once. Paradoxically, problems can also arise in longitudinal designs because of this same feature. One possible problem is that respondents may strive heroically to be consistent across interviews. This can be particularly troublesome if the study is designed to assess changes in respondents' attitudes! Although their attitudes have actually changed, people may report their original attitudes in an effort to appear consistent (perhaps they know researchers value reliability). Another potential problem is that the initial interview may sensitize respondents to the issue under investigation. For example, consider a longitudinal design used to assess students' concern about crime on campus. Once the study starts, participants may pay more attention to crime reports than they normally would. You might recognize this as an illustration of reactive measurement—people behaving differently because they know they are participating in a study.

Rather than trying to be heroically consistent in their eating attitudes and behaviors over time, Heatherton et al. (1997) noted that their participants may have been reluctant to report that they were having the same problems with eating as when they were in college. Thus, the decreases the researchers observed in problem eating during the 10-year period may be due to the fact that "women who are approaching their thirties may be embarrassed to admit they are experiencing problems typically associated with adolescence" (p. 124). When survey respondents are asked to report their attitudes and behaviors, researchers must be alert to reasons why their respondents' reports may not correspond to their actual behavior. We will return to this important issue later in this chapter.

QUESTIONNAIRES

Even if the sample of respondents was perfectly representative, the response rate was 100%, and the research design was elegantly planned and perfectly executed, the results of a survey will be useless if the questionnaire is poorly constructed. In this section we describe the most common survey research instrument, the questionnaire. To be useful, questionnaires should yield reliable and valid measures of demographic variables and of individual differences on self-report scales. Although there is no substitute for experience when it comes to preparing a good questionnaire, there are a few general principles of questionnaire construction with which you should be familiar. We describe six basic steps in preparing a questionnaire and then offer some more specific guidelines for writing and administering individual questions.

Questionnaires as Instruments

- Most survey research relies on the use of questionnaires to measure variables.
- Demographic variables describe the characteristics of people who are surveyed.
- The accuracy and precision of questionnaires requires expertise and care in their construction.
- Self-report scales are used to assess people's preferences or attitudes.

Key Concept }

The value of survey research (and any research) ultimately depends on the quality of the measurements that researchers make. The quality of these measurements, in turn, depends on the quality of the instruments used to make the measurements. The primary research instrument in survey research is the **questionnaire.** On the surface, a questionnaire may not look like the high-tech instruments used in much modern scientific research; but, when constructed and used properly, a questionnaire is a powerful scientific instrument for measuring different variables.

Demographic Variables   Demographic variables are an important type of variable frequently measured in survey research. Demographic variables are used to describe the characteristics of the people who are surveyed. Measures such as race, ethnicity, age, and socioeconomic status are examples of demographic variables. Whether we decide to measure these variables depends on the goals of our study, as well as on other considerations. Entwisle and Astone (1994), for example, provide a practical reason for including race and ethnicity as demographic variables in survey research. This practical reason is the ever-increasing diversity of the U.S. population. Entwisle and Astone (1994) point out that "the ethnic and racial diversity of the U.S. population is now projected to increase through the middle of the this century, so that by then the majority of the U.S. population will be persons whose ethnicity would now be classified as 'nonwhite'" (p. 1522). By asking respondents to identify their race, we are able to document the racial mix of our sample and, if related to our research questions, compare racial groups.

Measuring a demographic variable such as race may at first seem very easy. One straightforward method is simply to ask respondents to identify their race in an open-ended question: What is your race? _____ Such an approach may be straightforward, but the resulting measurement of race may not be satisfactory. For example, some respondents may mistakenly confuse "race" and "ethnicity." Important distinctions in identifying ethnic groups may go unrecognized by respondents and researchers. For instance, Hispanic does not identify a race; Hispanic designates all those whose country of origin is Spanish speaking. So, a person born in Spain would be classified as Hispanic. Latino is a term that is sometimes used interchangeably with Hispanic, but Latino designates people whose origin is from the countries of North and South America, excluding Canada and the United States. Distinctions like these can be

FIGURE 5.5   Although ethnic background is an important demographic variable, accurately classifying people on this variable is not an easy task.

confused. For example, a person known to the authors is of European Spanish heritage and correctly considers himself a Caucasian, and not Latino. His ethnicity is Hispanic.

In general, "quick and dirty" approaches to measurement in survey research tend to yield messy data that are hard to analyze and interpret. For example, many individuals identify themselves as "multi-racial"; however, if researchers fail to include this as a possible response option, the information from participants may be incorrect—or they may skip the question entirely. Entwisle and Astone (1994) recommend a deliberate—and effective—approach when measuring race. They outline a series of nine questions to measure a person's race. One of these questions is, What race do you consider yourself to be? Other questions seek information such as what countries the person's ancestors came from, and whether Latino respondents are Mexican, Puerto Rican, Cuban, or something else. This more detailed series of questions allows researchers to measure race less ambiguously, more accurately, and more precisely. We use this example of measuring race to illustrate a more general principle: *The accuracy and precision of questionnaires as survey-research instruments depends upon the expertise and care that go into their construction.*

Preferences and Attitudes   Individuals' preferences and attitudes are frequently assessed in surveys. For example, a marketing researcher may be interested in consumers' preferences for different brands of coffee, or a political group may be interested in potential voters' attitudes regarding controversial

---

BOX 5.3

SCALING INDIVIDUAL DIFFERENCES

Consider a researcher who is interested in measuring individuals' willingness to forgive others. If this researcher decides to use the Likert method, the first step would be to write items that reflect the construct or domain of interest, namely, willingness to forgive others. Typically, participants would next be asked to rate each of the items on a 5-point scale. They could indicate their rating, for example, by circling a number on the scale. One item that could be used to measure forgiveness is:

When people hurt me, I can usually forgive them.

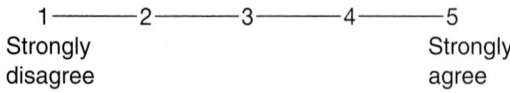

1————2————3————4————5
Strongly   Strongly
disagree   agree

Many such items are administered to a large group of people (at a minimum, 100), and each individual's responses are summed to derive a total score. The items that best represent the domain of interest (forgiveness) are then selected from the whole set of items by discarding those that don't discriminate individuals who are high on the dimension from individuals who are low (based on their total score). Each selected item should correlate well with the total scale score. Once the best items are chosen, an individual's scale score is obtained by summing her responses to these items. An important goal of scale development is reliability, and in the Likert method, each time the scale is used the researcher must demonstrate that the items in the scale consistently measure the domain of interest (reliability is discussed in greater detail in the next section). It is important to remember that not every 5-point rating scale represents a Likert scale. A scale qualifies as a Likert scale only if it follows the method for scale development that we just outlined.

---

public issues. Psychologists have long been interested in measuring people's thoughts and feelings on a vast array of topics, and often develop self-report scales for people to provide oral or written responses to items on the scale.

Self-report scales are commonly used to measure people's judgments about items presented on the scale (e.g., coffee, divorce, political candidates, life events) and to determine differences among people on some dimension presented on the scale (e.g., personality traits, amount of stress). For example, respondents may be asked to rate different life events according to how stressful they perceive the events to be. The researcher then may develop a list of life events that vary on the dimension of stressfulness. This type of scale focuses on differences among the items on the scale, not differences among individuals. To measure individual differences, respondents may be asked to report how often during the past year they experienced different stressful life events listed on a scale. A total stress score can be obtained for each individual by summing responses to the items on the scale. Individuals can then be compared according to the amount of stress experienced during the past year.[2] Box 5.3 describes the Likert method that is frequently used by researchers to develop individual differences scales.

---

[2]The area of psychological measurement concerned with scaling items or stimuli is known as psychophysics, and the area of measurement concerned with individual differences is referred to as psychometrics.

Self-report measures, often in the form of a questionnaire, are among the most frequently used tools in psychology. Given their importance, it is critical that these measures be developed carefully. Two critical characteristics of the measurements made using self-report questionnaires are essential characteristics of all measurements—reliability and validity.

Reliability and Validity of Self-Report Measures

- Reliability refers to the consistency of measurement, and is frequently assessed using the test-retest reliability method.
- Reliability is increased by including many similar items on a measure, by testing a diverse sample of individuals, and by using uniform testing procedures.
- Validity refers to the truthfulness of a measure: Does it measure what it intends to measure?
- Construct validity represents the extent to which a measure assesses the theoretical construct it is designed to assess; construct validity is determined by assessing convergent validity and discriminant validity.

Reliable self-report measures, like reliable observers or any other reliable measurements, are characterized by consistency. A reliable self-report measure is one that yields similar (consistent) results each time it is taken. Self-report measures must be reliable if they are to be used as a basis for making predictions. For example, measures of the stressfulness of an individual's life must be reliable if the stressfulness measure is to be used to predict the health problems that are related to stress. There are several ways to measure a test's reliability. One common method is to compute a *test-retest reliability*. Usually, test-retest reliability involves administering the same questionnaire to a large sample of people at two different times (hence, test and retest). For a questionnaire to yield reliable measurements, people need not obtain identical scores on the two administrations of the questionnaire, but a person's relative position in the distribution of scores should be similar at the two test times. The consistency of this relative positioning is determined by computing a correlation coefficient using the two scores on the questionnaire for each person in the sample. A desirable value for test-retest reliability coefficients is .80 or above, but the size of the coefficient will depend on factors such as the number and types of items.

As we just mentioned, the reliability of self-report measures is affected by the number of items on the questionnaire; in this case, more items are better. We are likely to have unreliable measures if we try to measure a baseball player's hitting ability based on a single time at bat or a person's attitude toward the death penalty based on a single question on a survey. The reliability of our measures will increase greatly if we average the behavior in question across a large number of observations—many at-bats and many survey questions (Epstein, 1979).

In general, measurements will also be more reliable when there is greater variability on the factor being measured among those individuals being tested. Often the goal of measurement is to determine the extent to which individuals differ. A sample of individuals who vary a great deal from one another is easier to differentiate reliably than are individuals who differ by only a small amount. Consider this example. Suppose we wish to assess soccer players' ability to pass the ball effectively to other players. We will be able to differentiate more reliably good players from poor players if we include in our sample a wider range of players—for example, professionals, high school players, and peewee players. It would be much harder to differentiate players reliably if we only tested professional players—they'd all be good! The range of skill level would not be that great. Thus, a test is often more reliable when administered to a diverse sample than when given to a restricted sample of individuals.

A third and final factor affecting reliability is related to the conditions under which the questionnaire is administered. Questionnaires will yield more reliable measurements when the testing situation is free of distractions and when clear instructions are provided for completing the questionnaire. You may remember times when your own test performance was hindered by noise or when you weren't sure what a question was asking.

The reliability of a survey measure is easier to determine and to achieve than the validity of a measure. The definition of validity is deceptively straightforward—a valid questionnaire measures what it is intended to measure. Have you ever heard students complain that questions on a test didn't seem to address the material covered in class? This is an issue of validity.

At this point, we will focus on construct validity, which is just one of the many ways in which the validity of a measurement is assessed. The *construct validity* of a measure represents the extent to which it measures the theoretical construct it is designed to measure. One approach to determining the construct validity of a test relies on two other kinds of validity: convergent validity and discriminant validity. These concepts can best be understood by considering an example.

Table 5.1 presents data showing how we might assess the construct validity of a measure of "life satisfaction." Lucas, Diener, and Suh (1996) note that psychologists are increasingly examining factors such as happiness, life satisfaction, self-esteem, optimism, and other indicators of well-being. However, it's not clear whether these different indicators all measure the same construct (e.g., well-being) or whether each is a distinguishable construct. Lucas and his

TABLE 5.1   EXAMPLE OF CONSTRUCT VALIDITY*

	SWLS	LS-5	PA
SWLS	(.88)		
LS-5	.77	(.90)	
PA	.42	.47	(.81)

*Data from Lucas et al. (1996), Table 3.
    Note: SWLS = Satisfaction with Life Scale; LS-5 = 5-item Life Satisfaction scale; PA = Positive Affect scale.

colleagues conducted several studies in which they asked individuals to complete questionnaire measures of these different indicators of well-being. For our purposes we will focus on a portion of their data from their third study, in which they asked participants to complete three scales: two life satisfaction measures, the Satisfaction with Life Scale (SWLS) and a 5-item Life Satisfaction measure (LS-5); and a measure of Positive Affect (PA). At issue in this example is whether the construct of life satisfaction—the quality of being happy with one's life—can be distinguished from being happy more generally (positive affect).

The data in Table 5.1 are presented in the form of a correlation matrix. A correlation matrix is an easy way to present a number of correlations. Look first at the values in parentheses that appear on the diagonal. These parenthesized correlation coefficients represent the test reliabilities of the three measures appearing in the table (Satisfaction with Life Scale, 5-item Life Satisfaction, and Positive Affect, respectively). As you can see, the three measures show good reliability (each is above .80). Our focus, however, is on measuring the construct validity of "life satisfaction," so let's look at what else is in Table 5.1.

It is reasonable to expect that scores on the Satisfaction with Life Scale (SWLS) should correlate with scores on the 5-item Life Satisfaction measure; after all, both measures were designed to assess the life satisfaction construct. In fact, Lucas et al. observed a correlation between these two measures of .77, which indicates that they correlate as expected. This finding provides evidence for *convergent validity* of the measures; the two measures converge (or "go together") as measures of life satisfaction.

The case for the construct validity of life satisfaction can be made even more strongly when the measures are shown to have discriminant validity. As can be seen in Table 5.1, the correlations between the Satisfaction with Life Scale (SWLS) and Positive Affect (.42) and between the 5-item Life Satisfaction measure (LS-5) and Positive Affect (.47) are lower. These findings show that life satisfaction measures do not correlate as well with a measure of another theoretical construct—namely, positive affect. The lower correlations between the life satisfaction tests and the positive affect test indicate that *different* constructs are being measured. Thus, there is evidence for *discriminant validity* of the life satisfaction measures because they seem to "discriminate" life satisfaction from positive affect—being satisfied with one's life is not the same as general happiness. The construct validity of life satisfaction gains support in our example because there is evidence for both convergent validity and discriminant validity.

Constructing a Questionnaire

- Constructing a questionnaire involves deciding what information should be sought and the type of questionnaire, writing a draft of the questionnaire, pretesting the questionnaire, and concluding with specifying the procedures for its use.
- The wording of questionnaires should be clear and specific using simple, direct, and familiar vocabulary.

- The order in which questions are asked on a questionnaire needs to be considered seriously because the order can affect respondents' answers.

Steps in Preparing a Questionnaire   Constructing a questionnaire that will yield reliable and valid measurements is a challenging task. In this section we suggest guidelines that can help you meet this challenge, especially if you are constructing a questionnaire for the first time as part of a research project you are doing. The following six steps can serve as a guide as you prepare your questionnaire:

1 Decide what information should be sought.
2 Decide what type of questionnaire should be used.
3 Write a first draft of the questionnaire.
4 Reexamine and revise the questionnaire.
5 Pretest the questionnaire.
6 Edit the questionnaire and specify the procedures for its use.

Step 1. The warning "Watch out for that first step!" is appropriate here. The first step in questionnaire construction—deciding what information is to be sought—should actually be the first step in planning the survey as a whole. This decision, of course, determines the nature of the questions to be included in the questionnaire. It is important to predict the likely results of the proposed questionnaire and then to decide whether these "findings" will answer the questions of the study. Surveys are frequently done under considerable time pressure, and inexperienced researchers are especially prone to impatience. Just remember that a poorly conceived questionnaire takes just as much time and effort to administer and analyze as does a well-conceived questionnaire. The difference is that a well-constructed questionnaire leads to interpretable results. The best that can be said for a poorly designed one is that it is a good way to learn how important careful deliberation is in the planning stages.

Step 2. Once the information to be sought from respondents has been clearly specified, the next step is to decide on the type of questionnaire to be used. For example, will it be self-administered, or will trained interviewers be using it? This decision is determined primarily by the survey method that has been selected. For instance, if a telephone survey is to be done, trained interviewers will be needed. In designing the questionnaire, one should also consider using items that have been prepared by other researchers. For example, there is no reason to develop your own instrument to assess racial prejudice if a reliable and valid one is already available. Besides, if you use items from a questionnaire that has already been used, you can compare your results directly with those of earlier studies.

Step 3. If you decide that no available instrument suits your needs, you will have to take the third step and write a first draft of your own questionnaire. Guidelines concerning the wording and ordering of questions are presented later in this section.

Step 4. The fourth step in questionnaire construction—reexamining and rewriting—is an essential one. Questions that appear objective and unambiguous to you may strike others as slanted and ambiguous. It is most helpful to have your questionnaire reviewed by experts, both those who have knowledge of survey research methods and those with expertise in the area on which your study is focused. For example, if you are doing a survey of students' attitudes toward the campus food service, it would be advisable to have your questionnaire reviewed by the campus food service director. When you are dealing with a controversial topic, it is especially important to have representatives of both sides of the issue screen your questions for possible bias.

Step 5. By far the most critical step in the development of an effective questionnaire is doing a pretest. A pretest involves actually administering the questionnaire to a small sample of respondents under conditions as much as possible like those to be used in the final administration of the survey. Pretest respondents must also be typical of those to be included in the final sample; it makes little sense to pretest a survey of nursing home residents by administering the questionnaire to college students. There is one way, however, in which a pretest does differ from the final administration of the survey. Respondents should be interviewed at length regarding their reactions to individual questions and to the questionnaire as a whole. This provides information about potentially ambiguous or offensive items.

   The pretest should also serve as a "dress rehearsal" for interviewers, who should be closely supervised during this stage to ensure that they understand and adhere to the proper procedures for administering the questionnaire. If major changes have to be made as a result of problems arising during the pretest, a second pretest may be needed to determine whether these changes solved the problems originally encountered.

Step 6. After pretesting is completed, the final step is to edit the questionnaire and specify the procedures to be followed in its final administration. To reach this final step successfully, it is important to consider guidelines for the effective wording of questions and for the ordering of questions.

Guidelines for the Effective Wording of Questions   Lawyers have long known that how a question is phrased has great impact on how that question is answered. Survey researchers need to be equally conscious of this principle. This point is illustrated in a survey Loftus (1979) conducted for the manufacturer of a leading headache remedy. She found that people reported having more headaches when they were asked, "Do you get headaches frequently and, if so, how often?" than when they were asked, "Do you get headaches occasionally and, if so, how often?" In a typical survey, only one wording is used for each question so, unfortunately, the extent of the influence of the wording of questions in a given survey can almost never be determined precisely.

Clark and Schober (1992) point out that respondents presume that the meaning of a question is obvious. This has important implications. For instance, when a question includes a vague word, respondents may interpret the word in various ways according to their individual biases and ideas of what is "obvious." Thus, words like "few" or "usually," or terms such as "energy crisis," may be interpreted differently by different individuals. Respondents also tend to assume that a word in a survey is used in the same way as in their subculture or culture. A recent example in popular culture is figuring out whether "bad" means "good." Clark and Schober (1992) cite as an example a surveyor who wanted to ask Mexican residents in the Yucatan the question, "How many children do you have?" When translated into Spanish, the surveyor used the word *niños* for children, but villagers in this area of Mexico treated *niños* as including living children and children who have died. Respondents also may reasonably assume that if the surveyor asks a question, then it is one that the respondent can answer. This assumption can lead respondents to give answers to questions that have no (valid) answers! For example, when asked to give opinions about nationalities that didn't exist, respondents nevertheless gave opinions.

Although it's clear that question wording in surveys can pose problems, the solution is less clear. *At a minimum, the exact wording of critical questions should always be reported along with the data describing respondents' answers.* The problem of the potential influence of the wording of questions is yet another illustration of why a multimethod approach is so essential in investigating behavior.

Survey researchers usually choose from two general types of questions when writing a questionnaire. The first type is a *free-response* (open-ended) question and the second type is a *closed* (multiple-choice) question. Free-response questions, like the essay questions on a classroom test, merely specify the area to be addressed in a response. For example, the question, "What are your views on the legalizing of abortion?" is a free-response question. By contrast, closed questions provide specific response alternatives. "Is police protection very good, fairly good, neither good nor bad, not very good, or not good at all?" is a closed question about the quality of police protection in a community.

The primary advantage of free-response questions is that they offer the respondent greater flexibility. However, this advantage is often more than offset by the difficulties that arise in recording and scoring responses to free-response questions. For example, extensive coding is frequently necessary to summarize rambling responses to free-response questions. Closed questions, on the other hand, can be answered more easily and quickly and fewer scoring problems arise. It is also much easier to summarize responses to closed questions because the answers are readily comparable across respondents. A major disadvantage of closed questions is that they reduce expressiveness and spontaneity. Further, the possibility exists that the respondent will have to choose a less than preferred response because no presented alternative really captures his or her views. Hence, the responses obtained may not accurately reflect the respondent's opinion.

Regardless of the type of question used, the *vocabulary should be simple, direct, and familiar to all respondents.* Questions *should be as clear and specific as possible. Double-barreled questions should be avoided.* An example of a double-barreled question is: "Have you suffered from headaches and nausea recently?" A person may respond "no" if both symptoms have not occurred at exactly the same time or may respond "yes" if either symptom has occurred. The solution to the problem of double-barreled questions is a simple one—rewrite them as separate questions. Survey questions should be as short as possible without sacrificing the clarity of the questions' meaning. Twenty or fewer words should suffice for most survey questions. *Each question should be carefully edited for readability and should be phrased in such a way that all conditional information precedes the key idea.* For example, it would be better to ask, "If you were forced to leave your present job, what type of work would you seek?" than to ask, "What type of work would you seek if you were forced to leave your present job?"

Leading or loaded questions should also be avoided in a questionnaire. *Leading* questions take the form, "Most people favor the use of nuclear energy. What do you think?" To avoid bias, it is better to mention all possible perspectives or to mention none. A survey question about attitudes toward nuclear energy could read, "Some people favor the use of nuclear energy, some people oppose the use of nuclear energy, and some people have no opinion one way or the other. What do you think?" or "What do you think about the use of nuclear energy?" *Loaded* questions are questions that contain emotion-laden words. For example, terms such as radical and racist should be avoided. To guard against loaded questions, it is best to have your questionnaire reviewed by individuals representing a range of social and political perspectives.

In summary, good questionnaire items should:

—use vocabulary that is simple, direct, and familiar to all respondents;
—be clear and specific;
—not involve leading, loaded, or double-barreled questions;
—be as short as possible (20 or fewer words);
—present all conditional information prior to the key idea; and
—be checked for readability.

Ordering of Questions   A crucial issue is deciding the order of the questions in a survey. The first few questions set the tone for the rest of the questionnaire, and determine how willingly and conscientiously respondents will work on subsequent questions. For self-administered questionnaires, it is best to begin with the most interesting set of questions in order to capture the respondent's attention. Demographic data should be obtained at the end of a self-administered questionnaire. For personal or telephone interviews, on the other hand, demographic questions are frequently asked at the beginning because they are easy for the respondent to answer and thus bolster the respondent's confidence. They also allow time for the interviewer to establish rapport before asking questions about more sensitive matters.

The order in which particular questions are asked can have dramatic effects, as illustrated in a study by Schuman, Presser, and Ludwig (1981). They found differential responding depending on the order of two questions concerning abortion, one general and one specific. The general question was: "Do you think it should be possible for a pregnant woman to obtain a legal abortion if she is married and does not want any more children?" The more specific question was: "Do you think it should be possible for a pregnant woman to obtain a legal abortion if there is a strong chance of a serious defect in the baby?" When the general question was asked first, 60.7% of respondents said "yes," but when the general question followed the specific question, only 48.1% of respondents said "yes." The corresponding values for the specific question were 84% and 83% agreement in the first and second positions, respectively. The generally accepted method for dealing with this problem is to use *funnel questions*, which means starting with the most general question and moving to more specific questions pertaining to a given topic.

The final aspect of the ordering of survey questions that we will consider is the use of *filter questions*—general questions asked of respondents to find out whether they need to be asked more specific questions. For example, the question, "Do you own a car?" might precede a series of questions about the costs of maintaining a car. In this instance, the respondents would answer the specific questions only if their response to the general question was "yes." If that answer was "no," the interviewer would not ask the specific questions (in a self-administered questionnaire, the respondent would be instructed to skip that section). When the filter questions involve objective information (e.g., "Are you over 65?"), their use is relatively straightforward. Caution must be exercised, however, in using behavioral or attitudinal questions as filter questions. Smith (1981) first asked respondents whether they approved of hitting another person in "any situations you can imagine." Logically, a negative response to this most general question should imply a negative response to any more specific questions. Nonetheless, over 80% of the people who responded "no" to the general question then reported that they approved of hitting another person in specific situations, such as in self-defense. Although findings such as this suggest that filter questions should be used cautiously, the need to demand as little of the respondent's time as possible makes filter questions an essential tool in the design of effective questionnaires.

A well-conducted survey is an efficient way to accomplish the research goals of description and prediction. When distributed to dozens if not hundreds of individuals, even a modest-sized questionnaire can quickly generate many thousands of responses to individual items. And, as we have seen, by using the Internet, researchers can literally obtain millions of responses in a short period of time. But there is a catch! How does one deal with this multitude of responses? The answer is: By careful planning!

Data analysis of responses obtained from questionnaires must be considered prior to writing the survey items. Will open-ended questions be used? Is the goal mainly descriptive; for example, are proportions or percentages of events in a population of interest? Is the primary goal correlational, for example, relating responses on one question to those of another? Will respondents use a yes-no response format? A yes-maybe-no format? Self-report scales? These response formats provide different kinds of data. As you have learned, qualitative data in the form of open-ended responses will require rules for coding and methods for getting intercoder reliabilities. Categorical data such as that obtained from a yes-no format yield nominal data, whereas scales are typically assumed to provide interval data (see Chapter 4 for comments on types of scales). These types of data must be approached differently when it comes to statistical analysis.

We can first repeat a message that you heard in a previous section of this chapter: It is important to anticipate the likely results of the proposed questionnaire and then to decide whether these "findings" will answer the questions of the survey. When "predicting" your results you will want to make sure that the results can be analyzed appropriately to answer your research question. In other words, *you should have an analysis plan prior to conducting the survey.* During the planning stage we suggest that you consult with experienced survey researchers regarding the correct statistical analyses.

Once again we refer you to Chapters 12 and 13 of this textbook to gain (or regain) familiarity with statistical procedures. Should your interest in conducting a survey lead you to look for relationships (correlations) among categorical (nominal) variables, you will need to go beyond this textbook. *The appropriate statistical analysis for examining relationships between nominal variables is the chi-square test of contingency.* An introduction to this test is found in nearly all introductory statistics books (e.g., Zechmeister & Posavac, 2003). If you are going to correlate responses to interval scales, then a Pearson-Product Moment correlation is appropriate. This type of analysis was introduced in Chapter 4 when we discussed interobserver reliability. We will have more to say about correlational analyses toward the end of this chapter. Procedures for calculating a Pearson *r* are found in Chapter 12.

Thinking Critically About Survey Research

Correspondence Between Reported and Actual Behavior

- Survey research involves reactive measurement because individuals are aware that their responses are being recorded.
- Social desirability refers to pressure respondents sometimes feel to respond as they "should" believe rather than how they actually believe.
- Researchers can assess the accuracy of survey responses by comparing these results with archival data or behavioral observations.

Regardless of how carefully survey data are collected and analyzed, the value of these data depends on the truthfulness of the respondents' answers to the survey questions. Should we believe that their responses on surveys reflect people's true thoughts, opinions, feelings, and behavior? The question of the truthfulness of verbal reports has been debated extensively, and no clear-cut conclusion has emerged. In everyday life, however, we regularly accept the verbal reports of others as valid. If a friend tells you she enjoyed reading a certain novel, you may ask why, but you do not usually question whether the statement accurately reflects your friend's feelings. There are some situations in everyday life, however, when we *do* have reason to suspect the truthfulness of someone's statements. When looking for a used car, for instance, we might not always want to trust the "sales pitch" we receive. Generally, however, we accept people's remarks at their face value unless we have reason to suspect otherwise. We apply the same standards to the information we obtain from survey respondents.

By its very nature, survey research involves reactive measurement. Respondents not only know their responses are being recorded, but they may also suspect their responses may prompt some social, political, or commercial action. Hence, pressures are strong for people to respond as they "should" believe and not as they actually believe. The term often used to describe these pressures is **social desirability** (the term "politically correct" refers to similar pressures). For example, if respondents are asked whether they favor giving help to the needy, they may say "yes" because they believe this is the most socially acceptable attitude to have. In survey research, as was true with observational research, the best protection against reactive measurement is to be aware of its existence.

Key Concept ⟩

Sometimes researchers can examine the accuracy of verbal reports directly. For example, Judd et al. (1991) describe research by Parry and Crossley (1950) wherein responses obtained by experienced interviewers were subsequently compared with archival records for the same respondents kept by various agencies. Their comparisons revealed that 40% of respondents gave inaccurate reports to a question concerning contributions to United Fund (a charitable organization), 25% reported they had registered and voted in a recent election (but they did not), and 17% misrepresented their age. A pessimist might find these figures disturbingly high, but an optimist would note that a majority of respondents' reports were accurate even when social desirability pressures were high, as in the question pertaining to charitable contributions.

Another way researchers can assess the accuracy of verbal reports is by directly observing respondents' behavior. An experiment done by Latané and Darley (1970) illustrates this approach. They found that bystanders are more likely to help a victim when the bystander is alone than when other witnesses are present. Subsequently, a second group of participants was asked whether the presence of others would influence the likelihood they would help a victim. They uniformly said that it would not. Thus, individuals' verbal reports *may not* correspond well to behavior. Research findings such as these should make us extremely cautious of reaching conclusions about people's behavior solely on the basis of verbal reports. Of course, we should be equally cautious of reaching

FIGURE 5.6   How people say they would respond to this type of situation does not always match what they actually do.

conclusions about what people think solely on the basis of direct observation of their behavior. The potential discrepancy between observed behavior and verbal reports illustrates again the wisdom of a multimethod approach in helping us identify and address potential problems in understanding behavior and mental processes (Figure 5.6).

We want to make one final point about the usefulness of survey results. The process of doing a survey has much in common with the process of writing an essay. You often begin with a grand topic that must be focused so that it can be covered manageably. As you narrow your focus, you may sometimes have the feeling that your original topic has been lost or at least made trivial. No essay can capture all aspects of a given topic, nor can a 20-item or even 200-item questionnaire. Survey research, like the rest of the scientific enterprise, is built on faith that compiling reliable findings in a series of limited studies will eventually lead to increased understanding of the important broader issues we face.

Correlation and Causality

- When two variables are related (correlated), we can make predictions for the variables; however, we cannot make inferences about the cause of the relationship.
- When a relationship between two variables can be explained by a third variable, the relationship is said to be "spurious."

• Correlational evidence, in combination with a multimethod approach, can help researchers identify potential causes of behavior.

Surveys are often used in correlational research, and correlational research is an excellent method for meeting the scientific goals of description and prediction. A study by Lubin and his colleagues (1988), for instance, illustrates how useful correlational studies can be in psychological research. They investigated correlations among measures of physical and psychological health in their survey of 1,543 adults living in the United States. Respondents rated their physical health and provided information about health-related factors such as how often they visit a physician and the nature and frequency of any medications they were taking. Each of the respondents also completed a self-administered questionnaire measuring both positive affect (e.g., happiness) and negative affect (e.g., depression). Measures of psychological health and physical health were found to be correlated. For example, positive affect was positively correlated with self-ratings of physical health; happier people were more healthy. Correlations like these can be useful for predicting physical and psychological health-related problems.

Correlational evidence provides a sound basis for prediction. However, the familiar maxim, "Correlation does not imply causation," reminds us that there are serious limitations that keep us from drawing causal inferences based solely on correlational evidence. For instance, there is a reliable correlation between being outgoing (socially active) and being satisfied with one's life (Myers & Diener, 1995). Based on this correlation alone, however, we could not argue convincingly that being more outgoing and socially active *causes* people to be more satisfied with their lives. Although it is possible that being outgoing causes people to be more satisfied with their lives, the "reverse" causal relationship also may be true: being satisfied with life may cause people to be more outgoing and socially active. The causal relationship could go either way—being more outgoing causes greater life satisfaction or being more satisfied with life causes people to be more outgoing. It is impossible to determine the correct causal direction simply by knowing the correlation between the two variables.

Not being able to determine the direction of the relationship in a correlation is only one challenge we face. It's possible that there is another causal interpretation for the correlation between the two variables. For example, it's possible that a third variable, having more friends, leads people to be more outgoing *and* more satisfied with their lives. A correlation that can be explained by a third variable is called a **spurious relationship** (Kenny, 1979). In this particular example, "number of friends" is a possible third variable that could account for the relationship between being outgoing and being satisfied with one's life. Individuals with more friends may be more likely to be outgoing and satisfied with life than people with fewer friends. This isn't to say that the original positive correlation between being outgoing and life satisfaction doesn't exist (it certainly does), it just means that other variables (e.g., number of friends) may explain *why* the relationship exists.

It is extremely important to understand why it is not possible to make a causal inference based only on the evidence provided by a correlation between

Key Concept

two variables. It is equally important to recognize that correlational evidence can be very useful in identifying potential causes of behavior. There are sophisticated statistical techniques that can be used to help with causal interpretations of correlational studies (see Box 5.4).

Anderson's (2001) summary of research related to the "heat hypothesis" provides a good example of how correlational findings can be useful in identifying causes. The heat hypothesis states that "hot temperatures can increase aggressive motives and behaviors" (p. 33). This hypothesis implies a causal relationship with increasing heat causing an increase in aggressive motives and behaviors. Anderson describes that the early evidence for this hypothesis was correlational.

BOX 5.4

A PATH CONNECTING CORRELATION AND CAUSALITY

Path analysis is one sophisticated statistical technique that can be used with correlational data (Baron & Kenny, 1986; Holmbeck, 1997). Path analysis involves the identification of mediator variables and moderator variables. A *mediator* variable is a variable that is used to explain the correlation between two variables. A *moderator* variable is a variable that affects the direction or strength of the correlation between two variables. A study by Valentiner, Holahan, and Moos (1994) nicely illustrates these two types of variables. The researchers carried out a correlational study to examine the relationship between parental support and students' adjustment to college. Parental support was measured by asking first-year students questions about their mother and father, such as: "Does she (he) really understand how you feel about things?" and "Is she (he) critical or disapproving of you?" They measured changes in well-being and distress over a 2-year period, and observed a correlation between parental support and changes in psychological adjustment. They found that students' perceptions of positive support from their parents were associated with greater well-being and less distress over the 2-year period. This relationship is called "direct" because one variable (parental support) is directly correlated with another variable (changes in adjustment); this is illustrated as Path a in Figure 5.7.

Valentiner and his colleagues sought to explain why this direct relationship exists. They predicted

that how students cope with stress might mediate, or help to explain, the relationship between parental support and adjustment. Specifically, they measured the extent to which these students coped using "approach coping" more than "avoidance coping" for "the 'most important problem' they experienced in the past 12 months" (p. 1096). Approach coping strategies involve active efforts to solve problems or change one's thinking about a

FIGURE 5.7 Illustration of direct (Path a) and indirect (Paths b and c) relationships between parental support and changes in psychological adjustment to college. Adapted from Figure 1 of Valentiner et at. (1994).

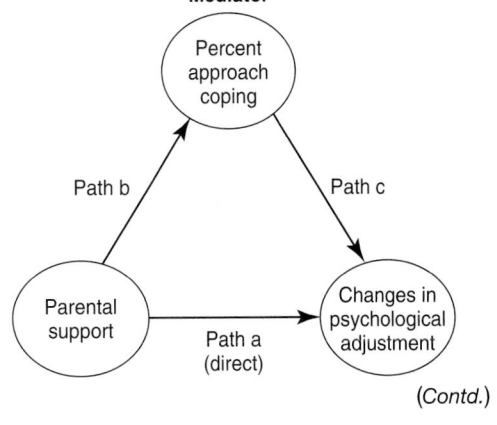

(Contd.)

problem, whereas avoidance coping strategies involve trying to forget the problem exists or behaving in ways that do not address the root of the problem (e.g., yelling "to let off steam"). Generally, approach coping is viewed as more adaptive than avoidance coping. Consistent with their predictions, Valentiner et al. found that parental support was positively correlated with the percent of approach coping students used; this is illustrated as Path b in Figure 5.7. Thus, students' perception that their parents are supportive was associated with more adaptive, approach coping.

This is only part of the story, however. Valentiner et al.'s next step was to show that approach coping is associated with positive changes in psychological adjustment (Path c in Figure 5.7). This is exactly what their correlations demonstrated. Students who used more approach coping than avoidance coping had improved well-being and less distress over the 2-year period. With this pattern of relationships, Valentiner and his colleagues were able to say that parental support was directly associated with students' adjustment (Path a), and also that approach coping partially mediated, or explained, the relationship between parental support and psychological adjustment (Paths b and c). Thus, one possible reason why parental support was associated with positive adjustment is because parental support also was associated with the use of adaptive, approach coping strategies. Said more formally, parental support is associated with psychological adjustment *indirectly,* through the mediating variable of coping strategies.

Valentiner et al. (1994) were also able to identify a moderator variable that affected the observed relationships between parental support, coping, and changes in students' adjustment. The moderator variable in their study was how controllable the participants thought their "most important problem" was. The sample was divided into two groups. One group included the students who thought the occurrence of their problem was controllable and the second group included students who thought the event's occurrence was uncontrollable. The correlational analyses were then repeated separately for each group of students

to determine if the same pattern of correlations would be obtained. *Researchers primarily seek to identify a moderator variable so that they can discover the conditions under which a relationship exists and the conditions under which the relationship is weaker or does not exist.*

What happened with students who reported their life event was *controllable?* A clear pattern of correlations emerged when life events were perceived as controllable. Perceptions of parental support were no longer directly related to changes in psychological adjustment (Path a). However, the indirect relationship between parental support and adjustment, through approach coping, was still observed (Paths b and c). Thus, for controllable problems, perceptions of parental support may help students to use more effective coping strategies, which are associated with positive changes in psychological adjustment.

Precisely the opposite pattern emerged for students who reported their event was *uncontrollable.* In these analyses, parental support directly predicted changes in students' psychological adjustment over the 2-year period (Path a). Now, however, the indirect path involving correlations with approach coping was not associated with students' adjustment (Paths b and c). How can it be that adaptive, approach coping was not associated with students' adjustment in the face of uncontrollable events? Valentiner et al. explain this rather unintuitive finding by arguing that when events are uncontrollable, coping strategies that emphasize active problem solving may be counterproductive—much like hitting your head against a brick wall. When events are uncontrollable, the best strategy may be to not try to solve the problem because it can't be solved. In this situation, perceptions of supportive parents seem to be more important for students' positive adjustment.

Path analysis and other sophisticated statistical techniques can greatly enhance our ability to interpret the results of correlational studies. It is important to remember, however, that we still can't make definite causal statements based on an analysis of mediator and moderator variables.

For example, more assaults occur during summer than during other months of the year. A third variable that could account for this correlation is activities people engage in. People are outside more in the summer and this could increase the opportunity for conflicts. The correlational evidence is not sufficient to confirm that heat causes aggressiveness.

More recent evidence for the heat hypothesis, however, has made it possible to move beyond the correlation and causation dilemma. Researchers investigating the heat hypothesis have made use of more sophisticated statistical techniques (called path analysis) that are now available for analyzing correlational studies (Baron & Kenny, 1986; Holmbeck, 1997). The early correlational findings have also led researchers to conduct experiments with animals and humans testing the heat hypothesis. This multimethod approach has provided much stronger evidence indicating that heat is not only correlated with aggressiveness but that heat can *cause* increased aggressiveness. Correlational evidence played a key role in leading investigators to pursue the heat hypothesis in terms of a causal relationship. It is true that correlational evidence is not a firm basis for a causal inference, but it is equally true that correlational evidence can be one of the first steps in identifying the causes of behavior.

Summary

Survey research provides an accurate and efficient means for describing people's characteristics (e.g., demographic variables) and their thoughts, opinions, and feelings. In addition, predictive relationships can be identified by assessing the covariation (correlation) among naturally occurring variables. Surveys differ in purpose and scope, but they generally involve sampling. Results obtained for a carefully selected sample are used to describe the entire population of interest. Surveys also involve the use of a predetermined set of questions, generally in the form of a questionnaire.

Sampling is a procedure whereby a specified number of elements are drawn from a sampling frame that represents an actual list of the possible elements in the population. Our ability to generalize from the sample to the population depends critically on the representativeness of the sample, the extent to which the sample has the same characteristics as the population. Representativeness is best achieved by using probability sampling rather than nonprobability sampling. In simple random sampling, the most common type of probability sampling, every element is equally likely to be included in the sample. Stratified random sampling is used when analysis of subsamples is of interest.

There are four general survey methods: mail surveys, personal interviews, telephone interviews, and Internet surveys. Mail surveys avoid problems of interviewer bias and are especially well suited for examining personal or embarrassing topics. The problem of response bias is a serious limitation of mail surveys. Personal interviews and phone surveys usually have higher response rates and provide greater flexibility. The phone survey is frequently used for brief surveys. Internet surveys are efficient, cost effective, and open new opportunities for survey researchers; however, they are also prone to sample biases and raise both methodological and ethical issues primarily due to the lack of control over the research environment.

Survey research is carried out according to an overall plan called a research design. There are three survey research designs: the cross-sectional design, the successive independent samples design, and the longitudinal design. Cross-sectional designs focus on describing the characteristics of a population or the differences between two or more populations at one point in time. Describing changes in attitudes or opinions over time requires the use of successive independent samples or longitudinal designs. The longitudinal design is generally preferred because it allows the researcher to assess changes for specific individuals and avoids the problem of noncomparable successive samples.

The primary instrument for survey research is the questionnaire. Questionnaires can be used to measure demographic variables or to assess people's preferences or attitudes. In order to construct questionnaires that will yield reliable and valid measurements, researchers must decide what information should be sought, what type of questionnaire to use, and what order of asking questions will be most effective. Most importantly, questions must be written so that they are clear, specific, and as unambiguous as possible.

Survey results, like those of other verbal reports, can be accepted at face value unless there is reason to do otherwise, such as pressures on respondents to give socially desirable responses. People's behavior does not always conform to what they say they would do, so survey research will never replace direct observation. However, survey research does provide an excellent way to begin to examine people's attitudes and opinions.

The greatest challenge in interpreting correlational evidence is understanding the relationship between correlation and causality. A correlation between two variables is not sufficient evidence for the existence of a causal relationship between the two variables. Correlational evidence can contribute, however, to identifying causal relationships when used in combination with sophisticated statistical techniques (such as analyses of mediators and moderators in path analysis) and the multimethod approach.

KEY CONCEPTS

correlational research
population
sample
representativeness
selection bias
nonprobability sampling
probability sampling
simple random sampling
stratified random sampling

response bias
interviewer bias
cross-sectional design
successive independent samples
  design
longitudinal design
questionnaire
social desirability
spurious relationship

REVIEW QUESTIONS

1 Briefly explain how correlational research differs from experimental research and describe the major goal of survey research.

2 Describe the information you would examine to determine whether survey results are biased because the sponsoring agency of the survey has a vested interest in how the results turn out.

3 What two characteristics do surveys have in common regardless of the purpose for which the survey has been done?

4 Explain why there is likely to be a serious threat to the interpretability of the results of a survey when a convenience sample is used.

5 Explain the relationship between the homogeneity of the population from which a sample is to be drawn and the size of a sample needed to ensure representativeness.

6 Explain why you would choose to use a mail survey, personal interviews, telephone interviews, or an Internet survey for your survey research project.

7 Explain why it is not possible to conclude that response bias has occurred in a survey research project simply by knowing that the return rate was 50%.

8 What are the major advantages and disadvantages of Internet surveys?

9 Describe the relationship that would need to exist among the samples in a successive independent samples design in order to be able to interpret group changes in attitudes over time.

10 You are interested in assessing the direction and extent of change over time in the opinions of individual respondents. Identify the survey research design you would choose and explain why you would make this choice.

11 Describe briefly one method for determining the reliability and one method for determining the validity of a self-report measure.

12 Describe three factors that affect the reliability of self-report measures in survey research.

13 How would you respond if someone told you that survey results were useless because people did not respond truthfully to questions on surveys?

14 Explain why "correlation does not imply causation" and explain how correlational evidence can be useful in identifying causes of behavior.

CHALLENGE QUESTIONS

1 Survey research is difficult to do well, and this can be especially the case when the topic is people's sexual attitudes and practices. For a book focusing in part on women's sexuality, an author mailed 100,000 questionnaires to women who belonged to a variety of women's groups in 43 states. These groups ranged from feminist organizations to church groups to garden clubs. The author's questionnaire included 127 essay questions. The author received responses from 4,500 women.

Findings in this survey included that 70% of respondents married five years or more reported having extramarital affairs and that 95% of respondents felt emotionally harassed by the men they love.

A The final sample in this study is large (4,500). Is this sufficient to assure the representativeness of the sample? If not, what survey research problem lessens the sample's representativeness?

(Contd.)

B Is it possible on the basis of your response to Part A of this question to argue that any conclusions drawn by the author from her data are incorrect? What could you do to determine whether the results were correct?

2 Two different national organizations that conduct research on higher education did independent surveys asking faculty how well prepared they thought their students were. The results of these two surveys drew attention when they were reported in the *Chronicle of Higher Education* because the findings from the two surveys were very different. Researchers from Research Foundation A found that nearly 75% of professors said that their students were "seriously underprepared." Researchers from Research Foundation B found that only 18.8% of the faculty they surveyed said that their students were "not at all prepared." Survey research findings can be expected to vary from one survey to another, but the large discrepancy found in these two surveys could make one wonder about the reliability and credibility of survey findings. Before reaching this conclusion, it is useful to consider several details of the two surveys. [Note: This question is based on a report from the *NCRIPTAL Update,* Spring 1990, Vol. 3, No. 1, pp. 2–3.]

A *Who was asked?* The original sample for Foundation A included 10,000 college professors who taught undergraduate and graduate students in all types of institutions. Of the original sample, 54.5% responded. Foundation B omitted research universities (25% of Foundation A's sample). Foundation B had a final sample of 2,311 (62% response rate). Approximately 90% of the final sample were teaching introductory-level students. *How might the characteristics of the samples surveyed by Foundations A and B affect the findings obtained in the two surveys?*

B *What was asked?* Foundation A asked its respondents: "The undergraduates with whom I have close contact are seriously underprepared in basic skills such as those required for written and oral communication." The responses for this statement were: strongly agree, agree with reservations, neutral, disagree with reservations, and disagree. Foundation B asked its respondents: "In their background preparation, students who enroll in this course

are most typically . . . ." The response choices were: not at all prepared, somewhat prepared, very well prepared, and extremely well prepared. *How might the nature of these questions affect the findings obtained in the two surveys?*

C *How were the results reported?* The findings for the Foundation A survey (75% of students seriously underprepared) were reported in the *Chronicle* by combining the response categories "strongly agree" and "agree with reservations." The findings for the Foundation B survey (18.8% of students not at all prepared) represented only respondents who chose the "not at all prepared" response category. *How do you think the results might look if the Foundation A estimate included only the respondents who chose the "strongly agree" response?*

3 A task force has been established at a small liberal arts college under the direction of the Dean of Students to examine the quality of students' experiences on their campus. The task force decided to do a survey to determine students' knowledge of and their perceptions of the fairness of the judicial system used to enforce the rules in the living units on campus. The questionnaire for the survey included personal questions asking students to describe their own experiences when they had violated college policies or when they had known other students who had violated college policies. A stratified random sample was drawn from the Registrar's list of full-time students living on and off campus. The sample size was 400 on a campus with 2,000 full-time students. Questionnaires were returned by 160 students for a response rate of 40%. One important finding from the survey was that over a third of the respondents rated the judicial system as unfair. The task force met to decide whether to include the survey findings such as this one in its final report to the Dean of Students.

A Was the initial sample of 400 students likely to be representative of the population of 2,000 full-time students? Why or why not?

B Identify a potential survey research problem that could be present in this study that would lead the task force to be concerned that the final sample was not representative of the population of 2,000 students.

C Using only the evidence that the response rate for the survey was 40%, the task force concluded that the final sample was not representative of the population of students. They further decided that the ratings of the judicial system as unfair by more than a third of the students was an incorrect overestimate. Do you agree that the finding represents an incorrect estimate? Why or why not?

D While the task force was meeting to discuss their final report, one member of the task force expressed the opinion that students' responses were unlikely to have been truthful and so the results of the survey were useless and should not be reported at all. The director of the task force calls on you to respond to this statement. What would you say?

4 Myers (2000) summarized the findings of numerous surveys done in Europe and North America that repeatedly show that married people report being happier and more satisfied with life than do people who are not married. Thus, a positive correlation between marriage and happiness is firmly established.

A Is it possible to confirm the direction of the causal relationship between marriage and happiness based on the correlation between them? Why or why not?

B Consider the following scenario that assumes that happiness leads people to marry rather than marriage leading people to be happy. In this scenario, the happiest people would marry sooner and more often, and thus progressively less happy people would move into marriage as people age. What should happen under this scenario to the reported happiness of married people and never-married people as people age?

C What implication would there be for the direction of the causal relationship between marriage and happiness if the reported happiness of married people and never-married people did not change as people get older?

Answer to Stretching Exercise

1. The first student researcher is proposing a stratified random sample in which 100 "Greek" and 100 "independent" students are sampled. In this plan the equal-sized strata would have representative samples for each stratum. A potentially serious flaw of this plan is that the overall sample would not represent the proportions of Greeks and independents in the population (25% and 75%, respectively). This would result in a biased sample because Greeks would be systematically overrepresented in the survey. The second student researcher is proposing a simple random sample of 100 students from the campus population. While this is likely to lead to a more representative sample, it will probably result in too few respondents in the "Greek" category (we'd expect about 25 Greeks) to adequately represent their viewpoint.

2. A preferred sampling plan would use a stratified random sample in which the sample sizes for Greeks and independents are proportional to the population values. With 200 students in the sample, we would select 150 students from the sampling frame of independent students and 50 students from the sampling frame of Greek students.

Answer to Challenge Question 1

A In general, larger sample sizes do make it more likely that the sample will be representative. The problem in this study is that the final sample (though large) represents a low response rate from the original sample of 100,000 (4.5%). The low response rate and the topic of the survey make it likely that a response bias is present in this survey such that the sample of 4,500 women cannot be considered representative.

B The likely problem of response bias does not make it possible to argue that the conclusions drawn by the author are incorrect. Neither can the author argue on the basis of this sample that the conclusions are correct. We simply cannot know based on this evidence whether the conclusions are correct or incorrect. There is at least one good way to determine if the results of this survey were correct. You would need to obtain from the literature the results of one or more surveys on women's sexual attitudes and practices. It would be essential that these other surveys had used representative samples of women. Then, you would compare the results of this survey with those of the other surveys. Only if the results of the present survey corresponded to those of the surveys with the representative samples would we consider the results of the present survey correct. Of course, you could also carry out your own survey, one that avoids the problems that are present in this survey, and determine whether your results are similar to those of this author-researcher!

CHAPTER SIX

Unobtrusive Measures of Behavior

CHAPTER OUTLINE

OVERVIEW

Key Concept }

We have described observational methods in which the researcher directly observes and records behavior in a natural setting (Chapter 4). We have also described how researchers can use survey-research methods to learn about people's thoughts and feelings by asking people directly about their opinions and attitudes (Chapter 5). In this chapter we consider methods that do not require direct observation or direct questioning of people. Researchers can gain important insights into people's behavior by examining physical traces of behavior (e.g., graffiti) and archival records (e.g., high school yearbooks). These indirect methods for investigating behavior are called **unobtrusive (nonreactive) measures.** When unobtrusive observation is used, the individuals being observed are not aware of the presence of the observer. When the researcher obtains data from physical traces or archival records, the method of gathering information is even more unobtrusive because the individuals being studied often are no longer present when the researcher is collecting the data. Although unobtrusive measures often yield important information in themselves, they also frequently provide a means of confirming or challenging the validity of conclusions reached using direct observation or surveys. Thus, unobtrusive measures can make important contributions to the multimethod approach to research.

The examination of *physical traces* produced by individuals' behavior represents one type of unobtrusive measure. Consider, for example, the possibility that Latin Americans differ from North Americans in their concern for punctuality. Possible cultural differences in a concern for "being on time" could be investigated using surveys that directly ask people about how often they are late for events, how they feel about concerts and sports events that start later than scheduled, and so on. One unobtrusive measure of people's concern for time, however, might be how accurately clocks are set. In fact, researchers found that public clocks (those located in banks) in a Brazilian city were less accurate than those in a similar-sized city in the United States (Levine, West, & Reis, 1980). Although there may be alternative explanations for this finding, differences in this physical-trace measure support the notion that cultural differences in concern for being on time do exist. Levine (1990) (whose research on pace of life we described in Chapter 2) also examined the accuracy of public clocks in cities and countries around the world. Levine found that measures of walking speed of a country's citizens (direct observation) correlated positively with the accuracy of the country's public clocks (unobtrusive measures).

Archival records are the public and private documents describing the activities of individuals, institutions, governments, and other groups. *Archival data* may be obtained by inspecting these archival records. For example, researchers have claimed that analyses of mortality data reveal a lower than expected frequency of deaths before important events, such as birthdays and religious holidays, and a higher than expected frequency of deaths after these important events (the death "dip/peak" hypothesis). The general procedure for investigating the relationship between death and important occasions is to examine archival data revealing the death dates of individuals in relation to certain important events (see, for example, Phillips, Van Voorhees, & Ruth, 1992; Schulz & Bazerman, 1980). Three major positive events have been examined by researchers: birthdays, national elections, and religious holidays. For instance, one of the early studies to offer data supporting a death-dip/peak hypothesis used birth dates and death dates of persons listed in the book *Four Hundred Notable Americans* (Schulz & Bazerman, 1980). Based on chance alone, one would expect that an individual's death is equally likely in any of the 12 months. However, the number of deaths during the month prior to the month of an individual's birth was found to be lower than the death rate for other months, thus supporting the death-dip/peak hypothesis. According to Schulz and Bazerman, a general explanation for this type of finding is that people somehow prolong their lives or delay death until a special event, such as a birthday, has been experienced.

Phillips and his colleagues demonstrated that a death dip/peak hypothesis is supported more for women than men (Phillips et al., 1992). Female mortality dips below normal the week before the birthday and peaks the week after, whereas male mortality peaks shortly before the birthday. The researchers suggested that for women birthdays act as a "lifeline," and for men birthdays act as a "deadline." Phillips has also shown support for the death dip/peak hypothesis as it relates to religious holidays. Mortality within a Jewish group showed the dip/peak pattern around the Jewish holiday of Passover (Phillips & King, 1988), and mortality within a Chinese group showed this pattern around the Harvest Moon Festival (Phillips & Smith, 1990).

Exactly how people might prolong their life is not particularly clear. One suggestion is that looking forward to a positive event creates a state of positive anticipation that precipitates beneficial neurochemical changes. Another possible explanation is that elderly persons are more likely to follow their health and medical regimens closely as an important date nears, so as to reduce the chances of dying before the event arrives.

In this chapter we present the rationale for using physical traces and archival data. Particular kinds of physical traces are identified and examples of their use in psychological studies are offered. Types of archives and the kinds of data that can be drawn from archival records are also reviewed. Several important advantages of the use of physical traces or archival data are highlighted. There are some limitations and problems with these unobtrusive measures, and they, too, are discussed.

Physical Traces

Rationale

- The problem of reactivity (people changing their behavior because they know they are being observed) does not arise when unobtrusive measures of behavior such as physical traces are used.
- The investigation of physical traces represents a valuable component of the multimethod approach to hypothesis testing.

As everyone who has read a few detective stories knows, examining physical evidence of past behavior can provide important clues to the characteristics of individuals and events. For example, the size of footprints in the ground says something about the size and age of the person who stepped there. The distance between footprints can indicate whether the person was walking or running.

Physical traces are especially valuable to researchers because they provide nonreactive measures of behavior (Webb et al., 1981). *A behavioral measure is reactive when participants' awareness of an observer affects the measurement process.* This is often the case when direct observations are made, and it is nearly always the case when surveys are conducted. Aware that their responses are being recorded, participants may behave in a way that does not correspond to their normal behavior. Survey data are particularly susceptible to reactive effects because respondents may give answers they feel the researcher wants to hear or may answer in a way that makes them (the respondents) look good. For instance, social scientists are well aware that responses to surveys asking about degree of political activity, such as past voting behavior, typically overestimate this activity (e.g., Endersby & Towle, 1996).

Physical-trace measures are nonreactive because they are obtained indirectly—the participant is often not present when the data are collected. Thus, unobtrusive measures are valuable alternatives to the reactive measures obtained via direct observation or surveys. In some studies it might be possible for a physical-trace measure to be the only measure of behavior. More commonly, physical traces are used in combination with other measures. As we emphasized in Chapter 1, researchers investigating a particular research question gain a great deal by including several different measures of behavior. A *multimethod approach* to examining a research question is recommended because it reduces the likelihood that research findings are due to some artifact of a single measurement process (Webb et al., 1981). There are few (if any) perfect measures in the social sciences. Therefore, the results of a study must be carefully scrutinized to determine whether some characteristic of the measurement instrument (such as its reactivity) has contributed to the results. Even then, it is possible that some artifact has been overlooked. The most persuasive argument supporting the validity of a particular research hypothesis is one based on evidence obtained by applying a combination of different measures.

Researchers investigating cultural differences in time perception used such a multimethod approach. They surveyed individuals living in Latin America and in the United States to find out how frequently their subjects were late for appointments and to discover their attitudes toward being late (Levine et al., 1980). Citizens of Brazil reported themselves more often late for appointments and expressed less regret at being late than did citizens of the United States. However, a bias in these responses could be present if people described themselves in a way that fit their cultural "image," rather than as they actually behaved. As we mentioned earlier, however, the researchers also found that public clocks were less accurate in Brazil than in the United States. Further, the researchers observed that watches worn by people in the United States deviated less from the correct time than watches worn by people in Brazil. The data obtained by examining public clocks and the watches worn by citizens of each country tended to confirm the validity of the survey responses and, in combination with the survey results, provided strong evidence for the research hypothesis.

Types of Physical Traces

- Two categories of physical traces are "use traces" and "products."
- Use traces reflect the physical evidence of use (or nonuse) of items, and can be measured in terms of natural or controlled use.
- By examining the products people own or the products produced by a culture, researchers test hypotheses about attitudes and preferences.

Key Concept }

Physical traces are the remnants, fragments, and products of past behavior. Two broad categories of physical traces are "use traces" and "products." *Use traces* are what the label implies—the physical evidence that results from use (or nonuse) of an item. Clock settings are an example of a physical-use trace. So are the remains of cigarettes in ashtrays and the marks made in textbooks. *Products* are the creations, constructions, or other artifacts of earlier behavior. Anthropologists are often interested in the surviving products of ancient cultures. By examining the types of vessels, paintings, and other artifacts that remain, the anthropologist can often describe precisely the pattern of behavior exhibited in a setting that is thousands of years old. Psychologists may also examine physical products in order to describe behavior or to test hypotheses. Psychologists who study animal behavior, for instance, may learn about the behavior of different species by examining the types of nests that are constructed. Newhagen and Ancell (1995) examined bumper stickers used by Black and White residents of a Washington, DC, suburb to investigate racial differences in degree of emotional expressiveness.

Use Traces   Physical-use traces are classified as either natural or controlled (planned). *Natural-use traces* are produced without any intervention by the investigator. Their appearance is the result of naturally occurring events. *Controlled-use* (or *planned-use*) *traces* result when there is some degree of intervention or manipulation by an investigator. A study by Friedman and Wilson (1975) illustrates the distinction between these two types of measures.

The investigators employed both controlled and natural accretion measures to investigate college students' use of textbooks. They affixed tiny glue seals between adjacent pages of textbooks before the students purchased the books for a course. At the end of the semester the investigators obtained the books from the students and recorded how many seals in the textbooks had been broken and where the broken seals were located. Because the researchers controlled the presence of glue seals in the books, this constituted a controlled-use trace. The investigators also analyzed the frequency and nature of underlining by

TABLE 6.1   EXAMPLES OF PHYSICAL-USE TRACES AND VARIABLES BEING MEASURED*

Trace	Variable
Natural-Use Traces	
Inscriptions (graffiti) on walls of public rest rooms	Sexual preoccupation
Fingerprints or smudges on pages of books	Book usage
Liquor bottles in trash cans	Alcohol consumption of households
Litter	Effectiveness of antilitter posters
Garbage	Food use and lifestyle
Locked/unlocked cars	Concern for property
Lengths of cigarette butts	Cultural differences in death rate due to cancer
Wear on floor or steps	Amount of foot traffic
Wear on library books	Frequency of use
Food consumed	Eating behavior
Spots (produced by rubbing) on statues or religious objects	Level of religious belief
Controlled-Use Traces	
Glue seals broken (seals inserted prior to distribution)	Index of specific pages read
Nose prints on windows of museum exhibit (windows wiped clean each night)	Popularity (frequency) and age (height of points) of viewers
Wear on children's shoes (measured at two points in time)	Activity level of children
Removal of "tear-away" tags on ads or notices	Interest in notice
Wear on mats or other floor coverings placed in specific areas	Amount of foot traffic
Change in statues or objects coated with substances sensitive to touching	Superstitious behavior

*From Webb et al. (1981).

students in the textbooks. Because underlining is typically associated with textbook use, the amount of underlining represents a natural-use measure. Analysis of these physical-use measures indicated that students more often read the chapters that appeared early in the book than those that appeared later in the book.

Table 6.1 includes examples of how physical-use traces can be used as unobtrusive measures of interesting variables. These measures either were used as part of an actual scientific study or represent suggestions by researchers of possible novel and nonreactive measures of behavior (see Webb et al., 1981). The examples given in Table 6.1 are organized according to whether the use traces are natural or controlled. As you examine the contents of Table 6.1, try to think of other possible physical traces that could serve as measures of the variables listed.

Products   Physical products have been examined less frequently in psychological studies than have physical-use traces. Nevertheless, this category of physical traces has been used in interesting and meaningful ways to test hypotheses about behavior. For example, researchers recently examined food-related products of both the United States and France to investigate what has been called the "French paradox" (Rozin, Kabnick, Pete, Fischler, & Shields, 2003). The term "French paradox" refers to the fact that the mortality rate from heart disease is much lower in France than the United States despite the fact that the French eat more fatty foods and less reduced-fat foods than Americans. Moreover, Americans are much more likely to be overweight or even obese than are the French. What accounts for these differences? The fact that the French drink much more red wine has been suggested as an explanation. Other explanations are genetic differences in metabolism and lower stress levels in France than the United States (see Rozin et al., 2003). Yet another possible explanation is that the French eat less, and Rozin et al. studied products of France and the United States, looking for evidence to support this hypothesis. They made on-site observations of portion sizes in comparable restaurants in France and the United States. In addition, they examined product sizes in French and American supermarkets. The researchers found that American portions were on average 25% greater than those in French restaurants, and food products on American supermarket shelves were generally larger. These findings provide evidence for yet another explanation of the French paradox—namely, that the French eat less and this contributes to their lower weight and lower mortality from heart disease.

Brandt (1972) points out that the products that people own provide important clues to their lifestyle and behavior patterns. What personality differences, for instance, are reflected in the purchase of different models of cars or in the extras and options that are ordered with a car? Besides serving as a measure of social status or personality, the products a person owns can be used to assess the validity of certain kinds of verbal reports. Are individuals' statements about their attitude toward energy conservation, for instance, related to the kinds of products they own and use?

Consider the American driving public's interest in bumper stickers. You probably have seen stickers that state, "Guns Don't Kill, People Do," or "Abortion Stops a Beating Heart." As Newhagen and Ancell (1995) point out, bumper stickers are unique in that they "allow for the expression of highly personal opinions about strongly held views to a large audience without any real commitment to interact with them" (p. 313). And, unlike graffiti, which is often illegal and socially undesirable, bumper stickers permit an acceptable outlet for the expression of public emotion. When Newhagen and Ancell analyzed bumper sticker messages of suburban Blacks and Whites in the Washington, DC, area, they found overall frequency of bumper sticker usage was highest in low-income areas regardless of race. High-income White neighborhoods showed most evidence of positive and intense stickers, whereas bumper stickers were least frequently observed and, when they were, the messages were the most

FIGURE 6.1   Bumper stickers are an unobtrusive measure of people's attitudes.

subdued, in high-income Black neighborhoods. The researchers suggested that the results illustrate examples of discretely different forms of public expression of emotion as a function of race and income. This conclusion seems to fit with Endersby and Towle's (1996) characterization of bumper stickers as reflecting "a form of identification and solidarity with a group sharing common beliefs" (p. 307).

Problems and Limitations

- Before concluding that a measure of physical traces is a valid indicator of behavior or attitudes, a researcher should make sure no sources of bias exist.
- Validity of physical-trace measures can be ascertained by examining converging evidence.

Physical measures offer a researcher valuable and sometimes novel means to study behavior, and the measures available are limited only by the ingenuity of the investigator. However, the validity of physical traces must be carefully examined and verified through independent sources of evidence. Bias can be introduced in the way physical-use traces are laid down and in the manner in which traces survive over time. Does a well-worn path to the right indicate people's interest in objects in that direction or simply a natural human tendency to turn right? Is the setting of clocks a good measure of people's

FIGURE 6.2 The classic "lost-letter technique" illustrates some of the problems with the analysis of physical traces (see text).

regard for punctuality, or do inaccurate clock settings indicate poor artisan-ship, inadequate maintenance, or irregular electrical service? To what extent is frequency of bumper sticker usage affected by the recent success of local sports teams?

Problems associated with the analysis of physical traces are illustrated in a classic study of honesty carried out using the "lost-letter technique" (see Merritt & Fowler, 1948). The investigators "accidentally" dropped postcards and envelopes at various locations in cities of the East and Midwest. Two types of envelopes were "lost." One contained a written message, and the other contained a lead slug the size of a 50-cent piece. All the letters were addressed and bore proper postage, but no return address was shown. Although 85% of the empty envelopes were returned, only 54% of the envelopes with a slug found their way to a mailbox. Further, more than 10% of the envelopes with a slug were re-turned after having been opened.

Before the researchers could conclude that the return rates represented a valid measure of the public's honesty (or dishonesty), several possible biases associated with this physical trace had to be considered. Postcards, for instance, were less likely than sealed envelopes to be returned. This difference may have been due, however, to the fact that postcards are more easily affected by the wind and other natural conditions than are larger envelopes. On the other hand, envelopes with a slug are heavier and less likely to be blown away—and these were still less likely to be returned. Letters that were dropped in certain locations (e.g., where many children are present) or at certain times of the day

---

BOX 6.1

LOST "LETTERS" ON THE INTERNET

Stern and Faber (1997) used the Internet to produce a "lost e-mail" version of the lost-letter technique. In one study the researchers investigated people's attitudes toward the 1996 presidential candidate, Ross Perot. The researchers sent messages that were supposed to look like misdirected e-mail messages to randomly selected e-mail addresses across the country. The messages went to "Steve" and asked for help with fund raising. The researchers were most interested in the e-mail replies when the original message mentioned that the fund raising was for Ross Perot. The returned messages indicated little support for Ross Perot. For instance, a number of people returning the Ross Perot message went out of their way to say they were voting for someone else, while none said they planned to vote for him.

The e-mail version of the lost-letter techniques raises ethical concerns that do not apply to the original version. For example, dropping letters on the street can be considered part of the public domain and the person's response is anonymous. A returned e-mail, on the other hand, typically includes the sender's e-mail address making an anonymous response impossible. How would you address these ethical concerns?

(e.g., just before nightfall) are also likely not to be returned for reasons other than the public's dishonesty or apathy.

The researchers avoided some possible biases associated with the lost-letter technique by the methods they used to "drop" the letters. They checked for other possible biases by directly observing a letter's fate. Their observations of a sample of dropped letters revealed that a letter was picked up 90% of the time by the first person who saw it, suggesting that dropped letters were soon in the hands of unknowing participants.

The consideration of possible biases in the lost-letter technique illustrates a more general principle. Whenever possible, supplementary evidence for the validity of physical traces should be obtained (see Webb et al., 1981). Alternative hypotheses for changes in physical traces must be considered, and data must be collected that allow alternative interpretations to be dismissed. Care must also be taken when comparing results across studies to make sure that measures are defined similarly. For example, when Newhagen and Ancell (1995) tallied bumper stickers, they included only those literally found on car bumpers; Endersby and Towle (1996) operationally defined bumper stickers as any message visible from the rear of the vehicle, which included rear window decals. Different operational definitions of a concept can easily lead to different results.

ARCHIVAL DATA

Rationale

- Archival data comprise the records or documents of the activities of individuals, groups, institutions, and governments.

STRETCHING EXERCISE

A researcher wishes to test the hypothesis that youth attending private high schools are not as "dirty-minded" as students attending public high schools. He chooses two schools (one a church-affiliated school and one public) that are located in the same neighborhood, approximately one mile apart. Both schools include grades 9 through 12. To test the hypothesis, the investigator decides to use both natural and controlled physical-use traces. Specifically, the researcher operationally defines "dirty-mindedness" as the number of obscene words (from a predetermined list) that are found in the restrooms of each school. The natural-use measure is simply the number of new target words appearing on the walls of the restrooms at the end of each week. As a measure of controlled use, the investigator obtains permission from the school authorities to place pads of paper and pencils in the toilet stalls of the restrooms at each school. On each pad of paper is written: "Leave me a note." At the end of each week the investigator replaces the pad with a fresh one and examines the pages that have been written on for the appearance of obscene words.

1 Comment on possible biases that could affect the validity of the physical-trace measures proposed in this study.
2 Frame questions that might be asked concerning the external validity of this study.
3 Suggest ways in which the investigator might use a multimethod approach to this problem.

- Archival data are used to test hypotheses as part of the multimethod approach, to establish the external validity of laboratory findings, and to assess the effects of natural treatments.
- Archival data represent a rich, plentiful source of observations for psychological studies.

When we were born, a record was made of our birth. Information on the birth record probably included the city and state in which we were born, the date and time of our birth, our parents' names, and our name. When we die, another record will be made. It will include such details as probable cause of death, date and time of death, and our age. In between these two events, innumerable records are made of our behavior. Physicians record visits. Hospitals keep a record of when we enter and when we leave. Schools record our grades and extracurricular activities. Our employer may record the number of times we are late or how often we fail to show up for work. Newspapers describe notable successes and failures. Local governments record when we get married and to whom, as well as when we buy a house and how much it costs. The federal government records, among other things, what we pay in income taxes.

Records are kept not only of individuals but also of countries, institutions, cities, and businesses. The gross national product of a country, its major exports and imports, the size of its defense budget, the distribution of its population, and the number of television sets owned by its populace are just a few of the facts that are frequently recorded. How much profit a company makes is part of its report to stockholders. Voting behaviors of state and federal legislators are recorded, as is the amount of money a city spends on social services. Analysis and interpretation of local and world events flood the media. The contents of the media and of documents and books (published and unpublished) are a source of information about current fads and prejudices, changing patterns of belief, and the ideas of important (and not so important) members of society. The Internet has increased both the number of records that are kept and the ease with which these records can be accessed by individuals.

Key Concept }

Archival data are obtained from records or documents recounting the activities of individuals or of institutions, governments, and other groups. As measures of behavior, archival data share some of the same advantages as physical traces. Archival data represent unobtrusive measures that provide a valuable alternative to direct observation and survey research. Like physical-trace measures, archival data can be used to check the validity of other measures as part of a multimethod approach to hypothesis testing. Research done by Frank and Gilovich (1988) provides an excellent illustration of the use of archival data in the context of a multimethod approach to hypothesis testing.

Frank and Gilovich (1988) investigated the strong cultural association that exists between the color black and "badness," or evil. They point out that you could always tell the good guys from the bad guys in vintage American Western movies. The good guys, of course, wore white hats and the bad guys wore black hats. The strong cultural association between black and badness is reflected in other ways. We speak of people being "blackballed," "blacklisted," "blackmailed," and a person's reputation's being "blackened." When terrible things happen it is a "black day." Black is seen in many cultures as the color of death. The good and bad sides of human nature are also contrasted using black-and-white images, as was illustrated by the characters of the famous *Star Wars* movies. Viewers of these classic films likely will remember the confrontation between the villain, Darth Vader (dressed completely in black), and the young hero, Luke Skywalker (dressed in white or light colors). Vader, unfortunately, had "gone over" to the dark side. (See also Meier et al., 2004, in Chapter 2, pp. 39–40.)

Frank and Gilovich wanted to find out if this strong cultural association between black and evil would affect the way people behave. Specifically, they asked whether professional sports teams that wear black uniforms are more aggressive than those that wear nonblack uniforms. Using archival data obtained from the central offices of the National Football League (NFL) and the National Hockey League (NHL), Frank and Gilovich analyzed penalty records of each major professional team in these sports between 1970 and 1986. As measures of aggressiveness they used yards penalized in the NFL and minutes that a player was assigned to the penalty box in the NHL. They chose these particular measures rather than simply counting the number of infractions because penalties for overaggressiveness are generally more severe (in yards or minutes) than are those for simple rule violations. The operational definition of a "black uniform" was that the colored version of the team's uniform (the one used typically for away games in the NHL and for home games in the NFL) was more than 50% black. (The dark blue uniforms of the Chicago Bears in the NFL were included among the black-uniform teams because many people mistakenly remember their uniforms as black.) The authors predicted that teams wearing black should be penalized more than would be expected simply by chance. And that's just what they found! Teams with black uniforms, such as Oakland, Chicago, and Cincinnati in the NFL, and Philadelphia, Pittsburgh, and Vancouver in the NHL, were reliably penalized more than many other teams that did not wear black uniforms. Thus, a clear connection between aggressiveness and wearing black uniforms was established.

What psychological processes might account for these effects? Frank and Gilovich suggest that both social-perception and self-perception processes are at work. They argue that social perception plays a role because others (specifically, referees) "see" players in black as more aggressive than players not wearing black and therefore award more penalties to players in black. Self-perception leads the players themselves to behave more aggressively when they put on black uniforms. Frank and Gilovich used a multimethod approach to provide support for their explanations based on the archival data by conducting two laboratory experiments. In one experiment, both college students and referees watched staged football games between teams wearing black or white uniforms and rated the players' aggressiveness. In a second experiment, students donned either black or white uniforms in anticipation of an athletic competition before choosing a game from a list of aggressive and nonaggressive games. In the first experiment, both referees and college students were more likely to rate a team wearing black as aggressive. The second experiment showed that students who donned black uniforms chose more aggressive games. By combining data obtained from archival analyses and laboratory experiments, Frank and Gilovich provide a strong case for their explanations of this interesting cultural phenomenon.

Archival data can also be used to test the external validity of laboratory findings. Researchers have used laboratory-based experiments to investigate *causal attributions:* the reasons people give for a certain outcome. A major finding from laboratory studies of causal attributions is that people make different attributions for their successes and failures. People tend to make internal attributions for their successes; they assume that the outcome is due to some characteristic within themselves. For failures, however, people tend to make external attributions; they assume that the outcome is due to something beyond their control. Lau and Russell (1980) analyzed the contents of the sports pages in eight daily newspapers in order to test whether results obtained from laboratory experiments were relevant to "real-world" settings. Lau and Russell's analysis of explanations given by sportswriters or team members for the outcome of baseball and football games supported the conclusion based on the lab findings. Specifically, they identified 594 explanations for success and failure involving 33 major sporting events. From the perspective of the winning team, 75% of the attributions were internal, whereas only 55% of the attributions of the losing team were internal.

Researchers can use archival data for two additional purposes—to test hypotheses about past behavior and to assess the effect of a natural treatment.

FIGURE 6.3 Archival records permit psychologists to study the "home advantage" in sports competitions.

For example, archival data play a central role in studies of the "home advantage" in sports competitions (see, for example, Courneya & Carron, 1992). Sports teams typically play "at home" and "away" over the course of a season and so researchers can ask how this difference affects a team's performance. The *home advantage* refers to the fact that in many sports competitions a team wins consistently more games played at home than it does games played away. Baumeister (1995) has investigated an interesting and somewhat counterintuitive finding that runs counter to the home advantage. Even though teams playing at home tend to win more consistently, they do not necessarily perform well in key games played at home, such as those that decide a championship. The "home choke" phenomenon, nevertheless, has not always found support through archival analyses (Schlenker, Phillips, Boniecki, & Schlenker, 1995a, 1995b).

Natural treatments are naturally occurring events that have significant impact on society at large or on particular members of society. Because it is not always possible to anticipate these events, researchers who want to assess their impact must use a variety of behavioral measures, including archival data. Acts of terrorism, drastic changes in the stock market, and the passage of new laws are examples of the kinds of events that may have important effects on behavior and that might be investigated using archival data. So, too, are the naturally occurring events of a natural life history, such as death or divorce of parents, a chronic illness, or marital difficulties.

In 1921, Lewis Terman began a longitudinal study of intelligence by recruiting more than 1,500 above average children in the San Francisco and Los Angeles schools (see Terman & Oden, 1947). The children, 856 boys and 672 girls, were preadolescents at the time and have been followed at 5- to 10-year intervals since that time. Friedman et al. (1995) have taken advantage of the archival data associated with Terman's study of gifted children to investigate "psychosocial and behavioral predictors of longevity." Friedman and his colleagues also interviewed surviving members of the original group of children for their study.

Friedman et al. (1995) used the archival data from Terman's study to examine the effect of parental divorce on longevity. There is considerable evidence in the psychology literature indicating that children who experience parental divorce or conflict have more conduct and behavioral problems, greater academic difficulties, and poorer health than children whose parents did not divorce (see Tucker et al., 1997). The question in the Friedman et al. (1995) study was whether divorce would also affect mortality rates. The sample of gifted children was relatively homogeneous in that the children were very bright (IQs greater than 135), nearly all White, and mostly middle-class. Nonetheless, the results for this group are clear; parental divorce is associated with premature death. Friedman et al. (1995) found that men from divorced homes were predicted to die at age 76, whereas those from intact homes were predicted to die at age 80; for women the corresponding predicted ages of death were 82 and 86. The reasons for this clear relationship between parental divorce and children's longevity are complex and not completely understood. For example, children from divorced homes were also more likely to be divorced themselves, men were more likely to die from physical injuries, and women from divorced homes smoke more (Tucker et al., 1997). Results of these archival analyses indicate, nevertheless, that "parental divorce sets off a negative chain of events, which contribute to a higher mortality risk among individuals from divorced homes" (Tucker et al., 1997, p. 389).

One final important reason for considering the use of archival data in research is simply because archival data are so plentiful. We noted earlier the extensive records that society keeps on individuals, groups, and institutions. We also described how researchers can now gain access to archival data more easily by using the Internet. Through careful analysis of archival information, researchers can gain evidence to test numerous hypotheses. There are practical advantages as well. Researchers can avoid the often lengthy data collection phase of research because archival data have already been collected. Archival records can even contain initial summary descriptions. Ethical concerns are also less worrisome because archival information is frequently part of the public record and is usually reported in a manner that does not identify individuals.

One goal of this chapter is to alert you to the rich resource that is available if you choose to analyze archival data when you are investigating psychological questions.

Types of Archival Data

- Types of archival data include running records, news media, and other types of records; archival data can consist of public or private documents.

The sheer diversity and extent of archival sources make their classification rather arbitrary. Records that are continuously kept and updated are frequently referred to as *running records*. Tax records and records of various government agencies are good examples, as are the myriad records of sports teams. Because of their continuous nature, running records are particularly useful in longitudinal studies or in the documentation of trends. Other records, such as personal documents, are more likely to be discontinuous or episodic (see Webb et al., 1981). Archival records can also be distinguished by the degree to which they are available for public inspection. Many records kept by government agencies are easily obtainable. Most records of private institutions and businesses, however, are not open to public scrutiny or can be obtained only after many requests and considerable patience on the part of the researcher.

The news media are yet another important source of archival data. Various records, ranging from stock market reports to crime statistics, are published in newspapers and reported on television and on the Internet. The content of media reports is also a form of archival record and is subject to analysis. Earlier we described how the contents of sports pages were used to test a theory of causal attribution. The placement of "Found" advertisements in the Lost and Found section of a newspaper can be used to measure public altruism (see Goldstein, Minkin, Minkin, & Baer, 1978). Researchers investigating the "French paradox" examined restaurant guides in Philadelphia and Paris, recording the number of references to "all-you-can-eat" buffets. There was no mention of all-you-can-eat options in Paris; there were 18 such cases in Philadelphia (Rozin et al., 2003).

Phillips (1977) used running records of motor vehicle fatalities kept by the California Highway Patrol and a measure of suicide publicity derived from California newspapers to determine whether there is a significant suicidal component to motor vehicle fatalities. He hypothesized that a substantial number of deaths arising from motor vehicle accidents are actually the result of individuals using their cars to commit suicide. To test this hypothesis, Phillips investigated whether motor vehicle fatalities would, like suicides in general, increase after a well-publicized suicide story. Components of the publicity measure included the daily circulation of each newspaper and the number of days the newspaper carried the suicide story. This publicity measure correlated significantly with changes in motor vehicle fatalities after each story. The number of motor vehicle fatalities increased significantly during the few days after a well-publicized suicide story, reaching a peak on day 3. This result is shown in Figure 6.4. Phillips did additional analyses to confirm that

FIGURE 6.4   Daily fluctuations in motor vehicle accident fatalities for a 2-week period before, during (Day 0), and after publication of suicide stories. (From Phillips, 1977.)

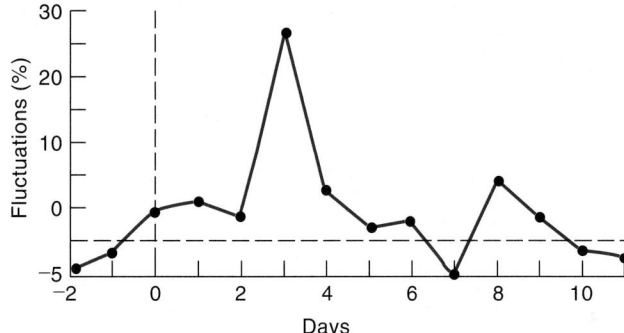

the pattern shown in Figure 6.4 was indeed associated with the publication of a suicide story. He compared changes in the frequency of motor vehicle fatalities during *experimental periods* (the week right after the story) with *control periods* that were free from suicide stories. The control periods were matched with the experimental periods in terms of day of the week, presence or absence of holidays, and time of the year. Phillips concluded that "suicide stories stimulate a wave of imitative suicides, some of which are disguised as motor vehicle accidents" (p. 1464).

Table 6.2 contains a list of selected sources of archival information and the nature of the data that might be obtained from them. The types of archival data shown in Table 6.2 are rather arbitrarily classified as running records, those pertaining to the media, and "other records," including records of businesses, schools, and other private institutions. Table 6.2 introduces you to the variety of archival data that can be obtained from archival sources. We will now discuss a critical type of analysis that is used in archival research—content analysis.

Content Analysis

- Content analysis refers to the process of making inferences based on objective coding of archival records.
- Steps for content analysis include identifying a relevant source of archival data, sampling data from the records, and then coding the contents of the records.
- Coding in content analysis involves classifying events and behaviors from archival records into clearly defined categories and recording the amount of time or words devoted to events and behaviors.
- Trained coders use rating scales to make qualitative judgments about the contents of archival records.

Identifying the many sources of archival data is important, but the usefulness of these sources depends ultimately on how their content is analyzed. In the

TABLE 6.2   SELECTED SOURCES OF ARCHIVAL INFORMATION AND ILLUSTRATIVE DATA FOR THREE TYPES OF ARCHIVES*

Source	Illustrative data
Running Records	
Congressional Record	Statements of position on particular issues
Telephone directories	Community ethnic group membership
Salaries of teachers or government employees	Community support
Government agency records (labor, commerce, agriculture departments)	Living trends
Judicial record	Uniformity in sentencing for antisocial behavior
Moody's Handbook	Corporate financial structure
Who's Who in America	Nature of cited accomplishments of successful people
Tax records	Regional differences in patterns of living
City budgets	Perceived value or extent of support of various activities
Media	
Society section of metropolitan newspaper	Upper-middle-class and lower-upper-class activities
Children's books on sale	Qualities of models (heroes and heroines)
Movie announcements in newspapers	Changing taboos and enticements
Want ads	Employer inducements
Obituary columns	Charity preferences
Published speeches	Political, social, economic attitudes
Newspaper headlines	Press bias
Other Records[†]	
Absentee and tardiness records	Work habits or motivation
Military reenlistment and longevity figures	Morale indicator
Production and other output figures	Performance of individuals, departments, and so on
Sales contest records	Selling effectiveness, effectiveness of incentive plans
Peanut sales at ball games	Excitement indicator (greater after than before seventh inning)
Air trip insurance figures	Public concern before and after air crashes
Sales of layettes by color (blue or pink)	Sex preference in different social classes
Actuarial records: birth, baptismal, death records; marriage licenses	Comparative demographic data (occupation, religion, time of day, cause of death, and so on)
Cemetery documents, burial-lot records	Family membership

*Adapted from Brandt (1972).
[†]Institutions, businesses, hospitals, schools, and so on; may or may not be open to public inspection.

simplest cases, only minimal analysis may be necessary. Recording the votes of state legislators may be as simple as transcribing vote tallies found in legislative documents or on government websites. In many cases, however, gleaning relevant data from an archival source can require careful procedures and relatively complex analysis of the source's content. Furthermore, problems of sampling, reliability, and validity are just as critical when analyzing archival sources as when analyzing data obtained from direct observation.

Key Concept

Content analysis can be generally defined as any technique that allows researchers to make inferences based on specific characteristics they objectively identify in messages (Holsti, 1969). Although content analysis is associated primarily with written communications, it may be used with any form of message, including television and radio programs, speeches, films, interviews, and e-mail messages. For instance, Weigel, Loomis, and Soja (1980) used content analysis to study race relations as depicted on prime-time television. They analyzed the frequency of appearances of Blacks and Whites on evening television shows carried by three major networks. In addition, they rated the quality of Black-White and White-White interactions.

In many content-analysis studies, the communication is written. The units of classification for *quantitative* analysis generally include single words, characters, sentences or paragraphs, themes, or particular items (Holsti, 1969). In a study of bereavement, for example, researchers performed a content analysis of interview transcripts of men who had lost a partner to AIDS (Pennebaker, Mayne, & Francis, 1997). Use of insight and causal words predicted emotional well-being a year later. When newspaper content is analyzed, a frequently used measure is space—for instance, number of column inches devoted to a particular topic. Phillips (1977) used this measure in his study of the relationship between publicized suicides and frequency of motor vehicle fatalities. When television or radio broadcasts are studied, time is often used as a unit of measurement. Weigel et al. (1980) measured both Black appearances and Black-White appearances in terms of the percentage of total human appearance time.

Qualitative measures are also used as part of content analysis. For example, Satterfield and Seligman (1994) used a qualitative measure to investigate the explanatory styles of George H.W. Bush (the 41st President) and Saddam Hussein during several historical periods of conflict, including the Persian Gulf Crisis. The particular measure used by these researchers is called the CAVE technique. The acronym CAVE stands for "content analysis of verbatim explanations." The CAVE guidelines help researchers identify causal statements in written or spoken verbatim messages. The statements can then be rated on dimensions of explanatory style. The content analysis of verbatim explanations by Bush and Hussein for periods preceding military actions or political conflicts produced an interesting result:

> When the leaders were pessimistic (relative to themselves), their subsequent actions were more cautious and passive. When the leaders were relatively optimistic, their subsequent actions were more aggressive and risky. (Satterfield & Seligman, 1994, p. 79)

Satterfield and Seligman appropriately acknowledge that the correlational nature of their study means they must "leave open the large class of third-variable accounts before concluding that explanatory style itself causes cautious versus risky actions" (p. 79). For instance, before a definitive conclusion regarding the

BOX 6.2

THREE BASIC STEPS IN CONTENT ANALYSIS

There are three basic steps in carrying out a content analysis: identifying a relevant archival source, sampling selections from the source, and coding units of analysis for quantitative and qualitative analyses.

Identifying a relevant source. The key to identifying a relevant archival source is defining what we mean by a *relevant* source. What is relevant, of course, depends on the goals of the study and the questions the researcher is asking. Simply stating the purpose of the study is sometimes sufficient to pinpoint an appropriate archival source. A researcher who sets out to study humor in tombstone messages or race relations on television has already identified the relevant archival source. In other situations the identification of relevant sources depends on the ingenuity of the researcher. Lau and Russell's (1980) choice to use the sports page to test the external validity of laboratory findings related to attribution represents an appropriate and clever identification of a relevant archival source. Similarly, Carroll and Russell (1997) identified relevant archival sources for their analysis of film actors' portrayal of emotions, such as disgust and fear, by selecting Hollywood films, such as *Ordinary People* (1980) and *Dead Poets Society* (1989), "noted for their realistic portrayal of modern life and for their highly emotional content" (p. 167).

Sampling selections from the archival source. The second step in content analysis involves the appropriate sampling of selections from the relevant archival source. As is the case when drawing samples for observational studies or for survey research, the goal of sampling is to obtain a representative sample. The extent to which the results of an archival study can be generalized depends on the representativeness of the sample that is used. For example, Terman's study of genius that we described earlier in the chapter was based on data collected from high IQ, mainly White, middle-class individuals. The same sample was used in the subsequent archival studies of longevity. The external validity of these longevity studies is necessarily less than it would be had the archival source included a more heterogeneous sample. Moreover, we might question the external validity of the findings of the longevity studies based on Terman's original sample for another reason. The impact of parental divorce on children's lives at the beginning of the 20th century, when divorce was less frequent and less socially acceptable, may well not be the same as it is today.

Coding units of analysis. The third and final step in performing a content analysis is *coding*. Similar to the scoring of narrative records (see Chapter 4), this step requires that relevant descriptive categories and appropriate units of measure be defined (see Holsti, 1969). As with the choice of the archival source itself, what determines a relevant descriptive category is related to the goals of the study. An analysis done by Weigel et al. (1980) in their study of race relations illustrates how the categories used in coding are tied to the study's goals. They defined four major categories: (1) human appearance time, (2) Black appearance time, (3) cross-racial appearance time, and (4) cross-racial interaction time. Each category was operationally defined. For instance, cross-racial interaction was defined as "the time during which black and white characters were engaged in active, on-screen interactions (talking, touching, or clear nonverbal communication)" (p. 886). The use of precise operational definitions permitted coders viewing the sample broadcasts to make reliable judgments of events.

FIGURE 6.5   Content analysis of cross-racial interactions between TV actors reveals how race relations are depicted in the American media.

relationship between explanatory style and political action can be reached, such issues as political demands on the leaders or cultural differences in rhetorical style need to be investigated further. Nevertheless, the data suggest that "shifts in explanatory style seem at least to signal corresponding shifts in aggressivity and risk taking" (p. 80). Archival research may help us better understand the psychological nature of political decision making and perhaps even help predict the course of world events.

The use of blind observers is one way to reduce observer bias in studies involving direct observation of behavior. Similarly, whenever it is possible to do so, those doing the coding or rating of archival sources should be blind to important aspects of the study, such as the main hypotheses, the source of the messages, and the immediate surrounding context. Judges in the Satterfield and Seligman (1994) study of explanatory style, for example, rated the world leaders' statements only after "all potentially biasing date information was removed" (p. 78) and after source material had been assigned random number codes. Measures of interjudge reliability also should be reported as part of a content analysis. (Measures of interobserver [interjudge] reliability are described in Chapter 4.)

Problems and Limitations

- Archival data may be biased due to selective deposit and selective survival.
- Selective deposit occurs when biases influence what information is recorded (deposited) in an archival record, or whether a record is made at all; selective survival occurs when archival records are missing or incomplete.
- Archival records are subject to errors and changes in record-keeping procedures.
- Although archival data are considered nonreactive, reactivity can influence the production of archival records; this is particularly true for public records.
- When interpreting the results of correlational analyses of archival data, researchers must be alert to the possibility of spurious relationships.

When discussing the validity of physical traces, we mentioned that biases may result from the way physical traces are established and from the manner in which they survive over time. These biases are referred to as selective deposit and selective survival, respectively, and they are no less a problem for archival records (see Webb et al., 1981). Either of these biases can impose severe limitations on the generality of research findings.

Key Concept

Problems of **selective deposit** arise when biases exist in the production of archival sources. For example, consider the possibility of selective deposit in the context of suicide notes. Osgood and Walker (1959) compared real suicide notes, ordinary letters, and faked suicide notes. A concern with the problem of selective deposit might lead us to ask whether the thoughts and feelings expressed in suicide notes are representative of all suicides. It happens that fewer than a fourth of all individuals who commit suicide leave notes, so it is possible that those who do leave notes are not representative of those who do not leave notes (Webb et al., 1981).

Problems of selective deposit may also arise when individuals associated with archival sources have the opportunity to edit and alter records before they are permanently recorded. Though the *Congressional Record* is ostensibly a spontaneous record of speeches and remarks made before the Congress, legislators actually have the opportunity to edit their remarks before they are published (Webb et al., 1981) and even to enter into the record documents and accounts that were never really read aloud. No doubt remarks that are, in hindsight, viewed as less than politically expedient are changed prior to publication in the *Congressional Record*. Researchers who use archival data must be aware of the biases that may occur when an archive is produced. Consider, for example, what types of biases might cause selective recording of crime statistics, income expense accounts, or sales figures.

Key Concept }

Problems associated with **selective survival** arise when records are missing or incomplete (something an investigator may or may not even be aware of). It is important to consider whether there are reasons to suspect systematic biases in the survival of certain records. Are documents missing that are particularly damaging to certain individuals or groups? Following a change of presidential administrations, are some types of archives destroyed or misplaced? Are "letters to the editor" representative of all letters that were received? Schoeneman and Rubanowitz (1985) cautioned that when analyzing the contents of advice columns, they could not avoid the possibility of a preselection bias because advice columnists print only a fraction of the letters they receive. As one prominent group of researchers has commented, when one examines archival data, "the gnawing reality remains that archives have been produced for someone else and by someone else" (Webb et al., 1981, p. 140).

Beyond the problems of selective deposit and survival, researchers face additional possible problems with archival sources that arise due to errors in record keeping and changes over time in the manner in which the records are kept. Researchers must be able to document that the record keeping was relatively constant and stable over the period of their study. When running records are kept, there is always the possibility that the definitions of categories have been changed midstream. An interesting example of unintended bias appears in the debate over the "home choke" hypothesis. Critics argue that the archival data do not support the hypothesis that sports teams choke in key games when playing at home (Schlenker et al., 1995a, 1995b). When defending the archival analyses supporting the hypothesis, Baumeister (1995) pointed out that during the archival period there had been a rule change for the World Series regarding the use of a designated hitter. The rule change favored the home team, and could have worked against the "home choke" hypothesis.

Archival data represent nonreactive measures of behavior, but their classification as nonreactive applies only to the analysis of archival data. Reactivity can be a problem at the time the archival record was produced. Statements made by public figures and printed in newspapers or reported by other media must be evaluated for possible reactivity. Politicians and others who are constantly exposed to media publicity no doubt learn how to "use" the media, and their public stance may not match their private views. Lau and Russell (1980) had to consider whether the public statements made by players and coaches about a team's performance were really the same as those they made in private. They concluded that differences between public and private statements of attribution no doubt existed but that these differences do not invalidate their generalization of laboratory findings to real-world settings. The only way to control for reactive effects in archival data is to be aware that they may exist and, when possible, to seek other forms of corroborative evidence.

The need to identify possible spurious relationships is yet another problem in the analysis of archival data. A *spurious relationship* exists when evidence falsely indicates that two or more variables are associated (see Chapter 5). False evidence can arise because of inadequate or improper statistical analysis. A spurious relationship linked to a statistical problem may exist in studies that claim a relationship between frequency of deaths and important occasions. Many people seem to endorse the view that individuals can somehow prolong their life in order to experience certain important events, such as birthdays. Based on their reanalysis of data from several studies, however, Schulz and Bazerman (1980) argue that the supportive evidence may be the result of statistical artifacts—for example, the way in which the period of time before and after a death was measured. Their reanalysis of the data eliminated any evidence for the death-dip hypothesis. But Schulz and Bazerman do not recommend that we abandon the death-dip hypothesis. Instead, they suggest that data supporting the death-dip hypothesis "may well be within reach if we use the proper methodologies and carefully select important events" (p. 261).

Spurious relationships most often occur when variables are accidentally or coincidentally related. As we saw in Chapter 5, this can happen when the correlation between two variables results from changes in another, usually unidentified, *third variable*. For instance, ice cream sales and crime rate are positively correlated. Before we conclude, however, that eating ice cream prompts people to commit crimes, it is important to consider the fact that both variables are likely affected by increases in temperature. Neither eating ice cream nor committing crime directly affects the other; they are correlated because of the third variable they share, temperature.

Several studies (e.g., Baron & Reiss, 1985) have been done to determine whether Phillips' (1983) finding of a relationship between heavyweight prize fights and homicides in the United States reflects a spurious relationship. Critics have questioned whether possible third variables might account for the relationship. Baron and Reiss, for instance, suggested that the third-day peak, which Phillips (1983) admitted he could not readily interpret, was due to the occurrence of holidays or weekends near prize-fight dates or even to fluctuations in the unemployment rate. In spite of questions such as these about possible third variables, extensive reanalysis of Phillips' original data tended to reaffirm a link between violence portrayed in the media and violence acted out in society (see Miller, Heath, Molcan, & Dugoni, 1991).

Researchers tend to be appropriately cautious in reaching final conclusions based solely on the outcome of an archival study (see, for example, Baumeister, 1995). Their cautiousness is due in large part to their recognition of how difficult it can be to identify and rule out possible spurious relationships. Gathering additional evidence from independent sources and subjecting the archival data to more than one kind of analysis is essential in dealing with spurious relationships. Even when these procedures are followed, however, it is hard to draw definitive conclusions from archival data alone. Archival data are most useful when they provide complementary evidence in a multimethod approach to the investigation of a phenomenon.

ETHICAL ISSUES AND UNOBTRUSIVE MEASURES

- Unobtrusive measures such as physical traces and archival data represent an important research method because psychologists can use them to fulfill their ethical obligation to improve individual and societal conditions.

The APA Ethics Code makes clear that "psychologists seek to promote accuracy, honesty, and truthfulness in the science," be "concerned about the ethical compliance of their colleagues' scientific and professional conduct," and commit themselves "to increasing scientific and professional knowledge of behavior and people's understanding of themselves and others and to the use of such knowledge to improve the condition of individuals, organizations, and society" (see Preamble, Principles B and C, of the APA Ethics Code; American Psychological Association, 2002, p. 1062). These are general ethical obligations, of course, that apply when scientists use any methodology. Nevertheless, several studies that we have reviewed in this chapter involving the use of unobtrusive measures provide excellent illustrations of these ethical principles. For instance, we have described research showing how psychologists have contributed meaningfully to our understanding of suicide, race relations, effects of parental divorce, conflict resolution, societal violence, sexual discrimination, and fair scientific practices. This research contributes "knowledge of behavior and people's understanding of themselves and others," and it also has the potential "to improve the condition of individuals, organizations, and society." These contributions arise from only one small sample of psychological research that deals with physical traces or archival data. This impressive list testifies to the ways in which psychologists strive to meet their ethical obligations to create positive change through their research.

It is important to remember that there may be a cost to society of not doing research (see Chapter 3). A better understanding of such social problems as violence, suicide, and race relations, for example, has the potential to improve many people's lives. Yet, ethical dilemmas arise when there are serious risks to participants that make certain kinds of research difficult to justify when considering a risk/benefit ratio. One potential resolution of this dilemma is to seek alternative methods of data collection that involve lower risk. Research involving the use of physical traces and archival data can be carried out on important psychological problems under conditions where ethical issues are often minimal relative to more intrusive methods. Thus, research using unobtrusive measures may represent an important methodology for investigating important social issues with less risk.

SUMMARY

Unobtrusive measures such as physical traces and archival data are important alternatives to direct observation and surveys. Physical traces are the remnants, fragments, and products of past behavior. Use traces can either result naturally, without any intervention by the investigator, or be planned by the investigator. Physical traces may provide important nonreactive (unobtrusive) measures of behavior and can be used as the sole dependent variable or in combination with other measures of behavior. Multimethod approaches to the study of behavior are particularly recommended because they reduce the chance that results are due to some artifact of the measurement process. In obtaining physical traces, an investigator must be aware of possible biases in the way in which traces accumulate or survive over time.

Archival data are found in records and documents that recount the activities of individuals, institutions, governments, and other groups. These sources of information are valuable because they provide a way of investigating the external validity of laboratory findings, assessing the effect of a "natural treatment" (such as divorce), and analyzing the content of communications. Archival records are nonreactive measures of behavior and, like physical traces, can be used in multimethod approaches to hypothesis testing. The analysis of archival data typically requires some form of content analysis, a process that can involve problems of sampling and coding that are not unlike those that arise in the analysis of narrative records (see Chapter 4). Problems of selective deposit and selective survival must be investigated when archival data are used, and evidence should be presented showing that observed relationships are not spurious.

Unobtrusive measures can be an important alternative to more intrusive methodologies, permitting psychologists to do research on important social issues with minimal risk to the participants.

KEY CONCEPTS

unobtrusive (nonreactive) measures	content analysis
physical traces	selective deposit
archival data	selective survival

REVIEW QUESTIONS

1   Why are physical traces and archival data especially attractive alternatives to the direct-observation and survey method of measuring behavior and attitudes?
2   Explain why researchers choose to use the multimethod approach to investigate a research question.

3   Identify the two kinds of physical-trace measures that are used by psychologists and briefly describe how they differ.

4   Explain how possible sources of bias can arise when physical-use traces are the dependent variable in a study, and how the validity of these measures can be verified.

5   Describe three reasons researchers use archival data in their research and provide a research example illustrating each of these reasons.

6   What two dimensions can be used to distinguish among the types of archival sources used by psychologists?

7   Briefly describe the three steps that are involved in carrying out a content analysis in archival research.

8   Explain the roles of selective deposit, selective survival, and reactivity in interpreting the results obtained using archival sources.

9   Explain two reasons why spurious relationships can arise in the analysis of archival data.

CHALLENGE QUESTIONS

1 Suggest one physical-trace measure and one source of archival data for each of the following variables. Be sure to specify an operational definition of each variable.
  A Public's interest in cultural events
  B Students' political attitudes
  C Community concern about crime
  D Citizens' attitudes toward their schools
  E Current fads in dress

2 For each of the following archival sources, specify two kinds of data that might be useful in a psychological study. Once again, be sure to specify the operational definition that could be used for the variable you have identified.
  A Weekly news magazine
  B Television soap operas
  C Classified section of newspaper
  D Annual city budgets
  E Student yearbooks
  F List of donors to a university
  G Television commercials

3 A bright female graduate student in psychology has been offered a job with both *Newsweek* and *Time*. The salary offers of the two companies are basically the same, and it appears that both the working conditions and the job responsibilities are similar. To help her decide which job to accept, she resolves to determine whether one magazine has a better attitude toward women than the other. She appeals to you to help her with a content analysis of these two news magazines. What specific advice would you give her regarding each of the following steps of her content analysis?
  A Sampling
  B Coding
  C Reliability
  D Quantitative and qualitative measures

4 An educational specialist was convinced that schoolyard fights among young boys were more violent than those among young girls. To gather evidence relevant to her hypothesis, she checked the records at the nurse's office of her school. She found that, of the 100 injuries resulting from fights which were reported to the school nurse, 75% involved boys and only 25% involved girls. The investigator was convinced on the basis of these findings that her hypothesis was correct. Think critically about her conclusion by considering how these very same findings could result if exactly the opposite of the investigator's hypothesis were true—namely, that fights among young girls are more violent. (Be sure to confine your response to the adequacy of the data that the investigator has presented to support her conclusion.)

Answer to Stretching Exercise

1. There could be a bias in the way the physical trace is laid down if students at the two schools have different expectations concerning the likelihood of disciplinary action for writing obscene words. Since the investigator is recording responses only once a week, either the custodial staff or other students and faculty (unaware of the purpose of the study) might try to remove the words from restroom walls and the "Leave me a note" pads. This potential bias in the way the messages survive over time would be especially troublesome if it differed at the two schools.

2. The external validity of this study could be questioned because comparisons between private and public schools are being made on the basis of only one school of each type from a particular geographical location with particular staff, and so on. The results of this study could be generalized, however, to schools that were similar to the two schools included in the study.

3. The physical-trace measures of this study could be supplemented by direct observations of youth at the two schools and by conducting a survey of the children at the two schools on their attitudes and behaviors. Important ethical concerns would need to be addressed, however, in attempting to do research on this topic in schools.

Answer to Challenge Question 1

An example of a physical-trace measure (PT) and a possible source of archival data (AD) are listed below for each of the variables. These examples represent only illustrations and not definitive answers. Operational definitions are only sketched here; they should be developed more fully through discussion in class.

A Public's interest in cultural events: (PT) amount of wear on floors at special exhibit in an Art Museum; (AD) attendance figures for theater and concerts in the past calendar year.

B Students' political attitudes: (PT) amount of refuse collected after political rallies on campus for different political groups; (AD) records of participation by students at local, state, and national conventions.

C Community concern about crime: (PT) number of dead bolt locks on front doors of houses; (AD) police records of all calls reporting "suspicious" activities in the community.

D Citizens' attitudes toward their schools: (PT) condition of playground facilities at elementary schools in the neighborhood; (AD) membership lists for parent-teacher organizations with the implication that active participation suggests positive attitudes.

E Fads in clothing: (PT) clothing donations to community agencies as an indicator of clothes that were previously in fashion; (AD) recent magazine, newspaper, and television advertisements for clothing as an indicator of current fashion.

PART THREE

Experimental Methods

CHAPTER SEVEN

Independent Groups Designs

CHAPTER OUTLINE

OVERVIEW

In Chapter 2 we introduced you to the four goals of research in psychology: description, prediction, explanation, and application. Psychologists use observational methods to develop detailed descriptions of behavior, often in natural settings. Survey research methods allow psychologists to describe people's attitudes and opinions. Psychologists are able to make predictions about behavior and mental processes when they discover measures and observations that covary (correlations). Description and prediction are essential to the scientific study of behavior, but they are not sufficient for understanding the causes of behavior. Psychologists also seek explanation—the "why" of behavior. We achieve scientific explanation when we identify the causes of a phenomenon. Chapters 7, 8, and 9 focus on the best available research method for identifying causal relationships—*the experimental method*. We will explore how the experimental method is used to test psychological theories as well as to answer questions of practical importance.

As we have emphasized, the best overall approach to research is the *multimethod approach*. We can be more confident in our conclusions when we obtain comparable answers to a research question after using different methods. Our conclusions are then said to have *convergent validity*. Each method has different shortcomings, but the methods have complementary strengths that overcome these shortcomings. The special strength of the experimental method is that it is especially effective for establishing cause-and-effect relationships.

In this chapter we discuss the reasons researchers conduct experiments and we examine the underlying logic of experimental research. We focus on a commonly used experimental design—the random groups design. We describe the procedures for forming random groups and the threats to interpretation that apply specifically to the random groups design. We describe the procedures researchers use to analyze and interpret the results they obtain in experiments, and we also explore how researchers establish the external validity of experimental findings. We conclude the chapter with consideration of two additional designs involving independent groups: the matched groups design and the natural groups design.

WHY PSYCHOLOGISTS CONDUCT EXPERIMENTS

- Researchers conduct experiments to test hypotheses about the causes of behavior.
- Experiments allow researchers to decide whether a treatment or program effectively changes behavior.

One of the primary reasons that psychologists conduct experiments is to make empirical tests of hypotheses they derive from psychological theories. For example, Pennebaker (1989) developed a theory that keeping thoughts and feelings about painful experiences might take a physical toll. According to this "inhibition theory," it's hard on the body to keep these experiences inside.

Pennebaker and his colleagues conducted many experiments in which they assigned one group of participants to write about traumatic emotional events and another group to write about superficial topics. Consistent with the hypotheses derived from the inhibition theory, participants who wrote about emotional topics had better health outcomes than participants who wrote about superficial topics. Not all the results, however, were consistent with the inhibition theory. For example, students asked to dance expressively about a trauma did not experience the same health benefits as students who danced and wrote about the trauma. Pennebaker and Francis (1996) did a further test of the theory and demonstrated that cognitive changes that occur through writing about emotional experiences were critical in accounting for the positive health outcomes.

Our brief description of experiments done to test the inhibition theory illustrates the general process involved when psychologists do experiments to test a hypothesis derived from a theory. If the results of the experiment are consistent with what is predicted by the hypothesis, then the theory receives support. On the other hand, if the results differ from what was expected, then the proposed explanation based on the theory may need to be modified and a new hypothesis developed and tested in another experiment. Testing hypotheses and revising theories based on the outcomes of experiments can sometimes be a long and painstaking process, much like combining the pieces to a puzzle to form a complete picture. The self-correcting interplay between experiments and proposed explanations is also a fundamental tool psychologists use to understand the causes of the ways we think, feel, and behave.

Besides providing empirical tests of hypotheses derived from theories, experiments can be used to test the effectiveness of a treatment or program. For instance, experiments are often used to test the effects of medical treatments for particular illnesses. This role of experiments in medicine has a long history (Thomas, 1992). Consider the fact that near the beginning of the 19th century, typhoid fever and delirium tremens were often fatal. The standard medical practice at that time was to treat these two conditions by bleeding, purging, and the administration of other similar "therapies." An experiment was performed to test the effectiveness of these supposedly beneficial treatments. One group was randomly assigned to receive the standard treatment (bleeding, purging, etc.), and a second group was randomly assigned to receive nothing but bed rest, good nutrition, and close observation. Thomas (1992) describes the results of this experiment as "unequivocal and appalling" (p. 9): The group given the standard medical treatment of the time did worse than the group left untreated. Treating such conditions using early 19th-century practices was worse than not treating them at all! Experiments such as these contributed to the insight that many medical conditions are self-limited; the illness runs its course, and patients recover on their own. People can also recover without treatment from many psychological disorders, a process known as spontaneous remission.

Well-conducted experiments can provide vital information about the effectiveness of treatments and programs in a wide variety of areas. Seligman and his associates, for example, initiated an impressive series of experiments looking at the effect of teaching cognitive and social problem-solving techniques on the prevention of childhood depression (e.g., Gillham, Reivich, Jaycox, & Seligman, 1995), a process they call "psychological immunization." Thus, experiments serve a useful purpose not only when we are testing theories but also when we are seeking solutions to society's problems.

LOGIC OF EXPERIMENTAL RESEARCH

- Researchers manipulate an independent variable in an experiment to observe the effect on behavior, as assessed by the dependent variable.
- Control is the essential ingredient of experiments; experimental control is gained through manipulation, holding conditions constant, and balancing.
- Experimental control allows researchers to make the causal inference that the independent variable *caused* the observed changes in the dependent variable.
- An experiment has internal validity when it fulfills the three conditions required for causal inference: covariation, time-order relationship, and elimination of plausible alternative causes.
- When confounding occurs, a plausible alternative explanation for the observed covariation exists, and therefore, the experiment lacks internal validity. Plausible alternative explanations are ruled out by holding conditions constant and balancing.

A true experiment involves the *manipulation* of one or more factors and the *measurement* (observation) of the effects of this manipulation on behavior. As you saw in Chapter 2, the factors the researcher controls or manipulates are called the *independent variables*. The measures used to observe the effect (if any) of the independent variables are called *dependent variables.*

Experiments are effective for testing hypotheses because they allow us to exercise a relatively high degree of control in a situation. Researchers use control in experiments to be able to state with confidence that the independent variable *caused* the observed changes in the dependent variable. The three conditions needed to make a causal inference are covariation, time-order relationship, and elimination of plausible alternative causes (see Chapter 2).

The covariation condition is met when we observe a relationship between the independent and dependent variables of an experiment. A time-order relationship is established when researchers manipulate an independent variable and *then* observe a subsequent difference in behavior (i.e., the change in behavior is contingent on the manipulation). Finally, elimination of plausible alternative causes is accomplished through the use of control procedures, most importantly, through *holding conditions constant* and *balancing.* When the three conditions for a causal inference are met, the experiment is said to have **internal validity,** and we can make the interpretation that the independent variable *caused* the difference in behavior as measured by the dependent variable. Let us first describe a research situation in which these conditions are *not* met. Then we'll describe a published experiment in which they are met; that is, the experiment can be said to have internal validity.

Key Concept

The conditions for causal inference are not met in a kind of research study that has been called a *one-group pretest-posttest design* (Campbell & Stanley, 1966). This design typically involves one group of participants who are singled out for treatment or intervention. Observations of behavior are made before (pretest) and after (posttest) the treatment. Such would be the case, for example, if children in one classroom were instructed using a new way of teaching mathematics (treatment) with relevant math tests given before and after the new method is introduced. This design can be described as:

Stage 1	Stage 2	Stage 3
O_1	X	O_2

where O_1 refers to the first observation of the group, or pretest; X indicates a treatment; and O_2 refers to the second observation, or posttest.

Although this particular research design is sometimes used in psychological research, the design has very little internal validity, and it is difficult to interpret any results from this type of research design. Can you see that this design does not control for factors that threaten the internal validity of the study? For example, should a difference between pretest and posttest measures be found, how do we know that this difference was not due to some event other than the treatment *(history threat)*, or that it simply was not due to the fact that the group of participants changed over time *(maturation threat)*? This particular design has so little going for it in terms of allowing cause-and-effect inferences that it is sometimes referred to as a "pre-experimental design," or one that serves as a "bad experiment" to illustrate possible threats to internal validity (see Campbell & Stanley, 1966). We will have much more to say about threats to internal validity later in this chapter and especially in Chapter 11 when we discuss research in natural settings. However, let us now examine a different research design, one that does have internal validity.

The logic of the experimental method and the application of control techniques that produce internal validity can be illustrated in an experiment investigating eyewitness behavior, which was conducted by Loftus and Burns (1982). Participants in their experiment viewed a film that contained a violent scene. Loftus and Burns were investigating the effect of witnessing a mentally shocking event on the participants' memory for information that was presented in the film seconds before the violent scene. The experiment was done at the University of Washington. The 226 students who volunteered to participate were tested in small groups, and each small group was randomly assigned to view one of two films. Approximately half of the students (115) were assigned to view a violent version of a film. Near the end of the film, these students saw a robber, while running to a getaway car, turn and fire a shot toward two men who were pursuing him. The shot hit a boy in the face, and the boy fell bleeding to the ground. The other half of the students viewed a nonviolent version of the film that was identical to the violent version until just before the shooting. At this point in the film, the camera switched back to inside the bank, where the students saw the bank manager telling the customers and employees what happened and asking them to remain calm. The violent and nonviolent versions of the film represent the two levels of the independent variable that was manipulated in the experiment.

After viewing the film, students in both groups answered 25 questions about events in the film. One question was critical: It asked for the number on the football jersey worn by a boy playing in the parking lot outside the bank. The boy wearing the jersey (see Figure 7.1) was visible for 2 seconds during the film—the 2 seconds before the shooting (violent version) or the 2 seconds before the scenes back in the bank (nonviolent version). The dependent variable was the students' response to the question about the jersey number. The version of the film participants saw did affect their recall. Just over 4% of the students correctly recalled the number in the violent condition, whereas nearly 28% did so in the nonviolent condition. Thus, Loftus and Burns concluded that a mentally shocking event can impair memory for details immediately preceding the event.

How did Loftus and Burns (1982) use the control techniques of holding conditions constant and balancing? In their experiment, several factors that could have affected the participants' memory were kept the same across the two conditions. The students viewed exactly the same film except for the critical incident; they were given the same experimental instructions at the beginning of the experiment and received the exact same questionnaire at the conclusion.

FIGURE 7.1   Black-and-white representation of scene viewed by students, showing boy with the number 17 on his football jersey. (From Loftus and Burns, 1982.)

Researchers use *holding conditions constant* to make sure that the independent variable is the *only* factor that differs systematically across the groups.

If the two groups had differed on a factor other than the film manipulation, then the results of the experiment would have been uninterpretable. For example, if the participants in the violent version had viewed a film depicting a boy in the background wearing a different jersey than that seen in the nonviolent version, then we wouldn't know whether the difference in recall was due to viewing the violent version of the film or to the fact that the jersey was different (e.g., a smaller or less distinct number). When the independent variable of interest and a different, potential independent variable are allowed to covary, a *confounding* is present. When there are no confoundings, an experiment has *internal validity*. When an experiment has internal validity, we are assured that changes in the independent variable caused the changes in the dependent variable.

Holding conditions constant is a control technique that researchers use to avoid confoundings. By holding constant the boy playing in the background and the jersey (among other things) in the two versions of the film, Loftus and Burns avoided confoundings by these factors. In general, a factor that is held constant cannot possibly covary with the intended independent variable. More importantly, a factor that is held constant does not change so it cannot possibly covary with the dependent variable either. Thus, researchers can rule out factors that are held constant as potential causes for the observed results.

It is important to recognize, however, that we choose to control only those factors we think might influence the behavior we are studying—what we consider *plausible* alternative causes. For instance, Loftus and Burns held the setting constant by testing all their participants in the same room, but it is unlikely they specifically controlled the room temperature to be constant between groups because room temperature probably would not affect memory (at least when varying only a few degrees). They also tested students in "small groups," but there was no apparent attempt to hold constant the size of the group. Again, it doesn't seem plausible that small variations in the size of groups watching the film would have an effect on recall. The point is that we control only those factors we believe are potentially relevant—that is, those additional factors that might affect the behavior of interest. Nevertheless, we should constantly remain alert to the possibility that there may be confounding factors in our experiments whose influence we had not anticipated or considered.

Key Concept }   In an **independent groups design,** each group of subjects represents a different condition as defined by the independent variable. The experiment on eyewitness behavior is an example of an independent groups design: The independent variable (i.e., version of the film) varied across different groups of participants. The particular independent groups design conducted by Loftus

Key Concept }   and Burns is called a **random groups design.** For an independent groups design to have internal validity, it is essential to balance individual differences among the different groups of the experiment. The control technique of balancing is required because not all factors we want to control can be held constant. That is, we must make sure that one group is not smarter, more motivated, more conscientious, contains more women, has fewer psychology majors, and so

STRETCHING EXERCISE

In this exercise you are to respond to the questions that appear after this brief description of a research report.

Students in a research methods class were the confederates and observers in a field experiment in which they examined people's responses when their personal space was invaded. The confederates invaded personal space by staring at the people they were observing. The participants were students who were walking alone past a bench along a path near the center of campus. The research methods students worked in pairs with one member of the pair sitting on the bench (the confederate) and the other member observing and timing the participants (the observer). Each team of students observed one participant in each of three conditions, and each team administered the conditions in a random order. The three conditions in the experiment all related to what the confederate sitting on the bench did. The confederates either were reading a newspaper held up in front of them or they stared at the participant as the participant approached the bench. In the third condition participants were observed with no one sitting on the bench. The observers made separate measurements of the time it took participants to walk up to the bench and away from the bench. The research methods students predicted that participants would walk faster when the confederate was staring at them. Contrary to their prediction, participants walked more slowly toward the bench in the staring condition than in the other two conditions. There was no difference among the three conditions in the walking speeds away from the bench.

1 What aspect of their experiment did the students control by using manipulation?
2 What aspect of their experiments did the students control by holding conditions constant?
3 What aspect of their experiment did the students control by using balancing?

forth, than another group. In the Loftus and Burns study of eyewitness behavior, if participants viewing the nonviolent film were also shown to be more attentive or have better recall ability than participants viewing the violent version, a plausible alternative explanation for the findings exists. It's possible that attentiveness (or memory ability) and not the version of the film could explain why participants in the nonviolent condition recalled more. (In the language of the researcher, a confounding would be present.) When individual differences such as attentiveness are balanced across the groups, however, we rule out the alternative explanation that the differences we obtain between the groups on the dependent variable are due to characteristics of the participants. Balancing in an independent groups design is accomplished by randomly assigning subjects to experimental conditions—hence, the name *random groups design.*

In the next section we will examine the random groups design more closely, and we will describe exactly how balancing through random assignment is accomplished in this design.

RANDOM GROUPS DESIGN

Random Assignment

- In the random groups design comparable groups of individuals are formed and the groups are treated the same in all respects except that each group receives only one level of the independent variable.

- The logic of the random groups design allows researchers to make causal inferences about the effect of the independent variable on the dependent variable.
- Random assignment to conditions is used to form comparable groups by balancing or averaging subject characteristics (individual differences) across the conditions of the independent variable manipulation.
- Block randomization balances subject characteristics and potential confoundings that occur during the time in which the experiment is conducted, and creates groups of equal size.

The simplest experiments involve one independent variable with two levels and one measure of the dependent variable. The effect of the independent variable is assessed by observing the difference in the dependent variable between these two levels. In the independent groups design, a different group of subjects participates in each level (i.e., the groups are independent of each other). In the experiment done by Loftus and Burns (1982), for example, one group of participants was assigned to view a violent version of a film while a second group of participants viewed a nonviolent version of the same film. Both groups' memory for details of the films was compared. The logic of the design is straightforward. The two groups are similar on all important characteristics at the start of the experiment. And, in the experiment itself, the two groups are treated the same except for the level of the independent variable (e.g., violent or nonviolent film). Thus, any difference in the performance (e.g., memory for details) of the two groups must be caused by the independent variable.

The experimental method allows researchers to interpret the effect of an independent variable. Comparable groups of individuals are formed and the groups are treated alike in all respects except that each group receives only one level of the independent variable. Logically, therefore, any differences in behavior of the two groups must be caused by the independent variable. Clearly, one key to the logic of the experimental method is forming comparable (similar) groups at the start of the experiment. In the *random groups design,* **random assignment** of subjects to conditions is used to form comparable groups prior to implementing the independent variable. The goal of random assignment to conditions is to establish equivalent groups of participants by balancing individual differences across the conditions. As we have seen, this was the procedure followed by Loftus and Burns in their study of eyewitness behavior. The random groups design may be described as follows:

Key Concept

Stage 1	Stage 2	Stage 3
R_1	X_1	O_1
R_2	X_2	O_1

where R_1 and R_2 refer to the random assignment of subjects to conditions (1 and 2) of the experiment; X_1 is one level of an independent variable (e.g., violent version of the film), and X_2 is a second level of the independent variable (e.g., nonviolent film), which in some cases may represent no treatment (control). An observation of behavior (O_1) in each group is then made. Unlike the one-group pretest-posttest design, the random groups design is an example of a good experiment.

The major benefit of randomly assigning subjects to groups is to balance or average out the characteristics of the students in the two groups. As we noted previously, if the groups of participants viewing the two versions of the film differed in their memory ability, then we could reasonably argue that the observed difference in memory for detail of the film was due simply to this characteristic of the participants rather than to the type of film they viewed. Because Loftus and Burns formed comparable groups by randomly assigning students to the conditions in their experiment, and because other important factors were held constant, the only factor that varied between the two groups was the manipulated independent variable. Therefore, the researchers were able to conclude that viewing the different versions of the film caused the difference in students' memory performance. Box 7.1 summarizes how Loftus and Burns applied the experimental method to their study of eyewitness behavior.

Key Concept }

A common procedure for carrying out random assignment is **block randomization.** First, let us describe exactly how block randomization is carried out, and then we will look at what it accomplishes. Suppose we have an experiment with five conditions. One "block" is made up of a random order of all five conditions.

One block of conditions	$\rightarrow$	Random order of conditions
A B C D E		C A E B D

BOX 7.1

SUMMARY OF THE LOFTUS AND BURNS EYEWITNESS EXPERIMENT

Overview of experimental procedure: College students are assigned to watch one of two different versions of a film. After viewing a film version, participants are asked questions about the content of the film.

Independent variable: Version of film viewed by participants (violent or nonviolent).
Dependent variable: Response to question about number on boy's jersey.
  Explanation of control procedures:
  Holding conditions constant: Students in the two groups viewed exactly the same film except for the critical incident, were given the same instructions at the beginning of the experiment, and received exactly the same questionnaire at the conclusion.

  Balancing: Individual differences among students were balanced through random assignment of students to different experimental conditions.
Explanation of experimental logic providing evidence for causality:
  Covariation: Participants' memory for film details was found to vary with experimental condition.
  Time-order relationship: The version of the film was manipulated prior to measuring retention.
  Elimination of plausible alternative causes: Control procedures of holding conditions constant and balancing individual differences through random assignment protected against confoundings.
  Conclusion: Viewing a mentally shocking event (the violent film version) caused memory impairment.
(Based on Loftus & Burns, 1982)

In block randomization, one subject is assigned to each condition in the block before a second subject is assigned to any one condition. That is, we assign subjects to conditions one block at a time. For example, if we want to have 10 subjects in each of five conditions, then there would be 10 blocks in the block-randomized schedule. Each block would consist of a random arrangement of the five conditions. You might think of this procedure as one where you take the first five people who show up for the experiment and assign each one randomly to one of the five conditions, then take the next five people and assign each to one of the five conditions, and so on, until you have done this 10 times. This procedure is illustrated below for the first 11 participants.

10 Blocks	Participants		Condition	
1) C A E B D	1) Cara	→	C	
2) E C D A B	2) Andy	→	A	
3) D B E A C	3) Jacob	→	E	First block
4) B A C E D	4) Molly	→	B	
5) A C E D B	5) Emily	→	D	
6) A D E B C	6) Eric	→	E	
7) B C A D E	7) Anna	→	C	
8) D C A E B	8) Laura	→	D	Second block
9) E D B C A	9) Sarah	→	A	
10) C E B D A	10) Lisa	→	B	
	11) Tom	→	D	

and so on for 50 participants

Block randomization is a very useful technique for randomly assigning subjects to groups because it produces groups that are of equal size while controlling for time-related variables. The number of observations in each group affects the reliability of the descriptive statistics for each group. It is desirable to have the reliability of these measures comparable across groups, and block randomization accomplishes this. Block randomization is also useful because experiments often take a substantial amount of time to complete. Participants can be affected by events that occur during the time the experiment is conducted. Block randomization helps to control for these time-related events because subjects are assigned to conditions one block at a time. Because one participant is tested in each condition within a block, equal numbers of subjects in all conditions of the experiment are likely to experience events that occur during the time when the experiment is being done. Block randomization also works to balance other time-related variables, such as changes in experimenters or even changes in the populations from which subjects are drawn. For example, a perfectly acceptable experiment could be done drawing students from both fall and spring semester classes if a block randomization schedule is used. The beauty of block randomization is that it will balance (or average) any characteristics of participants (including the effects of time-related factors) across the conditions of an experiment.

If you want to practice the procedure of block randomization, you can do Challenge Question 1A at the end of this chapter.

Threats to Internal Validity

- Randomly assigning intact groups to different conditions of the independent variable creates a potential confounding due to pre-existing differences among participants in the intact groups.
- Block randomization increases internal validity by balancing extraneous variables across conditions of the independent variable.
- Whether extraneous variables are controlled by balancing or by holding conditions constant influences the external validity and sensitivity of an experiment.
- Selective subject loss, but not mechanical subject loss, threatens the internal validity of an experiment.
- Placebo control groups are used to control for the problem of demand characteristics, and double-blind experiments control both demand characteristics and experimenter effects.

Key Concept

We've seen that *internal validity* is the degree to which differences in performance on a dependent variable can be attributed clearly and unambiguously to an effect of an independent variable, as opposed to some other uncontrolled variable. These uncontrolled variables are often referred to as **threats to internal validity.** These threats are possible causes of a phenomenon that serves as potential alternative explanations for a study's findings. In order to make a clear cause-and-effect inference about an independent variable, threats to internal validity must be controlled. We next describe problems in experimental research that can result in threats to internal validity, and methods to control these threats.

Testing Intact Groups   Random assignment is used to assure comparable groups in the random groups design. There are times, however, when noncomparable groups are formed even when random assignment appears to have been used. This problem occurs when intact groups (and not individuals) are randomly assigned to the conditions of an experiment. Intact groups are those that were formed prior to the start of the experiment. For example, the different sections of an introductory psychology course are intact groups. Students are not randomly assigned to different sections of introductory psychology (although sometimes scheduling classes seems random!). Students often choose to be in a particular section because of the time the class meets, the instructor, friends who will be in the class, and any number of other factors.

A confounding due to noncomparable groups can arise, however, when individuals differ systematically across the intact groups. For example, students who choose to take an 8 A.M. section may differ from students who prefer an

11 A.M. section. Random assignment of these intact groups to experimental conditions is simply not sufficient to balance the systematic differences among the intact groups. These systematic differences between the two intact groups are almost guaranteed to threaten the internal validity of the experiment. The solution to this problem is simple—do not use intact groups in a random groups design.

Balancing Extraneous Variables   A number of factors in an experiment may vary as a result of practical considerations when carrying out the study. For example, to complete an experiment more quickly, a researcher might decide to have several different experimenters test small groups of participants. The sizes of the groups and the experimenters themselves become potentially relevant variables that could confound the experiment. For example, if all the individuals in the experimental group are tested by one experimenter and all those in the control group are tested by another experimenter, the levels of intended independent variable become confounded with the two experimenters. We would not be able to determine whether an observed difference between the two groups was due to the independent variable or to the fact that different experimenters tested participants in the experimental and control groups.

Potential variables that are not directly of interest to the researcher but that could still be sources of confounding in the experiment are called *extraneous variables*. But don't let the term fool you! An experiment confounded by an extraneous variable is no less confounded than if the confounding variable were of considerable inherent interest. For example, Evans and Donnerstein (1974) studied one such extraneous variable—the differences between participants who volunteer early in the term and those who volunteer late in the term. Their results indicated that those who volunteer early are more academically oriented and are more likely to have an internal locus of control (i.e., they emphasize their own responsibility for their actions rather than external factors). Their findings suggest it would not be wise to test participants in the experimental condition at the beginning of the term and participants in the control condition at the end of the term, as this would potentially confound the independent variable with participants' locus of control, academic focus, and so on.

Block randomization provides an easy and effective way to control extraneous variables by balancing them across groups. All that is required is that entire blocks be tested at each level of the extraneous variable. For example, if there were four different experimenters, entire blocks of the block-randomized schedule would be assigned to each experimenter. Because each block contains all the conditions of the experiment, this strategy guarantees that each condition will be tested by each experimenter. Usually, we would assign the same number of blocks to each experimenter, but this is not essential. What is essential is that entire blocks be tested at each level of the extraneous variable, which, in this case, is the experimenters. The balancing act can become a bit tricky when there are several extraneous variables, but careful advance planning can avoid confounding by such factors.

Subject Loss We have emphasized that the logic of the random groups design requires that the groups in an experiment differ only because of the levels of the independent variable. We have seen that forming comparable groups of subjects at the beginning of an experiment is another essential characteristic of the random groups design. It is equally important that the groups be comparable except for the independent variable at the end of the experiment. When subjects begin an experiment but fail to complete it successfully, the internal validity of the experiment can be threatened. It is important to distinguish between two ways in which subjects can fail to complete an experiment: mechanical subject loss and selective subject loss (Underwood & Shaughnessy, 1975).

Key Concept **Mechanical subject loss** occurs when a subject fails to complete the experiment because of an equipment failure (in this case, the experimenter is considered part of the equipment). Mechanical subject loss can occur if a computer crashes, or if the experimenter reads the wrong set of instructions, or if someone inadvertently interrupts an experimental session. Mechanical loss is a less critical problem because the loss is not related to any characteristic of the subject. As such, mechanical loss should not lead to systematic differences between the characteristics of the subjects who successfully complete the experiment in the different conditions of the experiment. Mechanical loss can also reasonably be understood as the result of chance events that should occur equally across groups. Hence, internal validity is not typically threatened when subjects must be excluded from the experiment due to mechanical loss. When mechanical subject loss occurs, it should be documented. The name of the dropped subject and the reason for the loss should be recorded. The lost subject can then be replaced by the next subject tested.

Key Concept Selective subject loss is a far more serious matter. **Selective subject loss** occurs (1) when subjects are lost differentially across the conditions of the experiment; (2) when some characteristic of the subject is responsible for the loss; and (3) when this subject characteristic is related to the dependent variable used to assess the outcome of the study. Selective subject loss destroys the comparable groups that are essential to the logic of the random groups design, and can thus render the experiment uninterpretable. This problem can arise in a variety of experimental situations, for example, physiological studies involving surgical or drug treatments, memory experiments testing retention over days or weeks, and longitudinal designs in survey research (see Chapter 5).

We can illustrate the problems associated with selective subject loss by considering a fictitious but realistic example. Assume that the directors of a local fitness center decide to do an experiment to test the effectiveness of a one-month fitness program they have developed. They identify 80 people who are willing to volunteer for the experiment, and they randomly assign 40 to each of two groups. Random assignment to conditions is used to create comparable groups by balancing characteristics such as weight, fitness level, motivation, and so on across the two groups. Members of the control group are simply asked to come to the center at the end of the month. When they arrive, they are given a fitness test. Those in the experimental group participate in a vigorous fitness program for one month prior to the test at the end of the month. Assume all 40 control participants show up for the fitness test, but only 25 of the experimental participants stay with the rigorous fitness program for the full month. Also assume that the average fitness score for the 25 people remaining in the experimental group is significantly higher than the average score for the 40 people in the control group. Based on these findings, the directors of the fitness center make the claim that: "A scientifically based research study has shown that our program leads to better fitness."

Do you think the fitness center's claim is justified? It's not. This hypothetical study represents a classic example of selective subject loss, so the results of the study can't be used to support the fitness center's claim. The loss occurred differentially across conditions; participants were lost only from the experimental group. It is important to recognize that the differential loss in the two groups is not a problem because the groups ended up different in size. The results would have been interpretable if 25 people had been randomly assigned to the experimental group and 40 to the control group and all the individuals had completed the experiment. Selective subject loss is a problem because the 25 experimental participants who completed the fitness program are not likely to be comparable to the 40 control participants. The 15 experimental participants who could not complete the rigorous program are likely to have been less fit (even before the program began) than the 25 experimental participants who did complete the

FIGURE 7.2   Many people who begin a rigorous exercise program fail to complete it. In a sense, only the "fittest" survive, a situation that could cause problems of interpretation if different types of fitness programs were being compared.

program. The selective loss of participants in the experimental group has destroyed the comparable groups that were formed by random assignment at the beginning of the experiment. In fact, the final fitness scores of the 25 experimental participants might have been higher than the average in the control group even if they had not participated in the fitness program because they were more fit when they began! Thus, the subject loss in this experiment meets the other two conditions for selective subject loss. Namely, the loss is likely due to a characteristic of the participants—their original level of fitness—and this characteristic is relevant to the outcome of the study.

If selective subject loss is not identified until after the experiment is completed, little can be done except to chalk up the experience of having conducted an uninterpretable experiment. There are preventive steps that can be taken, however, when researchers realize in advance that selective loss may be a problem. One alternative is to administer a pretest and screen out subjects who are likely to be lost. For example, an initial test of fitness could have been given, and only those participants who scored above some minimal level would participate in the experiment. Screening participants in this way would involve a potential cost. The results of the study would likely apply only for people above the minimal fitness level. This cost may be well worth paying because an interpretable study of limited generality is still preferable to an uninterpretable study.

There is a second preventive approach that researchers can use when facing the possibility of selective subject loss. Researchers can give all subjects a pretest but then simply randomly assign all participants to one of the conditions. Then, if a subject is lost from the experimental group, a subject with a comparable pretest score can be dropped from the control group. In a sense, this approach tries to restore the comparability of the groups. Researchers must be able to anticipate possible factors that could be responsible for selective subject loss, and they must make sure that the pretest they use measures these factors. In our example, a fitness pretest would be preferable to a pretest of visual acuity (which is likely to be unrelated to subject loss in this study).

Placebo Control and Double-Blind Experiments   The final challenge to internal validity we will describe arises because of expectations held by both participants and experimenters. Demand characteristics represent one possible source of bias due to participants' expectations (Orne, 1962). *Demand characteristics* refer to the cues and other information that participants use to guide their behavior in a psychological study (see Chapter 4). For example, research participants who know they have been given alcohol may expect that they will experience certain effects, such as relaxation or giddiness. They may then behave consistent with these expectations rather than in response to the effects of the alcohol per se. Potential biases can also arise in experiments due to the expectations of the experimenters. The general term used to describe these biases is **experimenter effects** (Rosenthal, 1963). Experimenter effects may pose a problem if the experimenters treat subjects differently in the different groups of the

Key Concept }

experiment in ways other than those required to implement the independent variable. In an experiment involving alcohol, for instance, experimenter effects could occur if the experimenters read the instructions more slowly to participants who had been given alcohol than to those who had not. If experimenter effects do occur because experimenters treat participants differently in different groups, a confounding of the independent variable could result. Another way that experimenter effects can occur is if experimenters make biased observations when they know which treatment the subject has received. For example, biased observations due to experimenter effects might arise in the alcohol study if the experimenters were more likely to notice unusual motor movements or slurred speech among the "drinkers" (because they "expect" drinkers to behave this way). (See discussion of expectancy effects in Chapter 4).

Key Concept }

Researchers can never eliminate the problems of demand characteristics and experimenter effects, but there are special research designs that control these problems. Researchers use a **placebo control** group as one way to control demand characteristics A *placebo* (from the Latin word meaning, "I shall please") is a substance that looks like a drug or other active substance but is actually an inert, or inactive, substance. Some research even indicates that there can be therapeutic effects from the placebo itself (e.g., Kirsch & Sapirstein, 1998). Pishkin and Shurley (1983) used a placebo control group to control for demand characteristics in an experiment testing the effectiveness of two drugs (doxepin and hydroxyzine). The drugs were tested to determine if they reduce arousal levels of psychiatric patients in response to stress. The placebo participants were given capsules identical to the two drugs, but the placebo capsules contained only lactose, a sugar found in milk. None of the participants in the placebo control group realized their pill contained no medicine so all groups had the same "awareness" of taking a drug, and therefore, similar expectations. That is, the demand characteristics were similar for the groups—participants in both groups expected to experience effects of a drug. Any differences between the experimental groups and the placebo control group could legitimately be attributed to the actual effect of the drug taken by the experimental participants, and not the participants' expectations about receiving a drug.

Key Concept }

The use of placebo control groups in combination with a double-blind procedure can control for both demand characteristics and experimenter effects. In a **double-blind** procedure both the participant and the observer are blind to (unaware of) what treatment is being administered. In an experiment such as the Pishkin and Shurley (1983) study, two researchers would be needed to accomplish the double-blind procedure. The first researcher would prepare the drug capsules and code each capsule in some way; the second researcher would distribute the drugs to the participants, recording the code for each drug as it was given to an individual. This procedure ensures there is a record of which drug each person received, but neither the participant nor the experimenter who actually administers the drugs (and observes their effects) knows which treatment the participant received. Thus, experimenter expectancies about the effects of the treatment are controlled because the researcher who makes the observations is unaware of who received the treatment and who received the placebo. Similarly, demand characteristics are controlled because participants remain unaware of whether they received the drug or placebo.

Experiments that involve placebo control groups are a valuable research tool when it is important to assess the effectiveness of a treatment while controlling for demand characteristics. The use of placebo control groups, however, does raise special ethical concerns. The benefits of the knowledge gained using placebo control groups must be evaluated in light of the risks that are entailed when research participants who expect to receive a drug may instead receive a placebo. Typically, the ethics of this procedure are addressed in the informed consent procedure prior to the start of the experiment. Participants are told they may receive a drug or a placebo. Only individuals who consent to receiving either the placebo or the drug participate in the research. Should the experimental drug prove effective, then the researchers are ethically required to offer the treatment to participants in the placebo condition.

ANALYSIS AND INTERPRETATION OF EXPERIMENTAL FINDINGS

The Role of Data Analysis in Experiments

- Data analysis and statistics play a critical role in researchers' ability to make the claim that an independent variable has had an effect on behavior.
- The best way to determine whether the findings of an experiment are reliable is to do a replication of the experiment.

A good experiment, as is true of all good research, begins with a good research question. We have described how researchers use control techniques to design and implement an experiment that will allow them to gather interpretable evidence to answer their research question. This part of the research process is similar to what detectives do in a criminal investigation. Detectives carefully gather evidence to determine if the person they suspect is, in fact, the one who committed the crime. The most thorough investigation, however, is not sufficient to "make the case" that the suspect is guilty. Prosecuting attorneys must present the evidence to a jury and their case must be compelling enough to withstand the counterarguments presented by defense attorneys. Similarly, researchers cannot "make their case" by simply conducting a good experiment. They must also present the evidence in a convincing way to demonstrate that their findings support the conclusions they wish to draw based on that evidence. Data analysis and statistics play a critical role in the analysis and interpretation of experimental findings.

Robert Abelson in his book, *Statistics as Principled Argument* (1995), suggests that the primary goal of data analysis is to determine whether our observations support a claim about behavior. That is, can we "make the case" for our conclusion based on the evidence we have gathered in our experiment? We provide a more complete description of how researchers use data analysis and statistics in research in Chapters 12 and 13. Here we will introduce the central concepts of data analysis that apply to the interpretation of the results of experiments. But first let us mention one very important way that researchers can make their case concerning the results of their research.

The best way to determine whether the findings obtained in an experiment are reliable is to replicate the experiment and see if the same outcome is obtained. **Replication** means repeating the procedures used in a particular experiment in order to determine whether the same results will be obtained a second time. As you might imagine, an exact replication is almost impossible to carry out. The subjects tested in the replication will be different from those tested in the original study; the testing rooms, and experimenters also may be different. Nevertheless, replication is still the best way to determine whether a research finding is reliable. If we required, however, that the reliability of every experiment be established by replication, the process would be cumbersome and inefficient. Participants for experiments are a scarce resource, and doing a replication means we won't be doing an experiment to ask new and different questions about behavior. Data analysis and statistics provide researchers with an alternative to replication for determining whether the results of a single experiment can be used as evidence to make a claim about the effect an independent variable has on behavior.

Key Concept

Stat Tip

Data analysis of an experiment involves three stages: (1) getting to know the data, (2) summarizing the data, and (3) confirming what the data reveal. In the first stage we try to find out what is going on in the data set, look for errors, and make sure the data make sense. In the second stage we use descriptive statistics and graphical displays to summarize what was found. In the third stage we seek evidence for what the data tell us about behavior. What can we conclude? At this stage various statistical techniques may be used to help in our decision making.

In the following sections we provide only a brief introduction to these stages of data analysis. A more complete introduction to data analysis is found in Chapters 12 and 13 (see especially Box 12.1 in Chapter 12). These later chapters will become particularly important if you need to read and interpret the results of a psychology experiment published in a scientific journal or if you decide to carry out your own psychology experiment.

We will use the results of a name-learning experiment conducted by one of the authors to illustrate the process of data analysis. Learning and remembering the names of people we meet is an integral part of our everyday lives. Unfortunately, failing to remember people's names is also an all too common—and frustrating—aspect of our everyday experience. Cohen (1990) has suggested that names are more difficult to remember than other kinds of information because the names are arbitrary, meaningless, and difficult to associate with other information in memory. Landauer and Bjork (1978) introduced a mnemonic technique called expanding retrieval that could help people remember names.

FIGURE 7.3 A Study presentation with photo, name, and a personal description and three possible retrieval cues (photo only, description only, or photo with description) were used in a name recall experiment.

Expanding retrieval involves trying to recall a name you want to remember at increasing intervals after you have been introduced to a person.

One of the many experiments that have been done to test the effectiveness of expanding retrieval involved a situation in which students were asked to learn people's names while they were also trying to learn other information. The experiment attempted to simulate the social situation in which people try to learn names while engaged in conversation. In the experiment, college students were given a primary memory task of trying to learn 50 unrelated facts (the counterpart of a conversation). In the midst of the presentation of the facts, the participants were "introduced" to several people. After studying the facts and the names of the people, the participants were given memory tests for both the facts and the names.

An illustration of the "introduction" at the time of study and of the three cues used at recall are shown in Figure 7.3. During study, the participants were shown a photograph of the person and a brief description along with the person's name. At the time of the name recall test, there were three groups of 36 participants with each group given a different cue for recall of the names. The groups were given either just the photograph, just the brief description, or both the photograph and the brief description. The primary research question in this experiment was whether expanding retrieval would be effective when participants were concentrating on learning the facts. (It was!) For now, we will focus on the question of whether recall of the names varied depending upon which cue participants were given at the time of the memory test.

Describing the Results

- The two most common descriptive statistics that are used to summarize the results of experiments are the mean and standard deviation.
- Measures of effect size indicate the strength of the relationship between the independent and dependent variables, and they are not affected by sample size.

TABLE 7.1   MEAN RECALL, STANDARD DEVIATIONS, AND CONFIDENCE INTERVALS FOR THE THREE CONDITIONS OF A NAME-LEARNING EXPERIMENT

Retrieval cue conditions	N	Mean	SD	.95 Confidence interval
Photo	36	3.98	2.02	3.31–4.65
Description	36	2.40	1.84	1.79–3.01
Photo and description	36	3.80	1.71	3.23–4.37

Note: Maximum possible recall is 8.

- One commonly used measure of effect size, *d*, examines the difference between two group means relative to the average variability in the experiment.
- Meta-analysis uses measures of effect size to summarize the results of many experiments investigating the same independent variable or dependent variable.

Data analysis should begin with a careful inspection of the data set with special attention given to possible errors or anomalous data points. The next step is to describe what was found. At this stage the researcher wants to know, "What happened in the experiment?" To begin to answer this question researchers use *descriptive statistics.* The two most commonly reported descriptive statistics are the mean (a measure of central tendency) and the standard deviation (a measure of variability). The means and standard deviations for recall in the name-learning experiment are presented in Table 7.1. The means show that recall was highest in the photo condition (3.98) and lowest in the description condition (2.40). Recall in the condition with both cues (3.80) was closer to the recall in the photo condition than to that in the description condition. Knowing that the maximum recall in any condition was eight names, we can also say that participants recalled on average between one-third and one-half of the names.

In a properly conducted experiment, the standard deviation in each group should reflect only the individual differences among the subjects who have been randomly assigned to that group. Subjects in each group should be treated in the same way, and the level of the independent variable to which they've been assigned should be implemented in the same way for each subject in the group. The standard deviations shown in Table 7.1 indicate that there was variation around the mean recall in each group and that the variation was about the same in all three groups.

Key Concept

One important question that researchers ask when describing the results of an experiment is how large an effect the independent variable had on the dependent variable. Measures of **effect size** can be used to answer this question because they indicate the strength of the relationship between the independent and dependent variables. One advantage of measures of effect size is that they are not influenced by the size of the samples tested in the experiment. Measures of effect size take into account more than the mean difference between two conditions in an

Key Concept

experiment. The mean difference between two groups is always *relative* to the average variability in participants' scores. One frequently used measure of effect size is **Cohen's *d*.** Cohen (1992) developed criteria that are now widely accepted. Specifically, he suggested that *d* values of .20, .50, and .80 represent small, medium, and large effects of the independent variable, respectively. We can illustrate the use of Cohen's *d* as a measure of effect size by comparing only two re-call cues in the name-learning experiment outlined in Table 7.1, the photo cue and the description cue. The *d* value is .87 based on the difference between the mean recall in the photo condition (3.98) and the description condition (2.40). This *d* value allows us to say that the retrieval cue variable had a large effect on the recall of names in these two conditions. Effect size measures provide researchers with valuable information for describing the findings of an experiment.

Stat Tip

> Measures of central tendency and variability, as well as effect size, are de-scribed in Chapter 12. In that chapter we outline the computational steps for these measures and discuss their interpretation.

Key Concept

Researchers also use measures of effect size in a procedure called meta-analysis. **Meta-analysis** is a statistical technique used to summarize the effect sizes from several independent experiments investigating the same independent or dependent variable. Meta-analyses are used to answer questions like: Are there gender differences in conformity? What are the effects of class size on academic achievement? Is cognitive therapy effective in the treatment of depression? The results of individual experiments, no matter how well done, are not likely to be sufficient to provide answers to questions about such important general issues. We need to consider a body of literature (i.e., many experiments) pertaining to each issue. (See Hunt, 1997, for a good and readable introduction to meta-analysis.)

Meta-analysis allows us to draw stronger conclusions about the principles of psychology because these conclusions emerge only after looking at the relation-ships among the results of many individual experiments. Each strand con-tributes to the strength of a rope, but the rope is stronger than any strand. Similarly, each properly done experiment strengthens our confidence in a partic-ular psychological principle. The results of any individual experiment represent a strand in the stronger principles of psychology. For example, Rosenthal (1994a) used meta-analysis to summarize the results of 345 experiments on experimenter effects. Experimenter effects represent a specific instance of the more general cat-egory of interpersonal expectancy effects, which represent the effects of people's expectations on others' behavior. Table 7.2 presents the mean effect sizes for each of eight domains in which interpersonal expectancy effects have been studied. The mean effect size across all 345 studies is .70, greater than a medium effect using Cohen's (1992) scale. For four of the eight domains the mean effect size is greater than .80, indicating a large effect. Based on the results of Rosenthal's meta-analysis we can make the claim with more confidence for a general psy-chological principle: Interpersonal expectancies can influence people's behavior.

TABLE 7.2   ILLUSTRATION OF USE OF MEAN EFFECT SIZE IN META-ANALYSIS

Domain	*d*	Example of type of study
Laboratory interviews	.14	Effects of sensory restriction on reports of hallucinatory experiences
Reaction time	.17	Latency of word associations to certain stimulus words
Learning and ability	.54	IQ test scores, verbal conditioning (learning)
Person perception	.55	Perception of other people's success
Inkblot tests	.84	Ratio of animal to human Rorschach responses
Everyday situations	.88	Symbol learning, athletic performance
Psychophysical judgments	1.05	Ability to discriminate tones
Animal learning	1.73	Learning in mazes and Skinner boxes
Overall mean	.70	

Adapted from Rosenthal, R. (1994a). Interpersonal expectancy effects: A 30-year perspective. *Current Directions in Psychological Science, 3,* 176–179.

Meta-analyses provide an efficient and effective way to summarize the results of large numbers of experiments. Nevertheless, the sophisticated statistical techniques that are used in meta-analyses are powerful only when the data from the studies being analyzed have been gathered in appropriate ways. The results of meta-analyses can be misleading when experiments with poor internal validity are included. Thus, important questions regarding meta-analyses ask: Which experiments should be included in the meta-analysis? Will only experiments reported in journals with high editorial standards be included, or will the meta-analysis include research reports that have not undergone editorial review? In general, the methodological quality of the experiments included in the meta-analysis will determine its ultimate value (see Judd, Smith, & Kidder, 1991).

Confirming What the Results Reveal

- Researchers use inferential statistics to determine whether an independent variable has a reliable effect on a dependent variable.
- Two methods to make inferences based on sample data are null hypothesis testing and confidence intervals.
- Researchers use null hypothesis testing to determine whether mean differences among groups in an experiment are greater than the differences that are expected simply because of error variation.
- A statistically significant outcome is one that has a small likelihood of occurring if the null hypothesis were true.
- Researchers determine whether an independent variable has had an effect on behavior by examining whether the confidence intervals for different samples in an experiment overlap.

Perhaps the most basic claim that researchers want to make when they do an experiment is that the independent variable did have an effect on the dependent variable. Another way to phrase this claim is to say that researchers want to confirm that the independent variable *produced a difference in behavior.* Descriptive statistics alone are not sufficient evidence to confirm this basic claim.

To confirm whether the independent variable has produced an effect in an experiment, researchers use *inferential statistics.* Researchers need to use inferential statistics because of the nature of the control provided through random assignment in experiments. As we have previously described, random assignment does not eliminate the individual differences among subjects. Random assignment simply distributes the individual differences among subjects (comparably) across the groups of the experiment. That is, the differences among subjects are not allowed to vary systematically across groups. The nonsystematic variation due to differences among subjects within each group is called *error variation.* The presence of error variation poses a potential problem because the means of the different groups in the experiment may differ simply because of error variation and not because the independent variable has an effect. Thus, by themselves, the mean results of the best-controlled experiment do not permit a definite conclusion about whether the independent variable has produced a difference in behavior. Inferential statistics allow researchers to test whether differences between group means are due to an effect of the independent variable and not just due to chance (error variation). Researchers use two types of inferential statistics to make decisions about whether an independent variable has had an effect: null hypothesis testing and confidence intervals.

We realize that it may be frustrating to learn that the results of the best-controlled experiment often do not permit a definite conclusion about whether the independent variable produced a difference in behavior. In other words, what you have learned so far about research methods is not enough! Unfortunately, even with the tools of data analysis we still cannot give you a way to make *definite* conclusions about what produced a difference in behavior. But what we can give you is a way (actually, several ways) to make the best possible statement about what produced a difference. The conclusion will be based on a *probability*—namely, a probability that will help you to decide whether your effect is or is not simply due to chance. It is easy to get lost in the complexities of null hypothesis testing and confidence intervals, but keep in mind the following two critical points:

First and foremost, differences in behavior can arise simply due to chance (often referred to as *error variation*). What you want to know is, how likely it is that the difference you have observed is only due to chance (and not to the effect of your independent variable)? Actually, what you would really like to know is, how likely is it that your independent variable had an effect? However, we can't learn this information. As you will see, statistical inference is indirect (see, for example, Box 13.1 in Chapter 13).

Second, the data you have collected represent *samples* from a population; but in a sense, it is *populations* and not samples that really matter. (If only sample means mattered, then you could simply look at the sample means to see if they are different.) The mean performance for the samples in the various conditions of your experiment provides estimates that are used to *infer* the mean of the population. When you make statements of statistical inference, you are using the sample means to make decisions (inferences) about differences between (or among) population means. Once again we refer you to Chapter 13 for a more complete discussion of these issues.

Key Concept }

Key Concept }

Null Hypothesis Significance Testing (NHST)   Researchers most frequently use **null hypothesis significance testing (NHST)** to decide whether an independent variable has produced an effect in an experiment. Null hypothesis significance testing begins with the assumption that the independent variable has had *no* effect. If we assume that the null hypothesis is true, we can use probability theory to determine the probability that the difference we did observe in our experiment would occur "by chance." A **statistically significant** outcome is one that has only a small likelihood of occurring if the null hypothesis were true. A statistically significant outcome means only that the difference we obtained in our experiment is larger than would be expected if error variation alone (i.e., chance) were responsible for the outcome.

The outcome of an experiment is usually expressed in terms of the differences between the means for the conditions in the experiment. How do we know the probability of the obtained outcome in an experiment? Most often, researchers use inferential statistics tests such as the *t*-test or *F*-test. The *t*-test is used when there are two levels of the independent variable and the *F*-test is used when there are three or more levels of the independent variable. Each value of a *t*- or *F*-test has a probability value associated with it when the null hypothesis is assumed. This probability can be determined once the researcher has computed the value of the test statistic.

Just how small does the probability of our outcome need to be in order to be statistically significant? Scientists tend to agree that outcomes with probabilities (p) of less than 5 times out of 100 (or $p < .05$) are judged to be statistically significant. The probability value researchers use to decide that an outcome is statistically significant is called the *level of significance.* The level of significance is indicated by the Greek letter alpha (α).

We can now illustrate the procedures of null hypothesis testing to analyze the name-learning experiment we described earlier (see Table 7.1). The first research question we would ask is whether there was any *overall* effect of the independent variable of retrieval cue. That is, did the mean recall of names differ as a function of the three retrieval cues? The null hypothesis for this overall test is that there is no difference among the population means represented by the means of the experimental conditions (remember that the null hypothesis assumes no effect of the independent variable). The p value for the *F*-test that was computed for the effect of the retrieval cues in the name-learning experiment was $p = .001$. Because the p value for this *F*-test is less than the .05 level of significance, the overall effect of the retrieval cues was statistically significant. To interpret this outcome we would need to refer to the descriptive statistics for this experiment in Table 7.1. There we see that the mean recall for the three retrieval cues was different. For example, name recall was highest with the photo cue and lowest with the description cue. The statistically significant outcome of the *F*-test allows us to make the claim that the retrieval cues did produce a change in name recall.

Researchers want to make more specific claims about the effects of independent variables on behavior than that the independent variable did have an effect. *F*-tests of the overall differences among the means tell us that something happened in the experiment, but they don't tell us much about what did happen. To gain this more specific information about the effects of independent variables, researchers can use confidence intervals.

Using Confidence Intervals to Examine Mean Differences The confidence intervals for each of the three groups in the name-learning experiment are shown in Table 7.1. A confidence interval is associated with a probability (usually .95) that the interval contains the true population mean. The width of the interval tells us how precise our estimate is (the narrower the better). **Confidence intervals** can also be used to compare differences between two population means. We can use the .95 confidence intervals presented in Table 7.1 to ask more specific questions about the effects of the retrieval cues on name recall. We accomplish this by examining whether the confidence intervals for the different recall cue groups overlap. When the confidence intervals do not overlap, we can be confident that the population means for the two groups differ. For example, notice that the lowest estimate for the mean recall in the photo group is 3.31 and the highest estimate for the description group is 3.01. Thus, the confidence interval for the photo cue group does not overlap with the confidence interval for the description cue group. With this evidence we can make the claim that name recall with the photo cue was greater than recall with the description cue.

When we compare the confidence intervals for the photo group and the group that had both the photo and the description cues, however, we come to a different conclusion. The confidence intervals for these groups do overlap. Even though the sample means of 3.98 and 3.80 differ, we cannot conclude that the population means differ because of the overlap of the confidence intervals. We can offer the following rule of thumb for interpreting this result: If intervals overlap slightly, then we must acknowledge our uncertainty about the true mean difference and postpone judgment; if the intervals overlap such that the mean of one group lies within the interval of another group, we may conclude that the population means do not differ. In this case the overlap is such that the mean of the photo group lies within the interval for the photo-plus-description group. We will want to conclude that the population means do not differ; however, as we will see in the next section, what we really are saying is that we don't have sufficient evidence to state that they do, in fact, differ.

Key Concept

The logic and computational procedures for confidence intervals and for the *t*-test are found in Chapter 12. The *F*-test (in its various forms) is discussed in Chapter 13. Confidence intervals and rules for their interpretation are found in Chapter 12 (see especially Box 12.5).

What Data Analysis Can't Tell Us

We've already alluded to one thing that our data analysis can't tell us. Even if our experiment is internally valid and the results are statistically significant, we cannot say *for sure* that our variable had an effect (or did not have an effect). We must learn to live with probability statements. The results of our data analysis also can't tell us whether the results of our study have practical value or even if they are meaningful. It is easy to do experiments that ask trivial research questions (see Sternberg, 1997, and Chapter 1). It is also easy (maybe too easy!) to do a bad experiment. Bad experiments—that is, ones that lack internal validity—can easily produce statistically significant outcomes and nonoverlapping confidence intervals; however, the outcome will be uninterpretable.

When an outcome is statistically significant, we conclude that the independent variable produced an effect on behavior. Yet, as we have seen, our analysis does not provide us with certainty regarding our conclusion, even though we reached the conclusion "beyond a reasonable doubt." When an outcome is not statistically significant, we also cannot conclude with certainty that the independent variable did not have an effect. All we can conclude is that we do not have sufficient evidence to claim that the independent variable does have an effect. Determining that an independent variable has not had an effect can be even more crucial in applied research. For example, is a generic drug as effective as its brand name counterpart? The standards for experiments attempting to answer questions like these are higher than those for experiments seeking to confirm that an independent variable does have an effect. We describe these standards in Chapter 13.

Because researchers rely on probabilities to make decisions about the effects of independent variables, there is always some chance of making an error. There are two types of errors that can occur when researchers use inferential statistics. When we claim that an outcome is statistically significant and the null hypothesis is really true, we are making a Type I error. A *Type I error* is like a false alarm—saying that there is a fire when there is not. When we conclude that we have insufficient evidence to reject the null hypothesis and it is, in fact, false, we are making a *Type II error* (Type I and Type II errors are described more fully in Chapter 13). We would never make either of these errors if we could know for sure whether the null hypothesis was true or false. While being mindful of the possibility that data analysis can lead to incorrect decisions, we must also remember that data analysis can—and does—lead to correct decisions. The most important thing for researchers to remember is that inferential statistics can never replace replication as the ultimate test of the reliability of an experimental outcome.

ESTABLISHING THE EXTERNAL VALIDITY OF EXPERIMENTAL FINDINGS

- The findings of an experiment have external validity when they can be applied to other individuals, settings, and conditions beyond the scope of the specific experiment.

- In some investigations (e.g., theory-testing), researchers may choose to emphasize internal validity over external validity; other researchers may choose to increase external validity using sampling or replication.
- Conducting field experiments is one way that researchers can increase the external validity of their research in real-world settings.
- Partial replication is a useful method for establishing the external validity of research findings.
- Researchers often seek to generalize results about conceptual relationships among variables rather than specific conditions, manipulations, settings, and samples.

As you learned in Chapter 4, *external validity* refers to the extent to which findings from an experiment can be generalized to individuals, settings, and conditions beyond the scope of the specific experiment. A frequent criticism of highly controlled experiments is that they lack external validity. That is, the findings observed in a controlled laboratory experiment may describe what happens only in that specific setting, with the specific conditions that were tested, and with the specific individuals who participated. Consider again the Loftus and Burns (1982) experiment on the effects of a mentally shocking event on memory. Small groups of college students in this experiment viewed a film in a laboratory setting. The laboratory setting is ideally suited for exercising control procedures that insure the internal validity of an experiment. But, do these findings help us understand eyewitness behavior in a natural setting such as an actual bank? When a different type of traumatic event is involved? When the eyewitnesses are senior citizens? These are questions of external validity, and they raise a more general question. If the findings of laboratory experiments are so specific, what good are they to society?

One answer to this question is a bit unsettling, at least initially. Mook (1983) argued that, when the purpose of an experiment is to test a specific hypothesis derived from a psychological theory, the question of external validity of the findings is irrelevant. An experiment is often done to determine whether subjects *can* be induced to behave in a certain way. The question whether subjects *do* behave that way in their natural environment is secondary to the question raised in the experiment. The issue of the external validity of experiments is not a new one, as reflected in the following statement by Riley (1962, p. 413): "In general, laboratory experiments are not set up to imitate the most typical case found in nature. Instead, they are intended to answer some specific question of interest to the experimenter."

Of course, researchers often do want to obtain findings that they can generalize beyond the boundaries of the experiment itself. Researchers seeking to generalize their findings can include the characteristics of the situations to which they wish to generalize in their experiments. For example, Ceci (1993) described a research program that he and his colleagues conducted on children's eyewitness testimony. He described how their research program was motivated in part because previous studies on this topic did not capture all the

FIGURE 7.4   How similar can experiments be to real-life situations such as children testifying in court?

dimensions of an *actual* eyewitness situation. Ceci described how their research program included factors such as multiple suggestive interviews, very long retention intervals, and recollections of stressful experiences. Including these factors made the experiments more representative of situations that are actually involved when children testify.

Ceci (1993) also pointed out, however, that important differences remained between the experiments and real-life situations:

> High levels of stress, assaults to a victim's body, and the loss of control are characteristics of events that motivate forensic investigations. Although these factors are at play in some of our other studies, we will never mimic experimentally the assaultive nature of acts perpetrated on child victims, because even those studies that come closest, such as the medical studies, are socially and parentally sanctioned, unlike sexual assaults against children. (pp. 41–42)

As Ceci's comments reveal, in some situations, such as those involving eyewitness testimony about despicable acts, there may be important ethical constraints on establishing the external validity of experiments.

It may prove easier for researchers to include more representative samples of *situations* in psychology experiments than to include more representative samples of people. The external validity of psychological research findings is frequently questioned because of the nature of the "subjects." As you are aware, many studies in psychology involve college students who participate in experiments as part of their introductory psychology course. Dawes (1991), among others, argues that college students are a select group who may not always provide a good basis for building general conclusions about human behavior and mental processes. He suggests that the college environment tends to protect students from external problems, thereby enhancing their feeling of control over their lives. People living outside the college environment may not have the same sense of control that college students do. Thus, research on "locus of control" done with college students may not generalize to people living outside the college environment. In general, the arguments raised by Dawes and others should lead us to exercise care in generalizing conclusions from studies in which college students are participants.

Sue (1999) also raises concerns about the external validity of psychological research findings. He argues that the greater emphasis that researchers place on internal validity over external validity in their research lessens the attention paid to the representativeness of the people who are studied in psychological research. He further suggests that the emphasis on internal validity over external validity has hindered the development of research on ethnic minority groups. If psychologists believe that their research findings will generalize to populations other than those specifically tested in their research, there is little reason to cross-validate the findings by testing ethnic minority populations. Questions about the external validity of research findings based on the populations being studied are especially important in applied research. In medical research, for example, effective treatments for men may not be effective for women and effective treatments for adults may not be effective for children.

Field experiments, which we mentioned briefly in Chapter 4, are one way to increase the external validity of a research study. They can also yield practical knowledge. For example, Crusco and Wetzel (1984) investigated the effect of touching on restaurant customers. Female wait staff, working as confederates, touched restaurant customers on either the hand or the shoulder when returning change. The researchers speculated that a touch on the hand would produce positive feelings toward the server. They also hypothesized that a touch on the shoulder would be seen as a sign of dominance and therefore would not be viewed positively, especially by male diners. The researchers randomly assigned 114 diners to three levels of the independent variable: *Fleeting Touch,* when the wait staff person touched the diner's palm for 1/2 second when returning change; *Shoulder Touch,* when she placed her hand for 1 to 1½ seconds on the diner's shoulder as she gave back change; and *No Touch,* when no physical contact was made with the customers. The major dependent variable was the size of the tip. Both male and female diners gave a significantly larger tip after being touched than when not touched. Contrary to the researchers' expectations, however, the nature of the touch did not make a difference. Both male and female diners gave equally large tips when they were touched on the hand or the shoulder. Because this experiment was carried out in a natural setting, it is more likely to be representative of "real-world" conditions. Thus, we can be more confident that the results will generalize to other real-world settings than if an artificial situation had been created in the laboratory.

The external validity of experimental findings can be established through *partial replication.* Partial replications are commonly done as a routine part of the process of investigating the conditions under which a phenomenon reliably occurs. A partial replication can help to establish external validity by showing that a similar experimental result occurs when slightly different experimental procedures are used. Consider the same basic experiment done in both a large metropolitan public university and in a small rural private college; the participants and the settings in the experiments are very different. If the same results are obtained even with these different participants and settings, we can say the findings can be generalized across these two populations and settings. Notice that neither experiment alone has external validity; it is *the findings* that occur in *both* experiments that have external validity.

Researchers can also establish the external validity of their findings by doing *conceptual replications*. What we wish to generalize from any one study are conceptual relationships among variables, not the specific conditions, manipulations, settings, or samples (see Banaji & Crowder, 1989; Mook, 1983). Anderson and Bushman (1997) provide an example illustrating the logic of a conceptual replication. Consider that we did a study with 5-year-old children to determine if a specific insult ("pooh-pooh-head") induces anger and aggression. We could then do a replication to see if the same insult produces the same result with 35 year-old adults. As Anderson and Bushman state, the findings for 5-year-olds probably wouldn't be replicated with the 35-year-olds because "'pooh-pooh-head' just doesn't pack the same 'punch' for 5- and 35-year-old people" (p. 21). However, if we wish to establish the external validity of the idea that "insults increase aggressive behavior," we can use different words that are meaningful insults for each population.

When Anderson and Bushman (1997) examined variables related to aggression at the conceptual level, they found that findings from experiments conducted in laboratory settings and findings from correlational studies in "real-world" settings were very similar. They concluded that "artificial" laboratory experiments do provide meaningful information about aggression because they demonstrate the same conceptual relationships that are observed in real-world aggression. Furthermore, laboratory experiments allow researchers to isolate the potential causes of aggression and to investigate boundary conditions for when aggression will or will not occur.

What about when results in the lab and the real world disagree? Anderson and Bushman (1997) argue that these discrepancies, rather than evidence for the weakness of either method, should be used to help us refine our theories about aggression. That is, the discrepancies should make us recognize that different psychological processes may be at work in each setting. When we increase our understanding of these discrepancies, we will increase our understanding of aggression.

Establishing the external validity of each finding in psychology by performing partial replications or conceptual replications would be virtually impossible. But if we take arguments like those of Dawes (1991) and Sue (1999) seriously, as indeed we should, it would appear that we are facing an impossible task. How, for instance, could we show that an experimental finding obtained with a group of college students will generalize to groups of older adults, working professionals, less educated individuals, and so forth? Underwood and Shaughnessy (1975) suggest one possible approach worth considering. Their notion is that we should assume that behavior is relatively continuous across time, subjects, and settings unless we have reason to assume otherwise. Ultimately, the external validity of research findings is likely to be established more by the good judgment of the scientific community than by definitive empirical evidence.

MATCHED GROUPS DESIGN

- A matched groups design may be used to create comparable groups when there are too few subjects available for random assignment to work effectively.
- Matching subjects on the dependent variable task is the best approach for creating matched groups, but performance on any matching task must correlate with the dependent variable task.
- After subjects are matched on the matching task they should then be randomly assigned to the conditions of the independent variable.

To work effectively the random groups design requires samples of sufficient size to assure that individual differences among subjects will be balanced through random assignment. That is, the assumption behind the random groups design is that individual differences "average out" across groups. But how many subjects are required to assure that this averaging process works as it should? The answer is, "It depends." More subjects will be needed to average out individual differences when samples are drawn from a heterogeneous population than from a more homogeneous one.

We can be relatively confident that random assignment will not be effective in balancing the differences among subjects when small numbers of subjects are tested from heterogeneous populations. However, this is exactly the situation researchers face in several areas of psychology. For example, some developmental psychologists study newborn infants; others study the elderly. These psychologists often have available only limited numbers of participants, and both newborns and the elderly certainly represent diverse populations.

One alternative that researchers have in this situation is to administer all the conditions of the experiment to all the subjects, using a repeated measures design (to be discussed in Chapter 8). Nevertheless, some independent variables require separate groups of subjects for each level. For instance, suppose you wish to administer two types of postnatal care to different groups of premature infants. In this situation, and many others, you will need to test separate groups in your experiment.

The matched groups design is a good alternative when neither the random groups design nor repeated measures design can be used effectively. The logic

Key Concept

of the **matched groups design** is simple and compelling. Instead of trusting random assignment to form comparable groups, the researcher makes the groups equivalent by matching subjects. Once comparable groups have been formed based on the matching, the logic of the matched groups design is the same as that for the random groups design. In most uses of the matched groups design, a pretest task is used to match subjects. The challenge is to select a pretest task (also called a matching task) that equates the groups on a dimension that is relevant to the outcome of the experiment. *The matched groups design is useful only when a good matching task is available.*

The most preferred matching task is one that uses the same task that will be used in the experiment itself. For example, if the dependent variable in the experiment is blood pressure, participants should be matched on blood pressure prior to the start of the experiment. The matching is accomplished by measuring the blood pressure of all participants and then forming pairs or triples or quadruples of participants (depending on the number of conditions in the experiment) who have identical or similar blood pressures. Thus, at the start of the experiment, participants in the different groups will have, *on average,* equivalent blood pressure. Researchers can then reasonably attribute any group differences in blood pressure at the end of the study to the treatment (presuming other potential variables have been held constant or balanced).

In some experiments, the primary dependent variable cannot be used to match subjects. For example, consider an experiment that examines different approaches to solving a puzzle. If a pretest were given to see how long it took individuals to solve this puzzle, the participants would likely learn the solution to the puzzle during the pretest. If so, then it would be impossible to observe differences in the speed with which different groups of participants solved the puzzle in the experiment itself. In this situation the next best alternative for a matching task is to use a task from the same class or category as the experimental task. In our problem-solving experiment, participants could be matched on their performance when solving a different puzzle from the experimental puzzle. A less preferred, but still possible, alternative for matching is to use a task from a class different from the experimental task. For our problem-solving experiment, participants could be matched on some test of general ability, such as a test of spatial ability. When using these alternatives, however, researchers must confirm that performance on the matching task correlates with the performance on the task that is used in the experiment. In general, as the correlation between the matching task and the dependent variable decreases, the advantage of the matched groups design, relative to the random groups design, also decreases.

Even when a good matching task is available, matching is not sufficient to form comparable groups in an experiment. For example, consider an experiment comparing two different methods of caring for premature infants. The matched groups design would work well for this type of experiment. Six pairs of premature infants could be matched on their body weight and on measures such as their scores on an infant motor coordination test. This experiment illustrates the conditions when a matched groups design is most helpful—the need to test separate groups with only small numbers of participants and good matching tasks available. We began our discussion of the matched groups design by saying it is useful when we have too few participants to allow

FIGURE 7.5   Random assignment is not likely to be effective in balancing differences among subjects when small numbers of subjects from heterogeneous populations are tested (e.g., newborns). In this situation, researchers may want to consider the matched groups design.

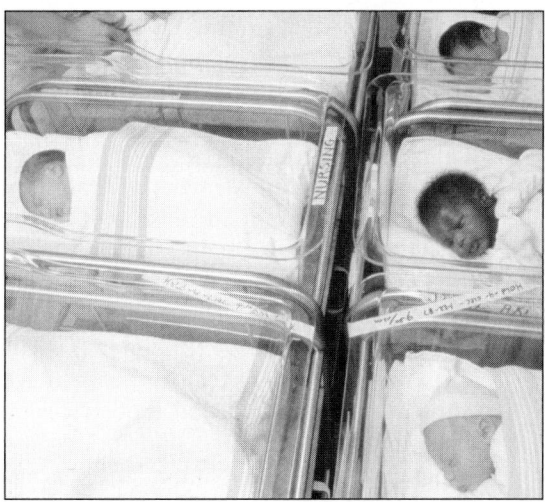

randomization to form comparable groups. The matched groups design serves a very important purpose by allowing us to form comparable groups on the significant dimensions reflected in good matching tasks (e.g., body weights of premature infants). There remain, however, potentially relevant characteristics of the participants beyond those measured by the matching task. For example, the two groups of premature infants may not be comparable in their general health or in their degree of parental attachment. It is important, therefore, to use random assignment in the matched groups design to try to balance other potential factors beyond the matching task. Specifically, after matching the infants on body weight and motor coordination, the pairs of infants would be randomly assigned to one of the two groups. In conclusion, *the matched groups design is a better alternative than the random groups design when a good matching task is available and when only a small number of subjects is available for an experiment that requires separate groups for each condition.*

NATURAL GROUPS DESIGN

- Individual differences variables (or subject variables) are selected rather than manipulated to form natural groups designs.
- The natural groups design represents a type of correlational research in which researchers look for covariations between natural groups variables and dependent variables.
- Causal inferences cannot be made regarding the effects of natural groups variables because plausible alternative explanations for group differences exist.

Key Concept

Researchers in many areas of psychology are interested in independent variables that are called **individual differences variables** or *subject variables*. An individual differences variable is a characteristic or trait that varies across individuals. Religious affiliation is an example of an individual differences variable. Researchers can't manipulate this variable by randomly assigning people to Catholic, Jewish, Muslim, Protestant, or other groups. Instead, researchers "control" the religious affiliation variable by systematically selecting individuals who *naturally* belong to these groups. Individual differences variables such as gender, introversion-extraversion, race, age, or aggressiveness are important independent variables in personality psychology, abnormal psychology, developmental psychology, and social psychology.

Key Concept

It is important to differentiate experiments involving independent variables whose levels are selected from those involving independent variables whose levels are manipulated. Experiments involving independent variables whose levels are selected—like individual differences variables—are called **natural groups designs.** The natural groups design is frequently used in situations in which ethical and practical constraints prevent us from directly manipulating independent variables. No matter how interested we might be in the effects of traumatic events such as major surgery on subsequent depression, we could not ethically perform major surgery on a randomly assigned group of introductory psychology students and then compare their depression symptoms with those of another group who did not receive surgery! Similarly, if we were interested in the relationship between divorce and emotional disorders, we could not randomly assign some people to get divorced. By using the natural groups design, however, we can compare people who have had surgery with those who have not. Similarly, people who have chosen to divorce can be compared with those who have chosen to stay married.

Researchers use natural groups designs to meet the first two objectives of the scientific method: description and prediction. For example, studies have shown that people who are separated or divorced are much more likely to receive psychiatric care than are those who are married, widowed, or have remained single. On the basis of studies like these we can describe divorced and married individuals in terms of emotional disorders, and we can predict which group is more likely to experience emotional disorders.

Serious problems can arise, though, when the results of natural groups designs are used to make causal statements. For instance, the finding that divorced persons are more likely than married persons to receive psychiatric care shows that these two factors covary. This finding could be taken to mean that divorce causes emotional disorders that lead to the need for psychiatric care. But, before we conclude that divorce *causes* emotional disorders, we must assure ourselves that the time-order condition for a causal inference has been met. Does divorce precede the emotional disorder or does the emotional disorder precede the divorce? A natural groups design does not tell us.

The natural groups design also poses problems when we try to satisfy the third condition for demonstrating causality, eliminating plausible alternative causes. The individual differences studied in the natural groups design are usually confounded—groups of individuals are likely to differ in many ways *in addition* to the variable used to classify them. For example, individuals who divorce and individuals who stay married may differ with respect to a number of characteristics other than their marital status. They may differ in their religious practices or financial circumstances. Any differences observed between divorced and married individuals may be due to these other characteristics, not divorce. The manipulation done by "nature" is rarely the controlled type we have come to expect in establishing the internal validity of an experiment.

There are approaches for drawing causal inferences in the natural groups design. One effective approach requires that individual differences be studied in combination with independent variables that can be manipulated. This combination of more than one independent variable in one experiment requires the use of a complex design, which we will describe in Chapter 9. For now, recognize that drawing causal inferences based on the natural groups design can be a treacherous enterprise. Although such designs are sometimes referred to as "experiments," there are important differences between an experiment involving an individual differences variable and an experiment involving a manipulated variable.

SUMMARY

Researchers conduct experiments to test hypotheses derived from theories, but experiments can also be used to test the effectiveness of treatments or programs in applied settings. The experimental method is ideally suited to identifying cause-and-effect relationships when the control techniques of manipulation, holding conditions constant, and balancing are properly implemented.

In Chapter 7 we focused on applying these control techniques in experiments in which different groups of subjects are given different treatments representing the levels of the independent variable. In the random groups design, the groups are formed using randomization procedures such that the groups are comparable at the start of the experiment. If the groups perform differently following the manipulation, it is presumed that the independent variable is responsible. Random assignment is the most common method of forming comparable groups. By distributing subjects' characteristics equally across the conditions of the experiment, random assignment is an attempt to ensure that the differences among subjects are balanced across groups in the experiment. The most common technique for carrying out random assignment is block randomization.

There are several threats to the internal validity of experiments that involve testing independent groups. Testing intact groups even when the groups are randomly assigned to conditions should be avoided because the use of intact groups is highly likely to result in a confounding. Extraneous variables, such as different rooms or different experimenters, must not be allowed to confound the independent variable of interest.

A more serious threat to the internal validity of the random groups design is involved when subjects fail to complete the experiment successfully. Selective subject loss occurs when subjects are lost differentially across the conditions and some characteristic of the subject that is related to the outcome of the experiment is responsible for the loss. We can help prevent selective loss by restricting subjects to those likely to complete the experiment successfully, or we can compensate for it by selectively dropping comparable subjects from the group that did not experience the loss. Demand characteristics and experimenter effects can be minimized through the use of proper experimental procedures, but they can best be controlled by using placebo control and double-blind procedures.

Data analysis and statistics provide an alternative to replication for determining whether the results of a single experiment can be used as evidence to make a claim that an independent variable has had an effect on behavior. Data analysis involves the use of both descriptive statistics and inferential statistics. Describing the results of an experiment typically involves the use of means, standard deviations, confidence intervals, and measures of effect size. Meta-analysis makes use of measures of effect size to provide a quantitative summary of the results of a large number of experiments on an important research problem.

Inferential statistics are important in data analysis because researchers need a way to decide whether the obtained differences in an experiment are due to chance or are due to the effect of the independent variable. Confidence intervals and null hypothesis testing are two effective statistical techniques researchers can use to analyze experiments. Statistical analysis cannot guarantee, however, that experimental findings will be meaningful or be of practical significance. Replication remains the ultimate test of the reliability of a research finding.

Researchers also strive to establish the external validity of their experimental findings. When testing psychological theories, researchers tend to emphasize internal validity over external validity. One effective approach for establishing the external validity of findings is to select representative samples of all dimensions on which you wish to generalize. By conducting field experiments researchers can increase the external validity of their research findings to real-world settings. Partial replications and conceptual replications are two more common ways that researchers use to establish external validity.

The matched groups design is an alternative to the random groups design when only a small number of subjects is available, along with a good matching task and when the experiment requires separate groups for each treatment. The biggest problem with the matched groups design is that the groups are equated only on the characteristic measured by the matching task. In the natural groups design, researchers select the levels of independent variables (usually individual differences or subject variables) and look for systematic relationships between these independent variables and other aspects of behavior. Essentially, the natural groups design involves looking for correlations between subjects' characteristics and their performance. Such correlational research designs pose problems in drawing causal inferences.

KEY CONCEPTS

internal validity	**replication**
independent groups designs	**effect size**
random groups design	**Cohen's *d***
random assignment	**meta-analysis**
block randomization	**null hypothesis significance**
threats to internal validity	**testing (NHST)**
mechanical subject loss	**statistically significant**
selective subject loss	**confidence interval**
experimenter effects	**matched groups design**
placebo control	**individual differences variable**
double-blind	**natural groups design**

REVIEW QUESTIONS

1 Describe two reasons why psychologists conduct experiments.
2 Describe how the control techniques of manipulation, holding conditions constant, and balancing contribute to meeting the three conditions necessary for a causal inference.
3 Explain why a research study conducted using the one-group pretest-posttest design has very little internal validity.
4 Explain why comparable groups are such an essential feature of the random groups design, and describe how researchers achieve comparable groups.
5 What preventive steps could you take if you anticipate that selective subject loss may pose a problem in your experiment?
6 Explain how placebo control and double-blind techniques can be used to control demand characteristics and experimenter effects.
7 Explain why meta-analysis allows researchers to draw stronger conclusions about the principles of psychology.
8 Explain what a statistically significant outcome of an inferential statistics test tells you about the effect of the independent variable in an experiment.
9 Explain what you could conclude if the confidence intervals did not overlap when you were testing for a difference between means for two conditions in an experiment.
10 Briefly describe four ways researchers can establish the external validity of a research finding.
11 Briefly explain the logic of the matched groups design and identify the three conditions under which the matched groups design is a better alternative than the random groups design.

12 How do individual differences variables differ from manipulated independent variables, and why does this difference make it difficult to draw causal inferences on the basis of the natural groups design?

CHALLENGE QUESTIONS

1 An experimenter is planning to do a random groups design experiment to study the effect of the rate of presenting stimuli on people's ability to recognize the stimuli. The independent variable is the presentation rate, and it will be manipulated at four levels: Very Fast, Fast, Slow, and Very Slow. The experimenter is seeking your help and advice with the following aspects of the experiment:

A The experimenter asks you to prepare a block-randomized schedule such that there will be four participants in each of the four conditions. To do this you can use the following random numbers that were taken from the random number table in the Appendix (Table A.1).

1-5-6-6-4-1-0-4-9-3-2-0-4-9-2-3-8-3-9-1
9-1-1-3-2-2-1-9-9-9-5-9-5-1-6-8-1-6-5-2
2-7-1-9-5-4-8-2-2-3-4-6-7-5-1-2-2-9-2-3

B The experimenter is considering restricting participants to those who pass a stringent reaction time test so as to be sure that they will be able to perform the task successfully with the Very Fast presentation rate. Explain what factors the experimenter should consider in making this decision, being sure to describe clearly what risks, if any, are taken if only this restricted set of participants is tested.

C The experimenter discovers that it will be necessary to test participants in two different rooms. How should the experimenter arrange the testing of the conditions in these two rooms so as to avoid possible confounding by this extraneous variable?

2 A researcher conducted a series of experiments on the effects of external factors that might influence people's persistence in exercise programs. In one of these experiments, the researcher manipulated three types of distraction while participants walked on a treadmill. The three types of distraction were concentrating on one's own thoughts (concentration group), listening to a tape of music (music group), and watching a video of people engaging in outdoor recreation (video group). The dependent variable was how strenuous the treadmill exercise was at the time the participant decided to end the session (the

incline of the treadmill was regularly increased as the person went through the session, thereby making the exercise increasingly strenuous). In an introductory psychology course, 120 students volunteered to participate in the experiment, and the researcher randomly assigned 40 students to each of the three levels of the distraction variable. The researcher expected that the mean strenuousness score would be highest in the video group, next highest in the music group, and lowest in the concentration group.

After only 2 minutes on the treadmill, each participant was given the option to stop the experiment. This brief time interval was chosen so that participants were given the option to stop before any of them could reasonably be expected to be experiencing fatigue. Data for the participants who decided to stop after only 2 minutes were not included in the analysis of the final results. Fifteen students chose to stop in the concentration group; ten stopped in the music group; and no students stopped in the video group. The results did not support the researcher's predictions. The mean strenuousness score for students who completed the experiment was highest for the concentration group ($n = 25$), next highest for the music group ($n = 30$), and lowest for the video group ($n = 40$).

A Identify a possible threat to the internal validity of this experiment and explain how this problem could account for the unexpected results of the study.

B Assume that a pretest measure was available for each of the 120 participants and that the pretest measured the degree to which each subject was likely to persist at exercise. Describe how you could use these pretest scores to confirm that the problem you identified in question 2A had occurred.

3 The newspaper headline summarizing research that had been reported in a medical journal read: "Study: Exercise Helps at Any Age." The research described in the article involved a 10-year study of nearly 10,000 men—and only men. The men were given a treadmill test between 1970 and 1989. Then they were given a second treadmill test 5 years after the

first test and their health was monitored for another 5 years. Men who were judged unfit on both treadmill tests had a death rate over the next 5 years of 122 per 10,000. Men judged fit on both treadmill tests had a 5-year death rate of only 40 per 10,000. Most interestingly, men judged unfit on the first treadmill test but fit on the second had a death rate of 68 per 10,000. The benefits of exercise were even greater when only deaths from heart attacks were examined. The benefits from exercise were present across a wide range of ages—thus, the headline.

A Why is the newspaper headline for this article potentially misleading?

B Why do you think the researchers tested only men?

C Identify two different ways of obtaining evidence that you could use to decide whether the results of this study could be applied to women. One of the ways would make use of already published research and the other way would require doing a new study.

4 An experiment was done to test the effectiveness of a drug that is being considered for possible use in the treatment of people who experience chronic anxiety. Fifty people who are chronically anxious are identified through a local health clinic and all 50 people give their informed consent to participate in the experiment. Twenty-five people are randomly assigned to the experimental group, and they receive the drug. The other 25 people are randomly assigned to the control group, and they receive a placebo. The participants in both groups are monitored by a physician and a clinical psychologist during the 6-week treatment period. After the treatment period, the participants provide a self-rating on a reliable and valid 20-point scale indicating the level of anxiety they are experiencing (higher scores indicate greater anxiety). The mean self-rating in the experimental group was 10.2 ($SD = 1.5$) and the mean rating in the control group was 13.5 ($SD = 2.0$). The .95 confidence interval for the mean self-rating in the experimental group was 9.9 to 10.5. The .95 confidence interval for the control group was 13.1 to 13.9.

A Explain why a double-blind procedure would be useful in this experiment and describe how the double-blind procedure could be carried out in this experiment.

B What information would you use to begin to describe "what happened" in this experiment?

C The probability associated with the test for the mean difference between the two groups was $p = .01$. What claim would you make about the effect of the treatment based on this probability? What claim would you make based on the estimates of the population means for the two groups in this experiment based on a comparison of the confidence intervals?

D The effect size for the treatment variable in this experiment is $d = .37$. What information does this effect size tell you about the effectiveness of the drug beyond what you know from the test of statistical significance and from comparing the confidence intervals?

Answer to Stretching Exercise

1   The students manipulated the independent variable in their study. There were three levels of the independent variable: no one sitting on the bench; confederate reading on the bench; and confederate sitting on the bench and staring at the participant.

2   The students held several factors constant: the path, the bench, and they observed only participants walking alone.

3   The teams of students balanced the characteristics of the participants across the three conditions by testing the conditions in a random order. The pairs of observers and confederates were also balanced across conditions because each pair observed one participant in each of the three conditions.

Answer to Challenge Question 1

A The first step is to assign a number from 1 to 4 to the respective conditions: 1 = Very Fast; 2 = Fast; 3 = Slow; and 4 = Very Slow. Then, using the random numbers, select four sequences of the numbers from 1 to 4. In doing this you skip any numbers greater than 4 and any number that is a repetition of a number already selected in the sequence. For example, if the first number you select is a 1, you skip all repetitions of 1 until you have selected all the numbers for the sequence of 1 to 4. Following this procedure and working across the rows of random numbers from left to right, we obtained the following four sequences for the four blocks of the randomized block schedule. The order of the conditions for each block is also presented. The block-randomized schedule specifies the order of testing the conditions for the first 16 participants in the experiment.

Block 1: 1-4-3-2 Very Fast, Very Slow, Slow, Fast

Block 2: 4-2-3-1 Very Slow, Fast, Slow, Very Fast

Block 3: 1-3-2-4 Very Fast, Slow, Fast, Very Slow

Block 4: 2-3-4-1 Fast, Slow, Very Slow, Very Fast

B The investigator is taking a reasonable step to avoid selective subject loss, but restricting participants to those who pass a stringent reaction time test entails the risk of decreased external validity of the obtained findings.

C The rooms can be balanced by assigning entire blocks from the block-randomized schedule to be tested in each room. Usually, the number of blocks assigned to each room is equal, but this is not essential. For effective balancing, however, several blocks should be tested in each room.

CHAPTER EIGHT

Repeated Measures Designs

CHAPTER OUTLINE

OVERVIEW

Thus far we have considered experiments in which subjects participate in only one condition of the experiment. They are randomly assigned to one condition in the random groups and matched groups designs, or they are selected to be in one group in natural groups designs. These independent groups designs are powerful tools for studying the effects of a wide range of independent variables. There are times, however, when it is more effective to have each subject participate in all the conditions of an experiment. These designs are called **repeated measures designs** (or within-subjects designs). In an independent groups design, there is a separate group that serves as a control for the group given the experimental treatment. In a repeated measures design, subjects *serve as their own controls* because they participate in both the experimental and control conditions.

Key Concept

We begin this chapter by exploring the reasons why researchers choose to use a repeated measures design. We then describe one of the central features of repeated measures designs. In repeated measures designs, participants can undergo changes during the experiment as they are repeatedly tested. Participants may improve with practice, for example, because they learn more about the task or because they become more relaxed in the experimental situation. They also may get worse with practice—for example, because of fatigue or reduced motivation. These temporary changes are called *practice effects*.

We described in Chapter 7 that individual differences among participants cannot be eliminated in the random groups design, but they can be balanced by using random assignment. Similarly, the practice effects that participants experience due to repeated testing in the repeated measures designs cannot be eliminated. Like individual differences in the random groups design, however, practice effects can be balanced across the conditions of a repeated measures design experiment. When practice effects are balanced, the effect of an independent variable in a repeated measures design experiment is interpretable. Balancing *does not eliminate* practice effects from repeated measures designs. Balancing works by *averaging out* the practice effects across conditions. By doing this, we avoid confounding practice effects with the conditions of the experiment.

Our primary focus in this chapter is to describe the techniques that researchers can use to balance practice effects. We also introduce data analysis procedures for repeated measures designs. We conclude the chapter with a consideration of problems that can arise in repeated measures designs.

WHY RESEARCHERS USE REPEATED MEASURES DESIGNS

- Researchers choose to use a repeated measures design in order to (1) conduct an experiment when few participants are available, (2) conduct the experiment more efficiently, (3) increase the sensitivity of the experiment, and (4) study changes in participants' behavior over time.

Researchers gain several advantages when they choose to use a repeated measures design. First, repeated measures designs require fewer participants, so these designs are ideal for situations in which only a small number of participants is available. Researchers who do experiments with children, the elderly, or special populations such as individuals with brain injuries frequently have a small number of participants available.

Researchers choose to use repeated measures designs even when sufficient numbers of participants are available for an independent groups design. The repeated measures designs often are more convenient and efficient. For example, Ludwig, Jeeves, Norman, and DeWitt (1993) conducted a series of experiments studying communication between the two hemispheres of the brain. The investigators measured how long it took participants to decide whether two briefly presented letters had the same name. The letters came from the set AaBb. Participants were to press the "match" key when the letters had the same name (AA, aa, Bb) and the "no match" key when the letters had different names (AB, ab, Ab). There were several different ways in which the pairs of letters were presented across four experiments, but there were two major conditions in these experiments. Either both letters were presented to one hemisphere (unilateral) or one letter of the pair was presented to each hemisphere (bilateral). Across four experiments, bilateral presentation led to faster response times than did unilateral presentation. In these experiments, two hemispheres were better than one!

Each trial in the Ludwig et al. (1993) experiment required only a few seconds to complete. They could have tested separate groups of participants for the unilateral and bilateral conditions, but this approach would have been horribly inefficient. It would have taken more time to instruct participants regarding the nature of the task than it would have to do the task itself! A repeated measures design in which each participant was tested on both unilateral and bilateral trials provided the experimenters with a far more convenient and efficient way to answer their question about how the brain processes information.

Key Concept

Another important advantage of repeated measures designs is that they are generally more sensitive than an independent groups design. The **sensitivity** of an experiment refers to the ability to detect the effect of the independent variable on the dependent variable even if the effect is a small one. An experiment is more sensitive when there is less variability in participants' responses within a condition of the experiment. That is, participants in any one condition will not all respond the same way. This *error variation* can be due to variations in the procedure each time the experiment is conducted or to individual differences in the participants. In general, participants in a repeated measures design will vary within themselves over time less than participants in a random groups design will vary from other participants. Another way to say this is that there is usually more variation *between* people than there is *within* people. Thus, error variation will generally be less in a repeated measures design. The less error variation, the easier it is to detect the effect of an independent variable. The increased sensitivity of repeated measures designs is especially attractive to researchers who are studying independent variables that have small (hard-to-see) effects on behavior.

Researchers also choose to use a repeated measures design because some areas of psychological research require its use. When the research question involves studying changes in participants' behavior over time, such as in a learning experiment or in a longitudinal design (see Chapter 5), a repeated measures design is needed. Further, whenever the experimental procedure requires that participants compare two or more stimuli relative to one another, a repeated measures design must be used. For example, a repeated measures design would have to be used if a researcher wanted to measure the minimum amount of light that must be added before participants could detect that a spot of light had become brighter. It would also be called for if a researcher wanted participants to rate the relative attractiveness of a series of photographs. Research areas such as psychophysics (illustrated by the light-detection experiment) and scaling (illustrated by the ratings of attractiveness) rely heavily on repeated measures designs. Journals such as *Perception & Psychophysics* and *Journal of Experimental Psychology: Human Perception and Performance* frequently publish results of experiments using repeated measures designs.

BOX 8.1

REPEATED MEASUREMENTS AND THE REPEATED MEASURES DESIGN

It is important to distinguish among different situations in which researchers test participants repeatedly. Researchers frequently measure participants on more than one occasion. There are important reasons for doing this, and these reasons usually have to do with the reliability of measurements. Researchers may obtain two (or more) measures of the same individual in order to establish the reliability (consistency) of a measure. For example, a group of participants may be given the same aptitude test on two different occasions in order to assess the *test-retest reliability* of the aptitude test. A correlation coefficient would likely be used to determine the reliability of the aptitude test. Another reason for testing participants repeatedly is to obtain a more stable and, hence, reliable measure of behavior. For example, consider a study of individuals' current level of depression based on a self-report inventory. An investigator who measures depression would probably not want to use a questionnaire that has only one item asking about depression. Rather, such a measure will be more reliable if it is based on people's responses to many different items asking about their current mood.

It is important to distinguish the repeated measures design from situations in which researchers test participants repeatedly either to determine the reliability of a test or to increase the reliability of measurements. In the repeated measures design, researchers are manipulating an independent variable to contrast participants' behavior in two or more conditions of an experiment. The critical repeated measurement in the repeated measures design is that each participant is measured in all conditions of the experiment.

THE ROLE OF PRACTICE EFFECTS IN REPEATED MEASURES DESIGNS

- Repeated measures designs cannot be confounded by individual differences variables because the same individuals participate in each condition (level) of the independent variable.
- Participants' performance in repeated measures designs may change across conditions simply because of repeated testing (and not because of the independent variable); these changes are called practice effects.
- Practice effects may threaten the internal validity of a repeated measures experiment when the different conditions of the independent variable are presented in the same order to all participants.
- There are two types of repeated measures designs (complete and incomplete) that differ in the specific ways in which they control for practice effects.

Defining Practice Effects

The repeated measures designs have another important advantage in addition to the ones we have already described. In a repeated measures design, the characteristics of the participants cannot confound the independent variable being manipulated in the experiment. The *same* participants are tested in all the conditions of a repeated measures design, so it is impossible to end up with brighter, healthier, or more motivated participants in one condition than in another condition. Stated more formally, *there can be no confounding by individual differences variables in repeated measures designs.* The absence of the potential for confounding by individual differences variables is a great advantage of the repeated measures designs. This does not mean, however, that there are no threats to the internal validity of experiments that are done using repeated measures designs.

One potential threat to internal validity arises because participants may change over time. The repeated testing of participants in the repeated measures design gives them practice with the experimental task. As a result of this practice, participants may get better and better at doing the task because they learn more about the task, or they may get worse at the task because of such factors as fatigue and boredom. The changes participants undergo with repeated testing in the repeated measures designs are called **practice effects.**

Key Concept

Kahneman, Frederickson, Schreiber, and Redelmeier (1993) used a repeated measures design in a series of experiments investigating people's perception of pain. Their findings showed that evaluations of pain are influenced most by the worst moments and the final moments of a painful experience. In other words, we judge how painful an experience was by judging how painful it was at the point of most intense pain and by how painful it was at the end of the experience. These two factors were shown to be more important in the perception of pain than the duration of the pain. We will use one of the experiments Kahneman et al. did to illustrate the nature of practice effects and the need to control for them in repeated measures designs.

FIGURE 8.1   There are both positive and negative effects of practicing a new skill. Repeating the same experience can lead to improvement, but it also can lead to fatigue, a decrease in motivation, and even boredom.

The experiment was done to determine the influence of the intensity of the pain in the final moments of the experience. There were two conditions in the experiment. In the first condition (short trial) students immersed one hand in cold water (14 degrees Celsius) for 60 seconds. In the second condition (long trial) the students also immersed their hand in 14-degree water for 60 seconds, but they then kept their hand immersed 30 seconds longer while the temperature of the water was gradually warmed (raised 1 degree) to 15 degrees. Each participant experienced both the short trial and the long trial only once. There was a 7-minute interval filled with another activity after each trial. One dependent variable was people's ratings of their degree of pain after each trial. The most important measure in the experiment, however, was the choice students made when they were asked to choose which trial they preferred to repeat.

The researchers found that the students' ratings of pain indicated that the 15-degree water was painful, but noticeably less painful than the 14-degree water. The students also rated the long trial as more painful overall than the short trial. Nonetheless, when students were asked which trial they preferred to repeat, 69% chose the more painful long trial. Kahneman et al. (1993) argued that the students chose the long trial because it was less painful in the final moments of the experience. The overall duration of the long trial was less critical in determining students' choice than was the fact that it was less painful at the end of their experience. To reach this intriguing insight the researchers had to control for practice effects in their experiment.

Suppose that Kahneman et al. (1993) had tested all the students by giving them the short trial first and then the long trial. If only one order had been used, the short trial would always be the first trial and the long trial would always be the second trial. Students might become more familiar with the sensations resulting from having their hand immersed in cold water as they move from one trial to the other. Or maybe they would be less apprehensive about possible pain after they had experience with one trial. There are many important ways in which the students could change over the two trials. These changes over the two trials represent practice effects. Practice effects and the two conditions of the experiment would be confounded if only one order had been used. If students rated the two conditions differently, we would not be able to interpret this difference. That is, we would not know whether the difference in ratings was due to the independent variable (short or long trial) or to the order (first or second) in which the conditions appeared.

Kahneman et al. (1993) controlled practice effects by balancing them across the two conditions. They administered the conditions in two different orders. Half of the students received the short trial followed by the long trial and half received the long trial followed by the short trial. Since both orders were used equally often, the students' preference to repeat the long trial rather than the short trial cannot be attributed to the long trial always having been presented last. The changes due to practice effects that occurred for the students from the first trial to the second trial are likely to fall equally on each of the two conditions because half the students experienced practice effects during a long trial, and half on a short trial. Any difference in performance, therefore, between the conditions is the result of the nature of the short and long trials and not the result of practice effects.

In general, practice effects should be balanced across the conditions in repeated measures designs so that practice effects "average out" across conditions. The key to conducting interpretable experiments using the repeated measures designs is learning to use appropriate techniques to balance practice effects. We will briefly introduce the two types of repeated measures designs before describing the use of specific balancing techniques.

The two types of repeated measures designs are the complete and the incomplete design. The specific techniques for balancing practice effects differ for the two repeated measures designs, but the general term used to refer to these balancing techniques is **counterbalancing.** In the *complete design*, practice effects are balanced for each participant. Balancing practice effects for each participant is accomplished by administering the conditions to each participant several

Key Concept

times, using different orders each time. Each participant can thus be considered a "complete" experiment. In the *incomplete design*, each condition is administered to each participant *only once*. The order of administering the conditions is varied across participants rather than for each participant, as is the case in the complete design. Practice effects in the incomplete design average out when the results are combined for all participants. This may seem a bit confusing at this point, but hopefully it will become clearer as we describe these types of designs more fully. Just keep in mind that a major goal when using a repeated measures design is to control for practice effects.

Balancing Practice Effects in the Complete Design

- Practice effects are balanced in complete designs within each participant using block randomization or ABBA counterbalancing.
- In block randomization, all of the conditions of the experiment (a block) are randomly ordered each time they are presented.
- In ABBA counterbalancing, a random sequence of all conditions is presented, followed by the opposite of the sequence.
- Block randomization is preferred over ABBA counterbalancing when practice effects are not linear, or when participants' performance can be affected by anticipation effects.

Research has shown that participants who view photographs depicting posed facial expressions of six basic human emotions (happiness, surprise, fear, sadness, anger, and disgust) can readily and accurately identify the expressed emotion. Sackeim, Gur, and Saucy (1978) used a repeated measures design to determine whether one side of our face expresses emotion more intensely than the other. They developed a photograph of a full face and a photograph of its mirror image. They then split both photographs down the middle making two composite photographs—one from the two versions of the left side of the face and one from the two versions of the right side. Illustrative photographs are presented in Figure 8.2. In the center is a photograph of a person expressing disgust. The two composite photographs made from the center photograph are presented on either side of the original. Does one of the two composites in Figure 8.2 look more disgusted than the other?

Participants were shown slides of photographs like those in Figure 8.2 and were asked to rate each slide on a 7-point scale indicating the intensity of the expressed emotion. The slides were presented individually for 10 seconds, and participants were then given 35 seconds to make their rating. The critical independent variable in the experiment was the version of the photograph depicting one of the emotions (left composite, original, or right composite). Each participant rated 54 slides: 18 left composites, 18 originals, and 18 right composites.

Participants' ratings of emotional intensity were consistently higher for the left composite than for the right composite. Does this finding match your judgment that the face in panel (a) in Figure 8.2 appears more disgusted than

FIGURE 8.2 (a) Left-side composite, (b) original, and (c) right-side composite of the same face. The face is expressing disgust. (From Sackeim et al., 1978.)

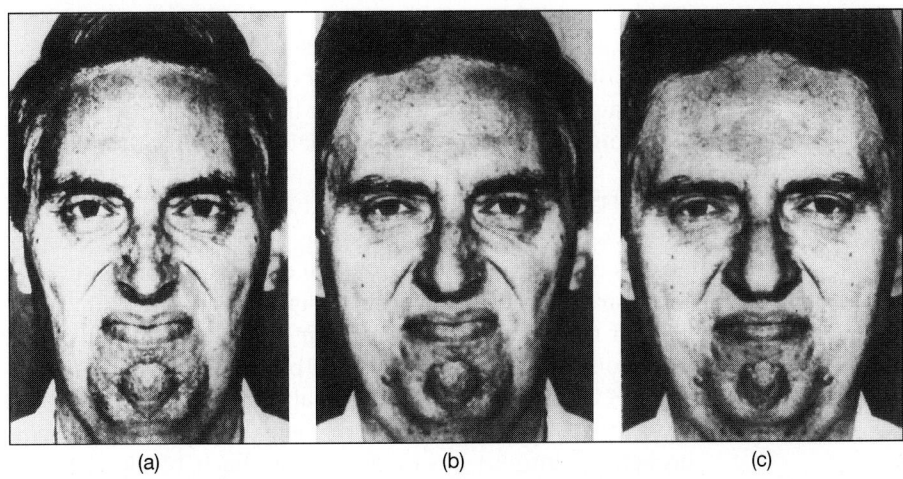

(a) (b) (c)

the face in panel (c)? Sackeim et al. interpreted these findings in terms of hemispheric specialization of the brain. In general, the left hemisphere controls the right side of the body and the right hemisphere controls the left side of the body. Thus, the left composite reflects control by the right hemisphere, and the right composite reflects control by the left hemisphere. The higher ratings of emotional intensity for the left composite photographs suggest that the right hemisphere may be more heavily involved than the left hemisphere in the production of emotional expression.

The interpretation of the differences in the ratings depends critically on the order in which the slides were presented to participants. Consider what could happen if all the original versions were presented first, followed by all the right composites, then by all the left composites. If you imagine yourself in this experiment making a rating for each of the slides in this long sequence (over 40 minutes), you will get a sense of what we mean by practice effects. Surely your attention, motivation, and experience in rating the emotionality of photographs will change as you work through the sequence of slides. If you gave higher ratings for the slides shown at the end of this long sequence, your ratings may reflect the intensity of your own emotions of boredom and fatigue rather than the intensity of the emotions actually depicted in the photographs. To avoid this possibility, Sackeim et al. used balancing techniques specifically developed for use with the complete design in repeated measures experiments. By using these balancing techniques, they ensured that each of the three versions of the photographs was equally likely to appear at any point in the long series of slides.

In the complete design, participants are given each treatment enough times to balance practice effects for each participant. When the task is simple enough and not too time consuming (such as judging the emotional intensity of photographs), it is possible to give one participant several experiences with each treatment. In fact, in some complete designs, only one or two participants are tested and each participant experiences literally hundreds of trials. More commonly, however, researchers use procedures like those used by Sackeim et al. That is, several participants are tested, and each participant is given each treatment only a relatively small number of times. Researchers have two choices in deciding how to arrange the order in which the treatments in a complete design are administered: block randomization and ABBA counterbalancing.

Block Randomization   We introduced block randomization in Chapter 7 as an effective technique for assigning participants to conditions in the random groups design. *Block randomization* can also be used to order the conditions for each participant in a complete design. For instance, Sackeim et al. administered each of the three versions of their photographs (left composite, original, and right composite) 18 times to each participant. The sequence of trials shown in Table 8.1 illustrates how block randomization could be used to arrange the order of the three conditions in their experiment. The sequence of 54 trials is broken up into 18 blocks of 3 trials. Each block of trials contains the three conditions of the experiment in random order. In general, *the number of blocks in a block-randomized schedule is equal to the number of times each condition is administered, and the size of each block is equal to the number of conditions in the experiment.*

   If a participant rated the photographs following the sequence in the block-randomized schedule shown in Table 8.1, it is unlikely that changes in the participant's attention, motivation, or experience with rating photographs would affect any one of the conditions more than any other. The practice effects can reasonably be expected to average out over the three experimental conditions. Determining the average position of each of the three conditions in the block-randomized sequence gives a rough indication of the balancing of practice effects. This can be done by summing the trial numbers on which each condition appears and dividing by 18. For instance, the original version of the photographs ("O") appeared on trials 1, 5, 8, 11, 13, 18, 21, 24, 27, 28, 33, 34, 39, 40, 44, 48, 49, and 53. The average position of the original photographs, therefore, was 27.6. The corresponding values for the left and right composite photographs are 27.7 and 27.2, respectively. That these average values are so similar tells us that any one version of the photographs was not more likely to appear at the beginning, middle, or end of the sequence of 54 trials.

   Block randomization is effective in balancing practice effects, but each condition must be repeated several times before we can expect practice effects to average out. We should not expect practice effects to be balanced after two or three blocks—any more than we would expect sample sizes of two or three in the random groups design to result in comparable groups. Fortunately, a technique is available to balance practice effects when it is not possible to administer each condition often enough for the averaging process of block randomization to work effectively.

TABLE 8.1 BLOCK-RANDOMIZED SEQUENCE OF 54 TRIALS IN AN EXPERIMENT
WITH THREE CONDITIONS ADMINISTERED 18 TIMES EACH

Trial	Conditions	Trial	Conditions
1	O	28	O
2	L	29	L
3	R	30	R
4	R	31	R
5	O	32	L
6	L	33	O
7	R	34	O
8	O	35	R
9	L	36	L
10	L	37	L
11	O	38	R
12	R	39	O
13	O	40	O
14	L	41	R
15	R	42	L
16	R	43	R
17	L	44	O
18	O	45	L
19	R	46	R
20	L	47	L
21	O	48	O
22	L	49	O
23	R	50	R
24	O	51	L
25	R	52	R
26	L	53	O
27	O	54	L

Note: The conditions are the three versions of the photographs used by Sackeim et al. (1978): L = left composite, O = original, R = right composite.

ABBA Counterbalancing In its simplest form, ABBA counterbalancing can be used to balance practice effects in the complete design with as few as two administrations of each condition. *ABBA counterbalancing* involves presenting the conditions in one sequence (i.e., A then B) followed by the opposite of that same sequence (i.e., B then A). Its name describes the sequences when there are only two conditions (A and B) in the experiment, but ABBA counterbalancing is not limited to experiments with just two conditions. Sackeim et al. could have presented the versions of their photographs according to the ABBA sequence outlined in the top row of Table 8.2 labeled "Condition." Note that in this case it literally would be ABCCBA since there are three conditions. The order of the three conditions on the first three trials is simply reversed for trials 4 to 6.

TABLE 8.2   ABBA COUNTERBALANCED SEQUENCE OF TRIALS IN AN EXPERIMENT WITH THREE
CONDITIONS (LEFT COMPOSITE, ORIGINAL, AND RIGHT COMPOSITE)

	Condition:	Trial 1 Left	Trial 2 Original	Trial 3 Right	Trial 4 Right	Trial 5 Original	Trial 6 Left
Practice effect (linear)		+0	+1	+2	+3	+4	+5
Practice effect (nonlinear)		0	+6	+6	+6	+6	+6

ABBA counterbalancing is appropriately used only when practice effects are linear. If practice effects are linear the same amount of practice effects is added to or subtracted from performance on each successive trial. The row of Table 8.2 labeled "Practice effect (linear)" illustrates how ABBA counterbalancing can balance practice effects. In this example, one "unit" of hypothetical practice effects is added to performance on each trial. Because there would be no practice effect associated with the first trial, the amount of practice added to Trial 1 in the table is zero. Trial 2 has one unit of hypothetical effects added because of participants' experience with the first trial; in Trial 3 there are two units added because of participants' experience with two trials, and so on.

We can get an idea of the influence of practice effects by adding up the values for each condition. For example, the left composite condition gets the least (0) and the greatest (+5) influence from practice effects; the right composite condition gets two intermediate amounts (+2 and +3). The sum of the hypothetical practice effects is +5 for both conditions. (What would the sum of the practice effects be for the original condition?) The ABBA cycle can be applied with any number of conditions, but there must be an even number of repetitions of each condition. ABBA counterbalancing balances practice effects even more effectively with larger numbers of repetitions of the cycle. Usually, however, ABBA counterbalancing is used when the number of conditions and the number of repetitions of each condition are relatively small.

Although ABBA counterbalancing provides a simple and elegant means to balance practice effects, it is not without limitations. For example, ABBA counterbalancing is ineffective when practice effects for a task are not linear. This is illustrated in the last row of Table 8.2, labeled "Practice effect (nonlinear)." In this example, the left composite receives a total of only six hypothetical units of practice effects, and the other two conditions receive a total of 12 units each. When practice effects involve abrupt initial changes followed by little change thereafter, researchers often ignore performance on the early trials and wait until the practice effects reach a "steady state." Reaching a steady state is likely to take several repetitions of each condition, so researchers tend to use block randomization to balance practice effects in these situations.

ABBA counterbalancing is also ineffective when anticipation effects can occur. *Anticipation effects* occur when a participant develops expectations about which condition should occur next in the sequence. The participant's response to that condition may then be influenced more by this expectation than by the actual experience of the condition itself. For example, consider a time-perception experiment in which the participant's task is to estimate the length of time that has passed between a signal presented on a computer screen indicating the start of an interval and another signal indicating the end of the interval. (Of course, participants have to be prevented somehow from marking off time during the interval by counting or rhythmically tapping.) If the time intervals in such an experiment are 12, 24, and 36 seconds, then one possible ABBA sequence of conditions could be 12-24-36-36-24-12. If this cycle were repeated several times, participants probably would recognize the pattern and expect a series of increasing and then decreasing intervals. Their time estimates might soon begin to reflect this pattern rather than their perception of each independent interval. If anticipation effects are likely, block randomization should be used rather than ABBA counterbalancing.

Balancing Practice Effects in the Incomplete Design

- Practice effects are balanced *across* subjects in the incomplete design rather than for each subject, as in the complete design.
- The rule for balancing practice effects in the incomplete design is that each condition of the experiment must be presented in each ordinal position (first, second, etc.) equally often.
- The best method for balancing practice effects in the incomplete design with four or fewer conditions is to use all possible orders of the conditions.
- Two methods for selecting specific orders to use in an incomplete design are the Latin Square and random starting order with rotation.
- Whether using all possible orders or selected orders, participants should be randomly assigned to the different sequences.

In the incomplete design, each participant is given each treatment *only once*. The results for any one participant, therefore, cannot be interpreted because the levels of the independent variable for each participant are perfectly confounded with the order in which those levels were presented. For instance, the first participant in an incomplete design experiment might be tested first in the experimental condition (E) and second in the control condition (C). Any differences in the participant's performance between the experimental and control conditions could be due to the effect of the independent variable *or* to the practice effects resulting from the EC order. To break this confounding of the order of conditions and the independent variable, we can administer different orders of the conditions to different participants. For example, we could administer the conditions of our incomplete design experiment to a second participant in the CE order, testing the control condition first and the experimental condition second. In this way, we could balance the effects of order across the two conditions using two participants instead of one.

To illustrate the techniques for balancing practice effects in the incomplete design, we will use an experiment by Erber (1991) on the effects of people's moods on their perceptions of other people. There were two stages in this experiment. In the first stage, participants read one of three stories about events in the life of a young female artist. These stories were previously shown to be effective in inducing positive, neutral, or negative moods in people. The story for the positive-mood condition included several events culminating in the artist's receiving a scholarship to college. The neutral-mood story described how the artist decided which college to attend. The negative-mood story described how the artist was overcome by a rare disabling illness at the end of her first year in college. Thus, after the first stage, participants are assumed to be in one of three moods: positive, neutral, or negative. (Note that in the first stage of the experiment each participant was in only one mood group—an independent groups design.)

The second stage of the experiment began at this point, and the participants believed that the second stage was a separate experiment. The participants were asked to rate the likelihood that each of four "target" individuals would engage in a particular behavior (welcoming a friend with a hug, getting depressed over the weather, and so on). For reasons that will become apparent, the descriptions of the four targets were based on somewhat contradictory traits. Each of the four "target people" was described as (1) either moody and warm; (2) pessimistic and understanding; (3) unselfish and unsociable; or (4) trustworthy and possessive. A repeated measures design was used to implement the independent variable of the target person. Specifically, an incomplete design was used in which each participant rated all four levels of the target person variable once.

Before describing the techniques that can be used to balance practice effects for an independent variable in the incomplete design, we will take a brief look at the results of the Erber study. The dependent variable in this study was the participants' ratings of the likelihood that the target people would engage in certain behaviors. The researcher hypothesized that these ratings would be influenced by *participants'* mood (positive, neutral, or negative) as manipulated in the first stage of the experiment. Because the target people were described using both a positive (e.g., warm) and a negative (e.g., moody) trait, the researchers wanted to see if the participants' mood would determine which of the two traits most influenced their ratings. For example, the participants' task was to rate how likely it was for someone described as "warm and moody" to engage in positive behavior, such as "welcoming a friend with a hug," or in negative behavior, such as "getting depressed over the weather." Welcoming someone with a hug is something a "warm" person might do, while getting depressed is something a "moody" person is more likely to do. Perhaps you can anticipate what happened in this experiment.

The results revealed that if a participant was in a positive mood, then a "warm and moody" person was rated as more likely to engage in positive behavior (e.g., welcoming with a hug) than in negative behavior (e.g., getting depressed over the weather). If the participant was in a negative mood, the same "warm and moody" individual was rated more likely to engage in negative behavior than in positive behavior. The effect of mood on ratings of negative behaviors was larger than was the effect of mood on ratings of positive behaviors. These findings (along with other findings reported in the study) indicate that mood can influence the way we perceive other people in important ways. One such influence, Erber (1991) argues, is that negative mood may facilitate the accessibility of negative information about others. In other words, if you're in a bad mood, you're more likely to accentuate someone's negative traits!

We turn our attention now to the balancing techniques that are used in the incomplete design. In an incomplete design it is essential that practice effects be balanced by varying the order in which the conditions are presented. The general rule for balancing practice effects in the incomplete design is a simple one: *Each condition of the experiment must appear in each ordinal position equally often.* Several techniques are available for satisfying this general rule. These techniques differ in what additional balancing they accomplish, but so long as the techniques are properly used, the basic rule will be met and the experiment will be interpretable. That is, if appropriate balancing is carried out, then we will be in a position to determine whether the independent variable, and not practice effects, influenced the participants' behavior.

All Possible Orders   The preferred technique for balancing practice effects in the incomplete design is to use all possible orders of the conditions. Each participant is randomly assigned to one of the orders. With only two conditions there are only two possible orders (AB and BA); with three conditions there are six possible orders (ABC, ACB, BAC, BCA, CAB, CBA). In general, there are $N!$ (which is read "N factorial") possible orders with N conditions, where $N!$ equals $N(N - 1)(N - 2) \ldots (N - [N - 1])$. As we just saw, there are six possible orders with three conditions, which is $3!$ ($3 \times 2 \times 1 = 6$). The number of required orders increases dramatically with increasing numbers of conditions. For instance, for only five conditions there are 120 possible orders, and for six conditions there are 720 possible orders. Because of this, the use of all possible orders is usually limited to experiments involving four or fewer conditions.

Because there were four target people in the Erber (1991) experiment, 24 sequences would be required to obtain all possible orders of the conditions. These sequences are presented in the left half of Table 8.3. Using all possible orders certainly meets the general rule of ensuring that all conditions appear in each ordinal position equally often. The first ordinal position shows this balancing most clearly: The first six sequences begin with the Moody-Warm (M) target, and each succeeding set of six sequences begins with one of the other three targets. The same pattern applies at each of the four ordinal positions. For example, the "M" target also appears six times in the second ordinal position, six times in the third ordinal position, and six times in the fourth ordinal position.

There is one other issue that must be addressed in deciding to use all possible orders. For this technique to be effective, it is essential that at least one participant be tested with each of the possible orders of the conditions. That is, at least one participant should receive the MPUT order, at least one should receive the MPTU order, and so on. Therefore, the use of all possible orders requires at least as many participants as there are possible orders. That is, if there are four conditions in the experiment, you must test 24 participants (or 48 or 72 or some other multiple of 24). This restriction makes it very important that you have a good idea of the number of potential participants available to you before testing the first participant.

Selected Orders   We have just described the preferred method for balancing practice effects in the incomplete design, all possible orders. There are times, however, when the use of all possible orders is not practical. For example, if we wanted to use the incomplete design to study an independent variable with seven levels, we would need to test 5,040 participants if we used all possible orders—one participant for each of the possible orders of the seven conditions (7! orders). We obviously need some alternative to using all possible orders if we are to use the incomplete design for experiments with five or more conditions.

Practice effects can be balanced by using just some of all the possible orders. The number of selected orders will always be equal to some multiple of the number of conditions in the experiment. For example, to do an experiment with one independent variable with seven levels, we need to select 7, 14, 21, 28, or some other multiple of seven orders to balance practice effects. The two basic variations of using selected orders are illustrated in Table 8.3. To allow you to compare the types of balancing more directly, we have illustrated the techniques for selected orders with the four-level independent variable from Erber's (1991) experiment that we described in the previous section.

The first type of balancing using selected orders is called the Latin Square. In a *Latin Square*, the general rule for balancing practice effects is met. That is, each condition appears at each ordinal position once. For example, just to the right of the center of Table 8.3, we can see that in the Latin Square, condition "M"

TABLE 8.3   ALTERNATIVE TECHNIQUES TO BALANCE PRACTICE EFFECTS IN AN INCOMPLETE REPEATED MEASURES DESIGN EXPERIMENT WITH FOUR CONDITIONS

								Selected orders							
								Latin Square				Random starting order with rotation			
All possible orders								Ordinal position				Ordinal position			
Ordinal position				Ordinal position											
1st	2nd	3rd	4th	1st	2nd	3rd	4th	1st	2nd	3rd	4th	1st	2nd	3rd	4th
M	P	U	T	U	M	P	T	M	P	U	T	P	U	T	M
M	P	T	U	U	M	T	P	P	T	M	U	U	T	M	P
M	U	P	T	U	P	M	T	T	U	P	M	T	M	P	U
M	U	T	P	U	P	T	M	U	M	T	P	M	P	U	T
M	T	P	U	U	T	M	P								
M	T	U	P	U	T	P	M								
P	M	U	T	T	M	P	U								
P	M	T	U	T	M	U	P								
P	U	M	T	T	P	M	U								
P	U	T	M	T	P	U	M								
P	T	M	U	T	U	M	P								
P	T	U	M	T	U	P	M								

Note: The four conditions are identified by the first letter of the first adjective describing each of the four target people in the Erber (1991) experiment: Moody-Warm (M), Pessimistic-Understanding (P), Unselfish-Unsociable (U), and Trustworthy-Possessive (T).

BOX 8.2

HOW TO CONSTRUCT A LATIN SQUARE

More than one valid Latin Square can be constructed for an experiment. A simple procedure for constructing a square *with an even number (N) of conditions* is as follows:

1 Randomly order the conditions of the experiment.
2 Number the conditions in your random order 1 through N.

>Thus, if you had $N = 4$ conditions (A,B,C,D) and the random order (from Step 1) was B, A, D, C, then B = 1, A = 2, D = 3, C = 4.

3 To generate the first row (first order of conditions), use the rule:

>$1, 2, N, 3, N − 1, 4, N − 2, 5, N − 3, 6$, etc.
>In our example, this would yield 1, 2, 4, 3.

4 To generate the second row (second order of conditions) add 1 to each number in the first row but with the understanding that 1 added to $N = 1$.

>We would then have 2, 3, 1, 4.

5 The third row (third order of conditions) is generated by adding 1 to each number in the second row and again $N + 1 = 1$.

>The third row would be 3, 4, 2, 1.

6 A similar procedure is carried out for each successive row.

Can you construct the fourth row in this 4×4 square?

7 Assign the conditions to their corresponding numbers as determined in Step 2.

The Latin Square for this example would be:

>B A C D
>A D B C
>D C A B
>C B D A

If there is an odd number of conditions, then two squares must be constructed. The first can be made according to the rule given above for even-numbered squares. The second square is generated by reversing the rows in the first square. For example, assume $N = 5$ and the first row of the first square is B A E C D. The first row of the second square would then be D C E A B. The two squares are joined to make a $N \times 2N$ square. In either case, even or odd, subjects should be assigned randomly to the rows of the square. Thus, you must have available at least as many subjects as there are multiples of rows. (Procedures for selecting or constructing Latin Squares are also described in Winer, Brown, and Michels [1991, pp. 674–679].)

---

appears exactly once in the first, second, third, and fourth ordinal positions. This is true for each condition. Additionally, in a Latin Square each condition precedes and follows each other condition exactly once. Examination of the Latin Square in Table 8.3 shows that the order "MP" appears once, as does the order "PM." The order "PU" appears once, as does the order "UP," and so on, for every combination of conditions. (The procedure for constructing a Latin Square is described in Box 8.2.)

The second balancing technique using selected orders requires you to begin with a random order of the conditions and to rotate this sequence systematically with each condition moving one position to the left each time (see the example on the right in Table 8.3). Using a random starting order with rotation effectively balances practice effects because, like the Latin Square, each condition appears in each ordinal position. However, the systematic rotation of the sequences means that each condition always follows and always precedes the *same* other conditions, which is not like the Latin Square technique. The simplicity of the random starting order with rotation technique and its applicability to experiments with more than four conditions are its primary advantages.

The use of all possible orders, Latin Squares, and random starting orders with rotation are equally effective in balancing practice effects because all three techniques ensure that each condition appears in each ordinal position equally often. Regardless of which technique one uses to balance practice effects, the sequences of conditions should be fully prepared prior to testing the first participant, and participants should be randomly assigned to these sequences.

DATA ANALYSIS OF REPEATED MEASURES DESIGNS

Describing the Results

- Data analysis for a complete design begins with computing a summary score (e.g., mean, median) for each participant.
- Descriptive statistics are used to summarize performance across all participants for each condition of the independent variable.

The first step in analyzing an experiment is preparing a matrix summarizing participants' performance in each condition of the experiment. In random groups designs, this means simply listing the scores of the participants tested in each of the conditions of the experiment and then summarizing these scores with descriptive statistics such as the mean and standard deviation. In an incomplete repeated measures design, each participant provides one score in each condition, but it is still relatively straightforward to summarize the scores for each condition. In doing so, you need to be careful as you "unwind" the various orders in which the participants were tested to be sure participants' scores are listed with the correct condition. Once all the scores for each condition have been listed together, means and standard deviations can be computed to describe performance in each condition.

An additional step needs to be taken when analyzing a complete repeated measures design. You must compute a score for each participant in each condition before you begin to summarize and describe the results. This additional step is necessary because each participant is tested in each condition more than once in a complete design. For example, five participants were tested in a time-perception experiment done as a classroom demonstration of a complete repeated measures design. The purpose of the experiment was not to test the accuracy of participants' time estimates compared with the actual interval lengths. Instead, the purpose of the experiment was to determine whether participants' estimates of time increased systematically with increasing lengths. In other words, could participants discriminate between intervals of different lengths?

Each participant in the experiment was tested six times on each of four interval lengths (12, 24, 36, and 48 seconds). Block randomization was used to

TABLE 8.4   DATA MATRIX TABLE FOR A REPEATED MEASURES DESIGN EXPERIMENT

	Data matrix			
	Interval length			
Participant	12	24	36	48
1	13	21	30	38
2	10	15	38	35
3	12	23	31	32
4	12	15	22	32
5	16	36	69	60
Mean (SD)	12.6 (2.0)	22.0 (7.7)	38.0 (16.3)	39.4 (10.5)

Note: Each value in the table represents the median of the participants' six responses at each level of the interval length variable.

determine the order in which the intervals were presented. Thus, each participant provided 24 time estimates, six estimates for each of the four interval lengths. Any one of the six estimates for a given time interval is contaminated by practice effects, so some measure that combines information across the six estimates is needed. Typically, the mean across the six estimates for each interval would be calculated for each participant to provide a single estimate of performance in each condition. As you may remember, however, extreme scores can influence the mean; it is quite possible that participants gave extreme estimates of the time intervals for at least one of the six tests of each interval. Thus, for this particular set of data, the median of the six estimates probably provides the best measure to reflect the participants' estimates of the time intervals. These median estimates (rounded to the nearest whole number) are listed in Table 8.4. (You may be used to seeing the mean and median as descriptive statistics summarizing a *group's* performance; however, as this example illustrates, these summary statistics also can be used to represent one *person's* performance when that performance is an "average" across trials or tests.)

Once an individual score for each participant in each condition has been obtained, the next step is to summarize the results across participants, using appropriate descriptive statistics. The mean estimate and standard deviation (SD) for each of the four intervals are listed in the row labeled "Mean (SD)" in Table 8.4. Even though the data for only five participants are included in the table, these mean estimates indicate that participants appear to have discriminated between intervals of different lengths, at least for intervals up to 36 seconds.

As we mentioned in Chapter 7, it is a good idea to include measures of effect size when describing the results of an experiment. A typical measure of effect size for a repeated measures design is the strength of association measure called eta squared (η^2). The value of eta squared for the time estimation experiment was .80. This value indicates that a large proportion of variation in participants' time estimates can be accounted for by the independent variable of interval length. You can find more information about the calculation of effect sizes and their interpretation in Chapters 12 and 13. In Chapter 13 we illustrate how to calculate eta squared using the data found in Table 8.4.

Confirming What the Results Reveal

- The general procedures and logic for null hypothesis testing and for confidence intervals for repeated measures designs are similar to those used for random groups designs.

Data analysis for experiments using repeated measures designs involves the same general procedures we described in Chapter 7 for the analysis of random groups design experiments. Researchers use null hypothesis testing and confidence intervals to make claims about whether the independent variable produced an effect on behavior. We will use the time-perception experiment to illustrate how researchers confirm what the data reveal when they use repeated measures designs.

The focus of the analysis of the time-perception experiment was on whether the participants could discriminate intervals of different lengths. We cannot make the claim that participants were able to discriminate intervals of varying lengths until we know that the mean differences in Table 8.4 are greater than would be expected on the basis of error variation alone. That is, even though it may *appear* that participants were able to discriminate between the different intervals, we do not know if their performance was different from that which would occur by chance. Thus, we must consider using analytical tools of null hypothesis testing and the construction of confidence intervals to help us make a decision about the effectiveness of the independent variable.

One distinctive characteristic of the analysis of repeated measures designs is the way in which error variation is estimated. We described in Chapter 7 that

---

STRETCHING EXERCISE

For this exercise you are to compute the mean for each level of the independent variable in this incomplete repeated measures design.

The table shows the orders in which three doses of a drug (0,50,100) were administered to six participants in an experiment. The values in parentheses represent the number of errors made by each participant in each condition on a problem-solving task. Use this table to describe the effect of the drug variable in this experiment.

Participant	Ordinal position		
	1	2	3
1	0(2)	50(9)	100(9)
2	0(7)	100(5)	50(3)
3	50(5)	0(3)	100(4)
4	50(8)	100(10)	0(6)
5	100(6)	0(8)	50(7)
6	100(8)	50(4)	0(4)

for the random groups design, individual differences among participants within the groups provides an estimate of error variation alone. In repeated measures designs, however, differences among participants are not just balanced—they are actually eliminated from the analysis. The ability to eliminate systematic variation due to participants in repeated measures designs makes these designs generally more sensitive than random groups designs. The source of error variation in the repeated measures designs is the differences in the ways the conditions affect different participants.

Stat Tip

The fact that error variation is estimated differently in a repeated measures design than it is in an independent groups design means that the calculation of the t-test and F-test used in null hypothesis testing also differs. Similarly, there is change in the way that confidence intervals are calculated. In Chapter 13 we use the data in Table 8.4 to show how both the F-test and confidence intervals are used in decision making as part of a repeated measures design. The null hypothesis for an analysis of the data in Table 8.4 is that the population means estimated by the sample means in Table 8.4 are the same across interval-length conditions. Having carried out an analysis of variance for these data (see Chapter 13), we can tell you that the probability associated with the F-test for the effect of interval length was $p = .0004$. Because this obtained probability is less than the conventional level of significance (.05), the effect of the interval length variable was statistically significant. Based on this outcome we can make the claim that participants' time estimates did differ systematically as a function of interval length. We already know from our calculation of the effect size (eta squared = .80) that it represents a large effect.

In Chapter 13 we used the same data to calculate .95 confidence intervals for the means seen in Table 8.4. The confidence intervals (in seconds) for the four conditions are: (12) 5.4–19.8; (24) 14.8–29.2; (36) 30.8–45.2; (48) 32.2–46.6. As you learned in Chapter 7 (see also Box 12.5), when intervals do not overlap we can claim that the population means estimated by the sample means are different. Does an inspection of these intervals tell you which means would be judged to be different? A convenient way to examine the relationship among confidence intervals is to plot them in a graph. For example, take a look at Figure 13.2 in Chapter 13, in which the intervals presented here are plotted around the sample means obtained in the time estimation experiment.

THE PROBLEM OF DIFFERENTIAL TRANSFER

- Differential transfer occurs when the effects of one condition persist and influence performance in subsequent conditions.
- Variables that may lead to differential transfer should be tested using a random groups design because differential transfer threatens the internal validity of repeated measures designs.

- Differential transfer can be identified by comparing the results for the same independent variable when tested in a repeated measures design and in a random groups design.

Researchers can overcome the potential problem of practice effects in repeated measures designs by using appropriate techniques to balance practice effects. There is a much more serious potential problem that can arise in repeated measures designs that is known as differential transfer (Poulton, 1973, 1975, 1982; Poulton & Freeman, 1966). **Differential transfer** arises when performance in one condition differs depending on the condition that precedes it.

Key Concept

Consider a problem-solving experiment in which two types of instructions are being compared in a repeated measures design. One set of instructions (A) is expected to enhance problem solving, whereas the other set of instructions (B) serves as the neutral control condition. It is reasonable to expect that participants tested in the order AB will be unable or unwilling to abandon the approach outlined in the A instructions when they are supposed to be following the B instructions. Giving up the "good thing" participants had under instruction A would be the counterpart of successfully following the admonition, "Don't think of pink elephants!" When participants fail to give up the instruction from the first condition (A) while they are supposed to be following instruction B, any difference between the two conditions is reduced. For those participants, after all, condition B was not really tried. The experiment becomes a situation in which participants are tested in an "AA" condition, not an "AB" condition.

In general, the presence of differential transfer threatens internal validity because it becomes impossible to determine if there are true differences between the conditions. It also tends to underestimate differences between the conditions and thereby reduces the external validity of the findings. *Therefore, when differential transfer could occur, researchers should choose an independent groups design.* Differential transfer is sufficiently common with instructional variables to advise against the use of repeated measures designs for these variables (Underwood & Shaughnessy, 1975). Unfortunately, differential transfer can arise in any repeated measures design. For instance, the effect of 50 units of marijuana may be different if administered after the participant has received 200 units than if administered after the participant has received the placebo (e.g., if the participant has an increased tolerance for marijuana after receiving the 200 doses). There are ways, however, to determine whether differential transfer is likely to have occurred.

The best way to determine whether differential transfer is a problem is to do two separate experiments (Poulton, 1982). The same independent variable would be studied in both experiments, but a random groups design would be used in one experiment and a repeated measures design in the other. The random groups design cannot possibly involve differential transfer because each participant is tested in only one condition. If the experiment using a repeated measures design shows the same effect of the independent variable as that shown in the random groups design, then there has likely been no differential transfer. If the two designs show different effects for the same independent variable, however, differential transfer is likely to be responsible for producing the different outcome in the repeated measures design. When differential transfer does occur, the results of the random groups design should be used to provide the best description of the effect of the independent variable.

SUMMARY

Repeated measures designs provide an effective and efficient way to conduct an experiment by administering all the conditions in the experiment to each participant. Repeated measures designs are useful when only very few participants are available or when an independent variable can be studied most efficiently by testing fewer participants several times. Repeated measures designs are generally more sensitive experiments. Finally, particular areas of psychological research (e.g., psychophysics) may require the use of repeated measures designs.

For any repeated measures design experiment to be interpretable, however, practice effects must be balanced. Practice effects are changes that participants undergo because of repeated testing. In a complete repeated measures design, practice effects are balanced for each participant. Block randomization and ABBA counterbalancing can be used to balance practice effects in a complete repeated measures design. ABBA counterbalancing should not be used, however, if practice effects are expected to be nonlinear or if anticipation effects are likely.

In an incomplete repeated measures design, each participant receives each treatment only once, and the balancing of practice effects is accomplished across participants. Techniques for balancing practice effects in an incomplete repeated measures design involve either the use of all possible orders or selected orders (the Latin Square and rotation of a random starting order).

The process of data analysis of the results of repeated measures designs is essentially the same as that for analyzing the results of random groups designs. The data are examined for errors and then summarized using descriptive statistics such as the mean, standard deviation, and measures of effect size. Null hypothesis testing and confidence intervals are used to make claims that the independent variable has produced an effect on behavior.

The most serious problem in any repeated measures design is differential transfer—when performance in one condition differs depending on which condition it follows. Procedures for detecting the presence of differential transfer are available, but there is little that can be done to salvage a study in which it occurs.

KEY CONCEPTS

repeated measures designs   counterbalancing
sensitivity   differential transfer
practice effects

Review Questions

1 Describe what is balanced in a random groups design and what is balanced in a repeated measures design.

2 Briefly describe four reasons why researchers would choose to use a repeated measures design.

3 Define sensitivity and explain why repeated measures designs are often more sensitive than random groups designs.

4 Distinguish between a complete design and an incomplete design for repeated measures designs.

5 What options do researchers have in balancing practice effects in a repeated measures experiment using a complete design?

6 Under what two circumstances would you recommend against the use of ABBA counterbalancing to balance practice effects in a repeated measures experiment using a complete design?

7 State the general rule for balancing practice effects in repeated measures experiments using an incomplete design.

8 Briefly describe the techniques that researchers can use to balance practice effects in the repeated measures experiments using an incomplete design. Identify which of these techniques is preferred and explain why.

9 Explain why an additional initial step is required to summarize the data for an experiment involving a complete repeated measures design.

10 Describe how researchers can determine if differential transfer has occurred in a repeated measures experiment.

CHALLENGE QUESTIONS

1 The following problems represent different situations in the repeated measures designs in which practice effects need to be balanced.

A Consider a repeated measures experiment using a complete design involving one independent variable. The independent variable in the experiment is task difficulty with three levels (Low, Medium, and High). You are to prepare an order for administering the conditions of this experiment so that the independent variable is balanced for practice effects. You are first to use block randomization to balance practice effects and then to use ABBA counterbalancing to balance practice effects. Each condition should appear twice in the order you prepare. (You can use the first row of the random number table (Table A.1) in the Appendix to determine your two random orders for block randomization.)

B Consider a repeated measures experiment using an incomplete design. The independent variable in the experiment is the font size in which a paragraph has been printed, and there are six levels (7, 8, 9, 10, 11, and 12). Present a table showing how you would determine the order of administering the conditions to the first six participants of the experiment. Be sure that practice effects are balanced for these participants.

(Contd.)

2 The pursuit rotor is a test of perceptual-motor coordination. It involves a turntable with a disk about the size of a dime embedded in it. The participant is given a pointer and is asked to keep the pointer on the disk while the turntable is rotating. The dependent variable is the percentage of time on each trial that the participant keeps the pointer on the disk. Learning on this task is linearly related to trials over many periods of practice, and the task generally takes a long time to master. A researcher wants to study the influence of time of day on the performance on this task with four different times (10 A.M., 2 P.M., 6 P.M., and 10 P.M.). The participants will receive a constant number of trials under each of the four conditions, and participants will be tested in one condition per day over four consecutive days. The researcher has 96 participants available.

A What design is being used for the time-of-day variable in this experiment?

B What design is included for the first condition given to each participant? How could the researcher use the results of the design included for the first condition given to each participant to test whether differential transfer had occurred?

3 The following table represents the order of administering the conditions to participants in a repeated measures experiment using an incomplete design in which the independent variable was the loudness of a tone to be detected by the participants while they were concentrating on another task. The three tones were extremely soft (ES), very soft (VS), and soft (S). The values in parentheses represent the number of times each participant detected the tone in each condition. Use this table, when necessary, to answer questions that follow.

Participant	Order of conditions		
1	ES (2)	VS (9)	S (9)
2	VS (3)	S (5)	ES (7)
3	S (4)	ES (3)	VS (5)
4	ES (6)	S (10)	VS (8)
5	VS (7)	ES (8)	S (6)
6	S (8)	VS (4)	ES (4)

A What method was used to balance practice effects in this experiment?

B Present the values you would use to describe the overall effect of the loudness variable. Include a verbal description of the effect along with the descriptive statistics that you use as a basis of your description.

C What claim would you make about the effect of the loudness variable if the probability associated with the F-test for the effect of the loudness variable was $p = .04$?

Answer to Stretching Exercise

The mean numbers of errors for each condition are computed by averaging the six values (one from each participant) for a given condition. For example, for the 0-dose condition the six values are 2, 7, 3, 6, 8, and 4. The mean for the 0-dose condition is 5.0; the mean for the 50-dose is 6.0; and the mean for the 100-dose condition is 7.0. These means indicate that the number of errors on the problem-solving task increased with increasing doses of the drug. Inferential statistics tests using null hypothesis testing or confidence intervals could be done to confirm whether the drug variable produced a reliable effect.

Answer to Challenge Question 1

A Assigning the values 1, 2, and 3 to the Low, Medium, and High conditions, respectively, and using the first row of the random number table (Table A.1) in the Appendix beginning with the first number in the row, the block-randomized sequence is: Low-High-Medium-Low-Medium-High. One possible ABBA counterbalanced sequence is: Low-Medium-High-High-Medium-Low.

B Because there are six conditions, all possible orders are not feasible. Therefore, either a Latin Square or a random starting order with rotation is needed to balance practice effects. A possible set of sequences using rotation is:

Participant	Position					
	1st	2nd	3rd	4th	5th	6th
1	8	10	11	9	7	12
2	10	11	9	7	12	8
3	11	9	7	12	8	10
4	9	7	12	8	10	11
5	7	12	8	10	11	9
6	12	8	10	11	9	7

CHAPTER NINE

Complex Designs

CHAPTER OUTLINE

OVERVIEW

Key Concept }

In Chapter 7 and Chapter 8 we focused on the basic experimental designs that researchers use to study the effect of an independent variable. We described how an independent variable could be implemented with a separate group of participants in each condition (independent groups designs) or with each participant experiencing all the conditions (repeated measures designs). We limited our discussion to experiments involving only one independent variable because we wanted you to concentrate on the basics of experimental research. Experiments involving only one independent variable are not, however, the most common type of experiment in current psychological research. Instead, researchers most often use **complex designs** in which two or more independent variables are studied simultaneously in one experiment.

Consider, for example, three experiments conducted by van Baaren and his colleagues (2004) to examine the role of mimicry in promoting prosocial behaviors, such as helping others. In each experiment, participants were interviewed individually by an experimenter who mimicked (copied) the participant's posture, body orientation (e.g., leaning forward or backward), and arm and leg positions while the participant described his or her reactions to 10 advertisements. The researchers disguised the true purpose of the experiment because participants may have altered their natural behavior if they knew the researchers were copying their behaviors to investigate helping. In order to understand the role of mimicry on behavior, you may want to try discreetly copying someone else's behavior while you have a conversation. Do you notice any difference in their behavior or attitude toward you?

In the first two experiments van Baaren et al. manipulated a single independent variable using a random groups design, which we discussed in Chapter 7. The researchers tested whether participants who were mimicked would be more helpful during the next phase of the study compared to the participants who were not mimicked. Thus, the single independent variable of mimicry had two levels, mimicry and nonmimicry. One group of participants was randomly assigned to be mimicked, and the other participants were not mimicked. Then the dependent variable was assessed. The experimenter "accidentally" dropped six pens, and noted whether each participant picked up the pens. The results indicated that *all* of the participants in the mimicry condition picked up the pens, whereas only 33% of the participants in the nonmimicry condition picked up the pens (a statistically significant effect of mimicry).[1] This finding supported the researchers' hypothesis that mimicry increases helpfulness.

---

[1]The "Stat Tip" in Chapter 5 identifies the *chi-square test of contingency* as the appropriate statistical analysis for examining the relationship between nominal (categorical) variables. In van Baaren et al.'s (2004) first two experiments, the two nominal variables were (1) the mimicry independent variable (mimicry, nonmimicry) and (2) whether the pens were picked up or not picked up. Their results indicated a strong association between mimicry and picking up pens and nonmimicry and not picking up pens.

In a second experiment, van Baaren and his colleagues tested whether participants would help a person other than the experimenter. Using the same mimicry independent variable and procedures, they recorded whether participants picked up pens dropped by a new, unfamiliar experimenter when she entered the room. The presence of the new experimenter was not a manipulated variable. After completing the "advertising" portion of the experiment, the new experimenter entered the room for *all* participants. Participants who were mimicked were more likely to pick up the new experimenter's pens (84%) than participants who were not mimicked (48%). van Baaren et al. concluded that mimicry enhances people's general prosocial orientation—that is, people who are mimicked become more helpful in general, and not just toward the person who mimicked their behavior.

In their third experiment, van Baaren et al. increased the efficiency of their research by using a *complex design* to examine two independent variables simultaneously. In their first two experiments they tested *indirectly* whether helping following mimicry differs for the two experimenters—the original experimenter who mimicked and a new experimenter. The third experiment tested the role of these two variables directly in a single experiment. One independent variable, mimicry, was the same as in the first two experiments. Participants were randomly assigned to be mimicked or not mimicked. For their second independent variable van Baaren et al. manipulated the experimenter who requested help. Participants were randomly assigned to hear the request from the original experimenter or from the new experimenter. Following the mimicry manipulation in this experiment, participants were given the opportunity to donate money they had earned for their research participation to a children's charity. Half of each group of mimicked and nonmimicked participants were asked to donate money by the original experimenter and half were asked for a donation by the new experimenter. To measure helping in this experiment, the dependent variable was the amount of money donated.

As indicated in the following diagram, this experiment involved four conditions: (1) mimicked participants with the original experimenter, (2) mimicked participants with the new experimenter, (3) nonmimicked participants with the original experimenter, and (4) nonmimicked participants with the new experimenter.

	Experimenter who requests donation	
Mimicry group	Original	New
Mimicked group	1	2
Nonmimicked group	3	4

In this complex design, the researchers used a random groups design for both independent variables; that is, participants were randomly assigned to the mimicry and experimenter conditions combined. Complex designs can also be called *factorial designs* because they involve factorial combination of independent variables. *Factorial combination* involves pairing each level of one independent variable with each level of a second independent variable. Mimicked participants' helping was tested either with the original experimenter or a new experimenter, and the same was true for nonmimicked participants. The number of conditions in a complex design is always equal to the product of the number of levels for each independent variable in the experiment. In the van Baaren et al. (2004) experiment there were two levels of mimicry and two levels of the experimenter variable, so there were four conditions ($2 \times 2 = 4$). If the experimenter variable (original, new) were tested with a third mimicry group (e.g., facial expressions mimicked), there would be six conditions in the experiment ($2 \times 3 = 6$).

Factorial combination in complex designs makes it possible to determine the effect of each independent variable alone (*main effect*) and the effect of the independent variables in combination (*interaction effect*). For example, as van Baaren et al. expected based on the findings from their first two experiments, participants who were mimicked donated more money to the children's charity compared to participants who were not mimicked. This represents a main effect of the mimicry variable. That is, "collapsed across" the two levels of the experimenter variable (original, new), mimicked participants helped more than did the nonmimicked participants. More importantly, the researchers were able to test directly whether helping after mimicry applied only to the experimenter who mimicked, or extended to the new experimenter. Inspection of the means for the amount of money donated suggests that the prosocial effect of mimicry was greater when the original experimenter requested the donation compared to when the new experimenter requested the donation. In other words, the effect of mimicry, compared to no mimicry, may lead to greater helping for the mimicker than for other people in the situation.[2] This type of effect, called an *interaction effect,* can be discovered only when two or more independent variables are included in the same experiment. In general, an **interaction effect** occurs when the effect of one independent variable differs depending on the level of a second independent variable.

Key Concept

Complex designs may seem a bit complicated at this point, but the concepts will become clearer as you progress through this chapter. We begin with a review of the characteristics of experimental designs that can be used to investigate

---

[2]Although the means in van Baaren et al.'s (2004) third experiment suggest an interaction between the mimicry and experimenter independent variables, their analysis indicated this effect was not statistically significant. It is likely, however, that they did not have a sufficient sample size in their experiment to detect the interaction effect. You may recall from Chapter 7 that this refers to a *Type II error.*

independent variables in a complex design. We then describe the procedures for producing, analyzing, and interpreting main effects and interaction effects. We introduce the analysis plans that are used for complex designs. We conclude the chapter by giving special attention to the interpretation of interaction effects in complex designs.

GUIDELINES FOR IDENTIFYING AN EXPERIMENTAL DESIGN

- Researchers use complex designs to study the effects of two or more independent variables in one experiment.
- In complex designs, each independent variable can be studied with an independent groups design or with a repeated measures design.

An experiment with a complex design has, by definition, more than one independent variable. Each independent variable in a complex design must be implemented using either an independent groups design or a repeated measures design according to the procedures described in Chapters 7 and 8. When a complex design has both an independent groups variable and a repeated measures variable it is called a *mixed design.* Before examining complex designs themselves, we need to review briefly the characteristics of the various experimental designs that can be used to study a single independent variable. You will be better able to understand descriptions of complex designs if you can quickly and accurately identify the independent variables, their levels, and the design used to implement each independent variable. Similarly, your ability to carry out your own experiments using complex designs will be enhanced if you can confidently select the most appropriate design for each independent variable in which you are interested.

The flowchart in Figure 9.1 summarizes the distinctions among experimental designs by taking you through a series of questions. The diagram will probably prove most useful to you when you are reading about a particular experiment in either your text or a journal article. As you identify each independent variable in an experiment, you can track the variable through Figure 9.1 to determine what design has been used to implement the independent variable. You should go through the flowchart in Figure 9.1 for each independent variable in a complex design. The first question at the top of the flowchart is the most critical one. The answer to the question, How many levels of the independent variable were administered to each participant?, determines whether an independent groups or repeated measures design has been used. Answering the subsequent questions for the independent groups designs will allow you to identify the particular type of design by examining the procedures used to form the groups. For the repeated measures designs, we have included questions to help you distinguish complete and incomplete repeated measures designs and to identify the appropriate balancing techniques for each type.

FIGURE 9.1   Flowchart for identifying experimental designs.

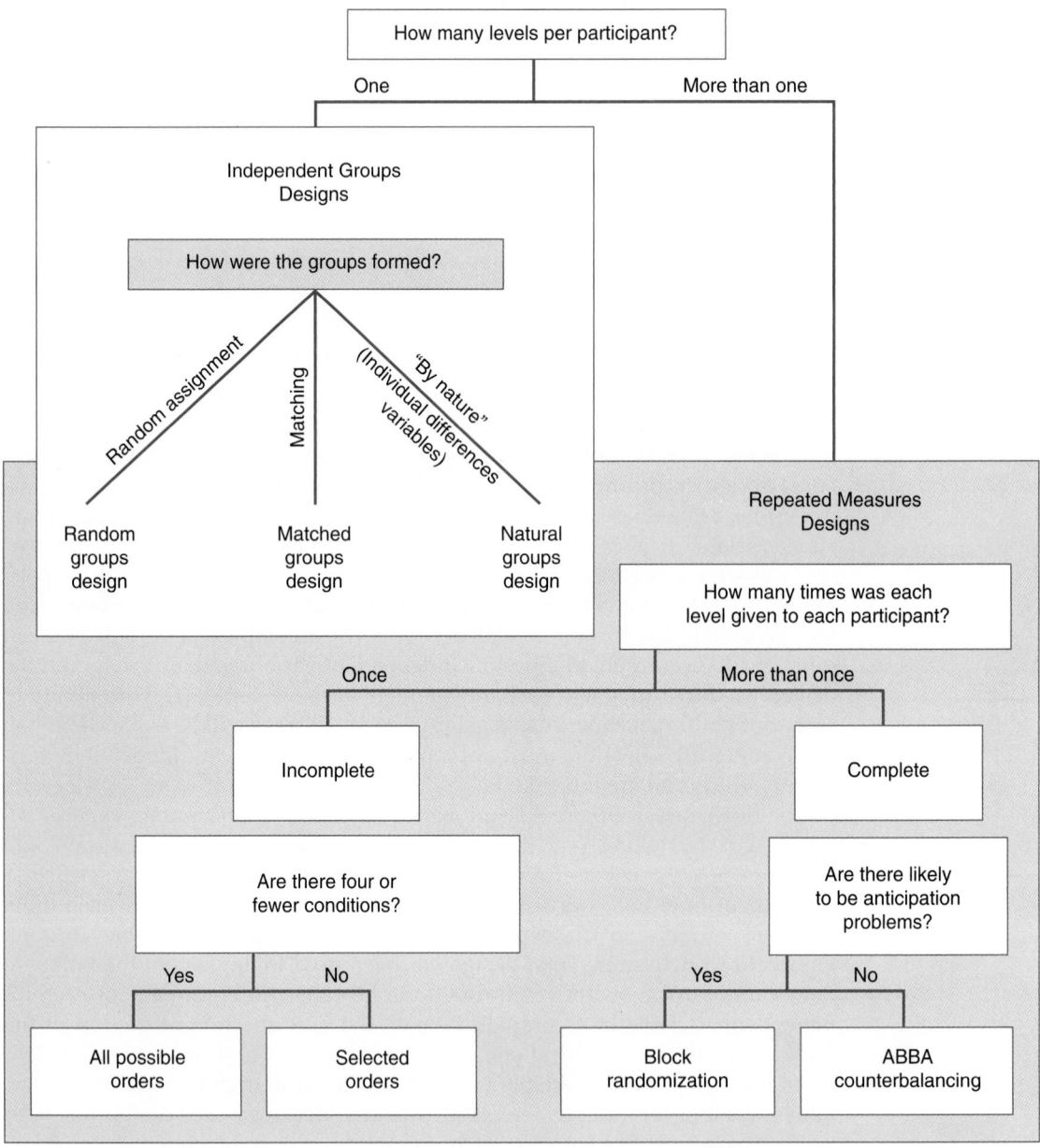

DESCRIBING EFFECTS IN A COMPLEX DESIGN

- The simplest complex design is a 2 × 2 design—two independent variables, each with two levels.
- The number of different conditions in a complex design can be determined by multiplying the number of levels for each independent variable (e.g., 2 × 2 = 4).
- More powerful and efficient complex designs can be created by including more levels of an independent variable or by including more independent variables in the design.

The simplest possible experiment involves one independent variable manipulated at two levels. Similarly, the simplest possible complex design involves two independent variables, each with two levels. Complex designs are identified by specifying the number of levels of each of the independent variables in the experiment. A 2 × 2 (which is read "2 by 2") design, then, identifies the most basic complex design. Conceptually, there is an unlimited number of complex designs because any number of independent variables can be studied and each independent variable can have any number of levels. In practice, however, it is unusual to find experiments involving more than four or five independent variables. Regardless of the number of independent variables, the number of conditions in a complex design can be determined by multiplying the number of levels of the independent variables. For instance, as we saw in van Baaren et al.'s (2004) third experiment of mimicry and the experimenter who requested help, there are two independent variables with each having two levels in a 2 × 2 design; thus, there are four conditions in a 2 × 2 design. In a 3 × 3 design there are two independent variables with three levels each so there are nine conditions. In a 3 × 4 × 2 design there are three independent variables with three, four, and two levels, respectively, and a total of 24 conditions. The primary advantage of all complex designs is the opportunity they provide for identifying interactions between independent variables.

Understanding the 2 × 2 design lays a foundation for understanding complex designs. The 2 × 2 design barely scratches the surface, however, when it comes to tapping the potential of complex designs. Complex designs can be extended beyond the 2 × 2 design in one of two ways. Researchers can add levels to one or both of the independent variables in the design, yielding designs such as the 3 × 2, the 3 × 3, the 4 × 2, the 4 × 3, and so on. Researchers can also build on the 2 × 2 design by increasing the number of independent variables in the same experiment. The number of levels of each variable can range from 2 to some unspecified upper limit. The addition of a third or fourth independent variable yields designs such as the 2 × 2 × 2, the 3 × 3 × 3, the 2 × 2 × 4, the 2 × 3 × 3 × 2, and so on.

The power and complexity of complex designs increase substantially when the number of independent variables in the experiment increases from two to three. In the two-factor design there can be only one interaction effect, but in the three-factor design each independent variable can interact with each of the other two independent variables and all three independent variables can interact together. Thus, the change from a two-factor to a three-factor design introduces the possibility of obtaining four different interaction effects. If the three independent variables are symbolized as A, B, and C, the three-factor design allows a test of the main effects of A, B, and C; two-way interaction effects of A × B, A × C, B × C; and the three-way interaction effect of A × B × C. The efficiency of an experiment involving three independent variables is remarkable. Complex designs are a very powerful tool in psychological research. The experiment described in Box 9.1 will give you a sense of just how powerful complex designs can be.

BOX 9.1

A WEIGHTY MATTER

Pingitore, Dugoni, Tindale, and Spring (1994) investigated possible discrimination against moderately obese people in a mock job interview. Participants in the experiment viewed videotapes of job interviews. In one of their experiments they used a 2 × 2 × 2 design. The first independent variable was the weight of the applicant (normal or overweight). The role of the applicant for the job in the videotapes was played by professional actors who were of normal weight. In the moderately obese conditions, the actors wore makeup and prostheses so that they appeared 20% heavier. The second independent variable in the experiment was the sex of the applicant (male or female). The third independent variable was the participants' concern about their own body (high or low). The degree of concern with one's own body was called the body-schema variable. It was based on the participants' satisfaction/dissatisfaction with their own bodies and the importance of body awareness to their self-concept. The dependent variable was the participants' rating on a 7-point scale of whether they would hire the applicant (1 = definitely not hire and 7 = definitely hire). A natural groups design was used to study the body-schema variable. Participants were randomly assigned to evaluate male or female applicants who were normal weight or moderately obese (random groups designs).

As a first step in describing the results of the Pingitore et al. (1994) study, we will examine an interaction effect of two independent variables that manipulated characteristics of the applicant: the applicant's weight and the applicant's sex. For normal weight applicants, male and female applicants were given very similar hiring ratings (means of 6.0 and 5.5 for males and females, respectively). For overweight applicants, however, mean hiring ratings were lower, especially the ratings of female applicants (means of 4.8 and 3.6 for males and females, respectively). The pattern of this interaction effect indicates that female applicants who are overweight may experience more job discrimination than male applicants who are overweight.

Pingitore et al. (1994) were able to refine their understanding of possible discrimination based on the applicant's weight even further when they included the independent variable of participants' body schema in their analysis. The interaction effect of the applicant's weight and sex described above occurred only with participants who were high in concern about their own bodies. That is, those high on the body-schema variable gave overweight female applicants especially low ratings. Participants who were low on the body-schema variable, on the other hand, gave lower ratings to overweight applicants, but their ratings for male and female applicants were about the same.

The results of the Pingitore et al. experiment for these three variables are shown in Figure 9.2. As you can see, displaying the means for a three-variable experiment requires a graph with more than one "panel." One panel of the figure shows the results for two variables at one level of the third variable and the other panel shows results for the same two variables at the second level of the third independent variable.

One way to summarize the Pingitore et al. (1994) findings shown in Figure 9.2 is to say that the interaction effect of the independent variables of the applicants' weight and the applicants' sex depended upon the participants' body schema. We call this type of finding a three-way (or triple)

interaction effect. As you can see, when we have a three-way interaction effect, all three independent variables must be taken into account when describing the results. In general, when there are two independent variables, an interaction effect occurs when the effect of one of the independent variables differs depending on the level of the second independent variable. *When there are three independent variables in a complex design, a three-way interaction effect occurs when the interaction of two of the independent variables differs depending on the level of the third independent variable.* The results shown in Figure 9.2 illustrate this well. The pattern of results for the first two independent variables (applicants' body weight and sex) differs depending on the level of the third variable (participants' body schema).

FIGURE 9.2 Illustration of an interaction effect for a 2 × 2 × 2 complex design.

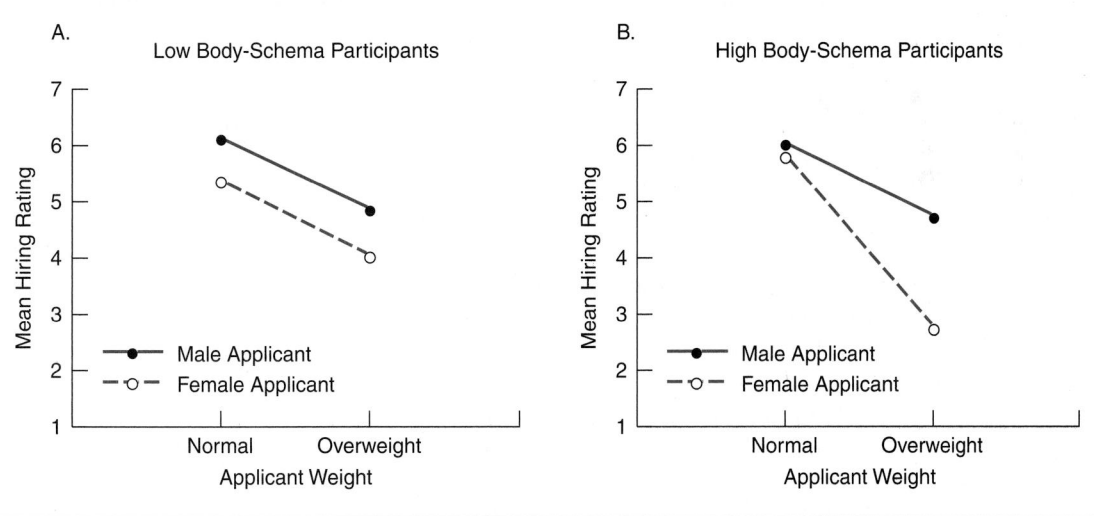

An Example of a 2 × 2 Design

The nature of main effects and interaction effects is essentially the same in all complex designs, but they can be seen most easily in a 2 × 2 design. Consider an experiment by Bazzini and Shaffer (1999). They used a 2 × 2 design to investigate the perceived attractiveness of potential dating partners. Clearly, the close relationships we have with other people, particularly our romantic partners, are very important aspects of our lives. We work hard to maintain these relationships and feel sadness and loss when these relationships end.

Bazzini and Shaffer investigated one important aspect of maintaining a relationship with a romantic partner—how individuals in a committed relationship respond to attractive *alternative* partners. Several previous experiments had demonstrated that individuals in committed relationships rate attractive prospects less favorably than individuals not in relationships. This finding has been interpreted as evidence that those in committed relationships evaluate potential partners negatively in order to maintain their relationship with their current partner. Bazzini and Shaffer argued, however, that it is also possible that individuals *not* in relationships enhance their ratings of the desirability of an attractive prospect. The purpose of Bazzini and Shaffer's experiment was to determine whether *relationship maintenance* (by individuals in committed relationships) or *relationship seeking* (by individuals not in committed relationships) can better explain attractiveness ratings of potential dating partners.

In Bazzini and Shaffer's (1999) experiment college students first completed a questionnaire about their current dating status. Based on their responses to this questionnaire, participants were classified as "exclusive daters" (individuals in a committed romantic relationship) or "nonexclusive daters" (individuals not in a committed relationship). Thus, a natural groups design was used to study their first variable, dating status, with two levels, exclusive and nonexclusive daters.

In a separate session, Bazzini and Shaffer asked these college students to read a hypothetical scenario in which they imagined themselves at a restaurant with their best same-sex friend. The scenario described a situation in which they encounter an "extremely attractive member of the opposite sex" who was described as either attracted to the participant or attracted to the participant's best friend (all of the participants were heterosexual). Students were randomly assigned to read one of the two scenarios. Thus, the second independent variable in Bazzini and Shaffer's experiment was the type of scenario with two levels: the stranger is attracted to the participant or the stranger is attracted to the friend.

Bazzini and Shaffer (1999) reasoned that individuals in exclusive relationships would experience the scenario in which the attractive stranger was attracted to them as a potential *threat* to their current relationship. The exclusive daters should not, however, feel that their current relationship is threatened when the stranger was attracted to the friend. Thus, exclusive daters were predicted to rate the desirability of the attractive stranger *lower* when the stranger was interested in them (to protect their own relationship) compared with when the stranger was interested in their friend. In contrast, Bazzini and Shaffer believed that nonexclusive daters would experience the scenario in which the attractive stranger was attracted to them as an *opportunity* for a new relationship. No such opportunity would be present for the nonexclusive daters when the stranger was attracted to the participant's friend. Thus, nonexclusive daters were predicted to rate the desirability of the attractive stranger *higher* when the attractive stranger was interested in them compared with when the stranger was interested in their friend.

TABLE 9.1   EXAMPLE OF A 2 × 2 DESIGN WITH AN INTERACTION

Dating status	Type of scenario		Means for dating status
	Stranger attracted to friend	Stranger attracted to participant	
Exclusive daters	9.77	9.25	9.52
Nonexclusive daters	10.00	11.13	10.54
Means for type of scenario	9.88	10.17	

Adapted from Bazzini and Shaffer (1999).

Bazzini and Shaffer used several dependent variables, but we will focus on only one, the participants' ratings of the stranger's romantic appeal. Bazzini and Shaffer summed participants' responses to three items (each rated on a 5-point scale) to derive a total "romantic interest" score that ranged from 3 to 15. The mean romantic interest ratings for participants in the four conditions of the experiment are presented in Table 9.1. We will use the data in this table to illustrate two critical concepts in complex designs: *main effects* and *interaction effects*.

Main Effects and Interaction Effects

- The overall effect of each independent variable in a complex design is called a main effect, and represents the differences among the average performance for each level of an independent variable collapsed across the levels of the other independent variable.
- An interaction effect between independent variables occurs when the effect of one independent variable differs depending on the levels of the second independent variable.

Key Concept }

In any complex factorial design it is possible to test predictions regarding the overall effect of each independent variable in the experiment while ignoring the effect of the other independent variable(s). The overall effect of an independent variable in a complex design is called a **main effect.** For example, the overall mean for exclusive daters (9.52) can be obtained by averaging the means of the attracted-to-friend and attracted-to-participant conditions for exclusive daters: $(9.77 + 9.25)/2 = 9.52$. Similarly, the mean of the nonexclusive daters can be computed to be 10.54.[3] *The means for a main effect represent the overall performance at each level of a particular independent variable collapsed across (averaged over) the*

[3]The simple averaging of the values within each row and column to obtain the means for the main effects is possible only when there are equal numbers of participants contributing to each mean in the table. For procedures to calculate weighted means when the cells of the table involve different sample sizes, see Keppel (1991).

STRETCHING EXERCISE

In this exercise you will have the opportunity to practice identifying main effects and interaction effects in 2 × 2 complex designs using only descriptive statistics.

In the spirit of practice makes perfect, let us now turn our attention to the exercise we have prepared to help you learn to identify main effects and interaction effects. Your task is to identify main effects and interaction effects in each of six complex design experiments (A through F). In each table or graph in this box, you are to determine whether the effect of each independent variable differs depending on the level of the other independent variable. In other words, is there an interaction effect? After checking for the interaction effect, you can also check to see whether each independent variable produced an effect when collapsed across the other independent variable. That is, is there a main effect of one or both independent variables? The exercise will be most useful if you also practice translating the data presented in a table (Figure 9.3) into a graph and those presented in graphs (Figures 9.4 and 9.5) into tables. The idea of the exercise is to become as comfortable as you can with the various ways of depicting the results of a complex design.

FIGURE 9.3   Mean number of correct responses as a function of task difficulty and anxiety level.

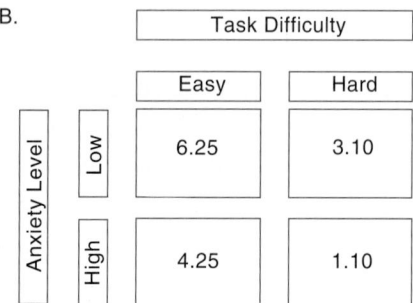

A.

		Task Difficulty	
		Easy	Hard
Anxiety Level	Low	3.34	3.34
	High	5.55	1.19

B.

		Task Difficulty	
		Easy	Hard
Anxiety Level	Low	6.25	3.10
	High	4.25	1.10

FIGURE 9.4   Mean number of aggressive responses as a function of type of media and content.

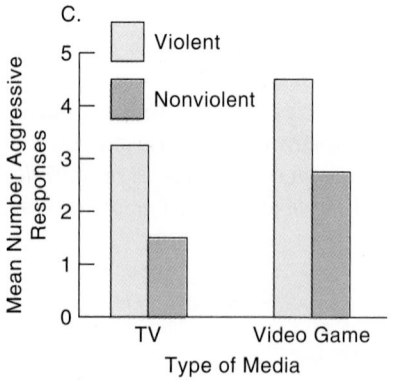

C.

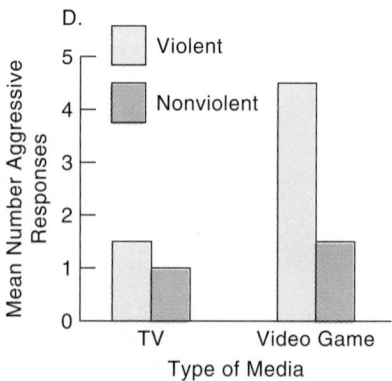

D.

FIGURE 9.5 Mean reaction time as a function of set size and response type.

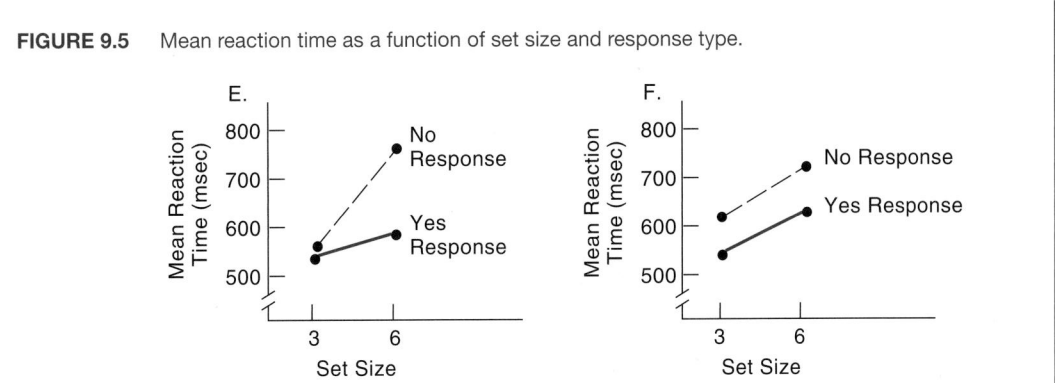

levels of the other independent variable. In this case we collapsed (averaged) over the type of scenario variable to obtain the means for the main effect of the dating status variable. The *main effect* of the dating status variable is the difference between the means for the two levels of the dating status variable (10.54 − 9.52 = 1.02). In the Bazzini and Shaffer experiment, the main effect of the dating status variable indicates that the overall ratings of romanic interest in the stranger were lower for exclusive daters (9.52) than for nonexclusive daters (10.54). Inferential statistics tests confirmed that the main effect of dating status was statistically significant in this experiment. Like the findings of previous research, however, the main effect of dating status can be interpreted either as the result of exclusive daters lowering their ratings due to relationship maintenance or of nonexclusive daters increasing their ratings due to relationship seeking. That is, we cannot determine which hypothesis is supported simply by examining the main effect of the dating status variable.

The most important aspect of Table 9.1 is that it reflects an interaction effect between the two independent variables, dating status and type of scenario. If only exclusive daters had been tested in the experiment (first row of Table 9.1), we would have concluded that the stranger was rated more negatively when attracted to the participant than when attracted to the friend. On the other hand, if only nonexclusive daters had been tested (second row of Table 9.1), we would have concluded that the stranger was rated more positively when attracted to the participant than when attracted to the friend. These results indicate that whether the stranger is rated more positively or negatively depends on the type of scenario. We describe the statistical analysis of interaction effects in complex designs in the next section, Analysis of Complex Designs. For now, it is sufficient if you recognize that *an interaction effect is likely to have occurred when the effect of one independent variable changes depending on the levels of the second independent variable.*

When one independent variable interacts with a second independent variable, the second independent variable must interact with the first one (that is, the order of the independent variables doesn't matter). For example, we described the interaction in Table 9.1 by stating that the effect of dating status depended on the type of scenario. The reverse is also true; the effect of the type of scenario depends on the dating status of the participants. The difference between the ratings of exclusive and nonexclusive daters was larger when the stranger was attracted to the participant than when the stranger was attracted to the friend.

Describing Interaction Effects

- Evidence for interaction effects can be identified using descriptive statistics presented in graphs (nonparallel lines) or tables (subtraction method), and the presence of an interaction effect is confirmed using inferential statistics.

How you choose to describe the results of an interaction effect depends on which aspect of the interaction effect you want to emphasize. For example, Bazzini and Shaffer (1999) emphasized the different effects that the type of scenario had on exclusive and nonexclusive daters to test their predictions based on relationship maintenance and relationship seeking. They found that the ratings of exclusive daters did not differ for the two scenarios, but that the ratings of nonexclusive daters were higher when the stranger was attracted to the participant than when the stranger was attracted to the friend. Bazzini and Shaffer interpreted these findings as support for relationship seeking but not for relationship maintenance. These findings also strongly indicate how the study of interaction effects in complex designs allows researchers to achieve greater understanding than is possible by doing experiments with only one independent variable.

There are three common ways to report a summary of the descriptive statistics in a complex design: tables, bar graphs, and line graphs. The procedures for preparing such tables and figures and the criteria for deciding which type of presentation to use are described in Chapter 14. In general, tables can be used for any complex design and are most useful when the exact values for each condition in the experiment need to be known. Bar graphs and line graphs, on the other hand, are especially useful for showing patterns of results without emphasizing the exact values. Line graphs are particularly useful for depicting the results of complex designs because an interaction effect can be seen so readily in a line graph. *Nonparallel lines in the graph suggest an interaction effect; parallel lines suggest no interaction effect.*

When the results of a 2 × 2 design are summarized in a table, it is easiest to assess the presence or absence of an interaction effect by using the *subtraction method.* The subtraction method involves comparing the differences between the means in each row (or column) of the table. If the differences are different, an interaction effect is likely. In applying the subtraction method, it is essential that the differences be calculated in the same direction. For example, to use the subtraction method for the data reported in Table 9.1, you could subtract the mean ratings for the two scenarios (attracted to friend and attracted to participant) for the exclusive daters (9.77 − 9.25 = .52) and then do the same for the nonexclusive daters ($10.00 - 11.13 = -1.13$). The sign of the obtained difference should also be carefully noted. The subtraction method shows you that these differences are different and, thus, an interaction effect between the two variables is likely.

ANALYSIS OF COMPLEX DESIGNS

- In a complex design with two independent variables, inferential statistics are used to test three effects: the main effects for each independent variable and the interaction effect between the two independent variables.
- Descriptive statistics are needed to interpret the results of inferential statistics.
- How researchers interpret the results of a complex design differs depending on whether a statistically significant interaction effect is present or absent in the data.

The analysis of complex designs builds on the logic used in the analysis of experiments with only one independent variable (see Chapters 7, 12, and 13). The first step in data analysis is to describe the results using descriptive statistics such as mean, standard deviation, and measures of effect size. Inferential statistics such as null hypothesis testing and confidence intervals are then used to confirm what the data reveal. On the basis of the descriptive and inferential statistics, researchers are able to make claims about what they have found. Data analysis of complex designs usually involves the use of the inferential statistics test, the analysis of variance (*F*-test), to determine the main effects of the independent variables and their interaction effect. In complex designs with two independent variables, there are three effects that can be identified. Each independent variable can produce a main effect, and the two independent variables can combine to produce an interaction effect.

Your task in the remaining section of this chapter is to understand data analysis as it is applied to complex designs, especially the manner in which an investigator interprets interaction effects and main effects. It may be helpful to read first the introduction that follows in this section, "Analysis of Complex Designs" and then to review the discussion of this topic in Chapter 13. The emphasis in both of these chapters is on the rationale and logic of these analyses, rather than on the nitty-gritty of computation. Fortunately, computers spare us the need to do the extensive calculations required of data produced in complex designs. On the other hand, computers cannot interpret the outcome of these calculations. That is where you come in. Go slowly; study this material carefully and be sure to examine the tables and figures that accompany this presentation.

The experiment we will use to illustrate the analysis plan for a complex design investigated stereotypic beliefs people have about others. Eagly and Steffen (1984) describe one such stereotype pertaining to beliefs about men and women: "women are more communal (selfless and concerned with others) and less agentic (self-assertive and motivated to master) than men" (p. 735). In a series of experiments testing college students, Eagly and Steffen examined whether the social roles that women and men hold may contribute to the gender stereotypes. That is, if women are more likely to be working at home caring for children and men more likely to be employed outside the home, then men may be seen as more agentic and women may be seen as more communal. Eagly and Steffen obtained results consistent with their social role interpretation.

One of your textbook author's research methods classes tried to replicate one of Eagly and Steffen's (1984) experiments. They reasoned that Eagly and Steffen's results might not replicate because of the changes that had occurred over the decades in men's and women's social roles. The experiment was a 2×3 design with six groups of participants. College students were given a brief description of a target person and were asked to rate the target on 18 different traits. The first independent variable was the sex of the target: male or female. The second independent variable was the role assigned to the target person; there were three levels: unspecified, employed, or home care. The description for the employed male target, for example, was "An average man who is employed full-time." The measure participants used to rate the targets included 18 bipolar trait adjectives like "Not at all Aggressive" at one end of the scale and "Very Aggressive" at the other end of the scale. The participants marked one of five points along the scale to indicate which point best described the target person for that scale. The lowest possible score on the trait measure was 18 (a value of 1 for all 18 adjectives) and the highest possible score on the measure was 90 (a value of 5 for all 18 adjectives). Targets rated higher on the measure were judged to have more agentic characteristics; targets rated lower were judged to have more communal characteristics. Fifteen participants were randomly assigned to each of the six conditions of the experiment.

The results of the replication experiment are presented in Figure 9.7. The nonparallel lines in the figure indicate that an interaction effect is present in this experiment. That is, the difference between the ratings for female and male targets varies with the different social roles. For the unspecified role, female targets are rated less agentic than are the male targets. This finding replicates a gender stereotype similar to that found by Eagly and Steffen (1984)—males are perceived as more agentic than females. For the employed role, however, female and male targets received comparable ratings, and both male and female employed targets were rated as agentic as the male target in the unspecified role. Similarly, for the home care role female and male targets were rated about the same and at about the same level as the female targets in the unspecified role. One way to summarize these findings is to say that if you are employed you are perceived to be more agentic (and more like a male) and if you are caring for children at home you are perceived as less agentic (and more like a female).

There are three potential *sources of systematic variation* in this experiment: the main effect of target sex, the main effect of social role, and the interaction effect between target sex and social role. We describe the specific procedures for using null hypothesis testing (and the *F*-test) and confidence intervals to analyze

FIGURE 9.6   Psychological research shows that stereotypes held about men's and women's roles in society affect how we view people in various occupations.

complex designs in Chapter 13. Here we will focus on how the main effects and interaction effect in a complex design are interpreted based on tests of statistical significance. A statistically significant effect in a complex design (as in any analysis) is an effect associated with a probability under the null hypothesis that is less than the accepted significance level of .05.

Inferential statistics tests can be used in conjunction with descriptive statistics to determine whether an interaction effect has, in fact, occurred in an experiment. The test for an interaction effect involves determining whether the effect of one independent variable differs across the levels of the other independent variable. In the gender stereotype experiment, the test of the interaction effect would be used to determine if the mean differences between males and females are different for the three different social roles. When the test of the interaction effect was done for this experiment, the interaction effect was statistically significant ($p = .0005$). Any claim we would make about the effects of either the target sex variable or the social role variable would need to take into

FIGURE 9.7   Illustration of an interaction effect in a complex design (2 × 3).

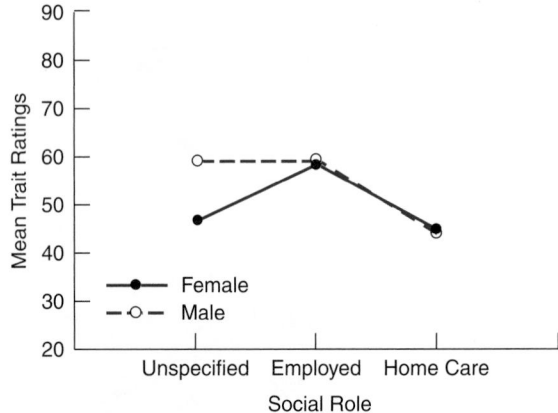

account the presence of this interaction effect. For example, any claim about the effect of target sex would depend on the level of the social role variable.

After examining the data for an interaction effect, researchers may examine the data for the presence of main effects of the independent variables. Using the means reported in Figure 9.7, we can compute the means for the main effect of target sex. The means were 54.0 for male targets and 49.0 for female targets (collapsed across social roles). The probability associated with the F-test for the main effect of target sex was $p = .0005$. Thus, the main effect of target sex was statistically significant. The means for the main effect of social role were 52.5 for the unspecified role, 57.5 for the employed role, and 44.5 for the home care role (collapsed across target sex). The main effect of social role was also statistically significant because the probability associated with the F-test was $p = .0005$.

Based on the results of the inferential statistics tests of the two main effects we now know that each of the independent variables in this experiment has produced a reliable effect on behavior. We need to be careful, however, about interpreting main effects of independent variables in a complex design. For example, based on the means for the statistically significant main effect of target sex, we might make the claim that male targets are rated more agentic than are female targets. Looking at Figure 9.7, however, we see that this claim is true only for the unspecified social role. For the employed and home care roles the mean ratings for male and female targets do not differ. *In general, main effects should be interpreted with caution whenever an interaction effect is present in an experiment.*

In a complex design, just as in an experiment with one independent variable, additional analyses may be needed to interpret the results. For example, in the gender stereotype experiment we might use confidence intervals to test the differences between the means for the two target genders for each of the social roles. The analysis plan for complex design experiments differs depending upon whether a statistically significant interaction effect is present in the experiment.

TABLE 9.2 GUIDELINES FOR THE ANALYSIS OF A TWO-FACTOR EXPERIMENT

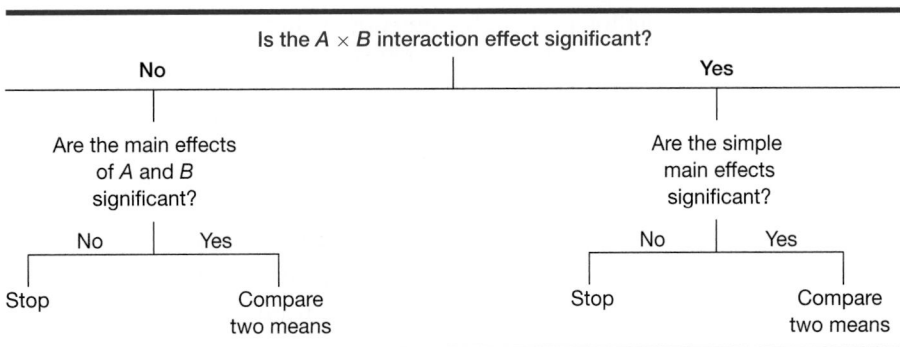

Table 9.2 provides guidelines for interpreting a complex design experiment when an interaction effect does occur and when one does not. We will illustrate both paths in Table 9.2 by describing an experiment in which there is a statistically significant interaction effect present and then describing a study in which the interaction effect is not statistically significant.

Analysis Plan with an Interaction Effect

- If the analysis of a complex design reveals a statistically significant interaction effect, the source of the interaction effect is identified using simple main effects analyses and comparisons of two means.
- A simple main effect is the effect of one independent variable at one level of a second independent variable.

One of the many approaches psychologists have tried to use to understand depression is based on investigating the differences between the thought patterns of depressed and nondepressed people. One aspect of this cognitive approach to depression deals with attributions, the causal explanations we use to try to account for our own behavior and the behavior of others. For example, depressed people exhibit a tendency to make attributions that are pessimistic, overgeneralized, and self-blaming. According to the cognitive approach, this tendency toward less optimistic thinking on the part of depressed people may be critically involved in causing the onset of depression, maintaining depression once it occurs, and alleviating depression by changing depressive thinking to be more optimistic. The study we will be using to illustrate the interpretation of the results of a complex design with an interaction effect represents one of the many experiments investigating the cognitive bases of depression.

Rodman and Burger (1985) investigated a particular phenomenon called the defensive-attribution effect. In previous experiments, nondepressed participants read a description of an accident in which a person suffered mild or severe consequences. These nondepressed individuals attributed more responsibility to the perpetrator in the severe than in the mild accident condition. One interpretation of this phenomenon is that people do not want to attribute the cause of a severe accident to chance. If they did attribute the accident to chance, they would be increasing the perceived possibility that they themselves could be involved in a severe accident. Their attribution of greater responsibility to the perpetrator in the severe accident is a defensive attribution, allowing them to perceive themselves as protected against a likelihood of future severe accidents. Rodman and Burger reasoned that depressed people might be less likely to show this type of defensive-attribution effect because their negative thinking would lead them to be less self-protective. Stated more formally, they tested the hypothesis that the defensive-attribution effect would decrease as a person's level of depression increased.

Rodman and Burger tested 56 college students in a 2 × 3 design. The first independent variable was the severity of the described accident (severe and nonsevere), and this was manipulated using the random groups design. The natural groups design was used for the second independent variable; students were selected on the basis of their scores on a paper-and-pencil test of depression to represent three groups: nondepressed, slightly depressed, and mildly depressed individuals. The dependent variable was a single item on a longer questionnaire that asked students to divide 100% among four potential sources of responsibility: each of the three drivers in the accident and uncontrollable "circumstances." The defensive-attribution effect would be reflected in a larger value assigned to uncontrollable circumstances (i.e., "chance") for the nonsevere than for the severe accident. (Remember that it is protective to avoid making attributions to uncontrollable circumstances for severe accidents.) The mean percentage values for this uncontrollable factor for each of the six conditions are presented in Table 9.3.

As Rodman and Burger had predicted, there was an interaction effect between the two independent variables: As degree of depression increases, the differences between the percentage values for severe and nonsevere accidents change. (You may wish to use the subtraction method to confirm this.) Nondepressed students show the defensive-attribution effect and mildly depressed students do not. Inferential statistics tests of these results using null hypothesis testing confirmed that the interaction effect was statistically significant.

TABLE 9.3   MEAN PERCENTAGE OF RESPONSIBILITY ATTRIBUTED
TO UNCONTROLLABLE CIRCUMSTANCES

Type of accident	Level of depression		
	Nondepressed	Slightly depressed	Mildly depressed
Severe	7.00 (9.2)	14.00 (16.1)	16.90 (16.0)
Nonsevere	30.50 (22.2)	16.50 (12.7)	3.75 (3.5)

Note: Standard deviations appear in parentheses. Adapted from Rodman and Burger (1985).

Once we have confirmed that there is an interaction of two independent variables, we must locate more precisely the source of that interaction. As outlined in Table 9.2, there are statistical tests specifically designed for tracing the source of a significant interaction. These tests are called simple main effects and comparisons of two means (see Chapter 13).

Key Concept

A **simple main effect** is the effect of one independent variable at *one level* of a second independent variable. We can illustrate the use of simple main effects by returning to the results of the Rodman and Burger experiment. There are five simple main effects in Table 9.3: the effect of the type of accident at each of the three levels of depression and the effect of the degree of depression at each of the two types of accidents. Rodman and Burger predicted that the defensive-attribution effect (the difference between the means for severe and nonsevere accidents) would decrease as severity of depression increased. Therefore, they chose to test the simple main effects of type of accident at each of the three levels of depression. They found, as predicted, that the simple main effect of type of accident was statistically significant for nondepressed students, but the simple main effects of type of accident for the slightly depressed and for the mildly depressed students were not statistically significant. When three or more means are tested in a simple main effect (as when testing the effect of the depression variable at each level of accident type), comparisons of means tested two at a time can be done to identify the source of the simple main effect (see Chapter 13).

Once an interaction effect has been thoroughly analyzed, researchers can also examine the main effects of each independent variable. As we mentioned earlier in this chapter, however, the main effects are of much less interest when we know that an interaction effect is statistically significant. For instance, the interaction effect in this experiment tells us that the effect of the type of accident varies depending on the level of depression. Once we know this, we have not added much when we learn that, overall, the nonsevere accident led to a higher mean percentage of responsibility attributed to uncontrollable circumstances than did the severe accident. Nonetheless, there are experiments in which the interaction effect and the main effects are all of interest.

Analysis Plan with No Interaction Effect

- If the analysis of a complex design indicates the interaction effect between independent variables is not statistically significant, the next step in the analysis plan is to determine whether the main effects of the variables are statistically significant.
- The source of a statistically significant main effect can be specified more precisely by performing comparisons of two means or using confidence intervals to compare means two at a time.

Dittmar, Berch, and Warm (1982) used a 3 × 3 design to test whether people who are deaf perform better on a visual-vigilance task than people who can hear. A visual-vigilance task requires a person to detect intermittent visual signals such as blips on a radar screen for a long period of time. Dittmar et al. expected

FIGURE 9.8   Results of a 3 × 3 complex design in which there was no interaction effect but there were two main effects. (Adapted from Dittmar et al., 1982.)

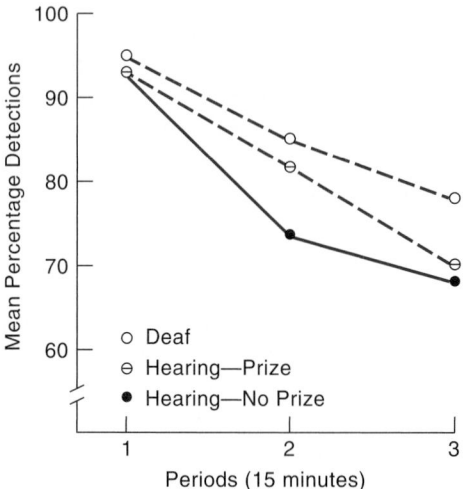

that deaf people would have an advantage on such a task because their deafness would keep them from being distracted. The group of deaf participants was offered a prize if their vigilance performance was the best in their group. Two additional groups of hearing people were tested to determine if the prize served as an incentive. One group of hearing people was offered a prize and the other group was not. These three groups represent the levels of the first independent variable in the experiment. The participants in all three groups were tested in a 45-minute session divided into three continuous 15-minute periods, and these three periods were the levels of the second independent variable. Note that this is a mixed factorial design in that the first independent variable is an independent groups variable and the second is a repeated measures variable.

The mean percentage of correct detections across the three periods for the three different groups of participants is presented in Figure 9.8. The interaction effect, or more accurately the lack of an interaction effect, can be seen in the figure. Although the three lines in the figure are not perfectly parallel, the mean percentage of correct detections appears to decrease in all three groups at approximately the same rate. Inferential statistics tests confirmed that there was not a statistically significant interaction effect in this experiment. The data shown in Figure 9.8 illustrate a more general principle of data analysis. *The pattern of the findings as shown by the descriptive statistics is not sufficient to decide whether an interaction effect is present in an experiment. Inferential statistics tests must be done to confirm what the data reveal.*

When the interaction effect is not statistically significant in an experiment, the next step is to examine the main effects of each independent variable (see Table 9.2). The results of the Dittmar et al. (1982) experiment are presented again in Table 9.4 to make it easier to determine the main effects. By collapsing

TABLE 9.4   MEAN PERCENTAGE OF CORRECT DETECTIONS ACROSS THREE PERIODS
OF A VIGILANCE TASK FOR DEAF AND HEARING PARTICIPANTS

	Period		
Group	1	2	3
Deaf	95	85	78
Hearing—Prize	93	82	70
Hearing—No Prize	93	74	68

Adapted from Dittmar et al. (1982).

(averaging) across the three vigilance periods, we can obtain the mean detection rates for each group (i.e., the main effect of the group variable). These means are 86.0, 81.7, and 78.3 for the Deaf, Hearing—Prize, and Hearing—No Prize groups, respectively. The group main effect was statistically significant. As indicated in Table 9.2, the source of a statistically significant main effect can be specified more precisely by comparing means two at a time. These comparisons can be done using *t*-tests or confidence intervals. For example, a comparison of performance in the Hearing—Prize and Hearing—No Prize groups (81.7 and 78.3) was not statistically significant, indicating that the presence of an incentive did not produce a difference between these two groups. However, the average performance of the two groups of hearing participants (80.0) was significantly lower than the performance of the deaf participants (86.0). These comparisons allow us to make two claims. First, deaf participants were better at the vigilance task than hearing participants. Second, the offer of a prize did not affect performance on the vigilance task for hearing participants.

We can also test for the main effect of the period variable using the means in Table 9.4. By collapsing across the three groups of participants, we obtain the means 93.7 (first period), 80.3 (second period), and 72.0 (third period) for the main effect of the period variable. The main effect of this variable was statistically significant, and visual inspection of the means reveals that performance decreased, on the average, over time. Comparisons of means considered two at a time could then be used to determine whether the decreases over each successive period (93.7 to 80.3 and 80.3 to 72.0) were statistically significant. The analysis of Dittmar et al.'s vigilance experiment illustrates that much can be learned from a complex design even when there is no statistically significant interaction effect.

INTERPRETING INTERACTION EFFECTS

Interaction Effects and Theory Testing

- Theories frequently predict that two or more independent variables interact to influence behavior; therefore, complex designs are needed to test theories.
- Tests of theories can sometimes produce contradictory findings. Interaction effects can be useful in resolving these contradictions.

Theories play a critical role in the scientific method. Complex designs greatly enhance researchers' ability to test theories because they can test for both main effects and interaction effects. For example, Bazzini and Shaffer (1999) examined hypotheses about the attractiveness of potential dating partners derived from a theory of interpersonal relationships. Prior to their study, research on the attractiveness of potential dating partners seemed to support the relationship-maintenance hypothesis. Because they used a complex design, Bazzini and Shaffer's data provided evidence to test both the relationship-maintenance hypothesis and the relationship-seeking hypothesis. The data for participants' romantic interest in the attractive stranger provided evidence regarding the relationship-maintenance hypothesis (for exclusive daters) and the relationship-seeking hypothesis (for nonexclusive daters). Bazzini and Shaffer predicted that exclusive daters may view an attractive stranger who is attracted to them more negatively in order to maintain and protect their current relationship. Contrary to this prediction, however, exclusive daters rated the stranger similarly when the stranger was described as attracted to them or to their friend. Bazzini and Shaffer stated that this finding "is not consistent with the notion that exclusive daters would seek to maintain or protect their existing relationship by devaluing the attributes of an attractive stimulus person who might pose a threat to their relationship" (p. 167). Thus, the relationship-maintenance hypothesis was not supported in their experiment.

In contrast, the findings for nonexclusive daters indicated support for the relationship-seeking hypothesis. Nonexclusive daters rated their romantic interest higher when the stranger was attracted to them rather than to their friend. As Bazzini and Shaffer (1999) stated, "they seemed to be bolstering their evaluations of the available target as if they were intrigued by the possibility of a new relationship" (p. 168). Bazzini and Shaffer's experiment illustrates how interaction effects obtained in a complex design allow us to make more sophisticated tests of psychological theories.

Bazzini and Shaffer's (1999) experiment also illustrates how interaction effects in complex designs can be useful for resolving contradictory findings. Previous research had supported the relationship-maintenance hypothesis, but Bazzini and Shaffer's results for the exclusive daters did not support relationship maintenance. In the previous research, participants responded to potential partners who were attracted to them and exclusive daters rated these potential partners more negatively than did nonexclusive daters. Bazzini and Shaffer replicated this finding for the conditions that involved potential partners attracted to the participant. By doing a complex design that included the independent variable of type of scenario (stranger attracted to participant and stranger attracted to friend), Bazzini and Shaffer were able to shed light on the contradictory findings regarding the relationship-maintenance hypothesis. More generally, complex designs can be extremely useful in tracking down the reasons for seemingly contradictory findings when theories are tested. The process can be a painstaking one, but it can also be very worthwhile.

Interaction Effects and External Validity

- When no interaction effect occurs in a complex design, the effects of each independent variable can be generalized across the levels of the other independent variable; thus, external validity of the independent variables increases.
- The presence of an interaction effect identifies boundaries for the external validity of a finding by specifying the conditions in which an effect of an independent variable occurs.

In Chapter 7 we discussed at some length the procedures for establishing the external validity of a research finding when an experiment involves only one independent variable. We described how partial replications could be done to establish external validity—that is, the extent to which our research findings may be generalized. We also discussed how field experiments allow researchers to examine independent variables in real-world settings. We can now examine the role of complex designs in establishing the external validity of a finding. As you might have suspected, the presence or absence of an interaction effect is critical in determining the external validity of the findings in a complex design.

When no interaction effect occurs in a complex design, we know that the effects of each independent variable can be generalized across the levels of the other independent variable. For instance, the Dittmar et al. (1982) study that we just described showed that detection performance declined across three 15-minute vigilance periods, but the decline occurred at approximately the same rate for hearing and deaf participants. That is, there was no interaction effect between the hearing variable (hearing or deaf) and the period variable. Thus, declining performance in a vigilance task can be generalized to both hearing and deaf people.

Of course, we cannot generalize our findings beyond the boundaries or conditions that were included in the experiment. For example, the absence of an interaction effect between the hearing variable and periods in the vigilance task does not allow us to conclude that detection performance would decline at the same rate if other groups were tested, such as young children or trained observers. Similarly, we do not know whether the same decline across periods would occur if there were short breaks after each observation period. We must also remember that not finding a statistically significant interaction effect does not necessarily mean that an interaction effect is not really present; we may not have performed an experiment with sufficient sensitivity to detect it.

As we have seen, the absence of an interaction effect increases the external validity of the effects of each independent variable in the experiment. Perhaps more important, the *presence* of an interaction effect identifies boundaries for the external validity of a finding. For example, when they tested exclusive daters, Bazzini and Shaffer (1999) found that the type of scenario (stranger attracted to participant *vs.* friend) had little effect on participants' ratings of the desirability of a potential dating partner. However, desirability ratings did differ for the two scenarios when nonexclusive daters were tested. This interaction effect clearly sets limits on the external validity of the effect that type of scenario has on desirability ratings. Given this finding, the best way to respond to someone's query regarding the general effect that the type of scenario has on potential dating partners' desirability is to say, "*It depends.*" In this case, it depends on whether exclusive or nonexclusive daters are tested. The presence of the interaction effect sets boundaries for the external validity, but the interaction effect also specifies what those boundaries are.

The possibility of interaction effects among independent variables should lead us to be cautious about saying that an independent variable does not have an effect on behavior. Independent variables that influence behavior are called relevant independent variables. In general, a **relevant independent variable** is one that influences behavior directly (results in a main effect) or produces an interaction effect when studied in combination with a second independent variable. Distinguishing between factors that affect behavior and those that do not is essential for developing adequate theories to explain behavior and for designing effective interventions to deal with problems in applied settings such as schools, hospitals, and factories (see Chapters 10 and 11).

Key Concept

There are several reasons why we should be cautious about identifying an independent variable as *irrelevant*. First, if an independent variable is shown to have no effect in an experiment, we cannot assume that this variable wouldn't have an effect if different levels of the independent variable had been tested. Second, if an independent variable has no effect in a single-factor experiment, this doesn't mean that it won't interact with another independent variable when used in a complex design. Third, the absence of a statistically significant effect may or may not mean that the effect is not present. Minimally, we would want to consider the sensitivity of our experiment and the power of our statistical analysis before deciding that we have identified an irrelevant variable. (See Chapter 13 for a discussion of the power of a statistical analysis.) For now, it is best if you avoid being dogmatic about identifying any independent variable as irrelevant.

Interaction Effects and Ceiling and Floor Effects

- When participants' performance reaches a maximum (ceiling) or a minimum (floor) in one or more conditions of an experiment, results for an interaction effect are uninterpretable.

Consider the results of a 3 × 2 experiment investigating the effects of increasing amounts of practice on performance during a physical-fitness test. There were six groups of participants in this plausible but hypothetical experiment. Participants were first given either 10, 30, or 60 minutes to practice, doing either easy or hard exercises. Then they took a fitness test using easy or hard exercises (the same they had practiced). The dependent variable was the percentage of exercises that each participant was able to complete in a 15-minute test period. Results of the experiment are presented in Figure 9.9.

The pattern of results in Figure 9.9 looks like a classic interaction effect; the effect of amount of practice time differed for the easy and hard exercises.

FIGURE 9.9   Illustration of a ceiling effect.

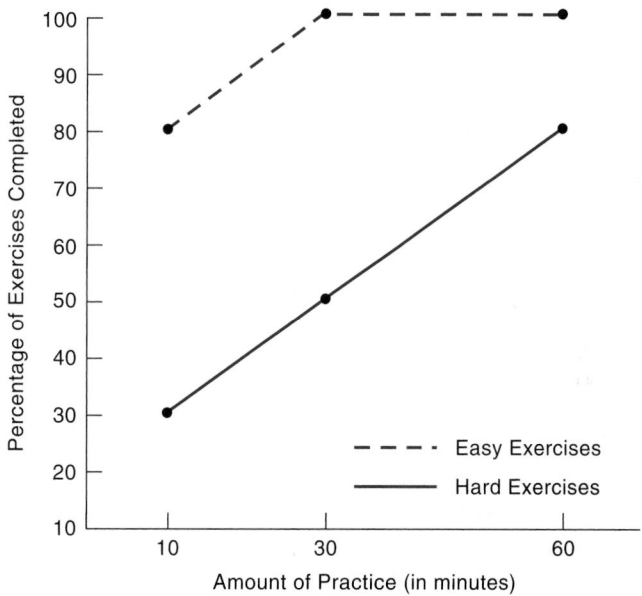

Increasing practice time improved test performance for the hard exercises, but performance leveled off after 30 minutes of practice with the easy exercises. If a standard analysis was applied to these data, the interaction effect would very likely be statistically significant. Unfortunately, this interaction effect would be essentially uninterpretable. For those groups given practice with the easy exercises, performance reached the maximum level after 30 minutes of practice, so no improvement beyond this point could be shown in the 60-minute group. Even if the participants given 60 minutes of practice had further benefited from the extra practice, the experimenter could not measure this improvement on the chosen dependent variable.

The preceding experiment illustrates the general measurement problem referred to as a ceiling effect. Whenever performance reaches a maximum in any condition of an experiment, there is danger of a **ceiling effect.** The corresponding name given to this problem when performance reaches a minimum (e.g., zero errors on a test) is a **floor effect.** Researchers can avoid ceiling and floor effects by selecting dependent variables that allow ample "room" for performance differences to be measured across conditions. For example, in the fitness experiment it would have been better to test participants with a greater number of exercises than anyone could be expected to complete in the time allotted for the test. The mean number of exercises completed in each condition could then be used to assess the effects of the two independent variables without the danger of a ceiling effect. It is important to note that ceiling effects also can pose a problem in experiments that don't involve a complex design. If the fitness experiment had included only the easy exercises, there would still be a ceiling effect in the experiment.

Key Concepts

Interaction Effects and the Natural Groups Design

- Researchers use complex designs to make causal inferences about natural groups variables when they test a theory for why natural groups differ.
- Three steps for making a causal inference involving a natural groups variable are to state a theory for why group differences exist, manipulate an independent variable that should demonstrate the theorized process, and test whether an interaction effect occurs between the manipulated independent variable and natural groups variable.

The natural groups design, which we described briefly in Chapter 7, is one of the most popular research designs in psychology. Groups of people are formed by selecting individuals who differ on some characteristic such as gender, age, introversion, extraversion, or aggressiveness. Researchers then look for systematic relationships between these individual differences variables and other aspects of behavior. The natural groups design is an effective one for establishing correlations between individuals' characteristics and their performance. As we also described in Chapter 7, however, the natural groups design is perhaps the most challenging design when it comes to drawing conclusions about the causes of behavior.

The difficulty in interpreting the natural groups design arises when we try to conclude that differences in performance are caused by the characteristics of the people we used to define the groups. For instance, consider an experiment in which participants are selected because of their musical training. One group of participants includes people with 10 or more years of formal musical training, and one group includes people with no formal training. Both groups are tested on their ability to remember the musical notation for simple 10-note melodies. Not surprisingly, the results of these tests show that those with musical training perform far better than those without such training.

We can conclude on the basis of these results that memory for simple melodies varies with (is correlated with) amount of musical training. But we cannot conclude that musical training *causes* superior memory performance. Why not? There are probably many additional ways in which people with 10 years of musical training differ from those without such training. The groups may differ in amount and type of general education, family background, socioeconomic status, and amount and type of experience they have had listening to music. Also, those with musical training may have generally better memories than those without such training, and their superior memory for simple melodies may reflect this general memory ability. Finally, those who sought out musical training may have done so because they had a special aptitude for music. Accordingly, they might have done better on the memory task even if they had not had any musical training. In short, there are many possible causes other than individual differences in musical training for the difference in memory performance that was observed.

There is a potential solution to the problem of drawing causal inferences based on the natural groups design (Underwood & Shaughnessy, 1975). The key to this solution is to develop a theory regarding the critical individual difference variable. For example, Halpern and Bower (1982) were interested in how memory for musical notation differs between musicians and nonmusicians. Halpern and Bower developed a theory of how musical training would influence the cognitive processing of musical notation by those who had such training. Their theory was based on a memory concept called "chunking." You can get some sense of the memory advantage provided by chunking if you imagine trying to memorize the following strings of 15 letters: HBOFBICNN-USAWWW. Chunking helps memory by changing the same string of letters to a series of five more easily remembered chunks: HBO-FBI-CNN-USA-WWW.

Halpern and Bower theorized that musical training led musicians to "chunk" musical notation into meaningful musical units, thereby reducing the amount of information they needed to remember in order to reproduce the notation for a simple melody. Furthermore, if this process were responsible for the difference between the memory performance of musicians and nonmusicians, then the difference between musicians and nonmusicians should be greater for melodies with good musical structure than for those with poor musical structure. Halpern and Bower manipulated the independent variable of musical structure to test their theory. To do this, they used three different types of melodies to test their groups of musicians and nonmusicians. They prepared sets of simple melodies whose notations had similar visual structures but that were either good, bad, or random in musical structure.

The critical test in Halpern and Bower's experiment was whether they would obtain an interaction effect between the two independent variables: musical training and type of melodies. Specifically, they expected that the difference in memory performance between musicians and nonmusicians would be largest for the melodies exhibiting good structure, next largest for the melodies exhibiting bad structure, and smallest for the random melodies. The results of Halpern and Bower's experiment conformed exactly to their predictions.

The obtained interaction effect allowed Halpern and Bower to rule out many alternative hypotheses for the difference in memory performance between musicians and nonmusicians. Such characteristics as amount and type of general education, socioeconomic status, and family background are not likely to explain why there is a systematic relationship between the structure of the melodies and the size of the difference in memory performance between musicians and nonmusicians. These potential alternative hypotheses cannot explain why there was little difference in the two groups' memory performance for random melodies. The interaction effect makes such simple correlational explanations much less plausible.

There are several steps that the investigator must take in carrying out the general procedure for drawing causal inferences based on the natural groups design.

Step 1: Develop a Theory   The first step is to develop a theory explaining why a difference should occur in the performance of groups that have been differentiated on the basis of an individual differences variable. For example,

Halpern and Bower theorized that musicians and nonmusicians differed in musical performance because of the way that these groups cognitively organize ("chunk") melodies.

Step 2: Identify a Relevant Variable to Manipulate   The second step is to select an independent variable that can be manipulated and that is presumed to influence the likelihood that this theoretical process will occur. Halpern and Bower suggested that type of musical structure was a variable associated with ease of chunking.

Step 3: Test for an Interaction   The most critical aspect of the recommended approach is to strive to produce an interaction effect between the manipulated variable and the individual differences variable. Thus, the relevant manipulated independent variable is applied to both natural groups. Halpern and Bower sought an interaction effect between the individual differences variable (musician vs. nonmusician) and the manipulated variable (type of musical structure) in a 2 × 3 complex design. The approach can be strengthened even further by testing predictions of interaction effects of three independent variables: two manipulated independent variables and the individual differences variable (see, for example, Anderson & Revelle, 1982).

SUMMARY

A complex design is one in which two or more independent variables are studied in the same experiment. A complex design involving two independent variables allows researchers to determine the overall effect of each independent variable (the main effect of each variable). More important, complex designs can be used to reveal the interaction effect between independent variables. Interaction effects occur when the effect of each independent variable depends on the level of the other independent variable.

The simplest possible complex design is the 2 × 2 design, in which two independent variables are both studied at two levels. The number of conditions in a factorial design is equal to the product of the levels of the independent variables (e.g., 2 × 3 = 6). Complex designs beyond the 2 × 2 can be even more useful for understanding behavior. Additional levels of one or both of the independent variables can be added to yield designs such as the 3 × 2, the 3 × 3, the 4 × 2, the 4 × 3, and so on. Additional independent variables can also be included to yield designs such as the 2 × 2 × 2, the 2 × 3 × 3, and so on. Experiments involving three independent variables are remarkably efficient. They allow researchers to determine the main effects of each of the three variables, the three two-way interaction effects, and the simultaneous interaction effect of all three variables.

When two independent variables are studied in a complex design, three potential sources of systematic variation can be interpreted. Each independent variable can produce a statistically significant main effect, and the two independent variables can combine to produce a statistically significant interaction effect. Interaction effects can be initially identified by using the subtraction method when the descriptive statistics are reported in a table, or by the presence of nonparallel lines when the results appear in a line graph. If the interaction effect does prove to be statistically significant, we can analyze the results further by examining simple main effects and, if necessary, comparisons of means considered two at a time. When no interaction effect arises, we examine the main effects of each independent variable, and we can use comparisons of two means or confidence intervals when necessary.

Complex designs play a critical role in the testing of predictions derived from psychological theories. Complex designs are also essential to resolve contradictions that arise when theories are tested. When a complex design is used and no interaction effect occurs, we know that the effects of each independent variable can be generalized across the levels of the other independent variable(s). When an interaction effect does occur, however, boundaries on the external validity of a finding can be clearly specified. The possibility of interaction effects requires that we expand the definition of a relevant independent variable to include those that influence behavior directly (produce main effects) and those that produce an interaction effect when studied in combination with another independent variable. Interaction effects that may arise because of measurement problems such as ceiling or floor effects must not be confused with interaction effects that reflect the true combined effect of two independent variables. Interaction effects can also be most helpful in solving the problem of drawing causal inferences based on the natural groups design.

KEY CONCEPTS

complex designs
interaction effect
main effect

simple main effect
relevant independent variable
ceiling and floor effects

REVIEW QUESTIONS

1 Identify the number of independent variables, the number of levels for each independent variable, and the total number of conditions for each of the following examples of complex design experiments: (a) 2×3 (b) 3×3 (c) $2 \times 2 \times 3$ (d) 4×3

2 Identify the conditions in a complex design when the following independent variables are factorially combined: (1) type of task with 3 levels (visual, auditory, tactile) and (2) group of children tested with 2 levels ("normal," developmentally delayed").

3 Use the Bazzini and Shaffer experiment on the attractiveness of potential dating partners to illustrate that there is one possible interaction effect in a 2×2 design but that there are two possible ways to describe the interaction effect.

4 Describe how you would use the subtraction method to decide whether an interaction effect was present in a table showing the results of a 2×2 complex design.

5 Describe the pattern in a line graph that indicates the presence of an interaction effect in a complex design.

6 Outline the steps in the analysis plan for a complex design with two independent variables when there is an interaction effect and when there is not an interaction effect.

7 Use an example to illustrate how a complex design can be used to test predictions derived from a psychological theory.

8 How is the external validity of the findings in a complex design influenced by the presence or absence of an interaction effect?

9 Explain why researchers should be cautious about saying that an independent variable does not have an effect on behavior.

10 Describe the pattern of descriptive statistics that would indicate a ceiling (or floor) effect may be present in a data set, and describe how this pattern of data may affect the interpretation of inferential statistics (e.g., F-test) for these data.

11 Explain how interaction effects in a complex design can be used as part of the solution to the problem of drawing causal inferences on the basis of the natural groups design.

CHALLENGE QUESTIONS

1 Consider an experiment in which two independent variables have been manipulated. Variable A has been manipulated at three levels, and Variable B has been manipulated at two levels.

A Draw a graph showing a main effect of Variable B, no main effect of Variable A, and no interaction effect between the two variables.

B Draw a graph showing no main effect of Variable A, no main effect of Variable B, but an interaction effect between the two variables.

C Draw a graph showing a main effect of Variable A, a main effect of Variable B, and no interaction effect between the A and B variables.

2 A researcher has used a complex design to study the effects of training (untrained and trained) and problem difficulty (easy and hard) on participants' problem-solving ability. The researcher tested a total of 80 participants, with 20 randomly assigned to each of the four groups resulting from the factorial combination of the two independent variables. The data presented below represent the percentage of the problems that participants solved in each of the four conditions.

Problem difficulty	Training	
	Untrained	Trained
Easy	90	95
Hard	30	60

A Is there evidence of a possible interaction effect in this experiment?

B What aspect of the results of this experiment would lead you to be hesitant to interpret an interaction effect if one were present in this experiment?

C How could the researcher modify the experiment so as to be able to interpret an interaction effect if it should occur?

3 A psychologist is interested in whether older people suffer a deficit with respect to their reaction time in processing complex visual patterns. Fifty 65-year-old people and 50 college-age young adults volunteer to participate in the experiment. The participants are tested using an embedded figures test. The psychologist presents a simple figure to each participant followed immediately by a complex pattern that contains the simple figure. The participant must indicate as quickly as possible the location of the simple figure in the complex pattern. Participants are timed from the onset of the complex pattern until they locate the simple pattern. As the psychologist had expected, the mean reaction times for the older adults were markedly longer than those for the young adults. By any standard the results were statistically significant.

A The psychologist claims based on these results that the differences in reaction times in this experiment were caused by a deficit in the older adults' ability to process complex information. You recognize that a complex design experiment would need to be done before he could conclude that older adults suffered a deficit in their processing of *complex* visual patterns. What additional reaction time test could the psychologist give to both groups in order to make his experiment into a complex design? Describe an outcome of the complex design experiment that would support the claim that older adults suffer a deficit in processing complex information and another outcome that would lead you to question the claim.

B Recognizing that his original study is flawed, the psychologist tries to use post hoc matching to try to equate his two groups. He decides to match on general health (i.e., the better your general health, the faster your reaction time). Although he cannot get an exact matching across groups he does find that when he looks only at the 15 healthiest older adults, their reaction times are only slightly longer than the mean for the young adults. Explain how this outcome would change the psychologist's conclusion concerning the effect of age on reaction time. Could the psychologist reach the general conclusion that older adults do not suffer a deficit in reaction time in this task? Why or why not?

Answer to Stretching Exercise

A interaction effect, main effect of task difficulty
B no interaction effect, main effects of task difficulty and anxiety level
C no interaction effect, main effects of type of media and content
D interaction effect, main effects of type of media and content
E interaction effect, main effects of response type and set size (additional statistical analyses are needed to test these effects)
F no interaction effect, main effects of response type and set size

Answer to Challenge Question 1

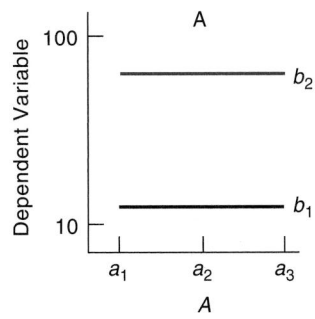
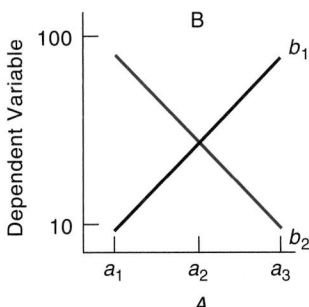
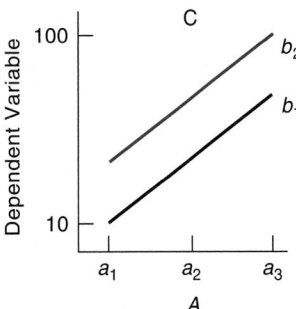

PART FOUR

Applied Research

CHAPTER TEN

Single-Case Designs and Small-n Research

CHAPTER OUTLINE

OVERVIEW

So far in this book we have emphasized *group methodology*—research designed to examine the average performance of one or more groups of participants. This was particularly evident in Chapters 7, 8, and 9 when we were considering experimental methods. In this chapter we introduce two alternative methodologies that emphasize the study of a single individual. We call *single-case research designs* to identify this kind of psychological research.

Single-case designs have been used since scientific psychology began in the 19th century. Psychophysical methods had their origin in the work of Gustav Fechner and were described in his 1860 book, *Elemente der Psychophysik*. Fechner, and countless other psychophysicists since, relied on data obtained through experiments with one or two individuals. Hermann Ebbinghaus is another major figure in the early history of psychology who used a single-case design. In fact, the single case that Ebbinghaus studied was himself. He was both the participant and the experimenter for the research he published in his monograph on memory in 1885. Over a period of many months he learned and then attempted to relearn hundreds of series of nonsense syllables. His data provided psychologists with the first systematic evidence of forgetting over time (see, for example, Zechmeister & Nyberg, 1982).

Cognitive psychologists have continued to rely on single-case research designs. For example, Linton (1978) followed in the tradition of Ebbinghaus when she investigated the retention of everyday events over a 6-year period by testing a single participant: herself. The study of expert performance, whether it be that of a ballet dancer, chess player, or musician, also relies heavily on small-*n* research (e.g., Ericsson & Charness, 1994). Single-case studies appear regularly in psychology journals, dealing with issues ranging from cognitive therapy for Vietnam veterans (Kubany, 1997) to the study of brain processes in amnesic patients (Gabrieli, Fleischman, Keane, Reminger, & Morrell, 1995).

In this chapter we discuss two specific single-case research methodologies, the case study method and single-subject experimental designs. The case study method is frequently associated with the field of clinical psychology, but investigators from other fields also make use of this important method. For example, neurologist Oliver Sacks (1985, 1995) captivated millions with his vivid case studies of individuals with peculiar, and rather fascinating, brain disorders. One of Sacks' best known books is *The Man Who Mistook His Wife for a Hat* (1985). In it, as the title indicates, we are introduced to a man who literally, when searching for his hat, seized his wife's head and tried to lift it off and put it on. These "clinical tales," as Sacks calls them, not only provide insights into the relationship between mind and brain, but also reveal how individuals adapt, cope, and succeed when faced with profound neurological deficits.

Case studies are frequently the source of valuable hypotheses about behavior and can be an important complement to more rigorously controlled approaches to understanding behavior. We will review the advantages and the disadvantages of the case study method.

Single-subject experimental designs are the second single-case methodology we will discuss in this chapter. We use the term *single-subject research designs* to identify this kind of psychological research, since the emphasis in this approach typically is on manipulations and interpretation for a single subject, even if a few subjects or a single "group" is observed.[1] Single-subject experimental designs are also frequently called "$N = 1$ experimental designs" or "small-*n* research designs." These designs are characteristic of approaches called the *experimental analysis of behavior* and *applied behavior analysis*. As you will see, these approaches represent basic and applied applications, respectively, of a small-*n* approach. Single-subject designs are more systematic and controlled than are case studies. We will examine the rationale behind the use of these designs and provide specific illustrations of the more common single-subject experimental designs. These experimental designs represent a special case of the repeated measures design introduced in Chapter 8.

THE CASE STUDY METHOD

Characteristics

- Case studies, intensive descriptions and analyses of individuals, lack the degree of control found in small-*n* experimental designs.
- Case studies are a source of hypotheses and ideas about normal and abnormal behavior.

Key Concept

A **case study** is an intensive description and analysis of a single individual. Case studies frequently make use of qualitative data, but this is not always the case (e.g., Smith, Harré, & Van Langenhove, 1995). Researchers who use the case study method obtain their data from several sources, including naturalistic observation (Chapter 4), interviews and psychological tests (Chapter 5), and even archival records (Chapter 6). A case study frequently describes the application and results of a particular treatment. For example, a clinical report of a case study may describe an individual's symptoms, the methods used to understand and treat the symptoms, and evidence for the treatment's effectiveness. Thus, case studies provide a potentially rich source of information about individuals.

However, treatment variables are rarely controlled systematically in case studies. Instead, several treatments may be applied simultaneously, and the psychologist may have little control over extraneous variables (e.g., home and work environments that influence the client's symptoms). Thus, *a fundamental characteristic of case studies is that they often lack a high degree of control*. Without

---

[1]In this edition we use the term *single-subject research design* rather than *single-case research design* because it is more commonly used to describe experimental studies using one subject, a few subjects, or a single group of subjects. Also, the term *single-case research* can be easily confused with *case study approach*. Note that "small-*n* research" refers to the small sample size (noted by *n*), and not simply the lowercase letter *n*.

control, it is difficult for researchers to make valid inferences about variables that influence the individual's behavior (including any treatment). Degree of control is one distinguishing feature between the case study method and single-subject experimental designs, with single-subject designs having a higher degree of control (see, for example, Kazdin, 1998).

The case study method has been used by child psychologists, memory researchers, and animal behaviorists, as well as by researchers in fields such as anthropology, criminology, neurology, and sociology. In actual practice, the form and content of case studies are extremely varied. Published case studies may be only a few printed pages long or may fill a book. For example, Kirsch (1978) described an attempt to implement "self-management training" with a woman experiencing low self-confidence and social inhibition. The case study, describing her treatment during nine therapy sessions and a 5-month follow-up, was presented in just four pages of one issue of the journal *Psychotherapy: Theory, Research and Practice*. In another case study, the personality psychologist Gordon W. Allport described the relationship between a mother and son as revealed in 301 letters that the mother wrote to friends. First reported in two consecutive issues of the *Journal of Abnormal and Social Psychology* (1946, Vol. 41, Nos. 3 and 4), this classic case study was published in 1965 as a 223-page book under the title *Letters from Jenny*.

Ruth Campbell's edited book, *Mental Lives* (1992), contains case studies of 15 individuals "with something 'abnormal' in the way they think, perceive, read, speak or remember" (p. 2). The focus of the book, however, is on what these cases reveal about normal cognitive functioning. For instance, Riddoch and Humphreys (1992) introduce us to Dennis, a 47-year-old man who experienced severe head trauma from a fall from a ladder. Dennis subsequently had difficulty recognizing familiar people (his own family) as well as common objects when he saw them (although his sight was good enough to watch TV). Dennis could recognize people, however, when he heard them speak and could identify common objects when he touched them. The authors of this case study use Dennis's experiences to teach us how visual recognition depends on stored knowledge. Emphasizing what we learn about normal behavior by examining unusual abnormal behaviors is, according to Campbell, what differentiates the case studies revealed in *Mental Lives* from those in other collections, such as those of Oliver Sacks. Sacks's collections of case studies focus mainly on vivid descriptions of individuals who have unusual brain disorders. As you can see, case studies serve many important purposes.

Many aspects of the case study method make it a unique means of studying behavior. It differs somewhat from more experimental approaches in terms of its goals, the methods used, and the types of information obtained (Kazdin, 1998). For example, the case study method is often characterized as "exploratory" in nature and a source of hypotheses and ideas about behavior (Bolgar, 1965). Experimental approaches, on the other hand, are frequently viewed as opportunities to test specific hypotheses. The case study method has sometimes been viewed as antagonistic to more controlled methods of investigation. A more appropriate perspective is suggested by Kazdin (1998), who sees the *case study method as interrelated with and complementary to other research methods in psychology.*

The case study method offers both advantages and disadvantages to the research psychologist (see, for example, Bolgar, 1965; Hersen & Barlow, 1976; Kazdin, 1998). Before reviewing its advantages and disadvantages, however, we will illustrate the method with a summary of an actual case study reported by Kirsch (1978), which was mentioned earlier. It is important that you read this slightly abbreviated version of a case study carefully because we will review it when discussing the advantages and disadvantages of the case study method.

CAN CLIENTS BE THEIR OWN THERAPISTS? A CASE STUDY ILLUSTRATION

This article reports on the use of self-management training (SMT), a therapeutic strategy which capitalizes on the advantages of brief therapies, while at the same time reducing the danger of leaving too many tasks not fully accomplished. . . . The essence of this approach involves teaching the client how to be his or her own behavior therapist. The client is taught how to assess problems along behavioral dimensions and to develop specific tactics, based on existing treatment techniques, for overcoming problems. As this process occurs, the traditional client-therapist relationship is altered considerably. The client takes on the dual role of client and therapist, while the therapist takes on the role of supervisor.

The case of Susan

Susan, a 28-year-old married woman, entered therapy complaining that she suffered from a deficient memory, low intelligence, and lack of self-confidence. The presumed deficiencies "caused" her to be inhibited in a number of social situations. She was unable to engage in discussions about films, plays, books, or magazine articles "because" she could not remember them well enough. She often felt that she could not understand what was being said in a conversation and that this was due to her low intelligence. She attempted to hide her lack of comprehension by

adopting a passive role in these interactions and was fearful lest she be discovered by being asked for more of a response. She did not trust her own opinions and, indeed, sometimes doubted whether she had any. She felt dependent on others to provide opinions for her to adopt.

Administering a Wechsler Adult Intelligence Scale (WAIS), I found her to have a verbal IQ of about 120, hardly a subnormal score. Her digit span (scale score 5 = 12, raw score 5 = 13) indicated that at least her short-term memory was not deficient. The test confirmed what I had already surmised from talking with her: that there was nothing wrong with her level of intelligence or her memory. After discussing this conclusion, I suggested that we investigate in greater detail what kinds of things she would be able to do if she felt that her memory, intelligence, and level of self-confidence were sufficiently high. In this way, we were able to agree upon a list of behavioral goals, which included such tasks as stating an opinion, asking for clarification, admitting ignorance of certain facts, etc. During therapy sessions, I guided Susan through overt and covert rehearsals of anxiety-arousing situations . . . structured homework assignments which constituted successive approximations of her behavioral goals, and had her keep records of her progress. In addition, we discussed negative statements which she was making to herself and which were not warranted by the available data (e.g., "I'm stupid"). I suggested that whenever she noticed herself making a statement of this sort, she counter it by intentionally saying more appropriate, positive statements to herself (e.g., "I'm not stupid—there is no logical reason to think that I am").

During the fifth session of therapy, Susan reported the successful completion of a presumably difficult homework assignment. Not only had she found it easy to accomplish, but, she reported, it had not aroused any anxiety, even on the first trial. . . . It was at this point that the nature of the therapeutic relationship was altered. During future sessions, Susan rated her progress during the week, determined what the next step should be, and devised her own homework assignments. My role became that of a supervisor of a student therapist, reinforcing her successes and drawing attention to factors which she might be overlooking.

After the ninth therapy session, direct treatment was discontinued. During the following month, I contacted Susan twice by phone. She reported feeling confident in her ability to achieve her goals. In particular, she reported feeling a new sense of control over her life. My own impressions are that she had successfully adopted a behavioral problem-solving method of assessment and had become fairly adept at devising strategies for accomplishing her goals.

Follow-up

Five months after termination of treatment, I contacted Susan and requested information on her progress. She reported that she talked more than she used to in social situations, was feeling more comfortable doing things on her own (i.e., without her husband), and that, in general, she no longer felt that she was stupid. She summarized by saying: "I feel that I'm a whole step or level above where I was."

I also asked her which, if any, of the techniques we had used in therapy she was continuing to use on her own. . . . Finally, she reported that on at least three separate occasions during the 5-month period following termination of treatment, she had told another person: "I don't understand that—will you explain it to me?" This was a response which she had previously felt she was not capable of making, as it might expose her "stupidity" to the other person.

Three months after the follow-up interview, I received an unsolicited letter from Susan (I had moved out of state during that time), in which she reminded me that "one of [her] imaginary exercises was walking into a folk dancing class and feeling comfortable; well, it finally worked."*

*Source: Kirsch, I. (1978). Teaching clients to be their own therapists: A case study illustration. *Psychotherapy: Theory, Research, and Practice, 15,* 302–305. (Reprinted by permission.)

Advantages of the Case Study Method

- Case studies provide new ideas and hypotheses, opportunities to develop new clinical techniques, and a chance to study rare phenomena.
- Scientific theories can be challenged when the behavior of a single case contradicts theoretical principles or claims, and theories can receive tentative support using evidence from case studies.
- Idiographic research (the study of individuals to identify what is unique) complements nomothetic research (the study of groups to identify what is typical).

Sources of Ideas About Behavior   Case studies provide a rich source of information about individuals and insights into possible causes of people's behavior. These insights, when translated into research hypotheses, can then be tested using more controlled research methods. This aspect of the case study method was acknowledged by Kirsch (1978) in discussing the successful psychotherapy with the woman named Susan. He stated that the "conclusions [of this case study] . . . should be viewed as tentative. It is hoped that the utility of [this technique] will be established by more controlled research" (p. 305). The case study method is a natural starting point for a researcher who is entering an area of study about which relatively little is known.

Opportunity for Clinical Innovation　The case study method provides an opportunity "to try out" new therapeutic techniques or to try unique applications of existing techniques. The use of self-management training (SMT) in psychotherapy represents a clinical innovation because Kirsch changed the typical client-therapist relationship. The SMT approach is based on teaching clients to be their own therapists—in other words, to identify problems and design behavioral techniques for dealing with them. The client is both client and therapist, while the therapist acts as supervisor. In a similar vein, Kubany (1997) reported the effect of a "marathon" 1-day cognitive therapy session with a Vietnam War veteran suffering from multiple sources of combat-related guilt. Therapy of this kind generally occurs over many hour-long sessions, but the fact that this intensive session appeared to be successful suggests a new way to conduct this type of clinical intervention.

Method to Study Rare Phenomena　Case studies are also useful for studying rare events. Some events appear so infrequently in nature that we can describe them only through the intensive study of single cases. Many of the case studies described in *Mental Lives* and in books by Oliver Sacks, for example, describe individuals with rare brain disorders. Other examples are found in the vivid case studies of so-called "feral children." These are children abandoned at an early stage who developed without significant human contact while living in the wild. Among the most celebrated case studies of a feral child is that of the "Wild Boy of Aveyron" (see, for example, *The Forbidden Experiment: The Story of the Wild Boy of Aveyron* [Shattuck, 1994]). Victor, as he came to be called, was captured in 1800 in the Aveyron district of France. Someone may have tried to kill him (as evidenced by the knife wound on his neck) and then abandoned him (perhaps had left him for dead) in the woods when he was about 5 years old. When he was captured, at about age 11 or 12, he was described as follows:

> He was human in bodily form and walked erect. Everything else about him suggested an animal. He was naked except for the tatters of a shirt and showed no modesty, no awareness of himself as a human person related in any way to the people who captured him. He could not speak and made only weird meaningless cries. (Shattuck, 1994, p. 5)

FIGURE 10.1   Only surviving picture of the "Wild Boy of Aveyron."

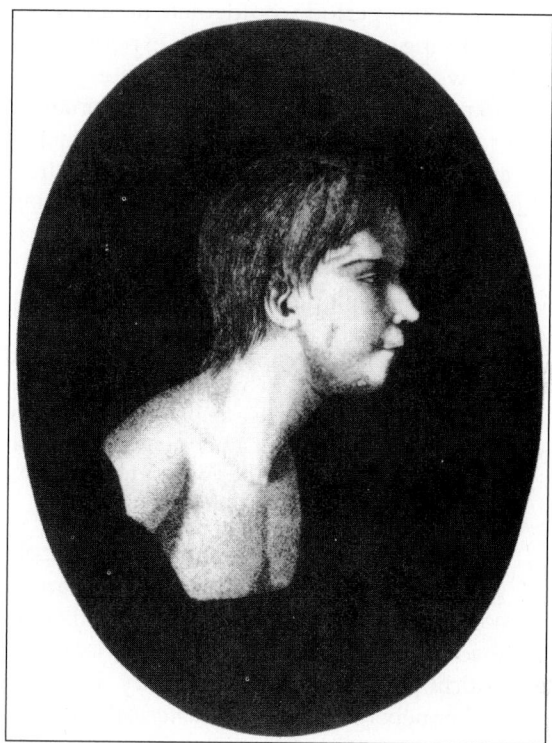

To many, Victor provided an opportunity to answer what were then (and still are today) burning questions about human nature. How are we different from animals? How do people learn language? What is "natural" and what is "cultural"? The story of Victor's reintroduction to society and his steps toward "humanity," under the tutelage of a devoted medical doctor and governess is compelling. The story in no way, however, provides definitive answers to those still burning questions. Rather, in one author's view, this story "obliges us to reflect on how to live with those unsolved questions" (Shattuck, 1994, p. 182). Such can be the power of the case study.

Challenge to Theoretical Assumptions   A theory that all Martians have three heads would quickly collapse if a reliable observer spotted a Martian with only two heads. The case study method can often advance scientific thinking by providing a "counterinstance": a single case that violates a general proposition or universally accepted principle (Kazdin, 1998). Consider, for example, the theory that human language development depends on exposure to normal language during a *critical period,* from about 2 years of age to puberty (suggested by Lenneberg, 1967). A human child deprived of language exposure during this period would, then, not be expected to acquire language. Of course, depriving a child of language experience for purposes of testing this hypothesis would be immoral. Yet, there are "nature's experiments." One such "experiment" involved a child, "Genie," discovered in 1970 who had been cruelly isolated from most human contact and normal language from about the age of 2 to age 13 (Curtiss, 1977). The circumstances surrounding Genie's imprisonment and abuse, as well as the attempts by psychologists and linguists to rehabilitate her, were chronicled by Rymer (1993). Genie's experiences represented an opportunity for scientists to test a critical-period theory of language development:

> At best, Genie could have provided a flawed endorsement of Lenneberg's theory. But she was capable of a ringing refutation. If Genie could not learn language, her failure would be attributed ambiguously—either to the truth of the critical-period hypothesis or to her emotional problems. If Genie did learn language in spite of all that had happened to her, how much stronger the rebuttal! (Rymer, 1993, pp. 121–122)

According to the psychologist most closely associated with Genie's language training, Genie showed some language development but it was never completely normal. This outcome challenges a "strong" version of Lenneberg's theory that language could not be learned at all without exposure during the critical period. Genie's case study does not refute, however, a "weak" version of Lenneberg's theory that *normal* language development would not appear after puberty without exposure during the critical period (Curtiss, 1977, p. 209).

Tentative Support for a Psychological Theory   Evidence from a case study can provide tentative support for a psychological theory. Although results of case studies are not used to provide *conclusive* evidence for a particular hypothesis, the outcome of a case study can sometimes provide important evidence in support of a psychological theory. The case of Genie is a good illustration since this case study provided important evidence in support of the weak version of Lenneberg's critical-period theory.

Another illustration of evidence from case studies providing support for a theory comes from the memory literature. In 1968, Atkinson and Shiffrin proposed a model of human memory that was to have considerable influence on research in this field. The model, which was based on principles of information processing, described both a short-term memory (STM) system and a long-term memory (LTM) system. Although results of numerous experiments provided evidence for this dual nature of our memory, Atkinson and Shiffrin considered the results of several case studies as "perhaps the most convincing demonstrations of a dichotomy in the memory system" (p. 97). These case studies involved patients who had been treated for epilepsy via surgical removal of parts of the brain within the temporal lobes, including a subcortical structure known as the hippocampus. Of particular importance to Atkinson and Shiffrin's theory was the case study of a patient known as H. M. (see Hilts, 1995; Scoville & Milner, 1957). Following the brain operation, H. M. was found to have a disturbing memory deficit. Although he could carry on a normal conversation and remember events for a short period of time, H. M. could not remember day-to-day events. He was able to read the same magazine over and over again without finding its contents familiar. It looked as though H. M. had an intact short-term memory system but could not get information into a long-term memory system. Subsequent testing of H. M. and patients with similar memory deficits revealed that the nature of this memory problem is more complex than originally suggested, but the case study of H. M. continues to be important whenever theories of human memory are discussed (for example, see Schacter, 1996).

Complement to the Nomothetic Study of Behavior   Psychology (like science in general) seeks to establish broad generalizations, "universal laws" that will apply to a wide population of organisms. As a consequence, psychological research is often characterized by studies that use the nomothetic approach. The

Key Concept

nomothetic approach involves large numbers of participants and it seeks to determine the "average" or typical performance of a group. This average may or may not represent the performance of any one individual in the group. Rather, a researcher hopes to be able to predict, on the basis of this mean performance, what organisms will be like "in general."

Some psychologists, notably Allport (1961), argue that a nomothetic approach is inadequate—that the individual is more than what can be represented by the collection of average values on various dimensions. Allport argues that the individual is both unique and lawful; the individual operates in accordance with internally consistent principles. Allport argues further that the study of the

Key Concept

individual, called an **idiographic approach** to research, is an important goal for psychological research (see also Smith et al., 1995).

Allport illustrates the need for an idiographic approach by desciting the task confronting the clinical psychologist. The clinician's goal "is not to predict the aggregate, but to foretell 'what any one man [sic] will do.' In reaching this ideal, actuarial predictions may sometimes help, universal and group norms are useful, but they do not go the whole distance" (p. 21). Allport suggests that our approach to understanding human nature should be neither exclusively nomothetic nor exclusively idiographic but should represent an "equilibrium" between the two. At the very least the idiographic approach, as represented by the case study method, permits the kind of detailed observation that has the power to reveal various nuances and subtleties of behavior that a "group" approach may miss. And, as you have seen, case studies have the ability to teach us about typical or average behavior by carefully studying individuals who are atypical.

STRETCHING EXERCISE

In this exercise you are to respond to the questions that follow this brief description.

One of your friends is taking an introductory psychology class this semester and she is describing to you over lunch her reactions to what happened in her class that morning. The topic for the day's class was adult development and the professor described two research studies related to marriage and divorce. The professor emphasized that both studies represented excellent research that had been done by leading experts in the field. The first study involved a large sample of married couples that had been randomly selected from a well-defined population. The results of this study indicated that slightly more than half of marriages end in divorce and that factors such as persistent conflict between spouses and a family history of divorce were reliable predictors of divorce. The professor highlighted the statistical analyses that confirmed the reliability of these predictors. The second study was a lengthy narrative description of a couple's experiences in therapy with a marriage and family counselor. The case study described how the couple had entered therapy seriously considering divorce but that they had decided after a year in therapy to stay married. The professor described several specific techniques the therapist had used while working with the couple to help them understand and deal with issues such as conflict in their marriage and a family history of divorce that put them at risk for divorce.

The class period ended before the professor had a chance to describe how the findings of these two studies were related and what conclusions about divorce could be drawn from them. How would you respond to the questions and concerns your friend had after this class?

1 One of your friend's questions is how can she decide which study's results to believe. The first study seems to say that marital conflict and a history of divorce lead to divorce, but the second study indicates that these factors need not lead to divorce. Your friend describes that she is inclined to believe the results of the second study. She finds the personal examples the professor described from the second study more compelling than the numbers he used to support the findings of the first study. What do you think?

2 Your friend also questions whether either of these studies will have implications for her own life experience. That is, can she tell based on the results of these studies whether she will experience a divorce if she someday chooses to get married. What do you think?

Disadvantages of the Case Study Method

- Researchers are unable to make valid causal inferences using the case study method because extraneous variables are not controlled and several "treatments" may be applied simultaneously in case studies.
- Observer bias and biases in data collection can lead to incorrect interpretations of case study outcomes.
- Whether results from a case study may be generalized depends on the variability within the population from which the case was selected; some characteristics (e.g., personality) vary more across individuals than others (e.g., visual acuity).

Difficulty of Drawing Cause-Effect Conclusions   You are well aware by now that one of the goals of science is to discover the causes of phenomena—to identify the specific factors that produce a particular event as unambiguously as possible. One disadvantage of the case study method is that cause-effect conclusions can rarely be drawn on the basis of results that are obtained from case studies. This disadvantage arises primarily because researchers are unable to control extraneous variables in case studies. Thus, the behavior changes that take place in case studies can be explained by several plausible alternative hypotheses.

Consider, for instance, the treatment of Susan through SMT reported by Kirsch (1978). Although Susan apparently benefited from the SMT therapy, can we be sure that SMT caused her improvement? Many illnesses and emotional disorders improve without treatment. Case study researchers must always consider the alternative hypothesis that individuals may have improved *without* treatment. In addition, several aspects of the situation may have been responsible for Susan's improvement. Her care was in the hands of a "clinical psychologist" who provided reassurance. Also, Susan may have changed her attitudes toward herself because of the insights of her therapist and the feedback she received from her test results, not because of SMT. The therapist also asked Susan, as part of her therapy, to rehearse anxiety-arousing situations covertly and overtly. This technique is similar to rehearsal desensitization, which may itself be an effective treatment (Rimm & Masters, 1979).

Because several treatments were used simultaneously we cannot argue convincingly that SMT was the unambiguous "cause" of Susan's improvement. As we have seen, Kirsch himself was sensitive to the limitations of the case study method and suggested that the inferences he drew based on the results of his study should be considered tentative until they were investigated more rigorously.

The case studies associated with feral children such as Victor, and abused and deprived children such as Genie, illustrate well the difficulty with isolating causal factors. We can only try to imagine the kinds of terror experienced by a child who is isolated and physically abused by an emotionally disturbed parent. How much of the failure to acquire normal language is the result of such emotional disturbance? What else don't we know about these children? Genie had been severely ill at age 14 months and an attending physician had commented that she showed signs of retardation (Curtiss, 1977). Was Genie destined to be developmentally delayed even without the horrible isolation she experienced? The data from case studies frequently leave us wondering about the causes of behavior.

Potential Sources of Bias   The outcome of a case study often depends on conclusions drawn by a researcher who is both participant and observer (Bolgar, 1965). That is, a therapist observes the client's behavior *and* participates in the therapeutic process. It is reasonable to assume that the therapist may be motivated to believe that the treatment helps the client. As a result, the therapist, even if well intentioned, may not accurately observe the client's behavior. The potential for biased interpretation is not peculiar to the case study method. We have previously considered the problems of observer bias (Chapter 4) and experimenter bias (Chapter 7).

The outcome of a case may be based mainly on the "impressions" of the observer (Hersen & Barlow, 1976). For example, Kirsch (1978) described the patient Susan's "feelings" about her ability to achieve her goals and told how she reported a "sense of control" over her life. He stated that his "impressions are that she successfully adopted a behavioral problem-solving method of assessment and had become fairly adept at devising strategies for accomplishing her goals" (p. 304). A serious weakness of the case study method is that interpretation of the outcome is based solely on the subjective impressions of the observer.

Bias can also occur in case studies when information is obtained from sources such as personal documents, session notes, and psychological tests. Archival records, as we described in Chapter 6, are open to several sources of bias. Further, when individuals provide information about themselves (self-reports), they may distort or falsify the information in order to "look good." This possibility existed in Susan's treatment. We have no way of knowing whether she exaggerated her self-reports of improvement. Another potential source of bias occurs when reports are based on individuals' memory. Cognitive psychologists have demonstrated repeatedly that memory can be inaccurate, particularly for events that happened long ago. Consider the following excerpt from a self-analysis by the well-known personality psychologist Alfred Adler (1973, pp. 179–180):

> Shortly after I went to a board[ing] school. I remember that the path to the school led over a cemetery. I was frightened every time and was exceedingly put out at beholding the other children pass the cemetery without paying the least attention to it, while every step I took was accompanied by a feeling of fear and horror. Apart from the extreme discomfort occasioned by this fear I was also annoyed at the idea of being less courageous than the others. One day I made up my mind to put an end to this fear of death. Again (as on my first resolve), I decided upon a treatment of hardening (Proximity of death!). I stayed at some distance behind the others, placed my school-bag on the ground near the wall of the cemetery and ran across it a dozen times, until I felt that I had mastered the fear. After that, I believe, I passed along this path without any fear.
>
> Thirty years after that I met an old schoolmate and we exchanged childhood reminiscences of our school days. It happened to occur to me that the cemetery was no longer in existence and I asked him what had happened to it remembering the great uneasiness it had at one time caused me. Astonished, my former schoolmate who had lived longer in that neighborhood than I had, insisted that there never had been a cemetery on the way to our school. Then I realized that the story of the cemetery had been but a poetic dress for my longing to overcome the fear of death.

Problem of Generalizing from a Single Individual   One of the most serious limitations of the case study method concerns the external validity of case study findings. To what extent can we generalize the findings for one individual to a larger population? Our initial response might be that the findings for one person cannot be generalized at all. Our ability to generalize from a single case, however, depends on the degree of variability in the population from which the case was selected. For example, psychologists who study visual perception are often able to generalize their findings based on the study of one individual. Vision researchers assume that visual systems in all humans are very similar. Therefore, only one or several cases may be used to understand how the visual system works. In contrast, other psychological processes are much more variable, such as learning, memory, emotions, personality, and mental health. When studying processes that vary greatly in the population, it is impossible to claim that what is observed in one individual will hold for all individuals.

Thus, even if we accept Kirsch's (1978) conclusion regarding the effectiveness of the SMT technique of psychotherapy, we do not know whether this particular treatment would be as successful for other individuals who might differ from the patient Susan in any of numerous ways, including intelligence, age, family background, and gender. As with findings from group methodologies, the important next step is to *replicate* the findings with additional individuals.

Thinking Critically About Testimonials Based on a Case Study

- Being mindful of the limitations of the case study method can be helpful when evaluating individuals' testimonials about the effectiveness of a particular treatment.

Case studies sometimes offer dramatic demonstrations of "new" findings or provide evidence for the "success" of a particular treatment. Consider advertisements for products you see in the media (e.g., infomercials). How many people who worry about their weight can resist the example of a formerly overweight individual who is shown to have lost considerable weight by using Product X. Evidence from case studies can be very persuasive. This is both an advantage and a disadvantage for the scientific community. Case studies demonstrating new or unusual findings may lead scientists to reconsider their theories or may lead them to new and fruitful avenues of research. Case studies, then, can help advance science.

The disadvantage of case studies, however, is that their findings are often accepted uncritically. Individuals eager to lose weight or be cured of an illness may not consider the limitations of case study evidence. Instead, the evidence offers a ray of hope for a cure. For people who have (or think they have) few alternatives, this grasping at straws may not be totally unreasonable. Too often, however, people do not consider (perhaps they do not want to consider) the reasons why a particular treatment would *not* work for them.

When we fail to consider the limitations of case study evidence we risk unfortunate consequences. For example, during the early 1980s considerable controversy surrounded the supposed cancer-curing drug laetrile (Sun, 1981). Few respectable scientists or medical researchers considered this drug to be beneficial in the treatment of cancer. Advocates of laetrile, however, presented case studies reporting positive results. Largely because of public pressure, the government carried out systematic and expensive tests of the drug under controlled conditions. Researchers did not find beneficial effects of the drug in controlled experiments. As others have commented, many patients who used laetrile instead of traditional therapies may have postponed or interrupted valid courses of treatment and thus contributed to the spread of their cancer.

SINGLE-SUBJECT (SMALL-*n*) EXPERIMENTAL DESIGNS

- In applied behavioral analysis, the methods developed within the experimental analysis of behavior are applied to socially relevant problems.

In the remainder of this chapter we will describe single-subject experimental (small-*n*) designs. These experimental designs have their roots in an approach to the study of behavior that was developed by B. F. Skinner in the 1930s. The approach is called an *experimental analysis of behavior*. It presents a unique behavioral view of human nature that not only contains prescriptions for the way psychologists should do research but also has implications for the way society should be organized. Several of Skinner's books, including *Walden Two*

FIGURE 10.2   Applied behavior analysis is an extension of B. F. Skinner's basic research on animal behavior.

and *Beyond Freedom and Dignity*, describe how the principles derived from an experimental analysis of behavior can be put to work to improve society.

In the experimental analysis of behavior (unlike the group methodologies discussed in previous chapters) it is often the case that the sample is a single subject or small *n*. Experimental control is demonstrated by arranging experimental conditions such that the individual's behavior changes systematically with the manipulation of an independent variable. As Skinner (1966, p. 21) commented,

> Instead of studying a thousand rats for one hour each, or a hundred rats for ten hours each, the investigator is likely to study one rat for a thousand hours. The procedure is not only appropriate to an enterprise which recognizes individuality, it is at least equally efficient in its use of equipment and of the investigator's time and energy. The ultimate test of uniformity or reproducibility is not to be found in the methods used but in the degree of control achieved, a test which the experimental analysis of behavior usually passes easily.

Often there is a minimum of statistical analysis associated with single-subject experimental designs. Conclusions regarding the effects of an experimental variable (treatment) typically are made by visually inspecting the behavioral record in order to observe whether behavior changes systematically with the introduction and withdrawal of the experimental treatment. Therefore, there is considerable emphasis on appropriately *defining, observing,* and *recording* behavior. Has the behavior been defined clearly and objectively so that it can be reliably observed and recorded? Will a continuous (cumulative) record of behavior be kept or will observations be made at regular intervals? Although frequency of responding is a common measure of behavior, duration of behavior or other characteristics are sometimes measured. Moreover, as you will see later in this chapter, statistical issues sometimes do arise, such as excessive variability in the behavioral record, and must be dealt with. A discussion of other statistical issues associated with single-subject research designs would necessarily go beyond our brief introduction.

In *applied behavior analysis*, the methods that are developed within an experimental analysis of behavior are applied to socially relevant problems. These applications are frequently referred to as *behavior modification* but when applied to clinical populations the term *behavior therapy* is preferred (Wilson, 1978). Behavior therapy is seen by many as a more effective approach to clinical treatment than that based on a psychodynamic model of therapy. Instead of seeking insight into the unconscious roots of problems, behavior therapy focuses on observable behavior. For example, self-stimulatory behaviors (e.g., prolonged body rocking, gazing at lights, or spinning) that often characterize autistic children may be conceptualized as behaviors under the control of reinforcement contingencies. In this way, clinicians and teachers may be able to control their frequency of occurrence by using behavior modification techniques (see Lovaas, Newsom, & Hickman, 1987). Numerous studies have been published showing how behavior modification and behavior therapy can be employed successfully to change the behavior of stutterers, normal and mentally impaired children and adults, psychiatric patients, and many others. Approaches based on applied behavior analysis have also been successfully used by school psychologists in educational settings (see Kratochwill & Martens, 1994). A primary source for these published studies is the *Journal of Applied Behavior Analysis.*

Characteristics of Single-Subject Experiments

- Researchers manipulate an independent variable in single-subject experiments; therefore, these designs allow more rigorous control than case studies.
- In single-subject experiments, baseline observations are first recorded to describe what an individual's behavior is like (and predicted to be like in the future) without treatment.
- Baseline behavior and behavior following the intervention (treatment) are compared using visual inspection of recorded observations.

Key Concept

The **single-subject experiment,** as its name suggests, typically focuses on an examination of behavior change in one individual or at most, a few individuals. However, as we will see later in this chapter, the behavior of a single "group" of individuals also may be the focus. In a single-subject experiment the researcher contrasts treatment conditions for one individual whose behavior is being continuously monitored. That is, the independent variable of interest (usually a treatment) is manipulated systematically for one individual. Single-subject experimental designs are an important alternative to the relatively uncontrolled case study method (Kazdin, 1982). Single-subject experiments also have advantages over multiple-group experiments as described in Box 10.1.

Key Concept

The first stage of a single-subject experiment is usually an observation stage, or **baseline stage.** During this stage researchers record the subject's behavior prior to any treatment. Clinical researchers typically measure the frequency of the target behavior within a unit of time, such as a day or an hour. For example, a researcher might record the number of times during a 10-minute interview that an excessively shy child makes eye contact, the number of headaches reported each week by a migraine sufferer, or the number of verbal pauses per minute made by a chronic stutterer. Using the baseline record, researchers are able to *describe* behavior before they provide treatment. Most importantly, the baseline allows researchers to *predict* what behavior will be like in the future without treatment (Kazdin, 1998). Of course, unless behavior is actually monitored researchers don't know for sure what future behavior will be like, but baseline measures allow them to predict what the future holds. Figure 10.3 illustrates this function of the baseline record. In this hypothetical example, all three measures of central tendency (mean, median, mode) converge in the prediction of future behavior. Actual observations of complex behaviors are likely not to demonstrate this uniformity, and researchers must consider the advantages and disadvantages of different measures of central tendency (see Chapter 12).

BOX 10.1

ADVANTAGES OF SINGLE-SUBJECT DESIGNS OVER GROUP DESIGNS: LESS CAN BE MORE

Single-subject experimental designs may be more appropriate than multiple-group designs for certain kinds of applied research (see Hersen & Barlow, 1976). One such situation is when research is directed toward changing the behavior of a specific individual. For example, the outcome of a group experiment may lead to recommendations about what treatments are effective "in general" in modifying behavior. It is not possible to say, however, what the effect of that treatment would be on any particular individual based on a group average. Kazdin (1982) summarizes this characteristic of single-subject experiments well, "Perhaps the most obvious advantage [of single-case experimental designs] is that the methodology allows investigation of the individual client and experimental evaluation of treatment for the client" (p. 482).

Another advantage of single-subject experiments over multiple-group experiments involves the ethical problem of withholding treatment that can arise in clinical research. In a multiple-group design, a potentially beneficial treatment must be withheld from individuals in order to provide a control group that satisfies the requirements of internal validity. Because single-subject experimental designs contrast conditions of "no-treatment" and "treatment" within the same individual, the problem of withholding treatment can be avoided. Moreover, investigators doing clinical research often have difficulty gaining access to enough clients to do a multiple-group experiment. For instance, a clinician may be able to identify only a few clients experiencing claustrophobia (excessive fear of enclosed spaces). The single-subject experiment provides a practical solution to the problem of investigating cause-effect conclusions when only a few participants are available.

Once researchers observe that the individual's behavior is relatively stable—that is, it exhibits little fluctuation between recording intervals—they introduce an intervention (treatment). The next step is to record the individual's behavior with the same measures used during the baseline stage. By comparing the behavior observed immediately following an intervention with the baseline performance, researchers are able to determine the effect of the treatment. The effect of the treatment is seen most easily using a graph of the behavioral record. How did behavior change, in other words, following the experimental treatment? Keep in mind that we can predict what behavior would be like without treatment; this is represented by the dashed line in Figure 10.3. By visually inspecting the difference between behavior following treatment and what was predicted would occur without treatment, we can infer whether the treatment effectively changed the individual's behavior. Traditionally, the analysis of single-subject experiments has not involved the use of tests of statistical significance, but there has been some controversy about this (Kratochwill & Brody, 1978). Later in this chapter we will discuss some of the problems that can arise when visual inspection is used to determine whether a treatment was effective (see also Kazdin, 1998).

FIGURE 10.3   Hypothetical example of baseline observations for the frequency of responses. Data in baseline stage (solid line) are used to predict the likely rate of responses in the future if treatment is not implemented (dashed line). (Adapted from Kazdin, 1998, p. 209.)

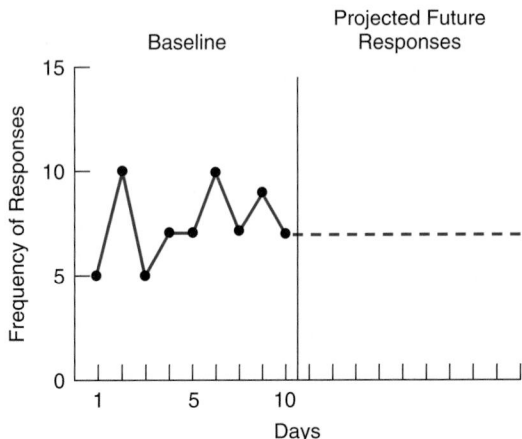

Although researchers have many design possibilities available (Hersen & Barlow, 1976; Kazdin, 1980), the most common single-subject designs are the ABAB and multiple-baseline designs (Kazdin, 1998).

Specific Experimental Designs

- In the ABAB design, baseline (A) and treatment (B) stages are alternated to determine the effect of treatment on behavior.
- Researchers conclude that treatment causes behavior change when behavior changes systematically with the introduction and withdrawal of treatment.
- Interpreting the causal effect of the treatment is difficult in the ABAB design if behavior does not reverse to baseline levels when treatment is withdrawn.
- Ethical considerations may prevent psychologists from using the ABAB design.
- In multiple-baseline designs, a treatment effect is shown when behaviors in more than one baseline change only following the introduction of a treatment.
- Multiple baselines may be observed across individuals, behaviors, or situations.
- Interpreting the causal effect of treatment is difficult in multiple-baseline designs when changes are seen in a baseline before an experimental intervention; this can occur when treatment effects generalize.

Key Concept   **The ABAB Design**   Researchers use the **ABAB design** to demonstrate that behavior changes systematically when they alternate "no-treatment" and "treatment" conditions. An initial baseline stage (A) is followed by a treatment stage (B), next by a return to baseline (A), and then by another treatment stage

(B). Because treatment is removed during the second A stage, and any improvement in behavior is likely to be reversed at this point, this design is also called a **reversal design.** The researcher using the ABAB design observes whether behavior changes immediately upon introduction of a treatment variable (first B), whether behavior reverses when treatment is withdrawn (second A), and whether behavior improves again when treatment is reintroduced (second B). If behavior changes following the introduction and withdrawal of treatment, the researcher gains considerable evidence that the treatment caused the behavior change.

Horton (1987) used an ABAB design to assess the effects of facial screening on the maladaptive behavior of a severely mentally impaired 8-year-old girl. Facial screening is a mildly aversive technique involving the application of a face cover (e.g., a soft cloth) when an undesirable behavior occurs. Previous research had shown this technique to be effective in reducing the frequency of

FIGURE 10.4   Applied behavior analysis is used to investigate methods of controlling maladaptive behavior of children and adults.

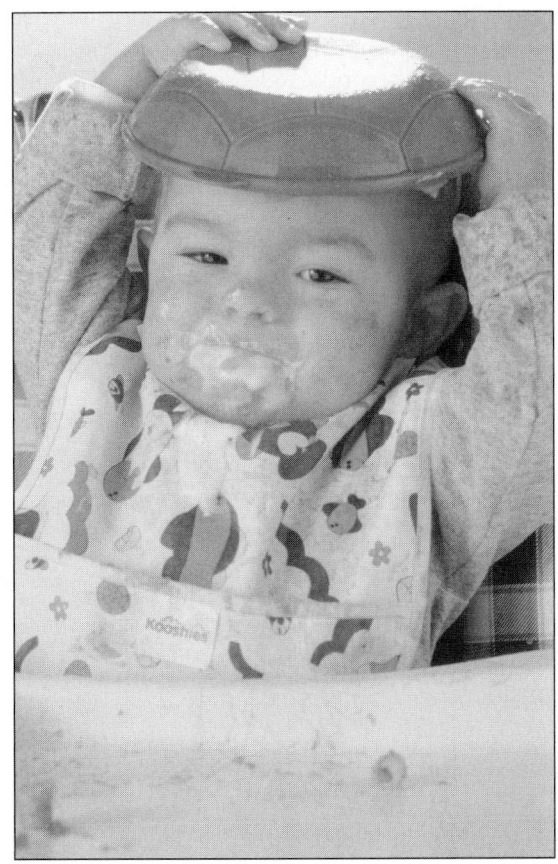

self-injurious behaviors such as face slapping. Horton sought to determine whether it would reduce the frequency of spoon banging by a young child at mealtime. The spoon banging prevented the girl from dining with her classmates at the school for exceptional children that she attended. The banging was disruptive not only because of the noise but because it often led her to fling food on the floor or resulted in her dropping the spoon on the floor.

A clear definition of spoon banging was made to distinguish it from normal scooping motions. Then, a paraprofessional was trained to make observations and to administer the treatment. A frequency count was used to assess the magnitude of spoon banging within each 15-minute eating session. During the initial, or baseline, period the paraprofessional recorded frequency and, with each occurrence of the response, said "no bang," gently grasped the girl's wrist, and returned her hand to her dish. The procedure was videotaped, and an independent observer viewed the films and recorded frequency as a reliability check. Interobserver reliability was approximately 96%. The baseline stage was conducted for 16 days.

The first treatment period began on Day 17 and lasted for 16 days. Each time spoon banging was observed, the paraprofessional continued to give the corrective feedback of "no bang" and returned the girl's hand to her dish. However, the paraprofessional now also pulled a terry-cloth bib over the girl's entire face for 5 seconds. Release from facial screening was contingent on the participant's not banging for 5 seconds. The first treatment phase was followed by a second baseline period and another treatment phase. Posttreatment observations were also made at 6, 10, 15, and 19 months.

Figure 10.5 shows changes in the frequency of the girl's spoon-banging behavior as a function of alternating baseline and treatment phases. Facial screening was not only effective in reducing this behavior during treatment

FIGURE 10.5 Frequency of spoon-banging responses across baseline, treatment, and follow-up phases of study. (Adapted from Horton, 1987.)

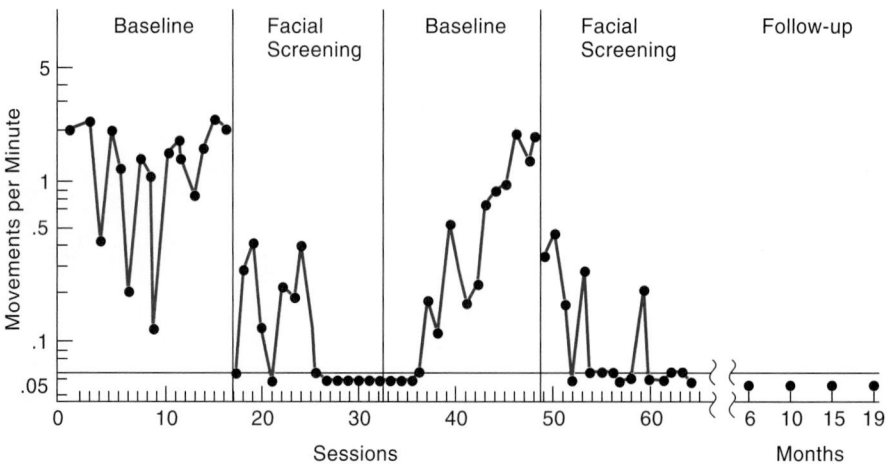

phases, follow-up observations revealed that the spoon banging was still absent months later. Following the final treatment phase, the girl no longer required direct supervision during mealtime at either school or home and was permitted to eat with her peers. There was clear evidence that the application of the facial screening was responsible for eliminating the spoon banging. The facial screening was the only treatment that was administered, and visual inspection of Figure 10.5 shows that behavior changed systematically with the introduction and withdrawal of treatment. The facial-screening technique was a successful procedure for controlling the maladaptive behavior of the young child when other, less intrusive procedures had failed.

Methodological Issues Associated with ABAB Designs A major methodological problem that sometimes arises in the context of an ABAB procedure can be illustrated by looking again at the results of the Horton (1987) study shown in Figure 10.5. In the second baseline stage, when application of the facial screening was withdrawn, spoon banging increased. That is, the improvement observed under the preceding treatment stage was reversed. What if the spoon-banging behavior had remained low even when the treatment was withdrawn? What can the researcher conclude about the effectiveness of the treatment when behavior in a second baseline stage does not revert to what it was during the

---

BOX 10.2

WHY REVERSAL MAY NOT OCCUR IN THE REVERSAL DESIGN

One reason the behavior may not revert back to the baseline level is that the behavior may not be expected logically to change once the treatment led to improvement. This occurs in situations in which the treatment involves teaching individuals new skills. For example, a researcher's treatment might be teaching a developmentally disabled individual how to commute to work. Once the skill is learned, it is unlikely to be "unlearned" (revert back to baseline) when the treatment is withdrawn. The solution to this problem is straightforward. Researchers should not use the ABAB design when they can logically expect that the target behavior would not revert back to baseline when treatment is withdrawn.

What other reasons are there for behavior not to return to baseline in the second stage? One possibility is that a variable *other than* the treatment variable caused behavior to change in the first shift from baseline to treatment stages. For example, the individual may receive increased attention from staff or friends during treatment. This increased attention—rather than the treatment—may cause behavior to improve. If the attention persists even though the specific treatment is withdrawn, the behavior change is likely to persist as well. This explanation suggests a confounding between the treatment variable and some other, uncontrolled factor (such as attention).

It is also possible that, although the treatment caused behavior to improve, other variables took over to control the new behavior. Again, we can consider the effect attention has on behavior. When family and friends witness a change in behavior, they may pay attention to the individual. Think of the praise people get when they have lost weight or quit smoking. Positive reinforcement in the form of attention may maintain the behavior change that was initiated by the treatment and so we would not expect behavior to return to baseline levels when the treatment was withdrawn.

initial baseline period? We describe reasons why behavior might not revert to the baseline level when the treatment is withdrawn in Box 10.2.

If for whatever reason behavior does not reverse back to baseline levels when treatment is withdrawn, researchers cannot conclude that the treatment caused the initial behavior change (Kazdin, 1980, 1998). The researcher must examine the situation carefully with the hope of identifying variables that might be confounding the treatment variable or replicate the procedure with different subjects (Hersen & Barlow, 1976).

Researchers can also face an ethical problem when using the ABAB design. Suppose the treatment seems to improve the individual's behavior relative to the baseline. Is it ethical to remove what appears to be a beneficial treatment to determine if the treatment actually caused the improvement? As you might imagine, withdrawing a beneficial treatment may not be justified in all cases. Some behaviors might be life-threatening or exceptionally debilitating, and it would not be ethical to remove treatment once a positive effect is observed. For example, some autistic children exhibit self-injurious behaviors such as head banging. If a clinical researcher succeeds in reducing the frequency of this behavior, it would be unethical to withdraw treatment to meet the requirements of the ABAB design. Fortunately, there is a single-case experimental design that does not involve withdrawal of treatment and that may be appropriate in such situations—the multiple-baseline design.

The Multiple-Baseline Design   The multiple-baseline design also makes use of baseline and treatment stages, but not by withdrawing a treatment as in the ABAB design. As the name suggests, researchers establish several baselines when using a multiple-baseline design. The multiple-baseline design demonstrates the effect of a treatment by showing that behaviors in more than one baseline change following the introduction of a treatment.

One example of the multiple-baseline design is to treat one person's behavior in different situations In this case, the first step in the multiple-baseline design is to record behavior (such as the aggressiveness of a child) as it normally occurs in several situations (such as at home, in the classroom, and at an after-school daycare facility). The researcher establishes the baseline frequency of the behavior in each situation (i.e., multiple baselines). Next the treatment is introduced in one of the situations (e.g., at home), *but not* in the other situations. The researcher continues to monitor behavior in all of the situations. A critical feature of the multiple-baseline design is that treatment is applied to only one baseline at a time. The behavior in the treated situation should improve; the behavior in the baseline situations should not improve. The next step is to apply the treatment in a second situation (treatment may continue in the first situation as well) but leave the third situation as a continuing baseline. Behavior should change only in the treated situation and not in the baseline situation. The final step is to administer the treatment in the third situation and again, the behavior should change when the treatment is administered in the third situation. The key evidence for the effectiveness of a treatment in the multiple-baseline design is the demonstration that behavior changes only when the treatment is introduced.

There are several variations on the multiple-baseline design, depending on whether multiple baselines are established for different individuals, for different behaviors in the same individual, or for the same individual in different situations. Although they sound complex, multiple-baseline designs are frequently used and easily understood. We will describe each type of multiple-baseline design using an applied research example.

Key Concept }

In the **multiple-baseline design across individuals,** baselines are first established for different individuals. When the behavior of each individual has stabilized, an intervention is introduced for one individual, then for another individual, later for another, and so on. As in all multiple-baseline designs, the treatment is introduced at a different time for each baseline (in this case for each individual). If the treatment is effective, then a change in behavior will occur immediately following the application of the treatment in each individual.

An example of the use of a multiple-baseline design across individuals comes from the field of sports psychology. Allison and Ayllon (1980) were interested in evaluating the effectiveness of a coaching method that involved several behavioral techniques on the acquisition of specific football, tennis, and gymnastic skills. Although they found that the method was effective for each sport, we will describe their test of the effectiveness of behavioral coaching for the acquisition of a football skill. The participants in this experiment were second-string members of a citywide football program chosen because they "completely lacked fundamental football skills" (p. 299).

The skill to be acquired in the Allison and Ayllon (1980) study was blocking. Blocking skill was defined operationally in terms of eight elements, ranging from the body's first being behind the line of scrimmage to maintaining body contact until the whistle was blown. Behavioral coaching involved specific procedures implemented by the team coach. The procedures included systematic verbal feedback, positive and negative reinforcement, and several other behavioral techniques. The experimenter first established baselines for several different members of the football team under "standard coaching" conditions. In the standard procedure, the coach used verbal instructions, provided occasional modeling or verbal approval, and, when execution was incorrect, "loudly informed the player and, at times, commented on the player's stupidity, lack of courage, awareness, or even worse" (p. 300). In short, it was an all-too-typical example of negative coaching behavior.

The experimenter and a second observer recorded the frequency of correct blocks made in sets of 10 trials. Behavioral coaching was begun, in accordance with the multiple-baseline design, at different times for each of four football players. Results of this intervention are shown in Figure 10.6. Across four individuals, behavioral coaching was shown to be effective in increasing the frequency of correctly executed blocks. The agreement between the two observers on blocking performance ranged from 84% to 94%, indicating that the observation of behavior was reliable. The skill execution changed for each

FIGURE 10.6   Multiple baselines showing percentage of football blocks executed correctly by four players as a function of standard coaching and behavioral coaching. (From Allison & Ayllon, 1980.)

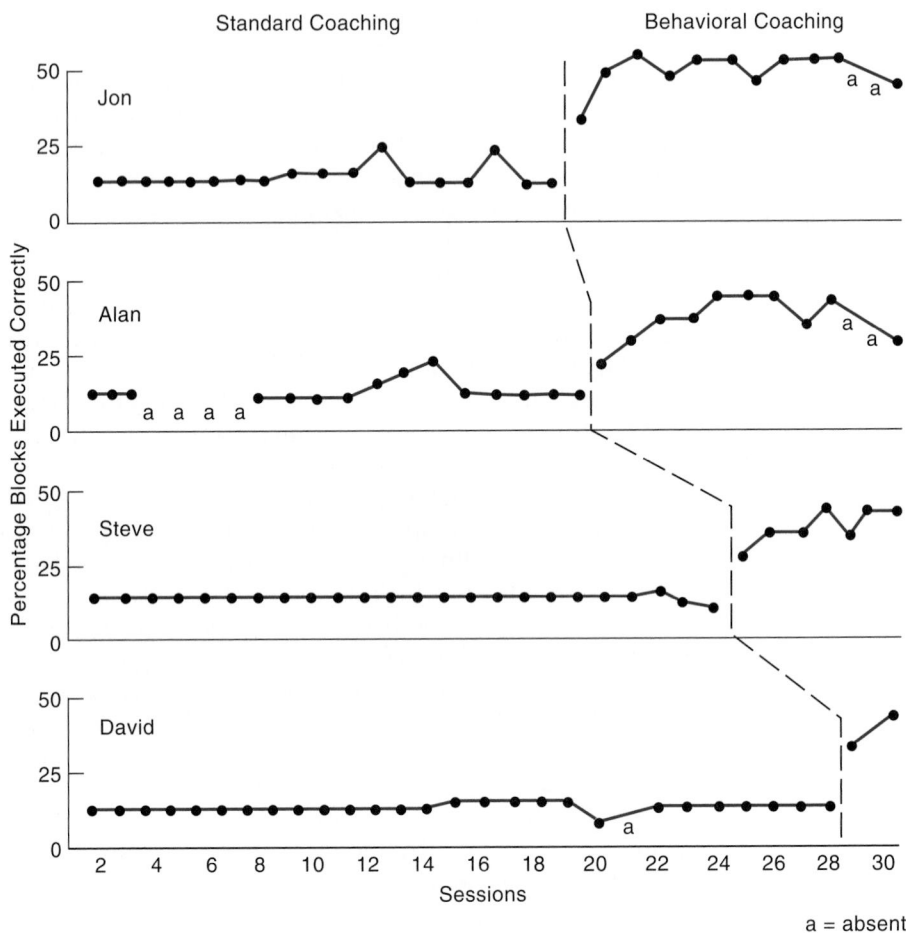

player at the point at which the behavioral coaching was introduced. Thus, there is evidence in this multiple-baseline design that the coaching method caused the change in each player's performance.

A second type of multiple-baseline design involves establishing two or more baselines by observing different behaviors in the same individual, a **multiple-baseline design across behaviors.** A treatment is directed first at one behavior, then at another, and so on. Evidence for a causal relationship between treatment and behavior is obtained if performance changes for each behavior immediately after the treatment is introduced. For example, Gena, Krantz, McClannahan, and Poulson (1996) attempted to teach several different socially appropriate affective behaviors to youths with autism. As the researchers noted, children with autism often show inappropriate affective behaviors, which limit their opportunities to communicate effectively with others and to develop interpersonal relationships.

Key Concept

Treatment included verbal praise and tokens (exchangeable for rewards) that were delivered contingent on appropriate affective responses in three or four different behavior categories. Target behaviors were selected from among the following: showing appreciation, talking about favorite things, laughing about absurdities, showing sympathy, and indicating dislike. Visual inspection of the behavioral records showed evidence for the effectiveness of the treatment. As required in the multiple-baseline design, the different affective behaviors changed immediately after introduction of the intervention for that behavior.

Key Concept

The third major variation on the multiple-baseline design involves establishing two or more baselines for an individual's behavior across different situations, a **multiple-baseline design across situations.** For example, as we described when we introduced the multiple-baseline design, a researcher might establish baselines showing the frequency of a child's aggressive behavior at home, in the classroom, and at an after-school day-care facility. As with other variations of this design, the treatment is applied at different times and the behavioral records are examined to determine whether behavior changes systematically with the introduction of treatment.

VanBiervliet, Spangler, and Marshall (1981) used a multiple-baseline design across situations to study the effect of changing the way meals were served in an institution for mentally impaired persons on the verbal interaction among the residents. The investigators suggested that the typical institutional method of serving meals did not encourage peer interaction and that an alternative procedure, serving "family style," would increase verbal interactions. Baselines for frequency of verbalizations of five residents were made for three different situations (actually, three meals)—dinner, lunch, and breakfast. Behavior change was assessed in two ways: (a) by averaging the number of vocalizations made by the five residents, and (b) by examining individual behavioral records. Both measures showed that frequency of verbal behavior increased at each meal following the change in the way meals were served.

Methodological Issues Associated with Multiple-Baseline Designs

- How many baselines are needed?

Often the first question to arise when one is doing an experiment using a multiple-baseline design is, "How many baselines do I need?" As with many other aspects of single-case research, there are no hard-and-fast rules. The bare minimum is clearly two baselines, but this is generally considered inadequate. Three or four baselines are recommended (Hersen & Barlow, 1976).

- What if behavior changes before the intervention?

Problems can arise in any of the types of multiple-baseline designs when changes in behavior are seen in a baseline before the treatment has been administered. The reasons for these premature changes in a baseline are not always clear. The logic of the multiple-baseline designs depends critically on the changes in behavior occurring directly after the introduction of the treatment. Thus, when changes in baseline performance occur prior to treatment, it makes it hard to conclude that the treatment was effective. If the pretreatment changes occur in only one of several baselines (especially if there is a plausible explanation for the change based on procedural or situational factors), the multiple-baseline design can still be interpreted with some confidence. For instance, Kazdin and Erickson (1975) used a multiple-baseline design across individuals to help severely mentally impaired individuals respond to instructions. Participants who followed instructions were reinforced with candy-coated cereal and praise, and this intervention was introduced in each of four small groups at different points in time. Performance changed directly with the application of the positive reinforcement procedure in three groups, but not in the fourth. In this group, which had the longest baseline, behavior gradually improved prior to the intervention. The researchers reasonably suggested that this occurred because individuals in this group saw other participants comply with instructions and then imitated the treated participants' behavior.

- What if the treatment generalizes to other behaviors or situations?

A problem sometimes seen in multiple-baseline designs occurs when changes in one behavior *generalize* to other behaviors or situations. For example, when researchers successfully increased the amount of verbal interaction of mentally impaired persons at their dinner meal, it would not be too surprising if the residents began to talk more at other meals. The increased interaction at other meals might have been prompted by the sight of food being served or the act of sitting down beside an acquaintance. In fact, VanBiervliet et al. (1981) did not observe generalization across meals, so the effect of the mealtime intervention was clearly demonstrated.

In dealing with possible problems of generalization, researchers need to keep in mind the maxim, "An ounce of prevention is worth a pound of cure." If altering the behavior of one individual is likely to affect the behaviors of others, if behavior in one situation is likely to influence behavior in another situation, or if changing one type of behavior is likely to affect other behaviors, then multiple-baseline designs may need to be modified or perhaps abandoned altogether (Kazdin, 1998). Unfortunately, anticipating when changes will occur simultaneously in more than one baseline is not always easy, but these problems appear to be relatively infrequent exceptions to the effects usually seen in a multiple-baseline design (Kazdin, 1998). What is clear, however, is that concluding that a treatment is effective using a multiple-baseline design requires that behavior changes directly following the introduction of the treatment in each baseline.

Problems and Limitations Common to All Single-Subject Designs

- Interpreting the effect of a treatment can be difficult if the baseline stage shows excessive variability or increasing or decreasing trends in behavior.
- The problem of low external validity with single-subject experiments can be reduced by testing small groups of individuals.

Problems with Baseline Records   An ideal baseline record and response to an intervention are shown in panel A of Figure 10.7. Behavior during baseline is very stable, and behavior changes immediately following the introduction of treatment. If this were the outcome of the first stages of either an ABAB or a multiple-baseline design, we would be headed in the direction of showing that our treatment is effective in modifying behavior. However, consider the baseline and treatment stages shown in panel B of Figure 10.7. Although the desired behavior appears to increase in frequency following an intervention, the baseline shows a great deal of variability. It is difficult to know whether the treatment produced the change or behavior just happened to be on the upswing. In general, it is hard to decide whether an intervention was effective when there is excessive variability in the baseline.

There are several ways to deal with the problem of excessive baseline variability. One way is to look for factors in the situation that might be producing the variability and that could be removed. The presence of a particular staff member, for instance, might be causing changes in the behavior of a psychiatric patient. Another approach is to "wait it out"—to continue taking baseline measures until behavior stabilizes. It is, of course, not possible to predict when and if this might occur. Introducing the intervention before behavior has stabilized, however, would jeopardize a clear interpretation of the outcome. A final way to deal with excessive variability is to average data points. By charting a behavioral record using averages of several points, researchers can sometimes reduce the "appearance" of variability (Kazdin, 1978).

FIGURE 10.7   Examples of behavioral records showing possible relationships between baseline and intervention phases of a behavior modification program. The arrow indicates the start of an intervention.

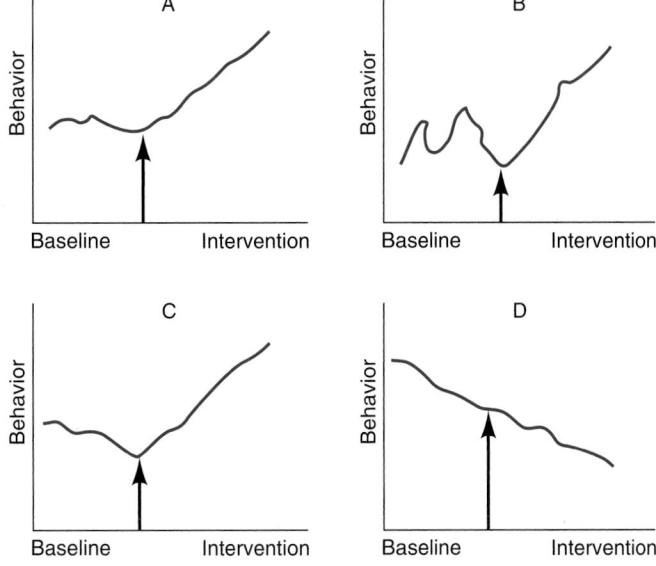

Panel C of Figure 10.7 illustrates another potential problem that can arise when baselines show an increasing or decreasing trend. If the goal of the intervention was to increase frequency of behavior, the decreasing trend shown in panel C poses no problem of interpretation. An intervention that reversed the decreasing trend can be taken as evidence that the treatment was effective. If the goal of the intervention were to be to reduce the frequency of a behavior, however, the problem would be more serious. This situation is illustrated in panel D. Here we see a decreasing trend in the baseline stage and continued reduction of frequency in the treatment stage. It would be difficult to know whether the treatment had an effect because the decrease following the intervention could be due to the intervention or to a continuation of the baseline trend. When an intervention is expected to have an effect in the same direction as a baseline trend, the change following the intervention must be much more marked than that shown in panel D to support a conclusion that the treatment had been effective (Kazdin, 1978). This problem becomes even more troubling because a treatment effect in a single-subject design is usually judged by visually inspecting the behavioral record. It is often difficult to say what constitutes a "marked" change in the behavioral record (see, for example, Parsonson & Baer, 1992). It is an especially good idea in these circumstances to complement the observations of the target behavior with other means of evaluation such as making comparisons with "normal" individuals or asking for subjective evaluations from others familiar with the individual.

Questions of External Validity   A frequent criticism of the use of single-subject research designs is that the findings have limited external validity. In other words, the single-subject experiment appears to have the same limitation as the case study method. Because each person is unique, it can be argued that there is no way of knowing whether the effect of a particular intervention will generalize to other individuals. There are several reasons, however, why the external validity of findings from single-subject experiments may not be as limited as it seems.

First, the types of intervention used in single-subject experiments are often potent ones and frequently produce dramatic and sizable changes in behavior (Kazdin, 1978). Consequently, these types of treatments are often found to generalize to other individuals. Other evidence for the generality of effects based on single-subject experiments comes from the use of multiple-baseline designs. A multiple-baseline design across individuals, for example, is often able to show that a particular intervention was successful in modifying the behavior of several individuals. Similarly, multiple baselines across situations and behaviors can attest to the external validity of a treatment effect.

Perhaps the best way to establish the external validity of a treatment effect in a single-subject experiment is to test a "single group" of subjects. The procedures associated with single-subject designs are sometimes used with small groups of individuals (i.e., small-n). We have already seen two examples of this.

VanBiervliet et al. (1981) showed that changes in a mealtime procedure were effective in increasing the average frequency of verbalizations of five mentally impaired individuals who were treated simultaneously. Similarly, Kazdin and Erickson (1975) found that positive reinforcement improved responsiveness to instructions in small groups of mentally impaired individuals. In both experiments, the researchers were able to demonstrate that a treatment was, on average, effective for a small group of participants as well as for individuals in the group. In a sense, the treatment effect was replicated several times across members of a group. Single-subject experiments like these offer impressive evidence for both internal and external validity.

SUMMARY

Two important single-case research designs are the case study and the single-subject experiment, or small-*n* design. The case study method can be an important source of hypotheses about behavior, can provide an opportunity for clinical innovation (e.g., trying out new approaches to therapy), can permit the intensive study of rare phenomena, can challenge theoretical assumptions, and can provide tentative support for a psychological theory. The intensive study of individuals that is the hallmark of the case study method is called idiographic research, and it can be viewed as complementary to the nomothetic approach (seeking general laws or principles) that is also characteristic of psychology. Problems arise when the case study method is used to draw cause-effect conclusions, or when biases in the collection of, or interpretation of, data are not identified. The case study method also involves potential problems of generalizing findings based on the study of a single individual. Moreover, the "dramatic" results obtained from some case studies, though they may give scientific investigators important insights, are frequently accepted as valid by people who are not aware of the limitations of this method.

B. F. Skinner developed the experimental analysis of behavior. Applied behavior analysis seeks to apply principles derived from an experimental analysis of behavior to socially relevant problems. The major methodology of these approaches is the single-subject experiment, or small-*n* research. Although there are many kinds of single-subject designs, the most common are the ABAB design and the multiple-baseline design.

An ABAB design, or reversal design, allows a researcher to confirm a treatment effect by showing that behavior changes systematically with conditions of no treatment (baseline) and treatment. Methodological problems arise in this design when behavior that changed during the first treatment (B) stage does not reverse when treatment is withdrawn during the second baseline (A) stage. When this occurs, it is difficult to establish that the treatment, rather than some other factor, was responsible for the initial change. One may encounter ethical problems when using the ABAB design if a treatment that has been shown to be beneficial is withdrawn during the second baseline stage.

A multiple-baseline design demonstrates the effectiveness of a treatment by showing that behaviors across more than one baseline change as a consequence of the introduction of a treatment. Baselines are first established across different individuals, or across behaviors or across situations in the same individual. Methodological problems arise when behavior does not change immediately with the introduction of a treatment or when a treatment effect generalizes to other individuals, other behaviors, or other situations.

Problems of excessive baseline variability as well as of increasing or decreasing baselines sometimes make it difficult to interpret the outcome of single-subject designs. The problem of excessive baseline variability can be approached by seeking out and removing sources of variability, by extending the time during which baseline observations are made, or by averaging data points to remove the "appearance" of variability. Increasing or decreasing baselines may require the researcher to obtain other kinds of evidence for the effectiveness of a treatment. Finally, the single-subject design is often criticized for its lack of external validity. However, because treatments typically produce substantial changes in behavior, these changes can often be easily replicated in different individuals. The use of single "groups" of subjects (small-*n* research) can also provide immediate evidence of generality across subjects.

Key Concepts

case study
nomothetic approach
idiographic approach
single-subject experiment
baseline stage

ABAB design (reversal design)
multiple-baseline design (across
   individuals, across behaviors,
   across situations)

Review Questions

1 Identify and give an example of each of the advantages of the case study method.
2 Distinguish between a nomothetic and an idiographic approach to research.
3 Identify and give an example of each of the disadvantages of the case study method.
4 What is the major limitation of the case study method in drawing cause-effect conclusions?
5 Under what conditions might a single-subject design be more appropriate than a multiple-group design?
6 Distinguish between baseline and intervention stages of a single-subject experimental design.
7 Why is an ABAB design also called a reversal design?
8 What problems are specifically associated with an ABAB design?
9 Outline the general procedures and logic that are common to all the major forms of multiple-baseline designs.
10 What methodological problems are specifically associated with multiple-baseline designs?

11 What methodological problems must be addressed in all single-subject experimental designs?

12 What evidence supports the external validity of single-subject experimental designs?

CHALLENGE QUESTIONS

1 A case study showing how "mud therapy" was successful in treating an individual exhibiting excessive anxiety was reported in a popular magazine. The patient's symptoms included having trouble sleeping, loss of appetite, extreme nervousness when in groups of people, and general feelings of arousal that led the individual always to feel "on edge" and fearful. The California therapist who administered the mud therapy was known for this treatment, having appeared on several TV talk shows. He first taught the patient a deep relaxation technique and a "secret word" to repeat over and over in order to block out all disturbing thoughts. Then the patient was asked to lie submerged for two hours each day in a special wooden "calm tub" filled with mud. During this time the patient was to practice the relaxation exercises and to concentrate on repeating the secret word whenever the least bit of anxiety was experienced. The therapy was very costly, but after six weeks the patient reported to the therapist that he no longer had the same feelings of anxiety that he had had before. The therapist pronounced him cured and attributed the success of the treatment to immersion in the calming mud. The conclusion drawn by the author of the magazine article describing this therapy was that "it is a treatment that many people could benefit from." On the basis of your knowledge of the limitations of the case study method, answer the following questions:

  A What possible sources of bias were there in the study?

  B What alternative explanations can you suggest for the successful treatment?

  C What potential problem arises from studying only one individual?

2 A 5-year-old child frequently gets skin rashes, and the mother has been told by her family doctor that the problem is due to "something" that the child eats. The doctor suggests that she "watch carefully" what the child eats. The mother decides to approach this problem by recording each day whether the child has a rash and what the child has eaten the day before. She hopes to find some relationship between eating a particular food and the presence or absence

of the rash. Although this approach might help discover a relationship between eating certain foods and the appearance of the rash, a better approach might be one based on the logic and procedures associated with single-subject designs. Explain how the mother might use such an alternative approach. Be specific and point to possible problems that may arise in this application of behavioral methodology.

3 During the summer months you find employment in a camp for mildly mentally impaired children. As a counselor you are asked to supervise a small group of children, as well as to look for ways to improve their attention to various camp activities that take place indoors (e.g., craft making and sewing). You decide to explore the possibility of using a system of rewards (M&M candies) for "time on task." You realize that the camp director will want evidence of the effectiveness of your intervention strategy as well as some assurance that it will work with other children in the camp. Therefore you are to:

  A Plan an intervention strategy based on reinforcement principles that has as its goal an increase in the time children spend on a camp activity.

  B Explain what behavioral records you will need to keep and how you will determine whether your intervention has produced a change in the children's behavior. You will need, for example, to specify exactly when and how you will measure behavior, as well as to justify your use of a particular design to carry out your "experiment."

  C Describe the argument you will use to convince the director that your intervention strategy (assuming that it works) will work with other, similar children.

4 A teacher asks your help in planning a behavioral intervention that will help manage the behavior of a problem child in his classroom. The child does not stay at her desk when asked to do so, does not remain quiet during "quiet times," and exhibits other behaviors that disrupt the teaching environment. Explain specifically how a positive reinforcer, such as candy or small toys, might be used as part of a multiple-baseline across behaviors design to improve the child's behavior.

Answer to Stretching Exercise

1   You may be inclined to agree with your friend. Personal examples are often more compelling than quantitative evidence. In evaluating these two studies, however, it is important to recognize that they represent two different approaches to doing research. The first study represents the nomothetic approach, which relies on the study of large groups and tends to use quantitative measures to describe the groups. The second study represents the idiographic approach, which involves the intensive study of individual cases and more qualitative description. After recognizing these differences in the two approaches, careful examination of the findings indicate that there is no need to choose between the two studies. The first study does indicate that slightly more than half of marriages end in divorce, but this means that slightly less than half of all marriages do not end in divorce. The second study indicates that even marriages that are at risk for divorce because of such factors as conflict and a family history of divorce do not necessarily end in divorce. The second study suggests that it may take additional effort to overcome these risk factors. For example, the couple considering divorce when they entered therapy were willing to spend a year in therapy to work on their marriage. The findings of these two studies illustrate the more general idea that nomothetic and idiographic research can complement rather than compete with each other.

2   Your friend's second question is an example of a more general question that students of psychology often ask (and should ask). Namely, what does all this research evidence have to do with me? The findings of these two studies do provide potentially useful information for your friend as she considers her future. The first study tells us that divorce does occur frequently and that certain factors have been identified as indicators of when divorce is more likely to occur. The second study tells us that marriages can succeed even when these risk factors are present. This information can be useful because it provides evidence from systematic and controlled study that complements what we can learn from our own experience. Your friend will not be able to determine based on these findings whether she will, in fact, divorce should she choose to marry. More generally, the findings of psychological research cannot yet tell us the answer to Gordon Allport's question of what any one person will do.

Answer to Challenge Question 1

A   One source of bias in this case study was that the same individual served as therapist and as researcher with the commensurate problems of observer bias. A second source of bias is that the therapist based his conclusion solely on the self-reports of the patient.

B   The successful treatment may have resulted from the relaxation technique alone; the use of the "secret word" in the face of anxiety; attention the patient received from the therapist; or even the high cost of the treatment.

C   The major problem that arises from studying one individual is a potential lack of external validity.

CHAPTER ELEVEN

Quasi-Experimental Designs and Program Evaluation

CHAPTER OUTLINE

Overview

In the most general sense, an experiment is a test; it is a procedure we use to find out something that we don't yet know. In this sense we experiment when we add new ingredients to a chili recipe in order to see whether they improve its taste. We experiment with new ways to catch fish by changing the lures we use. We experiment when we take a different route to our job in order to find a faster way to commute. As you no doubt recognize, however, these kinds of informal "experiments" are much different from the experiments that are typically carried out in psychological research. Experimental methods, unlike other research techniques such as observation and surveys, are viewed as the most efficient way to determine causation. But determining causation is not always easy, and in the last few chapters you were introduced to the complexity of the task facing researchers who seek to understand a phenomenon by discovering what caused it.

In this chapter we continue our discussion of experimental methods, but we focus on experiments as they are conducted in natural settings such as hospitals, schools, or businesses. You will see that the task of drawing cause-effect conclusions in these settings often becomes even more difficult, and that new problems arise when an investigator leaves the confines of the laboratory to do experiments in natural settings.

There are many reasons why researchers do experiments in natural settings. One reason for these "field experiments" is to test the external validity of a laboratory finding (see Ch. 7). That is, we seek to find out if a treatment effect observed in the laboratory works in a similar way in another setting. Other reasons for experimenting in natural settings are more practical. Doing experiments in natural settings allows researchers to achieve an important goal of the scientific method. That is, research in natural settings is likely to associated with attempts to improve conditions under which people live and work. The government may experiment with a new tax system or a new method of job training for the economically disadvantaged. Schools may experiment by changing lunch programs, after-school care, or curricula. A business may experiment with new product designs, methods of delivering employee benefits, or flexible work hours. In these cases, as is true in the laboratory, it is important to determine whether the "treatment" caused a change. Did a change in the way patients are admitted to a hospital emergency room cause patients to be treated more quickly and efficiently? Did a college energy conservation program cause a decrease in energy consumption? Knowing whether a treatment was effective permits us to make important decisions about continuing the treatment, about spending additional money, about investing more time and effort, or about changing the present situation on the basis of our knowledge of the results. Research that seeks to determine the effectiveness of changes made by institutions, government agencies, and other organizations is one goal of *program evaluation*.

In this chapter we describe obstacles to doing experiments in natural settings, and we discuss ways of overcoming these obstacles so that experiments are done whenever possible. Nevertheless, experiments are sometimes not feasible outside the laboratory. In these cases, experimental procedures that only approximate the conditions of laboratory experiments must be considered. We discuss several of these quasi-experimental techniques. We conclude the chapter by providing a brief introduction to the logic, procedures, and limitations of program evaluation.

TRUE EXPERIMENTS

Characteristics of True Experiments

- In true experiments, researchers manipulate an independent variable with treatment and comparison condition(s) and exercise a high degree of control (especially through random assignment to conditions).

Although many everyday activities (such as altering the ingredients of a recipe) might be called experiments, we would not consider them "true" experiments in the sense in which experimentation has been discussed in this textbook. Analogously, many "social experiments" carried out by the government and those that are conducted by company officials or educational administrators are also not true experiments. *A true experiment is one that leads to an unambiguous outcome regarding what caused an event.*

True experiments exhibit three important characteristics:

1 In a true experiment some type of intervention or treatment is implemented.

2 True experiments are marked by the high degree of control that an experimenter has over the arrangement of experimental conditions, assignment of participants, systematic manipulation of independent variables, and choice of dependent variables. The ability to assign participants randomly to experimental conditions is often seen as the most critical defining characteristic of the true experiment (Judd et al., 1991).

3 Finally, true experiments are characterized by an appropriate comparison. Indeed, the experimenter exerts control over a situation to establish a proper comparison to evaluate the effectiveness of a treatment. In the simplest of experimental situations, this comparison is one between two comparable groups that are treated exactly alike except for the variable of interest.

When the conditions of a true experiment are met, any differences in a dependent variable that arise can logically be attributed to the differences between levels of the independent variable. There are differences, however, between true experiments done in natural settings and experiments done in a laboratory. A few of the most important differences are described in Box 11.1.

Obstacles to Conducting True Experiments in Natural Settings

- Researchers may experience difficulty obtaining permission to conduct true experiments in natural settings and gaining access to participants.

BOX 11.1

DIFFERENCES BETWEEN EXPERIMENTS IN THE LAB AND IN NATURAL SETTINGS

Experiments that are conducted outside the laboratory are likely to differ in a number of significant ways from those done in the laboratory. Not every experiment in a natural setting differs from laboratory experiments in all of these ways, of course. But if you are thinking of doing research in a natural setting, we urge you to consider the following critical issues.

Control

More than anything else, the scientist is concerned with control. Only by controlling those factors that are assumed to influence a phenomenon can we make a decision about what caused it. For instance, the random assignment of participants to conditions of an experiment is a method of control used to balance individual differences across conditions. Or, researchers can hold other factors constant that are likely to influence a phenomenon. In a natural setting, a researcher may not always have the same degree of control as in a laboratory over assignment of participants or over the conditions of an experiment. A researcher may even be asked to evaluate whether an intervention was effective without having been involved in the planning or conduct of the "experiment." This kind of "after-the-fact" evaluation is especially difficult because those conducting the study may not have considered important factors in the planning and execution of the intervention.

External validity

The high degree of control in the "artificial" environment of the laboratory that increases the internal validity of research often decreases the external validity of the findings. Experiments in natural settings may therefore need to be done in order to establish the external validity of a laboratory finding. When an experiment is done primarily to test a specific psychological theory, however, the external validity of a laboratory finding may not be all that important (e.g., Mook, 1983). In contrast, the external validity of research done in natural

settings is often very important. This is especially true when social experimentation serves as the basis for large-scale social changes, such as trying out new ways to curb drunk driving or new procedures for registering voters. Will the results of a program that is judged to be beneficial for curbing drunk driving in a Midwestern state generalize to states in other areas of the country? Does a course found to improve students' critical thinking skills at one college also "work" at other colleges? These are, of course, questions about the external validity of research findings.

Goals

Experimentation in natural settings often has different goals from those of laboratory research (see Chapter 2). Laboratory research frequently represents *basic research* with the single goal of understanding a phenomenon—of determining how "nature" works. It may be done to gain knowledge merely for knowledge's sake. *Applied research* is also directed toward discovering the reasons for a phenomenon, but it is likely to be done only when knowing the reasons for an event will lead to changes that will improve the present situation. Experimentation in natural settings, therefore, is more likely to have practical goals.

Consequences

Sometimes experiments are conducted that have far-reaching impact on communities and society, affecting large numbers of people. The Head Start program for disadvantaged children and the "Sesame Street" television show were social experiments designed to improve the education of literally hundreds of thousands of children across the nation. Social experiments are also carried out on a smaller scale in natural settings such as in local schools or businesses. Experiments in businesses may be carried out with the eventual goal of reducing the number of employees or in other ways affecting the quality of employees' lives. Clearly, these examples of society's

FIGURE 11.1 As a social experiment, "Sesame Street" was designed to improve the education of hundreds of thousands of children.

"experiments," are likely to have consequences of greater immediate impact than those of laboratory research. Moreover, as is true of all experiments, the consequences are not always those that were anticipated.

In order to draw meaningful conclusions about the effects of these experiments, we must consider the design and implementation of these "treatments" and do the best we can to assess whether the treatments worked. This is especially important because, as we have seen, the consequences of such experiments frequently are so great in terms of money spent and the number of people whose lives are affected. By contrast, the immediate consequences of a laboratory experiment can be substantial, but they are much more likely to be minimal. They may directly affect only the lives of a few researchers and of those relatively few participants recruited to participate. Both laboratory experiments and experiments in natural settings are valuable tools for researchers. Like all tools, however, they are best used when we understand their strengths and limitations.

- Although random assignment is perceived by some as unfair because it may deprive individuals of a new treatment, it is still the best way and fairest way to determine if a new treatment is effective.

Experimental research is an effective tool for solving problems and answering practical questions. Nevertheless, two major obstacles often arise when we try to carry out experiments in natural settings. The first problem is obtaining permission to do the research from individuals in positions of authority. Unless they believe that the research will be useful, school board presidents and government and business leaders are unlikely to support research financially or otherwise. The second, and often more pressing, obstacle to doing experiments in natural settings is the problem of access to participants. This problem can prove especially troublesome if participants are to be randomly assigned to either a treatment group or a comparison group.

Random assignment to conditions appears unfair at first—after all, random assignment requires that a potentially beneficial treatment be withheld from at least some participants. Suppose that a new approach to the teaching of foreign languages was to be tested at your college or university. Suppose further that, when you went to register for your next semester's classes, you were told that you would be randomly assigned to one of two sections taught at the time you selected—one section involving the old method and one involving the new method. How would you react? Your knowledge of research methods tells you that the two methods must be administered to comparable groups of students and that random assignment is the best way to ensure such comparability. Nonetheless, you might be tempted to feel that random assignment is not fair, especially if you are assigned to the section using the old (old-fashioned?) method. Let's take a closer look at the fairness of random assignment.

If those responsible for selecting the method of foreign language instruction already knew that the new method was more effective than the old method at schools such as yours, there would be little justification for testing the method again. Under such circumstances we would agree that withholding the new method from students in the control group would be unjust. If we do not know whether the new method is better, however, any approach other than conducting a true experiment will leave us in doubt about the new method's effectiveness. Random assignment to treatments—call it a "lottery" if you prefer—may be the fairest procedure for assigning students to sections. The old method of instruction, after all, was considered effective before the development of the new method. If the new method proves less effective, random assignment will have actually "protected" the control participants from receiving an ineffective treatment.

There are ways to offer a potentially effective treatment to all participants while still maintaining comparable groups. One way is to alternate treatments. For example, Atkinson (1968) randomly assigned students to receive computer-assisted instruction in either English or math (the "treatment") and then tested both groups in English and math. Each group served as a control for the other on the test for which its members had not received computer-assisted instruction. After completing the experiment, both groups could then be given computer-assisted instruction in the subject matter to which they had not been previously exposed. Thus, all participants received all potentially beneficial treatments.

Establishing a proper control group is also possible if there is more demand for a service than an agency can meet. People who are waiting to receive the service can become a *waiting list control group*. It is essential, however, that people be assigned to the waiting list randomly. People who are "first in line" are no doubt different on important dimensions from those who arrive last (e.g., more eager for treatment). Random assignment is necessary to distribute these characteristics in an unbiased way between treatment and comparison groups.

There will always be circumstances in which random assignment simply cannot be used. For example, in clinical trials involving tests of new medical treatments, it may be extremely difficult to get patients to agree to be randomly assigned to either the treatment group or the control (no treatment) group. As you will see, *quasi-experimental designs* can be used in these situations. The logic and procedures for these quasi-experimental designs will be described later in this chapter.

Threats to Internal Validity Controlled by True Experiments

- Threats to internal validity are confounds that serve as plausible alternative explanations for a research finding.
- Major classes of threats to internal validity include history, maturation, testing, instrumentation, regression, selection, subject attrition, and additive effects with selection.

Key Concept

Prior to doing an experiment, we want to consider what major classes of possible explanations can be ruled out by our experimental procedure. Only by controlling all possible alternative explanations can we arrive at a definite causal inference. In previous chapters, we referred to various uncontrolled factors that threaten the internal validity of an experiment as confounding factors (they are also called confounds). Several types of confounds were identified in earlier chapters (see especially Chapter 7). Campbell and Stanley (1966; Cook & Campbell, 1979; see also Shadish, Cook, & Campbell, 2002)[1] have identified eight classes of confounds that they call **threats to internal validity.** You have already been introduced to some of these; others will be new. After reviewing these major threats to internal validity, we will be able to judge the extent to which various experimental procedures control for these kinds of alternative explanations of a treatment effect.

---

[1]In their revision of the classic Cook and Campbell (1979) text on quasi-experimentation, Shadish et al. (2002) add "ambiguous temporal precedence" as a ninth major threat to internal validity. Specifically, although cause must precede effect, the fact that A comes before B does not by itself justify claiming that A causes B; moreover, some causation may be bidirectional. We have not added this threat to our list because we believe that (a) this issue has been partially dealt with when introducing the logic of the experimental method, and (b) a discussion leads students beyond a test of simple unidirectional effects found in most experiments. Finally, Shadish et al. provide reasons why the term "additive" rather than "interactive" is preferred when identifying possible threats due to the combination of selection and threats such as instrumentation or maturation. Accordingly, we changed our terminology from previous editions when discussing these combinatorial effects.

History   The occurrence of an event other than the treatment can threaten internal validity if it produces changes in the research participants' behavior. A true experiment requires that participants in the experimental group and in the control group be treated the same (have the same history of experiences while in the experiment) except for the treatment. In the laboratory, this is usually accomplished by balancing or holding conditions constant. When doing experiments in natural settings, the researcher may not always be able to exercise the degree of control associated with laboratory settings, so confounding due to history can be a threat to internal validity. For example, suppose that you set out to test whether a college-level critical thinking course did, in fact, change students' thinking. And suppose further that your test was simply to examine students' performance on a critical thinking test at the beginning of the critical thinking course and then again at the end of the course. Without an appropriate comparison group, **history** would be a threat to internal validity if events other than the treatment (i.e., the critical thinking course) occurred that might improve the critical thinking abilities of the students. For instance, suppose that many students taking this course also took it upon themselves to access a website designed to teach critical thinking that wasn't required for the course. The students' history that now included the website experience would confound the treatment and therefore pose a threat to the internal validity of the study.

Key Concept }

Maturation   Participants in an experiment necessarily change as a function of time. They grow older, become more experienced, and so forth. Change associated with the passage of time per se is called maturation. For example, suppose a researcher is interested in assessing children's learning over a school year using a new teaching technique. Without a proper comparison a researcher might attribute the changes in performance between the beginning and the end of the school year of a group of schoolchildren to the effect of the teaching intervention when, in reality, the changes were simply due to a **maturation** threat to validity.

Key Concept }

Testing   Taking a test generally has an effect on subsequent testing. Consider, for example, the fact that many students often improve from the initial test in a course to the second test. During the first test the students gain familiarity with the testing procedure and with the instructor's expectations. This familiarity then affects their performance on the second test. Likewise, in the context of a psychology experiment in which more than one test is given (e.g., in a pretest-posttest design), **testing** is a threat to internal validity if the effect of a treatment cannot be separated from the effect of testing. Can you see how an attempt to assess the effect of a critical thinking course would be problematic if the assessment is simply the students' scores on a pretest and a posttest?

Key Concept }

Instrumentation   Changes over time can take place not only in the participants of an experiment (e.g., maturation or increased familiarity with testing), but also in the instruments used to measure the participants' performance. This is most clearly a possibility when human observers are used to assess behavior. For instance, observer bias can result from fatigue, expectations, and other characteristics of observers. Unless controlled for, these changes in the observers represent an **instrumentation** threat to internal validity by providing alternative explanations for differences in behavior between one observation period and another. Mechanical instruments also may change with repeated use. A researcher known to the authors once found that a machine used to present material in a learning experiment was not working the same at the end of the experiment as it was at the beginning. Measures made near the end of the experiment differed from those made at the beginning of the experiment. Thus, what looked like a learning effect was really just a change in the instrument used to measure learning.

Regression   Statistical **regression** is always a problem when individuals have been selected to participate in an experiment because of their "extreme" scores. Extreme scores on one test are not likely to be as extreme on a second test. In other words, a very, very bad performance, or a very, very good performance (both of which we have all experienced), is likely to be followed by a performance that is not quite so bad, or not quite so good, respectively. Consider, for instance, your best ever performance on a classroom examination. What did it take to "nail" this test? It took no doubt a lot of hard work. But it is also likely that some luck was involved. Everything has to work just right to produce an extremely good performance. If we are talking about an exam, then it is likely that the material tested was that which you just happened to study the hardest, or the test format was one you particularly like, or it came at a time when you were feeling particularly confident, or all of these and more. Particularly good performances are "extreme" because they are inflated (over our usual or typical performance) by chance. Similarly, an especially bad test performance is likely to have occurred because of some bad luck. When tested again (following either a very good or a very bad performance), it is simply not likely that chance factors will "gang up" the same way to give us that super score or that very poor score. We will likely see a performance closer to the average of our overall scores. This phenomenon frequently is called *regression to the mean.*

Now, consider an attempt to raise the academic performance of a group of college students who have performed very poorly during their first semester of college (the "pretest"). Participants are selected because of their extreme performance (in this case, extremely poor performance). Let us assume that a treatment (e.g., a 10-hour study skills workshop) is then applied. Statistical regression is a threat to internal validity because we would expect these students to perform slightly better after the second semester (the "posttest") *without any treatment* simply due to statistical regression. An unknowing researcher may mistakenly confuse this "regression effect" with a "treatment effect."

Key Concept

Key Concept

Key Concept }

Subject Attrition   A threat to internal validity occurs when participants are lost from an experiment, for example, when participants drop out of the research project. The **subject attrition** threat to internal validity rests on the assumption that the loss of participants changes the nature of a group from that established prior to the introduction of the treatment—for example, by destroying the equivalence of groups that had been established through random assignment. This might occur, for instance, if an experimental task is very difficult and causes some experimental participants to become frustrated and to drop out of the experiment. Participants who are left in the experimental group will differ from those who dropped out (and possibly from those in a control group) if for no other reason than that they were able to do the task (or at least stuck it out).

Key Concept }

Selection   When, from the outset of a study, differences exist between the kinds of individuals in one group and those in another group in the experiment, there is a threat to internal validity due to **selection.** That is, the people who are in the treatment group may differ from people in the comparison group in many ways other than their group assignment. In the laboratory, this threat to internal validity is generally handled by balancing participant characteristics through random assignment. When one is doing experiments in natural settings, there are often many obstacles to randomly assigning participants to treatment and comparison conditions. These obstacles prevent doing a true experiment and hence present a possible threat to internal validity due to selection.

Additive Effects with Selection   Individual threats to internal validity such as maturation can be a source of additional concern because they can combine with the selection threat to internal validity. Specifically, when comparable groups are not formed by random assignment, there are possible problems due to additive effects of (1) selection and maturation, (2) selection and history, and (3) selection and instrumentation. For example, additive effects of selection and maturation could occur if first-year students in college who served as an experimental group were compared with sophomores who served as a control group. Changes in students that occur during their first year (as students gain familiarity with the college environment) might be presumed to be greater than the changes that occur during the second or sophomore year. These differences in maturation rates might explain any observed differences between the experimental and control groups, rather than the differences being due to the experimental intervention.

An additive effect of selection and history results when events occurring in time have a different effect on one group of participants than on another. This is particularly a problem when intact groups are compared. Perhaps due to events that are peculiar to one group's situation, an event may have more of an impact on that group than on another. Consider, for example, research involving an investigation of the effectiveness of an AIDS awareness campaign involving two college campuses (one treatment and one control). Nationwide media attention to this problem might reasonably be assumed to affect students on both campuses equally. However, if a prominent student with AIDS died at one college during this period, and the story was featured in the college newspaper, we would assume that students at this student's college would be affected differently from those at the other. In terms of assessing the effect of an AIDS awareness campaign, this situation would represent an additive effect of selection and history.

Finally, an additive effect of selection and instrumentation might occur if a test instrument is relatively more sensitive to changes in one group's performance than to changes in another's. This occurs, for instance, when ceiling or floor effects are present. Such is the case when a group scores initially so low on an instrument (floor effect), that any further drop in scores cannot be reliably measured, or so high (ceiling effect) that any more gain cannot be assessed. As you can imagine, a threat to internal validity would be present if an experimental group showed relatively no change (due to floor or ceiling effects), while a control group changed reliably because its mean performance was initially near the middle of the measurement scale.

One of the great advantages of true experiments is that they *control* for all these threats to internal validity. As Campbell (1969) emphasizes, true experiments should be conducted when possible, but if they are not feasible, quasi-experiments should be conducted. "We must do the best we can with what is available to us" (p. 411). Quasi-experiments represent the best available compromise between the general aim of gaining valid knowledge regarding the effectiveness of a treatment and the realization that true experiments are not always possible.

Problems That Even True Experiments May Not Control

- Threats to internal validity that can occur in any study include contamination, experimenter expectancy effects, and novelty effects.
- Contamination occurs when information about the experiment is communicated between groups of participants, which may lead to resentment, rivalry, or diffusion of treatment.
- Novelty effects occur when people's behavior changes simply because an innovation (e.g., a treatment) produces excitement, energy, and enthusiasm.
- Threats to external validity occur when treatment effects may not be generalized beyond the particular people, setting, treatment, and outcome of the experiment.

Before considering specific quasi-experimental procedures, we should point out that even true experiments may not control for all possible threats to the interpretation of an experimental outcome. Although major threats to internal validity are eliminated by the true experiment, there are some additional threats that the investigator who is working in natural settings must guard against. We will use the term *contamination* to describe one general class of threats to

---

BOX 11.2

EXPERIMENTAL CONTAMINATION

There are several possible effects resulting from communication between groups of experimental participants. These include: (1) *resentment* on the part of individuals receiving less desirable treatments, (2) *rivalry* among groups receiving different treatments, or (3) a general *diffusion of treatments* across the groups (see Cook & Campbell, 1979; Shadish et al., 2002).

- *Resentment.* Consider a situation in which individuals have been randomly assigned to a control group. Further, assume that control group participants learn that "other" participants are receiving a beneficial treatment. What do you think might be the reaction of the control participants? One possibility is that the control participants will feel resentful and demoralized. As Cook and Campbell explain, in an industrial setting the person receiving the less desirable treatment may retaliate by lowering productivity. In an educational setting teachers or students might "lose heart" or become angry. This effect of "leaked" information about a treatment may make a treatment look better than it ordinarily would because of the lowered performance of the control group that responds with resentment.

- *Rivalry.* Another possible effect that may occur when a control group learns about another group's good fortune is a spirit of competition or rivalry. That is, a control group might become motivated to reduce the expected difference between itself and the treatment group. As Cook and Campbell point out, this may be likely when intact groups (such as departments, work crews, branch offices, and the like) are assigned to various conditions. Realizing that another group will look better depending on how much it distinguishes itself from the control group, participants comprising the control group may be motivated to "try harder" so as not to look bad by comparison.

- *Diffusion of treatments.* Yet another possible effect of contamination is diffusion of treatments. According to Cook and Campbell, this occurs when participants in a control group use information given to others to help them change their own behavior. For example, control participants may use the information given to participants in the treatment group to imitate the behavior of individuals who were given the treatment. Of course, this reduces the differences between the treated and untreated groups and affects the internal validity of the experiment.

Key Concept }

internal validity. **Contamination** occurs when there is communication of information about the experiment between groups of participants. Contamination can lead to several unwanted effects as described in Box 11.2.

True experiments can also be affected by threats due to *experimenter expectancy effects.* Effects due to experimenter expectancies occur when an experimenter unintentionally influences the results. Systematic errors in interpretation or mistakes in recording data can be the result of experimenter expectancy effects. Observer bias occurs when researchers' biases and expectancies lead to errors in observing, identifying, recording, and interpreting behavior. [Various ways to control observer or experimenter effects were outlined in Chapter 4 and Chapter 7 (e.g., using a double-blind procedure).]

Key Concept }

Novelty effects can occur when an innovation, such as an experimental treatment, is introduced (Shadish et al., 2002). For example, if little in the way of change or innovation has occurred for some time at a work site, employees may become excited or energized by the novelty (or newness) of their work environment when an intervention is introduced. Employees' newfound enthusiasm may account for the "success" of the intervention, rather than the intervention itself. The opposite of a novelty effect can occur as a *disruption effect*, in which an innovation, perhaps with new work procedures, disrupts employees' work to such an extent they cannot maintain their typical effectiveness.

One specific novelty effect has been labeled the *Hawthorne effect*. This refers to changes in people's behavior brought about by the interest that "significant others" show in them. The effect was named after events occurring at the Hawthorne plant of the Western Electric Company in Cicero, Illinois, near Chicago, between 1924 and 1932 (Roethlisberger, 1977). Studies were conducted to examine the relationship between productivity and conditions of the workplace. In one experiment, the amount of lighting in the plant was varied and worker performance was examined. Results revealed that *both* experimental and control groups increased their productivity during the study. Although there is some controversy surrounding the exact factors responsible for this effect (e.g., Parsons, 1974), a Hawthorne effect generally refers to a change in behavior that results from participants' awareness that someone is interested in them.

As one example of the Hawthorne effect, consider a study in which prisoners are chosen to participate in research examining the relationship between changes in prison cell conditions and attitudes toward prison life. If positive changes in prisoners' attitudes are obtained, the results could be due to the actual changes in cell conditions that were made, or they could be due to an increase in morale because prisoners saw the prison administration as expressing concern for them. Researchers working in natural settings must be conscious of the fact that changes in participants' behavior may be partially due to their awareness that others are interested in them. Thus, you can see that a Hawthorne effect represents a specific kind of reactivity (i.e., an awareness that one is being observed), which we discussed in previous chapters (especially Chapter 4).

In addition to problems resulting from threats to internal validity, true experiments can be weakened by *threats to external validity*. External validity depends mainly on how representative our sample is of the persons, settings, and times to which we want to generalize. Representativeness is normally achieved through random sampling. Because random sampling is used so infrequently (see Shadish et al., 2002), however, we can rarely say that our sample of participants, or the situation in which we are making observations, or the times during which we test individuals are representative samples of all persons, settings, treatments, or outcomes. Therefore, the investigator must be aware of possible interactions between the independent variable of an experiment and, for example, the type of individual or the nature of the setting that is involved in the experiment. Is a difference, for instance, between an experimental group and a control group that is observed with volunteers from an inner-city school in the winter also likely to be found when nonvolunteers are tested in a suburban school in the spring of the year?

Cook and Campbell describe several approaches to evaluating threats to external validity; the most important is attempting to determine the representativeness of the sample. *They point out, however, that in the last analysis the best test of external validity is replication.* That is, they recommend that establishing external validity is an empirical question. Thus, the question of external validity is best answered by repeating the experiment with different types of participants, in different settings, with different treatments, and at different times. Occasionally partial replications can be "built into" an experiment—for example, by selecting more than one group to participate. For example, testing schoolchildren from a lower socioeconomic group and a higher socioeconomic group in an experiment designed to determine the effectiveness of a new educational program would provide evidence of the generality of the treatment's effectiveness across these two socioeconomic groups.

QUASI-EXPERIMENTS

- Quasi-experiments provide an important alternative when true experiments are not possible.
- Quasi-experiments lack the degree of control found in true experiments; most notably, quasi-experiments typically lack random assignment.
- Researchers must seek additional evidence to eliminate threats to internal validity when they do quasi-experiments rather than true experiments.
- The one-group pretest-posttest design is called a pre-experimental design or a bad experiment because it has so little internal validity.

Key Concept

A dictionary will tell you that one definition of the prefix *quasi-* is "resembling." Quasi-experiments involve procedures that *resemble* those that are characteristic of true experiments. Generally speaking, **quasi-experiments** include some type of intervention or treatment and they provide a comparison, but they lack the degree of control found in true experiments. Just as randomization is the hallmark of true experiments, so *lack of randomization* is the hallmark of quasi-experiments. As Campbell and Stanley (1966) explain, quasi-experiments arise when researchers lack the control necessary to perform a true experiment.

Quasi-experiments are recommended when true experiments are not feasible. Some knowledge about the effectiveness of a treatment is more desirable than none. The list of possible threats to internal validity provided by Campbell and Stanley (1966; Shadish et al., 2002), which we reviewed earlier, can be used as a checklist in deciding just how good that knowledge is. Moreover, the investigator must be prepared to look for additional kinds of evidence that might rule out a threat to internal validity that is not specifically controlled in a quasi-experiment. For example, suppose that a quasi-experiment does not control for a history threat that would be eliminated by a true experiment. The investigator may be able to show that the history threat is implausible based on a logical analysis of the situation or based on evidence provided by a supplementary analysis. If the investigator can show that the history threat is implausible, then a stronger argument can be made for the internal validity of the quasi-experiment. Researchers must recognize the specific shortcomings of quasi-experimental procedures and they must work like detectives to provide whatever evidence they can to overcome these shortcomings. As we begin to consider the appropriate uses of quasi-experiments, we need to acknowledge that there is a great difference between the power of the true experiment and that of the quasi-experiment. *Before facing the problems of interpretation that result from quasi-experimental procedures, the researcher should make every effort possible to approximate the conditions of a true experiment.*

Perhaps the most serious limitation researchers face in doing experiments in natural settings is that they are frequently unable to assign participants randomly to conditions. This occurs, for instance, when an intact group is singled out for treatment and when administrative decisions or practical considerations prevent randomly assigning participants. For example, children in one classroom or school and workers at a particular plant represent intact groups that might receive a treatment or intervention without the possibility of randomly assigning individuals to conditions. If we assume that behavior of a group is measured both before and after treatment, such an "experiment" can be described as follows:

$$O_1 \; X \; O_2$$

where O_1 refers to the first observation of a group, or pretest, X indicates a treatment, and O_2 refers to the second observation, or posttest.

STRETCHING EXERCISE

In this exercise we ask you to consider possible threats to internal validity in this brief description of a one-group pretest-posttest design.

A psychologist interested in the effect of a new therapy for depression recruited a sample of 20 individuals who sought relief from their depression. At the beginning of the study he asked all participants to complete a questionnaire about their symptoms of depression. The mean depression score for the sample was 42.0 (the highest possible score is 63.0), indicating severe depressive symptoms. [Individuals who are not depressed typically score in the 0 to 10 range on this measure.] During the next 16 weeks the psychologist treated participants in the study with the new treatment. At the end of the treatment the participants completed the depression questionnaire again. The mean score for the posttest was 12.0, indicating that, on average, participants'

depression symptoms were dramatically reduced and indicated only mild depression. The psychologist concluded that the treatment was effective; that is, the treatment caused their depressive symptoms to improve.

Cause-and-effect statements, such as the one made by this psychologist, are essentially impossible to make when the one-group pretest-posttest design is used. To understand why this is true, we ask you to think of potential threats to internal validity in this study.

1 How might a *history* effect threaten the internal validity of this study?
2 Explain how *maturation* likely plays a role in this study.
3 Are *testing* and *instrumentation* threats likely in this study?
4 Explain how *statistical regression* might influence the interpretation of these findings.

As we described in Chapter 7, this *one-group pretest-posttest* design represents a pre-experimental design or more simply may be called a bad experiment. Any obtained difference between the pretest and posttest scores could be due to the treatment *or* to any of several threats to internal validity, including history, maturation, testing, and instrumentation threats (as well as experimenter expectancy effects and novelty effects). The results of a bad experiment are inconclusive with respect to the effectiveness of a treatment. Fortunately, there are quasi-experiments that improve upon this pre-experimental design.

The Nonequivalent Control Group Design

- In the nonequivalent control group design, a treatment group and a comparison group are compared using pretest and posttest measures.
- If the two groups are similar in their pretest scores prior to treatment but differ in their posttest scores following treatment, researchers can more confidently make a claim about the effect of treatment.
- Threats to internal validity due to history, maturation, testing, instrumentation, and regression can be controlled in a nonequivalent control group design.

Key Concept

The one-group pretest-posttest design can be modified to create a quasi-experimental design with greatly superior internal validity if two conditions are met: (1) there exists a group "like" the treatment group that can serve as a comparison group, and (2) there is an opportunity to obtain pretest and posttest measures from individuals in both the treatment and the comparison groups. Campbell and Stanley (1966) call a quasi-experimental procedure that meets these two conditions a **nonequivalent control group design.** Because a comparison group is selected on bases other than random assignment, we cannot assume that individuals in the treatment and control groups are equivalent on all important characteristics (a selection threat arises). Therefore it is essential that a pretest be given to both groups to assess their similarity on the dependent measure. A nonequivalent control group design can be outlined as follows:

$$O_1 \; X \; O_2$$

- - - - - -

$$O_1 \quad O_2$$

The dashed line indicates that the treatment and comparison groups were not formed by assigning participants randomly to conditions.

By adding a comparison group, threats to internal validity due to history, maturation, testing, instrumentation, and regression can be controlled. A brief review of the logic of experimental design will help show why this occurs. We wish to begin an experiment with two similar groups; then one group receives the treatment and the other does not. If the two groups' posttest scores differ following treatment, we first must rule out alternative explanations before we can claim that treatment caused the difference. If the groups are truly compara-ble, and both groups have similar experiences, then we can assume that history, maturation, testing, instrumentation, and regression effects occur to both groups equally. Thus, we may assume that both groups change naturally at the same rate (maturation), experience the same effect of multiple testing, or are exposed to the same external events (history). If these effects are experienced in the *same* way by both groups, they cannot possibly be used to account for group *differences* on posttest measures. Therefore, they no longer are threats to internal validity. Thus, researchers can gain a tremendous advantage in their ability to make causal claims simply by adding a comparison group. These causal claims, however, depend critically on forming comparable groups at the start of the study, and assuring that the groups then have comparable experiences, except for the treatment. Because this is difficult to realize in practice, as we'll see, threats to internal validity due to additive effects with selection typically are not eliminated in this design.

As you approach the end of a course on research methods in psychology, you might appreciate learning about the results of a nonequivalent control group design that examined the effect of taking a research methods course on reason-ing about real-life events (VanderStoep & Shaughnessy, 1997). Students enrolled in two sections of a research methods course (and who happened to be using an edition of this textbook!) were compared with students in two sections of a developmental psychology course on their performance on a test emphasizing methodological reasoning about everyday events. Students in both kinds of classes were administered tests at the beginning and at the end of the semester. Results revealed that research methods students showed greater improvement than did students in the control group. Taking a research methods course im-proved students' ability to think critically about real-life events.

With that bit of encouraging news in mind, let us now examine in detail another study using a nonequivalent control group design. This will give us the opportunity to review both the specific strengths and limitations of this quasi-experimental procedure.

Quasi-experiments often assess the overall effectiveness of a treatment that has many components; follow-up research may then determine which components are critical for achieving the treatment effect.

Langer and Rodin (1976) hypothesized that environmental changes associ-ated with old age contribute, in part, to feelings of loss, inadequacy, and low self-esteem among the elderly. Of particular importance is the change that oc-curs when elderly persons move into a nursing home. Although they usually care for the elderly quite adequately in physical terms, nursing homes often provide what Langer and Rodin call a "virtually decision-free" environment. The elderly are no longer called on to make even the simplest decisions, such as what time to get up, whom to visit, what movie to watch, and the like. In a nursing home, many or most of these everyday decisions are made for the elderly, leaving them with little personal responsibility and choice.

To test the hypothesis that the lack of opportunity to make personal decisions contributes to the psychological and even the physical debilitation sometimes seen in the elderly, Langer and Rodin carried out a quasi-experiment in a Connecticut nursing home. The independent variable was the type of communication given to two groups of nursing home residents. One group was given a communication stressing the many decisions that the patients needed to make regarding how their rooms were arranged, visiting, care of plants, movie selection, and so forth. These residents were also given a small plant as a gift (if they decided to accept it) and told to take care of it as they wished. This was the responsibility-induced condition. The second group of residents, the comparison group, was also called together for a meeting, but the communication given to this group stressed the staff's responsibility for them. These residents also received a plant as a gift (whether they chose to have one or not) and were told that the nurses would water and care for the plants for them.

Residents of the nursing home had been assigned to a particular floor and room on the basis of availability, and some residents had been there for a long time. As a consequence, randomly assigning residents to the two communication groups was impractical—and probably undesirable from the administration's point of view. Therefore the two communications were given to residents on two different floors of the nursing home. These floors were chosen, in the words of the authors, "because of similarity in the residents' physical and psychological health and prior socioeconomic status, as determined from evaluations made by the home's director, head nurses, and social worker" (Langer & Rodin, p. 193). The floors were randomly assigned to one of the two treatments. In addition, questionnaires were given to residents 1 week before and 3 weeks after the communications. The questionnaires contained items that related to "how much control they felt over general events in their lives and how happy and active they felt" (p. 194). Furthermore, staff members on each floor were asked to rate the residents, before and after the experimental communications, on such traits as alertness, sociability, and activity. The investigators also included a clever posttest measure of social interest by holding a competition that asked participants to guess the number of jelly beans in a large jar. Residents entered the contest if they wished by simply filling out a piece of paper giving their estimate and name. Thus, there were a number of dependent variables to assess the residents' perceptions of control, happiness, activity, interest level, and so forth.

The Langer and Rodin study nicely illustrates the procedures of a nonequivalent control group design. Moreover, differences between pretest and posttest measures showed that the residents in the responsibility-induced group were generally happier, more active, and more alert following the treatment than were residents in the comparison group. Behavioral measures such as frequency of movie attendance also favored the responsibility-induced group, and, although 10 residents from this group entered the jelly bean contest, only 1 resident from the comparison group participated! The investigators point to possible practical implications of these findings. Specifically, they suggest that some of the negative consequences of aging can be reduced or reversed by giving the aged the opportunity to make personal decisions and to feel competent.

Before turning to the specific limitations associated with this design, let us call your attention to another feature of the Langer and Rodin study, one that characterizes many experiments in natural settings. The treatment in the Langer and Rodin study actually had several components. For example, residents were encouraged by the staff to make decisions about a number of different things (e.g., movies, rooms, etc.) and they were offered a plant to take care of. The experiment evaluated, however, the treatment "package." That is, the effectiveness of the overall treatment was assessed and not individual components of the treatment. We only know (or at least we assume based on the evidence) that the treatment with all its components worked; we don't necessarily know whether the treatment would work with fewer components or whether one component is more critical than others.

Research in natural settings is often characterized by treatments with many components. Moreover, the initial goal of such research is often to assess the overall effect of the treatment "package." Finding evidence for an overall treatment effect, therefore, may be only the first stage in a research program if we want to identify the critical elements of a treatment. There may be practical as well as theoretical benefits to such identification. On practical grounds, should research reveal that only some of the treatment's features are critical to the effect, then perhaps the less critical features could be dropped. This may make the treatment more cost effective and more likely to be adopted and carried out. From a theoretical standpoint, it is important to determine whether components of the treatment specified by the theory as being critical are, indeed, the critical components. When you hear about research showing an overall treatment effect you might think about how additional research could reveal what specific components are critical to the treatment's effect.

To interpret the findings in quasi-experimental designs, researchers examine the study to determine if any threats to internal validity are present. The threats to internal validity that must be considered when using the non-equivalent control group design include additive effects with selection, differential regression, observer bias, contamination, and novelty effects. Although groups may be comparable on a pretest measure, this does not ensure that the groups are comparable in all possible ways that are relevant to the outcome of the study.

According to Cook and Campbell (1979), the nonequivalent control group design generally controls for all major classes of potential threats to internal validity except those due to additive effects of (1) selection and maturation, (2) selection and history, (3) selection and instrumentation, and (4) those due to differential statistical regression. We will explore how each of these potential sources of invalidity might pose problems for Langer and Rodin's interpretation of their findings. We will then explain how Langer and Rodin offered both logical argument and empirical evidence to refute the possible threats to the internal validity of their study. We will also examine how experimenter bias and problems of contamination were controlled. Finally, we will comment briefly on challenges of establishing external validity that are inherent in the nonequivalent control group design.

An important initial finding in Langer and Rodin's study was that the residents in the two experimental groups did not differ significantly on the pretest measures. It would not have been surprising to find a difference between the two groups before the treatment was introduced because the residents were not randomly assigned to conditions. Even when pretest scores show no difference between groups, however, we cannot assume that the groups are "equivalent" (Campbell & Stanley, 1966). We will explain why we cannot conclude that the groups are equivalent in the discussion that follows.

Selection-Maturation Effect   An additive effect of selection and maturation occurs when individuals in one group grow more experienced, more tired, or more bored at a faster rate than individuals in another group (Shadish et al., 2002). A selection-maturation effect is more likely to be a threat to internal validity when the treatment group is self-selected (the members deliberately sought out exposure to the treatment) and when the comparison group is from a different population from the treatment group (Campbell & Stanley, 1966). Langer and Rodin selected their groups (but not individuals) randomly from the same population of individuals. Consequently, their design more closely approaches a true experiment than it would if individuals in the two groups came from different populations (Campbell & Stanley, 1966). A selection-maturation effect would have been more likely, for example, if residents in a nursing home were compared with those attending a sheltered workshop program for the elderly, or if residents on different floors of a nursing facility require different levels of care.

The possibility of a selection-maturation effect is one reason why we cannot conclude the groups are equivalent (comparable) even when pretest scores are the same on average for the treatment and control groups. The natural growth rate of two groups from different populations might be different, but the pretest may have been taken at a time when both groups happened to be about the same. This problem is illustrated in Figure 11.3. The normal rate of change is greater in Group A than in Group B, but the pretest is likely to show that the groups do not differ. Because of the differential growth rate, however, the groups would probably show a difference at the posttest that could be

FIGURE 11.3   Possible differential growth rates for two groups (A and B) in the absence of treatment.

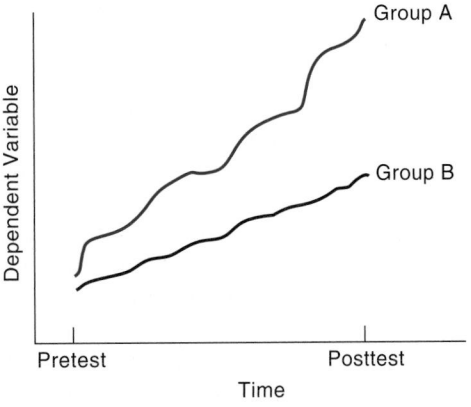

mistaken for a treatment effect. There is a second, and more general, reason why we cannot conclude that groups are comparable based only on the absence of a difference between the groups on the pretest. The pretest is likely to measure respondents on only one measure, or at best on a few measures. The mere fact that individuals do not differ on one measure does not mean they don't differ on other measures that are relevant to their behavior in this situation.

Is there any reason to suspect a selection-maturation effect in the Langer and Rodin study? That is, would it be reasonable to expect that residents on the treatment floor would change naturally at a faster rate than would patients on the no-treatment floor? Several kinds of evidence suggest that this would not be the case. First, the procedure the nursing home used to assign residents to the two floors was basically random, and the floors were assigned randomly to the treatment and no-treatment conditions. Langer and Rodin also reported that the residents of the two floors were, on the average, equivalent on measures such as socioeconomic status and length of time at the nursing home. Finally, although it is not sufficient evidence in itself, residents on the two floors did not differ on the pretest measures. Thus, the evidence strongly indicates that there was not a threat to the internal validity of the Langer and Rodin study due to the additive effects of selection and maturation.

Selection-History Effect   Another threat to internal validity that is not controlled in the nonequivalent control group design is the additive effect of selection and history. Cook and Campbell (1979) refer to this problem as *local history effects*. This problem arises when an event other than the treatment affects one group and not the other. Local history, for example, could be a problem in the Langer and Rodin study if an event affecting the residents' happiness and alertness occurred on one floor of the nursing home but not on the other. You can probably imagine a number of possibilities. A change in nursing staff on one floor, for instance, might bring about either an increase or a decrease in residents' morale, depending on the nature of the change and the relationship between the behavior of a new nurse and that of the previous one. Problems of local history become more problematic the more the settings of the individuals in the treatment and comparison groups differ. Langer and Rodin do not specifically address the problem of local history effects.

Selection-Instrumentation Effect   A threat due to the combination of selection and instrumentation occurs when changes in a measuring instrument are more likely to be detected in one group than they are in another. Floor or ceiling effects, for instance, could make it difficult to detect changes in behavior from pretest to posttest. If this is more of a problem in one group than in another, a selection-instrumentation effect is present. Shadish et al. (2002) point out that this threat to internal validity is more likely to be a problem the greater the nonequivalence of the groups and the closer the group scores are to the end of the scale. Because Langer and Rodin's groups did not differ on the pretest, and because performance of the groups did not suggest floor or ceiling effects on the measurement scales that were used, this threat to internal validity seems implausible in their study.

Differential Statistical Regression   The final threat to internal validity that is not controlled in the nonequivalent control group design is differential statistical regression (Shadish et al., 2002). As we described earlier, regression toward the mean is to be expected when individuals are selected on the basis of extreme scores (the poorest readers, the workers with the lowest productivity, the patients with the most severe problems). *Differential regression* can occur when regression is more likely in one group than in another. For example, consider a nonequivalent control group design in which the participants with the most serious problems comprise the treatment group. It is possible, even likely, that regression would occur for this group. The changes from pretest to posttest may be mistakenly interpreted as a treatment effect if regression is more likely in the treatment group than in the control group. Because the groups in the Langer and Rodin study came from the same population and there is no evidence that one group's pretest scores were more extreme than another's, a threat to internal validity due to differential statistical regression is not plausible in their study.

Expectancy Effects, Contamination, and Novelty Effects   Langer and Rodin's study could also have been influenced by three additional threats to internal validity that can even affect true experiments—expectancy effects, contamination, and novelty effects. If observers in their study had been aware of the research hypothesis, it is possible that they inadvertently might have rated residents as being better after the experimental communication than before. This observer bias, or expectancy effect, appears to have been controlled, however, because all the observers were kept unaware of the research hypothesis. Langer and Rodin were also aware of possible contamination effects. Residents in the control group might have become demoralized if they learned that residents on another floor were given more opportunity to make decisions. In this case, the use of different floors of the nursing home was advantageous; Langer and Rodin indicate that "there was not a great deal of communication between floors" (1976, p. 193). Thus, contamination effects do not seem to be present, at least on a scale that would destroy the internal validity of the study.

Novelty effects would be present in the Langer and Rodin study if residents on the treatment floor gained enthusiasm and energy as a result of the innovative responsibility-inducing communication. Thus, this new enthusiasm may explain any treatment effects, rather that treatment residents' increased responsibility. In addition, the special attention given the treatment group may have produced a Hawthorne effect in which residents on the treated floor felt better about themselves. It is difficult to rule out completely novelty effects or a Hawthorne effect in this study. According to the authors, however, "there was no difference in the amount of attention paid to the two groups" (p. 194). In fact, communications to both groups stressed that the staff cared for them and wanted them "to be happy." Thus, without additional evidence to the contrary, we can conclude that the changes in behavior Langer and Rodin observed were due to the effect of the independent variable and not to the effect of an extraneous variable that the investigators failed to control.

What should be apparent at this point is that for an investigator to decide whether an independent variable "worked" in the context of a particular experiment, he or she must be something of a detective. Evidence for and against the interpretation that the treatment actually caused behavior to change must be systematically collected and carefully weighed. For example, as we have seen in our analysis of the Langer and Rodin study, the various threats to the internal validity of the nonequivalent control group design must be examined in light of the actual outcomes of the pretest and posttest scores. The plausibility of a particular threat may be assessed to a large degree by examining the observed pattern of outcomes (see Shadish et al., 2002).

As Cook and Campbell (1979, pp. 55–56) explain:

> Estimating the internal validity of a relationship is a deductive process in which the investigator has to systematically think through how each of the internal validity threats may have influenced the data. Then, the investigator has to examine the data to test which relevant threats can be ruled out. In all of this process, the researcher has to be his or her own best critic, trenchantly examining all of the threats he or she can imagine. When all of the threats can plausibly be eliminated, it is possible to make confident conclusions about whether a relationship is probably causal. When all of them cannot, perhaps because the appropriate data are not available or because the data indicate that a particular threat may indeed have operated, then the investigator has to conclude that a demonstrated relationship between two variables may or may not be causal.

The Issue of External Validity

- Similar to internal validity, the external validity of research findings must be critically examined.
- The best evidence for the external validity of research findings is replication with different populations, settings, and times.

We must make the same systematic inquiry into the external validity of a quasi-experiment that we did into its internal validity. What evidence is there that the particular pattern of results is restricted to a particular group of participants, setting, or time? For example, although Langer and Rodin suggest that certain changes be made in the way the elderly are cared for, we might question whether the effectiveness of the responsibility-inducing communication would hold for all elderly residents, for all types of nursing facilities, and at different times. That the particular nursing home selected by Langer and Rodin was described as "rated by the state of Connecticut as being among the finest care units" (1976, p. 193) suggests that the residents, facilities, and staff might be different from those found in other facilities. For instance, if residents at this particular nursing home were relatively more independent before coming to the home than residents at other homes (perhaps because of differences in socioeconomic status), then the changes experienced upon moving into a home might have had greater impact on them. Consequently, the opportunity to be more independent of staff might be more important to these residents relative to residents in other homes. Similarly, if staff members at this home were more competent than those at other homes, they might be more effective in communicating with the residents than would the staff members at other homes.

In the last analysis, the investigator must be ready to *replicate* an experimental finding with different populations, settings, and times in order to establish external validity. The deductive process applied to questions of internal validity must also be used to examine a study's external validity. Moreover, *we must be ready to live with the fact that one study is not likely to answer all questions about a research hypothesis.*

A second quasi-experiment, a **simple interrupted time-series design,** is possible when researchers can observe changes in a dependent variable for some time before and after a treatment is introduced (Shadish et al., 2002). The essence of this design is the availability of periodic measures before and after a treatment has been introduced. The simple interrupted time-series design can be outlined in the following way:

$$O_1 O_2 O_3 O_4 O_5 \ X \ O_6 O_7 O_8 O_9 O_{10}$$

The simple interrupted time-series design can be used to assess the effect of a treatment in situations such as when a new product has been introduced, a new social reform instituted, or a special advertising campaign begun. Campbell (1969) investigated the effect of a social policy change in Connecticut in the mid-1950s. The governor had ordered a crackdown on speeding, and Campbell made use of an interrupted time-series design to determine the effect of this order on traffic fatalities. Campbell was able to obtain a wealth of archival data to use as pretreatment and posttreatment measures because statistics related to traffic accidents are regularly kept by state agencies. Besides number of fatalities, Campbell looked at number of speeding violations, number of

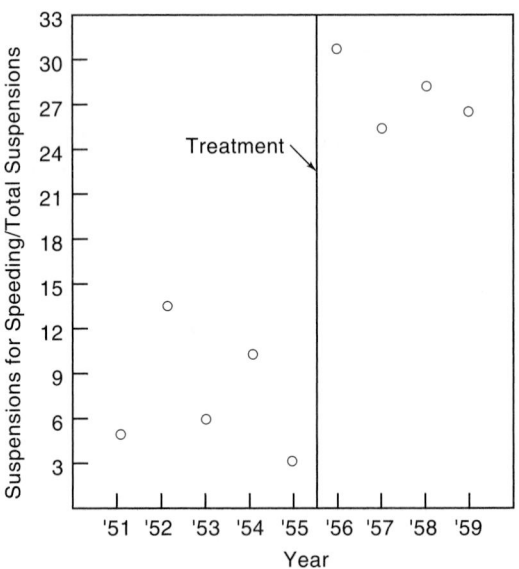

drivers having their licenses suspended, and other measures related to driving behavior. Figure 11.4 shows the percentage of suspensions of licenses for speeding (as a percentage of all license suspensions) before and after the crackdown. There is a clear discontinuity in the graph that coincides with the onset of the treatment. This discontinuity provides evidence for an effect of the treatment. Indeed, *a discontinuity in the time series is the major evidence of an effect of treatment.*

As Campbell points out, only abrupt changes in the time graph can be interpreted because gradual changes are indistinguishable from normal fluctuations over time. Unfortunately, changes often are not nearly so dramatic as those seen in Figure 11.4. In fact, Campbell's analysis of traffic fatalities over the same time period did reveal evidence for an effect of the crackdown, but the change in traffic fatalities was not as abrupt as that associated with suspension of drivers' licenses (see Campbell, 1969, Figure 2).

A variation of the interrupted time-series design was used to assess the effect of avoiding the "dread risk of flying" following the terrorist attack on the United States on September 11, 2001 (Gigerenzer, 2004). The rationale for this study was as follows. People tend to fear "dread risks," which are defined as "low-probability, high-consequence events, such as the terrorist attack on September 11, 2001" (Gigerenzer, 2004, p. 286). If Americans, in order to avoid the dread risk of flying, instead drove to their destinations, then an increase in traffic fatalities would be expected. To test this hypothesis, Gigerenzer (2004) examined data from the U.S. Department of Transportation for the three

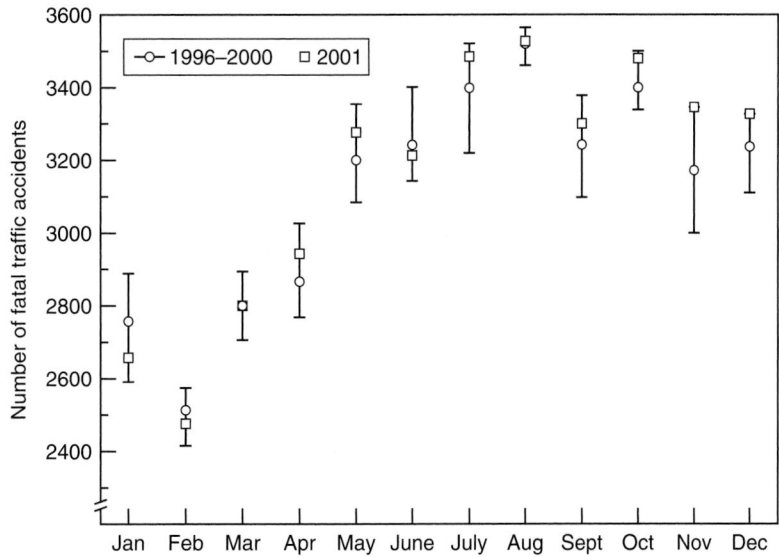

months following September 11, 2001. Data also were analyzed for the five years prior to that date. The mean number of fatalities in these preceding years was compared with the numbers after September 11, 2001. The results of this analysis are seen in Figure 11.5.

The graph shows fatal traffic accidents for all 12 months of the year for both the preceding five years (circles depict the means in the graphed line) and for the year 2001 (depicted by squares). In addition, the highest and lowest values for each month in the preceding five years are shown (the bars around each mean). The data for fatalities during October, November, and December reveal that in the year 2001, the number of fatal traffic accidents was as high or higher than the highest value for the preceding five years. On the basis of these data (and statistical analyses) Gigerenzer (2004) was able to conclude that traffic fatalities increased by 353 people in October, November, and December 2001. He attributed this increase to Americans' dread fear of flying following the events of 9/11. Gigerenzer compared this increase of 353 deaths to the 266 passengers and crew who were killed in the four plane crashes (and of course many more on the ground). The researcher suggested that "if the public were better informed about psychological reactions to catastrophic events, and the potential risk of avoiding risk," perhaps this "psychologically motivated toll" could be prevented (p. 287).

Although results of the interrupted time-series design and other quasi-experimental designs are sometimes able to be interpreted on the basis of visual inspection (see, for example, Figure 11.4), statistical analyses are often needed. Gigerenzer (2004), for example, used a chi-square test of statistical significance to demonstrate that there was a statistically significant increase in the frequency of fatalities following September 11, 2001, compared to the previous years. We previously mentioned the chi-square test in Chapters 5 and 9. In other situations more sophisticated analyses may need to be conducted. For more information readers are referred to Shadish et al.'s (2002) text, *Experimental and Quasi-Experimental Designs for Generalized Causal Inference.*

Campbell and Stanley (1966) summarize the problem facing researchers using the simple interrupted time-series design: "The problem of internal validity boils down to the question of plausible competing hypotheses that offer likely alternate explanations of the shift in the time series other than the effect of X" (p. 39). An effect of history is the main threat to internal validity in this type of design (Shadish et al., 2002). For instance, is it possible that some factor other than avoiding "dread risk" was responsible for the increase in fatal traffic accidents depicted in Figure 11.5?

Particularly threatening to the internal validity of the time-series design are influences of a cyclical nature, including seasonal variation (Cook & Campbell, 1979). For instance, when analyzing the effect of the Connecticut governor's crackdown on speeding, Campbell (1969) gathered data from neighboring states in order to rule out possible regional trends due to weather in order to strengthen his case for the effect of this particular social policy change.

Instrumentation must also be considered a threat to internal validity in the simple interrupted time-series design (Shadish et al., 2002). When new programs or new social policies are instituted, for example, there are often accompanying changes in the way records are kept or in the procedures used to collect information. A program intended to reduce crime may lead authorities to modify their definitions of particular crimes or to become more careful when observing and reporting criminal activities. Nevertheless, for an instrumentation threat to be plausible, the changes in instrumentation must be shown to have occurred at *exactly* the time as the intervention (Campbell & Stanley, 1966).

Threats to internal validity due to maturation, testing, and regression are controlled in the simple interrupted time-series design. None of these threats can be ruled out when only a single pretest and posttest measure is available. These threats are nearly eliminated, however, by the presence of multiple observations both before and after treatment. For example, an effect of maturation would not normally be expected to show a sharp discontinuity in the time series, although this might be possible in some situations (Campbell & Stanley, 1966).

Threats to external validity in the simple interrupted time-series design must be examined carefully. When pretreatment observations of behavior are based on multiple tests, then it is very likely that an effect of the treatment may be restricted to those individuals who have had these multiple test experiences.

Moreover, the interrupted time-series design generally involves testing only a single group that has not been randomly selected. This characteristic leaves open the possibility that the results are limited to people with characteristics similar to those who took part in the study.

Time Series with Nonequivalent Control Group

Key Concept

- In a time series with nonequivalent control group design, researchers make a series of observations before and after treatment for both a treatment group and a comparable comparison group.

The internal validity of the interrupted time-series design can be enhanced greatly by including a control group following the procedures we described earlier for the nonequivalent control group design. For the **time series with nonequivalent control group design** the researcher must find a group that is comparable to the treatment group and that allows a similar opportunity for multiple observations before and after the time that the treatment is adminis- tered to the experimental group. This design is outlined as follows:

$$O_1 O_2 O_3 O_4 O_5 \; X \; O_6 O_7 O_8 O_9 O_{10}$$

$$O_1 O_2 O_3 O_4 O_5 \quad O_6 O_7 O_8 O_9 O_{10}$$

As before, a dashed line is used to indicate that the control group and the ex- perimental group were not randomly assigned. The interrupted time series with nonequivalent control group design permits researchers to rule out many threats due to history. As was mentioned earlier, Campbell (1969) used traffic fatality data obtained from neighboring states to provide a comparison with traffic fatality data following the crackdown on speeding in Connecticut. Although traffic fatalities in Connecticut showed a decline immediately follow- ing the crackdown, data from comparable states did not exhibit any such decline. This finding tends to rule out claims that the decrease in traffic fatalities in Connecticut were due to factors such as favorable weather conditions, improved automobile design, or any other factors that were likely shared by Connecticut and the neighboring states.

As we have seen previously, archival data, rather than direct observation, frequently provide the basis for time-series designs. McSweeney's (1978) study of the effect of charging for directory assistance calls provides a partic- ularly good illustration of the use of archival data in a time-series design with nonequivalent control group. Directory assistance calls cost the tele- phone company money, and they pay these expenses by charging more for other services. McSweeney (1978) noted that an intervention that would effectively reduce the frequency of these unnecessary calls would benefit both the telephone company and the consumer.

In 1974, officials at Cincinnati Bell Telephone Company initiated charges for local directory assistance calls in excess of three per month. Subscribers were charged 20 cents for each additional call. The exact number of customers affected by the service charge for local directory assistance could not be known, but it was estimated that it affected more than a million users. The effect of this intervention could be assessed using a time-series analysis because the telephone company keeps extensive archival records. Furthermore, a simple time series could be expanded by using a nonequivalent control group. McSweeney chose to use the long-distance directory assistance calls that were made from outside the Cincinnati area as the comparison group (no charge was made for these calls). From data provided by Cincinnati Bell administrative records, McSweeney created the time-series graph shown in Figure 11.6. The frequency of local calls decreased dramatically after the charge was initiated; directory assistance calls from outside the area continued to increase gradually. The clear discontinuity in the time series associated with the treatment group, in conjunction with the absence of any decrease in calls by the comparison group, provides nearly incontrovertible evidence that the effect was due to the

FIGURE 11.6   Number of local and long-distance directory assistance calls placed per average business day before and after charges were introduced. (From McSweeney, 1978.)

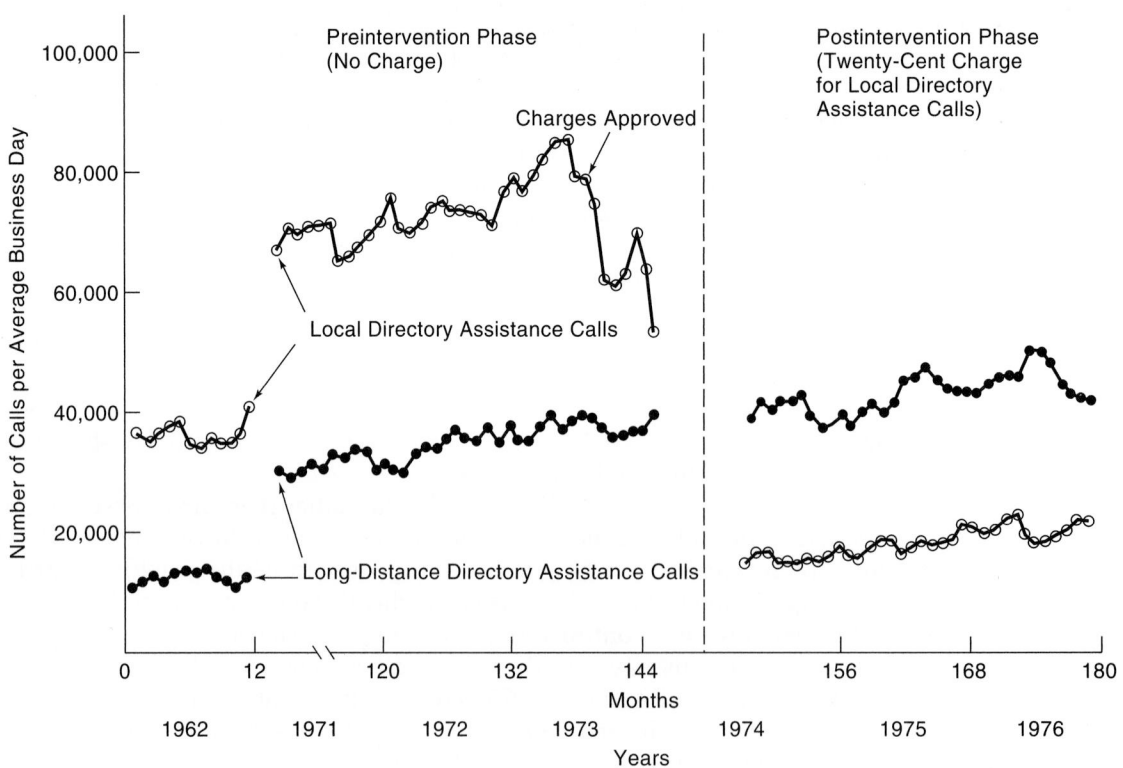

intervention made by the telephone company. A subsequent analysis showed that the decrease in local directory assistance calls resulted in an average savings of 65 cents on the telephone bill of each individual residential consumer.

PROGRAM EVALUATION

- Program evaluation is used to assess the effectiveness of human service organizations and provide feedback to administrators about their services.
- Program evaluators assess needs, process, outcome, and efficiency of social services.
- The relationship between basic research and applied research is reciprocal.
- Despite society's reluctance to use experiments, true experiments and quasi-experiments can provide excellent approaches for evaluating social reforms.

Organizations that produce goods have a ready-made index of success. If a company is set up to make microprocessors, its success is ultimately determined by its profits from the sale of microprocessors. At least theoretically, the efficiency and effectiveness of the organization can be easily assessed by examining the company's financial ledgers. Increasingly, however, organizations of a different sort play a critical role in our society. Because these organizations typically provide services rather than goods, Posavac and Carey (2003) refer to them as human service organizations. For example, hospitals, schools, police departments, and government agencies provide a variety of services ranging from emergency room care to fire prevention inspections. Because profit making is not their goal, some other method must be found to distinguish between effective and ineffective agencies. One useful approach to assessing the effectiveness of human service organizations is program evaluation.

Key Concept

Posavac and Carey (2003, p. 1) define **program evaluation** as a

> . . . collection of methods, skills, and sensitivities necessary to determine whether a human service is needed and likely to be used, whether the service is sufficiently intense to meet the unmet needs identified, whether the service is offered as planned, and whether the service actually does help people in need at a reasonable cost without unacceptable side effects.

The definition of program evaluation includes several components; we will take up each of these components in turn. Posavac and Carey emphasize, however, that the overarching goal of program evaluation is *providing feedback regarding human service activities*. Program evaluations are designed to provide feedback to the administrators of human service organizations to help them decide what services to provide to whom, and how to provide them most effectively and efficiently. Program evaluation represents an integrative discipline that draws on political science, sociology, economics, education, and psychology. We are discussing program evaluation at the end of this chapter on research in natural settings because it represents perhaps the most large-scale application of the principles and methods we have been describing throughout this book.

Posavac and Carey (2003) identify four questions that are asked by program evaluators. These questions are about needs, process, outcome, and efficiency. An assessment of *needs* seeks to determine the unmet needs of the people for whom an agency might provide a service. Consider, for example, a city government that has received a proposal to institute a program of recreational activities for senior citizens in the community. The city would first want to determine whether senior citizens actually need or want such a program. If the senior citizens do want such a program, the city would further want to know what kind of program would be most attractive to them. The methods of survey research are used extensively in studies designed to assess needs. Administrators can use the information obtained from an assessment of needs to help them plan what programs to offer.

Once a program has been set up, program evaluators may ask questions about the *process* that has been established. Observational methods are often useful in assessing the processes of a program. Programs are not always implemented the way they were planned, and it is essential to know what actually is being done when a program is implemented. If the planned activities were not being used by the senior citizens in a recreational program designed specifically for them, it might suggest that the program was inadequately implemented. An evaluation that provides answers to questions about process, that is, about how a program is actually being carried out, permits administrators to make adjustments in the delivery of services in order to strengthen the existing program (Posavac & Carey, 2003).

The next set of questions a program evaluator is likely to ask involves the *outcome*. Has the program been effective in meeting its stated goals? For example, do senior citizens now have access to more recreational activities, and are they pleased with these activities? Are these particular activities preferred over other activities? The outcome of a community-watch program designed to curb neighborhood crime might be evaluated by assessing whether there were actual decreases in burglaries and assaults following the implementation of the program. It is possible to use archival data like those described in Chapter 6 to carry out evaluations of outcome. For example, examining police records in order to document the frequency of various crimes is one way to assess the effectiveness of a community-watch program. Evaluations of outcome may also involve both experimental and quasi-experimental methods for research in natural settings. An evaluator may, for example, use a nonequivalent control group design to assess the effectiveness of a school reform program by comparing students' performance in two different school districts, one with the reform program and one without.

The final questions evaluators might ask is about the *efficiency* of the program. Most often, questions about efficiency relate to the cost of the program. Choices often have to be made among possible services that a government or other institution is capable of delivering. Information about how successful a program is (outcome evaluation) and information about the program's cost (efficiency evaluation) are necessary if we want to make informed decisions about continuing the program, how to improve it, whether to try an alternative program, or to cut back on the program's services.

Earlier in this chapter and in Chapter 2 we described differences between *basic and applied research*. Program evaluation is perhaps the extreme case of applied research. The purpose of program evaluation is practical, not theoretical. Nevertheless, even in the context of blatantly practical goals, a case can be made for a reciprocal relationship between basic and applied research (see Box 11.1). Writing in the *International Journal of Psychology*, Salomon (1987) argues that each domain of research serves the other in an ongoing circular way. Salomon's model is illustrated in Figure 11.7. Specifically, Salomon argues that basic research provides us with certain abstractions (e.g., scientifically based principles) that express certain regularities in nature. When these principles are examined in the complex and "dirty" world where they supposedly apply, new complexities are recognized and new hypotheses are called for. These new complexities are then tested and evaluated in the lab before being tried out again in the real world.

Salomon points to the work of Ellen Langer as a concrete example of this circular relationship. She identified a decline in elderly people's health once they entered nursing homes (see Langer, 1989; Langer & Rodin, 1976, described in this chapter). These naturalistic observations led her to develop a theory of mindfulness, which she has tested under controlled experimental conditions and which has implications for more general theories of cognitive development

Applied
Research

Affects and
modifies

Leads to

Deductive
Theory

Human and Social
World

Guides

Interprets and
explains

Basic
Research

and of education (see, for example, Langer, 1989, 1997; Langer & Piper, 1987). The theory provides a guide for her applied work—designing new models of nursing homes. Tests of the practical effects of changes in the care given by nursing homes on the residents' health and well-being will undoubtedly lead to modifications of her theory of mindfulness.

According to Campbell (1969), it is important for public officials involved with social experiments to emphasize the importance of the problem rather than the importance of the solution. Instead of pushing for one certain cure-all (which, in most cases, has little opportunity for success), officials must be ready to execute reform in a manner that permits the clearest evaluation and must be prepared to try different solutions if the first one fails. Public officials must, in other words, be ready to use the experimental method to identify society's problems and to determine effective solutions.

Campbell's (1969) idea that social reforms and experimental methods be routinely brought together has had some impact on social policymakers, but it is still underutilized (see Berk et al., 1987 and Box 11.3). The reasons are some of the same ones initially identified by Campbell. Nevertheless, without social experimentation, especially that which makes use whenever possible of randomized field experiments, policymakers and the community at large may believe a treatment works when it doesn't or vice versa. Such incorrect decisions lead us to allocate money and resources to ineffective programs.

Not too many years ago, a show called "Scared Straight" was aired on national television. It described a juvenile education program implemented at Rahway State Prison in New Jersey. The program involved taking youthful offenders into a prison to meet with selected convicts from the inmate population. The goal was to inform juveniles about the reality of prison life and, thereby, the program leaders hoped, dissuade them from further illegal activity. Unsubstantiated claims were made for the effectiveness of the program, including some suggesting a success rate as high as 80% to 90% (see Locke, Johnson, Kirigin-Ramp, Atwater, & Gerrard, 1986). The Rahway program is just one of several similar programs around the country. But do these programs really work?

Several evaluation studies of the exposure-to-prison programs produced mixed results, including positive findings, findings of no difference between control and experimental participants, as well as results suggesting that the program may actually increase juvenile crime among some types of delinquents. There is a possibility that less hardened juvenile offenders may increase their criminal activity after meeting the prisoners. It has been suggested that because these less hardened offenders have recently begun a lifestyle wherein they are being recognized and reinforced by their peers for their toughness, this image is also reinforced by the tough image often projected by the prisoners. On the other hand, more frequent juvenile offenders, who have achieved a level of status among their peers for some period of time, may be more threatened by the prospects of prison life because it would mean loss of that status (see Locke et al., 1986).

Perhaps the greatest difference between basic research and program evaluation lies in the political and social realities surrounding program evaluation. Governments at both local and national levels regularly propose, plan, and execute various types of social reforms. Tax relief programs, work incentive programs, educational reforms, police reforms, and medical care for senior citizens are just a few of the types of social reform programs that a government might initiate. Unfortunately, as the late Donald Campbell (1969), a past president of the American Psychological Association, pointed out, the outcome of these social reforms often cannot be meaningfully evaluated. Did a change in police techniques lead to less crime? Are more elderly people gaining access to public transportation after a reduction in fares? Does a work incentive program take more people off the unemployment rolls? The answers to such questions often cannot be found, said Campbell, because most social reforms are instituted in a political climate that is not ready for hardheaded evaluation. What public official, for instance, wants to be associated with a program that failed? As Campbell suggested, there is "safety under the cloak of ignorance" (pp. 409–410). Furthermore, many social reforms are begun under the assumption that they are certain to be successful. Otherwise why spend all that tax money? For many public administrators it is advantageous to leave that assumption in people's minds rather than face the truth about what happened.

Campbell (p. 409) put forth the argument that:

The United States and other modern nations should be ready for an experimental approach to social reform, an approach in which we try out new programs, in which we learn whether or not these programs are effective, and in which we retain, imitate, modify, or discard them on the basis of apparent effectiveness on the multiple imperfect criteria available.

Social scientists need to convince administrators to use true experiments, if at all possible, or quasi-experiments at the very least, when instituting new social programs. For example, a randomization procedure, perhaps based on public lottery, could be used to decide which group receives a pilot program or gains access to scarce resources. Groups not receiving the program or the available resources would become comparison groups. The effect of a social "treatment" could then be meaningfully evaluated. At present, decisions regarding who gets what are often influenced by particular interest groups—as the result of intense lobbying, for example—or made on the basis of political favoritism.

Attempts to evaluate the effectiveness of this significant social program provide good examples of the difficulties inherent in evaluation research: the difficulty of randomly assigning participants, of getting administrators to cooperate with experimental procedures, and of dealing with loss of participants during the evaluation. Nevertheless, program evaluation based on sound experimental methodology offers policymakers at all levels (institution, community, city, state, federal) the information that can help them make more informed choices among possible treatments for social problems. Because resources inevitably are in short supply, it is critical that resources be put to the best possible use.

Our hope is that your knowledge of research methods will allow you to participate knowledgeably and perhaps contribute constructively to the ongoing debate concerning the role of experimentation in society.

Experimentation in natural settings differs in many ways from experimentation in psychology laboratories. The reasons for doing experiments in natural settings include testing the external validity of laboratory findings and assessing the effects of "treatments" aimed at improving conditions under which people work and live.

Campbell and others have argued that society must be willing to take an experimental approach to social reform—one that will allow the clearest evaluation of the effectiveness of new programs. In many situations (for instance, when available resources are scarce), true experiments involving randomization of individuals to treatment and no-treatment conditions are recommended. However, if a true experiment is not feasible, quasi-experimental procedures are the next best approach. Quasi-experiments differ from true experiments in that fewer plausible rival hypotheses for an experimental outcome are controlled. When specific threats to the internal validity of an experiment are not controlled, then the experimenter, by logically examining the situation and by collecting additional evidence, must seek to rule out these threats to internal validity.

A particularly strong quasi-experimental procedure is the nonequivalent control group design. This procedure generally controls for all major threats to internal validity except those associated with additive effects of (1) selection and history, (2) selection and maturation, (3) selection and instrumentation, and (4) threats due to differential statistical regression. In addition to the major threats to internal validity, an experimenter must be sensitive to possible contamination resulting from communication between groups of participants. Problems of experimenter expectancy effects (observer bias); questions of external validity; and novelty effects, including the Hawthorne effect, are potential problems in all experiments, whether conducted in the laboratory or in the field.

When it is possible to observe changes in a dependent measure before and after a treatment is administered, one can carry out a simple interrupted time-series design. The researcher using this design looks for an abrupt change (discontinuity) in the time series that coincides with the introduction of the treatment. The major threat to internal validity in this design is history—some event other than the treatment may have been responsible for the change in the time series. Instrumentation also can be a problem, especially when the treatment represents a type of social reform that may lead to changes in the way records are kept or data collected. By including a control group that is as similar as possible to the experimental group, one can strengthen the internal validity of a simple time-series design. A time series with nonequivalent control group, for example, controls for many possible history threats.

A particularly important goal of research in natural settings is program evaluation. Professionals other than psychologists (such as educators, political scientists, and sociologists) are often involved in this process. Types of program evaluation include assessment of needs, process, outcome, and efficiency. Perhaps the most serious constraints on program evaluation are the political and social realities that surround it. The reluctance of public officials to seek an evaluation of social reforms is often an obstacle to be overcome. Nevertheless, social scientists have called on program evaluators to make themselves available to human services organizations. By answering this call, we may help change society in a way that will bring the most effective services to those most in need.

KEY CONCEPTS

threats to internal validity
   history
   maturation
   testing
   instrumentation
   regression
   subject attrition
   selection
   contamination
   novelty effects

quasi-experiments
nonequivalent control group design
simple interrupted time-series
   design
time series with nonequivalent
   control group design
program evaluation

REVIEW QUESTIONS

1 Identify two reasons why it might be especially important to carry out experiments in natural settings.

2 Explain how laboratory experiments and those in natural settings differ in control, external validity, goals, and consequences.

3 Describe the three distinguishing characteristics of true experiments, and identify how the independent variable can be defined in terms of these characteristics.

4 What obstacles do researchers have to overcome when they try to carry out experiments in natural settings?

5 Identify two procedures that permit researchers to assign participants randomly to conditions while still giving all participants access to the experimental treatment.

6 Describe and explain the consequences of the three ways in which participants in a control group might respond when contamination occurs.

7 Explain how novelty effects, including the Hawthorne effect, may influence a researcher's interpretation of the effectiveness of an experimental treatment.

8 What do Cook and Campbell (1979) consider the best test of external validity?

9 Explain why it is essential to use a pretest in the nonequivalent control group design.

10 Explain how one threat to internal validity is controlled in the nonequivalent control group design, and describe a threat to internal validity that is not controlled in this design.

11 Identify two reasons why we cannot conclude that the treatment and control groups in a nonequivalent control group design are equivalent even when the pretest scores are the same for both groups.

12 Explain the difference between a history threat to internal validity and what is called a "local history effect" in the nonequivalent control group design.

13 What is the major evidence for an effect of the treatment in a simple interrupted time-series design, and what are the major threats to internal validity in this design?

14 Explain how the addition of a nonequivalent control group to a simple interrupted time-series design reduces the threat to the internal validity of the design.

15 Describe what type of information is being sought when evaluators ask each of the four questions typically addressed in program evaluation.

CHALLENGE QUESTIONS

1 A quasi-experiment was used to determine whether multimedia instruction is effective. Two sections of introductory psychology were taught by the same instructor both in the early afternoon. In one section (the treatment group) the instructor used multimedia instruction. In the other section the instructor covered the same material but did not use multimedia instruction. Students did not know when they registered for the course whether multimedia instruction would be used, but the students were not randomly assigned to sections. Students' knowledge of the course material was assessed using two forms of a comprehensive introductory psychology test. The comprehensive test can be considered a reliable and valid test that can be used to compare the effectiveness of the instruction in the two sections. The students in both sections were tested on the second day of class (the pretest) and at the final (the posttest). Different forms of the test were used at the pretest and at the posttest.

A What quasi-experimental design is used in the study?

B The instructor initially considered doing a true experiment rather than a quasi-experiment. Comment critically on the fairness of random assignment if you were arguing in favor of doing a true experiment to test the effectiveness of multimedia instruction.

C Explain why the quasi-experimental design used by the instructor is more effective than if the instructor had tested only students who had received multimedia instruction. Identify one threat to internal validity that was controlled in this study

that would not have been controlled if only students who received multimedia instruction had been tested.

2 A psychologist published a book describing the effects of divorce on men, women, and children. She was interested in the effects of divorce that occurred 10 years after the divorce. She found that even 10 years after a divorce half of the women and one-third of the men were still intensely angry. Although half the men and women described themselves as happy, 25% of the women and 20% of the men remained unable to "get their lives back on track." In only 10% of the divorced families did both the former husbands and wives have happy, satisfying lives a decade later. Finally, more than half of the children of divorce entered adulthood as underachieving and self-deprecating men and women. These findings were based on a 15-year study of 60 divorced couples and their 131 children living in Marin County, California (an affluent suburban area including mostly well-educated people). Explain how the use of a quasi-experimental design would have been helpful in order to specify which of the reported results are due to the effects of divorce.

3 The police force of a large city had to decide between two different approaches to keeping the officers on the force informed about the changes in laws. An enlightened administrator of this force decided to put the two approaches to test in a research study. She decided to do a true experiment and she assigned 30 officers randomly to each of the two programs for a period of 6 months. At the end of this time all the officers who successfully completed the training

under the two approaches were given a final test on their knowledge of the law. The 20 officers who completed Program A showed a reliably higher mean score on this test than did the 28 officers who completed Program B. The administrator wisely chose not to accept these results as decisive evidence of the effectiveness of the two programs. Using only the data reported in this problem, explain why she made this decision. Next, explain how her decision would have been different if only 20 officers completed both programs (from the original 30 assigned to each) and there was still a sizable difference favoring Program A. Be sure to mention any limitations on the conclusions she could reach concerning the overall effectiveness of these programs.

4 A small undergraduate college with a new physical fitness center decided to introduce a health enhancement program for faculty and staff. The program is designed to take one semester to complete with three 1-hour sessions per week. Comment critically on each of the following questions regarding the evaluation of this program.

A How might an assessment of needs have played a role in planning the program?

B What questions about the process of the program would be useful once the program was underway to help ensure that the evaluation of the outcome of the program could be interpreted appropriately?

C Explain how you would test the effectiveness of the proposed program if it were not possible to do a true experiment.

Answers to the Stretching Exercise

1 History is a threat when an event other than the treatment can explain the participants' improvement. For example, participants may have read self-help books, tried herbal supplements, talked to friends or pastors, or experienced any number of potentially beneficial "treatments." Any of these other events may have caused the depression to improve, rather than the psychologist's treatment.

2 Maturation occurs when participants naturally change over time. One of the things we know about depression is that it tends to improve with time. Therefore, the participants' improvement may reflect natural decreases in depression over time, rather than the effect of the treatment.

3 A testing threat occurs when a first administration of a test influences subsequent testing. In this study, participants may have remembered their earlier responses on the depression measure, and perhaps in an effort to demonstrate they improved, chose responses that indicated less depression at posttest (even if they didn't feel less depressed). An instrumentation threat occurs when the measure used to assess thoughts, feelings, and behavior changes over time. Because the same questionnaire was used for both the pretest and posttest, this threat is less likely.

4 Statistical regression is possible when participants are selected because they are extreme on a pretest measure. In this study, participants were selected because they are depressed—they scored high on a measure of depression. It's possible that the lower scores at posttest indicated improvement because of statistical regression to the mean, not because of the effects of treatment.

Answer to Challenge Question 1

A The nonequivalent control group design was used in this study.

B Students may perceive random assignment to the two sections as unfair because they would not have a choice about which section they would take. If we do not know whether multimedia instruction is effective, then random assignment is the best and fairest method to determine whether multimedia instruction is effective.

C If only the students who had received multimedia instruction had been tested, the design of the study would have been a single group pretest-posttest design. There are several threats to the internal validity of a pretest-posttest single group design. That is why it is referred to as a pre-experimental design or a bad experiment. One possible threat in this study is maturation; that is, students are likely (we hope) to increase in knowledge of introductory psychology by the end of the course in which they are enrolled even if multimedia instruction had not been used. The non-equivalent control group design used in this study controls for this threat because any increase due to maturation will likely be the same for both groups. A greater increase from the pretest to the posttest for the group given multimedia instruction can be interpreted as an effect of the instruction.

Analyzing and Reporting Research

Data Analysis and Interpretation: Part I. Describing Data, Confidence Intervals, Correlation

The primary goal of data analysis is to determine whether our observations support a claim about behavior (Abelson, 1995). The claim may be that children of drug-addicted mothers exhibit more learning difficulties than those born to drug-free mothers, or that a program intended to prevent depression has worked. Whatever the claim, our case must be prepared with careful attention given to the quality of the evidence and to the way it is presented. When a quantitative research study is conducted, the evidence is primarily the numerical data we collected. To prepare a convincing argument, we need to know what to look for in these data, how to summarize that information, and how best to evaluate the information.

Data, of course, do not come out of thin air; we can assume results were obtained using a particular research method (e.g., observation, survey, experiment). If serious errors were made in the data collection stage, then there may be nothing we can do to "save" the data and it may be best to start again. Thus, we need to ensure that the data for the analysis were gathered after giving careful consideration to the statement of the research hypothesis (i.e., our tentative claim about behavior), the choice of a proper research design to test that hypothesis, selection of appropriate response measures, and assessment of statistical power. And, of course, we want to make sure that the data were collected in a manner that minimizes the contribution of demand characteristics, experimenter biases, confoundings, or other artifacts of the research situation. In short, we seek data from a "good" research study, one that is internally and externally valid, sensitive, and reliable (see Chapters 7–9).

Key Concepts }

Trusting we have obtained data based on a sound research study, what should we do next? There are three distinct, but related **stages of data analysis: getting to know the data, summarizing the data,** and **confirming what the data reveal** (see Box 12.1). Whether conducting an observational study (see Chapter 4) or an experiment (see Chapters 7 to 9) based on quantitative data, the first two stages of data analysis, *getting to know the data* and *summarizing the data*, proceed in much the same way. When conducting a survey (see Chapter 5) or other research study in which evidence for covariation between two variables is sought, data summary proceeds somewhat differently. We will use several research examples to illustrate the stages of data analysis, including those that focus on mean performance of one or more groups as well as those that emphasize the correlation between variables.

There are different, but complementary, approaches to the third stage of analysis, *confirming what the data tell us*. One approach makes use of confidence intervals to provide evidence for the range and precision of estimation of population parameters. Another relies on null hypothesis significance testing (NHST). Both of these approaches were briefly introduced in Chapter 7, and, as we said, these approaches are related; however, there are important differences and we will introduce them first separately and then show how information from both approaches might be combined in the final analysis story. In this

The three major stages of data analysis can be described as follows:

I **Getting to Know the Data:** In the first stage we want to become familiar with the data. This is an exploratory or investigative stage (Tukey, 1977). We inspect the data carefully, get a feel for it, and even, as some have said, "make friends" with it (Hoaglin, Mosteller, & Tukey, 1991, p. 42). Questions we ask include, What is going on in this number set? Are there errors in the data? Do the data make sense or are there reasons for "suspecting fishiness" (Abelson, 1995, p. 78)? Visual displays of distributions of numbers are important at this stage. What do the data look like? Only when we have become familiar with the general features of the data, have checked for errors, and have assured ourselves that the data make sense, should we proceed to the second stage.

II **Summarizing the Data:** In the second stage we seek to summarize the data in a meaningful way. The use of descriptive statistics and creation of graphical displays are important at this stage. How should the data be organized? Which ways of describing and summarizing the data are most informative? What happened in this study as a function of the factors of interest? What trends and patterns do we see? Which graphical display best reveals these trends and patterns? When the data are appropriately summarized, we are ready to move to the confirmation stage.

III **Confirming What the Data Reveal:** In the third stage we decide what the data tell us about behavior. Do the data confirm our tentative claim (research hypothesis) made at the beginning of the study? What can we claim based on the evidence? Sometimes we look for a categorical, yes-no judgment, and act as judge and jury to render a verdict. Do we have evidence to convict? Yes or no: Is the effect real? At this stage we may use various statistical techniques to counter arguments that our results are simply "due to chance." Null hypothesis testing, when appropriate, is performed at this stage of analysis. Our evaluation of the data, however, need not always lead us to a categorical judgment about the data (e.g., Schmidt, 1996). We don't, in other words, have to attempt a definitive statement about the "truth" of the results. Our claim about behavior may be based on an evaluation of the probable range of effect sizes for the variable of interest. What, in other words, is likely to happen when this variable is present? Confidence intervals are particularly recommended for this kind of evaluation (e.g., Cohen, 1995; Hunter, 1997; Loftus, 1996).

The confirmation process actually begins at the first or exploratory stage of data analysis, when we first get a feel for what our data are like. As we examine the general features of the data we start to appreciate what we found. In the summary stage we learn more about trends and patterns among the observations. This provides feedback that helps to confirm our hypotheses. The final step in data analysis is called the confirmation stage to emphasize that it is typically at this point when we come to a decision about what the data mean. Information obtained at each stage of data analysis, however, contributes to this confirmatory process (e.g., Tukey, 1977).

chapter we discuss confidence intervals and in Chapter 13, NHST. In Chapter 13 we also discuss the important concept of statistical power and its relationship to confidence intervals and NHST.

When data analysis is completed, we must construct a coherent narrative that explains our findings, counters opposing interpretations, and justifies our conclusions.

Making a convincing argument for a claim about behavior requires more than simply analyzing the data. A good argument requires a good story. A trial attorney, in order to win a case, must not only call a jury's attention to the facts of a case, but also must be able to weave those facts into a coherent and logical story. If the evidence points to the butler, then we want to know "why" the butler (and not the cook) might have done it. Abelson (1995, p. 13) makes a similar point regarding a research argument:

> High-quality evidence, embodying sizeable, well-articulated and general effects, is necessary for a statistical argument to have maximal persuasive impact, but it is not sufficient. Also vital are the attributes of the research story embodying the argument.

Consequently, when data analysis is completed, we must construct a coherent narrative that explains our findings, counters opposing interpretations, and justifies our conclusions. In Chapters 13 and 14 we'll return to the analysis story when we introduce guidelines to help you develop an appropriate narrative for your research study.

COMPUTER-ASSISTED DATA ANALYSIS

- Researchers typically use computers to carry out the statistical analysis of data.
- Carrying out statistical analyses using computer software requires that the researcher must have a good knowledge of research design and statistics.

Most researchers have ready access to computers that include appropriate software to carry out the statistical analysis of data sets. The ability to set up and carry out an analysis using a statistical software package and to interpret the output are essential skills that must be learned by researchers. Some of the more popular software packages are known by abbreviations like BMDP, SAS, SPSS, and STATA. You likely have access to one or more of these programs on the computers in your psychology department or at your campus computer center.

Carrying out statistical analyses using computer software requires that the researcher have a good knowledge of research design and statistics. In Chapters 7, 8 and 9 we introduced various experimental designs. This knowledge is essential if you wish to use computer-assisted analysis. A computer is not able to determine what research design you used or the rationale behind the use of that design (although some of the more user-friendly programs provide prompts to guide your thinking). To carry out computer-assisted data analysis, you must enter information such as the type of design that was used (e.g., random groups or repeated measures); the number of independent variables (e.g., single factor or multifactor); the number of levels of each independent variable; and the number of dependent variables and the level of measurement employed for each. You must also be able to articulate your research hypotheses and to plan appropriate statistical tests of your research hypotheses. A contacted 24 mothers who had one child about 70 months old and one child approximately 40 months old. The details of the study need not concern us except to note that homes of the participants were visited four times, with only a few days separating the experimental sessions. The researcher found that sessions 3 and 4 for one family were separated by 2 months instead of a few days. Scheduling difficulties with this family had caused the unintended longer interval between sessions. Further inspection during the initial data analysis stage revealed that this family's data consistently produced outliers. Haden (1998) decided not to include the data obtained from this family in further analyses and she explained in the Method section of her published article the circumstances and rationale leading to her decision to exclude this family's data from her study.

In the first stage of data analysis we also want to look for ways to describe the distribution of scores meaningfully. What is the dispersion (variability) like? Are the data skewed or relatively normally distributed? One of the goals of this first stage of analysis is to determine whether the data require transformation prior to proceeding. Transforming data is a process of "re-expression" (Hoaglin, Mosteller, & Tukey, 1983). Examples of relatively simple transformations include those that express inches as feet, degrees Fahrenheit as Celsius, or number correct as percent correct. More sophisticated statistical transformations are also sometimes useful.

The best way to get a feel for a set of data is to construct a picture of it. An advantage of computer-aided data analysis is that we can quickly and easily plot data using various display options (e.g., frequency polygons, histograms) and just as easily incorporate changes of scale (e.g., inches to feet) to see how the data picture is altered. Minimally, by experimenting with different ways to visualize our data set we become more familiar with it. Which visual representation reveals the most about our data? What do we learn about our data when we compare plots with the axes defined differently? Is a polygon or histogram more informative? A picture is not only worth a proverbial 1,000 words, but also it can quickly summarize 1,000 numbers. As we become more familiar with different pictures of our data, we learn that some pictures are better than others.

The data from the Zechmeister et al. (1995) vocabulary study represented the number of correct meanings identified out of a possible 191. Because participants without knowledge of the correct answer can be correct by chance on multiple-choice tests, a standard correction for guessing was applied to individual responses. However, two typographical errors appeared in the booklets given to the older adult group and so these items were deleted from further analysis. Also, examination of the test booklets revealed that several of the older participants omitted a page when working through the test booklet. Thus, the number of possible words was reduced for these individuals. Because of these problems, the data were transformed to percentage correct to account for differences in the total number of possible responses among participants.

After cleaning the data set, the researchers obtained the following data in the first stage of the analysis. These data are expressed in terms of percentage correct multiple-choice performance for college students and older adults.

College ($n = 26$): 59, 31, 47, 43, 54, 42, 38, 44, 48, 57, 42, 48, 30, 41, 59, 23, 62, 27, 53, 51, 39, 38, 50, 58, 56, 45.

Elderly ($n = 26$): 70, 59, 68, 68, 57, 66, 78, 78, 64, 43, 53, 83, 74, 69, 59, 44, 73, 65, 32, 60, 54, 64, 82, 62, 62, 78.

Key Concept

Stem-and-Leaf Displays   A **stem-and-leaf display** is particularly useful for visualizing the general features of a data set and for detecting outliers (Tukey, 1977). A stem-and-leaf display obtains its name through the convention of using leading digits in a numerical array as "stems" and trailing digits as "leaves."

The following is a stem-and-leaf display for the college student data from our example vocabulary study:

2*	3
2	7
3*	01
3	889
4*	12234
4	5788
5*	0134
5	67899
6*	2

The leading digits are the first or tens' digits (e.g., 2-, 3-, 4-,) and the trailing digits are just that, those that trail the leading or most significant digits; in this example the trailing digits are the units' or ones' digits (e.g., -5, -6, -8). The display is made by arranging the leading digits in a vertical array beginning with the smallest at the top. A leading digit is followed, in ascending order, by as many trailing digits as appear in the distribution. Each line in the display is a stem followed by its leaves (Tukey, 1977). For example, the stem 3 in the above display has three leaves, 8,8,9, indicating that the numbers 38, 38, and 39 appear in the distribution. By convention, when many numbers are displayed, or when the entire data set contains only a few leading digits, a leading digit followed by an asterisk(*) is frequently used to indicate the first half of an interval (see Tukey, 1977). For example, 5* would be the stem for leaves 0,1,2,3, and 4 (i.e., numbers 50–54); the leading digit 5 (without the *) would be the stem for leaves 5,6,7,8,9 (i.e., numbers 55–59). In the above display, for instance, the stem 2* has one leaf, 3, and the stem 2 has one leaf, 7, corresponding to the numbers 23 and 27, respectively.

There also may be more than one leading digit. For example, if scores varied between 50 and 150, single leading digits would be used for numbers less than 100 (8-, 9-, etc.), and two leading digits for numbers equal to or greater than 100 (10-, 11-, 12-, etc.).

As you might see, a stem-and-leaf display is something of a histogram on its side. It has an advantage over a histogram, however, in that each value is displayed; thus, specific item information is not lost, as occurs when a histogram is formed using class intervals (Howell, 2002). The most important advantage of a stem-and-leaf display is that it can clearly reveal the shape of the distribution and the presence, if any, of outliers.

Look carefully at the stem-and-leaf display for the vocabulary data of the 26 college students. What do you see? Is the general shape of the distribution "normal" (i.e., symmetrical and "bell-shaped") or skewed (i.e., asymmetrical with scores trailing off in one direction)? Is there a lot of dispersion or do the numbers tend to "center" around a particular value? Are anomalous values present? We suggest that the stem-and-leaf display for these data reveals that the data are concentrated around the 40 and 50 percentages with the distribution somewhat negatively skewed (note how the "tail" trails off toward the low or negative end of the distribution). Outliers do not seem to be present (e.g., there are no single-digit percentages or percentages beyond the 60s).

It can be particularly revealing to display two stem-and-leaf displays side-by-side when comparing two groups of data. Consider the display pictured below. The same stems are used with trailing digits in one distribution increasing from right to left (e.g., 997 5) and leaves in the other distribution ascending (on the same line) from left to right (e.g., 5 67899). This indicates that the first distribution had scores of 57, 59, and 59, and the second distribution had scores of 56, 57, 58, 59, and 59. Side-by-side stem-and-leaf displays might be meaningfully used, for instance, to compare responses to a questionnaire item when a researcher is comparing two groups that differ in socioeconomic status, age, gender, or in some other meaningful way.

A side-by-side stem-and-leaf display for the two conditions of the vocabulary study looks like this:

Older adults		College students
	2*	3
	2	7
2	3*	01
	3	889
43	4*	12234
	4	5788
43	5*	0134
997	5	67899
44220	6*	2
98865	6	
430	7*	
888	7	
32	8*	

Look at the display on the left, the one for the older participants. How would you characterize it? The data seem to be somewhat normally distributed, although an extreme score, an outlier, appears to be present. The "32" doesn't seem to belong with the rest of the data. (There are ways to operationalize outliers in terms of their distance from the middle of the distribution and some computer programs will do this automatically.) Without additional information about the nature of the respondent (e.g., amount of medication taken that day, or possible reading problems) the experimenters could find no reason to exclude this score from the study. The presence of this possible outlier necessarily increases the amount of variability present in this group relative to what it would be without this score. Nevertheless, we must acknowledge that some data sets are naturally going to be more variable than others. For example, the older adults in this study simply may represent a more heterogeneous group of individuals than those in the college student sample. (There is a moral here: Obtain as much relevant information about your participants as is conveniently possible at the time you collect data. An extreme score has to be treated as a true score unless you know the score is extreme due to error or to circumstances unrelated to the study.)

Now look at what the side-by-side stem-and-leaf display reveals about both distributions. You should immediately see that scores in the groups overlap to some degree, but there are many more scores above 60 in the older group than in the college group. This "picture" of the data begins to confirm the idea that the older adults performed better overall than the college students on this test of vocabulary size.

Conclusion   In the first stage of data analysis—the process of getting to know our data—we should identify:

(a) the nature and frequency of any errors in the data set, and, if errors were present, whether corrections could be made or data need to be dropped;

(b) anomalous values, including outliers, and if they are present, what reasons there might be for the presence of these values and what should be done about them (retained or dropped);

(c) the general features and shape of the distribution of numbers; and

(d) alternate ways to more meaningfully express the data.

Stage 2: Summarizing the Data

- Measures of central tendency include the mean, median, and mode.
- Important measures of dispersion or variability are the range and standard deviation.
- The standard error of the mean is the standard deviation of the theoretical sampling distribution of means and is a measure of how well we have estimated the population mean.
- Effect size measures are important because they provide information about the strength of the relationship between the independent variable and the dependent variable that is independent of sample size.
- An important effect size measure when comparing two means is Cohen's *d*.

Data can be effectively summarized numerically, pictorially, or verbally. Good descriptions of data frequently use all three modes. In this chapter we will focus mainly on ways to summarize data numerically, that is, using descriptive statistics, although we do present some graphs. Information about drawing graphs to summarize data is also found in Chapter 14. Verbal description of data also is a major topic of Chapter 14 (see especially guidelines for writing the Results section of a research report).

The data from the vocabulary study will be summarized using measures of central tendency, dispersion, standard error of the mean, and effect size.

Key Concepts }

Central Tendency   Measures of central tendency include the mean, median, and mode. These **measures of central tendency** do just what their name implies: they indicate the score that the data tend to center around. The **mode** is the crudest measure of central tendency: it simply indicates the score in the frequency distribution that occurs most often. If two scores in the distribution occur with higher frequency than do other scores in the distribution, and if these two scores occur at different locations in the frequency distribution, this distribution is said to be bimodal (i.e., to have two modes).

Key Concept }

The **median** is defined as the middle point in the frequency distribution. It is calculated by ranking all the scores from lowest to highest and identifying the value that splits the distribution into two halves, each half having the same number of values. Consider the following data set: 4, 5, 6, 7, 8, 8. For these data the median would be 6.5. When there are an even number of values the median is defined as the average of the two middle numbers [in this case $(6 + 7)/2 = 6.5$]. When there are an odd number of values the median is, by convention, the middle value when numbers are arranged in ascending or descending order. For the number set, 4, 5, 6, 17, 18, the median is 6. Note that the median would still be 6 if the highest value was 180, not 18. The median is the best measure of central tendency when the distribution includes extreme scores because it is less influenced than is the mean by the extreme scores.

Key Concept }

The **mean** is the most commonly reported measure of central tendency and is determined by dividing the sum of the scores by the number of scores contributing to that sum. The mean of a population is symbolized as μ (Greek letter mu); the mean of a sample is indicated by M when reported in text, for example, in a Results section. (The symbol $\overline{X}$ [read "X bar"] is typically used in statistical formulas.) The mean should always be reported as a measure of central tendency unless there are extreme scores in the distribution. When people speak of an "average" score, they usually are referring to the arithmetic mean. For the data set, 4, 5, 6, 7, 8, 8, the mean is:

$$\overline{X} = \frac{\Sigma X}{N} = \frac{38}{6} = 6.33$$

where:

Σ = "sum of"

X = individual (raw) score

N = number of values in data set

Measures of central tendency for the two groups in the vocabulary study are:

	College	Older adult
Mean (*M*)	45.58	64.04
Median	46.00	64.50
Mode	38,42,48,59	78

As you can see, the mean performance of the college group is much lower than the mean or average performance of the older adults. This confirms what we saw in the side-by-side stem-and-leaf display: the older group performed better overall on the average than did the college group. Note that the mean and median in each group are similar; thus, even though we identified an extreme score in the older sample when looking at the stem-and-leaf display, the presence of this score does not seem to have "thrown off" the mean as a measure of central tendency. There is more than one mode in the college data, each appearing twice; the most frequent score in the older group is 78, and it appeared only three times. As you can see, the mode is not particularly helpful in summarizing these small data sets.

Key Concepts

Dispersion or Variability Whenever you report a measure of central tendency, it should always be accompanied by an appropriate **measure of dispersion (variability).** Measures of central tendency indicate the value in a frequency distribution on which scores tend to "center"; measures of dispersion indicate the breadth or variability of the distribution.

The crudest measure of dispersion (the counterpart of the mode) is the **range.** The range is determined by subtracting the lowest score in the distribution from the highest score. For example, in a small distribution made up of the scores 1,3,5,7 the range would be equal to 7–1, or 6.

Key Concept

The most commonly used measure of dispersion (the counterpart of the mean) is the **standard deviation.** The standard deviation tells you approximately how far on the average a score is from the mean. It is equal to the square root of the average squared deviations of scores in the distribution about the mean. The standard deviation is defined as:

$$\sqrt{\frac{\Sigma(X - \overline{X})^2}{N - 1}}$$

where:

X = individual (raw) score

$\overline{X}$ = sample mean

N = sample size

Σ = "sum of"

For reasons that need not concern us here the average of the squared deviations about the mean involves division by $N - 1$ rather than N so as to provide an unbiased estimate of the population standard deviation based on the sample. The standard deviation of a population is symbolized as σ (Greek letter sigma); the standard deviation of a sample of scores is indicated as *SD* when appearing in text, but it is often symbolized as *s* in statistical formulas. The variance, a measure of dispersion that is important in the calculation of various inferential statistics, is the square of the standard deviation, that is, s^2.

Measures of variability for the two vocabulary groups are:

	College	Older adult
Range	23–62	32–83
Variance (s^2)	109.45	150.44
Standard deviation (*SD* or *s*)	10.46	12.27

Note that the stem-and-leaf display showed greater dispersion among the older adults; with the *SD* we have a number to reflect that characteristic of the distribution.

Standard Error of the Mean   In doing inferential statistics, we use the sample mean as a point estimate of the population mean. That is, we use a single value ($\overline{X}$) to estimate (infer) the population mean (μ). It is often helpful to be able to determine how much error there is in estimating μ on the basis of $\overline{X}$. The central limit theorem in mathematics tells us that if we draw an infinite number of samples of the same size and we compute $\overline{X}$ for each of these samples, the mean of these samples means ($\mu_{\overline{X}}$) will be equal to the population mean (μ), and the standard deviation of the sample means will be equal to the population standard deviation (σ) divided by the square root of the sample size (N). The standard deviation of this theoretical sampling distribution of the mean is called the **standard error of the mean** ($\sigma_{\overline{X}}$) and is defined as:

Key Concept

$$\sigma_{\overline{X}} = \frac{\sigma}{\sqrt{N}}$$

Key Concept

Typically, we do not know the standard deviation of the population so we estimate it using the sample standard deviation (s). Then we may obtain an **estimated standard error of the mean** using the formula:

$$s_{\overline{X}} = \frac{s}{\sqrt{N}}$$

Small values of $s_{\overline{X}}$ suggest that we have a good estimate of the population mean, and large values of $s_{\overline{X}}$ suggest that we have only a rough estimate of the population mean. The formula for the standard error of the mean indicates that our ability to estimate the population mean on the basis of a sample depends on the size of the sample (large samples lead to better estimates) and on the variability in the population from which the sample was drawn, as estimated by the sample standard deviation (the less variable the scores in a population, the better our estimate of the population mean will be). As we will show later, the standard error of the mean plays an important role in the construction of confidence intervals and is frequently displayed along with sample means in a figure summarizing results of a research study. It is symbolized as *SE* when reporting results in a research manuscript.

Measures of Effect Size When we do an experiment we are interested in determining whether the independent variable had an effect and, if it did, how much of an effect there was. The concept of effect size was introduced in Chapter 7. Measures of *effect size* or what are more generally called measures of "effect magnitude" (see Kirk, 1996) are important because they provide information about the strength of the relationship between the independent variable and the dependent variable that is independent of sample size.

One commonly used measure of effect size in experimental research when comparisons are made between two means is called Cohen's *d*. It is a ratio that measures the difference between the means for the levels of the independent variable divided by the within-group standard deviation. Remember that the standard deviation tells us approximately how far, on the average, scores vary from a group mean. It is a measure of the "dispersal" of scores around a mean and, in the case of the within-group standard deviation, tells us about the degree of "error" due to individual differences (i.e., how individuals vary in their responses). The standard deviation serves as a useful metric to assess a difference between means. That is, the "size" of the effect of the independent variable (the difference between group means for the independent variable) is always in terms of the average amount of dispersal of scores occurring in an experiment.

The effect size measure, *d*, defined as the difference between sample means divided by the common population standard deviation, is called Cohen's *d* after the late statistician Jacob Cohen [see Cohen (1988) for more information about *d*].

$$\text{Cohen's } d = \frac{\overline{X}_1 - \overline{X}_2}{\sigma}$$

The population standard deviation (σ) is obtained by pooling the within-group variability across groups and dividing by the total number (N) of scores in both groups. A formula for the common population standard deviation using sample variances is:

$$\sigma = \sqrt{\frac{(n_1 - 1)s_1^2 + (n_2 - 1)s_2^2}{N}}$$

where:

n_1 = sample size of Group 1

n_2 = sample size of Group 2

$s_1^2 = $ variance of Group 1

$s_2^2 = $ variance of Group 2

$N = n_1 + n_2$

If there is a lot of within-group variability (i.e., the within-group standard deviation is large), the denominator for d is large. To be able to observe the effect of the independent variable, given this large within-group variability, the difference between two group means must be large. When the within-group variability is small (the denominator for d is small), the same difference between means will reflect a larger effect size. Because effect sizes are presented in standard deviation units, they can be used to make meaningful comparisons of effect sizes across experiments using different dependent variables. For example, an effect size from a study of vocabulary knowledge that compared college students and older adults on tests emphasizing discrimination of word meanings (i.e., multiple-choice tests) and an effect size from a study contrasting performance of two similar groups using recall of word definitions could be directly compared. Such comparisons form the bases of *meta-analyses,* which seek to summarize the effect of a particular independent variable across many different studies (see Chapter 7).

There are some guidelines to help us interpret d ratios. J. Cohen (1992) provided a useful classification of effect sizes with three values—small, medium, and large. He describes the rationale for his classification of effect size (ES) as follows:

> My intent was that medium ES represent an effect likely to be visible to the naked eye of a careful observer. (It has since been noted in effect-size surveys that it approximates the average size of observed effects in various fields.) I set small ES to be noticeably smaller than medium but not so small as to be trivial, and I set large ES to be the same distance above medium as small was below it. Although the definitions were made subjectively, with some minor adjustments, these conventions . . . have come into general use. (p. 156)

Each of the classes of effect size can be expressed in quantitative terms; for example, a medium effect for a two-group experiment is a d of .50; a small and large effect are ds of .20 and .80, respectively. These expressions of effect magnitude are especially useful when comparing results from similar studies.

It is important to note that researchers define the standardized difference between means in slightly different ways (see, for example, Cohen, 1988; Kirk, 1996; Rosenthal, 1991). Which measure of effect size to use is a decision left up to the investigator. But, given the differences in measures appearing in the psychology literature, *it is very important to identify in a research report precisely how a measure of effect size was calculated.*

An effect size for the vocabulary study using Cohen's d is:

$$d = \frac{\overline{X}_1 - \overline{X}_2}{\sigma} = \frac{64.04 - 45.58}{\sqrt{\dfrac{(26 - 1)(150.04) + (26 - 1)(109.45)}{52}}} = 1.65$$

To interpret the value of 1.65, we can use J. Cohen's (1992) classification of effect sizes of $d = .20$ for a small effect size, $d = .50$ for a medium effect size, and $d = .80$ for a large effect size. Because our value is larger than .80, we can conclude that "age" had a large effect on vocabulary knowledge.

Conclusion   In the second, summary stage of data analysis, we should identify:

(a) the central tendency (e.g., mean) of each condition or group in the study;

(b) measures of dispersion (variability), such as the range and standard deviation, for each condition of the study;

(c) the effect size for each of the major independent variables; and

(d) how to best present pictorial summaries of the data (e.g., figure showing mean performance across conditions).

Note: Although a graph showing mean performance in the two groups of the vocabulary study could be drawn, a figure usually is not needed when only two group means are involved. Pictorial summaries become more important when summarizing the results of studies with more than two groups.

Stage 3: Using Confidence Intervals to Confirm What the Data Reveal

• An important approach to confirming what the data are telling us is to construct confidence intervals for the population parameter, such as a mean or difference between two means.

Key Concept

In the third stage of data analysis we seek to confirm impressions of the evidence obtained as we familiarized ourselves with the data and obtained summary measures. A major approach in this third stage is the calculation of a **confidence interval for a population parameter.** A confidence interval (CI) may be calculated for a single population mean or population mean difference. We first review the use of confidence intervals for one population mean. Then we introduce confidence intervals for the difference between two population means and discuss the interpretation of intervals when there are three or more means.

Confidence intervals may already be familiar to you under a different name. Have you not heard reports in the media of survey results based on a sample of respondents? And with these reports have you sometimes heard a "margin of error" presented? In Box 12.2 we review the concept of margin of error and its relation to a confidence interval.

Confidence Intervals for a Single Mean   The mean of a random sample from a population is a point estimate of the population mean. However, we can expect variability among sample means from one situation to another due to random variation. The standard error of the mean ($s_{\bar{X}}$) provides information

BOX 12.2

THE MARGIN OF ERROR IN SURVEY RESULTS

As you learned in Chapter 5, survey research relies heavily on sampling. Survey research is conducted when we would like to know the characteristics of a population (e.g., preferences, attitudes, demographics), but often it is impractical to survey the entire population. Responses from a sample are used to describe the larger population. Well-selected samples will provide good descriptions of the population, but it is unlikely that the results for a sample will describe the population exactly. For example, if the average age in a classroom of 33 college students is 26.4, it is unlikely that the mean age for a sample of 10 students from the class will be exactly 26.4. Similarly, if it were true that 65% of a city's population favor the present mayor and 35% favor a new mayor, we wouldn't necessarily expect an exact 65:35 split in a sample of 100 voters randomly selected from the city population. We expect some "slippage" due to sampling, some "error" between the actual population values and the estimates from our sample. At issue, then, is how accurately the responses from the sample represent the larger population.

It is possible to estimate the margin of error between the sample results and the true population values. Rather than providing a precise estimate of a population value (e.g., "65% of the population prefer the present mayor"), the margin of error presents a range of values that are likely to contain the true population value (e.g., "between 60% and 70% of the population prefer the present mayor"). What specifically is this range?

The margin of error provides an estimate of the difference between the sample results and the population values due simply to chance or random factors. The margin of error gives us the range of values we can expect due to sampling error—remember that we expect some error; we don't expect to describe the population exactly. Let us assume that a poll of many voters is taken and a media spokesperson gives the following report: "Results indicate that 63% of those sampled favor the incumbent, and we can say with 95% confidence that the poll has a margin of error of 5%." The reported margin of error with the specified level of confidence (usually 95%) indicates that the percentage of the actual population who favor the

incumbent is estimated to be found in the interval between 58% and 68% (5% is subtracted from and added to the sample value of 63%). It's important to remember, however, that we usually don't know the true population value. The information we get from the sample and the margin of error is the following: 63% of the *sample* favor the incumbent, and we are 95% confident that if the entire population were sampled, between 58% and 68% of the *population* would favor the incumbent. This can be represented on a graph by plotting the value obtained for the sample (63%), with error bars representing the margin of error. Figure 12.1 displays error bars around the sample estimate.

Margins of error are routinely included in media reports of national surveys. The goal of these surveys is to tell you with a "margin of error" what the true population value is. Similarly, the goal of many scientific studies is to tell you the margin of error, now usually called a confidence interval, for an estimate of a population value.

FIGURE 12.1   Error bars are used to represent the margin of error for the estimate of the population value.

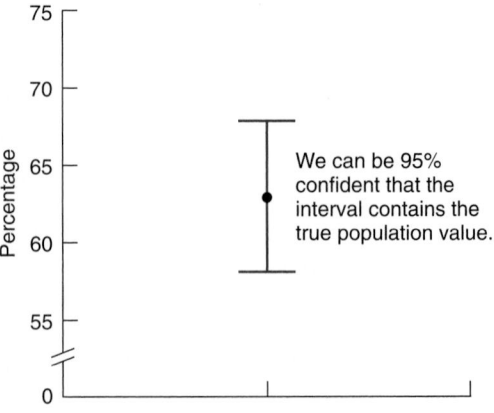

about the "normal" range of sampling error. In computing a confidence interval we specify a range of values which we state with a certain degree of confidence includes the population mean. As you may suspect, the larger the interval we specify, the greater our confidence that the mean will be included; but larger intervals give us less specific information about the exact value of the population mean. As a compromise, researchers have agreed that the 95% confidence interval and the 99% confidence interval are the best intervals to use when an interval estimate of the population mean is desired.

The confidence interval is centered about our point estimate ($\overline{X}$) of the population mean and the boundaries of the 95% confidence interval can be calculated using the following formulas:

$$\text{Upper limit of 95\% confidence interval: } \overline{X} + [t_{.05}][s_{\overline{X}}]$$

$$\text{Lower limit of 95\% confidence interval: } \overline{X} - [t_{.05}][s_{\overline{X}}]$$

We have already described procedures for computing the sample mean ($\overline{X}$) and the estimated standard error of the mean ($s_{\overline{X}}$). The unfamiliar symbols in the two equations for the limits of the 95% confidence interval are t and .05.

You may recognize the alpha (α) level of .05 from other psychology courses. It is typically associated with inferential tests of statistical significance (i.e., NHST), and we will have much more to say about alpha levels in Chapter 13. In the case of confidence intervals, $\alpha = (1 - \text{level of confidence})$, expressed as a proportion. So, for the 95% confidence interval, $\alpha = (1 - .95) = .05$ and for the 99% confidence interval, $\alpha = (1 - .99) = .01$.

The t statistic included in the equation is defined by the number of degrees of freedom, and the statistical significance of t can be determined by looking in Appendix Table A.2. For a single sample mean, the degrees of freedom are $N - 1$. You will learn more about the t statistic in Chapter 13 when we discuss NHST. At this point let us simply concentrate on the calculation and proper interpretation of a confidence interval using the above formulas.

An example will illustrate how we obtain a confidence interval for a single mean. Suppose you obtained a random sample of students at your university and measured their intelligence using a brief but valid and reliable measure of this construct. Assume thirty students ($N = 30$) were tested and the mean intelligence score was 115 with a sample standard deviation of 14. The population of students is represented by the thousands of students attending your university. And while the sample mean is a good point estimate of the population mean (i.e., our best guess of the population mean), we must acknowledge that if another random sample of 30 students was selected and tested the sample mean would not likely be exactly 115. There will be some slippage, or "error," due to this random process. Recall that the standard error of the mean is one measure of the error in estimation.

Rather than rely simply on a point estimate of the population mean, we can obtain an interval estimate by finding the 95% confidence interval for the population mean using the formulas presented earlier. We first calculate the estimated standard error of the mean:

$$s_{\overline{X}} = \frac{s}{\sqrt{N}} = \frac{14}{\sqrt{30}} = \frac{14}{5.48} = 2.55$$

Next, we obtain the critical t value. Because there were 30 students, the degrees of freedom associated with the t statistic are $30 - 1$ or 29. Using Table A.2 we can find that the value of t with alpha of .05 and 29 degrees of freedom is 2.04. Using the formulas for the confidence interval we have:

Upper limit of 95% confidence interval $= 115 + [2.04][2.55]$

Lower limit of 95% confidence interval $= 115 - [2.04][2.55]$

Upper limit $= 115 + 5.20 = 120.20$

Lower limit $= 115 - 5.20 = 109.80$

We may state that there is a .95 probability that the interval, 109.80 to 120.20, contains ("has captured") the population mean (see Box 12.3).

The narrower the interval the better is our interval estimate of the population mean. You can see by examining the formulas for the upper and lower limits that the width of the interval depends on both the t statistic and the standard error of the mean. Both of these values are related to sample size such that each decreases as sample size increases; however, increases in sample size have the most effect on the standard error. Consider that doubling the sample size in the above example would produce a standard error of 1.81 ($14/\sqrt{60}$) and consequently a much narrower confidence interval. *The bottom line: Increasing sample size will improve the interval estimate of the mean.*

Confidence Intervals for a Comparison Between Two Independent Group Means   The procedure and logic for constructing confidence intervals for a difference between means is similar to that for setting confidence intervals for a single mean. Because our interest is now in the difference between the population means (i.e., "the effect" of our independent variable) we substitute $\overline{X}_1 - \overline{X}_2$ for $\overline{X}$ and use the standard error of the difference between means rather than the standard error of the mean. The 95% confidence interval for the difference between two population means is defined as:

$$CI\,(95\%) = (\overline{X}_1 - \overline{X}_2) \pm (t_{.05})(s_{\overline{X}_1 - \overline{X}_2})$$

where t is found in Table A.2 with degrees of freedom equal to $[(n_1 + n_2) - 2]$ at alpha $= .05$.

The standard error of the difference between means is calculated as:

$$s_{\overline{X}_1 - \overline{X}_2} = \sqrt{\left[\frac{(n_1 - 1)s_1^2 + (n_2 - 1)s_2^2}{n_1 + n_2 - 2}\right]\left[\frac{1}{n_1} + \frac{1}{n_2}\right]}$$

BOX 12.3

INTERPRETING CONFIDENCE INTERVALS FOR A SINGLE MEAN: RINGS AND STAKES

Having calculated the .95 confidence interval for a population mean we may state that:

The odds are 95/100 that the obtained confidence interval contains the true population mean.

As Mulaik, Raju, and Harshman (1997) point out, the confidence interval either does or does not contain the true mean. A .95 probability associated with the confidence interval for a mean refers to the probability of capturing the true population mean if we were to construct many confidence intervals based on different random samples of the same size. That is, confidence intervals around the sample mean tell us what happens if we were to repeat this study under the same conditions (e.g., Estes, 1997). In 95 of 100 replications we would expect to capture the true mean with our confidence intervals.

Having calculated the 95% confidence interval for a population mean we should NOT state that:

The odds are 95/100 that the true mean falls in this interval.

This statement may seem to be identical to the statement above. It isn't. Keep in mind that the value in which we are interested is fixed, a constant; it is a population characteristic or parameter. Intervals are not fixed; they are characteristics of sample data. Intervals are constructed from sample means and measures of dispersion that are going to vary from study to study and consequently, so do confidence intervals.

Howell (2002) provides a nice analogy to help understand how these facts relate to our interpretation of confidence intervals. He suggests we think of the parameter (e.g., the population mean) as a stake and confidence intervals as rings. From the sample data the researcher constructs rings of a specified width that are tossed at the stake. When using the 95% confidence interval, the rings will encircle the stake 95% of the time and will miss it 5% of the time. "The confidence statement is a statement of the probability that the ring has been on target; it is not a statement of the probability that the target (parameter) landed in the ring" (Howell, 2002, p. 208).

As an illustration, let us calculate the confidence limits for the difference between the two means in our example vocabulary research study. The critical *t* value for alpha set at .05 is found in Table A.2 with degrees of freedom equal to $26 + 26 - 2$, or 50. This value is 2.009. We can obtain the standard error of the difference between two means by:

$$s_{\bar{X}_1 - \bar{X}_2} = \sqrt{\left[\frac{(26-1)109.45 + (26-1)150.44}{26 + 26 - 2}\right]\left[\frac{1}{26} + \frac{1}{26}\right]} = 3.16$$

Therefore, the 95% confidence interval for the population mean difference is:

$$CI(95\%) = 18.46 \pm (2.009)(3.16)$$

$$= 18.46 \pm 6.35$$

Thus, the upper limit is 18.46 + 6.35 = 24.81, and the lower limit is 18.46 − 6.35 = 12.11. Thus, we have .95 confidence that the interval 12.11 to 24.81 contains the true population difference for percentage correct on the vocabulary test when comparing older adults and college students.

We are now in a position to model a statement of results for the analysis of mean performance in two groups based on confidence intervals for the effect of the independent variable in the vocabulary study.

> The mean performance on the multiple-choice vocabulary test for college students was 45.58 (SD = 10.46); the mean of the older group was 64.04 (SD = 12.27). Older participants in this study had a greater vocabulary size than did the younger participants. There is a .95 probability that the obtained confidence interval, 12.11 to 24.81, contains the true population mean difference (SE = 3.16).

Note that the value of zero (0.0) is not within the interval. This is important when interpreting confidence intervals for the difference between two means (see Box 12.4).

Confidence Intervals for a Comparison Between Two Means in a Repeated Measures Design   Thus far we have considered experiments involving two independent groups of subjects. As you are aware, experiments also can

---

BOX 12.4

INTERPRETING CONFIDENCE INTERVALS FOR A DIFFERENCE BETWEEN TWO MEANS: LOOKING FOR ZERO

Having calculated a 95% confidence interval for the difference between two means, we can state that:

The odds are 95/100 that the obtained confidence interval contains the true population mean difference or absolute effect size.

The width of the confidence interval provides information about effect size. By using confidence intervals we obtain information about the probable effect size of our independent variable. Obtained effect sizes vary from study to study as characteristics of samples and procedures differ. The confidence interval "specifies a probable range of magnitude for the effect size" (Abelson, 1997, p. 130). It indicates that the effect size likely could be as small as the value of the lower boundary and as large as the value of the upper boundary. Researchers are sometimes amazed to see just how large an interval is needed to specify an effect size with a high degree of confidence (e.g.,

Cohen, 1995). Thus, the narrower the width of the confidence interval the better job we have done at estimating the true effect size of our independent variable. Of course, the size (width) of the confidence interval is directly related to sample size. By increasing sample size we get a better idea of exactly what our effect looks like.

It is important to determine if the confidence interval for a mean difference includes the value of zero. *When zero is included in the confidence interval, we must accept the possibility that the two population means do not differ.* Thus, we cannot conclude that an effect of the independent variable is present. Remember, confidence intervals give us a probable range for our effect. If zero is among the probable values, then we should admit our uncertainty regarding the presence of an effect (e.g., Abelson, 1997). You will see in Chapter 13 that this situation is similar to that when a nonsignificant result is found using NHST.

be carried out by having each subject participate in each condition of the experiment or by "matching" subjects on some measure related to the dependent variable (e.g., IQ scores, weight, etc.). Such experiments are called matched groups designs, within-subjects designs, or repeated measures designs (see Chapter 8). For example, suppose a cognitive psychologist wants to compare people's performance on two different puzzles. Rather than asking two different groups of people to work on each puzzle, she might ask just one group of people to work on both puzzles. (Procedures for presenting materials in a repeated measures design were described in Chapter 8.) All the participants would then provide a score on both puzzles. As you will see, the difference between their scores serves as the measure of interest in a repeated measures design.

Procedures for assessing effect size in a matched groups or repeated measures design are somewhat more complex than those we reviewed for an independent groups design (see Cohen, 1988; and Rosenthal & Rosnow, 1991, for information pertaining to the calculation of d in these cases). One suggestion is to calculate an effect size measure as if the study was an independent groups design and apply Cohen's guidelines (i.e., .20, .50, .80) as before (e.g., Zechmeister & Posavac, 2003).

Confidence intervals, too, can be constructed for the population mean difference in a repeated measures design involving two conditions. However, the underlying calculations change for this situation. Specifically, when each subject is in both conditions of the experiment, t is based on difference scores (see Chapter 13). A difference score is obtained by subtracting the two scores provided by each subject. The mean of the difference scores ("D bar") is defined as:

$$\overline{D} = \Sigma D / N$$

where D = a difference score, and N is the number of difference scores (i.e., number of pairs of scores). Note that $\overline{D} = \overline{X}_1 - \overline{X}_2$.

The standard error of the difference scores ($s_{\overline{D}}$) is defined as:

$$s_{\overline{D}} = \frac{s_D}{\sqrt{N}} \quad \text{where } s_D \text{ is the standard deviation of difference scores}$$

Critical values of t are obtained by consulting Appendix Table A.2 with degrees of freedom equal to $N - 1$. Note that in this case N refers to the number of participants or pairs of scores in the experiment.

The confidence interval for the difference between two means in a repeated measures design can be defined as:

$$CI = \overline{D} \pm (t_{.05})(s_{\overline{D}})$$

In order to illustrate confidence intervals for repeated measures designs, let us follow up on the example of the cognitive psychologist who gave people two different puzzles to solve. Assume that time (seconds) to complete the puzzles was the dependent variable. If 9 people were tested, we can consider the following hypothetical results:

Participant	(Seconds) Puzzle #1	(Seconds) Puzzle #2	D	D^2
1	10	16	6	36
2	18	15	−3	9
3	9	17	8	64
4	14	15	1	1
5	18	15	−3	9
6	11	19	8	64
7	16	18	2	4
8	10	9	−1	1
9	13	19	6	36
			$\Sigma D = 24$	$\Sigma D^2 = 224$

Note that to obtain difference scores (D) that times are subtracted consistently in the same direction (e.g., time for puzzle #2 − time for puzzle #1). The mean of the difference scores is:

$$\overline{D} = \Sigma D/N = 24/9 = 2.67$$

The standard deviation of the difference scores (s_D) is defined as:

$$s_D = \sqrt{\frac{\Sigma D^2 - \frac{(\Sigma D)^2}{N}}{N-1}} = \sqrt{\frac{224 - \frac{24^2}{9}}{8}} = \sqrt{\frac{160}{8}} = \sqrt{20} = 4.47$$

Thus, the standard error of the mean differences ($s_{\overline{D}}$) for these data is:

$$s_{\overline{D}} = \frac{s_D}{\sqrt{N}} = \frac{4.47}{\sqrt{9}} = \frac{4.47}{3} = 1.49$$

The 95% confidence interval for the population mean difference can be calculated as:

$$CI = \overline{D} \pm (t_{.05})(s_{\overline{D}})$$

The value of $t_{.05}$ is found in Table A.2 with 8 degrees of freedom and alpha equal to .05. This value is 2.31.

$$95\% \ CI = (2.67) \pm (2.31)(1.49) = 2.67 \pm 3.44, \text{ or } -.77 \text{ to } 6.11$$

Note that 0.0 is within the confidence interval. Given these data, we cannot conclude that there is a difference in mean (population) times for solving the two puzzles (see Box 12.4).

Confidence Intervals for a Comparison Among Several Independent Group Means   To illustrate the use of confidence intervals to analyze and interpret results when there are more than two means, we consider a study on how infants "grasp the nature of pictures" (DeLoache, Pierroutsakos, Uttal, Rosengren, & Gottlieb, 1998). Have you ever wondered whether infants understand that a picture of an object is not the same thing as the object itself? DeLoache and her colleagues were intrigued by research demonstrating that infants as young as 5 months seem to recognize the similarity between objects and their pictures, but also seem to recognize they're not the same. However, these research findings do not correspond well to anecdotes of infants' behavior toward pictures in which infants and young children try to grasp or pick up the objects represented in pictures, and even try to step into a picture of a shoe! These anecdotal reports suggest that infants and children treat pictured objects as if they are real objects, despite the two-dimensional representation in the picture. In four studies, DeLoache et al. examined "to what extent infants would treat depicted objects as if they were real objects" (p. 205).

Although we will focus on the results presented for DeLoache et al.'s (1998) fourth study, it is helpful to highlight the findings from their first three studies. In Study 1, a structured observation, ten 9-month-old infants were observed as they explored a picture book with "eight highly realistic color photographs of individual objects (common plastic toys)" (p. 206). The results indicated that each infant manually explored at least one picture and 8 of the 10 infants tried to grasp a pictured object at least once (the average was 3.7 attempts). In their second study, the investigators sought to make sure that infants could distinguish between pictured objects and their real-life counterparts. In this study, eight 9-month-olds were presented with the pictured object and the real object simultaneously. Overwhelmingly, the infants reached first for the object instead of the picture (86% of the trials), indicating that infants' grasping at pictures in Study 1 was not because the infants could not discriminate between two- and three-dimensional objects. The purpose of Study 3 was to determine the external validity of these findings by observing the grasping of pictures by "Beng infants from severely impoverished and largely nonliterate families living in a rural village in the West African nation of Côte d'Ivoire (Ivory Coast)" (p. 207). (See Figure 12.2.) The results indicated that Beng infants manually explored and grasped at the pictures (including pictures of objects common in the Beng community) in the same way as American infants.

The purpose of the fourth study was to determine how children's behavior toward pictures changes with age. Three age groups were tested: 9-month-olds, 15-month-olds, and 19-month-olds. Each group had 16 children, 8 girls and 8 boys. In addition to observing children's behaviors of investigating the pictures with their hands (grasping and other investigative behaviors), the researchers also coded instances of pointing at pictured objects. Their results for infants' investigative behaviors are shown in Figure 12.3.

The independent variable, age of the children, is a natural groups design with three levels: 9 months, 15 months, and 19 months. This variable appears on the horizontal axis (*x*-axis). The dependent variable was number of investigative behaviors and the mean number of these behaviors appears on the vertical axis (*y*-axis). As you can see in Figure 12.3, the mean number of investigative

FIGURE 12.2   Infants' understanding of the nature of pictures was examined by observing how they investigate and point to pictured objects. (From DeLoache et al., 1998; used with permission.)

behaviors is highest for 9-month-olds, and much lower for 15-month-olds and 19-month-olds. The other important piece of information in the figure is the "bars" that surround each mean. We can use these bars to make decisions about whether there was an effect of the independent variable, age.

The bars around each mean in Figure 12.3 represent confidence intervals. As you have learned, confidence intervals tell us about the range of values we can expect for a population value. We cannot estimate the population value

FIGURE 12.3   Mean number of investigative behaviors with 95% confidence intervals for 9-month-olds, 15-month-olds, and 19-month-olds. (From DeLoache et al., 1998; used with permission.)

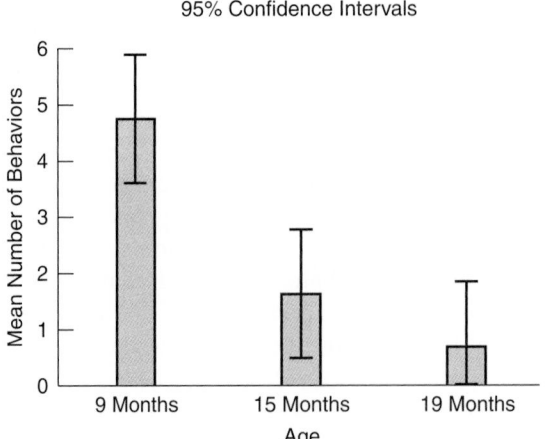

precisely because of sampling error, but we can estimate a range of probable values. The smaller the range of values expressed in our confidence interval, the better is our estimate of the population value. Each of the bars in Figure 12.3 represents a 95% confidence interval. However, the calculation of this interval in a multigroup study differs slightly from that when only one mean is present. Specifically, when calculating the estimated standard error of the mean we may make use of the pooled variance from all the groups in the study. Let us illustrate.

The formula for the 95% confidence interval is the same as it was when there was only one mean:

$$\text{Upper limit of 95\% confidence interval: } \overline{X} + [t_{.05}][s_{\overline{X}}]$$

$$\text{Lower limit of 95\% confidence interval: } \overline{X} - [t_{.05}][s_{\overline{X}}]$$

However, the calculation of $s_{\overline{X}}$ differs from that with one mean; so, too, does the calculation of the degrees of freedom for the critical value of t. To estimate the standard error of the mean we may pool the variances from the various groups to obtain one measure of variability. In this case we pool the information from as many groups as we have in the study. When the comparison involves two or more means from independent groups, the standard error of the mean is calculated as follows. First, we find the standard deviation based on the pooled variance:[1]

$$s_{\text{pooled}} = \sqrt{\frac{(n_1 - 1)s_1^2 + (n_2 - 1)s_2^2 + (n_3 - 1)s_3^2 + \cdots}{(n_1 - 1) + (n_2 - 1) + (n_3 - 1) + \cdots}}$$

When sample sizes are equal, the estimated standard error is then defined as:

$$s_{\overline{X}} = \frac{s_{\text{pooled}}}{\sqrt{n}} \quad \text{where } n = \text{sample size for each group}$$

Degrees of freedom are then calculated as $k(n - 1)$, where k is equal to the number of independent groups.

Looking again at Figure 12.3, we can see that for 9-month-olds, the mean number of investigative behaviors for the sample was 4.75. The expression $[t_{.05}][s_{\overline{X}}]$ in the equation for the 95% confidence interval in this analysis is 1.14. We can be 95% confident that the interval 3.61 and 5.89 (4.75 ± 1.14) contains the population mean for 9-month-olds. Thus, the sample of 16 nine-month-old infants in this study is used to estimate the average number of investigative behaviors that would be demonstrated if the larger population of 9-month-olds was tested in this situation. For 15-month-olds, the mean number of investigative behaviors was 1.63, and we can be 95% confident that the interval between

---

[1]The pooled estimate of the population standard deviation is equivalent to the square root of the mean square error in a between-groups analysis of variance (ANOVA). That is, $s_{\text{pooled}} = \sqrt{MS_{\text{error}}}$. See Chapter 13 for discussion of ANOVA.

Key Concept

In a correlational study our primary interest is not in the difference between the means but in the relationship between the sets of scores. The major descriptive techniques for correlational data are the construction of a **scatterplot** and the calculation of a *correlation coefficient*. A scatterplot describes the relationship between the two sets of scores. The correlation coefficient provides a quantitative summary of the relationship observed in the scatterplot. It is important to examine carefully the scatterplot before attempting to interpret a correlation coefficient. We first illustrate the construction of scatterplots and then show how a correlation coefficient is obtained and interpreted.

Drawing a Scatterplot The nature of a correlation can be represented graphically using a scatterplot. Scores for the two variables are represented on the x-axis and y-axis. Each individual has a value (or score) for each variable (e.g., ratings of worry and concentration difficulty). A scatterplot shows the intersecting points for each pair of scores. The magnitude or degree of correlation is seen in a scatterplot by determining how well the points correspond to a straight line; stronger correlations more clearly resemble a straight line of points. Figure 12.5 shows three different scatterplots. The correlation is stronger in the first (*a*) and third (*c*) panels than in the second (*b*) panel because the points in (*a*) and (*c*) more closely approximate a straight line.

The direction of a correlation can be seen in the scatterplot by noting how the points are arranged. When the pattern of points seems to move from the lower left corner to the upper right [panel (*a*)], the correlation is positive (low scores on the x-axis go with low scores on the y-axis and high scores on the x-axis go with high scores on the y-axis). When the pattern of points is from the upper left to the lower right [panel (*c*)], the correlation is negative (low scores on the x-axis go with high scores on the y-axis and high scores on the x-axis go with low scores on the y-axis).

FIGURE 12.5 Three scatterplots illustrating a positive (*a*), zero (*b*), and negative (*c*) correlation between scores on two variables: X and Y.

(a) Positive relationship (b) Zero relationship (c) Negative relationship

Assume that 20 college students provided responses to the two questions we described above. Assume further that the data were carefully inspected for errors and any anomalies and that the data were judged to be clean.

We wish to find out whether scores on one measure are related to (i.e., "go with") scores on the second measure. Is reported worry about grades related to self-reported difficulty concentrating on exams? To find out we can construct a scatterplot showing the relationship between the scores. To do this we first identify each person's responses on the two 10-point scales. Data from our hypothetical study look like this:

Respondent	Worry (X)	Concentration difficulty (Y)
1	7	5
2	4	4
3	5	3
4	6	7
5	2	2
6	3	4
7	5	7
8	4	5
9	8	6
10	9	8
11	6	6
12	5	3
13	4	4
14	6	5
15	2	4
16	6	8
17	5	4
18	7	8
19	8	4
20	7	9

A scatterplot is constructed by drawing a graph showing the intersection of the two measures from each respondent. The axes on the graph represent the two measures of interest. By convention, the measure of the behavior that "comes first" or that is used to predict the second behavior is placed on the horizontal or x-axis. The second behavior or that which is predicted by the first is placed on the vertical or y-axis. In many situations such a decision is easy. If you were correlating volunteers' blood alcohol levels and a measure of their performance on a driving simulator, we would easily see that alcohol was first consumed and then simulated driving performance was measured. Blood alcohol levels would be used to predict performance on a driving simulator. In other situations the decision is less easy. Does worry about grades come before difficulty concentrating on exams? Or does difficulty concentrating on exams lead to worry about grades? We believe a case could be made for either.

FIGURE 12.6   Two examples of nonlinear relationships between two variables: X and Y.

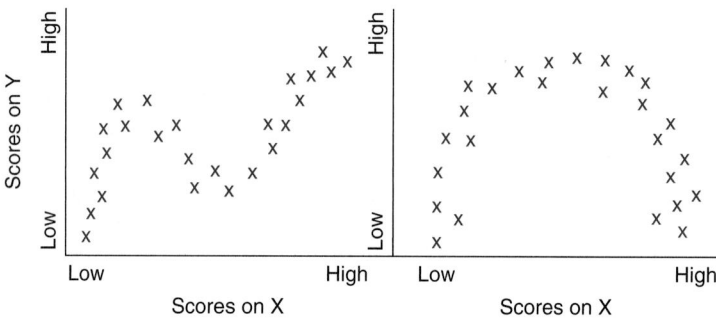

Key Concept ➤ We want to examine the scatterplot for possible trends. More specifically, we look to see if there is evidence of a **linear trend** in the scatterplot. Simply, a linear trend is one that may be summarized by a straight line. As you have seen, scatterplots (*a*) and (*c*) in Figure 12.5 show evidence of a linear trend. It is also possible to see no trend in the scatterplot. In this case, scores on one measure are just as likely to go with low, middle, or high scores on the second measure. If there is no discernible trend in the graph, as in the middle panel of Figure 12.5, then we can conclude there is no relationship between the sets of scores. Note that in this case we are not able to use our knowledge of scores on one measure to make predictions about scores on the second measure.

Finally, it is also possible to see a relationship in the scatterplot, but one that is not linear. Figure 12.6 provides two examples of nonlinear relationships between variables. We may judge these relationships to be interesting and even worthy of further investigation; however, a nonlinear relationship poses serious problems of interpretation for a correlation coefficient. Consequently, if the trend in the scatterplot is nonlinear, a correlation coefficient should not be calculated. Outliers in a scatterplot also pose problems when interpreting a correlation coefficient.

Figure 12.7 shows a scatterplot describing the relationship between scores on the worry (X) and concentration difficulty (Y) measures from our hypothetical survey. Since we really don't know in this case which factor "comes first," we have arbitrarily put the measure of worry on the *x*-axis and the measure of concentration difficulty on the *y*-axis in the scatterplot found in Figure 12.7. That is, we are using the measure of worry to predict the measure of concentration. Can you see a trend in the scatterplot? Is it generally linear?

Calculating a Correlation Coefficient   The direction and strength of a correlation are determined by computing a *correlation coefficient*. The correlation coefficient is a quantitative index of how well we are able to predict one set of scores (e.g., concentration ratings) using another set of scores (e.g., worry

FIGURE 12.7   Scatterplot showing relationship between scores on self-report measure of degree of worry about grades (X) and self-report measure of difficulty concentrating during an exam (Y).

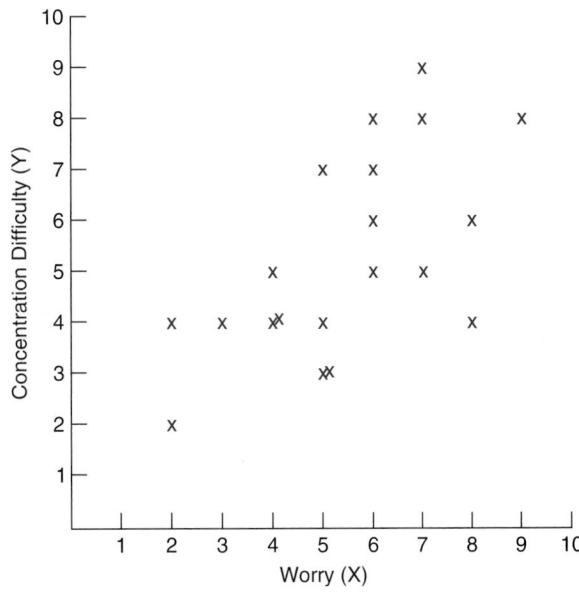

ratings). A correlation coefficient expresses the relationship between two variables in terms of both the direction and the magnitude of that relationship.

Key Concept

The direction of a correlation coefficient can be either positive or negative. A **positive correlation** indicates that, as the values for one measure increase, the values for the other measure also increase [see panel (*a*) in Figure 12.5]. As we've seen, measures of smoking and lung disease are positively correlated (more smoking, more lung disease). Another predictive relationship concerns Scholastic Aptitude Test (SAT) scores: SAT scores and college students' first-semester GPAs are positively correlated. Thus, we can predict that students with higher SAT scores should have higher first-semester GPAs, and students with lower SAT scores should have lower first-semester GPAs. With correlations, the "reverse" prediction can be made too. If we know only the first-semester GPAs of students, we can "predict" what their SAT scores were prior to entering college. Students with higher GPAs would be more likely to have higher SAT scores, and students with lower GPAs would be likely to have lower SAT scores.

Key Concept

In a **negative correlation,** as the value of one measure increases, the value of the other measure decreases [see panel (*c*) in Figure 12.5]. A national survey of high school seniors showed a negative correlation between the amount of time spent watching TV and the number of correct answers on an academic achievement test (Keith, Reimers, Fehrmann, Pottebaum, & Aubrey, 1986). Students who spent more time watching TV answered fewer questions correctly on an achievement test. What about the reverse prediction? Based on this finding, if you knew that a student scored very high on the achievement test, would you predict that the student had spent "a lot" of time or "a little" time watching TV?

Is the relationship between measures of worry and concentration difficulty seen in Figure 12.7 positive or negative?

The magnitude (degree) of a correlation coefficient can range in absolute values from 0.0 to 1.00. A value of 0.0 indicates there is no correlation and there is no basis for making predictions. The relationship between intelligence and mental illness, for example, exhibits a zero correlation; we cannot predict the likelihood that a person will become mentally ill by knowing the person's IQ (nor can we predict a person's IQ based on his or her mental health). A value of +1.00 indicates a perfect positive correlation, and a value of −1.00 indicates a perfect negative correlation. When a correlation coefficient is either +1.00 or −1.00, all the points in the scatterplot fall on a straight line and we can make predictions with absolute confidence. Values between 0 and 1.00 indicate predictive relationships of intermediate strength and, therefore, we have less ability to predict confidently. Remember, the sign of the correlation signifies only its direction; a correlation coefficient of −.46 indicates a stronger (more predictive) relationship than one of +.20. (*Note:* In practice, only the sign of negative correlation coefficients is indicated; a coefficient without a plus or minus sign is treated as positive, that is, +.20 = .20.)

A formula for calculating the most commonly used correlation coefficient, the Pearson Product-Moment Correlation Coefficient, r, is:

$$ r = \frac{\Sigma XY - \dfrac{(\Sigma X)(\Sigma Y)}{N}}{\sqrt{\left[\Sigma X^2 - \dfrac{(\Sigma X)^2}{N}\right]\left[\Sigma Y^2 - \dfrac{(\Sigma Y)^2}{N}\right]}} $$

where

X = raw scores for the first variable

Y = raw scores for the second variable

ΣXY = sum of the cross products of X and Y; that is, multiply each X and Y and then sum these products

N = number of pairs of scores

Using the above formula, the correlation coefficient for the relationship between worry and concentration difficulty based on the 20 students in our hypothetical study is .62. As indicated in the scatterplot in Figure 12.7, low scores on the worry measures tend to go with low scores on the concentration measure, and high scores with high scores. We may state that the two variables are positively related. More specifically, we can say that the more students worry, the more likely they are to have difficulty concentrating during exams. But can we say that worrying *causes* students to have difficulty concentrating?

Correlation and Causality   As you may recall from our discussion of correlations in Chapters 4 and 5, "correlation does not imply causation." Knowing that two variables are correlated does not allow us to infer that one causes the other (even if one precedes the other in time). It may be that worry about grades causes concentration difficulty during exams, or that the experience of difficulty while concentrating during exams causes worry about grades. In addition, a *spurious relationship* exists when a third variable can account for the positive correlation between worry about grades and concentration difficulty during exams. For example, number of hours employed might serve as a third variable that can account for this relationship. As number of hours employed increases, students might experience greater concern about grades and greater difficulty concentrating during exams.

Conclusion   A Pearson Product-Moment Correlation Coefficient may be used to summarize the relationship between two variables. It is important, however, to inspect the scatterplot of the two variables prior to calculating a Pearson r to make sure that the relationship is best summarized with a straight line, that is, that there is a linear trend. As the correlation coefficient approaches 1.00, the relationship between the two variables observed in the scatterplot approaches a straight line, and our ability to predict one variable based on knowledge of another increases.

Stage 3: Constructing a Confidence Interval for a Correlation

- We can obtain a confidence interval estimate of the population correlation, ρ, just as we did for the population mean, μ.

A Pearson r calculated from a sample is an estimate of the correlation in the population just as a sample mean is an estimate of a population mean (μ). The population correlation is symbolized with the Greek letter rho (ρ). Moreover, just as a sample mean is subject to sampling error or variation from sample to sample, so, too, is a correlation coefficient. Thus, in some situations we may wish to obtain an interval estimate of the population value, ρ, just as we did for the population value, μ. In other words, we can calculate a confidence interval for ρ. We will leave this topic, however, for books providing more comprehensive treatment of statistical procedures (e.g., Zechmeister & Posavac, 2003).

SUMMARY

There are three distinct, but related stages of data analysis: getting to know the data, summarizing the data, and confirming what the data reveal. In the first stage we want to become familiar with the data, inspecting them carefully, checking for errors and anomalous values. We want to be particularly sensitive to the presence of outliers, extreme values that just don't seem to go with the other values. Creating a stem-and-leaf display is a good way to visualize the distribution of numbers in a data set and to detect outliers. In the second stage we want to summarize the data set using descriptive statistics and graphical displays. Measures of central tendency (mean, median, mode) and measures of dispersion or variability (range and standard deviation) are particularly useful at this point. When a study involves the effect of an independent variable on a dependent variable, it is important to describe "how much of an effect" the independent variable had on the dependent variable. Measures of effect size are important when concluding meta-analyses, which summarize the effect of a particular variable across many different studies. An important effect size measure when two means are compared is Cohen's *d*.

In the third stage of data analysis, confirming what the data reveal, we determine what we may reasonably claim based on the evidence obtained in our study. There are two complementary approaches to this stage of analysis: null hypothesis significance testing (NHST) and the construction of confidence intervals. Both approaches rely on estimates of sampling variability to help a researcher make decisions about the true values of population parameters. Although the mean of a random sample is a good point estimate of the population mean, there will be variation ("error") in this estimate from sample to sample due to random or chance factors. The estimated standard error of the mean assesses how well a sample mean estimates the population mean. NHST focuses the researcher on the probability that the obtained results are "due to chance." A confidence interval specifies a range of values that have a certain probability (usually 95%) of containing a population value (e.g., the population mean). Confidence intervals are directly analogous to the "margin of error" that you may have heard in media reports of survey results. The narrower the interval the better is our estimate of the population value; increasing sample size will improve the interval estimate.

Confidence intervals for the difference between two means provide evidence for the difference between the population means represented by the two sample means in a study. The width of the interval yields information concerning the probable effect size of an independent variable. When constructing confidence intervals for a difference between two means, if the interval includes the value of zero then we do not want to say that an effect is present. In other words, if zero is within the interval we should admit our uncertainty regarding the effect of the variable. Confidence intervals can be constructed for both independent groups and repeated measures designs.

When there are three or more means, confidence intervals are constructed for each mean. Conclusions about differences between means in a multigroup study are made by examining whether intervals overlap. When intervals do not overlap we can be confident that the population means estimated by these sample means do in fact differ. However, when intervals overlap, we do NOT say that there is no difference between population means; rather, we must admit uncertainty about the true difference and wait until more research is done.

A correlational study is frequently carried out when the researcher's goal is that of prediction, for example, when predicting test performance from a paper-and-pencil measure of test anxiety. A correlation exists when two different measures of the same people, events, or things vary together. Just as we do when a study involves a comparison between means, the data from a correlational study should be carefully inspected and summarized. A scatterplot describes the relationship between two sets of scores; a correlation coefficient produces a quantitative summary of the relationship observed in the scatterplot. More specifically, the correlation coefficient describes how well the data in the scatterplot fit a straight line. The value of a correlation coefficient may vary from −1.00 to +1.00. The sign of the correlation coefficient (− or +) indicates the direction of the relationship; the absolute value of the coefficient (0.0 to 1.00) indicates the magnitude of the relationship. The closer the correlation coefficient approaches 1.00 (positive or negative), the more the points in the scatterplot fall on a straight line, and the stronger is the relationship.

A positive correlation exists when values for one measure increase as values on a second measure increase. In a negative correlation, as values of one measure increase, values on a second measure decrease. Knowing that there is a relationship (correlation) between two measures permits a researcher to predict scores on one measure based on knowledge of scores on a second measure. The closer the correlation coefficient is to 1.00, the better is the ability to predict. It is important to keep in mind that correlation alone is not evidence for a causal relationship between variables: correlation does not imply causality.

KEY CONCEPTS

stages of data analysis
   getting to know the data
   summarizing the data
   confirming what the data reveal
stem-and-leaf display
measures of central tendency
   mode
   median
   mean
measures of dispersion (variability)
   range

standard deviation
standard error of the mean
estimated standard error of the
   mean
confidence interval for a population
   parameter
scatterplot
linear trend
positive correlation
negative correlation

REVIEW QUESTIONS

1 Identify the three major stages of data analysis and indicate what specific things a researcher typically will be looking to do at each stage.

2 What does a researcher attempt to do when constructing an "analysis story" to go with the results of a study?

3 Why must a researcher have a good knowledge of research methodology and statistical procedures to be able to use computer software to analyze results of a study?

4 Construct a stem-and-leaf display for the following set of numbers; then, report what you have learned by examining the data in this way. 36,42,25,26,26,21,22,43,40,69,21, 21,23,31,32,32,34,37,37,38,43,20,21,24,23,42,24,21,27,29,34,30,41,25,28.

5 Calculate the mean, median, and mode for the following data set: 7,7,2,4,2,4,5,6,4,5. Describe the advantages and disadvantages of the three measures of central tendency: mean, median, mode.

6 Calculate the standard deviation for the data set in Question 5. What does the standard deviation as a measure of variability tell you?

7 What does the estimated standard error of the mean tell you about a sample mean?

8 A study was done to investigate a newly created drug to increase memory performance. The study was done with rats. The dependent measure was number of errors made while learning a maze after being injected with the memory drug or a saline solution (control). Rats were randomly assigned to either the memory-enhancing drug or the control. A total of 30 rats was tested; there were 15 in each group. The mean (and standard deviation) for the drug group was 11.7 (4.7); that of the control group was 15.1 (5.1). (Lower numbers mean better performance.) What is the effect size for this study?

9 Why is a confidence interval also called a "margin of error"?

10 A random sample of 25 students was asked their opinion of the food service in the college dining hall. Students used a 7-point scale (1 = *horrible*, 7 = *great*) to indicate their opinion. The mean rating for the 25 students was 4.7 with a standard deviation (s) of 1.2.

   A What is the 95% confidence interval for the population mean?

   B Describe in words what the confidence interval tells you about the population mean.

11 What is the 95% confidence interval for the difference between the two means reported in Question 8? What is the correct interpretation of this interval?

12 How do you use confidence intervals to reach a conclusion about differences among means in a study with three or more means?

13 When inspecting data depicted in a scatterplot, why is it important to look for a linear trend in the data?

14 A researcher investigates whether there is a relationship between vocabulary size and performance on a reading comprehension test. Each of 15 sixth grade students is given both a vocabulary test and a reading comprehension test (both tests are scored in terms of percentage correct). The results for the 15 school children are (with vocabulary scores given first): 44,67; 24,33; 67,45; 75,54; 34,45; 88,79; 57,67; 44,32; 87,95; 77,67; 87,78; 54,67; 90,78; 36,55; 79,91. Draw a scatterplot and calculate a correlation coefficient for these data.

15 Explain whether you could use the correlation you computed in Question 14 to support the claim that increasing vocabulary size causes increases in reading comprehension.

CHALLENGE QUESTIONS

1 A cognitive psychologist investigates the effect of four presentation conditions on the retention of a lengthy passage describing the Battle of Gettysburg. Let us simply denote the presentation conditions as A, B, C, and D. Sixty-four ($N = 64$) college students are randomly assigned in equal numbers to the four conditions ($n = 16$). Memory is tested after students hear the passage read aloud one time. The dependent

variable is number of idea units recalled in the immediate written recall of the passage. The mean recall and standard deviation for each of the four presentation conditions are as follows:

	A	B	C	D
M	16.4	29.9	24.6	19.5
SD	4.6	7.1	5.9	6.3

A Calculate the 95% confidence intervals for the population means estimated by the four sample means.

B Interpret the pattern of confidence intervals by stating what we may conclude about the differences between the various population means.

2 A developmental psychologist investigates the effect of mothers' carrying behavior on infant sleep patterns. Specifically, the investigator solicits help from 40 mothers of newborns. The psychologist trains 20 mothers in a carrying method that presses the newborn's head against the mother's breast; the other 20 mothers are not instructed in a particular carrying method. All mothers are trained to record the number of hours their newborn sleeps each 24-hour period. Records are kept for 3 months in both groups. The mean 24-hour sleep period for infants in the instructed group was 12.6 (SD = 5.1); in the uninstructed group the mean was 10.1 (SD = 6.3).

A Calculate the 95% confidence interval for the difference between the two means.

B What may be said about the effect of training based on an examination of the confidence interval for this experiment?

C What is the effect size for this experiment? Interpret the effect size measure based on Cohen's guidelines for small, medium, and large effects.

3 A researcher asks college students to play a demanding video game while listening to classical music and while listening to hard rock. All of the 10 students in the experiment play the video game for 15 minutes under each of the music conditions. Half of the students play while listening first to classical music and then to hard rock music; the other half perform with the types of music in the reverse order (see Chapter 8 for information on counterbalancing in a repeated measures design). The dependent variable is the number of correct "hits" in the game over the 15-minute period. The scores for the 10 students are:

Student	Classical	Hard rock
1	46	76
2	67	69
3	55	51
4	63	78
5	49	66
6	76	67
7	58	63
8	75	75
9	69	78
10	77	85

A Calculate the means for each condition. What trend do you see in the comparison of means?

B Calculate the standard error of the difference scores.

C Find the 95% confidence interval for the difference between the two means in this repeated measures design.

D State a conclusion regarding the effect of type of music on performance given the analysis of these results.

4 A social psychologist seeks to determine the relationship between a paper-and-pencil measure of prejudice and people's attitudes toward racial profiling as a crime deterrent. At the beginning of the semester students in a general psychology class are asked to complete six different questionnaires. Among the questionnaires is a measure of prejudice. Later in the semester students are invited to take part in an experiment examining attitudes about criminal behavior and law enforcement tactics. As part of the experiment students complete a questionnaire asking about attitudes toward racial profiling as a crime deterrent. The researcher wishes to find out if scores on the prejudice measure obtained earlier will predict people's attitudes about racial profiling. Higher scores on the prejudice measure indicate greater prejudice and higher scores on the profiling scale indicate greater support for racial profiling. Scores on both measures are obtained for 22 students as follows:

Student	1	2	3	4	5	6	7	8	9	10	11
Prejudice	19	15	22	12	9	19	16	21	24	13	10
Profiling	7	6	9	6	4	7	8	9	5	5	7

Student	12	13	14	15	16	17	18	19	20	21	22
Prejudice	12	17	23	19	23	18	11	10	19	24	22
Profiling	4	8	9	10	10	5	6	4	8	8	7

(Contd.)

A Draw a scatterplot showing the relationship between these two measures.

B Inspect the scatterplot and comment on the presence or absence of a linear trend in the data.

C Calculate a correlation coefficient for these data and comment on the direction and strength of the relationship.

D On the basis of the correlational analysis the researcher concludes that prejudicial thinking causes people to support racial profiling by law enforcement agencies. Comment on this conclusion based on what you know about the nature of correlational evidence.

Answer to Challenge Question 1

A Begin by calculating s_{pooled} for the four groups, being sure to note that the problem provides the standard deviation for each group and the formula for spooled makes use of the variances. Thus each standard deviation must be squared before multiplying by n − 1. The value of s_{pooled} is 6.04. The estimated standard error of the mean ($s_{\overline{X}}$) is, therefore, $6.04/\sqrt{n}$ or 1.51. The critical value of t at the .05 level is 2.00 (60 *df*) from Table A.2. The confidence intervals for the means are:

A 16.4 ± (2.00)(1.51) = 13.38 to 19.42

B 29.9 ± (2.00)(1.51) = 26.88 to 32.92

C 24.6 ± (2.00)(1.51) = 21.58 to 27.62

D 19.5 ± (2.00)(1.51) = 16.48 to 22.52

B (HINT: It may be helpful to draw a figure with columns representing the mean performance in each group and bars around the means corresponding to the confidence intervals. You may also want to review the information found in Box 12.5.) It can be seen that the A interval overlaps only the D interval. The C and D intervals overlap. Although the observed pattern of group means is our best estimate of the locations of the population values, the confidence intervals also provide information about the precision of our estimates. On the basis of these data we may conclude that the population mean estimated by sample mean A differs from the population means represented by B and C. We will want to withhold judgment about the difference between A and D. We may also conclude that population means B and D differ, but admit we are uncertain about the true difference between B and C.

CHAPTER THIRTEEN

Data Analysis and Interpretation: Part II. Tests of Statistical Significance and the Analysis Story

CHAPTER OUTLINE

OVERVIEW

In Chapter 12 we introduced the three major stages of data analysis: *getting to know the data, summarizing the data, and confirming what the data tell us*. In the final stage of data analysis we evaluate whether we have sufficient evidence to make a claim about behavior. What, given these data, can we say about behavior? This stage is sometimes called *confirmatory data analysis* (e.g., Tukey, 1977). At this point we seek confirmation for what the data are telling us. In Chapter 12 we emphasized the use of confidence intervals to confirm what the data tell us. In this chapter we continue our discussion of confirmatory data analysis by focusing on tests of statistical significance, or what is more formally known as *null hypothesis significance testing* (NHST).

NHST is the most common approach to performing confirmatory data analysis. Nevertheless, tests of statistical significance have received persistent criticism (e.g., Cohen, 1995; Hunter, 1997; Loftus, 1991, 1996; Meehl, 1967; Schmidt, 1996), and for good reason. Researchers have been misusing (and misinterpreting) them for decades, all the time ignoring warnings that they were doing so (e.g., Finch, Thomason, & Cumming, 2002). There are critics who suggest we discard NHST altogether (e.g., Hunter, 1997; Schmidt, 1996). However, the majority of experts suggest that we continue to use NHST but be cautious about its use (e.g., Abelson, 1995, 1997; Chow, 1988; Estes, 1997; Greenwald, Gonzalez, Harris, & Guthrie, 1996; Hagen, 1997; Krueger, 2001; Mulaik et al., 1997). Whatever the outcome of this debate within the psychology community, there is nearly universal agreement on the need (a) to understand exactly what it is that NHST can and cannot do, and (b) to increase our use of alternative methods of data analysis, especially the use of confidence intervals and the reporting of effect sizes. Sometimes these alternative techniques will supplant NHST, at other times they will complement NHST.

In what immediately follows we first provide an overview of NHST. Next we discuss the important concepts of experimental sensitivity and statistical power. Then we illustrate the NHST approach to data analysis using the same data we used in Chapter 12 to construct confidence intervals for the difference between two means. By using the same data we can contrast the information obtained from NHST with that provided by confidence intervals. We point out what we can and cannot say based on NHST and suggest that information obtained from NHST can complement information obtained with confidence intervals. Finally, we provide some recommendations for you to follow when evaluating evidence for a claim about behavior involving two means and illustrate how to create an analysis story for your study.

The most common technique of confirmatory data analysis associated with studies involving more than two groups is a form of NHST called *analysis of variance (ANOVA)*. The rationale for using an ANOVA, the computational procedures associated with ANOVA, and the interpretation of ANOVA results are discussed in the second half of this chapter.

Null Hypothesis Significance Testing (NHST)

- Null hypothesis testing is used to determine whether mean differences among groups in an experiment are greater than the differences that are expected simply because of error variation.
- The first step in null hypothesis testing is to assume that the groups do not differ—that is, that the independent variable did not have an effect (the null hypothesis).
- Probability theory is used to estimate the likelihood of the experiment's observed outcome, assuming the null hypothesis is true.
- A statistically significant outcome is one that has a small likelihood of occurring if the null hypothesis is true.
- Because decisions about the outcome of an experiment are based on probabilities, Type I (rejecting a true null hypothesis) or Type II (failing to reject a false null hypothesis) errors may occur.

Key Concept

Statistical inference is both inductive and indirect. It is inductive because we draw general conclusions about populations on the basis of the specific samples we test in our experiments, as we do when constructing confidence intervals. However, unlike the approach using confidence intervals, this form of statistical inference is also indirect because it begins by assuming the null hypothesis. The **null hypothesis (H_0)** is the assumption that the independent variable has had no effect. Once we make this assumption, we can use probability theory to determine the likelihood of obtaining this difference (or a larger difference) observed in our experiment *IF* the null hypothesis were true. If this likelihood is small, we reject the null hypothesis and conclude that the independent variable did have an effect on the dependent variable. Outcomes that lead us to reject the null hypothesis are said to be *statistically significant.* A statistically significant outcome means only that the difference we obtained in our experiment is larger than would be expected if error variation alone (i.e., chance) were responsible for the outcome (see Box 13.1).

Key Concept

A statistically significant outcome is one that has only a small likelihood of occurring if the null hypothesis were true. But just how small is small enough? Although there is no definitive answer to this important question, the consensus among members of the scientific community is that outcomes associated with probabilities of less than 5 times out of 100 (or .05) if the null hypothesis were true are judged to be statistically significant. The probability we elect to use to indicate an outcome is statistically significant is called the **level of significance.** The level of significance is indicated by the Greek letter alpha (α). Thus, we speak of the .05 level of significance, the .10 level, or the .01 level, which we report as $\alpha = .05$, $\alpha = .10$, $\alpha = .01$, respectively.

Just what do our results tell us when they are statistically significant? The most useful information we gain is that we know that something interesting has happened. More specifically, we know that the smaller the exact probability of the observed outcome, the greater is the probability that an exact replication

BOX 13.1

HEADS OR TAILS? TOSSING COINS AND NULL HYPOTHESES

Perhaps you can appreciate the process of statistical inference by considering the following dilemma. A friend, with a sly smile, offers to toss a coin with you to see who pays for the meal you just enjoyed at a restaurant. Your friend just happens to have a coin ready to toss. Now it would be convenient if you could directly test whether your friend's coin is biased (by asking to look at it). Not willing to appear untrusting, however, the best you can do is test your friend's coin indirectly by assuming it is not biased and seeing if you consistently get outcomes that differ from the expected 50:50 split of heads and tails. If the coin does not exhibit the ordinary 50:50 split (after many trials of flipping the coin), you might surmise that your friend is trying, by slightly underhanded means, to get you to pay for the meal. Similarly, we would like to make a direct test of statistical

significance for an obtained outcome in our experiments. The best we can do, however, is to compare our obtained outcome with the expected outcome of no difference between frequencies of heads and tails. *The key to understanding null hypothesis testing is to recognize that we can use the laws of probability to estimate the likelihood of an outcome only when we assume that chance factors are the sole cause of that outcome.* This is not different from flipping your friend's coin a number of times to make your conclusion. You know that, based on chance alone, 50% of the time the coin should come up heads, and 50% of the time it should be tails. After many coin tosses, anything different from this probable outcome would lead you to conclude that something other than chance is working—that is, your friend's coin is biased.

will produce a statistically significant finding. But we must be careful what we mean by this statement. Researchers sometimes mistakenly say that when a result occurs with $p < .05$ that "this outcome will be obtained 95/100 times if the study is repeated." This is simply not true. Simply achieving statistical significance (i.e., $p < .05$) does not tell us about the probability of replicating the results. For example, a result just below .05 probability (and thus statistically significant) has only about a 50:50 chance of being statistically significant (i.e., $p < .05$) if replicated exactly (Greenwald et al., 1996). On the other hand, knowing the exact probability of the results does convey information about what will happen if a replication were done. The smaller the exact probability of an initial finding, the greater the probability that an exact replication will produce a statistically significant ($p < .05$) finding (e.g., Posavac, 2002). Consequently, and as recommended by APA, *always report the exact probability of results when carrying out NHST.*

You must choose the level of significance before you begin your experiment, not after you have done the statistical analysis. Choosing the level of significance before doing the analysis allows you to avoid the temptation of using the probability of your obtained outcome as the level of significance you would have chosen. Strictly speaking, there are only two conclusions possible when you do an inferential statistics test: you either *reject* the null hypothesis or you *fail to reject* the null hypothesis. Note that we did *not* say that one alternative is to accept the null hypothesis. Let us explain.

When we conduct an experiment and observe the effect of the independent variable is not statistically significant, we do not reject the null hypothesis. However, we do not necessarily accept the null hypothesis of no difference either. There may have been some factor in our experiment that prevented us from observing an effect of the independent variable (e.g., ambiguous instructions to subjects, poor operationalization of the independent variable). As we will show later, too small a sample often is a major reason why a null hypothesis is not rejected. Although we recognize the logical impossibility of proving that a null hypothesis is true, we also must have some method of deciding which independent variables are not worth pursuing. NHST can help with that decision. A result that is not statistically significant suggests we should be cautious about concluding that the independent variable influenced behavior in more than a trivial way. At this point you will want to seek more information, for example, by noting the size of the sample and the effect size (see next section, Experimental Sensitivity and Statistical Power).

There is a troublesome aspect to the process of statistical inference and our reliance on probabilities for making decisions. No matter what decision you reach, and no matter how carefully you reach it, there is always some chance you are making an error. The two possible "states of the world" and the two possible decisions an experimenter can reach are listed in Table 13.1. The two "states of the world" are that the independent variable either does or does not have an effect on behavior. The two possible correct decisions the researcher can make are represented by the upper-left and lower-right cells of the table. If the independent variable does have an effect, the researcher should reject the null hypothesis; if it does not, the researcher should fail to reject the null hypothesis.

The two potential errors (Type I error and Type II error) are represented by the other two cells of Table 13.1. These errors arise because of the probabilistic nature of statistical inference. When we decide an outcome is statistically significant because the outcome's probability of occurring under the null hypothesis is less than .05, we acknowledge that in 5 out of every 100 tests, the outcome could occur even if the null hypothesis were true. The level of significance, therefore, represents the probability of making a **Type I error:** rejecting the null hypothesis when it is true. The probability of making a Type I error can be reduced simply by making the level of significance more stringent, perhaps .01. The problem with this approach is that it increases the likelihood of making a **Type II error:** failing to reject the null hypothesis when it is false.

Key Concepts

TABLE 13.1 POSSIBLE OUTCOMES OF DECISION MAKING WITH INFERENTIAL STATISTICS

	States of the world	
	Null hypothesis is false.	Null hypothesis is true.
Reject null hypothesis	Correct decision	Type I error
Fail to reject null hypothesis	Type II error	Correct decision

The problem of Type I errors and Type II errors should not immobilize us, but it should help us understand why researchers rarely use the word "prove" when they describe the results of an experiment that involved tests of statistical significance. Instead, they describe the results as "consistent with the hypothesis," or "confirming the hypothesis," or "supporting the hypothesis." These more tentative statements are a way of indirectly acknowledging that the possibility of making a Type I error or a Type II error always exists. The .05 level of significance represents a compromise position that allows us to strike a balance and avoid making too many of either type of error. The problem of Type I errors and Type II errors also reminds us that *statistical inference can never replace replication as the best test of the reliability of an experimental outcome.*

EXPERIMENTAL SENSITIVITY AND STATISTICAL POWER

- Sensitivity refers to the likelihood that an experiment will detect the effect of an independent variable when, in fact, the independent variable truly has an effect.
- Power refers to the likelihood that a statistical test will allow researchers to reject correctly the null hypothesis of no group differences.
- The power of statistical tests is influenced by the level of statistical significance, the size of the treatment effect, and the sample size.
- The primary way for researchers to increase statistical power is to increase sample size.
- Repeated measures designs are likely to be more sensitive and to have more statistical power than independent groups designs because estimates of error variation are likely to be smaller in repeated measures designs.
- Type II errors are more common in psychological research using NHST than are Type I errors.
- When results are not statistically significant (i.e., $p > .05$), it is incorrect to conclude that the null hypothesis is true.

Key Concept

The *sensitivity of an experiment* is the likelihood that it will detect an effect of the independent variable if the independent variable does, indeed, have an effect (see Chapter 8). An experiment is said to have sensitivity; a statistical test is said to have **power**. The power of a statistical test is the probability that the null hypothesis will be rejected when it is false. The null hypothesis is the hypothesis of "no difference," and, thus, is false and should be rejected when the independent variable has made a difference. Recall that we defined a Type II error as the probability of failing to reject the null hypothesis when it is false. Power can also be defined as 1 minus the probability of a Type II error.

Power tells us how likely we are to "see" an effect that is there and is an estimate of the study's replicability. Because power tells us the probability of rejecting a false null hypothesis, we know how likely we are to miss a real effect. For instance, if a result is not significant and power is only .30, we know that a study with these characteristics detects an effect equal to the size we observed only 3 out of 10 times. Therefore, 7 of 10 times we do this study we will miss seeing the effect. In this case we may want to suspend judgment until the study can be redone with greater power.

The power of a statistical test is determined by the interplay of three factors: the level of statistical significance, the size of the treatment effect, and the sample size (Keppel, 1991). For all practical purposes, however, *sample size is the primary factor that researchers use to control power*. The differences in sample size that are needed to detect effects of different sizes can be dramatic. For example, Cohen (1988) reports the sample sizes needed for an independent groups design experiment with one independent variable manipulated at three levels. It takes a sample size of 30 to detect a large treatment effect; it takes a sample size of 76 to detect a medium treatment effect; and it takes a sample size of 464 to detect a small treatment effect. It thus takes over 15 times more participants to detect a small effect than it does to detect a large effect!

Using repeated measures experiments can also affect the power of the statistical analyses researchers use. As described in Chapter 8, repeated measures experiments are generally more sensitive than are independent groups experiments. This is because the estimates of error variation are generally smaller in repeated measures experiments. The smaller error variation leads to an increased ability to detect small treatment effects in an experiment. And that is just what the power of a statistical analysis is—the ability to detect small treatment effects when they are present.

When introducing NHST we suggested that making a so-called Type I error is equivalent to alpha (.05 in this case). Logically, to make this kind of error, the null hypothesis must be capable of being false. Yet, critics argue that the null hypothesis defined as zero difference is "always false" (e.g., Cohen, 1995, p. 1000) or, somewhat more conservatively is "rarely true" (Hunter, 1997, p. 5). If an effect is always, or nearly always, present (i.e., there is more than a zero difference between means), then we can't possibly (or at least hardly ever) make a mistake by claiming that an effect is there when it is not. Following this line of reasoning, the only error we are capable of making is a Type II error (see Hunter, 1997; Schmidt & Hunter, 1997), that is, saying a real effect is not there. This type of error, largely due to low statistical power in many psychological studies, typically is much greater than .05 (e.g., Cohen, 1990; Hunter, 1997; Schmidt & Hunter, 1997). Let us suggest that Type I errors do occur if the null hypothesis is taken literally, that is, if there really is a literally zero difference between the population means or if we believe that in some situations it is worth testing an effect against a hypothesis of no difference (see Abelson, 1997; Mulaik et al., 1997). As researchers we must be alert to the fact that in some situations it may be important not to conclude an effect is present when it is not, at least not to more than a trivial degree (see Box 13.2).

Type II errors are likely when power is low, and low power has characterized many studies in the literature: *the most common error in psychological research using NHST is a Type II error*. Just because we did not obtain statistical significance does not mean that an effect is not present (e.g., Schmidt, 1996). In fact, one

---

BOX 13.2

DO WE EVER ACCEPT THE NULL HYPOTHESIS?

Despite what we have said thus far, there may be some instances in which researchers will choose to accept the null hypothesis (rather than simply fail to reject it). Yeaton and Sechrest (1986, pp. 836–837) argue persuasively that findings of no difference are especially critical in applied research. Consider some questions they cite to illustrate their point: Are children who are placed in day-care centers as intellectually, socially, and emotionally advanced as children who remain in the home? Is a new, cheaper drug with fewer side effects as effective as the existing standard in preventing heart attacks?

These important questions clearly illustrate situations in which accepting the null hypothesis (no effect) involves more than a theoretical issue—life and death consequences rest on making the correct decision. Frick (1995) argues that never accepting the null hypothesis is neither desirable nor practical for psychology. There may be occasions when we want to be able to state with confidence that there is no (meaningful) difference (see also Shadish et al., 2002).

---

important reason for obtaining a measure of effect size is that we can compare the obtained effect with that found in other studies, whether or not the effect was statistically significant. This is the goal of meta-analysis (see Chapter 7). Although a nonsignificant finding does not tell us that an effect is absent, assuming that our study was conducted with sufficient power, a nonsignificant finding may indicate that an effect is so small that it isn't worth worrying about.

To determine the power of your study *before* it is conducted, you must first estimate the effect size anticipated in your experiment. An examination of the effect sizes obtained in previous studies for the independent variable of interest should guide your estimate. Once an effect size is estimated, you must then turn to "power tables" to obtain information about the sample size you should use in order to "see" the effect. These steps for conducting a power analysis are described more fully in the Appendix where a power table for comparing two means is found. *When you have a good estimate of the effect size you are testing, it is strongly recommended that you perform a power analysis before doing a research study.*

Power tables are also used after the fact. When a study is completed and the finding is not statistically significant the APA *Publication Manual* (2001) recommends that the power of your study be reported. In this way you communicate to other researchers what was the likelihood of detecting an effect that was there. If that likelihood was low then the research community may wish to suspend judgment regarding the meaning of your findings until a more powerful replication of your study is carried out. On the other hand, a statistically nonsignificant result from a study with sufficient power may suggest to the research community that this is an effect not worth pursuing. Instructions for doing this type of power analysis are also found in the Appendix.

NHST: COMPARING TWO MEANS

- The appropriate inferential test when comparing two means obtained from different groups of subjects is a *t*-test for independent groups.
- A measure of effect size should always be reported when NHST is used.
- The appropriate inferential test when comparing two means obtained from the same subjects (or matched groups) is a repeated measures (within-subjects) *t*-test.

We now illustrate the use of NHST when comparing the difference between two means. First, we consider a research study involving two independent means. The data for this study are from the vocabulary study of Zechmeister et al. (1995) that we described in Chapter 12. Next we consider a situation where there are two dependent means, that is, when a repeated measures design was used.

Independent Groups

Key Concept

Recall that a study was conducted in which the vocabulary size of college students and older adults was assessed. The appropriate inferential test for this situation is a **t-test for independent groups.** We may use this test to evaluate the difference between the mean percent multiple-choice performance of the college and older adult samples. We can define t for independent groups as the difference between sample means $(\overline{X}_1 - \overline{X}_2)$ divided by the standard error of the mean difference $(s_{\overline{X}_1 - \overline{X}_2})$. That is,

$$t = \frac{\overline{X}_1 - \overline{X}_2}{s_{\overline{X}_1 - \overline{X}_2}} \quad \text{where} \quad s_{\overline{X}_1 - \overline{X}_2} = \sqrt{\left[\frac{(n_1 - 1)s_1^2 + (n_2 - 1)s_2^2}{n_1 + n_2 - 2} \right] \left[\frac{1}{n_1} + \frac{1}{n_2} \right]}$$

Using this formula, the obtained t was 5.84. An alpha of .05 had been chosen prior to doing the analysis. Table A.2 of the Appendix shows critical values of t associated with various degrees of freedom (df). The obtained t of 5.84 is larger than the critical t value with 50 df (the $df = N - 2$, where N equals the sum of the two sample sizes, $n_1 + n_2$); thus, the obtained t can be said to be statistically significant.[1]

Statistical software programs typically provide the actual probability of an obtained t as part of the output, thus circumventing the need to consult a table of t values. In fact, the *Publication Manual* of the American Psychological Association (2001) advises that the exact probability be reported. When the exact

---

[1]The critical t value for 50 df is not found in Appendix Table A.2. When this occurs it is appropriate to compare the obtained t with the critical t associated with the next lowest number of degrees of freedom. In Table A.2, the value associated with 40 df is 2.02. The obtained value of 5.84 is clearly larger than this value. As pointed out in the text, when statistical analysis is done using computer software packages the exact probability is given automatically. This exact probability should always be reported.

probability is less than .001 (e.g., $p = .0004$), statistical software programs frequently report the exact probability as .000. (This was the case for the analysis reported above.) Of course, the exact probability is not .000 but something less than .001. Because in this situation a researcher does not know exactly what that probability is, one solution is to report the obtained probability as $p \leq .0005$ since a value larger than .0005 would have been rounded to .001.

Therefore, for the vocabulary experiment we have been discussing, the result of the inferential statistics test can be summarized as follows:

$$t(50) = 5.84, \; p \leq .0005$$

In Chapter 12 we showed how an effect size, d, can be calculated for a comparison between two means. *A measure of effect size should always be reported when NHST is used.* You may recall that in Chapter 12 we calculated d for the vocabulary study as 1.65. Cohen's d also can be calculated from the outcome of the independent groups t-test according to the following formula:

$$d = \frac{2t}{\sqrt{df}} \quad \text{(see Rosenthal \& Rosnow, 1991).}$$

That is,

$$d = \frac{2(5.84)}{\sqrt{50}} = \frac{11.68}{7.07} = 1.65$$

Repeated Measures Designs

Thus far we have considered experiments involving two independent groups of subjects. As you are aware, experiments can also be carried out by having each subject participate in each condition of the experiment or by "matching" subjects on some measure related to the dependent variable (e.g., IQ scores, weight, etc.). Such experiments are called matched groups (see Chapter 7), within-subjects designs or repeated measures designs (see Chapter 8). The logic of NHST is the same in a repeated measures design as it is in an independent groups design. However, the t-test comparing two means takes on a different form in a repeated measures design. The t-test in this situation is typically called a direct-difference t or **repeated measures (within-subjects) t-test.** When each subject is in both conditions of the experiment t is defined as:

Key Concept

$$t = \frac{\overline{D}}{s_{\overline{D}}}$$

where

$\overline{D}$ = mean of difference scores or $(\Sigma D)/N$

$s_{\overline{D}}$ = standard error of difference scores, that is, $s_{\overline{D}}$

$$s_{\overline{D}} = s_D/\sqrt{N}$$

where

s_D = standard deviation of difference scores and

N = number of difference scores (i.e., number of pairs of scores)

The numerator of the repeated measures t is the mean of the difference scores ($\overline{D}$) and is algebraically equivalent to the difference between the sample means (i.e., $\overline{X}_1 - \overline{X}_2$). Statistical significance is determined by consulting a table of critical values of t with df equal to $N - 1$ (see Appendix Table A.2). In this case N refers to the number of participants or pairs of scores in the experiment. You interpret the obtained t as you would the t obtained in an independent groups design.

As noted in Chapter 12, assessing effect size in a matched groups or repeated measures design is somewhat more complex for an independent groups design (see Cohen, 1988; and Rosenthal & Rosnow, 1991, for information pertaining to the calculation of d in these cases).

STATISTICAL SIGNIFICANCE AND SCIENTIFIC OR PRACTICAL SIGNIFICANCE

- We must recognize the fact that statistical significance is not the same as scientific significance.
- We also must acknowledge that statistical significance is not the same as practical or clinical significance.

Tests of statistical significance are an important tool in the analysis of research findings. We must be careful, however, to interpret statistically significant findings correctly (see Box 13.3). We must also be careful not to confuse a statistically significant finding with a scientifically significant finding. Whether the results of a study are important to the scientific community will depend on the nature of the variable under study (the effects of some variables are simply more important than those of others), how sound the study is (statistically significant findings can be produced with poorly done studies), and other criteria such as effect size (see, for example, Abelson, 1995).

Similarly, the practical or clinical significance of a treatment effect depends on factors other than statistical significance. These include the external validity associated with the study, the size of the effect, and various practical considerations (including financial ones) associated with a treatment's implementation. Even a statistically significant outcome showing a large effect size is not a guarantee of its practical or clinical significance. A very large effect might be obtained as a part of a study that does not generalize well from the laboratory to the real world (i.e., has low external validity); thus, the results may be of little value to the applied psychologist. Moreover, a relatively large treatment effect that does generalize well to real-world settings may never be applied because it is too costly, too difficult to implement, too controversial, or too similar in its effects to existing treatments.

It is also possible that, given enough power, a small effect size will be statistically significant. Small effect sizes may not be practically important outside the laboratory. As we described in Chapter 7, external validity is an empirical

BOX 13.3

WHAT WE SHOULD **NOT** SAY WHEN A RESULT IS STATISTICALLY SIGNIFICANT ($p < .05$)

- We cannot specify the exact probability for the real difference between the means. For example, it is wrong to say that the probability is .95 that the observed difference between the means reflects a real (true) mean difference in the populations.

The outcome of NHST reveals the probability of a difference this great by chance (given these data) assuming the null hypothesis is true. It does not tell us about probabilities in the real world (e.g., Mulaik et al., 1997). If results occur with a probability less than our chosen alpha level (e.g., .05), then all we can conclude is that the outcome is not likely to be a chance event in this situation.

- Statistically significant results do not demonstrate that the research hypothesis is correct. (For example, the data from the vocabulary study do not prove that older adults have greater vocabulary knowledge than do younger adults.)

NHST (as well as confidence intervals) cannot prove that a research hypothesis is correct. A statistically significant result is (reasonably) sometimes said to "provide support for" or to "give evidence for" a hypothesis, but it alone cannot prove that the research hypothesis is correct. There are a couple of important reasons why. First, NHST is a game of probabilities; it provides answers in the form of likelihoods that are never 1.00 (e.g., *p* greater or less than .05). There is always the possibility of error. If there is "proof" it

is only "circumstantial" proof. As we have seen, the research hypothesis can only be tested indirectly by referring to the probability of these data assuming the null hypothesis is true. If the probability that our results occurred by chance is very low (assuming a true null hypothesis), we may reason that the null hypothesis is really not true; this does not, however, mean our research hypothesis is true. As Schmidt and Hunter (1997, p. 59) remind us, researchers doing NHST "are focusing not on the actual scientific hypothesis of interest." Second, evidence for the effect of an independent variable is only as good as the methodology that produced the effect. The data used in NHST may or may not be from a study that is free of confounds or experimenter errors. It is possible that another factor was responsible for the observed effect. (For example, suppose that the older adults in the vocabulary study, but not the college students, had been recruited from a group of expert crossword puzzle players.) As we have mentioned, a large effect size can easily be produced by a bad experiment. Evidence for a research hypothesis must be sought by examining the methodology of a study as well as considering the effect produced on the dependent variable. *Neither NHST, confidence intervals, nor effect sizes tell us about the soundness of a study's methodology.*

question. It is important to conduct a study under conditions similar to those in which the treatment will be used in order to see whether a finding is practically significant. We are not likely to carry out such an empirical test, however, if the effect size is small (although see Rosenthal [1990] for important exceptions).

RECOMMENDATIONS FOR COMPARING TWO MEANS

We offer the following recommendations when evaluating the data from a study looking at the difference between two means. First, keep in mind the final goal of data analysis: to make a case based on our observations for a claim about behavior. In order to make the best case possible you will want to explore various alternatives for data analysis. Don't fall into the trap of thinking that there is one and only one way to provide evidence for a claim about behavior. When there is a choice (and there almost always is), as recommended by the APA's Task Force on Statistical Inference (Wilkinson et al., 1999), use the simplest possible analysis. Second, when using NHST be sure to understand its limitations and what the outcome of NHST allows you to say. Always consider reporting a measure of effect magnitude when using NHST, and also a measure of power, especially when a nonsignificant result is found. Although there will be some situations when effect size information is not warranted—for example, when testing a theoretical prediction of direction only (e.g., Chow, 1988), these situations are relatively rare. In many research situations, and in nearly all applied situations, effect size information is an important, even necessary, complement to NHST. Finally, researchers must "break the habit" of relying solely on NHST and consider reporting confidence intervals for effect sizes in addition to, or even rather than, *p* values associated with results of inferential tests. The APA *Publication Manual* (2001, p. 22) strongly recommends the use of confidence intervals.

REPORTING RESULTS WHEN COMPARING TWO MEANS

We are now in a position to model a statement of results that takes into account the information gained from all three stages of data analysis, the complementary evidence obtained by using confidence intervals (Chapter 12) and NHST, and the recommendations of the APA *Publication Manual* (2001) regarding reporting results (see especially pp. 20–26 of the *Manual*).

Reporting Results of the Vocabulary Study We may report the results as follows:

> The mean performance on the multiple-choice vocabulary test for college students was 45.58 ($SD = 10.46$); the mean of the older group was 64.04 ($SD = 12.27$). With alpha set at .05, this difference was statistically significant, $t(50) = 5.84$, $p \leq .0005$. Older participants in this study had a greater vocabulary size than did the younger participants. The effect size based on Cohen's *d* was 1.65. There is a .95 probability that the obtained confidence interval, 12.11 to 24.81, contains the true population mean difference.

Commentary Descriptive statistics in the forms of means and standard deviations summarize "what happened" in the experiment as a function of the independent variable (age). As recommended by the APA *Publication Manual* the alpha level for NHST is stated prior to reporting the obtained *p* value. Because the exact probability was less than .001, results are reported at $p \leq .0005$, but note that exact probabilities are to be reported when .001 or greater. The exact probability conveys information about the probability of an exact replication (Posavac, 2002). That is, we know that the results are "more reliable" than if a larger exact p value was obtained. This information is not found when only confidence intervals are reported. The sentence beginning, "Older participants in this study . . ." summarizes in words what the statistical analysis revealed. It is always important to tell your reader directly what the analysis shows. This becomes increasingly important as the number and complexity of analyses performed and reported in a research study increase. An effect size (i.e., d) is also reported as recommended by the APA *Publication Manual*. This information is valuable to researchers doing meta-analyses and who wish to compare results of studies using similar variables. On the other hand, confidence intervals provide a range of possible effect sizes in terms of actual mean differences and not a single value such as Cohen's d. Because zero is not within the interval we know that the outcome would be statistically significant at the .05 level (see Chapter 12). However, as the APA *Manual* emphasizes, confidence intervals provide information about precision of estimation and location of an effect that is not given by NHST alone. Recall from Chapter 12 that the smaller the confidence interval the more precise is our estimate.

Note: As mentioned in Chapter 12, a figure usually is not needed when only two group means are involved. Pictorial summaries such as graphs become more important when summarizing the results of experiments with more than two groups. If a figure were drawn showing the mean performance in the groups, then the statement of results should refer to the figure. (See Chapter 14.)

Power Analysis   When we know the effect size we can determine the statistical power of an analysis. Power, as you will recall, is the probability that a statistically significant effect will be obtained. Suppose that a previous study of vocabulary size contrasting younger and older adults produced an effect size of .50, a medium effect according to Cohen's (1988) rule of thumb. We can use the power tables created by Cohen (1988) to determine the number of participants needed in a test of mean differences to "see" an effect of size .50 with alpha .05. (See Table A.4 in the Appendix.) The table identifies the power associated with various effect sizes as a function of sample size. Looking at the power table we see that the sample size (in each group) of a two-group study would have to be about 64 to achieve power of .80 (for a two-tailed test). Looking for a medium effect size we would need a total of 128 (64×2) participants to obtain statistical significance in 8 of 10 tries. Had Zechmeister et al. been looking for a medium effect, their vocabulary study would have been underpowered. As it turns out, anticipating a large effect size, a sample size of 26 was appropriate to obtain power .80.

If the result is not statistically significant, then an estimate of power should be reported. If, for example, using an independent groups design the outcome had been $t(28) = 1.96, p > .05$, with an effect size of .50, we can determine the power of the study after the fact. Assuming equal size groups in the study we know that there were 15 subjects in each group ($df = n_1 + n_2 - 2$, or $28 = 15 + 15 - 2$). An examination of Appendix Table A.4 reveals that power for this study is .26. A

STRETCHING EXERCISE
A TEST OF (YOUR UNDERSTANDING OF) THE NULL HYPOTHESIS TEST

As should be apparent by now, understanding, applying, and interpreting results of NHST is no easy task. Even seasoned researchers occasionally make mistakes. To help you avoid mistakes we provide a true-false test based on the information presented thus far about NHST.

Assume that an independent groups design was used to assess performance of participants in an experimental and control group. There were 12 participants in each condition and results of NHST with alpha set at .05 revealed: $t(22) = 4.52$, $p = .006$. True or false? The re-

searcher may reasonably conclude on the basis of this outcome that:

1 The null hypothesis should be rejected.
2 The research hypothesis has been shown to be true.
3 The results are of scientific importance.
4 The probability that the null hypothesis is true is only .006.
5 The probability of finding statistical significance at the .05 level if the study were replicated is greater than if the exact probability had been .02.

Answers: (1) T, (2) F, (3) F, (4) F, (5) T.

---

statistically significant outcome would be obtained in only about 1 of 4 attempts with this sample size and when a medium (.50) effect must be found. In this case, researchers would need to decide if practical or theoretical decisions should be made on the basis of this result, or if "more research is needed."

DATA ANALYSIS INVOLVING MORE THAN TWO CONDITIONS

Thus far we have discussed the stages of data analysis in the context of an experiment with two conditions, that is, two levels of one independent variable. What happens when we have more than two levels (conditions), or, as is often the case in psychology, more than two independent variables? The most frequently used statistical procedure for analyzing results of psychology experiments in these situations is the analysis of variance (ANOVA).

We illustrate how ANOVA is used to test null hypotheses in four specific research situations: single-factor analysis of independent groups designs; single-factor analysis for repeated measures designs; two-factor analysis for independent groups designs; and two-factor analysis for mixed designs. We recommend that, before proceeding, you review the information presented in Chapters 7, 8, and 9 that describes these research designs.

ANOVA FOR SINGLE-FACTOR INDEPENDENT GROUPS DESIGN

- Analysis of variance (ANOVA) is an inferential statistics test used to determine whether an independent variable has had a statistically significant effect on a dependent variable.

- The logic of analysis of variance is based on identifying sources of error variation and systematic variation in the data.
- The *F*-test is a statistic that represents the ratio of between-group variation to within-group variation in the data.
- The results of the initial overall analysis of an omnibus *F*-test are presented in an analysis of variance summary table; comparisons of two means can then be used to identify specific sources of systematic variation in an experiment.
- Although analysis of variance can be used to decide whether an independent variable has had a statistically significant effect, researchers examine the descriptive statistics to interpret the meaning of the experiment's outcome.
- Effect size measures for independent groups designs include eta squared (η^2) and Cohen's *f*.
- A power analysis for independent groups designs should be conducted prior to implementing the study in order to determine the probability of finding a statistically significant effect and power should be reported whenever nonsignificant results based on NHST are found.
- Comparisons of two means may be carried out to identify specific sources of systematic variation contributing to a statistically significant omnibus *F*-test.

Key Concept

Key Concept

Overview   Statistical inference requires a test to determine whether or not the outcome of an experiment was statistically significant. The most commonly used inferential statistics test in the analysis of psychology experiments is the **ANOVA.** As its name implies, the analysis of variance is based on analyzing different sources of variation in an experiment. In this section we will briefly introduce how the analysis of variance is used to analyze experiments that involve independent groups with one independent variable, or what is called a **single-factor independent groups design.** Although ANOVA is used to analyze the results of either random groups or natural groups designs, the assumptions underlying ANOVA strictly apply only to the random groups design.

There are two sources of variation in any random groups experiment. First, variation within each group can be expected because of individual differences among subjects who have been randomly assigned to a group. The variation due to individual differences cannot be eliminated, but this variation is presumed to be balanced across groups when random assignment is used. In a properly conducted experiment, the differences among subjects within each group should be the only source of error variation. Participants in each group should be given instructions in the same way, and the level of the independent variable to which they've been assigned should be implemented in the same way for each member of the group (see Chapter 7).

The second source of variation in the random groups design is variation between the groups. If the null hypothesis is true (no differences among groups), any observed differences among the means of the groups can be attributed to error variation (e.g., the different characteristics of the participants in the groups). As we've seen previously, however, we don't expect sample means to be exactly identical. Fluctuations produced by sampling error make it likely that the means will vary somewhat—this is error variation. Thus, the variation among the different group means, when the null hypothesis is assumed to be true, provides a second estimate of error variation in an experiment. If the null hypothesis is true, this estimate of error variation *between* groups should be similar to the estimate of error variation *within* groups. Thus, the random groups design provides two independent estimates of error variation, one within the groups and one between the groups.

Now suppose that the null hypothesis is false. That is, suppose the independent variable has had an effect in your experiment. If the independent variable has had an effect, should the means for the different groups be the same or different? You should recognize that they should be different. An independent variable that has an effect on behavior should produce systematic differences in the means across the different groups of the experiment. That is, the independent variable should introduce a source of variation among the groups of the experiment—it should cause the groups to vary. This systematic variation will be added to the differences in the group means that are already present due to error variation. That is, between-group variation will increase.

The *F*-Test   We are now in a position to develop a statistic that will allow us to tell whether the variation due to our independent variable is larger than would be expected on the basis of error variation alone. This statistic is called *F*; it is named after Ronald Fisher, the statistician who developed the test. The

Key Concept

conceptual definition of the **F-test** is the following:

$$F = \frac{\text{Variation between groups}}{\text{Variation within groups}} = \frac{\text{Error variation} + \text{systematic variation}}{\text{Error variation}}$$

If the null hypothesis is true, there is no systematic variation between groups (no effect of the independent variable) and the resulting *F*-test has an expected value of 1.00 (since error variation divided by error variation would equal 1.00). As the amount of systematic variation increases, however, the expected value from the *F*-test becomes greater than 1.00.

The analysis of experiments would be easier if we could isolate the systematic variation produced by the independent variable. Unfortunately, the systematic variation between groups comes in a "package" along with error variation. Consequently, the value of the *F*-test may sometimes be larger than 1.00 simply because our estimate of error variation between groups happens to be larger than our estimate of error variation within groups (i.e., the two estimates should be similar but can differ due to chance factors). How much greater than 1.00 does the *F* statistic have to be before we can be relatively sure that it reflects true systematic variation due to the independent variable? Our earlier discussion of statistical significance provides an answer to this question. To be statistically significant, the *F* value needs to be large enough so that its probability of occurring if the null hypothesis were true is less than our chosen level of significance, usually .05.

We are now ready to apply the principles of NHST and the procedures of ANOVA to analyze a specific experiment.

Analysis of Single-Factor Independent Groups Design   The first step in doing an inferential statistics test like the *F*-test is to state the research question the analysis is intended to answer. Typically, this takes the form of, "Did the independent variable have any overall effect on performance?" Once the research question is clear, the next step is to develop a null hypothesis for the analysis. The experiment we will discuss as an example examines the effect on memory retention of several kinds of memory training. There are four levels (conditions) of this independent variable and, consequently, four groups of participants. Each sample or group represents a population. The initial overall

Key Concept

analysis of the experiment is called an **omnibus *F*-test.** The null hypothesis for such omnibus tests is that all the population means are equal. Remember that the null hypothesis assumes no effect of the independent variable. The formal statement of a null hypothesis (H_0) is always made in terms of population characteristics. These population characteristics are indicated by Greek letters, and the population mean is symbolized as μ ("mu"). We can use a subscript for each mean to represent the levels of the independent variable). Our null hypothesis then becomes:

$$H_0: \mu_1 = \mu_2 = \mu_3 = \mu_4$$

The alternative to the null hypothesis is that one or more of the means of the populations are not equal. In other words, the alternative hypothesis (H_1) states that H_0 is wrong; there is a difference somewhere. The alternative hypothesis becomes:

$$H_1: \text{NOT } H_0$$

If the type of memory training does have an effect on retention (i.e., if the independent variable produces systematic variation), then we will want to reject the null hypothesis.

The data in Table 13.2 represent the number of words correctly recalled (out of a possible 20) on a retention test in an experiment investigating memory training techniques. Five participants were randomly assigned to each of four groups (defined by the method of study that individuals were instructed to use to learn the words in preparation for the memory test). The control method involved no specific instructions, but in the three experimental groups participants were instructed to study by making up a story using the to-be-remembered words (story method), to use visual imagery (imagery method), or to use rhymes to remember the words (rhyme method). The independent variable being

TABLE 13.2 NUMBER OF WORDS RECALLED IN A MEMORY EXPERIMENT

				Instruction (A)				
Subject	Control (a_1)	Subject	Story (a_2)	Subject	Imagery (a_3)	Subject	Rhymes (a_4)
1	12	6	15	11	16	16	14
2	10	7	14	12	16	17	14
3	9	8	13	13	13	18	15
4	11	9	12	14	12	19	12
5	8	10	12	15	15	20	12
Mean	10.0		13.2		14.4		13.4
Standard deviation	1.6		1.3		1.8		1.3
Range	8–12		12–15		12–16		12–15

manipulated is instruction, and it can be symbolized by the letter "A." The levels of this independent variable can be differentiated by using the symbols, $a_1, a_2, a_3,$ and a_4 for the four respective groups. The number of participants within each group is referred to as n; in this case, $n = 5$. The total number of individuals in the experiment is symbolized as N; in this case, $N = 20$.

An important step in the analysis of any experiment is to set up a data matrix like the one in Table 13.2. The number of correct responses is listed for each person in each of the four groups with each participant identified with a unique subject number. In order to understand the results of an experiment it is essential to summarize the data prior to examining the outcome of the ANOVA. Below the data matrix the mean, range (minimum and maximum scores), and standard deviation are provided for each group.

Before examining the "significance" of any inferential test, try to get an impression of what the summary statistics are telling you. Look to see if there is a visible "effect" of the independent variable; that is, see if there is substantial variation among the means. By examining the ranges and standard deviations, get a sense of the variability in each group. (Remember, the less scores vary around their sample means the better the chance of seeing an effect that is present.) The range, or difference between the minimum and maximum values, is useful in identifying floor and ceiling effects. Is the variability among the groups similar? We want the variation to be relatively homogeneous as wide discrepancies in within-group variability can create interpretation problems when using ANOVA.

Our examination of the summary statistics reveals that there appears to be systematic variation among the means; the largest difference is seen between the Control (10.0) and the Imagery Group (14.4). All the experimental means are larger than the Control mean. Note that the range is similar for all the groups; the standard deviations, too, are fairly similar. This attests to the homogeneity (similarity) of variance among the groups. (Many computer programs provide

TABLE 13.3   ANALYSIS OF VARIANCE SUMMARY TABLE FOR MEMORY EXPERIMENT

Source	Sum of squares	df	Mean square	F-ratio	p
Group	54.55	3	18.18	7.80	0.002
Error	37.20	16	2.33		
Total	91.75	19			

a test of "homogeneity of variance" along with the ANOVA output.) Moreover, an inspection of the highest scores in each group shows that ceiling effects are not a problem in this data set (as total possible was 20).

The next step in an analysis of variance is to do the computations to obtain the estimates of variation that make up the numerator and denominator of the F-test. Calculations for F-tests are best done using a computer. We will focus, therefore, on interpreting the results of the computations. The results of an analysis of variance are presented in *Analysis of Variance Summary Table* (see Table 13.3).

Interpreting the ANOVA Summary Table   The summary table for the omnibus F-test for the independent groups design used to investigate the effect of memory training is found in Table 13.3. Remember that there were four groups of size $n = 5$ and, thus, overall $N = 20$. It is critically important you know what the ANOVA summary table contains. Thus, we examine the components of the summary table before looking at the outcome of the F-test for the experiment.

The left column of the summary table lists the two sources of variation described earlier. In this case the independent variable of the training group ("Group") is a source of variation between the groups, and the within-groups differences provide an estimate of error variation. The total variation in the experiment is the sum of the variation between and within groups. The third column is the degrees of freedom (df). In general, the statistical concept of degrees of freedom is defined as the number of entries of interest minus one. Since there are 4 levels of the training independent variable, there are 3 df between groups. There are 5 participants within each group, and so there are 4 df ($n - 1$) within each of the 4 groups. Because all 4 groups are the same size, we can determine the within-groups df by multiplying the df within each group by the number of groups (4×4) for 16 df. The total df is the number of subjects minus one ($N - 1$), or the sum of df between groups plus df within groups ($3 + 16 = 19$).

The sums of squares (SS) and the mean square (MS) are computational steps in obtaining the F statistic. The MS between groups (row 1) is an estimate of systematic variation plus error variation, and is calculated by dividing the SS between groups by the df between groups ($54.55/3 = 18.18$). The MS within groups (row 2) is an estimate of error variation only, and is computed by dividing the SS within groups by the df within groups ($37.20/16 = 2.33$). The F-test is calculated by dividing the MS between groups by the MS within groups ($18.18/2.33 = 7.80$).

We are now ready to use the information in the summary table to test for the statistical significance of the outcome in the memory training experiment. You may anticipate the conclusion already, knowing that when the null hypothesis is assumed to be true (i.e., no effect of the independent variable), the estimate of systematic variation plus error variation (numerator of the F-test) should be approximately equal to the estimate of error variation only (denominator of the F-test). As we see here, the estimate of systematic variation plus error variation (18.18) is quite a bit larger than the estimate of error variation alone (2.33).

The obtained F value in this analysis (7.80) appears in the second to last column of the summary table. The probability of obtaining an F as large as 7.80 if the null hypothesis were true is shown in the last column of the summary table (0.002). The obtained probability of .002 is less than the level of significance ($\alpha = .05$), so we reject the null hypothesis and conclude that the overall effect of memory training is statistically significant. The results of NHST using ANOVA would be summarized in your research report as:

$$F(3, 16) = 7.80, p = .002$$

An F statistic is identified by its degrees of freedom. In this case there are 3 df between groups and 16 df within groups (i.e., 3, 16). Note that the exact probability (i.e., .002) is reported because it gives us information about the probability of replication.

Just what have we learned when we find a statistically significant outcome in an analysis of variance testing an omnibus null hypothesis? In one sense, we have learned something very important. We are now in a position to state that manipulating the independent variable produced a change in performance (i.e., participants' memory for the to-be-remembered words). In another sense, merely knowing our outcome is statistically significant tells us little about the nature of the effect of the independent variable. The descriptive statistics (in our example, the mean number of words recalled as reported in Table 13.2) allow us to describe the nature of the effect. Note that only by examining the pattern of group means do we begin to learn what happened in our experiment as a function of the independent variable. *Never try to interpret a statistically significant outcome without referring to the corresponding descriptive statistics.*

Although we know that the omnibus F-test was statistically significant, we do not know the degree of relationship between the independent and dependent variable, and thus we should consider calculating an effect size for our independent variable. Based on the omnibus test alone we also are unable to state which of the group means differed significantly. Fortunately, there are analysis techniques that allow us to locate more specifically the sources of systematic variation in our experiments. One approach that is highly recommended is the use of confidence intervals (see Chapter 12). Confidence intervals can provide evidence for the pattern of population means estimated by our samples (see especially Box 12.5). Another technique is that of comparing two means. We first discuss an effect size measure for the independent groups ANOVA, as well as power analysis for this design, and then turn our attention to comparisons of two means.

Calculating Effect Size for Designs with Three or More Independent Groups

Key Concept

We mentioned earlier that the psychology literature contains many different measures of effect magnitude, which depend on the particular research design, test statistic, and other peculiarities of the research situation (e.g., Cohen, 1992; Kirk, 1996; Rosenthal & Rosnow, 1991). When we know one measure of effect magnitude, we usually can translate it to another, comparable measure without too much difficulty. An important class of effect magnitude measures that applies to experiments with more than two groups is based on measures of "strength of association" (Kirk, 1996). What these measures have in common is that they allow estimates of the proportion of total variance accounted for by the effect of the independent variable on the dependent variable. A popular strength of association measure is **eta squared** or η^2. It is easily calculated based on information found in the ANOVA Summary Table (Table 13.3) for the omnibus *F*-test (although many computer programs automatically provide eta squared as a measure of effect size). Eta squared is defined as:

$$\frac{\text{Sum of squares between groups}}{\text{Total sum of squares}}$$

In our example (see Table 13.3),

$$\text{eta squared } (\eta^2) = \frac{54.55}{[(54.55) + (37.20)]} = .59$$

Eta squared can also be computed directly from the *F*-ratio for the between-groups effect when the ANOVA table is not available (see Rosenthal & Rosnow, 1991, p. 441):

$$\text{eta squared } (\eta^2) = \frac{(F)(df \text{ effect})}{[(F)(df \text{ effect})] + (df \text{ error})}$$

or, in our example,

$$\text{eta squared } (\eta^2) = \frac{(7.80)(3)}{[(7.80)(3)] + 16} = .59$$

Key Concept

Another measure, designed by J. Cohen, for designs with three or more independent groups is *f* (see Cohen, 1988). It is a standardized measure of effect size similar to *d*, which we saw was useful for assessing effect sizes in a two-group experiment. However, unlike *d*, which defines an effect in terms of the difference between two means, **Cohen's *f*** defines an effect in terms of a measure of dispersal among group means. Both *d* and *f* express the effect relative to (i.e., "standardized" on) the within-population standard deviation. Cohen has provided guidelines for interpreting *f*. Specifically, he suggests that small, medium, and large effects sizes correspond to *f* values of .10, .25, and .40. The calculation of *f* is not easily accomplished using the information found in the ANOVA

Summary Table (Table 13.3), but it can be obtained without too much difficulty once eta squared is known (see Cohen, 1988), as:

$$f = \sqrt{\frac{\eta^2}{1 - \eta^2}}$$

or, in our example,

$$f = \sqrt{\frac{.59}{1 - .59}} = 1.20$$

We can thus conclude that memory training accounted for .59 of the total variance in the dependent variable and produced a standardized effect size, f, of 1.20. Based on Cohen's guidelines for interpreting f (.10, .25, .40), it is apparent that memory training had a large effect on recall scores.

Assessing Power for Independent Groups Designs

Once the effect size is known we can obtain an estimate of power for a specific sample size and degrees of freedom associated with the numerator (between-groups effect) of the F-ratio. In our example, we set alpha at .05; the experiment was done with $n = 5$ and $df = 3$ for the between-groups effect (number of groups minus 1). The effect size, f, associated with our data set is very large (1.20), and there really is no good reason to conduct a power analysis for this large effect which was statistically significant. Thus, let's consider a somewhat different outcome.

Assume that the ANOVA in our example yielded a nonsignificant F and effect size was $f = .40$, still a large effect according to Cohen's guidelines. An important question to answer is: What was the power of our experiment? How likely were we to see an effect of this size given an alpha of .05, a sample size of $n = 5$, and $df = 3$ for our effect? Consulting the abbreviated power table in the Appendix (see Table A.5), we find that under these conditions power was .26. In other words, the probability of obtaining statistical significance in this situation was only .26. In only approximately one-fourth of the attempts under these conditions would we obtain a significant result. The experiment was clearly underpowered and it is unreasonable to make much of the fact that NHST did not reveal a significant result. To do so would ignore the very important fact that the effect of our independent variable was, in fact, large.

Although learning about power after the fact can be important, particularly when we obtain a nonsignificant outcome based on NHST, ideally power analysis should be conducted prior to an experiment in order to reveal the a priori (from the beginning) probability of finding a statistically significant effect. An experimenter who begins an experiment knowing that power is only .26 would appear to be wasting time and resources given that the odds of *not* finding a significant effect are .74. Let us assume, therefore, that the experiment has not yet been conducted and that the investigator examined the literature on memory training and found that a large effect was often obtained by previous researchers in this area. Let us further assume that the researcher wants power to be .80 in the experiment. Because power is typically increased by increasing sample size, the researcher will want to find out what the sample size should be in order to find a large effect with power .80.

To find the sample size needed to see a large effect in 8 of 10 tries we use the power table to find *n* with *df* = 3 under the effect size heading of .40. Table A.5 in the Appendix shows that to achieve power of .80 we would need about 18 participants in each condition of the experiment. The researcher should take this information into consideration before doing the experiment.

Comparing Means in Multiple-Group Experiments

As we noted, knowing that "something happened" in a one-factor, multiple-group experiment is often not all that interesting. We generally do research, or at least we should, with more specific hypotheses in mind than "this variable will have an effect" on the dependent variable. Neither the results of the omnibus *F*, nor a measure of overall effect size, tell us which means are significantly different from which other means. We cannot, for instance, look at the four means in our memory experiment and judge that the "imagery" mean is significantly different from the "story" mean. The results of the omnibus *F* simply tell us there is variation present among all the groups that is larger than would be expected by chance in this situation.

We can suggest two complementary ways to learn more about what happened in a multiple-group, single-factor experiment. One approach is to examine the probable pattern of population means by calculating 95% confidence intervals for the mean estimates in our experiment. This approach was illustrated in Chapter 12 when we showed how confidence intervals could be used to compare means in a multiple-group experiment. Confidence intervals can be used to make decisions about the probable differences among population means that are estimated by the means of our experimental groups. These decisions are made by examining whether confidence intervals overlap, and if they do, to what degree they overlap (see especially Box 12.5). Remember that the width of the confidence intervals provides information about the precision of our estimates.

Key Concept

A second approach makes use of NHST and focuses on a small set of two-group comparisons in order to specify the source of the overall effect of our independent variable. A **comparison of two means** allows the researcher to focus on a particular difference of interest. These comparisons can be quite sophisticated, for example, comparing the average of two or more groups in an experiment with the mean of another group or the average of two or more other groups. However, most of the time we will be interested in the difference between just two means that are represented by individual groups. These two-mean comparisons are usually made after we have determined that our omnibus *F*-test is statistically significant.

One approach for carrying out comparisons of two means is to use a *t*-test; however, there is a slight modification in the way that *t* is calculated when comparing means in a multiple-group experiment. Specifically, we want to use a *pooled variance* estimate based on the within-group variation estimate (MS_{error}) found in our omnibus *F*-test. That is, our variance estimate uses information obtained from *all* the groups in our experiment, and not just the two groups of interest. Therefore, the formula for this *t*-test is:

$$t = \frac{\overline{X}_1 - \overline{X}_2}{\sqrt{[MS_{error}]\left[\frac{1}{n_1} + \frac{1}{n_2}\right]}}$$

The value for the MS_{error} is obtained from the ANOVA Summary Table of our omnibus *F*-test, and the degrees of freedom for our comparison *t*-test are those associated with the MS_{error} [or $k(n - 1)$, where k = number of groups]. For example, the *MS* within groups (error) for the analysis reported in Table 13.3 is 2.33 with 16 degrees of freedom [$4(5 - 1) = 16$].

One comparison of two means we could make for the memory experiment is to compare the mean performance for the memory training groups (combined) and the control group. The mean retention for the three memory training groups is 13.67 ($n = 15$), and the mean for the control group is 10.00 ($n = 5$). We can ask, does memory training, regardless of type (i.e., story, imagery, rhymes), lead to better memory retention than no memory training (control)? The null hypothesis is that the two population means do not differ (and the sample means differ by chance alone). When the appropriate values are substituted into the formula for *t* given above, we observe a statistically significant effect, $t(16) = 4.66, p = .0003$.[2] Thus, memory training in this experiment, regardless of type, resulted in better memory retention for the words compared to no training. You can see that this statement is more specific than the statement we could make based on the omnibus *F* test, in which we could only say that the variation across the four conditions of the experiment was larger than that expected based on chance alone. Our discussion of the confidence intervals for these means in the next section will help you to determine whether it would be useful to conduct additional two-mean comparisons among the three memory training conditions.

Cohen's *d* may be calculated for comparisons of two means using the results of the *t*-test. The formula for Cohen's *d* in this situation is:

$$d = \frac{2(t)}{\sqrt{df_{error}}}$$

[2]Often the *t*-tests for comparisons of two means following an omnibus *F*-test can be easily calculated by hand using the formula provided above. The probability (*p*) associated with the computed value of *t* can then be determined in one of two ways: (1) compare the observed *t* to the critical values of *t* found in Appendix A.2, or (2) use a computer program that allows users to enter the *df* and *t* values for a one- or two-tailed test to obtain the exact probability associated with those values (e.g., try the website at http://math.uc.edu/~brycw/classes/148/tables.htm).

For the comparison between the three memory training groups and the control group, substituting into the formula the value of (4.66) and with 16 df_{error}, the effect size, d, is 2.33. According to Cohen's criteria for effect sizes, this can be interpreted as a large effect of memory instruction relative to no instruction.

We can conclude this section on analyzing mean differences in a multiple-group experiment by reviewing the complementary information obtained by using confidence intervals and NHST. Because each approach adds unique kinds of information, an argument can be made for using both confidence intervals and NHST in this situation. The use of confidence intervals allows us to make decisions about the probable pattern of population means across all the conditions of our experiment. The width of the interval tells us how precisely we have estimated the population mean. When using a t-test we are seeking to make a decision about rejecting or not rejecting the null hypothesis with a specific probability (e.g., $p = .001$). As noted previously, the exact probability associated with the outcome of NHST can be important when interpreting results (e.g., Posavac, 2002). The lower the exact probability, the greater is the likelihood that an exact replication would permit rejecting the null hypothesis at $p < .05$ (see Zechmeister & Posavac, 2003). Minimally, we want to report the lowest probability for statistical significance for which we have information. (Computers automatically give the exact probability of our test result.)

The results of the t comparison also permit us to contrast results with previous studies in two ways. First, we can note whether our experiment's findings for statistical significance are similar to those observed in a previous experiment. That is, did we *replicate* a statistically significant finding? Second, we can calculate an effect size (e.g., Cohen's d) for this two-mean comparison that may be compared with effects obtained in previous experiments, perhaps as part of a meta-analysis. Neither of these contrasts is easy to do using confidence intervals. That is, unlike NHST, confidence intervals do not provide an exact probability associated with a difference seen in our experiment and the calculation of an effect size is more directly carried out following a t-test (see Chapter 12).

In summary, we encourage you to look at your data and differences between means using more than one statistical technique, seeking evidence for "what happened" from different approaches to data analysis.

Reporting Results of a Single-Factor Independent Groups Experiment

We are now ready to model a statement of results based on the recommendations of the APA *Publication Manual* (2001) (see especially pp. 20–26 of the *Manual*). The report includes information obtained from both the construction of confidence intervals (Chapter 12) and NHST. A report of the results of the memory training study might take this form:

> The effects of memory training on retention of words was examined. Mean recall (out of a possible 20 words) was determined for each of the four instructional conditions, each with five participants ($N = 20$): story method, imagery method, rhyme method, and control (no specific instructions). These means (and sample

standard deviations) were, for each of the conditions: story, 13.2 (1.3); imagery, 14.4 (1.8); rhyme, 13.4 (1.3); control, 10.0 (1.6). Mean recall differed significantly among the four instruction conditions, $F(3, 16) = 7.80$, $p = .002$, $\eta^2 = .59$. A comparison of two means was performed to contrast the overall mean recall of the three memory training groups with that of the control group. Retention of words was greater for participants in the memory training groups (13.7) compared to the control group, $t(16) = 4.66$, $p < .01$. The effect size, d, for this comparison was 2.33, indicating a large effect of memory training relative to no training. The 95% confidence interval for the mean of each group is shown in Figure 13.1. The confidence interval for the control group does not overlap the intervals for the instructional groups. However, the intervals among the three training conditions overlap substantially (including the sample means within these intervals), indicating the population means for the three instructional conditions are not likely to differ. This pattern indicates that instructions to use specific memory techniques, regardless of type of technique, were successful in increasing memory retention relative to a noninstructed control group.

Commentary   In the first sentence of the report we find information about the purpose of the experiment, the overall number of participants (20), the number of levels of the independent variable, how levels were defined (and their names), and the size of each group (5). Descriptive statistics are then provided for each group. The width of the confidence intervals calls our attention to the precision of estimation (or lack of) of the population means for each group as well as the likely pattern of population means. The construction of confidence intervals follows the procedure outlined in Chapter 12. Because the square root of the MS_{error} from the ANOVA summary table is equivalent to s_{pooled} we can define the 95% confidence interval as:

$$95\% \; CI = \overline{X} \pm \left[\sqrt{(MS_{error}/n)}\right](t_{crit})$$

FIGURE 13.1   Means and 95% confidence intervals for the memory training experiment.

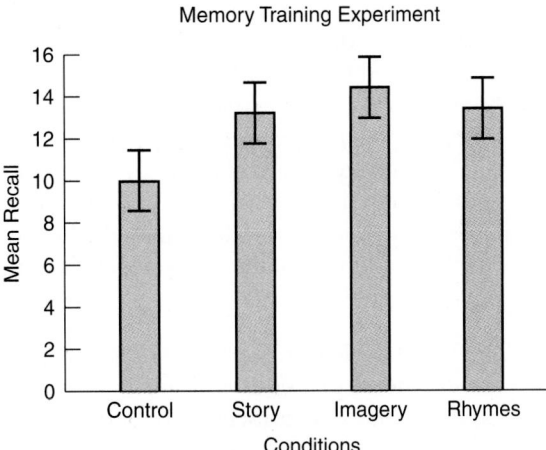

where t_{crit} is the value for t with degrees of freedom associated with the MS_{error}.

In our example, the degrees of freedom for MS_{error} are 16 (see ANOVA Summary Table) and t_{crit} at the .05 level (two-tailed test) is 2.12. Therefore,

$$95\% \ CI = \overline{X} \pm \left[\sqrt{(2.32/5)}\right](2.12) = \overline{X} \pm (\sqrt{.464})(2.12) = \overline{X} \pm (.68)(2.12)$$

$$= \overline{X} \pm 1.44$$

As shown in Figure 13.1, intervals overlap among the three training conditions but do not overlap with the control interval. The report of the omnibus F is accompanied by both the exact probability for the F-test and an effect size measure, eta squared. Neither of these pieces of information can be obtained from an examination of the confidence intervals. This information is repeated for the comparison of two means, which focuses on the comparison between the performance of the experimental groups and the control group. Usually only one effect size measure is reported and, as you saw, we chose d, although one might reasonably prefer eta squared. Finally, the final sentence summarizes the results of the experiment for the reader.

It may be useful in some situations to perform additional comparisons of two means, for example, contrasting the difference between one or more of the experimental groups and the control group. However, in this case, an examination of the confidence intervals in Figure 13.1 suggests that, since intervals overlap substantially among the three training conditions but none overlaps with the control interval, we may reasonably conclude that each specific training procedure differed from the control and the training conditions did not differ from one another (see Chapter 12).

REPEATED MEASURES ANALYSIS OF VARIANCE

- The general procedures and logic for null hypothesis testing using repeated measures analysis of variance are similar to those used for independent groups analysis of variance.
- Before beginning the analysis of variance for a complete repeated measures design, a summary score (e.g., mean, median) for each participant must be computed for each condition.
- Descriptive data are calculated to summarize performance for each condition of the independent variable across all participants.
- The primary way that analysis of variance for repeated measures differs is in the estimation of error variation, or residual variation; residual variation is the variation that remains when systematic variation due to the independent variable and subjects is removed from the estimate of total variation.

The analysis of experiments using repeated measures designs involves the same general procedures used in the analysis of independent groups design experiments. The principles of NHST are applied to determine whether the differences obtained in the experiment are larger than would be expected on the basis of error variation alone. The analysis begins with an omnibus analysis of variance to determine whether the independent variable has produced any systematic variation among the levels of the independent variable. Should this omnibus analysis prove statistically significant, confidence intervals and comparisons of two means can be made to find the specific source of the systematic variation—that is, to determine which specific levels differed from each other. We have already described the logic and procedures for this general analysis plan for experiments that involve independent groups designs. We will focus in this section on the analysis procedures specific to repeated measures designs. Our example will be the time-perception experiment described in Chapter 8.

Summarizing the Data   Recall that in a repeated measures design, each participant experiences every condition of the experiment. In a complete design, each participant experiences every condition more than once; in an incomplete design, each participant experiences every condition exactly once. In Chapter 8 we described an experiment in which participants estimated the duration of four time intervals (12, 24, 36, and 48 seconds) in a complete repeated measures design. For example, on a single trial, participants experienced a randomly determined time interval (e.g., 36 seconds) and then were asked to estimate the duration of the interval.

The first step for analyzing these data is to prepare a data matrix that allows you to summarize participants' performance in each condition of the experiment. In a complete design, this requires that you first calculate for each participant a score to summarize each individual's performance in each condition. This summary statistic balances the practice effects associated with any one particular trial across the trials for a condition. In the time-estimation experiment, participants experienced each condition six times; thus, with four conditions in the experiment, each participant made 24 estimates. A median was used to summarize each participant's performance in each of the four conditions. Typically a mean would be calculated to summarize a participant's score within a condition, but recall that a mean is influenced by extreme scores. Participants' time estimates are likely to have extreme values on some trials (e.g., due to inattention). The median scores for five participants are presented in the top portion of Table 13.4. For example, the median amount of time estimated by the first participant for the 12-second interval condition, across six trials, was 13 seconds. The next step in summarizing the data is to calculate descriptive statistics across the participants for each of the conditions. The means and standard deviations (in parentheses) for each condition also appear in Table 13.4.

The focus of the analysis was on whether the participants could discriminate intervals of different lengths. As you have probably already realized, we cannot confirm the participants' ability to discriminate intervals of varying lengths until we know that the mean differences in Table 13.4 are greater than would be expected on the basis of error variation alone. That is, even though it may appear that participants were able to discriminate between the different intervals

TABLE 13.4   DATA MATRIX AND ANALYSIS OF VARIANCE SUMMARY TABLE FOR A REPEATED
MEASURES DESIGN EXPERIMENT

	Data matrix			
	Interval length			
Participant	12	24	36	48
1	13	21	30	38
2	10	15	38	35
3	12	23	31	32
4	12	15	22	32
5	16	36	69	60
Mean (SD)	12.6 (2.0)	22.0 (7.7)	38.0 (16.3)	39.4 (10.5)

Note: Each value in the table represents the median of the participants' six responses at each level of the interval length variable.

Source of variation	df	SS	MS	F	p
Subjects	4	1553.5	—	—	—
Interval length	3	2515.6	838.5	15.6	.000
Residual (error variation)	12	646.9	53.9		
Total	19	4716.0			

when examining the means, we do not know if their performance was different from that which would occur by chance. The null hypothesis for an omnibus analysis of variance for the data in Table 13.4 is that the population means estimated for each interval are the same. To perform an *F*-test of this null hypothesis, we need an estimate of error variation plus systematic variation (the numerator of an *F*-test). The variation among the mean estimates across participants for the four intervals provides the information we need for the numerator. Even if these five participants had been tested on only one interval length several times, we would not expect their mean estimates to be identical. Thus, we know the mean estimates we have for each level of the interval variable reflect error variation as well. We also know, however, that if the different interval lengths did systematically affect the participants' judgments, then the mean estimates for the intervals would reflect this systematic variation. To complete the *F*-test, we also need an estimate of error variation alone (the denominator of the *F*-test). See Box 13.4.

The source of error variation in the repeated measures designs is the differences in the ways the conditions affect different participants. Perhaps the best way to describe the way we get these estimates is to say that we do it "by default." We first determine how much total variation there is in our experiment. Then we subtract the two potential sources of systematic variation: the independent variable and subjects. The remainder is called residual variation, and it

---

BOX 13.4

ESTIMATING ERROR AND SENSITIVITY IN A REPEATED MEASURES DESIGN

One distinctive characteristic of the analysis of repeated measures designs is the way in which error variation is estimated. We described earlier that for the random groups design individual differences among participants that are balanced across groups provide the estimate of error variation that becomes the denominator of the *F*-test. Because individuals participate in only one condition in these designs, differences among participants cannot be eliminated—they can only be balanced. In repeated measures designs, on the other hand, there is systematic variation among participants. Some participants consistently perform better across conditions, and some participants consistently perform worse. Because each

individual participates in each condition of repeated measures designs, however, differences among participants contribute equally to the mean performance in each condition. Accordingly, any differences among the means for each condition in repeated measures designs cannot be the result of systematic differences among participants. In repeated measures designs, however, differences among participants are not just balanced—they are actually eliminated from the analysis. *The ability to eliminate systematic variation due to participants in repeated measures designs makes these designs generally more sensitive than random groups designs.*

---

represents our estimate of error variation alone. As was the case in the random groups design when we used variation within groups as our estimate of error variation alone, residual variation serves as the denominator for the *F*-test in repeated measures designs (i.e., as an estimate of error variation alone).

Interpreting the ANOVA Summary Table   The analysis of variance summary table for this analysis is presented in the lower portion of Table 13.4. The computations of a repeated measures analysis of variance would be done using a statistical software package on a computer. Our focus now is on interpreting the values in the summary table and not on how these values are computed. Table 13.4 lists the four sources of variation in the analysis of a repeated measures design with one manipulated independent variable. Reading from the bottom of the summary table up, these sources are: (1) total variation, (2) residual variation, (3) variation due to interval length (the independent variable), and (4) variation due to subjects.

As in any summary table, the most critical pieces of information are the *F*-test for the effect of the independent variable of interest and the probability associated with that *F*-test assuming the null hypothesis is true. The important *F*-test in Table 13.4 is the one for interval length. The numerator for this *F*-test is the mean square (MS) for interval length; the denominator is the residual MS. There are four interval lengths, so there are 3 degrees of freedom (df) for the numerator. There are 12 df for the residual variation. We can obtain the df for the residual variation by subtracting the df for subjects and for interval length from the total $df(19 - 4 - 3 = 12)$. The obtained F of 15.6 has a probability under the null hypothesis of .000, which is less than the .05 level of significance we have chosen

FIGURE 13.2   Means and 95% confidence intervals for the time-perception experiment.

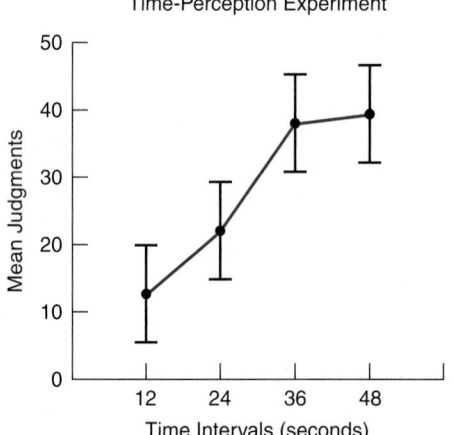

as our criterion for statistical significance. So we reject the null hypothesis and conclude that the interval length was a source of systematic variation. This means that we can conclude that the participants' estimates did differ systematically as a function of interval length.

Figure 13.2 shows 95% confidence intervals around the means in the time-perception experiment. The procedure for constructing these intervals is the same as that for the independent groups experiment. Intervals were constructed using the MS_{error} (residual) in the omnibus ANOVA (as recommended by Loftus & Masson, 1994). That is,

$$95\% \ CI = \overline{X} \pm \left[\sqrt{(MS_{error}/n)}\right](t_{crit})$$

where t_{crit} is the value of t with the degrees of freedom associated with the MS_{error} (residual). The interpretation of confidence intervals in the repeated measures design is the same as that of the independent groups design (see Chapter 12).

Effect Size Measures   As we mentioned previously, it is a good idea to include measures of effect size for your analyses. A typical measure of effect size for a repeated measures design is the strength of association measure called eta squared (η^2). It may be calculated by dividing the sum of squares for the within-subjects effect by the combined sums of squares for the within-subjects effect and residual or error. For our sample study,

$$\text{eta squared} \ (\eta^2) = \frac{SS_{effect}}{SS_{effect} + SS_{error}} = \frac{2515.6}{2515.6 + 646.9} = .795$$

This indicates the proportion of variance accounted for by the independent variable.

In some cases, the omnibus analysis of variance would be followed by comparisons of two means (such as comparing the mean for each interval to the mean for the succeeding interval) to determine more exactly that mean estimates increased with increasing interval lengths. Once again, the logic of these two-mean comparisons corresponds to the logic we considered for comparisons in the random groups design. The decision to perform these comparisons will be influenced by the specific hypotheses being tested in the experiment and by knowledge gained from an examination of confidence intervals surrounding the means. (See Keppel [1991], however, for a discussion of the complications that can arise in doing two-mean comparisons in repeated measures designs.)

Two-Factor Analysis of Variance for Independent Groups Designs

The two-factor analysis of variance for independent groups designs is used for the analysis of experiments in which each of two independent variables was manipulated at two or more levels. The logic of complex designs with two independent variables and the conceptual basis for the analysis of these experiments are described in Chapter 9. In Chapter 9 you also learned to describe both main effects and interaction effects. We will focus in this chapter on the computer-assisted analysis of a factorial design that involves F-tests for the main effect of A, the main effect of B, and the interaction effect, A × B. The two-factor analysis for independent groups is applicable to experiments in which both independent variables are manipulated using a random groups design, in which both independent variables represent the natural groups design, or in which one independent variable represents the natural groups design and the other represents the random groups design. The analysis of a complex design proceeds somewhat differently depending on whether the omnibus F-test does or does not reveal an interaction effect. We first consider the analysis plan when an interaction effect is detected.

Analysis of a Complex Design with an Interaction Effect

- If the omnibus analysis of variance reveals a statistically significant interaction effect, the source of the interaction effect is identified using simple main effects analyses and comparisons of two means.
- A simple main effect is the effect of one independent variable at one level of a second independent variable.
- If an independent variable has three or more levels, comparisons of two means can be used to examine the source of a simple main effect by comparing means two at a time.
- Confidence intervals may be drawn around group means to provide information regarding the precision of estimation of population means.

We discussed an experiment in Chapter 9 by Rodman and Burger (1985) in which college students were asked to read about a car accident. One independent variable was the severity of the described accident (severe and nonsevere). Students were randomly assigned to read one of these two descriptions. A natural groups design was used for the second independent variable. Students were selected on the basis of their scores on a paper-and-pencil test of depression to represent three groups: nondepressed, slightly depressed, and mildly depressed individuals. Thus, the experiment was a 2 × 3 design.

As we described in Chapter 9, Rodman and Burger investigated a phenomenon called the defensive attribution effect. Attributions refer to the causal explanations we use to try to account for our own behavior and the behavior of others. In previous experiments, nondepressed participants who read a description of an accident in which a person suffered mild or severe consequences attributed more responsibility to the perpetrator in the severe than in the mild accident condition. It appears that nondepressed individuals do not want to attribute the cause of a severe accident to chance. To do so would increase the perceived possibility that they themselves could be involved in a severe accident. The attribution of greater responsibility to the perpetrator in the severe accident is called defensive attribution. Nondepressed individuals "defended" or protected themselves against thinking that they would be involved in future severe accidents. Because depressed individuals tend to exhibit negative thinking, Rodman and Burger reasoned that they might be less likely to show this defensive attribution effect. That is, they would be less likely to defend themselves against thinking that there is a possibility that it could happen to them.

Rodman and Burger hypothesized that the defensive-attribution effect would decrease as a person's level of depression increased. The major dependent variable in their study was a single item on a longer questionnaire that asked students to divide 100% among four potential sources of responsibility for the accident: each of the three drivers in the accident and uncontrollable "circumstances" (i.e., chance). The defensive-attribution effect would be reflected in a larger value assigned to uncontrollable circumstances for the nonsevere than for the severe accident.

The mean percentage values for this uncontrollable factor for each of the six conditions are presented in Table 13.5. We described the analysis of these data in Chapter 9. An analysis of variance summary table for a complex design with two independent variables includes four sources of variation: the main effects

TABLE 13.5   MEAN PERCENTAGE OF RESPONSIBILITY ATTRIBUTED TO UNCONTROLLABLE CIRCUMSTANCES

Type of accident	Level of depression		
	Nondepressed	Slightly depressed	Mildly depressed
Severe	7.00 (9.2)	14.00 (16.1)	16.90 (16.0)
Nonsevere	30.50 (22.2)	16.50 (12.7)	3.75 (3.5)

Note: Standard deviations appear in parentheses. Adapted from Rodman and Burger (1985).

of each independent variable, the interaction effect of the two independent variables, and the within-group error. For example, in the Rodman and Burger experiment there could be a main effect of Type of Accident and a main effect of Level of Depression. The effect of primary interest in the Rodman and Burger experiment, however, was the predicted interaction effect between the two independent variables. Moreover, an ANOVA revealed that this interaction effect was statistically significant. As you can see in Table 13.5, the interaction effect arises because the differences between the percentage values for severe and nonsevere accidents changed as the degree of depression increased. Specifically, nondepressed students showed the defensive-attribution effect and mildly depressed students did not.

Once we have confirmed that there is an interaction of two independent variables, we must locate more precisely the source of that interaction effect. There are statistical tests specifically designed for tracing the source of a significant interaction effect. These tests are called simple main effects and comparisons of two means (see Keppel, 1991).

A *simple main effect* is the effect of one independent variable at one level of a second independent variable. In fact, one definition of an interaction effect is that the simple main effects across levels are different. We can illustrate the use of simple main effects by returning to the results of the Rodman and Burger experiment. There are five simple main effects in Table 13.5. Three of the simple main effects are represented by the effect of the type of accident (severe, nonsevere) at each of the three levels of depression considered separately. The other two simple main effects are represented by the effect of depression level (nondepressed, slightly depressed, mildly depressed) at each of the two levels of accident type. The defensive attribution effect refers to the difference between the means for severe and nonsevere accidents, and Rodman and Burger predicted that this effect of the type of accident would decrease as the level of depression increased. Therefore, it was appropriate for Rodman and Burger to analyze the simple main effect of accident type at each level of depression to test their prediction. They found, as predicted, that the simple main effect of the type of accident was statistically significant for nondepressed students. That is, this group of nondepressed students demonstrated different attributions to uncontrollable (chance) circumstances for severe and nonsevere accidents. In contrast, the simple main effects for type of accident were not statistically significant for the slightly depressed and the mildly depressed students. Thus, for the two groups of slightly and mildly depressed students, there was no difference in their attribution to chance for severe and nonsevere accidents.

Two of the simple main effects in the Rodman and Burger (1985) study each involve three means. One can also examine how nondepressed, slightly depressed, and mildly depressed students differed in their attributions for severe accidents and how these three groups differed in their attributions for nonsevere accidents. That is, if statistical analysis reveals a significant simple main effect, then one concludes that there is a difference among the means (e.g., among the three groups for severe accidents). The next step, then, is to conduct comparisons of two means to analyze simple main effects more fully (see Keppel, 1991). That is, once a simple main effect involving more than two levels of a variable has been shown to be statistically significant, comparisons of two means can be done to determine the nature of the differences among the levels. In this procedure, means within the simple main effect are compared two at a time in order to identify the source of differences among levels. As you can see, two-mean comparisons only make sense when there is a simple main effect for an independent variable with three or more levels. With two levels, a simple main effect compares the difference between the two means and no additional comparisons are necessary.

Once an interaction effect has been thoroughly analyzed, researchers can also examine the main effects of each independent variable. In general, however, main effects are less interesting when an interaction effect is statistically significant. For example, in the Rodman and Burger (1985) experiment, we learned that the effect of the type of accident on participants' attributions to uncontrollable circumstances depended on individuals' level of depression. Based on the analyses of main effects, we do not learn much more of interest when we add that, overall, participants attributed a higher mean percentage of responsibility to uncontrollable circumstances for nonsevere accidents compared to severe accidents. Nonetheless, there are experiments in which the interaction effect and the main effects are all of interest.

Analysis with No Interaction Effect

- If an omnibus analysis of variance indicates the interaction effect between independent variables is not statistically significant, the next step is to determine whether the main effects of the variables are statistically significant.
- The source of a statistically significant main effect can be specified more precisely by performing comparisons that compare means two at a time and by constructing confidence intervals.

When the interaction effect is not statistically significant, the next step is to examine the main effects of each independent variable. If the overall main effect for an independent variable is not statistically significant, then there is nothing more to do. However, if a main effect is statistically significant, there are several approaches a researcher may take. For example, if there are three or more levels of the independent variable, the source of a statistically significant main effect can be specified more precisely by performing comparisons of two means. (Of course, if there are but two levels, an additional comparison is not needed.) Yet another approach is to construct confidence intervals around the group means (see Chapter 12). You may see that these analyses are similar to the analyses we described for a single-factor independent groups design. The difference for the complex design is that the data for one independent variable are collapsed across the levels of other independent variables.

Effect Sizes for Two-Factor Design with Independent Groups

A common measure of effect size for a complex design using ANOVA is eta squared (η^2), or proportion of variance accounted for, which was discussed earlier in the context of single-factor designs. In calculating eta squared, it is recommended that we focus only on the effect of interest (see Rosenthal & Rosnow, 1991). Specifically, eta squared can be defined as:

$$\eta^2 = \frac{SS_{\text{effect of interest}}}{SS_{\text{effect of interest}} + SS_{\text{within}}} \quad \text{(see Rosenthal \& Rosnow, 1991, p. 352)}.$$

Thus, eta squared may be obtained for each of the three effects in an A × B design.

As noted above (and see Rosenthal & Rosnow, 1991), when the sums of squares for the effects are not available, eta squared can be computed using the following formula:

$$\eta^2 = \frac{(F)(df_{\text{effect}})}{(F)(df_{\text{effect}}) + (df_{\text{error}})}$$

ROLE OF CONFIDENCE INTERVALS IN THE ANALYSIS OF COMPLEX DESIGNS

The analysis of a complex design can be aided by the construction of confidence intervals for the means of interest. For example, each mean in a 2 × 3 design can be bracketed with a confidence interval following the procedures outlined in Chapter 12 and earlier in this chapter. Recall that the formula is:

$$\text{Upper limit of 95\% confidence interval: } \overline{X} + [t_{.05}][s_{\overline{X}}]$$

$$\text{Lower limit of 95\% confidence interval: } \overline{X} - [t_{.05}][s_{\overline{X}}]$$

When sample sizes are equal, the estimated standard error is defined as:

$$s_{\overline{X}} = \frac{s_{\text{pooled}}}{\sqrt{n}} \quad \text{where } n = \text{sample size for each group.}$$

Because the square root of the MS_{error} from the ANOVA Summary Table is equivalent to s_{pooled} we can define the 95% confidence interval as:

$$95\% \; CI = \overline{X} \pm (t_{.05})\left[\sqrt{(MS_{\text{error}}/\sqrt{n})}\right]$$

where $t_{.05}$ is defined by the degrees of freedom associated with the MS_{error}.

To illustrate the use of confidence intervals in the analysis of a complex design we will use the results of a hypothetical 2 × 3 independent groups design. Suppose that in this experiment participants are asked to perform a motor task with their dominant hand or their nondominant hand. Furthermore, one-third of the group of participants are randomly assigned to a 60-second delay between trials, another third to a 30-second delay, and the final third of the participants are assigned to a 0-second delay between trials. The dependent variable is the number of correct responses on the motor task. Variable A is Hand Dominance with 2 levels (dominant and nondominant hand). Variable B is Delay Between the Trials with 3 levels (0, 30, and 60 seconds). The means for each of the six groups in this experiment are presented below. There were 5 participants in each group ($n = 5$). It may be helpful to graph the means to reveal the nature of the interaction effect. The omnibus F-test revealed that the interaction effect was statistically significant, $F(2, 24) = 12.34, p \leq .0005$ (as were both main effects).

		Delay (B)		
		0 sec (b_1)	30 sec (b_2)	60 sec (b_3)
	Dom (a_1)	19.0	19.0	20.0
Hand (A)				
	NonDom (a_2)	10.6	15.8	18.2

The MS_{error} for this hypothetical experiment was 2.45 ($df = 24$). Thus, the pooled standard error of the mean is equal to:

$$\left(\sqrt{MS_{error}}/\sqrt{n}\right) = (\sqrt{2.45}/\sqrt{5}) = \sqrt{.49} = .70$$

Consulting Appendix Table A.2, we find that the critical t value for 24 df is 2.06. The 95% CIs for the six groups in this experiment are:

$$a_1b_1 = \overline{X} \pm (2.06)(.70) = 19.0 \pm 1.44 = 17.56 - 20.44$$
$$a_1b_2 = \overline{X} \pm (2.06)(.70) = 19.0 \pm 1.44 = 17.56 - 20.44$$
$$a_1b_3 = \overline{X} \pm (2.06)(.70) = 20.0 \pm 1.44 = 18.56 - 21.44$$
$$a_2b_1 = \overline{X} \pm (2.06)(.70) = 10.6 \pm 1.44 = 9.16 - 12.04$$
$$a_2b_2 = \overline{X} \pm (2.06)(.70) = 15.8 \pm 1.44 = 14.36 - 17.24$$
$$a_2b_3 = \overline{X} \pm (2.06)(.70) = 18.2 \pm 1.44 = 16.76 - 19.64$$

Figure 13.3 shows the confidence intervals around the six means in the hypothetical experiment. An examination of the CIs tells us about the precision of our estimates. We want to examine the interval width and the probable pattern of *population* means by looking to see if the intervals around the sample means overlap, and, if so, to what degree they overlap. Recall that a rule of thumb for interpreting confidence intervals suggests that if the intervals around means do not overlap then the two means would likely be statistically significant if tested using NHST (see Box 12.5 in Chapter 12).

Based on these 95% confidence intervals, the interaction effect indicates that the effect of the hand-dominance variable varies depending on the level of the

FIGURE 13.3 Mean number of correct responses as a function of the delay between trials (in seconds) and hand used to perform motor task (dominant, nondominant). The 95% confidence interval is shown around each mean.

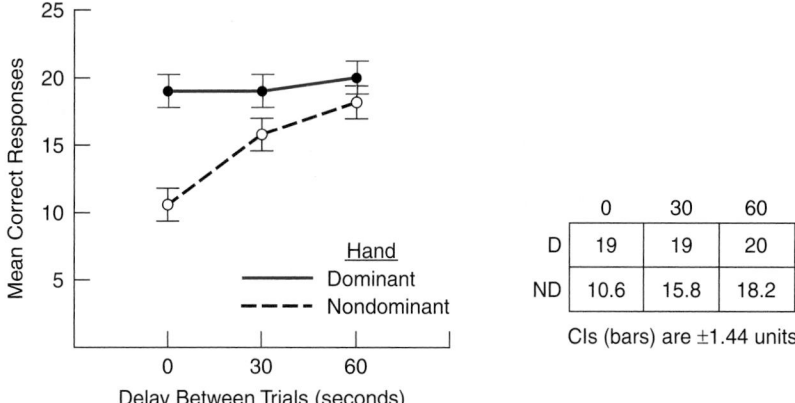

delay variable. In the 0-second and 30-second delay conditions, the number of correct responses is greater for the dominant hand compared to the nondominant hand. This difference in motor-task performance when comparing dominant and nondominant hands is greatest for the 0-second delay between trials, followed by the 30-second delay condition. There may be no difference in motor-task performance between groups using the dominant and the nondominant hand when there is a 60-second delay between trials (i.e., the confidence intervals overlap); additional data are needed before a firm conclusion may be made.

The second way to explain the interaction effect is to describe the effect of the delay variable for each level of hand dominance. For the dominant hand condition, the 95% confidence intervals overlap across the three levels of time delay, and each of the three sample means are included within the three confidence intervals representing the delay levels. Thus, we can reasonably conclude that the delay variable does not affect motor-task performance for participants who use their dominant hand. In contrast, the number of correct responses within the nondominant hand condition varies as a function of the delay variable. The 95% confidence intervals indicate fewer correct responses in the 0-second condition compared to the 30-second and the 60-second delay conditions, but that performance in these latter two conditions may not differ (the results are inconclusive).

Two-Factor Analysis of Variance for a Mixed Design

The two-factor analysis of variance for a mixed design is appropriate when one independent variable represents either the random groups or natural groups design and the second independent variable represents the repeated measures design. The first independent variable is called the between-subjects factor

Care must be taken when analyzing a mixed design to use the appropriate error term for analyses beyond those listed in the summary table (i.e., simple main effects, comparisons of two means). For example, if a significant interaction effect is obtained, it is recommended that simple main effects be analyzed by treating each simple effect as a single-factor ANOVA at that level of the second independent variable. If, for instance, we had obtained a significant interaction effect between group and presentation frequency in our sample experiment, a simple main effect for the intentional group would involve carrying out a repeated measures ANOVA for only that group (see Keppel, 1991, for more information on these comparisons).

Effect size estimates in a mixed design also frequently make use of eta squared, that is, an estimate of proportion of variance accounted for by the independent variable. As in the independent groups design (see above) eta squared is defined as the *SS* effect divided by the *SS* effect plus the *SS* error for that effect.

REPORTING RESULTS OF A COMPLEX DESIGN

Reporting results of a complex design follows the general form of a report for a single-factor ANOVA but giving special attention to the nature of an interaction effect when it is present. The following are important elements of a report of the results of a complex design:

—description of variables and definition of levels (conditions) of each;
—summary statistics for cells of the design matrix in text, table, or figure, including when appropriate, confidence intervals for group means;
—report of *F*-tests for main effects and interaction effect with exact probabilities;
—effect size measure for each effect;
—statement of power for nonsignificant effects;
—simple main effects analysis when interaction effect is statistically significant;
—verbal description of statistically significant interaction effect (when present), referring reader to differences between cell means across levels of the independent variables;
—verbal description of statistically significant main effect (when present), referring reader to differences among cell means collapsed across levels of the independent variables;
—comparisons of two means, when appropriate, to clarify sources of systematic variation among means contributing to main effect;
—conclusion that you wish reader to make from the results of this analysis.

An example of a Results section can be found in the Sample Research Report in Chapter 14.

SUMMARY

Statistical tests based on null hypothesis significance testing (NHST) are commonly used to perform confirmatory data analysis in psychology. NHST is used to determine whether differences produced by independent variables in an experiment are greater than what would be expected solely on the basis of error variation (chance). The null hypothesis is that the independent variable did not have an effect. A statistically significant outcome is one that has a small probability of occurring if the null hypothesis were true. Two types of errors may arise when doing NHST. A Type I error occurs when a researcher rejects the null hypothesis when it is true. The probability of a Type I error is equivalent to alpha or the level of significance, usually .05. A Type II error occurs when a false null hypothesis is not rejected. Type II errors can occur when a study does not have enough power to correctly reject a null hypothesis. The primary way researchers increase power is by increasing sample size. By using power tables researchers may estimate, before a study is conducted, the power needed to reject a false null hypothesis, and, after a study is completed, the likelihood of detecting the effect that was found. The exact probability associated with the result of a statistical test should be reported.

The appropriate statistical test for comparing two means is the *t*-test. When the difference between two means is tested, an effect size measure, such as Cohen's *d*, should also be reported. The APA *Publication Manual* strongly recommends that confidence intervals be reported as well as the results of NHST. When reporting the results of NHST, it is important to keep in mind that statistical significance (or nonoverlapping confidence intervals) is not the same as scientific or practical significance. Moreover, neither NHST, confidence intervals, nor effect sizes, tell us about the soundness of a study's methodology. That is, none of these measures alone may be used to state that the alternative hypothesis (that the independent variable did have an effect) is correct. Only after we have examined carefully the methodology used to obtain the data for an analysis will we want to venture a claim about what influenced behavior.

Analysis of variance (ANOVA) is the appropriate statistical test when comparing three or more means. The logic of ANOVA is based on identifying both error variation and sources of systematic variation in the data. An *F*-test is constructed that represents error variation and systematic variation (if any) divided by error variation alone. Results of the overall analysis, called an omnibus *F*-test, are reported in an ANOVA Summary Table. A large *F*-ratio provides evidence that the independent variable had an effect. Effect size measures for a single-factor independent groups design include Cohen's *f* and eta squared (η^2). Comparisons of two means may be conducted following results of an omnibus *F*-test in order to more clearly specify the sources of systematic variation contributing to a significant omnibus *F*-test. Confidence intervals, too, may be meaningfully used to complement an ANOVA conducted with data from a multiple-group study and should be reported when the results of NHST are summarized.

A two-factor ANOVA is appropriate when a researcher examines simultaneously the effect on behavior of two or more independent variables in a complex design. When one independent variable represents an independent groups variable (random or natural groups) and another is a repeated measures within-subjects variable, we speak of a mixed design. An omnibus *F*-test is carried out to assess both main effects and the interaction effect of variables. When a statistically significant interaction effect is found, the source of the interaction effect may be pursued by conducting simple main effects. A simple main effect is the effect of an independent variable at only one level of a second independent variable. Confidence intervals, too, may be used to help understand the effect of an independent variable in a complex design. A commonly used measure of effect size in a complex design is eta squared.

KEY CONCEPTS

null hypothesis (H$_0$)
level of significance
Type I error
Type II error
power
t-test for independent groups
repeated measures
   (within-subjects) *t*-test
ANOVA

single-factor independent groups
   design
F-test
omnibus *F*-test
eta squared (η^2)
Cohen's *f*
comparison of two means

REVIEW QUESTIONS

1 What does it mean to say that the results of a statistical test are "statistically significant"?

2 Differentiate between Type I and Type II errors as they occur when carrying out NHST.

3 What three factors determine the power of a statistical test? Which factor is the primary one that researchers can use to control power?

4 Why is a repeated measures design likely to be more sensitive than a random groups design?

5 Describe one advantage and one limitation of using measures of effect size.

6 Why may a statistically significant result be neither scientifically nor practically significant?

7 Outline briefly the logic of the *F*-test.

8 Distinguish between the information you gain from an omnibus *F*-test and from comparisons of two means.

9 What is the primary way that a repeated measures ANOVA differs from that of an ANOVA for independent groups?

10 How does a simple main effect differ from an overall main effect?

CHALLENGE QUESTIONS

1 A researcher conducts an experiment comparing two methods of teaching young children to read. An older method is compared with a newer one and the mean performance of the new method was found to be greater than that of the older method. The results are reported as, $t(120) = 2.10, p = .04(d = .34)$.

A Is the result statistically significant?

B How many participants were there in this study?

C Based on the effect size measure, d, what may we say about the size of the effect found in this study?

D The researcher states that on the basis of this result the newer method is clearly of practical significance when teaching children to read and should be implemented right away. How would you respond to this statement?

E What would the construction of confidence intervals add to our understanding of these results?

2 A social psychologist compares three kinds of propaganda messages on college students' attitudes toward war on terrorism. Ninety ($N = 90$) students are randomly assigned in equal numbers to the three different communication conditions. A paper-and-pencil attitude measure is used to assess students' attitudes toward the war after they are exposed to the propaganda statements. An ANOVA is carried out to determine the effect of the three messages on student attitudes. The ANOVA Summary Table is found below:

Source	Sum of squares	df	Mean square	F	p
Commun- ication	180.10	2	90.05	17.87	0.000
Error	438.50	87	5.04		

A Is the result statistically significant? Why or why not?

B What effect size measure can be easily calculated from these results? What is the value of that measure?

C How could doing comparisons of two means contribute to the interpretation of these results?

D Although the group means are not provided, it is possible from these data to calculate the width of the confidence interval for the means based on the pooled variance estimate. What is the width of the confidence interval for the means in this study?

3 A developmental psychologist gives 4th, 6th, and 8th grade children two types of critical thinking tests. There are 28 children tested at each grade level; 14 received one form (A or B) of the test. The dependent measure is the percentage correct on the tests. The mean percentage correct for the children at each grade level and for the two tests is as follows:

Test	4th	6th	8th
Form A	38.14	63.64	80.21
Form B	52.29	68.64	80.93

The ANOVA Summary Table for this experiment is as follows:

Source	Sum of squares	df	Mean square	F	p
Grade	17698.95	2	8849.48	96.72	.000
Test	920.05	1	920.05	10.06	.002
Grade × Test	658.67	2	329.33	3.60	.032
Error	7136.29	78	91.49		

A Draw a graph showing the mean results for this experiment. Based on your examination of the graph, would you suspect a statistically significant interaction effect between the variables? Explain why or why not.

B Which effects were statistically significant? Describe verbally each of the statistically significant effects.

C What are the eta squared values for the main effects of grade and test?

D What further analyses could you do to determine the source of the interaction effect?

E What is the simple main effect of Form for each level of Grade?

F Calculate confidence intervals for the six means in the experiment and draw them around the means in your graph of these results.

Answer to Challenge Question 1

A Yes. The obtained probability of this result assuming the null hypothesis is true is less than .05, the conventional level of significance.

B The degrees of freedom (*df*) are reported to be 120. For an independent groups *t*-test, $df = n_1 + n_2 - 2$. Thus, there must have been 122 participants.

C Cohen's guidelines suggest that an effect size of .20 is a small effect, .50 a medium or average effect, and .80 a large effect. An effect size of .34 is a small effect.

D The results of NHST do not speak directly to practical significance. If the newer method is much more expensive, too time-consuming to implement, or requires resources (e.g., new reading materials) that are not immediately available, then the practical significance of this finding (at least in the short run) is likely to be small. This may be especially the case because the effect size is rather small. Also, the fact that $p = .04$ suggests that the probability of replicating this statistically significant finding at the .05 level is not that high. Finally, we would want to examine carefully the methodology of the study to determine that the study was sound, free of confounds and experimenter errors.

E Constructing a confidence interval for the difference between the two population means would provide evidence of the size of the difference between these methods and indicate (based on examining the width of the interval) the precision of the estimation of the difference between two population means.

CHAPTER FOURTEEN

Communication in Psychology

CHAPTER OUTLINE

INTRODUCTION

Scientific research is a public activity. A clever hypothesis, an elegant research design, meticulous data collection procedures, reliable results, and an insightful theoretical interpretation of the findings are not useful to the scientific community unless they are made public. As one writer suggests most emphatically, "Until its results have gone through the painful process of publication, preferably in a refereed journal of high standards, scientific research is just play. Publication is an indispensable part of science" (Bartholomew, 1982, p. 233). Bartholomew (1982) expresses a preference for a "refereed" journal because refereed journals involve the process of *peer review*. Submitted manuscripts are reviewed by other researchers ("peers") who are experts in the specific field of research addressed in the paper under review. These peer reviewers decide whether the research is methodologically sound and whether it makes a substantive contribution to the discipline of psychology. These reviews are then submitted to a senior researcher who serves as editor of the journal. It is the editor's job to decide which papers warrant publication. Peer review is the primary method of quality control for published psychological research.

There are many journals in which psychologists can publish their research. *Psychological Science, Memory & Cognition, Child Development, Journal of Personality and Social Psychology, Psychological Science in the Public Interest* and *Journal of Clinical and Consulting Psychology* are but a few of the many psychology journals. As we mentioned, editors of these journals make the final decisions about which manuscripts will be published. Their decisions are based on (a) the quality of the research and (b) the effectiveness of its presentation in the written manuscript, as assessed by the editor and the peer reviewers. Thus both content and style are important. Editors seek the best research, clearly described. The editors of the 26 primary journals of the American Psychological Association reviewed about 6,000 (5,978) manuscript submissions in 2003. Journal editors set rigorous standards; *only about one of every three (68% rejection rate) submitted manuscripts is accepted for publication* (American Psychological Association, 2003).

Editorial review and the publication process can take a long time. Up to a year (and sometimes longer) may elapse between when a paper is submitted and when it finally appears in the journal. The review of the manuscript can take several months before a decision whether to accept the paper is made. Several months are also required for the publication process between the time the paper is accepted and when it is actually published in the journal. To provide a more timely means of reporting research findings, professional societies such as the American Psychological Association, the American Psychological Society, the Psychonomic Society, the Society for Research in Child Development, and regional societies such as the Eastern, Midwestern, Southeastern, and Western Psychological Associations sponsor conferences at which researchers give brief oral presentations or present posters describing their recent work. Such conferences provide an opportunity for timely discussion and debate among investigators interested in the same research questions. Research that is "in press" (i.e., waiting completion of the publication process) may be discussed, thus giving conference attendees a preview of important, but yet-to-be-published, research findings.

Researchers often must obtain financial support in the form of a grant from a government or private agency in order to carry out their research. Grants are awarded on the basis of a competitive review of research proposals. Research proposals also typically are required of graduate students when preparing a master's thesis or dissertation. A faculty committee then reviews the proposal before the thesis or dissertation research is begun. So, too, undergraduate students often are required to prepare a research proposal as part of a research methods or laboratory class in psychology. Finally, researchers at all levels will find that research proposals are required by IRBs in order to assess the ethical nature of proposed research at an institution (see Chapter 3). Research proposals require a slightly different style and format from a journal article that reports results of a completed study. We provide suggestions for preparing a research proposal later in this chapter.

What do journal articles, oral presentations, and research proposals have to do with you? If you attend graduate school in psychology, you will likely have to describe your research using all three of these types of scientific communication. Even if you do not pursue a professional career in psychology, the principles of good written and oral research reports are applicable to a wide variety of employment situations. For example, a memo to your department manager describing the outcome of a recent sale may have much the same content and format as a short journal article. Of more immediate concern, you may have to prepare a research proposal and write or deliver a research report in your research methods course. This chapter will help you do these things well.

The primary source for scientific writing in psychology is the fifth edition of the *Publication Manual* (2001) of the American Psychological Association. Editors and authors use this manual to ensure a consistent style across the many different journals in psychology. The manual is an invaluable resource for almost any question pertaining to the style and format of a research manuscript. It includes chapters on the content and organization of a manuscript; the expression of ideas and reducing bias; APA editorial style; reference list format including referencing electronic media; manuscript preparation for journal articles and other published research; and on manuscript acceptance and production including guidelines for electronic submission of manuscripts. The manual also includes information about APA policies governing journals and their editorial management as well as information about ethical issues in scientific writing (see our discussion of this in Chapter 3). APA acknowledges that neither editorial style nor the technology of publishing is static. The APA website [www.apastyle.org] provides updates to the *Publication Manual* and the latest changes in APA style and in APA policies and procedures.

Throughout this chapter we have drawn heavily on the *Publication Manual* (2001).[1] This chapter is intended primarily to help you complete successfully the writing you will be doing in your research methods course. It is not intended as a substitute for the *Publication Manual* (2001). If you are planning advanced study in psychology, we recommend that you add the *Publication Manual of the American Psychological Association* (2001) to your personal library. APA also provides helpful resources such as *Mastering APA Style: Student's Workbook and Training Guide* (2001) by H. Gelfand and C. J. Walker. (You can order APA books from the APA website [www.apa.org] or from American Psychological Association, Book Order Department, P.O. Box 92984, Washington, DC 20090-2984.)

Formal communication among researchers through journal articles and convention presentations is not sufficient to sustain the collaborative nature of science. Informal communication is vital to doing research. Research ideas are often formulated in research team meetings or in informal conversations with colleagues. Researchers routinely collaborate at a distance using the Internet and discuss their research using e-mail. Researchers also access electronic databases through the Internet. The Internet has given researchers the ability to access and disseminate information related to their research more quickly and more extensively.

THE INTERNET AND RESEARCH

Access to the Internet has already become an indispensable tool for research psychologists, especially for communication via electronic mail (e-mail). The Internet also serves students and professional psychologists in many other important ways, including as a vehicle for conducting original research (see, for example, Azar, 1994a; 1994b; Birnbaum, 2000; Kardas & Milford, 1996; Kelley-Milburn & Milburn, 1995). We describe here a few of the more important ways that psychologists use the Internet in research.

For many researchers *e-mail* is their primary means of communication with colleagues, journal editors, research collaborators, directors of granting agencies, and other professionals. Have a question about an article you just read? Ask the author by sending an e-mail message. E-mailing is simple, efficient, and convenient. The first author of your textbook, for example, can be reached by sending an e-mail message to John J. Shaughnessy (Hope College) [shaughnessy@hope.edu]

There is also a home page on the Web dedicated to this textbook, which can be accessed for student resources (e.g., practice tests) and information about the authors, changes in editions, additional resources for doing psychological research, and errors or omissions in the current edition, publisher's address, ordering information, etc. Visit our page [www.mhhe.com/shaughnessy7].

Discussion groups, called "Listservs," allow interested individuals to discuss psychological issues in which they share an interest. The group consists of a "list" of "subscribers" who wish to contribute to an ongoing discussion. List members are immediately "served" any message posted by a subscriber. (If you subscribe to a large Listserv you will likely need to access and edit your e-mail frequently or you may find your mailbox stuffed with messages.) There are hundreds of Listservs on the Internet that link researchers around the world discussing a wide variety of topics, including addiction, religion, and women's studies. Some Listservs are open to anyone who wishes to take part in the discussion, including those who only want to participate passively ("lurk"). Other Listservs are open only to individuals with certain credentials (e.g., members of a particular APA division). APA also sponsors discussion groups for students (psycSTUDENTS) that can be accessed through their website [www.apa.org].

Databases on the Internet are just that: electronic data files that are stored on the Internet and that can be accessed electronically. Databases related to medicine, alcoholism, and opinion polls are available, to mention but a few. Databases are particularly useful when doing archival research (see Chapter 6) and time-series analyses (Chapter 11). Large databases, in which data for hundreds of variables and large numbers of participants are available, have become important to many researchers who seek to answer research questions in psychology (e.g., in clinical, social, and developmental psychology). Electronic access to databases frees researchers from the expense and time needed to collect data that may already exist in databases, thereby eliminating wasteful duplication of researchers' and participants' efforts.

Electronic access to journals is now common, and electronic submission of manuscripts is now the norm for journals and for conferences. The wide availability of Internet access and e-mail has facilitated the review process, such that the manuscript submission, peer reviews, and editorial feedback to authors can be completed using the Internet. In addition, some journals are offered exclusively as *electronic journals*. Subscribers receive articles in their electronic mailboxes and readers can electronically submit their comments on the articles. *Psycoloquy, Psyche,* and *Prevention and Treatment* are examples of electronic journals. Whether submitted to electronic journals or journals that are printed, authors seeking publication of their manuscript in respected journals should expect peer review of their research.

Original research, as you saw in earlier chapters, can also be done electronically. To repeat a comment made in Chapter 1: The Web allows practically any type of psychological research that uses computers as equipment and humans as participants (Krantz & Dalal, 2000; see especially Kraut et al., 2004, for helpful information about doing online research). How useful you will find the Internet in planning and conducting research will depend both on your specific needs and on your ability to use the Internet. If you are just beginning, we again recommend Fraley's guide, *How to Conduct Behavioral Research Over the Internet* (2004; New York: Guilford Press).

GUIDELINES FOR EFFECTIVE WRITING

Learning to write well is like learning to swim, drive a car, or play the piano. Improvement is unlikely to result solely from reading about how the activity is to be done. Heeding expert advice, though, can help a person get off to a good start. Effective writing begins with having something worthwhile to say, and then being willing to work hard to say it in the best way possible. One key to writing well is getting critical feedback from writing "coaches"—teachers, friends, editors, and even yourself. Lee Cronbach (1992), author of several of the most widely cited articles in the *Psychological Bulletin*, summarizes these ideas well.

> My advice must be like the legendary recipe for jugged hare, which begins, "First catch your hare." First, have a message worth delivering. Beyond that, it is care in writing that counts. . . . Rework any sentence that lacks flow or cadence, any sentence in which first-glance reading misplaces the emphasis, and any sentence in which comprehension comes less than instantly to that most knowledgeable of readers, the writer of the sentence. At best, technical writing can aspire to literary virtues—a change of pace from abstract thesis to memorable example, from brisk to easeful, from matter-of-fact to poetic. (p. 391)

Professional writer Jack Ridl provides the first maxim for effective writing: "Write, not assuming that you will be understood, but trying to avoid being misunderstood." Good writing, like good driving, is best done defensively. Assume that whatever can be misunderstood will be! To avoid these writing accidents, we offer the following tips to consider *before* you begin writing.

- **KNOW YOUR AUDIENCE.** If you assume your readers know more than they actually do, you will leave them confused. If you underestimate your readers, you risk boring them with unnecessary details. Either risk increases the likelihood that what you have written will not be read. But if you must err, it is better to underestimate your readers. For example, when you prepare a research report in a psychology class you might reasonably assume that your intended audience is your instructor. Writing for your instructor might lead you to leave a lot out of your paper because, after all, you assume your instructor knows all that anyway. It would probably be better to consider students in another section of your research methods course as your audience. This might result in your including more detail than necessary, but it will be easier for your instructor to help you learn to "edit out" the nonessential material than to "edit in" essential material that you have omitted. Whatever audience you choose, be sure to make the selection before you begin to write, and keep your audience in mind every step of the way.
- **IDENTIFY YOUR PURPOSE.** Journal articles fall within the general category of expository writing. *Webster's Dictionary* defines exposition as "discourse designed to convey information or explain what is difficult to understand." *The principal purposes of a journal article are to describe and to convince.* You want first to describe what you have done and what you have found, and second to convince the reader that your interpretation of these results is an appropriate one.

- **WRITE CLEARLY.** The foundation of good expository writing is clarity of thought and expression. The *Publication Manual* (2001) clearly outlines the road to clarity:

  > You can achieve clear communication, which is the prime objective of scientific reporting, by presenting ideas in an orderly manner and by expressing yourself smoothly and precisely. By developing ideas clearly and logically and leading readers smoothly from thought to thought, you make the task of reading an agreeable one. (p. 31)

The *Publication Manual* cites three avenues to clarity:

1 economy of expression,
2 precision, and
3 adherence to grammatical rules.

- **BE CONCISE.** If you say only what needs to be said, you will achieve economy of expression. Short words and short sentences are easier for readers to understand. The best way to eliminate wordiness is by editing your own writing across successive drafts and asking others to edit drafts of your paper.
- **BE PRECISE.** Precision in using language means choosing the right word for what you want to say. The *Publication Manual* (2001) contains sage advice regarding precision of expression:

  > Make certain that every word means exactly what you intend it to mean. Sooner or later most authors discover a discrepancy between the meaning they attribute to a term and its dictionary definition. In informal style, for example, *feel* broadly substitutes for *think* or *believe*, but in scientific style such latitude is not acceptable. (pp. 36–37)

- **FOLLOW GRAMMATICAL RULES.** Adherence to grammatical rules is absolutely necessary for good writing because failure to do so distracts the reader and can introduce ambiguity. It also makes you, the writer, look bad, and, as a consequence, can serve to weaken your credibility (and your argument) with your reader. Economy of expression, precision, and adherence to grammatical rules do not guarantee effective writing. They do, however, greatly increase the likelihood that your writing will be effective.
- **WRITE FAIRLY.** As a writer you should also strive to choose words and use constructions that acknowledge people fairly and without bias. The American Psychological Association has outlined its policy regarding bias in the language authors use (*Publication Manual*, 2001).

  > As a publisher, APA accepts authors' word choices unless those choices are inaccurate, unclear, or ungrammatical. As an organization, APA is committed both to science and to the fair treatment of individuals and groups, and this policy requires authors of APA publications to avoid perpetuating demeaning attitudes and biased assumptions about people in their writing. Constructions that might imply bias against persons on the basis of gender, sexual

orientation, racial or ethnic group, disability, or age should be avoided. Scientific writing should be free of implied or irrelevant evaluation of the group or groups being studied. (p. 61)

The *Publication Manual* (2001) describes several guidelines to achieve unbiased communication:

1 Describe the person or persons at the appropriate level of specificity. For example, the phrase *men and women* is more accurate than the generic term *man* when referring to all human adults. "Chinese Americans" or "Mexican Americans" would be a more specific reference for participants in a study than would be Asian Americans or Hispanic Americans.

2 Be sensitive to the labels we use to refer to people, for example, terms we use to refer to people's racial or ethnic identity. One of the best ways to follow this guideline is to avoid labeling people whenever possible. A label that is perceived by the labeled group as pejorative should never be used. In trying to follow this guideline it is important to remember that preferences for labeling groups of individuals change with time and that people within a group disagree about what label is preferred.

3 "Write about the people in your study in a way that acknowledges their participation" (p. 65). One way to accomplish this is to describe the people who participated in your study using more descriptive terms such as *college students* or *children* rather than the more impersonal term, *subjects*. Active voice is better than passive voice in acknowledging participation—"the students completed the survey" is preferred over "the survey was administered to the students." The *Publication Manual* (2001) includes several good applications and illustrations of these guidelines to the labeling of persons based on their gender, sexual orientation, racial and ethnic identity, disabilities, and age.

- **WRITE AN INTERESTING REPORT.** The *Publication Manual* (2001) provides useful advice about the overall tone of scientific writing:

  Although scientific writing differs in form from literary writing, it need not and should not lack style or be dull. In describing your research, present the ideas and findings directly, but aim for an interesting and compelling manner that reflects your involvement with the problem. (p. 10)

One way to try to achieve an appropriate tone in writing your research reports is to strive to tell a good story about your research. Good research makes for good stories; and well-told stories are good for advancing research.

STRUCTURE OF A RESEARCH REPORT

The structure of a research report serves complementary purposes for the author and for the reader. The structure provides an organization that the author can use to present a clear description of the research and a convincing interpretation of the findings. In this sense, the structure of a research report parallels the structure of a Shakespearean play. In a Shakespearean play, both the playwright and the audience share certain expectations about what should occur in each act as the play unfolds. For example "the stage is set" in the first act, and the climax can be expected in the third act. Similarly, in a research report both author and reader share expectations about the content of each section of the report. As in a play, the reader of a research report can expect to find certain information in each section. If you want to know how an experiment was done, you would look in the Method section; if you want information about the analysis of the data in the study, you would refer to the Results section. The structure is not intended to shackle the playwright or the author. It simply provides a vehicle to make it easier for the audience to focus on the particular point being made in the play or the research report.

A research report consists of the following sections:

Title Page
Abstract
Introduction ⎱
Method   ⎰ Body of
Results   ⎰ Report
Discussion ⎱
References
Appendixes
Author Note
Footnotes

The body of the report is made up of four sections: Introduction, Method, Results, and Discussion (the four acts of the "play"). The title page and the abstract are like the playbill you see before the play itself begins, and the References, Appendixes, and Notes are analogous to the credits. In this chapter we will provide descriptions of the content and format of each of these sections; more complete descriptions are provided in the *Publication Manual* (2001). Neither this chapter nor the *Publication Manual* will suffice for teaching you how to write a research report. The best preparation for that is to read journal articles reporting research in an area of psychology that interests you. Ultimately, however, you will develop the skills for writing research reports only by actually writing them.

Title Page

The first page of a research report is the title page. It indicates what the research is about (i.e., the title), who did the research (i.e., the authors), where the research was done (i.e., authors' affiliation), and a brief heading to indicate to readers what the article is about (the "running head"). An illustration of a correctly typed title page and succeeding pages of a research report are presented in the Sample Research Report at the end of this chapter. The sample paper includes notes to highlight several important aspects of the final typed draft of a research report.

its position at the beginning of the paper. Thus, the first paragraph of the Introduction section begins immediately below the title (see Sample Research Report). The introduction serves three primary objectives:

1 to introduce the problem being studied and to indicate why the problem is an important one to study;

2 to describe the theoretical implications of the study and to summarize briefly the relevant background literature related to the study; and

3 to describe the purpose, rationale, and design of the present study with a logical development of the predictions or hypotheses guiding the research.

The order in which you address these objectives in your paper may vary, but the order we describe here is a common one. The *Publication Manual* (2001) describes the common purpose shared by all three objectives. "A good introduction, by summarizing the relevant arguments and the data, gives the reader a firm sense of what was done and why" (p. 16).

The second objective of the introduction includes a summary of related research studies. This review is not intended to provide an exhaustive literature review. Instead, you should carefully select those studies that are most directly related to your research. In summarizing these selected studies, you should emphasize whatever details of the earlier work will best help the reader understand what you have done and why. You must acknowledge the contributions of other researchers to your understanding of the problem. Of course, if you quote directly from another person's work, you must use quotation marks (see Chapter 3 for advice about citing others' work).

More commonly, however, reference is made to the work of other researchers in one of two ways. Either you refer to the authors of the article you are citing by their last names, with the year in which the paper was published appearing in parentheses immediately after the names, or you make a general reference to their work and follow it with both the names and the year of publication in parentheses. For example, if you were citing a study by Lorna Hernandez Jarvis and Patricia V. Roehling that was published in 2003 you would write either "Jarvis and Roehling (2003) found . . ." or "Recent research (Jarvis & Roehling, 2003) showed that . . . ." Complete bibliographical information on the Jarvis and Roehling paper, including the journal title, volume number, and specific pages, would appear in the References section. Footnotes are not used to cite references in a research report in psychology.

You should include in your paper only those references that you have actually read. If you read a paper by Barney (2002) in which the research of Ludwig (2000) is described, you should not cite the Ludwig paper unless you have actually read that paper. Instead, you should use some form such as "Ludwig (2000), as reported by Barney (2002), found that . . ." You should use this approach for two reasons. The first and most obvious one is that you should accurately report what you have read. If this appeal to scholarly integrity does not suffice, you should recognize the risk you are taking. If Barney (2002) has misreported the work of Ludwig (2000) and you repeat this misrepresentation, you are equally subject to criticism. The general rule is simple: Cite only what you have read. (See also Chapter 3.)

Tips on Writing the Introduction In order to write an effective introduction, be sure you can answer the following four questions *before* beginning to write:

- "Why is this problem important?
- How do the hypothesis and the experimental design relate to the problem?
- What are the theoretical implications of the study, and how does the study relate to previous work in the area?
- What are the theoretical propositions tested, and how were they derived?" (*Publication Manual*, p. 16).

Searching the Psychological Literature   In the long run, the best way to develop ideas for research and to become familiar with the relevant literature is to read the journals in your area of interest on a regular basis. If you are just beginning to do research in psychology, you may not have had a chance to read the research literature widely or to have settled on a principal area of interest in psychology. Even if you have identified your primary interest area, you may want to explore research from a literature different from the one that you are used to reading. For example, you may have an idea for an experiment and you may wonder whether the experiment has already been done. Or you may have read an article describing an experiment on which you would like to base an experiment, and you may be interested in finding other studies related to this topic. An important source for additional reading on your topic is the References section of the article. Whatever your topic or research question, there undoubtedly will come a time when you need to search the psychological literature. Resources for searching the psychological literature are available to help you answer these types of questions.

The foundation of present-day methods of searching the psychological literature is *Psychological Abstracts*. The American Psychological Association has published *Psychological Abstracts* since 1927. The abstracts, taken from over 1,000 national and international periodicals, are published monthly in the *Psychological Abstracts*. These abstracts are organized under general categories, such as "Physical and Psychological Disorders." Searching the printed *Psychological Abstracts* was a time-consuming and cumbersome task. Electronic databases have made the task of searching the psychological literature much less labor intensive.

The primary online database for searching the psychological literature is PsycINFO. PsycINFO can be accessed through online databases such as *FirstSearch* and *InfoTrac*. Check with your local library staff to find out what online services are available to you. An electronic database makes it possible to scan the titles and abstracts of articles in the database and to identify all those that contain particular keywords. The most effective approach to this type of search is to have intersecting keywords, both of which need to be present before the computer will "flag" an article. For example, a student was interested in conducting a survey to determine the incidence of rapes and other sexual assaults on dates (i.e., date rapes). The student used the keyword RAPE and the letter string DAT to guide her search. She chose the letter string DAT in order to catch such variants as DATE, DATES, and DATING. This intersection led to the identification of 75 references, 73 of which were written in English.

The major advantage of searching electronic databases is that they provide quick access to large amounts of information. There are, however, a few potential problems. One possible problem is that the likelihood that you will obtain all the relevant references you are seeking is directly dependent on the quality of the search you do. When it comes to electronic databases, what you search is what you get. After searching such vast databases multiple times with different keywords, we may become unduly confident that we have identified "all that there is on the subject." However, it is possible that *pertinent information can be missed in any given search of an electronic database.* Keywords can also prove tricky. The string DAT identified all studies using the word DATA, so a number of the student's references provided data about rape—but not solely in the context of dating. These potential problems are not problems with the *use* of electronic databases; they are problems for the *users* of electronic databases. When electronic databases are used properly, the advantages of searching the psychological literature using PsycINFO far outweigh their disadvantages. Joswick (1994) provides recommendations for electronic searches for those who want to move beyond the basics.

Method

The second major section of the body of a research report is the Method section. The Method section starts on the same page on which the introduction ends. It is separated from the introduction with a double-spaced centered heading (Method), and the text of the Method section begins one double-spaced line below the heading (see Sample Research Report). The introduction has provided a broad outline of the research you have done; the method fills in the nitty-gritty details. The *Publication Manual* presents a straightforward description of the goals of the Method section:

> The Method section describes in detail how the study was conducted. Such a description enables the reader to evaluate the appropriateness of your methods and the reliability and the validity of your results. It also permits experienced investigators to replicate the study if they so desire. (p. 17)

Writing a good Method section can be difficult. It sounds easy because all you have to do is describe exactly what you have done. But if you want to get a sense of how challenging this can be, just try to write a clear and interesting paragraph describing how to tie your shoelaces.

Tips on Writing the Method Section   The key to writing a good Method section is organization. Fortunately, the structure of this section is so consistent across research reports that a few basic subsections provide the pattern of organization you need for most research reports. Before describing the content of these subsections, however, we must address the question that students writing their first research report ask most frequently: "How much detail should I include?" The quality of your paper will be adversely affected if you include either too much or too little detail. The rule stated in the *Publication Manual* seems simple enough: "Include in these subsections only the information essential to comprehend and replicate the study" (p. 18). As we have said before, the best way to learn how to follow this rule is to read the Method sections of journal articles and to write your own research reports. Be sure to get feedback from your instructor concerning the appropriate level of detail for your research reports.

The three most common subsections of the Method section are participants, materials (apparatus), and procedure. Each of these subsections is introduced by an italicized subheading that usually begins at the left margin (see Sample Research Report). The *Publication Manual* (p. 18) aptly summarizes the purpose and the content of the *participants* subsection.

> Appropriate identification of research participants and clientele is critical to the science and practice of psychology, particularly for assessing the results (making comparisons across groups); generalizing the findings; and making comparisons in replications, literature reviews, or secondary data analyses.
>
> When humans are the subjects of the study, report the procedures for selecting and assigning them and the agreements and payments made. Report major demographic characteristics such as sex, age, and race/ethnicity, and, where possible and appropriate, characteristics such as socioeconomic status, disability status, and sexual orientation. When a particular demographic characteristic is an experimental variable or is important for the interpretation of results, describe the group specifically—for example, in terms of national origin, level of education, health status, and language preference and use.
>
> When animals are the subjects, report the genus, species, and strain number or other specific identification, such as the name and location of the supplier and the stock designation.
>
> Give the total number of subjects and the number assigned to each experimental condition. If any did not complete the experiment, state how many and explain why they did not continue. (pp. 18–19)

The *apparatus* or *materials* subsection is not always included in a research report. If the only equipment you used is paper, pencils, and a computer, it is better to include this information in the procedure subsection than in a separate apparatus section. On the other hand, if the apparatus or materials played a central role in the study, a separate subsection is useful. If complex or custom-made equipment has been used, a diagram or drawing is helpful for both the reader and the writer of an apparatus subsection. In general, the label *apparatus* is used when mechanical equipment is described. The label *materials* is used when less mechanical instruments, such as a paper-and-pencil questionnaire, have been constructed or used. If you use equipment or materials developed by another investigator, you should cite the work of that investigator, but you should also include the general characteristics of the materials in your own report.

The *procedure* subsection is the most critical component of the Method section. In this subsection you describe what happened from the beginning to the end of the sessions in which you tested your participants. As the previous sentence implies, the organization of the procedure subsection is usually chronological. You should begin writing this subsection by outlining the important steps in testing participants in each group of your study. Next you can either describe the procedure for each group in turn or describe the procedures common to all groups and then point out the distinguishing features of each group. Whichever organization you choose (you may not learn which works best until you have tried to write both), it is best to begin writing only after you have prepared a checklist of the important features of your procedure. The instructions given to participants should be presented in paraphrase form unless they define an experimental manipulation, in which case they should be reported verbatim. The *Publication Manual* recommends that the Method section, and especially the procedure subsection, "should tell the reader *what* you did and *how* you did it in sufficient detail so that a reader could reasonably replicate your study" (p. 20).

Results

The centered heading, Results, introduces this third major section of the body of a research report. The Results section begins on the same page on which the Method section ends with a double space separating the heading from the end of the Method section and another double space after the heading (see Sample Research Report). Like the third act of a dramatic play, the Results section contains the climax of the research report—the actual findings of the study. For many students, though, the excitement of describing the climax is blunted by concern about the necessity of reporting statistical information in the Results section. The best way to alleviate this concern, of course, is to develop the same command of statistical concepts that you have of other concepts. An excellent way to begin would be to read Chapters 12 and 13. Another helpful first step is to adopt a simple organizational structure to guide your writing of the Results section.

You should use your Results section to answer the questions you raised in your introduction. However, the guiding principle in the Results section is to "stick to the facts, just the facts." You will have the opportunity to move beyond just the facts when you get to the Discussion section.

Reporting Statistics   The *Publication Manual* provides an excellent overview of the objectives of a Results section:

> The Results section summarizes the data collected and the statistical or data analytic treatment used. Report the data in sufficient detail to justify the conclusions. Mention all relevant results, including those that run counter to the hypothesis. Do not include individual scores or raw data, with the exception, for example, of single-case designs or illustrative samples. Discussing the implications of the results is not appropriate here. (p. 20)

TABLE 14.1   STRUCTURE OF A TYPICAL PARAGRAPH IN THE RESULTS SECTION

1. State the purpose of the analysis.
2. Identify the descriptive statistic to be used to summarize results.
3. Present a summary of this descriptive statistic across conditions in the text itself, in a table, or in a figure.
4. If a table or figure is used, point out the major findings on which the reader should focus.
5. Present the reasons for, and the results of, confidence intervals, effect sizes, and inferential statistics tests.
6. State the conclusion that follows from each test, but do not discuss implications. These belong in the Discussion section.

Sample paragraph

To examine retention as a function of instructions given at the time of study, the number of words recalled by each participant in each instruction condition was determined. Words were scored as correct only if they matched a word that had appeared on the target list. Misspelled words were accepted if the spelling was similar to a target item. Mean numbers of words recalled (with the corresponding standard deviations) were: 15.6 (1.44); 15.2 (1.15); and 10.1 (1.00) in the bizarre imagery condition, the standard imagery condition, and the control condition, respectively. The 95% confidence intervals were: bizarre imagery, 13.18–18.02; standard imagery, 12.78–17.62; control, 7.68–12.52. Overall, the mean differences were statistically significant, $F(2, 72) = 162.84$, $p \leq .0005$, $MSE = 1.47$, eta squared $(\eta^2) = .82$. Comparisons of the confidence intervals revealed that both the imagery conditions differed from the control condition, but that two imagery conditions did not differ. In conclusion, retention by participants instructed to use imagery was higher than that by participants given no specific study instructions, but retention did not differ for the two types of imagery instructions.

One way to meet these objectives is to use an organizational structure that is typical of paragraphs in the Results section. This structure is outlined in Table 14.1, and an illustration of a paragraph from the Results section of a published article appears after the table.

Tips on Writing a Good Results Section   We suggest you follow these steps when writing your Results section.

- *Step 1.* A Results section paragraph begins by stating the purpose of the analysis. The reason(s) for doing an analysis should be stated succinctly; often, no more than a phrase is necessary. In the sample paragraph, for example, the purpose of the analysis is, "to examine retention as a function of the instructions given at the time of study." There are two reasons for making the purpose for each analysis explicit. It helps your reader follow the logic of your analysis plan. And, perhaps more importantly, it ensures that you will never try to report an analysis whose purpose you do not understand.
- *Step 2.* The second step in writing a Results section paragraph is to identify the descriptive statistic that will be used to summarize the results for a given dependent variable. For example, you might use the mean numbers of words recalled, as in the sample paragraph. Other

possible descriptive statistics that could be used to summarize the results in each condition of your experiment are the median reaction time or the cumulative number of responses per minute.

- *Step 3*. The third step is to present a summary of this descriptive statistic across conditions. Measures of central tendency should be accompanied by corresponding measures of variability such as reporting a standard deviation along with each mean. A measure of effect size is also strongly recommended. If there are only two or three conditions in your experiment, this summary can be presented in the text itself. For instance, you could summarize the results of a two-group study by saying, "The mean number of correct responses for the experimental group was 10.5 ($SD = 2.1$), whereas that for the control group was 8.2 ($SD = 1.8$). The effect size (d) was 1.20." More commonly, however, you will have more data to summarize and you will need to present your findings in either a table or a figure (graph). We will describe the procedures for constructing tables and figures later in this section. The *Publication Manual* gives good advice regarding the use of tables and figures:

  > To report the data, choose the medium that presents them most clearly and economically. Tables provide exact values and, if well prepared, can present complex data and analyses in a format that is familiar to the reader (e.g., ANOVA tables). Figures of professional quality attract the reader's eye, provide a quick visual impression, and best illustrate complex relationships and general comparisons but are not intended to be as precise as tables.
  >
  > Summarizing the results and the analysis in tables or figures instead of text may be helpful; for example, a table may enhance the readability of complex sets of analysis of variance results. Avoid repeating the same data in several places and using tables for data that can be easily presented in a few sentences in the text. (p. 21)

- *Step 4*. We should not expect a table or figure to be self-sufficient. Your reader will need help to gain as much information as possible from a table or figure. You are in the best position to offer this help because you are the person most familiar with your results. You should direct your reader's attention to the highlights of the data in the table or figure, focusing especially on those aspects of the results that are consistent (or discrepant) with the hypotheses you proposed in the introduction. Usually the same data are not reported in both a table and a figure. Whichever you choose, be sure to highlight in the text itself the critical results that the table or figure reveals.

- *Step 5*. The fifth step in writing a paragraph of the Results section is to present the results of inferential statistical tests. Three pieces of information should always be reported with any inferential statistics test: the name of the test (usually indicated by a symbol such as t, r, or F); the degrees of freedom for the test (presented in parentheses after the test is identified); and the value of the test statistic that you obtained. The exact probability of the test outcome should be reported whenever possible along with measures of effect size. The *Publication Manual* makes a strong case for why it is very important to report confidence intervals. (See also Chapters 12 and 13.)

> The reporting of confidence intervals (for estimates of parameters, for functions of parameters such as differences in means, and for effect sizes) can be an extremely effective way of reporting results. Because confidence intervals combine information on location and precision and can often be directly used to infer significance levels, they are, in general, the best reporting strategy. The use of confidence intervals is therefore strongly recommended. (p. 22)

For instance, you might see, "The 95% confidence interval for the control condition was 4.5 to 6.4 and that for the experimental condition was 7.2 to 9.1. The effect of the drug variable was statistically significant, $F(1, 64) = 7.15$, $p \leq .0005$. The effect size (d) was .85."

- *Concluding Step.* The final step in writing a paragraph in the Results section is to state a brief conclusion that follows from each test you report. For example, consider a study in which the mean number correct in the experimental group is 10 and that in the control group is 5 and the confidence intervals for these two means do not overlap. An appropriate concluding statement would be: "The control group did worse than the experimental group." In this simple example the conclusion may seem obvious, but appropriate concluding statements are essential, especially for more complex analyses.

Each paragraph of the Results section follows the structure outlined in Table 14.1. The idea is not to overload your reader with statistics. The challenge is to select those findings that are most critical, being sure to report all the data pertinent to the questions raised in your introduction. Before concluding our discussion of the Results section, we will briefly describe the basic procedures for constructing tables and figures, two key tools in reporting results effectively.

Presenting Data in Tables   Tables are an effective and efficient means for presenting large amounts of data in concise form. The table should supplement and not duplicate information in the text of the paper, but it should be well integrated into the text. The tables in a research report are numbered consecutively. Numbering the tables makes it easy to refer to them in the text by their numbers. Each table should also have a brief explanatory title, and the columns and rows of the table should be labeled clearly. The data entries in the table should all be reported to the same degree of precision (i.e., all values should have the same number of decimal places), and the values should be consistently aligned with the corresponding row and column headings. An appropriately constructed table appears in the Sample Research Report at the end of this chapter.

Presenting Data in Figures   Figures, like tables, are a concise way to present large amounts of information. A figure has two principal axes: the horizontal axis, or x-axis, and the vertical axis, or y-axis. Typically, the levels of the independent variable are plotted on the x-axis and those of the dependent variable are plotted on the y-axis. When there are two or more independent variables, the levels of the

FIGURE 14.1   Mean number of words recalled (of a possible ten) as a function of serial position within blocks, cuing (C = Cued; NC = Noncued), and instructional condition.

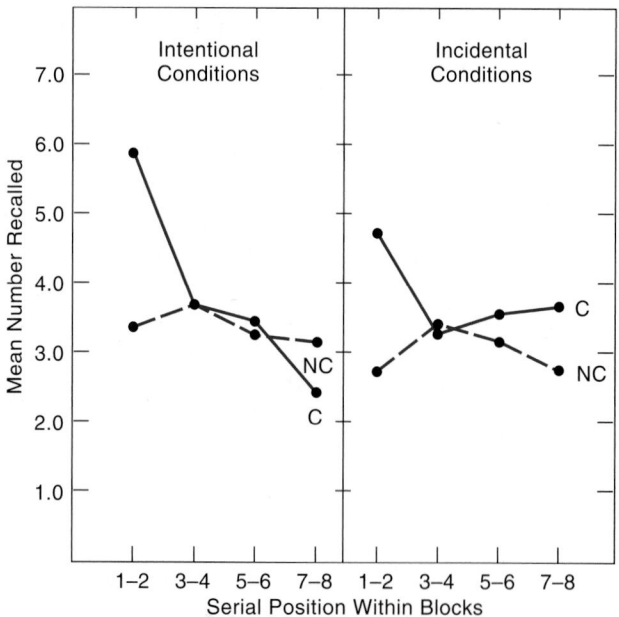

second and succeeding independent variables serve as labels for the data within the figure or are indicated in a figure legend. In Figure 14.1 the values of the dependent variable (mean number recalled) are plotted on the y-axis, the levels of one independent variable (serial position) are indicated on the x-axis. The levels of the second independent variable (cued [C] or noncued [NC]) label the data within the figures, and the levels of the third independent variable (instructions) serve as the headings for each of the two separate panels of the figure.

Two general types of figures are commonly used in psychology: line graphs and bar graphs. The most common type of figure is the line graph like the one shown in Figure 14.1. When the independent variable plotted on the x-axis is a nominal-scale variable, however, a bar graph is often used. For example, if you were plotting the mean GPA (dependent variable) of students enrolled in different academic majors (independent variable), you could use a bar graph. An illustration of a bar graph is presented in Figure 14.2.

There are alternative ways to construct useful graphic presentations. All figures must include certain features, however. The x- and y-axes must be clearly labeled, with each label printed next to the corresponding axis. Selected points (called grid points) on each axis must be identified with labeled grid marks, and the grid labels are always printed horizontally. The grid scale for the x- and y-axes should be chosen such that the plotted data are legible and span the entire illustration. The figures and the captions for the figures appear separately in a manuscript submitted for publication (see Sample Research Report).

FIGURE 14.2   Proportion recognition errors made by two groups of college students after rating verbal items for either familiarity or meaning. The items were nonwords (NW) and words appearing less than one time, one through ten times and more than forty times per million in the Thorndike-Lorge count.

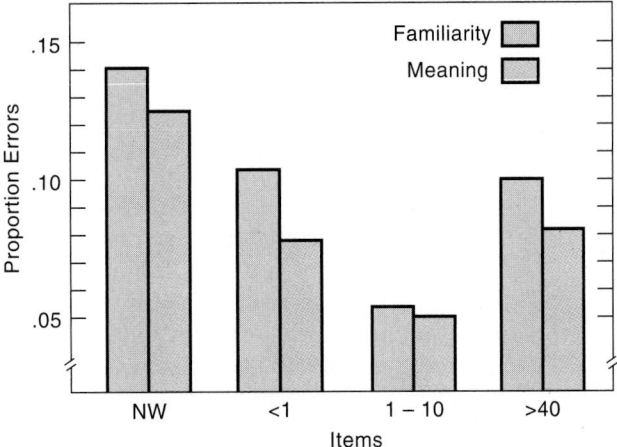

Discussion

The fourth section of the body of your report, the Discussion, begins with a centered heading (see Sample Research Report). The Discussion section (like the Method and Results sections) begins on the same page on which the previous section ended. The Discussion section, unlike the Results section, contains "more than just the facts." In the words of the *Publication Manual:*

> After presenting the results, you are in a position to evaluate and interpret their implications, especially with respect to your original hypothesis. You are free to examine, interpret, and qualify the results, as well as to draw inferences from them. (p. 26)

(*Note:* When the results are relatively brief and discussion is straightforward and also not very lengthy, the two sections can be combined in a Results and Discussion section in some research reports.)

The Discussion begins with a succinct statement of the essential findings. You should give particular attention to how your findings support or refute your original hypotheses. You do not repeat the descriptive statistics in this summary, nor do you necessarily refer to the statistical analyses of the findings. The *Publication Manual* provides good advice about what to do and not to do after the succinct summary of the findings:

> Similarities and differences between your results and the work of others should clarify and confirm your conclusions. Do not, however, simply reformulate and repeat points already made; each new statement should contribute to your position and to the reader's understanding of the problem. Acknowledge limitations, and address alternative explanations of results. (p. 26)

The Discussion is written in a tone and style consistent with the introduction. Be careful, however, to keep the statements you make in the discussion consistent with the data reported in the results. For instance, you should not report that one group did better than another if the difference between the means for these groups was not reliable—at least not without some qualification of what you mean by "better."

As just noted from the *Publication Manual*, the Discussion includes a description of how your findings relate to the relevant literature, most of which you will have cited in the Introduction. If your results are not consistent with your original hypotheses, you should suggest an explanation for these discrepancies. Such post hoc (after-the-fact) explanations should be considered tentative at best. If the reasons for your results are unclear, you should not hesitate to say so. It sometimes is necessary and helpful to include a paragraph describing limitations or problems in the research. One good way to identify limitations or problems is to try to anticipate criticisms of your study that others might make.

If appropriate, conclude the Discussion by proposing additional research that should be done on the problem you are investigating. Strive to be specific about what research should be done and why it needs to be done. That is, be sure to explain what the new research should reveal that we do not already know. The reader will not learn much if you say, "It would be interesting to do this experiment with younger participants." The reader can learn much more if you explain how you would expect the results to differ with younger participants and what you would conclude if the results of the proposed experiment were to turn out as expected. Remember, the watchword in proposing new research is to be specific. Your emphasis when writing your report should definitely be on quality, not quantity.

Tips on Writing the Discussion Section   Again, the *Publication Manual* gives good advice for authors beginning to write their Discussion section: "In this section you might address the following sorts of issues:

- Problem choice: Why is this problem important?
- Level of analysis: How can the findings be linked to phenomena at more complex and less complex levels of analysis?
- Application and synthesis: If the findings are valid and replicable, what real-life psychological phenomena might be explained or modeled by the results? Are applications warranted on the basis of this research?

The responses to these questions are the core of your contribution and justify why readers outside your own specialty should attend to your findings. These readers should receive clear, unambiguous, and direct answers." (p. 27)

References

We have already described the procedure for citing references within the body of a research report by using the name(s) of the author(s) and the date of

TABLE 14.2   ILLUSTRATION OF FORMAT OF REFERENCE CITATIONS

Journal article

Loftus, E. F., & Burns, T. E. (1982). Mental shock can produce retrograde amnesia. *Memory & Cognition, 10*, 318–323.

Book

Posavac, E. J., & Carey, R. G. (2003). *Program evaluation* (6th ed.). Englewood Cliffs, NJ: Prentice Hall.

Chapter in an edited book

Weiss, J. M. (1977). Psychological and behavioral influences on gastrointestinal lesions in animal models. In J. D. Maser & M. E. P. Seligman (Eds.), *Psychopathology: Experimental models* (pp. 232–269). San Francisco: W. H. Freeman.

Article in electronic journal

Kirsch, I., & Sapirstein, G. (1998). Listening to prozac but hearing placebo: A meta-analysis of antidepressant medication. *Prevention and Treatment* [On-line serial], *1*. Available: journals.apa.org/prevention/volume1/pre0010002a.html.

publication. The References section, which appears with a centered heading on a separate page after the discussion (see Sample Research Report), includes the complete citation for each reference. "Just as data in the paper support interpretations and conclusions, so reference citations document statements made about the literature" (*Publication Manual*, p. 28).

There are four types of references that will cover almost all those needed for most research reports: journal articles, books, chapters in edited books, and Internet sources. The format for each of these reference types is illustrated in Table 14.2. As this table shows, all lines but the first line of each reference are indented (hanging indent). Like the rest of the manuscript, references should be typed double-spaced. The journal article reference includes the authors, the year of publication, the title of the article, the name of the journal, the volume number, and the page numbers. The book citation includes the authors, the copyright date, the title, the city in which the book was published, and the publisher. The reference for a chapter in an edited volume includes the author of the chapter, the date, the chapter title, the editors of the book, the title of the book, page numbers of the chapter, the city of publication, and the publisher. The citation to an electronic journal identifies the specific Internet address.

When citing information from the Internet, especially websites, it is critical that you give the reader the specific information required to locate the source. Be aware, however, that Internet addresses change regularly, as does the information that is found in them. It is recommended (e.g., Harnack & Kleppinger, 1997) that you indicate the date you accessed a website, for example in parentheses following the citation. You can check the APA website [www.apastyle.org] for changes in the format for citing Internet sources and for the latest information in APA style and publication policies and procedures.

You can save your readers much aggravation if you follow the reference formats closely and proofread your reference list carefully. The references are listed in alphabetical order by the last name of the first author of each article. If there are two articles by the same author(s), they are arranged in ascending order by year of publication.

Appendixes

Appendixes are rare in published research articles, but they are a bit more common in students' research reports. When they are intended for a published article, each appendix begins on a separate manuscript page and they appear at the end of the paper following the references. (*Note:* Instructors may require you to submit an appendix including your raw data, the worksheets for a statistical analysis, or the computer printout of the analyses. The appendix can also be used to provide a verbatim copy of the instructions to participants or a list of the specific materials used in an experiment.) Each appendix is identified by letter (A, B, C, and so on), and any reference to the appendix in the body of the text is made using this letter. For instance, you might write, "The complete instructions can be found in Appendix A."

Author Note

The *Publication Manual* provides a concise description of the contents of an author note:

> The author note (a) identifies the departmental affiliation of each author, (b) identifies sources of financial support, (c) provides a forum for authors to acknowledge colleagues' professional contributions to the study and personal assistance, and (d) tells whom the interested reader may contact for further information concerning the article. (p. 29)

The author note appears on a separate page under the centered heading "Author Note" immediately after the References section, or after the appendixes, if there are any (see Sample Research Report).

Footnotes

Because they are not used for citing references, footnotes are rare in journal articles and even more rare in students' research reports. When footnotes appear in the text they are of two types: content footnotes and copyright permission footnotes. Content footnotes supplement or expand upon the text material. Copyright permission footnotes acknowledge the source of extensive quotations. Footnotes (of both kinds) are numbered consecutively in the text. In the printed or typed manuscript, footnotes appear on a separate page following the References section under the centered heading "Footnotes" (see Sample Research Report).

Order of Manuscript Pages

The pages of your research report should be numbered consecutively in the following order:

Title Page
Abstract
Text (Introduction, Method, Results, Discussion)
References (start on a separate page)
*Appendixes (start each on a separate page)
Author Note (start on a separate page)
*Footnotes (list together, starting on a separate page)
Tables (start each on a separate page)
Figure Captions (list together, starting on a separate page)
Figures (place each on a separate page)

*Appear only infrequently in journal articles.

ORAL PRESENTATIONS

Research psychologists regularly attend professional conventions at which they present brief oral descriptions of their research. Similarly, students may give oral presentations of their research either in class or at a department research symposium involving students from a number of different classes or at undergraduate research conferences. All of these settings share one characteristic—the time allowed for the presentation is usually no more than 10 to 15 minutes. In this length of time it is impossible to provide the detailed description that is included in a journal article. In general, as noted in the *Publication Manual,* "Material delivered verbally should differ from written material in its level of detail, organization, and presentation" (p. 329). To reach your audience the *Publication Manual* recommends that you:

> Omit most of the details of scientific procedures, because a listener cannot follow the same level of detail as a reader. The audience wants to know (a) what you studied and why, (b) how you went about the research (give a general orientation), (c) what you discovered, and (d) the implications of your results. A verbal presentation should create awareness about a topic and stimulate interest in it; colleagues can retrieve the details from a written paper, copies of which you may want to have available. (pp. 329–330)

A colleague of ours in the biology department has developed five principles that he distributes to his students to help them prepare the oral presentation required in his class. Like all good maxims these five sound simple enough, but they are all too frequently ignored even by experienced researchers.

Five Principles for Effective Oral Presentations

- AVOID THE TEMPTATION TO TELL EVERYTHING YOU KNOW IN 10 MINUTES. This temptation can best be avoided by limiting your presentation to one or two main points. What are the important "take-home messages"? The brief time available for an oral presentation is barely sufficient to allow you to present the evidence supporting these main points. There simply will not be time to discuss any side issues.

- CULTIVATE A GOOD PLATFORM PRESENCE. This can best be achieved by developing public speaking skills. Most people need a written copy of their presentation in front of them while they are presenting, but your presentation will be more effective if you can appear not to be reading. Many people speak too quickly in front of an audience, particularly if they are reading; it is best to use simple, direct sentences presented at a moderate rate. Most important, speak loudly and clearly.
- USE EFFECTIVE VISUAL AIDS. The use of effective visual aids can help your listeners follow your presentation. Slides, overhead transparencies, and electronic presentations must be distinct enough to be seen clearly at a distance. The successful use of audiovisual aids is a skill and it can be improved with practice. Be sure that whatever visual aids you use are as close to self-explanatory as you can make them.
- LEAVE TIME FOR QUESTIONS. You need to keep in mind the fourth principle, leaving time for questions, because most professional conferences and classroom presentations will require that you reserve time for questions. Although questions from the audience can be somewhat intimidating, the opportunity for questions gives your listeners a chance to become actively involved in your presentation.
- PRACTICE YOUR TALK BEFORE A CRITICAL AUDIENCE BEFORE YOU GIVE IT. This final principle is perhaps the most important. Practicing your talk before an audience is more beneficial than simply rehearsing the talk over and over by yourself. Such private rehearsal is a good way to prepare for your "dress rehearsal," but it is no substitute for practicing before others.

These five principles provide a good coaching manual for oral presentations. The best way to develop this skill, however, is to deliver as many oral presentations as possible under "game conditions." Practice may not make perfect, but it is the best route we know to improvement.

RESEARCH PROPOSALS

In the last section of this chapter we discuss writing again—but this time the writing of research proposals. As we mentioned at the beginning of this chapter, researchers must often seek financial support for their research by submitting grant proposals to private or government agencies. Students in research methods classes are also sometimes required to submit proposals describing research they might do. Even if a written proposal is not required, only a foolhardy researcher would tackle a research project without careful prior consideration of related literature, possible practical problems, workable statistical analyses of the data, and eventual interpretation of the expected results. This careful prior consideration will help you develop a research proposal that is feasible and one that can be analyzed and interpreted appropriately.

The purpose of a research proposal is to ensure a workable experimental design that, when implemented, will result in an interpretable empirical finding of significant scientific merit. No research proposal, no matter how carefully prepared, can guarantee important results. Researchers learn early in their careers about Murphy's Law. In essence, Murphy's Law states, "Anything that can go wrong will go wrong." Nonetheless, it is worthwhile to develop a research proposal, if only to avoid the research problems that are avoidable.

A written research proposal follows the general format of a journal article, but the headings of the various sections are slightly different. The proposal should include the following main sections:

Introduction
Method
Expected Results and Proposed Data Analysis Plan
Conclusions
References
Appendix
Information for Institutional Review Board

An abstract is not included in a research proposal. The introduction of a research proposal is likely to include a more extensive review of the relevant literature than is required for a journal article. The statement of the research problem and the logical development of hypotheses in a research proposal are the same as required in a journal article. Similarly, the Method section in the proposal should be as close as possible to the one that will accompany the finished research. Thus our remarks about the format and content of the Method section of a research report apply equally to the writing of a proposal.

The section of the proposal entitled "Expected Results and Proposed Data Analysis Plan" should include a brief discussion of the anticipated results of the research. In most cases the exact nature of the results will not be known. Nevertheless, you will always have some idea (in the form of a hypothesis or prediction) of the outcome of the research. The Expected Results section may include tables or figures of the results as you expect (hope) that they will come out. The results that are most important to the project should be highlighted. A proposed data analysis plan for the expected results should be in this section. For example, if you are proposing a complex design, you would need to indicate which effects you will be testing and what statistical tests you will use. Reasonable alternatives to the expected results should also be mentioned, as well as possible problems of interpretation that will arise if the results deviate from the research hypothesis. The body of a research proposal ends with a Conclusions section that provides a brief statement of the conclusions and implications based on the expected results.

The References section should be in exactly the same form as the one you would submit with the final report. An appendix should complete the research proposal and should include a list of all materials that will be used in doing the experiment. In most cases this will mean that a copy of the instructions to participants will be included, as well as the type of apparatus used, a list of the materials or a description of the materials, and so on. For example, if you are doing a study involving students' memory for lists of words, the following must be included in the appendix: actual lists with randomizations made, type of apparatus used for presentation, instructions to participants for all conditions, and randomizations of conditions.

Finally, a research proposal should include material to be submitted to an Institutional Review Board (IRB) or similar committee designed to review the ethics of the proposed research (see Chapter 3).

A SAMPLE RESEARCH REPORT

First few words of title appear before page number.

5 spaces

→ False Recall   1

→ Running head: FALSE MEMORIES

Type flush with left margin.

Type running head all caps.

Number pages consecutively, beginning with title page.

False Recall and Recognition of List Items Following Delay

Jeanne S. Zechmeister and Eugene B. Zechmeister

Loyola University of Chicago

Use upper and lower case for title, name, and affiliation (centered).

Note:
Use one-inch margins at the top, bottom, right, and left of all pages.

No paragraph indentation for abstract.

Center, do not italicize.

Include initials only in Abstract.

False Recall   2

↓

Abstract

Whether false memories persist over a delay was investigated using H. L. Roediger and K. B. McDermott's (1995) false memory procedure. College students ($N = 19$) studied 12 15-item lists and either recalled items immediately or following a 90-s delay. A first recognition test immediately followed recall of lists; a second test occurred 2 days later. The proportion of correctly recalled list items decreased with the 90-s delay, whereas the proportion of falsely recalled critical items increased. The overall proportion of items recognized as "old" was greater for false critical items than for correct list items, but both false recognition and correct recognition decreased over the 2-day period. These findings are compared to other studies that examined false memories following delays.

Abstract should be a single paragraph not exceeding 120 words.

Note:
    Double-space between all lines of the manuscript. There should be no more than 27 lines of text on each page.
    When using a word processor, use left justification only (not full). Use italics for statistical symbols and infrequently otherwise, and use one font size throughout the manuscript.

Leave one space at end of all sentences, and after all commas, colons, and semicolons.

Title appears centered on page 3, with first letter of major words in caps.

False Recall   3

False Recall and Recognition of List Items Following Delay

Roediger and McDermott (1995) captured the attention of memory researchers by reminding us of the importance of examining participants' errors in recall and that these errors can sometimes be quite predictable. Moreover, these "false memories" are relevant to ongoing debates about false memories that may occur in more natural settings (e.g., clinics, courtrooms). Roediger and McDermott, and many others, have demonstrated that false memories are easily created and that participants' phenomenological experience of these memories mimics their memories for actual events (e.g., Mather, Henkel, & Johnson, 1997; Norman & Schacter, 1997; Payne, Elie, Blackwell, & Neuschatz, 1996). The purpose of the present study was to replicate Roediger and McDermott's (1995) findings and to extend their findings by examining the persistence of false memories following delays. If false memories persist following delays, important implications exist regarding courtroom testimony and recovered memories in therapy. For example, memory retrieval in these cases follows varying periods of delay and the accuracy of these memories may thus be questioned.

In this false memory paradigm word lists are constructed such that each word is highly associated with a critical, not-presented word. For example, participants may hear the words *bed*, *rest*, *awake*, *tired*, *dream*, etc., but never the critical word, *sleep*. False recall and recognition for the word *sleep* is quite high. Underwood (1965) proposed that an implicit associative response (IAR) occurs when participants study an associated word. For example, when participants hear "bed" they may think of "sleep" (the IAR). With the next word, "rest," they again may experience "sleep" as an IAR, and so on. When their memory is tested participants may have difficulty discriminating the

Identify all authors (surnames only) the first time you cite a source (five or fewer authors).

List multiple sources in alphabetical order, separated by a semicolon.

Indent every paragraph using the tab key (set at five to seven spaces or 1/2 inch).

Abbreviated terms are first spelled out, followed by the abbreviation in parentheses.

Use Latin abbreviations (such as e.g. and i.e.) only in parentheses.

Use numbers to express amounts 10 and above, and when numbers are grouped for comparison with numbers 10 and above.

An "s" (with no period) is the abbreviation for second.

Use number for units of time or measure.

Note: Use past tense to describe the study.

Flush with left margin, italicized, only first letter in caps.

Always use words to express numbers that begin a sentence.

False Recall   4

IAR from the presented items, resulting in false recall or recognition. An alternative account relies on the extent to which the lists of associated words activate a schema for the words (e.g., a "sleep" schema). According to this account, recall after a delay may be based on memory for the schema rather than the actual list presentation.

In the present study participants listened to 12 lists comprised of 15 words that were associated to a critical, not-presented word. Participants were randomly assigned to recall 4 of the 12 lists in either an immediate-recall condition or following a 90-s delay in a single trial of free recall. When not recalling words (and during the 90-s delays) participants completed distractor tasks consisting of math problems. Additionally, two recognition tests were administered. The first recognition test followed the presentation and recall of the 15 lists; the second was 2 days later.

We hypothesized that the proportions of correct recall and false recall would not differ in the immediate-recall condition because of participants' inability to differentiate their memory for the presented words from the IARs generated for the critical items. In the delayed-recall condition, we expected the proportion of false items recalled to be greater than the proportion of correct items recalled because of participants' activation of a schema for the list to aid recall. This activation was assumed to lead to recall of the highly associated, critical item. Furthermore, we anticipated that correct recall would decrease over time but false recall would increase with the delay. Similar predictions were made for participants' recognition of correct list items and false critical items.

Method

Center, no italics, only the first letter in caps.

Participants

Nineteen students (16 women, 3 men) from a research methods in psychology

Note: Method, Results, and Discussion sections do not begin on new page (unless coincidentally).

Note: "Data" is plural.

Indented, and italicized paragraph heading, followed by a period. Only first letter of first word in caps.

Use words to express numbers less than 10.

False Recall   5

class at Loyola University of Chicago participated as part of a class project. Data for one student were omitted from all analyses because the student attempted recall for the wrong lists; recognition data for two students were omitted from analyses because they missed the second class session in which the experiment was conducted.

Materials

Word lists. We used 12 15-item word lists from Roediger and McDermott's (1995) study. They constructed 24 lists by selecting 15 words that were highly associated with a critical word that was not presented. Words were ordered such that the strongest associates were presented first, followed by more weakly associated words. For example, the list for the critical word, *needle*, was *thread, pin, eye, sewing, sharp, point, prick, thimble, haystack, thorn, hurt, injection, syringe, cloth,* and *knitting.* Six lists in the present study were identified by Roediger and McDermott as having a high likelihood of creating false memories (identified by the critical item): chair, mountain, needle, rough, sleep, sweet. The other six lists used in the present study for recall were randomly selected from their remaining lists (identified by the critical item): bread, cold, doctor, foot, music, slow.

Participants recalled words from 4 of the 12 lists in a single trial of free recall. In order to rule out the possibility that proportions of correct and false recall would be determined by the particular lists used for the recall task, the four recall lists were counterbalanced. The 12 lists were randomly divided into three sets of four lists, with the provision that two lists in each set have high likelihoods for creating false memories. Participants were randomly assigned to recall words for four lists. Seven participants recalled the chair, bread, slow, and sleep lists; seven participants recalled the needle,

False Recall   6

foot, doctor, and rough lists, and four participants recalled the sweet, music, cold, and

mountain lists.

   Distractor task. Participants completed a distractor task consisting of math

problems when not recalling words and during the 90-s delay. We generated 20 pages

of math problems. Each page had six complex math problems involving addition,

subtraction, multiplication, and division.

   Recall packets. We created six different packets to manipulate the recall condition

(immediate, delayed) and counterbalance the lists used for recall. Four pages

presented recall instructions based on those used by Roediger and McDermott (1995):

"Please write down as many words from the list that you remember. A good strategy is

to write down the last few items first, then the rest of the words in any order." Twenty

pages had math problems. Between each page was a colored sheet of paper, which

masked the participants' next task (recall or math problems). The order of the 24 pages

depended on whether participants were in the immediate- or delayed-recall condition

and which list set participants were assigned to recall. For example, the "music" list was

presented first. Following the presentation of the list, participants assigned to recall the

music list in the immediate condition opened their packet to a page with recall

instructions; all other participants opened their packet to a page of math problems. After

90 s, a tone signaled participants to turn to the next white page (following the colored

sheet). If assigned to recall the music list in the delayed-recall condition, participants'

next sheet had recall instructions; all other participants received math problems. This

sequence was followed for the remaining 11 word lists.

   Recognition tests. Participants completed two different recognition tests, the first

Place periods or commas within quotation marks.

followed the presentation and recall of lists (immediate), the second was 2 days later

(delayed). Because three list sets were used for recall (to counterbalance recall lists

across participants), we created three versions of the first recognition test (session 1)

and three versions of the second recognition test (session 2). Following Roediger and

McDermott's terminology, recognition-test items that were presented during the recall

portion of the study are referred to as "studied," and new distractor items are referred to

as "not studied." Each 72-item recognition test consisted of six different types of items:

10 Studied/Recalled items (5 each from two of the four lists participants were asked to

recall); 2 corresponding critical items for these lists; 20 Studied/Not Recalled items (5

each from four of the eight lists participants did not recall); 4 corresponding critical

items for these lists; 30 Not Studied Distractor items (5 each from six lists that were not

presented); and 6 corresponding critical items for the distractor lists (these lists also

were from Roediger & McDermott, 1995). The five items selected from the word lists for

each recognition test were the first, third, fifth, seventh, and ninth words. The 72 words

on each list were randomly ordered. Participants made recognition judgments using a

4-point scale (1 = *sure new*, 2 = *probably new*, 3 = *probably old*, and 4 = *sure old*).

Procedure

A 2 (condition) X 2 (memory type) mixed factorial design was used for the recall

portion of the experiment. Students were randomly assigned to either the immediate-

recall condition or the delayed-recall condition; thus, the condition variable was

manipulated as a random groups design. Memory type was a repeated measures

variable with two levels: correct and false memory. The recognition portion of the

experiment was a repeated measures independent variable. Participants completed the

A comma separates authors' surnames and year of publication when citation is within parentheses.

Use ampersand to indicate "and" for references within parentheses.

Italicize the anchors of a scale.

Numbers are used to indicate the levels of a design. Include one space to left and right of multiplication sign.

False Recall   8

first recognition test immediately following the presentation and recall of word lists and completed the delayed recognition test 2 days later. The dependent variables were proportion of correct and false recall and proportion of correct and false recognition.

The experiment was conducted during two scheduled class periods. In the first session, lasting 50 min, the experimenter gave students a consent form and a packet that corresponded to their condition when they entered the class (students were randomly assigned to conditions prior to their arrival). A participant number appeared on top of the packet. Instructions requested students not to open their packet. After students read and signed their consent form, they listened to tape-recorded instructions for the study. Following this, the experimenter stopped the tape recorder and asked if there were any questions. Tape-recorded word lists were then presented. The random order of the lists was as follows (identified by the critical item): music, needle, sleep, doctor, slow, mountain, rough, bread, sweet, cold, chair, and foot. Words were presented at the rate of approximately one word every 1½ s. Following the list presentation, participants heard a tone informing them to turn to the next white page. They then either recalled list items or completed math problems for 90 s. A tone then signaled participants to turn to the next white page. This page instructed them to recall the list items or complete math problems. This procedure was followed for all 12 lists.

After the study and recall phase of the experiment, the experimenter distributed the first recognition test and asked participants to record their participant number on the top of the recognition test. After completing the recognition test, participants were asked to write their participant number in their notebook; they were then dismissed. At the beginning of the next class session (2 days later), participants reported their number

"min" (without a period) is the abbreviation for minute.

Note: Words are not hyphenated at the end of a line.

Note: Always double-space. Do not insert extra spaces between sections. Center, no italics.

and they were given the corresponding second recognition test. Each recognition test took approximately 5 min to complete. The instructor then fully debriefed participants regarding the purpose of the experiment.

Results

Results are presented first for participants' recall and then for their recognition of list items. The dependent variables were proportion of correct recall/recognition and proportion of false recall/recognition. Proportion of correct recall was determined by counting the number of words participants correctly recalled and dividing by 60 (the total number of list items they were asked to recall). Proportion of false recall was determined by counting the number of critical items falsely recalled and dividing by 4 (the total number of critical items for the four lists participants recalled).

Similar proportions were computed for recognition data. For ease of comparisons, participants' recognition responses were collapsed such that ratings of 1 or 2 indicated judgments that the word was "new" (i.e., not presented during the recall portion of the study), and ratings of 3 or 4 indicated the word was "old" (i.e., presented during the recall portion). The number of items judged "old" for each type of word (e.g., studied, recalled; not studied distractor) was counted and divided by the total number of words of that type presented on the recognition test.

Recall

Mean proportions for correct and false recall were entered into a 2 (condition) X 2 (memory type) mixed-design analysis of variance (ANOVA). Across the two recall conditions the proportion of falsely recalled critical items (M = .60, SD = .23) tended to be greater than the proportion of correctly recalled list items (M = .48, SD = .12), F(1,

M is the abbreviation for arithmetic mean.

SD is the abbreviation for standard deviation.

MSE is the abbreviation for Mean Square Error.

Italicize all statistical terms.

Do not capitalize names of conditions.

Footnotes appear on a separate page near end of manuscript (not at bottom of the page).

Do not abbreviate "Figure." Figure caption and figure appear on separate pages at end of manuscript.

Degrees of freedom for statistical tests are reported in parentheses (with no space after statistical term).

False Recall   10

16) = 4.38, p = .053 (MSE = .03, effect size r = .47).[1] The observed power to detect this large effect with the small sample size (n = 9 per condition), at alpha = .05, was estimated to be only .50. The main effect of condition was not significant, $F(1, 16)$ = .10, p > .05 (MSE = .02, r = .10, power = .06). As predicted, however, recall condition and memory type interacted to influence participants' recall, $F(1, 16)$ = 9.50, p < .01 (MSE = .03, r = .61). Comparisons of means revealed that recall differed in the immediate- and delayed-recall conditions in the predicted direction (see Figure 1). Participants in the immediate-recall condition did not differ in their proportions of correct recall and false recall, $F(1, 8)$ = .41, p > .05 (MSE = .036, r = .22, power = .09); however, participants in the delayed-recall condition were more likely to recall a greater proportion of false critical items than correct list items, $F(1, 8)$ = 16.57, p < .005 (MSE = .024, r = .82).[2]

A second set of comparisons of means examined the effect of delay for each type of recall. As expected, the proportion of correctly recalled list items decreased following delay and the proportion of false recall increased following delay (see Figure 1). For correct list items, participants in the delayed-recall condition recalled fewer items than participants who recalled list items immediately, $t(16)$ = 2.08, p = .054 (MSE = .03). The effect size (d) was 1.04, indicating a very large effect of immediate- vs. delayed-recall on participants' correct recall (see Cohen, 1988). In contrast, the proportion of falsely recalled critical items increased following the 90-s delay relative to the immediate-recall condition, $t(16)$ = 2.33, p = .033 (MSE = .03). The effect size (d) was 1.16, indicating a very large effect of recall condition (immediate, delayed) on participants' false recall.

Recognition

Across two testing sessions separated by 2 days, we examined the proportion of items recognized as "old" as a function of whether items were correct list items or false critical items and whether the items were recalled (vs. not recalled) during the recall portion of the experiment (see Table 1).[3] Distractor items were excluded from the analyses because the proportion of these items judged "old" was generally low across item type and sessions, $M = .18$ ($SD = .12$). Main effects were observed for the time, memory type, and recalled/not recalled variables. As expected, memory for the items decreased over the 2-day period, as the proportion of all items recognized as "old" decreased at Time 2 ($M = .71$, $SD = .14$) relative to Time 1 ($M = .87$, $SD = .11$), $F(1, 14) = 16.40$, $P < .005$ ($MSE = .04$, $r = .73$). Additionally, the main effect of memory type indicated that participants rated a higher proportion of false critical items "old" ($M = .85$, $SD = .11$) than correct list items ($M = .73$, $SD = .13$), $F(1, 14) = 14.72$, $P < .005$ ($MSE = .026$, $r = .71$). Thus, in terms of proportions, false recognition was greater than correct recognition at Time 1 and Time 2. Finally, the proportion of items judged "old" was greater for lists participants were asked to recall ($M = .87$, $SD = .09$) relative to lists they did not recall ($M = .71$, $SD = .14$), $F(1, 14) = 23.57$, $p < .001$ ($MSE = .032$, $r = .79$). This is the "testing effect" identified by Roediger and McDermott (1995), in which rehearsal during the recall portion of the experiment increases subsequent recognition.

There was also a Time X Recalled/Not Recalled interaction effect, $F(1, 14) = 7.49$, $p < .05$ ($MSE = .024$, $r = .59$). This interaction indicated that recognition of words for recalled lists was slightly higher at Time 1 ($M = .90$, $SD = .07$) relative to Time 2 ($M = .83$, $SD = .16$), $F(1, 15) = 3.22$, $p < .10$ ($MSE = .013$, $r = .42$, power = .39). In contrast,

Table appears on separate page near end of manuscript.

Note use of spaces and punctuation when typing statistics.

Variable names in caps when they appear with a multiplication sign.

Capitalize nouns that are followed by a number.

recognition of words from not-recalled lists dropped significantly at Time 2 (M = .60, SD = .18) relative to Time 1 (M = .83, SD = .18), $F(1, 15)$ = 18.63, p < .005 (MSE = .023, r = .74). Thus, rehearsal of the lists (through recall) increased the proportion of correct items and false critical items recognized as "old" even after a 2-day period, relative to lists that were not rehearsed.

As noted above, we observed differential effects of delay on the proportion recall of correct list items and false critical items. However, a similar effect was not observed for recognition data, as the Time X Memory Type interaction effect was not statistically significant, $F(1, 14)$ = .028, p > .05 (MSE = .014). The effect size, r, for this interaction was quite small (.04, power = .05). Thus, the 2-day delay between the recognition tests resulted in similar decreases in the proportions of correct list items and false critical items that were recognized as "old."

Note: Make sure you use the "greater than" or "less than" sign correctly.

Center, no italics.

Discussion

Participants recalled list items in a single trial of free recall immediately after list presentation or following a 90-s filled delay. The proportion of correctly recalled list items decreased as a function of delay, but the proportion of false critical items recalled increased following the 90-s delay. Participants' recognition of correct list items and false critical items was tested following a 2-day delay. In terms of proportions, false recognition of critical items was greater than correct recognition of list items at Time 1 and Time 2, but recognition for both types of items decreased over the 2-day period. A testing effect occurred such that correct and false recognition were greater for lists participants had attempted recall relative to lists not recalled. The effects of rehearsal persisted over the 2-day period. In general, delay produced large effect sizes for both

Year of publication in parentheses after author's surname.

Do not use contractions such as "wasn't."

Year of publication is not repeated within a paragraph if it is clear that the same study is being described.

Year of publication appears in parentheses even when reference has appeared previously in manuscript.

Use "et al." following surname of first author for work with three or more authors.
Note: First citation to this work lists all authors (see p. 3).

recall and recognition.

McDermott (1996) used a 30-s filled delay to examine the effects of delay on participants' recall of correct list items and false critical items. Although she observed a decrease in correct recall following delay, her participants' false recall of critical items was not affected by delay. In contrast, we observed an increase in the proportion of false critical items recalled following a 90-s delay. One reason for this discrepancy may be derived from our differing findings for correct list recall. In McDermott's study the proportion of correct list items recalled following a 30-s delay was .50; in our study, the proportion of correct recall following a 90-s delay was .39. To the extent that a longer delay increased participants' forgetting of correct list items in our study, they may have had to rely more on schema-based recall, which we hypothesized to increase the occurrence of false memories. Alternatively, discrimination between IARs and memory for list items may become more difficult with longer delays. As a result, greater proportions of false recall would be expected (as was observed). This explanation is corroborated by McDermott's findings that after a 2-day delay, the proportion of falsely recalled critical items was greater than the proportion of correctly recalled items (similar to our findings for recognition). Thus, in both studies, participants demonstrated high levels of false recall that persisted over time.

Payne et al. (1996) examined participants' recognition memory for correct list items and false critical items in immediate (2 min) and delayed (24 hr) conditions. Similar to our recognition data, Payne et al. observed that false critical items were recognized with higher likelihood at both testing sessions than correct list items. However, they also observed an interaction between item type (correct, false) and "hr" (with no period) is the abbreviation for hour.

retention (immediate, delayed) for their recognition data that we did not. They observed more forgetting for correct list items than false critical items over the 24-hr period, whereas over our 2-day period we observed similar decreases for correct list items and false critical items. Differences in the retention interval (24 vs. 48 hr), the number of word lists (16 vs. 12), or other procedural differences may account for this discrepancy.

The findings of this study and those of other recent studies indicate that false memories are frequent and persist following delays. Moreover, there is accumulating evidence to suggest that false memories for highly associated information may exceed correct memory over time. These data are limited to individuals' recall for highly associated list items. Important areas for future research include false memories for natural categories such as people and events. Also, it is not clear to what extent individuals' emotions may affect correct and false recall. This question is particularly relevant to the issue of false memory in the emotionally charged situations of eyewitness testimony and therapy.

Note: References section begins on a new page immediately after the Discussion section.

Italicize titles of books. Only first letter of first word and word following a colon in caps.

Publisher of book.

Use ampersand before last author's name.

First letter of questionnaire names in caps.

Use initials for first and middle names.

Period after year of publication (in parentheses).

Page numbers.

Use lower case for titles of articles and book chapters (except first word and word after a colon).

Italicize journal name and volume number. Capitalize first letter of major words in journal name. Use comma after journal name and volume number.

Use hanging indents for each reference entry.
Center, no italics.

False Recall   15

References

Cohen, J. (1988). *Statistical power analysis for behavioral sciences* (2nd ed.).

New York: Academic Press.

Keppel, G. (1991). *Design and analysis: A researcher's handbook* (3rd ed.).

Englewood Cliffs, NJ: Prentice-Hall.

Mather, M., Henkel, L. A., & Johnson, M. J. (1997). Evaluating characteristics of

false memories: Remember/know judgments and Memory Characteristics

Questionnaire compared. *Memory & Cognition, 25,* 826-837.

McDermott, K. B. (1996). The persistence of false memories in list recall. *Journal*

of Memory and Language, 35, 212-230.

Norman, K., & Schacter, D. L. (1997). False recognition in younger and older

adults: Exploring the characteristics of illusory memories. *Memory & Cognition,*

25, 838-848.

Separate authors' names with a comma.

Payne, D. G., Elie, C. J., Blackwell, J. M., & Neuschatz, J. S. (1996). Memory

illusions: Recalling, recognizing, and recollecting events that never occurred.

Journal of Memory and Language, 35, 261-285.

Roediger, H. L., & McDermott, K. B. (1995). Creating false memories: Remembering

words not presented in lists. *Journal of Experimental Psychology: Learning,*

Memory, and Cognition, 21, 803-814.

Underwood, B. J. (1965). False recognition produced by implicit verbal

responses. *Journal of Experimental Psychology, 70,* 122-129.

Note: List references in alphabetical order using first author's surname. Double-space references, no extra space between references.

Center, no italics

↓

Author Note

Authors' department affiliations in first paragraph.

Jeanne S. Zechmeister, Department of Psychology; Eugene B. Zechmeister, Department of Psychology.

Acknowledge people who assisted with the research and manuscript preparation.

Portions of this research were presented at the Annual Meeting of the Psychonomic Society, November 1996. The authors thank the students in the first author's Research Methods in Psychology course at Loyola University of Chicago who participated in and discussed this study, and John J. Shaughnessy for his suggestions for this manuscript.

Last paragraph in Author Note specifies author's address for correspondence. Use this form exactly with your name and address.

Send correspondence concerning this manuscript to Jeanne S. Zechmeister, Department of Psychology, Loyola University of Chicago, 6525 N. Sheridan Road, Chicago, IL 60626; e-mail: jzechme@luc.edu.

Footnotes

[1] The effect size, *r*, was derived from ANOVA output that presented η^2 as a measure of effect size. η^2 represents the proportion of variance in the dependent variable that is accounted for by the independent variable. η^2 is analogous to r^2 in analyses involving one *df* for the effect. The square root of η^2 represents *r*, the magnitude of linear relationship between two variables. Cohen (1988) offers the following guidelines for interpreting the size of an effect using *r*: small effect, *r* = .10; medium effect, *r* = .25; large effect, *r* = .40.

[2] Simple main effect analyses were calculated by treating the comparison as a one-way ANOVA, as recommended by Keppel (1991) for mixed designs.

[3] We also examined whether immediate- vs. delayed-recall conditions influenced recognition in the ANOVA. Because this variable did not produce any statistically significant effects in the recognition analyses, it will not be discussed further.

Note: Use footnotes sparingly in manuscript.

Type flush with left margin.

Line separates title from body of table.

Center column headings over appropriate columns.

Line separates headings from table data.

Line at end of table data.

Table "notes" are typed flush with left margin.

Table title, italicized, with first letters of major words in caps.

False Recall   18

Table 1

Mean Proportions for Recognizing Items as "Old" at Time 1 and Time 2 (48-hr Delay)

	Studied and recalled	Studied and not recalled	Distractor
Correct list items			
Time 1	.84	.79	.19
	(.12)	(.17)	(.12)
Time 2	.76	.56	.18
	(.22)	(.16)	(.16)
False critical items			
Time 1	.97	.88	.28
	(.12)	(.20)	(.13)
Time 2	.91	.64	.17
	(.20)	(.24)	(.10)

Note. Standard deviations are in parentheses. "Recalled" and "Not Recalled" refer to whether participants were asked to recall list items at Time 1, not whether these items were produced by participants during recall.

Note: Use double-space in table. Place only one table on a page.

Center, no italics.

Flush with left margin. Do not abbreviate "Figure."

False Recall   19

↓
Figure Caption

Figure 1. Mean proportions of correct and false recall in the immediate- and delayed-

recall conditions.

Note: More than one figure caption may appear on a "Figure Captions" page.

The figure itself appears on a separate page at end of manuscript. If there is more than one figure, each appears on a separate page.

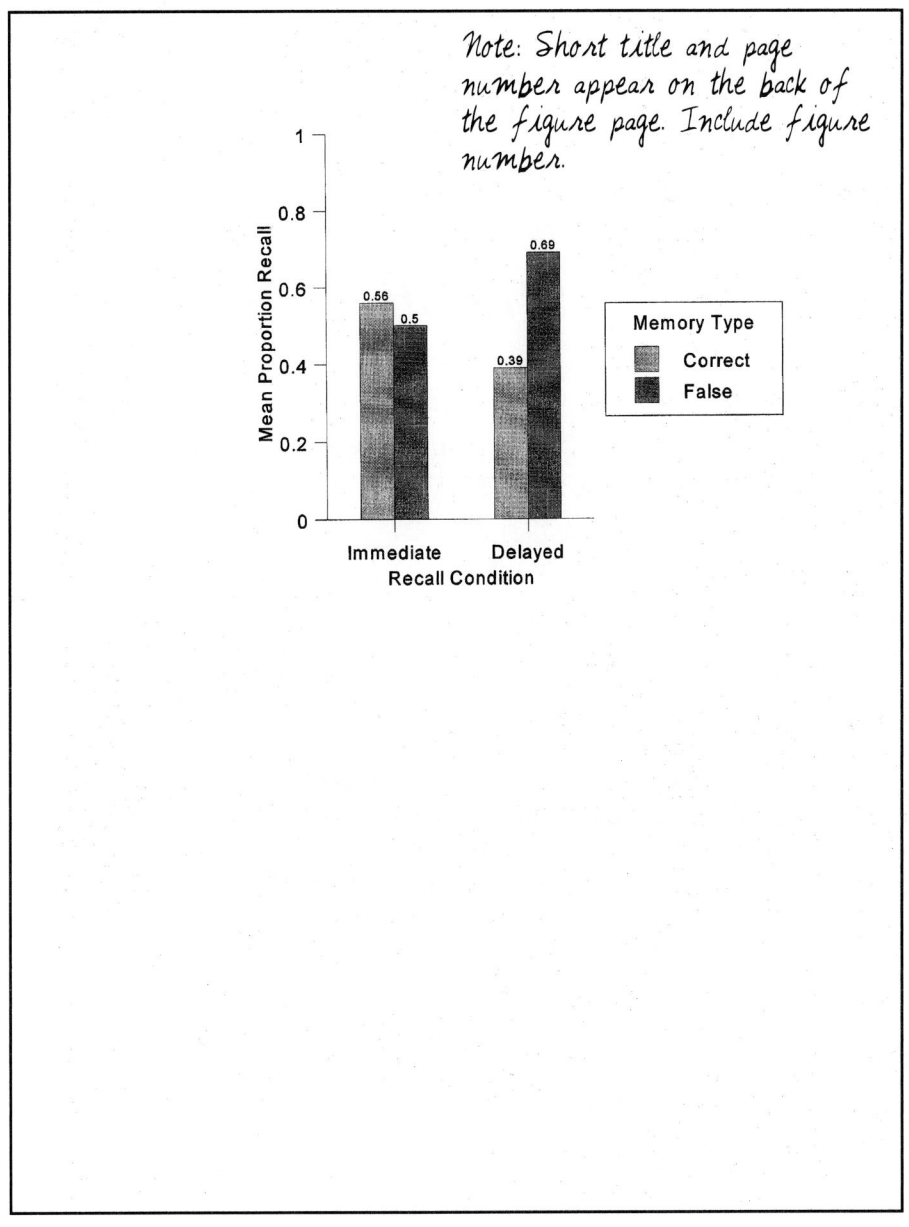

Note: Short title and page number appear on the back of the figure page. Include figure number.

appendix

Statistical Tables

APPENDIX OUTLINE

TABLE A.1 TABLE OF RANDOM NUMBERS*

Col. line	(1)	(2)	(3)	(4)	(5)	(6)	(7)	(8)	(9)	(10)	(11)	(12)	(13)	(14)
1	10480	15011	01536	02011	81647	91646	69179	14194	62590	36207	20969	99570	91291	90700
2	22368	46573	25595	85393	30995	89198	27982	53402	93965	34095	52666	19174	39615	99505
3	24130	48360	22527	97265	76393	64809	15179	24830	49340	32081	30680	19655	63348	58629
4	42167	93093	06243	61680	07856	16376	39440	53537	71341	57004	00849	74917	97758	16379
5	37570	39975	81837	16656	06121	91782	60468	81305	49684	60672	14110	06927	01263	54613
6	77921	06907	11008	42751	27756	53498	18602	70659	90655	15053	21916	81825	44394	42880
7	99562	72905	56420	69994	98872	31016	71194	18738	44013	48840	63213	21069	10634	12952
8	96301	91977	65463	07972	18876	20922	94595	56869	69014	60045	18425	84903	42508	32307
9	89579	14342	63661	10281	17453	18103	57740	84378	25331	12566	58678	44947	05585	56941
10	85475	36857	53342	53988	53060	59533	38867	62300	08158	17983	16439	11458	18593	64952
11	28918	69578	88231	33276	70997	79936	56865	05859	90106	31595	01547	85590	91610	78188
12	63553	40961	48235	03427	49626	69445	18663	72695	52180	20847	12234	90511	33703	90322
13	09429	93969	52636	92737	88974	33488	36320	17617	30015	08272	84115	27156	30613	74952
14	10365	61129	87529	85689	48237	52267	67689	93394	01511	26358	85104	20285	29975	89868
15	07119	97336	71048	08178	77233	13916	47564	81506	97735	85977	29372	74461	28551	90707
16	51085	12765	51821	51259	77452	16308	60756	92144	49442	53900	70960	63990	75601	40719
17	02368	21382	52404	60268	89368	19885	55322	44819	01188	65255	64835	44919	05944	55157
18	01011	54092	33362	94904	31273	04146	18594	29852	71585	85030	51132	01915	92747	64951
19	52162	53916	46369	58586	23216	14513	83149	98736	23495	64350	94738	17752	35156	35749
20	07056	97628	33787	09998	42698	06691	76988	13602	51851	46104	88916	19509	25625	58104
21	48663	91245	85828	14346	09172	30168	90229	04734	59193	22178	30421	61666	99904	32812
22	54164	58492	22421	74103	47070	25306	76468	26384	58151	06646	21524	15227	96909	44592
23	32639	32363	05597	24200	13363	38005	94342	28728	35806	06912	17012	64161	18296	22851
24	29334	27001	87637	87308	58731	00256	45834	15298	46557	41135	10367	07684	36188	18510
25	02488	33062	28834	07351	19731	92420	60952	61280	50001	67658	32586	86679	50720	94953
26	81525	72295	04839	96423	24878	82651	66566	14778	76797	14780	13300	87074	79666	95725
27	29676	20591	68086	26432	46901	20849	89768	81536	86645	12659	92259	57102	80428	25280
28	00742	57392	39064	66432	84673	40027	32832	61362	98947	96067	64760	64584	96096	98253
29	05366	04213	25669	26422	44407	44048	37937	63904	45766	66134	75470	66520	34693	90449
30	91921	26418	64117	94305	26766	25940	39972	22209	71500	64568	91402	42416	07844	69618
31	00582	04711	87917	77341	42206	35126	74087	99547	81817	42607	43808	76655	62028	76630
32	00725	69884	62797	56170	86324	88072	76222	36086	84637	93161	76038	65855	77919	88006
33	69011	65795	95876	55293	18988	27354	26575	08625	40801	59920	29841	80150	12777	48501
34	25976	57948	29888	88604	67917	48708	18912	82271	65424	69774	33611	54262	85963	03547
35	09763	83473	93577	12908	30883	18317	28290	35797	05998	41688	34952	37888	38917	88050
36	91567	42595	27958	30134	04024	86385	29880	99730	55536	84855	29080	09250	79656	73211
37	17955	56349	90999	49127	20044	59931	06115	20542	18059	02008	73708	83517	36103	42791
38	46503	18584	18845	49618	02304	51038	20655	58727	28168	15475	56942	53389	20562	87338
39	92157	89634	94824	78171	84610	82834	09922	25417	44137	48413	25555	21246	35509	20468
40	14577	62765	35605	81263	39667	47358	56873	56307	61607	49518	89696	20103	77490	18062
41	98427	07523	33362	64270	01638	92477	66969	98420	04880	45585	46565	04102	46880	45709
42	34914	63976	88720	82765	34476	17032	87589	40836	32427	70002	70663	88863	77775	69348
43	70060	28277	39475	46473	23219	53416	94970	25832	69975	94884	19661	72828	00102	66794
44	53976	54914	06990	67245	68350	82948	11398	42878	80287	88267	47363	46634	06541	97809
45	76072	29515	40980	07391	58745	25774	22987	80059	39911	96189	41151	14222	60697	59583
46	90725	52210	83974	29992	65831	38857	50490	83765	55657	14361	31720	57375	56228	41546
47	64364	67412	33339	31926	14883	24413	59744	92351	97473	89286	35931	04110	23726	51900
48	08962	00358	31662	25388	61642	34072	81249	35648	56891	69352	48373	45578	78547	81788
49	95012	68379	93526	70765	10592	04542	76463	54328	02349	17247	28865	14777	62730	92277
50	15664	10493	20492	38391	91132	21999	59516	81652	27195	48223	46751	22923	32261	85653

*Source: Table of 105,000 Random Decimal Digits, Statement no. 4914, File no. 261-A-1, Interstate Commerce Commission, Washington, D.C. May 1949.

TABLE A.2   SELECTED VALUES FROM THE *t* DISTRIBUTION*

Instructions for use: To find a value of *t*, locate the row in the left-hand column of the table corresponding to the number of degrees of freedom (*df*) associated with the standard error of the mean, and select the value of *t* listed for your choice of α (nondirectional). The value given in the column labeled $\alpha = .05$ is used in the calculation of the 95% confidence interval, and the value given in the column labeled $\alpha = .01$ is used to calculate the 99% confidence interval.

df	$\alpha = .05$	$\alpha = .01$	df	$\alpha = .05$	$\alpha = .01$
1	12.71	63.66	18	2.10	2.88
2	4.30	9.92	19	2.09	2.86
3	3.18	5.84	20	2.09	2.84
4	2.78	4.60	21	2.08	2.83
5	2.57	4.03	22	2.07	2.82
6	2.45	3.71	23	2.07	2.81
7	2.36	3.50	24	2.06	2.80
8	2.31	3.36	25	2.06	2.79
9	2.26	3.25	26	2.06	2.78
10	2.23	3.17	27	2.05	2.77
11	2.20	3.11	28	2.05	2.76
12	2.18	3.06	29	2.04	2.76
13	2.16	3.01	30	2.04	2.75
14	2.14	2.98	40	2.02	2.70
15	2.13	2.95	60	2.00	2.66
16	2.12	2.92	120	1.98	2.62
17	2.11	2.90	Infinity	1.96	2.58

*This table is adapted from Table 12 in *Biometrika Tables for Statisticians,* vol. 1 (3d ed.), New York: Cambridge University Press, 1970, edited by E. S. Pearson and H. O. Hartley, by permission of the *Biometrika* Trustees.

TABLE A.3 CRITICAL VALUES OF THE *F*-DISTRIBUTION*

Instructions for use: To find the critical value of *F*, locate the cell in the table formed by the intersection of the row containing the degrees of freedom associated with the denominator of the *F*-ratio and the column containing the degrees of freedom associated with the numerator of the *F*-ratio. The numbers listed in boldface type are the critical values of *F* at $\alpha = .05$; the numbers listed in Roman type are the critical values of *F* at $\alpha = .01$. As an example, suppose we have adopted the 5% level of significance and wish to evaluate the significance of an *F* with $df_{num} = 2$ and $df_{denom} = 12$. From the table we find that the critical value of $F(2, 12) = 3.89$ at $\alpha = .05$. If the obtained value of *F* equals or exceeds this critical value, we will reject the null hypothesis; if the obtained value of *F* is smaller than this critical value, we will not reject the null hypothesis.

Degrees of freedom for numerator

	1	2	3	4	5	6	7	8	9	10	12	15	20	24	30	40	60	Infinity
1	**161**	**200**	**216**	**225**	**230**	**234**	**237**	**239**	**241**	**242**	**244**	**246**	**248**	**249**	**250**	**251**	**252**	**254**
	4052	4999	5403	5625	5764	5859	5928	5981	6022	6056	6106	6157	6209	6325	6261	6287	6313	6366
2	**18.5**	**19.0**	**19.2**	**19.2**	**19.3**	**19.3**	**19.4**	**19.4**	**19.4**	**19.4**	**19.4**	**19.4**	**19.4**	**19.4**	**19.5**	**19.5**	**19.5**	**19.5**
	98.5	99.0	99.2	99.2	99.3	99.3	99.4	99.4	99.4	99.4	99.4	99.4	99.4	99.5	99.5	99.5	99.5	99.5
3	**10.1**	**9.55**	**9.28**	**9.12**	**9.01**	**8.94**	**8.89**	**8.85**	**8.81**	**8.79**	**8.74**	**8.70**	**8.66**	**8.64**	**8.62**	**8.59**	**8.57**	**8.53**
	34.1	30.8	29.5	28.7	28.2	27.9	27.7	27.5	27.4	27.2	27.0	26.9	26.7	26.6	26.5	26.4	26.3	26.1
4	**7.71**	**6.94**	**6.59**	**6.39**	**6.26**	**6.16**	**6.09**	**6.04**	**6.00**	**5.96**	**5.91**	**5.86**	**5.80**	**5.77**	**5.75**	**5.72**	**5.69**	**5.63**
	21.2	18.0	16.7	16.0	15.5	15.2	15.0	14.8	14.7	14.6	14.4	14.2	14.0	13.9	13.8	13.8	13.6	13.5
5	**6.61**	**5.79**	**5.41**	**5.19**	**5.05**	**4.95**	**4.88**	**4.82**	**4.77**	**4.74**	**4.68**	**4.62**	**4.56**	**4.53**	**4.50**	**4.46**	**4.43**	**4.26**
	16.3	13.3	12.1	11.4	11.0	10.7	10.5	10.3	10.2	10.0	9.89	9.72	9.55	9.47	9.38	9.29	9.20	9.02
6	**5.99**	**5.14**	**4.76**	**4.53**	**4.39**	**4.28**	**4.21**	**4.15**	**4.10**	**4.06**	**4.00**	**3.94**	**3.87**	**3.84**	**3.81**	**3.77**	**3.74**	**3.67**
	13.8	10.9	9.78	9.15	8.75	8.47	8.26	8.10	7.98	7.87	7.72	7.56	7.40	7.31	7.23	7.14	7.06	6.88
7	**5.59**	**4.74**	**4.35**	**4.12**	**3.97**	**3.87**	**3.79**	**3.73**	**3.68**	**3.64**	**3.57**	**3.51**	**3.44**	**3.41**	**3.38**	**3.34**	**3.30**	**3.23**
	12.2	9.55	8.45	7.85	7.46	7.19	6.99	6.84	6.72	6.62	6.47	6.31	6.16	6.07	5.99	5.91	5.82	5.65
8	**5.32**	**4.46**	**4.07**	**3.84**	**3.69**	**3.58**	**3.50**	**3.44**	**3.39**	**3.35**	**3.28**	**3.22**	**3.15**	**3.12**	**3.08**	**3.04**	**3.01**	**2.93**
	11.3	8.65	7.59	7.01	6.63	6.37	6.18	6.03	5.91	5.81	5.67	5.52	5.36	5.28	5.20	5.12	5.03	4.86
9	**5.12**	**4.26**	**3.86**	**3.63**	**3.48**	**3.37**	**3.29**	**3.23**	**3.18**	**3.14**	**3.07**	**3.01**	**2.94**	**2.90**	**2.86**	**2.83**	**2.79**	**2.71**
	10.6	8.02	6.99	6.42	6.06	5.80	5.61	5.47	5.35	5.26	5.11	4.96	4.81	4.73	4.65	4.57	4.48	4.31
10	**4.96**	**4.10**	**3.71**	**3.48**	**3.33**	**3.22**	**3.14**	**3.07**	**3.02**	**2.98**	**2.91**	**2.85**	**2.77**	**2.74**	**2.70**	**2.66**	**2.62**	**2.54**
	10.0	7.56	6.55	5.99	5.64	5.39	5.20	5.06	4.94	4.85	4.71	4.56	4.41	4.33	4.25	4.17	4.08	3.91
11	**4.84**	**3.98**	**3.59**	**3.36**	**3.20**	**3.09**	**3.01**	**2.95**	**2.90**	**2.85**	**2.79**	**2.72**	**2.65**	**2.61**	**2.57**	**2.53**	**2.49**	**2.40**
	9.65	7.21	6.22	5.67	5.32	5.07	4.89	4.74	4.63	4.54	4.40	4.25	4.10	4.02	3.94	3.86	3.78	3.60
12	**4.75**	**3.89**	**3.49**	**3.26**	**3.11**	**3.00**	**2.91**	**2.85**	**2.80**	**2.75**	**2.69**	**2.62**	**2.54**	**2.51**	**2.47**	**2.43**	**2.38**	**2.30**
	9.33	6.93	5.95	5.41	5.06	4.82	4.64	4.50	4.39	4.30	4.16	4.01	3.86	3.78	3.70	3.62	3.54	3.36
13	**4.67**	**3.81**	**3.41**	**3.18**	**3.03**	**2.92**	**2.83**	**2.77**	**2.71**	**2.67**	**2.60**	**2.53**	**2.46**	**2.42**	**2.38**	**2.34**	**2.30**	**2.21**
	9.07	6.70	5.74	5.21	4.86	4.62	4.44	4.30	4.19	4.10	3.96	3.82	3.66	3.59	3.51	3.43	3.34	3.17
14	**4.60**	**3.74**	**3.34**	**3.11**	**2.96**	**2.85**	**2.76**	**2.70**	**2.65**	**2.60**	**2.53**	**2.46**	**2.39**	**2.35**	**2.31**	**2.27**	**2.22**	**2.13**
	8.86	6.51	5.56	5.04	4.69	4.46	4.28	4.14	4.03	3.94	3.80	3.66	3.51	3.43	3.35	3.27	3.18	3.00
15	**4.54**	**3.68**	**3.29**	**3.06**	**2.90**	**2.79**	**2.71**	**2.64**	**2.59**	**2.54**	**2.48**	**2.40**	**2.33**	**2.29**	**2.25**	**2.20**	**2.16**	**2.07**
	8.68	6.36	5.42	4.89	4.56	4.32	4.14	4.00	3.89	3.80	3.67	3.52	3.37	3.29	3.21	3.13	3.05	2.87
16	**4.49**	**3.63**	**3.24**	**3.01**	**2.85**	**2.74**	**2.66**	**2.59**	**2.54**	**2.49**	**2.42**	**2.35**	**2.28**	**2.24**	**2.19**	**2.15**	**2.11**	**2.01**
	8.53	6.23	5.29	4.77	4.44	4.20	4.03	3.89	3.78	3.69	3.55	3.41	3.26	3.18	3.10	3.02	2.93	2.75
17	**4.45**	**3.59**	**3.20**	**2.96**	**2.81**	**2.70**	**2.61**	**2.55**	**2.49**	**2.45**	**2.38**	**2.31**	**2.23**	**2.19**	**2.15**	**2.10**	**2.06**	**1.96**
	8.40	6.11	5.18	4.67	4.34	4.10	3.93	3.79	3.68	3.59	3.46	3.31	3.16	3.08	3.00	2.92	2.83	2.65
18	**4.41**	**3.55**	**3.16**	**2.93**	**2.77**	**2.66**	**2.58**	**2.51**	**2.46**	**2.41**	**2.34**	**2.27**	**2.19**	**2.15**	**2.11**	**2.06**	**2.02**	**1.92**
	8.29	6.01	5.09	4.58	4.25	4.01	3.84	3.71	3.60	3.51	3.37	3.23	3.08	3.00	2.92	2.84	2.75	2.57

Degrees of freedom for denominator

(Continued)

TABLE A.3   CRITICAL VALUES OF THE *F*-DISTRIBUTION* (*Concluded*)

		1	2	3	4	5	6	7	8	9	10	12	15	20	24	30	40	60	Infinity
										Degrees of freedom for numerator									
Degrees of freedom for denominator	19	4.38	3.52	3.13	2.90	2.74	2.63	2.54	2.48	2.42	2.38	2.31	2.23	2.16	2.11	2.07	2.03	1.98	1.88
		8.18	5.93	5.01	4.50	4.17	3.94	3.77	3.63	3.52	3.43	3.30	3.15	3.00	2.92	2.84	2.76	2.67	2.49
	20	4.35	3.49	3.10	2.87	2.71	2.60	2.51	2.45	2.39	2.35	2.28	2.20	2.12	2.08	2.04	1.99	1.95	1.84
		8.10	5.85	4.94	4.43	4.10	3.87	3.70	3.56	3.46	3.37	3.23	3.09	2.94	2.86	2.78	2.69	2.61	2.42
	22	4.30	3.44	3.05	2.82	2.66	2.55	2.46	2.40	2.34	2.30	2.23	2.15	2.07	2.03	1.98	1.94	1.89	1.78
		7.95	5.72	4.82	4.31	3.99	3.76	3.59	3.45	3.35	3.26	3.12	2.98	2.83	2.75	2.67	2.58	2.50	2.31
	24	4.26	3.40	3.01	2.78	2.62	2.51	2.42	2.36	2.30	2.25	2.18	2.11	2.03	1.98	1.94	1.89	1.84	1.73
		7.82	5.61	4.72	4.22	3.90	3.67	3.50	3.36	3.26	3.17	3.03	2.89	2.74	2.66	2.58	2.49	2.40	2.21
	26	4.23	3.37	2.98	2.74	2.59	2.47	2.39	2.32	2.27	2.22	2.15	2.07	1.99	1.95	1.90	1.85	1.80	1.69
		7.72	5.53	4.64	4.14	3.82	3.59	3.42	3.29	3.18	3.09	2.96	2.81	2.66	2.58	2.50	2.42	2.33	2.13
	28	4.20	3.34	2.95	2.71	2.56	2.45	2.36	2.29	2.24	2.19	2.12	2.04	1.96	1.91	1.87	1.82	1.77	1.65
		7.64	5.45	4.57	4.07	3.75	3.53	3.36	3.23	3.12	3.03	2.90	2.75	2.60	2.52	2.44	2.35	2.26	2.06
	30	4.17	3.32	2.92	2.69	2.53	2.42	2.33	2.27	2.21	2.16	2.09	2.01	1.93	1.89	1.84	1.79	1.74	1.62
		7.56	5.39	4.51	4.02	3.70	3.47	3.30	3.17	3.07	2.98	2.84	2.70	2.55	2.47	2.39	2.30	2.21	2.01
	40	4.08	3.23	2.84	2.61	2.45	2.34	2.25	2.18	2.12	2.08	2.00	1.92	1.84	1.79	1.74	1.69	1.64	1.51
		7.31	5.18	4.31	3.83	3.51	3.29	3.12	2.99	2.89	2.80	2.66	2.52	2.37	2.29	2.20	2.11	2.02	1.80
	60	4.00	3.15	2.76	2.53	2.37	2.25	2.17	2.10	2.04	1.99	1.92	1.84	1.75	1.7	1.65	1.59	1.53	1.39
		7.06	4.98	4.13	3.65	3.34	3.12	2.95	2.82	2.72	2.63	2.50	2.35	2.20	2.12	2.03	1.94	1.84	1.60
	120	3.92	3.07	2.68	2.45	2.29	2.17	2.09	2.02	1.96	1.91	1.83	1.75	1.66	1.61	1.55	1.50	1.43	1.25
		6.85	4.79	3.95	3.48	3.17	2.96	2.79	2.66	2.56	2.47	2.34	2.19	2.03	1.95	1.86	1.76	1.66	1.38
	INFINITY	3.84	3.00	2.60	2.37	2.21	2.10	2.01	1.94	1.88	1.83	1.75	1.67	1.57	1.52	1.46	1.39	1.32	1.00
		6.63	4.61	3.78	3.32	3.02	2.80	2.64	2.51	2.41	2.32	2.18	2.04	1.88	1.79	1.70	1.59	1.47	1.00

*This table is abridged from Table 18 in *Biometrika Tables for Statisticians,* vol. 1 (3d ed.), New York: Cambridge University Press, 1970, edited by E. S. Pearson and H. O. Hartley, by permission of the *Biometrika* Trustees.

TABLE A.4 POWER TABLE FOR COMPARISON BETWEEN TWO MEANS (INDEPENDENT GROUPS) WITH ALPHA = .05 (TWO-TAILED TEST)

Note: The table shows the power associated with various effect sizes (.10–1.00) as a function of sample size for an independent groups *t*-test ($\alpha = .05$, two-tailed test). Effect size is based on Cohen's *d*. The table may be used to assess power post hoc, that is, after a study has been completed. For example, when $n = 20$ in *each group* and the effect size is medium (.50), power is .33. (Decimal points have been omitted in table.) For the same sample size and a large effect size (.80), power is .69. The table may also be used in planning an experiment. Suppose that an examination of the literature suggests that the effect you are looking for is about .60, slightly greater than a medium effect size according to Cohen's (1988) rule of thumb. What sample size is needed to see this effect with power = .80? Looking at the column for this size effect (.60), you will see that power increases as sample size increases until .84 power is achieved when sample size is 50. To obtain power = .80 we can estimate that sample size for each group should be about 45 (by interpolating between sample size 40 and 50). What sample size is needed to see this effect with power = .70? You should see that sample size must be 35 in each group to achieve power = .70. (Based on Cohen, 1988, pp. 36–37.)

Effect size (d)

n	.10	(Small) .20	.30	.40	(Medium) .50	.60	.70	(Large) .80	1.00
10	06	07	10	13	18	24	31	39	56
15	06	08	12	18	26	35	45	56	75
20	06	09	15	23	33	45	58	69	87
25	06	11	18	28	41	55	68	79	93
30	07	12	21	33	47	63	76	86	97
35	07	13	23	38	54	70	82	91	98
40	07	14	26	42	60	75	87	94	99
50	08	17	32	50	70	84	93	98	*
60	08	19	37	58	77	90	97	99	*
80	10	24	47	71	88	96	99	*	*
100	11	29	56	80	94	99	*	*	*

TABLE A.5   POWER TABLE FOR ANALYSIS OF VARIANCE FOR INDEPENDENT GROUPS WITH ALPHA = .05

Note: The table shows the power associated with various effect sizes (.05–.50) as a function of sample size in each group in an independent groups design. Effect size is assessed using Cohen's *f* (see Chapter 12). Power is summarized separately for an experiment with independent groups of 2, 3, 4, and 5. The table may be used to assess power post hoc, after a study is completed. For example, assume that an experiment was conducted with 3 groups ($n = 30$) and an analysis of variance performed on the data. Assume further that the effect size based on *f* was .40, a large effect according to Cohen's (1988) rule of thumb. What was the power associated with this test? Looking at that portion of the table that reveals power values for 3 groups ($df = 2$), and under the column .40, you can see that power = .93 when sample size is 30. (Decimal points have been omitted in the table.) The table also may be used to plan an experiment by determining the sample size needed to see an effect of a specific magnitude. Suppose that a review of previous studies revealed that on the average an effect size of .30 was obtained for the variable of interest. What sample size would be needed in a 4-group experiment to see an effect of this size with power = .80? Looking at the power values for an independent groups experiment with 4 groups, and under the effect size column .30, you will see that power increases as sample size increases and is .84 when sample size for each group is 30. Power is .76 when $n = 25$; thus we can interpolate to estimate that sample size for each group should be about 28 to achieve power = .80. If the effect size we are seeking is .10, a small effect size according to Cohen, you can see that power is only .22 even when sample size is 60. (Based on Cohen, 1988, pp. 311–318.)

2 Groups ($df = 1$)

				Effect size (*f*)					
		(Small)			(Medium)			(Large)	
n	.05	.10	.15	.20	.25	.30	.35	.40	.50
5	05	06	07	08	11	13	16	20	29
10	05	07	09	13	18	25	32	40	57
15	06	08	12	18	26	36	47	57	76
20	06	09	15	23	34	46	59	70	88
25	06	10	18	29	42	56	69	80	94
30	06	11	21	34	49	64	77	87	97
35	07	12	24	39	55	71	83	92	99
40	07	14	27	43	61	77	88	95	99
50	07	16	32	52	71	85	94	98	*
60	08	19	38	60	79	91	97	99	*

3 Groups ($df = 2$)

				Effect size (*f*)					
		(Small)			(Medium)			(Large)	
n	.05	.10	.15	.20	.25	.30	.35	.40	.50
5	05	06	07	09	11	14	17	22	32
10	05	07	10	14	20	27	35	45	64
15	06	08	13	20	29	40	52	64	84
20	06	09	16	26	38	52	66	78	93
25	06	10	19	32	47	63	77	87	98
30	06	12	22	37	55	71	85	93	99
35	07	13	26	43	62	79	90	96	*
40	07	15	29	48	68	84	94	98	*
50	08	18	36	58	79	92	98	99	*
60	08	21	42	67	86	96	99	*	*

TABLE A.5   POWER TABLE FOR ANALYSIS OF VARIANCE FOR INDEPENDENT GROUPS
WITH ALPHA = .05 (*Concluded*)

4 Groups (*df* = 3)

				Effect size (*f*)				
		(Small)			(Medium)			(Large)	
n	.05	.10	.15	.20	.25	.30	.35	.40	.50
5	05	06	07	09	12	16	21	26	40
10	06	07	10	16	23	33	44	56	78
15	06	09	14	23	36	50	65	78	94
20	06	10	18	31	47	65	79	90	99
25	06	12	23	39	58	76	89	96	*
30	07	13	27	46	67	84	94	98	*
35	07	15	31	54	75	90	97	99	*
40	07	17	36	60	81	94	99	*	*
50	08	19	40	65	85	96	99	*	*
60	09	22	47	74	91	98	*	*	*

5 Groups (*df* = 4)

				Effect size (*f*)				
		(Small)			(Medium)			(Large)	
n	.05	.10	.15	.20	.25	.30	.35	.40	.50
5	05	06	07	10	13	17	22	29	44
10	06	07	11	17	25	36	48	61	83
15	06	09	15	25	39	55	70	82	96
20	06	11	20	34	52	70	84	93	99
25	07	12	24	43	63	81	92	98	*
30	07	14	29	51	73	88	96	99	*
35	07	16	34	65	80	93	98	*	*
40	08	18	39	68	86	96	99	*	*
50	08	21	44	71	90	98	*	*	*
60	09	24	52	80	95	99	*	*	*

*Indicates that power is greater than .995.

Glossary

ABAB design (reversal design) A single-subject experimental design in which an initial baseline stage (A) is followed by a treatment stage (B), a return to baseline (A), and then another treatment stage (B); the researcher observes whether behavior changes on introduction of the treatment, reverses when the treatment is withdrawn, and improves again when the treatment is reintroduced.

alpha See **level of significance.**

ANOVA The analysis of variance, or ANOVA, is the most commonly used inferential test for examining a null hypothesis when comparing more than two means in a single-factor study, or in studies with more than one factor (i.e., independent variable). The ANOVA test is based on analyzing different sources of variation in an experiment.

applied research Research that seeks knowledge that will improve a situation. See also **basic research.**

archival data Source of evidence based on records or documents relating the activities of individuals, institutions, governments, and other groups; used as an alternative to or in conjunction with other research methods.

attrition See **subject attrition.**

baseline stage First stage of a single-subject experiment in which a record is made of the individual's behavior prior to any intervention.

basic research Research that seeks knowledge to increase understanding of behavior and mental processes and to test theories. See also **applied research.**

block randomization The most common technique for carrying out random assignment in the random groups design; each block includes a random order of the conditions and there are as many blocks as there are subjects in each condition of the experiment.

case study An intensive description and analysis of a single individual.

causal inference Identification of the cause or causes of a phenomenon, by establishing covariation of cause and effect, a time-order relationship with cause preceding effect, and the elimination of plausible alternative causes.

ceiling (and floor) effect Measurement problem whereby the researcher cannot measure the effects of an independent variable or a possible interaction effect because performance has reached a maximum (minimum) in any condition of the experiment.

central tendency See **measures of central tendency.**

coding The initial step in data reduction, especially with narrative records, in which units of behavior or particular events are identified and classified according to specific criteria.

Cohen's d A frequently used measure of effect size in which the difference in means for two conditions is divided by the average variability of participants' scores (within-group standard deviation). Based on Cohen's guidelines, d values of .20, .50, and .80 represent small, medium, and large effects, respectively, of an independent variable.

Cohen's f A measure of effect size when there are more than two means that defines an effect relative to the degree of dispersion among group means. Based on Cohen's guidelines, an f value of .10, .25, and .40 defines a small, medium, and large effect size, respectively.

comparison of two means A statistical technique that can be applied (usually after obtaining a statistically significant omnibus F-test) to locate the specific source of systematic variation in an experiment by comparing means two at a time.

complex design Experiment in which two or more independent variables are studied simultaneously.

confidence intervals Indicate the range of values which we can expect to contain a population value with a specified degree of confidence (e.g., 95%).

confidence interval for a population parameter A range of values around a sample statistic (e.g., sample mean) with specified probability (e.g., .95) that the population parameter (e.g., population mean) has been captured within that interval.

confirming what the data reveal In the third stage of data analysis the researcher determines what the data tell us about behavior. Statistical techniques are used to counter arguments that the results are simply "due to chance."

confounding Occurs when the independent variable of interest systematically covaries with a second, unintended independent variable.

construct A concept or idea used in psychological theories to explain behavior or mental processes; examples include aggression, depression, intelligence, memory, and personality.

contamination Occurs when there is communication of information about the experiment between groups of participants.

content analysis Any of a variety of techniques for making inferences by objectively identifying specific characteristics of messages, usually written communications but may be any form of message; used extensively in the analysis of archival data.

control Key component of the scientific method whereby the effect of various factors possibly responsible for a phenomenon are isolated; three basic types of control are manipulation, holding conditions constant, and balancing.

correlation Exists when two different measures of the same people, events, or things vary together; the presence of a correlation makes it possible to predict values on one variable by knowing the values on the second variable.

correlation coefficient Statistic indicating how well two measures vary together; absolute size ranges from 0.0 (no correlation) to 1.00 (perfect correlation); direction of covariation is indicated by the sign of the coefficient, a plus (+) indicating that both measures covary in the same direction and a minus (−) indicating that the variables vary in opposite directions.

correlational research Research to identify predictive relationships among naturally occurring variables.

counterbalancing A control technique for distributing (balancing) practice effects across the conditions of a repeated measures design. How counterbalancing is accomplished depends on whether a complete or an incomplete repeated measures design is used.

cross-sectional design Survey research design in which one or more samples of the population are selected and information is collected from the samples at one time.

data reduction Process in the analysis of behavioral data whereby results are meaningfully organized and statements summarizing important findings are prepared.

debriefing Process following a research session through which participants are informed about the rationale for the research in which they participated, about the need for any deception, and about their specific contribution to the research. Important goals of debriefing are to clear up any misconceptions and to leave participants with a positive feeling toward psychological research.

deception Intentionally withholding information from a participant about significant aspects of a research project or presenting misinformation about the research to participants.

demand characteristics Cues and other information used by participants to guide their behavior in a psychological study, often leading participants to do what they believe the observer (experimenter) expects them to do.

dependent variable Measure of behavior used by the researcher to assess the effect (if any) of the independent variable.

differential transfer Potential problem in repeated measures designs when performance in one condition differs depending on which of two other conditions precedes it.

double-blind Both the participant and the observer are kept unaware (blind) of what treatment is being administered.

effect size Index of the strength of the relationship between the independent variable and dependent variable that is independent of sample size.

empirical approach Approach to acquiring knowledge that emphasizes direct observation and experimentation as a way of answering questions.

estimated standard error of the mean An estimate of the true standard error obtained by dividing the sample standard deviation by the square root of the sample size.

eta squared (η^2) A measure of the strength of association (or effect size) based on the proportion of variance accounted for by the effect of the independent variable on the dependent variable.

ethnocentrism An attempt to understand the behavior of individuals in different cultures based solely on experiences in one's own culture.

experiment A controlled research situation in which scientists manipulate one or more factors and observe the effects of this manipulation on behavior.

experimenter effects Experimenters' expectations that may lead them to treat subjects differently in different groups or to record data in a biased manner.

external validity The extent to which the results of a research study can be generalized to different populations, settings, and conditions.

factorial design See **complex design.**

field experiment Procedure in which one or more independent variables is manipulated by an observer in a natural setting to determine the effect on behavior.

floor effect See **ceiling effect.**

F-test In the analysis of variance, or ANOVA, the ratio of between-group variation and within-group or error variation.

getting to know the data In this first stage of data analysis the researcher inspects the data for errors and outliers and generally becomes familiar with the general features of the data.

Hawthorne effect See **novelty effects.**

history The occurrence of an event other than the treatment that can threaten internal validity if it produces changes in the research participants' behavior.

hypothesis A tentative explanation for a phenomenon.

idiographic approach Intensive study of an individual, with an emphasis on both individual uniqueness and lawfulness.

independent groups design Each separate group of subjects in the experiment represents a different condition as defined by the level of the independent variable.

independent variable Factor for which the researcher manipulates at least two levels in order to determine its effect on behavior.

individual differences variable A characteristic or trait that varies consistently across individuals, such as level of depression, age, intelligence, gender. Because this variable is formed from pre-existing groups (i.e., it occurs "naturally") an individual differences variable is sometimes called a natural groups variable. Another term sometimes used synonymously with individual differences variable is subject variable.

informed consent Explicitly expressed willingness to participate in a research project based on clear understanding of the nature of the research, of the consequences of not participating, and of all factors that might be expected to influence willingness to participate.

instrumentation Changes over time can take place not only in the participants of an experiment, but also in the instruments used to measure the participants' performance. These changes due to instrumentation can threaten internal validity if they cannot be separated from the effect of the treatment.

interaction effect When the effect of one independent variable differs depending on the level of a second independent variable.

internal validity Degree to which differences in performance can be attributed unambiguously to an effect of an independent variable, as opposed to an effect of some other (uncontrolled) variable; an internally valid study is free of confounds.

interobserver reliability Degree to which two independent observers are in agreement.

interrupted time-series design See **simple interrupted time-series design** and **time series with nonequivalent control group design.**

interviewer bias Occurs when the interviewer tries to adjust the wording of a question to fit the respondent or records only selected portions of the respondent's answers.

level of significance The probability when testing the null hypothesis that is used to indicate whether an outcome is statistically significant. Level of significance, or alpha, is equal to the probability of a Type I error.

linear trend A trend in the data that is appropriately summarized by a straight line.

longitudinal design Research design in which the same sample of respondents is interviewed (tested) more than once.

main effect Overall effect of an independent variable in a complex design.

matched groups design Type of independent groups design in which the researcher forms comparable groups by matching subjects on a pretest task and then randomly assigning the members of these matched sets of subjects to the conditions of the experiment.

maturation Change associated with the passage of time *per se* is called maturation. Changes participants undergo in an experiment that are due to maturation and not due to the treatment can threaten internal validity.

mean The arithmetic mean, or average, is determined by dividing the sum of the scores by the number of scores contributing to that sum. The mean is the most commonly used measure of central tendency.

measurement scale One of four levels of physical and psychological measurement: nominal (categorizing), ordinal (ranking), interval (specifying distance between stimuli), and ratio (having an absolute zero point).

measures of central tendency Measures such as the mean, median, and mode, that identify a score that the data tend to center around.

measures of dispersion (variability) Measures such as the range and standard deviation that describe the degree of dispersion of numbers in a distribution.

mechanical subject loss Occurs when a subject fails to complete the experiment because of equipment failure or because of experimenter error.

median The middle point in a distribution, above which half the scores fall and below which half fall.

meta-analysis Analysis of results of several (often, very many) independent experiments investigating the same research area; the measure used in a meta-analysis is typically effect size.

minimal risk A research participant is said to experience minimal risk when probability and magnitude of harm or discomfort anticipated in the research are not greater than that ordinarily encountered in daily life or during the performance of routine tests.

mode The score that appears most frequently in the distribution.

multimethod approach Approach to hypothesis testing that seeks evidence by collecting data using several different research procedures and measures of behavior; a recognition of the fact that any single observation of behavior can result from some artifact of the measuring process.

multiple-baseline design (across individuals, across behaviors, across situations) A single-subject experimental design in which the effect of a treatment is demonstrated by showing that behaviors in more than one baseline change as a consequence of the introduction of a treatment; multiple baselines are established for different individuals, for different behaviors in the same individual, or for the same individual in different situations.

$N = 1$ designs See **single-subject experiment.**

narrative record Record intended to provide a more or less faithful reproduction of behavior as it originally occurred.

natural groups design Type of independent groups design in which the conditions represent the selected levels of a naturally occurring independent variable, for example, the individual differences variable age.

naturalistic observation Observation of behavior in a more or less natural setting without any attempt by the observer to intervene.

negative correlation A relationship between two variables in which values for one measure increase as the values of the other measure decrease.

nomothetic approach Approach to research that seeks to establish broad generalizations or laws that apply to large groups (populations) of individuals; the average or typical performance of a group is emphasized.

nonequivalent control group design Quasi-experimental procedure in which a comparison is made between control and treatment groups that have been established on some basis other than through random assignment of participants to groups.

nonprobability sampling A sampling procedure in which there is no way to estimate the probability of each element's being included in the sample; a common type is convenience sampling.

novelty effects Threats to internal validity of a study that occur when people's behavior changes simply because an innovation (e.g., a treatment) produces excitement, energy, and enthusiasm; a Hawthorne effect is a special case of novelty effects.

null hypothesis (H$_0$)   Assumption used as the first step in statistical inference whereby the independent variable is said to have had no effect.

null hypothesis significance testing (NHST)   A procedure for statistical inference used to decide whether a variable has produced an effect in a study. NHST begins with the assumption that the variable has no effect (see **null hypothesis**), and probability theory is used to determine the probability that the effect (e.g., a mean difference between conditions) observed in a study would occur simply by error variation ("chance"). If the likelihood of the observed effect is small (see **level of significance**), assuming the null hypothesis is true, we infer the variable produced a reliable effect (see **statistically significant**).

observer bias   Systematic errors in observation often resulting from the observer's expectancies regarding the outcome of a study (i.e., expectancy effects).

omnibus *F*-test   The initial overall analysis based on ANOVA.

operational definition   Procedure whereby a concept is defined solely in terms of the observable procedures used to produce and measure it.

participant observation   Observation of behavior by someone who also has an active and significant role in the situation or context in which behavior is recorded.

physical traces   Source of evidence that is based on the remnants, fragments, and products of past behavior; used as an alternative to or in conjunction with other research methods.

placebo control   Procedure by which a substance that resembles a drug or other active substance but that is actually an inert, or inactive, substance is given to participants.

plagiarism   Presentation of another's ideas or work without clearly identifying the source.

population   Set of all the cases of interest.

positive correlation   A relationship between two variables in which values for one measure increase as the values of the other measure also increase.

power   Probability in a statistical test that a false null hypothesis will be rejected; power is related to the level of significance selected, the size of the treatment effect, and the sample size.

practice effects   Changes that participants undergo with repeated testing. Practice effects are the summation of both positive (e.g., familiarity with a task) and negative (e.g., boredom) factors associated with repeated measurement.

privacy   Right of individuals to decide how information about them is to be communicated to others.

probability sampling   Sampling procedure in which the probability that each element of the population will be included in the sample can be specified.

program evaluation   Research that seeks to determine whether a change proposed by an institution, government agency, or other unit of society is needed and likely to have an effect as planned or, when implemented, to actually have an effect.

quasi-experiments   Procedures that resemble characteristics of true experiments, for example, that some type of intervention or treatment is used and a comparison is provided, but are lacking in the degree of control that is found in true experiments.

questionnaire   A set of predetermined questions for all respondents that serves as the primary research instrument in survey research.

random assignment   Most common technique for forming groups as part of an independent groups design; the goal is to establish equivalent groups by balancing individual differences.

random groups design   Most common type of independent groups design in which subjects are randomly selected or randomly assigned to each group such that groups are considered comparable at the start of the experiment.

random sampling   See **simple random sampling.**

range   The difference between the highest and lowest number in a distribution.

reactivity   Influence that an observer has on the behavior under observation; behavior influenced by an observer may not be representative of behavior that occurs when an observer is not present.

regression (to the mean)   Statistical regression can occur when individuals have been selected to participate in an experiment because of their "extreme" scores. Statistical regression is a threat to internal validity because individuals selected from extreme groups would be expected to have less extreme scores on a second test (the "posttest") *without any treatment* simply due to statistical regression.

relevant independent variable   Independent variable that has been shown to influence behavior, either directly, by producing a main effect, or indirectly, by resulting in an interaction effect in combination with a second independent variable.

reliability A measurement is reliable when it is consistent.

repeated measures designs Research designs in which each subject participates in all conditions of the experiment (i.e., measurement is repeated on the same subject).

repeated measures (within-subjects) *t*-test An inferential test for comparing two means from the same group of subjects or from two groups of subjects "matched" on some measure related to the dependent variable.

replication Repeating the exact procedures used in an experiment to determine whether the same results are obtained.

representativeness A sample is representative to the extent that it has the same distribution of characteristics as the population from which it was selected; our ability to generalize from sample to population is critically dependent on representativeness.

response bias Threat to the representativeness of a sample that occurs when some participants selected to respond to a survey systematically fail to complete the survey (e.g., due to failure to complete a lengthy questionnaire or to reply with a request to participate in a phone survey).

reversal design See **ABAB design.**

risk/benefit ratio Subjective evaluation of the risk to a research participant relative to the benefit both to the individual and to society of the results of the proposed research.

sample Something less than all the cases of interest; in survey research, a subset of the population actually drawn from the sampling frame.

scatterplot A graph showing the relationship between two variables by indicating the intersection of two measures obtained from the same person, thing, or event.

scientific method Approach to knowledge that emphasizes empirical rather than intuitive processes, testable hypotheses, systematic and controlled observation of operationally defined phenomena, data collection using accurate and precise instrumentation, valid and reliable measures, and objective reporting of results; scientists tend to be critical and, most importantly, skeptical.

selection Selection is a threat to internal validity when, from the outset of a study, differences exist between the kinds of individuals in one group and those in another group in the experiment.

selection bias Threat to the representativeness of a sample that occurs when the procedures used to select a sample result in the over- or underrepresentation of a significant segment of the population.

selective deposit Bias that results from the way physical traces are laid down and the way archival sources are produced, edited, or altered, as they are established; when present, the bias severely limits generality of research findings.

selective subject loss Occurs when subjects are lost differentially across the conditions of the experiment as the result of some characteristic of each subject that is related to the outcome of the study.

selective survival Bias that results from the way physical traces and archives survive over time; when present, the bias severely limits the external validity of research findings.

sensitivity Refers to the likelihood in an experiment that the effect of an independent variable will be detected when that variable does, indeed, have an effect; sensitivity is increased to the extent that error variation is reduced (e.g., by holding variables constant rather than balancing them).

simple interrupted time-series design Quasi-experimental procedure in which changes in a dependent variable are observed for some period of time both before and after a treatment is introduced.

simple main effect Effect of one independent variable at one level of a second independent variable in a complex design.

simple random sampling (random selection) Type of probability sampling in which each possible sample of a specified size in the population has an equal chance of being selected.

single-factor independent groups design An experiment that involves independent groups with one independent variable.

single-subject experiment A procedure that focuses on behavior change in one individual by systematically contrasting conditions within that individual while continuously monitoring behavior.

situation sampling Random or systematic selection of situations in which observations are made with the goal of representativeness across circumstances, locations, and conditions.

small-*n* research See **single-subject experiment.**

social desirability Pressures on survey respondents to answer as they think they should respond in accordance with what is most socially acceptable, and not in accordance with what they actually believe.

spurious relationship What exists when evidence falsely indicates that two or more variables are associated.

stages of data analysis Three stages of data analysis are: getting to know the data, summarizing the data, and confirming what the data reveal.

standard deviation The most commonly used measure of dispersion that indicates approximately how far on the average scores differ from the mean.

standard error of the mean The standard deviation of the sampling distribution of means.

statistically significant When the probability of an obtained difference in an experiment is smaller than would be expected if error variation alone were assumed to be responsible for the difference, the difference is statistically significant.

stem-and-leaf display A technique for visualizing both the general features of a data set and specific item information by creating leading digits as "stems" and trailing digits as "leaves."

stratified random sampling Type of probability sampling in which the population is divided into subpopulations called strata and random samples are drawn from each of these strata.

structured observation Variety of observational methods using intervention in which the degree of control is often less than in field experiments; frequently used by clinical and developmental psychologists when making behavioral assessments.

subject attrition A threat to internal validity occurs when participants are lost from an experiment, for example, when participants drop out of the research project. The loss of participants changes the nature of a group from that established prior to the introduction of the treatment—for example, by destroying the equivalence of groups that had been established through random assignment.

successive independent samples design Survey research design in which a series of cross-sectional surveys is done and the same questions are asked of each succeeding sample of respondents.

summarizing the data In this second stage of data analysis the researcher uses descriptive statistics and graphical displays to summarize the information in a data set. Trends and patterns in the data set are described.

testing Taking a test generally has an effect on subsequent testing. Testing can threaten internal validity if the effect of a treatment cannot be separated from the effect of testing.

theory Logically organized set of propositions that serves to define events, describe relationships among events, and explain the occurrence of these events; scientific theories guide research and organize empirical knowledge.

threats to internal validity Possible causes of a phenomenon that must be controlled so a clear cause-effect inference can be made.

time sampling Selection of observation intervals either systematically or randomly with the goal of obtaining a representative sample of behavior.

time series with nonequivalent control group design (See also **simple interrupted time-series design.**) Quasi-experimental procedure that improves on the validity of a simple time-series design by including a nonequivalent control group; both treatment and comparison groups are observed for a period of time both before and after the treatment.

***t*-test for independent groups** An inferential test for comparing two means from different groups of subjects.

Type I error The probability of rejecting the null hypothesis when it is true, equal to the level of significance, or alpha.

Type II error The probability of failing to reject the null hypothesis when it is false.

unobtrusive (nonreactive) measures Measures of behavior that eliminate the problem of reactivity because observations are made in such a way that the presence of the observer is not detected by those being observed.

validity The "truthfulness" of a measure; a valid measure is one that measures what it claims to measure.

variability See **measures of dispersion.**

References

Abelson, R. P. (1995). *Statistics as principled argument.* Hillsdale, NJ: Erlbaum.

Abelson, R. P. (1997). On the surprising longevity of flogged horses: Why there is a case for the significance test. *Psychological Science, 8,* 12–15.

Adair, J. G., Dushenko, T. W., & Lindsay, R. C. L. (1985). Ethical regulations and their impact on research practice. *American Psychologist, 40,* 59–72.

Adjang, O. M. J. (1986). Exploring the social environment: A developmental study of teasing in chimpanzees. *Ethology, 73,* 136–160.

Adler, A. (1973). *Practice and theory of individual psychology* (P. Radin., Trans.). Totowa, NJ: Littlefield, Adams.

Adler, T. (1991, December). Outright fraud rare, but not poor science. *APA Monitor,* 11.

Allison, M. G., & Ayllon, T. (1980). Behavioral coaching in the development of skills in football, gymnastics, and tennis. *Journal of Applied Behavior Analysis, 13,* 297–314.

Allport, G. W. (1946). Letters from Jenny. *Journal of Abnormal and Social Psychology, 41,* 3–4.

Allport, G. W. (1961). *Pattern in growth and personality.* New York: Holt, Rinehart and Winston.

Allport, G. W. (1965). *Letters from Jenny.* New York: Harcourt, Brace & World.

Altmann, J. (1974). Observational study of behavior: Sampling methods. *Behavior, 48,* 1–41.

Ambady, N., & Rosenthal, R. (1993). Half a minute: Predicting teacher evaluations from thin slices of nonverbal behavior and physical attractiveness. *Journal of Personality and Social Psychology, 64,* 431–441.

American Psychiatric Association. (2000). *Diagnostic and statistical manual of mental disorders* (4th ed., Text Revision). Washington, DC: Author.

American Psychological Association. (2001). *Publication manual* (5th ed). Washington, DC: Author.

American Psychological Association. (2002). Ethical principles of psychologists and code of conduct. *American Psychologist, 57,* 1060–1073.

Anderson, C. A. (2001). Heat and violence. *Current Directions in Psychological Science, 10,* 33–38.

Anderson, C. A., Berkowitz, L., Donnerstein, E., Huesmann, L. R., Johnson, J. D., Linz, D., Malamuth, N. M., & Wartella, E. (2003). The influence of media violence on youth. *Psychological Science in the Public Interest, 4,* 81–110.

Anderson, C. A., & Bushman, B. J. (1997). External validity of "trivial" experiments: The case of laboratory aggression. *Review of General Psychology, 1,* 19–41.

Anderson, C. R. (1976). Coping behaviors as intervening mechanisms in the inverted-U stress-performance relationship. *Journal of Applied Psychology, 61,* 30–34.

Anderson, J. R. (1990). *The adaptive character of thought.* Hillsdale, NJ: Erlbaum.

Anderson, J. R. (1993*). Rules of the mind.* Hillsdale, NJ: Erlbaum.

Anderson, J. R., & Milson, J. R. (1989). Human memory: An adaptive perspective. *Psychological Review, 96,* 703–719.

Anderson, K. J., & Revelle, W. (1982). Impulsivity, caffeine, and proofreading: A test of the Easterbrook hypothesis. *Journal of Experimental Psychology: Human Perception and Performance, 8,* 614–624.

Anglin, J. M. (1993). Vocabulary development: A morphological analysis. *Monographs of the Society for Research in Child Development, 58* (10, Serial No. 238).

Atkinson, R. C. (1968). Computerized instruction and the learning process. *American Psychologist, 23,* 225–239.

Atkinson, R. C., & Shiffrin, R. M. (1968). Human memory: A proposed system and its control processes. In K. W. Spence & J. T. Spence (Eds.), *The psychology of learning and motivation, Vol. 2* (pp. 89–195). New York: Academic Press.

Azar, B. (1994a, August). Computers create global research lab. *APA Monitor, 1,* 16.

Azar, B. (1994b, August). Research made easier by computer networks. *APA Monitor,* 16.

Banaji, M. R., & Crowder, R. G. (1989). The bankruptcy of everyday memory. *American Psychologist, 44,* 1185–1193.

Barker, R. G., Wright, H. F., Schoggen, M. F., & Barker, L. S. (1978). Day in the life of Mary Ennis. In R. G. Barker et al. (Eds.), *Habitats, environments, and human behavior* (pp. 51–98). San Francisco: Jossey-Bass.

Baron, J. N., & Reiss, P. C. (1985). Same time, next year: Aggregate analyses of the mass media and violent behavior. *American Sociological Review, 50,* 347–363.

Baron, R. M., & Kenny, D. A. (1986). The moderator-mediator variable distinction in social psychological research: Conceptual, strategic, and statistical considerations. *Journal of Personality and Social Psychology, 51,* 1173–1182.

Barsalou, L. W. (1999). Perceptual symbol systems. *Behavioral and Brain Sciences, 22,* 577–660.

Bartholomew, G. A. (1982). Scientific innovation and creativity: A zoologist's point of view. *American Zoologist, 22,* 227–335.

Baumeister, R. F. (1995). Disputing the effects of championship pressures and home audiences. *Journal of Personality and Social Psychology, 68,* 644–648.

Baumeister, R. F., Campbell, J. D., Krueger, J. I., & Vohs, K. D. (2003). Does high self-esteem cause better performance, interpersonal success, happiness, or healthier lifestyles? *Psychological Science in the Public Interest, 4,* 1–44.

Baumrind, D. (1985). Research using intentional deception: Ethical issues revisited. *American Psychologist, 40,* 165–174.

Bazzini, D. G., & Shaffer, D. R. (1999). Resisting temptation revisited: Devaluation versus enhancement of an attractive suitor by exclusive and nonexclusive daters. *Personality and Social Psychology Bulletin, 25,* 162–176.

Behnke, S. (2003). Academic and clinical training under APA's new ethics code. *Monitor on Psychology, 34,* 64.

Berk, R. A., Boruch, R. F., Chambers, D. L., Rossi, P. H., & Witte, A. D. (1987). Social policy experimentation: A position paper. In D. S. Cordray & M. W. Lipsey (Eds.), *Evaluation Studies Review Annual,* Vol. 11 (pp. 630–672). Newbury Park, CA: Sage.

Bickman, L. (1976). Observational methods. In C. Selltiz, L. S. Wrightsman, & S. W. Cook (Eds.), *Research methods in social relations* (pp. 251–290). New York: Holt, Rinehart and Winston.

Birnbaum, M. H. (2000). Decision making in the lab and on the Web. In M. H. Birnbaum (Ed.), *Psychological experiments on the Internet* (pp. 3–34). San Diego, CA: Academic Press.

Blanchard, F. A., Crandall, C. S., Brigham, J. C., & Vaughn, L. A. (1994). Condemning and condoning racism: A social context approach to interracial settings. *Journal of Applied Psychology, 79,* 993–997.

Blanck, P. D., Bellack, A. S., Rosnow, R. L., Rotheram-Borus, M. J., & Schooler, N. R. (1992). Scientific rewards and conflicts of ethical choices in human subjects research. *American Psychologist, 47,* 959–965.

Bolgar, H. (1965). The case study method. In B. B. Wolman (Ed.), *Handbook of clinical psychology* (pp. 28–39). New York: McGraw-Hill.

Bond, C. F., Jr., & Titus, L. J. (1983). Social facilitation: A meta-analysis of 241 studies. *Psychological Bulletin, 94,* 265–292.

Boring, E. G. (1954). The nature and history of experimental control. *American Journal of Psychology, 67,* 573–589.

Brainerd, C. J. (1978). *Piaget's theory of intelligence.* Englewood Cliffs, NJ: Prentice-Hall.

Brandt, R. M. (1972). *Studying behavior in natural settings.* New York: Holt, Rinehart and Winston: University Press of America, 1981.

Bröder, A. (1998). Deception can be acceptable. *American Psychologist, 53,* 805–806.

Brown, R., & Kulik, J. (1977). Flashbulb memories. *Cognition, 5,* 73–99.

Buchanan, T. (2000). Potential of the Internet for personality research. In M. H. Birnbaum (Ed.), *Psychological experiments on the Internet* (pp. 121–139). San Diego, CA: Academic Press.

Bushman, B. J., & Cantor, J. (2003). Media ratings for violence and sex: Implications for policymakers and parents. *American Psychologist, 58,* 130–141.

Bushman, B. J., & Phillips, C. M. (2001). If the television program bleeds, memory for the advertisement recedes. *Current Directions in Psychological Science, 10,* 43–47.

Campbell, A. (1981). *The sense of well-being in America.* New York: McGraw-Hill.

Campbell, D. T. (1969). Reforms as experiments. *American Psychologist, 24,* 409–429.

Campbell, D. T., & Stanley, J. C. (1966). *Experimental and quasi-experimental designs for research.* Chicago: Rand McNally.

Campbell, R. (Ed.). (1992). *Mental lives: Case studies in cognition.* Oxford: Blackwell.

Candland, D. K. (1993). *Feral children and clever animals.* New York: Oxford University Press.

Carroll, J. M., & Russell, J. A. (1997). Facial expressions in Hollywood's portrayal of emotion. *Journal of Personality and Social Psychology, 72,* 164–176.

Caspi, A., Begg, D., Dickson, N., Harrington, H., Langley, J., Moffitt, T. E., & Silva, P. A. (1997). Personality differences predict health-risk behaviors in young adulthood: Evidence from a longitudinal study. *Journal of Personality and Social Psychology, 73,* 1052–1063.

Ceci, S. J. (1993). Cognitive and social factors in children's testimony. Master lecture presented at the American Psychological Association Convention.

Chambers, J. H., & Ascione, F. R. (1987). The effects of prosocial and aggressive videogames on children's donating and helping. *Journal of Genetic Psychology, 148,* 499–505.

Chastain, G., & Landrum, R. E. (1999). *Protecting human subjects: Departmental subject pools and institutional review boards.* Washington, DC: American Psychological Association.

Chernoff, N. N. (2002, December). Nobel Prize winner pushes economic theory despite hurdles. *APS Observer, 15,* 9–10.

Chow, S. L. (1988). Significance test or effect size? *Psychological Bulletin, 103,* 105–110.

Christensen, L. (1988). Deception in psychological research: When is its use justified? *Personality and Social Psychology Bulletin, 14,* 664–675.

Clark, H. H., & Schober, M. F. (1992). Asking questions and influencing answers. In J. M. Tanur (Ed.), *Questions about questions: Inquiries into the cognitive bases of surveys.* New York: Russell Sage Foundation.

Cohen, G. (1990). Why is it difficult to put names to faces? *British Journal of Psychology, 81,* 287–297.

Cohen, J. (1988*). Statistical power analysis for the behavioral sciences* (2nd ed.). Hillsdale, NJ: Erlbaum.

Cohen, J. (1990). Things I have learned (so far). *American Psychologist, 45,* 1304–1312.

Cohen, J. (1992). A power primer. *Psychological Bulletin, 112,* 155–159.

Cohen, J. (1995). The earth is round ($p < .05$). *American Psychologist, 49,* 997–1003.

Cohen, N. J., McCloskey, M., & Wible, C. G. (1990). Flashbulb memories and underlying cognitive mechanisms: Reply to Pillemer. *Journal of Experimental Psychology: General, 119,* 97–100.

Cook, T. D., & Campbell, D. T. (1979). *Quasi-experimentation: Design and analysis issues for field settings.* Chicago: Rand McNally.

Coon, D. J. (1992). Testing the limits of sense and science: American experimental psychologists combat spiritualism, 1880–1920. *American Psychologist, 47,* 143–151.

Cordaro, L., & Ison, J. R. (1963). Psychology of the scientist: X. Observer bias in classical conditioning of the planarian. *Psychological Reports, 13,* 787–789.

Courneya, K. S., & Carron, A. V. (1992). The home advantage in sport competitions: A literature review. *Journal of Sport & Exercise Psychology, 14,* 13–27.

Cronbach, L. J. (1992). Four *Psychological Bulletin* articles in perspective. *Psychological Bulletin, 12,* 389–392.

Crossen, C. (1994). *Tainted truth: The manipulation of fact in America.* New York: Simon & Schuster.

Crusco, A. H., & Wetzel, C. G. (1984). The Midas touch: The effects of interpersonal touch on restaurant tipping. *Personality and Social Psychology Bulletin, 10,* 512–517.

Csikszenmihalyi, M., & Larson, R. W. (1987). Validity and reliability of the experience-sampling method. *Journal of Nervous and Mental Disorders, 175,* 526–533.

Curtiss, S. R. (1977). *Genie: A psycholinguistic study of a modern-day "wild child."* New York: Academic Press.

Dallam, S. J., Gleaves, D. H., Cepeda-Benito, A., Silberg, J. L., Kraemer, H. C., & Spiegel, D. (2001). The effects of child sexual abuse: Comment on Rind, Tromovitch, and Bauserman (1998). *Psychological Bulletin, 127,* 715–733.

Dawes, R. M. (1991, June). *Problems with a psychology of college sophomores.* Paper presented at the Third Annual Convention of the American Psychological Society, Washington, DC.

de Blois, S. T., Novak, M. A., & Bond, M. (1998). Object permanence in orangutans (*Pongo pygmaeus*) and squirrel monkeys (*Saimiri sciureus*). *Journal of Comparative Psychology, 112,* 137–152.

Delespaul, P. A. E. G. (1995). *Assessing schizophrenia in daily life: The experience sampling method.* Rijkjaniversiteit van Limburg (Maastricht, The Netherlands).

DeLoache, J. S., Pierroutsakos, S. L., Uttal, D. H., Rosengren, K. S., & Gottlieb, A. (1998). Grasping the nature of pictures. *Psychological Science, 9,* 205–210.

Dickie, J. R. (1987). Interrelationships within the mother-father-infant triad. In P. W. Berman, & F. A. Pedersen (Eds.), *Men's transitions to parenthood: Longitudinal studies of early family experience* (pp. 113–143). Hillsdale, NJ: Erlbaum.

Diener, E., & Crandall, R. (1978). *Ethics in social and behavioral research.* Chicago: The University of Chicago Press.

Dittmar, M. L., Berch, D. B., & Warm, J. S. (1982). Sustained visual attention in deaf and hearing adults. *Bulletin of the Psychonomic Society, 19,* 339–342.

Dolan, C. A., Sherwood, A., & Light, K. C. (1992). Cognitive coping strategies and blood pressure responses to real-life stress in healthy young men. *Health Psychology, 11,* 233–240.

Eagly, A. H., & Steffen, V. J. (1984). Gender stereotypes stem from the distribution of women and men into social roles. *Journal of Personality and Social Psychology, 46,* 735–754.

Eibl-Eibesfeldt, I. (1975). *Ethology: The biology of behavior.* New York: Holt, Rinehart and Winston.

Endersby, J. W., & Towle, M. J. (1996). Tailgate partisanship: Political and social expression through bumper stickers. *The Social Science Journal, 33,* 307–319.

Entwisle, D. R., & Astone, N. M. (1994). Some practical guidelines for measuring youth's race/ethnicity and socioeconomic status. *Child Development, 65,* 1521–1540.

Epley, N., & Huff, C. (1998). Suspicion, affective response, and educational benefit as a result of deception in psychology research. *Personality and Social Psychology Bulletin, 24,* 759–768.

Epstein, S. (1979). The stability of behavior: On predicting most of the people much of the time. *Journal of Personality and Social Psychology, 37,* 1097–1126.

Erber, R. (1991). Affective and semantic priming: Effects of mood on category accessibility and inference. *Journal of Experimental Social Psychology, 27,* 480–498.

Ericsson, K. A., & Charness, N. (1994). Expert performance: Its structure and acquisition. *American Psychologist, 49,* 725–747.

Estes, W. K. (1997). On the communication of information by displays of standard errors and confidence intervals. *Psychonomic Bulletin & Review, 4,* 330–341.

Evans, R., & Donnerstein, E. (1974). Some implications for psychological research of early versus late term participation by college students. *Journal of Research in Personality, 8,* 102–109.

Feeney, D. M. (1987). Human rights and animal welfare. *American Psychologist, 42,* 593–599.

Festinger, L., Riecken, H., & Schachter, S. (1956). *When prophecy fails.* Minneapolis: University of Minnesota Press.

Fidler, F., Thomason, N., Cumming, G., Finch, S., & Leeman, J. (2004). Editors can lead researchers to confidence intervals, but can't make them think. *Psychological Science, 15,* 119–126.

Finch, S., Thomason, N., & Cumming, G. (2002). Past and future American Psychological Association guidelines for statistical practice. *Theory & Psychology, 12,* 825–853.

Fine, M. A., & Kurdek, L. A. (1993). Reflections on determining authorship credit and authorship order on faculty-student collaborations. *American Psychologist, 48,* 1141–1147.

Fisher, C. B., & Fryberg, D. (1994). Participant partners: College students weigh the costs and benefits of deceptive research. *American Psychologist, 49,* 417–427.

Fossey, D. (1981). Imperiled giants of the forest. *National Geographic, 159,* 501–523.

Fossey, D. (1983). *Gorillas in the mist.* Boston: Houghton-Mifflin.

Fowler, R. D. (1992). Report of the chief executive officer: A year of building for the future. *American Psychologist, 47,* 876–883.

Fraley, R. C. (2004). *How to conduct behavioral research over the Internet.* New York: Guilford Press.

Frame, C. L., & Strauss, C. C. (1987). Parental informed consent and sample bias in grade-school children. *Journal of Social and Clinical Psychology, 5,* 227–236.

Frank, M. G., & Gilovich, T. (1988). The dark side of self- and social perception: Black uniforms and aggression in professional sports. *Journal of Personality and Social Psychology, 54,* 74–85.

Frick, R. W. (1995). Accepting the null hypothesis. *Memory & Cognition, 23,* 132–138.

Friedman, H. S., Tucker, J. S., Schwartz, J. E., Tomlinson-Keasy, C., Martin, L. R., Wingard, D. L., & Criqui, M. H. (1995). Psychosocial and behavioral predictors of longevity: The aging and death of the "Termites." *American Psychologist, 50,* 69–78.

Friedman, M. P., & Wilson, R. W. (1975). Application of unobtrusive measures to the study of textbook usage by college students. *Journal of Applied Psychology, 60,* 659–662.

Fromm, E. (1998). Lost and found half a century later: Letters by Freud and Einstein. *American Psychologist, 53,* 1195–1198.

Gabrieli, J. D. E., Fleischman, D. A., Keane, M. M., Reminger, S. L., & Morrell, F. (1995). Double dissociation between memory systems underlying explicit and implicit memory in the human brain. *Psychological Science, 6,* 76–82.

Geller, E. S., Russ, N. W., & Altomari, M. G. (1986). Naturalistic observations of beer drinking among college students. *Journal of Applied Behavior Analysis, 19,* 391–396.

Gena, A., Krantz, P. J., McClannahan, L. E., & Poulson, C. L. (1996). Training and generalization of affective behavior displayed by youth with autism. *Journal of Applied Behavioral Analysis, 29,* 291–304.

Gigerenzer, G. (2004). Dread risk, September 11, and fatal traffic accidents. *Psychological Science, 15,* 286–287.

Gigerenzer, G., Krauss, S., & Vitouch, O. (2004). The null ritual: What you always wanted to know about significance testing but were afraid to ask. In D. Kaplan (Ed.), *The Sage handbook of quantitative methodology for the social sciences* (pp. 391–408). Thousand Oaks, CA: Sage.

Gillham, J. E., Reivich, K. J., Jaycox, L. H., & Seligman, M. E. P. (1995). Prevention of depressive symptoms in school children: Two-year follow-up. *Psychological Science, 6,* 343–351.

Glaser, J., Dixit, J., & Green, D. P. (2002). Studying hate crime with the Internet: What makes racists advocate racial violence? *Journal of Social Issues, 58,* 177–193.

Goldstein, R. S., Minkin, B. L., Minkin, N., & Baer, D. M. (1978). Finders, keepers?: An analysis and validation of a free-found-ad policy. *Journal of Applied Behavior Analysis, 11,* 465–473.

Golombok, S., Perry, B., Burston, A., Murray, C., Mooney-Somers, J., Stevens, M., & Golding, J. (2003). Children with lesbian parents: A community study. *Developmental Psychology, 39,* 20–33.

Goodall, J. (1987). A plea for the chimpanzees. *American Scientist, 75,* 574–577.

Goodman, S. H., Lahey, B. B., Fielding, B., Dulcan, M., Narrow, W., & Regier, D. (1997). Representativeness of clinical samples of youths with mental disorders: A preliminary population-based study. *Journal of Abnormal Psychology, 106,* 3–14.

Gosling, S. D., Vazire, S., Srivastava, S., & John, O. P. (2004). Should we trust Web-based studies? A comparative analysis of six preconceptions about Internet questionnaires. *American Psychologist, 59,* 93–104.

Grammer, K., Schiefenhoevel, W., Schleidt, M., Lorenz, B., & Eibl-Eibesfeldt, I. (1988). Patterns on the face: The eyebrow flash in crosscultural comparison. *Ethology, 77,* 279–299.

Greenwald, A. G., Gonzalez, R., Harris, R. J., & Guthrie, D. (1996). Effect sizes and p values: What should be reported and what should be replicated? *Psychophysiology, 33,* 175–183.

Griffin, J. H. (1960). *Black like me.* New York: New American Library.

Haden, C. A. (1998). Reminiscing with different children: Relating maternal stylistic consistency and sibling similarity in talk about the past. *Developmental Psychology, 34,* 99–114.

Hagen, R. L. (1997). In praise of the null hypothesis statistical test. *American Psychologist, 52,* 15–24.

Haggbloom, S. J., Warnick, R., Warnick, J. E., Jones, V. K., Yarbrough, G. L., Russell, T. M., et al. (2002). The 100 most eminent psychologists of the 20th century. *Review of General Psychology, 6,* 139–152.

Halpern, A. R., & Bower, G. H. (1982). Musical expertise and melodic structure in memory for musical notation. *American Journal of Psychology, 95,* 31–50.

Harlow, H. F., & Harlow, M. K. (1966). Learning to love. *American Scientist, 54,* 244–272.

Harnack, A., & Kleppinger, E. (1997). *Online! A reference guide to using Internet sources.* New York: St. Martin's Press.

Hartup, W. W. (1974). Aggression in childhood: Development perspectives. *American Psychologist, 29,* 336–341.

Hay, D. F., Pawlby, S., Angold, A., Harold, G., & Sharp, D. (2003). Pathways to violence in the children of mothers who were depressed postpartum. *Developmental Psychology, 39,* 1083–1094.

Heath, L., & Davidson, L. (1988). Dealing with the threat of rape: Reactance or learned helplessness? *Journal of Applied Social Psychology, 18,* 1334–1351.

Heatherton, T. F., Mahamedi, F., Striepe, M., Field, A. E., & Keel, P. (1997). A 10-year longitudinal study of body weight, dieting, and eating disorder symptoms. *Journal of Abnormal Psychology, 106,* 117–125.

Heatherton, T. F., Nichols, P., Mahamedi, F., & Keel, P. K. (1995). Body weight, dieting, and eating disorder symptoms among college students 1982 to 1992. *American Journal of Psychiatry, 152,* 1623–1629.

Hersen, M., & Barlow, D. H. (1976). *Single-case experimental designs: Strategies for studying behavior change.* New York: Pergamon Press.

Hilts, P. J. (1995). Memory's ghost: The nature of memory and the strange tale of Mr. M. New York: Simon & Schuster.

Hippler, H. J., & Schwarz, N. (1987). Response effects in surveys. In H. J. Hippler, N. Schwarz, & S. Sudman (Eds.), *Social information processing and survey methodology* (pp. 102–122). New York: Springer-Verlag.

Hoaglin, D. C., Mosteller, F., & Tukey, J. W. (Eds.). (1983). *Understanding robust and exploratory data analysis.* New York: Wiley.

Hoaglin, D. C., Mosteller, F., & Tukey, J. W. (Eds.). (1991). *Fundamentals of exploratory analysis of variance.* New York: Wiley.

Holden, C. (1987). Animal regulations: So far, so good. *Science, 238,* 880–882.

Hollon, S. D., Thase, M. E., & Markowitz, J. C. (2002). Treatment and prevention of depression. *Psychological Science in the Public Interest, 3,* 39–77.

Holmbeck, G. N. (1997). Toward terminological, conceptual, and statistical clarity in the study of mediators and moderators: Examples from the child-clinical and pediatric psychology literatures. *Journal of Consulting and Clinical Psychology, 65,* 599–610.

Holsti, O. R. (1969). *Content analysis for the social sciences.* Reading, MA: Addison-Wesley.

Horton, S. V. (1987). Reduction of disruptive mealtime behavior by facial screening. *Behavior Modification, 11,* 53–64.

Howell, D. C. (2002). *Statistical methods for psychology* (5th ed.). Belmont, CA: Wadsworth.

Hughes, H. M., & Haynes, S. N. (1978). Structured laboratory observation in the behavioral assessment of parent-child interactions: A methodological critique. *Behavior Therapy, 9,* 428–447.

Hunt, M. (1997). *How science takes stock: The story of meta-analysis.* New York: Russell Sage Foundation.

Hunter, J. E. (1997). Needed: A ban on the significance test. *Psychological Science, 8,* 3–7.

Jenni, D. A., & Jenni, M. A. (1976). Carrying behavior in humans: Analysis of sex differences. *Science, 194,* 859–860.

Johnson, D. (1990). Animal rights and human lives: Time for scientists to right the balance. *Psychological Science, 1,* 213–214.

Joswick, K. E. (1994). Getting the most from PsycLIT: Recommendations for searching. *Teaching of Psychology, 21,* 49–53.

Judd, C. M., Smith, E. R., & Kidder, L. H. (1991). *Research methods in social relations* (6th ed.). Fort Worth, TX: Holt, Rinehart and Winston.

Kagan, J., Reznick, J. S., & Snidman, N. (1988). Biological bases of childhood shyness. *Science, 240,* 167–171.

Kahneman, D. (2003). A perspective on judgment and choice: Mapping bounded rationality. *American Psychologist, 58,* 697–720.

Kahneman, D., Fredrickson, B. L., Schreiber, C. A., & Redelmeier, D. A. (1993). When more pain is preferred to less: Adding a better end. *Psychological Science, 4,* 401–405.

Kahneman, D., & Tversky, A. (1973). On the psychology of prediction. *Psychological Review, 80,* 237–251.

Kardas, E. P., & Milford, T. M. (1996). *Using the Internet for social science research and practice.* Belmont, CA: Wadsworth.

Kaschak, M. P., & Moore, C. F. (2000). On the documentation of statistical analyses in the "Clicky-Box" era. *American Psychologist, 55,* 1511–1512.

Kassin, S. A., & Kiechel, K. L. (1996). The social psychology of false confessions: Compliance, internalization, and confabulation. *Psychological Science, 7,* 125–128.

Kazdin, A. E. (1978). Methodological and interpretive problems of single-case experimental designs. *Journal of Consulting and Clinical Psychology, 46,* 629–642.

Kazdin, A. E. (1980). *Behavior modification in applied settings* (rev. ed.). Homewood, IL: Dorsey Press.

Kazdin, A. E. (1982). Single-case experimental designs. In P. C. Kendall & J. N. Butcher (Eds.), *Handbook of research methods in clinical psychology* (pp. 416–490). New York: Wiley.

Kazdin, A. E. (1998). *Research designs in clinical psychology.* Boston: Allyn and Bacon.

Kazdin, A. E., & Erickson, L. M. (1975). Developing responsiveness to instructions in severely and profoundly retarded residents. *Journal of Behavior Therapy and Experimental Psychiatry, 6,* 17–21.

Keith, T. Z., Reimers, T. M., Fehrmann, P. G., Pottebaum, S. M., & Aubrey, L. W. (1986). Parental involvement, homework, and TV time: Direct and indirect effects on high school achievement. *Journal of Educational Psychology, 78,* 373–380.

Keller, F. S. (1937). *The definition of psychology.* New York: Appleton-Century-Crofts.

Kelley-Milburn, D., & Milburn, M. A. (1995). Cyberpsych: Resources for psychologists on the Internet. *Psychological Science, 6,* 203–211.

Kelman, H. C. (1967). Human use of human subjects: The problem of deception in social psychological experiments. *Psychological Bulletin, 67,* 1–11.

Kelman, H. C. (1972). The rights of the subject in social research: An analysis in terms of relative power and legitimacy. *American Psychologist, 27,* 989–1016.

Kenny, D. A. (1979). *Correlation and causality.* New York: Wiley.

Keppel, G. (1991). *Design and analysis: A researcher's handbook* (3rd ed.). Englewood Cliffs, NJ: Prentice-Hall.

Kidd, S. A. (2002). The role of qualitative research in psychological journals. *Psychological Methods, 7,* 126–138.

Kidd, S. A., & Kral, M. J. (2002). Suicide and prostitution among street youth: A qualitative analysis. *Adolescence, 37,* 411–430.

Kimble, G. A. (1989). Psychology from the standpoint of a generalist. *American Psychologist, 44,* 491–499.

Kimmel, A. J. (1996). *Ethical issues in behavioral research: A survey.* Cambridge, MA: Blackwell.

Kimmel, A. J. (1998). In defense of deception. *American Psychologist, 53,* 803–805.

Kirk, R. E. (1996). Practical significance: A concept whose time has come. *Educational and Psychological Measurement, 56,* 746–759.

Kirkham, G. L. (1975). Doc cop. *Human Behavior, 4,* 16–23.

Kirsch, I. (1978). Teaching clients to be their own therapists: A case-study illustration. *Psychotherapy: Theory, Research and Practice, 15,* 302–305.

Kirsch, I., & Sapirstein, G. (1998). Listening to prozac but hearing placebo: A meta-analysis of antidepressant medication. *Prevention and Treatment -* [On-line serial], *1.* Available: journals.apa.org/prevention/volume1/pre0010002a.html.

Kohlberg, L. (Ed.). (1981). *The philosophy of moral development: Essays on moral development* (Vol I). San Francisco: Harper & Row.

Kohlberg, L. (Ed.). (1984). *The philosophy of moral development: Essays on moral development* (Vol II). San Francisco: Harper & Row.

Krantz, J. H., & Dalal, R. (2000). Validity of Web-based psychological research. In M. H. Birnbaum (Ed.), *Psychological experiments on the Internet* (pp. 35–60). San Diego, CA: Academic Press.

Kratochwill, T. R., & Brody, G. H. (1978). Single subject designs: A perspective on the controversy over employing statistical inference and implications for research and training in behavior modification. *Behavior Modification, 2,* 291–307.

Kratochwill, T. R., & Martens, B. K. (1994). Applied behavior analysis and school psychology. *Journal of Applied Behavior Analysis, 27,* 3–5.

Kraut, R., Olson, J., Banaji, M. R., Bruckman, A., Cohen, J., & Couper, M. (2004). Psychological research online: Report of Board of Scientific Affairs' Advisory Group on the conduct of research on the Internet. *American Psychologist, 59,* 105–117.

Krueger, J. (2001). Null hypothesis significance testing: On the survival of a flawed method. *American Psychologist, 56,* 16–26.

Kubany, E. S. (1997). Application of cognitive therapy for trauma-related guilt (CT-TRG) with a Vietnam veteran troubled by multiple sources of guilt. *Cognitive and Behavioral Practice, 4,* 213–244.

LaFrance, M., & Mayo, C. (1976). Racial differences in gaze behavior during conversations: Two systematic observational studies. *Journal of Personality and Social Psychology, 33,* 547–552.

Lakatos, I. (1978). *The methodology of scientific research.* London: Cambridge University Press.

Lakoff, G., & Johnson, M. (1999). *Philosophy in the flesh: The embodied mind and its challenges to western thought.* New York: Basic Books.

Landauer, T. K., & Bjork, R. A. (1978). Optimum rehearsal patterns and name learning. In M. M. Gruneberg, P. E. Morris, & R. N. Sykes (Eds.), *Practical aspects of memory* (pp. 625–632). London: Academic Press.

Landers, S. (1988, September). Adolescent study presents dilemma. *APA Monitor, 6.*

Langer, E. J. (1989). *Mindfulness.* Reading, MA: Addison-Wesley.

Langer, E. J. (1997). *The power of mindful learning.* Reading, MA: Addison-Wesley.

Langer, E. J., & Piper, A. I. (1987). The prevention of mindlessness. *Journal of Personality and Social Psychology, 53,* 280–287.

Langer, E. J., & Rodin, J. (1976). The effects of choice and enhanced personal responsibility for the aged: A field experiment in an institutional setting. *Journal of Personality and Social Psychology, 34,* 191–198.

Larson, R. (1989). Beeping children and adolescents: A method for studying time use and daily experience. *Journal of Youth and Adolescence, 18,* 511–530.

Larson, R. W., Richards, M. H., Moneta, G., Holmbeck, G., & Duckett, E. (1996). Changes in adolescents' daily interactions with their families from ages 10 to 18: Disengagement and transformation. *Developmental Psychology, 32,* 744–754.

Latané, B., & Darley, J. M. (1970). *The unresponsive bystander: Why doesn't he help?* New York: Appleton-Century-Crofts.

Lau, R. R., & Russell, D. (1980). Attributions in the sports pages. *Journal of Personality and Social Psychology, 39,* 29–38.

LeBlanc, P. (2001, September). "And mice." (Or tips for dealing with the animal subjects review board). *APS Observer, 14,* 21–22.

Lenneberg, E. H. (1967). *Biological foundations of language.* New York: Wiley.

Levine, R. V. (1990). The pace of life. *American Scientist, 78,* 450–459.

Levine, R. V., West, L. J., & Reis, H. T. (1980). Perceptions of time and punctuality in the United States and Brazil. *Journal of Personality and Social Psychology, 38,* 541–550.

Linton, M. (1978). Real world memory after six years: An *in vivo* study of very long term memory.

In M. M. Gruneberg, P. E. Morris, & R. N. Sykes (Eds.), *Practical aspects of memory* (pp. 69–76). New York: Academic Press.

Locke, T. P., Johnson, G. M., Kirigin-Ramp, K., Atwater, J. D., & Gerrard, M. (1986). An evaluation of a juvenile education program in a state penitentiary. *Evaluation Review, 10,* 281–298.

Loftus, E. F. (1979). *Eyewitness testimony.* Cambridge, MA: Harvard University Press.

Loftus, E. F. (2003, August). Loftus: The need to defend scientific freedom. *APS Observer, 16,* 1, 32.

Loftus, E. F., & Burns, T. E. (1982). Mental shock can produce retrograde amnesia. *Memory & Cognition, 10,* 318–323.

Loftus, G. R. (1991). On the tyranny of hypothesis testing in the social sciences. *Contemporary Psychology, 36,* 102–105.

Loftus, G. R. (1996). Psychology will be a much better science when we change the way we analyze data. *Current Directions in Psychological Science, 5,* 161–171.

Loftus, G. R., & Masson, M. E. J. (1994). Using confidence intervals in within-subject designs. *Psychonomic Bulletin & Review, 1,* 476–490.

Lovaas, O. I., Newsom, C., & Hickman, C. (1987). Self-stimulatory behavior and perceptual reinforcement. *Journal of Applied Behavior Analysis, 20,* 45–68.

Lubin, B., Zuckerman, M., Breytspraak, L. M., Bull, N. C., Gumbhir, A. K., & Rinck, C. M. (1988). Affects, demographic variables, and health. *Journal of Clinical Psychology, 44,* 131–141.

Lucas, R. E., Diener, E., & Suh, E. (1996). Discriminant validity of well-being measures. *Journal of Personality and Social Psychology, 71,* 616–628.

Ludwig, T. E., Jeeves, M. A., Norman, W. D., & DeWitt, R. (1993). The bilateral field advantage on a letter-matching task. *Cortex, 29,* 691–713.

Lyle, J., & Hoffman, H. R. (1972). Children's use of television and other media. In E. A. Rubenstein, G. A. Comstock, & J. P. Murray (Eds.), *Television and social behavior: Vol. 4. Television in day-to-day life: Patterns of use* (pp. 129–256). Washington, DC: U.S. Government Printing Office.

MacCoun, R. (2002, December). Why a psychologist won the Nobel Prize in economics. *APS Observer, 15,* 1, 8.

Madigan, C. M. (1995, March 19). *Hearing it right: Small turnout spoke.* Chicago Tribune, pp. 1–2.

Maestripieri, D., & Carroll, K. A. (1998). Child abuse and neglect: Usefulness of the animal data. *Psychological Bulletin, 123,* 211–223.

Marx, M. H. (1963). The general nature of theory construction. In M. H. Marx (Ed.), *Theories in contemporary psychology* (pp. 4–46). New York: Macmillan.

McCallum, D. M. (2001, May/June). "Of men . . ." (Or how to obtain approval from the human subjects review board). *APS Observer, 14,* 28–29, 35.

McGrew, W. C. (1972). *An ethological study of children's behavior.* New York: Academic Press.

McGuire, W. J. (1997). Creative hypothesis generating in psychology: Some useful heuristics. *Annual Review of Psychology, 48,* 1–30.

McKinney, J. D., Mason, J., Perkerson, K., & Clifford, M. (1975). Relationship between classroom behavior and academic achievement. *Journal of Educational Psychology, 67,* 198–203.

McNally, R. J., Bryant, R. A., & Ehlers, A. (2003). Does early psychological intervention promote recovery from posttraumatic stress? *Psychological Science in the Public Interest, 4,* 45–79.

McSweeney, A. J. (1978). Effects of response cost on the behavior of a million persons: Charging for directory assistance in Cincinnati. *Journal of Applied Behavior Analysis, 11,* 47–51.

Medvec, V. H., Madey, S. F., & Gilovich, T. (1995). When less is more: Counterfactual thinking and satisfaction among Olympic medalists. *Journal of Personality and Social Psychology, 69,* 603–610.

Meehl, P. E. (1967). Theory-testing in psychology and physics: A methodological paradox. *Philosophy of Science, 34,* 103–115.

Meehl, P. E. (1978). Theoretical risks and tabular asterisks: Sir Karl, Sir Ronald, and the slow progress of soft psychology. *Journal of Consulting and Clinical Psychology, 46,* 806–834.

Meehl, P. E. (1990a). Appraising and amending theories: The strategy of Lakatosian defense and two principles that warrant it. *Psychological Inquiry, 1,* 108–141.

Meehl, P. E. (1990b). Why summaries of research on psychological theories are often uninterpretable. *Psychological Reports, 66,* 195–244 (Monograph Supplement 1-V66).

Meier, B. P., Robinson, M. D., & Clore, G. L. (2004). Why good guys wear white: Automatic inferences about stimulus valence based on brightness. *Psychological Science, 15,* 82–87.

Merritt, C. B., & Fowler, R. G. (1948). The pecuniary honesty of the public at large. *Journal of Abnormal and Social Psychology, 43,* 90–93.

Miles, M. B., & Huberman, A. M. (1994). *Qualitative data analysis* (2nd ed.). Thousands Oaks, CA: Sage.

Milgram, S. (1974). *Obedience to authority.* New York: Harper & Row.

Milgram, S. (1977, October). Subject reaction: The neglected factor in the ethics of experimentation. *Hastings Center Report.*

Milgram, S., Liberty, H. J., Toledo, R., & Wackenhut, J. (1986). Response to intrusion into waiting lines. *Journal of Personality and Social Psychology, 51,* 683–689.

Miller, G. A., & Wakefield, P. C. (1993). On Anglin's analysis of vocabulary growth. *Monographs of the Society for Research in Child Development, 58* (10, Serial No. 238).

Miller, J. D. (1986, May). Some new measures of scientific illiteracy. Paper presented at the meeting of the American Association for the Advancement of Science, Philadelphia.

Miller, N. E. (1985). The value of behavioral research on animals. *American Psychologist, 40,* 423–440.

Miller, T. Q., Heath, L., Molcan, J. R., & Dugoni, B. L. (1991). Imitative violence in the real world: A reanalysis of homicide rates following championship prize fights. *Aggressive Behavior, 17,* 121–134.

Mook, D. G. (1983). In defense of external invalidity. *American Psychologist, 38,* 379–387.

Mosteller, F., & Hoaglin, D. C. (1991). Preliminary examination of data. In D. C. Hoaglin, F. Mosteller, & J. W. Tukey (Eds.), *Fundamentals of exploratory analysis of variance* (pp. 40–49). New York: Wiley.

Mulaik, S. A., Raju, N. S., & Harshman, R. A. (1997). There is a time and place for significance testing. In L. L. Harlow, S. A. Mulaik, & J. H. Steiger (Eds.), *What if there were no significance tests?* (pp. 65–115). Mahwah, NJ: Erlbaum.

Musch, J., & Reips, U. (2000). A brief history of Web experimenting. In M. H. Birnbaum (Ed.), *Psychological experiments on the Internet* (pp. 61–87). San Diego, CA: Academic Press.

Myers, D. G. (1999). *Social psychology* (6th ed.). New York: McGraw-Hill.

Myers, D. G. (2000). The funds, friends, and faith of happy people. *American Psychologist, 55,* 1–12.

Myers, D. G., & Diener, E. (1995). Who is happy? *Psychological Science, 6,* 10–19.

National Research Council. (1996). *Guide for the care and use of laboratory animals.* A report of the Institute of Laboratory Animal Resources committee. Washington, DC: National Academy Press.

Neisser, U., & Harsch, N. (1992). Phantom flashbulbs: False recollections of hearing the news about *Challenger.* In E. Winograd & U. Neisser (Eds.), *Affect and accuracy in recall: Studies of "flashbulb memories"* (pp. 9–31). New York: Cambridge University Press.

Neisser, U. (1967). *Cognitive psychology.* New York: Appleton-Century-Crofts.

Newburger, E. C. (2001, September, U.S. Census Bureau). *Home computers and Internet use in the United States: August 2000.* Retrieved June 1, 2004 from http:// www.census.gov/prod/2001pubs/ p23-207.pdf.

Newhagen, J. E., & Ancell, M. (1995). The expression of emotion and social status in the language of bumper stickers. *Journal of Language and Social Psychology, 14,* 312–323.

Nosek, B. A., Banaji, M. R., & Greenwald, A. G. (2002). E-Research: Ethics, security, design, and control in psychological research on the Internet. *Journal of Social Issues, 58,* 161–176.

Novak, M. A. (1991, July). "Psychologists care deeply" about animals. *APA Monitor, 4.*

Ondersma, S. J., Chaffin, M., Berliner, L., Cordon, I., Goodman, G. S., & Barnett, D. (2001). Sex with children is abuse: Comment on Rind, Tromovitch, and Bauserman (1998). *Psychological Bulletin, 127,* 707–714.

Orne, M. T. (1962). On the social psychology of the psychological experiment: With particular reference to demand characteristics and their implications. *American Psychologist, 17,* 776–783.

Ortmann, A., & Hertwig, R. (1997). Is deception necessary? *American Psychologist, 52,* 746–747.

Ortmann, A., & Hertwig, R. (1998). The question remains: Is deception acceptable? *American Psychologist, 53,* 806–807.

Osgood, C. E., & Walker, E. G. (1959). Motivation and language behavior: A content analysis of suicide notes. *Journal of Abnormal and Social Psychology, 59,* 58–67.

Park, C. L., Armeli, S., & Tennen, H. (2004). Appraisal-coping goodness of fit: A daily Internet study. *Personality and Social Psychology Bulletin, 30,* 558–569.

Parry, H. J., & Crossley, H. M. (1950). Validity of responses to survey questions. *Public Opinion Quarterly, 14,* 61–80.

Parsons, H. M. (1974). What happened at Hawthorne? *Science, 183,* 922–932.

Parsonson, B. S., & Baer, D. M. (1992). The visual analysis of data, and current research into the stimuli controlling it. In T. R. Kratochwill & J. R. Levin (Eds.), *Single-case research design and analysis* (pp. 15–40). Hillsdale, NJ: Erlbaum.

Pennebaker, J. W. (1989). Confession, inhibition, and disease. In L. Berkowitz (Ed.), *Advances in experimental social psychology* (Vol. 22, pp. 211–244). New York: Academic Press.

Pennebaker, J. W., & Francis, M. E. (1996). Cognitive, emotional, and language processes in disclosure. *Cognition and Emotion, 10,* 601–626.

Pennebaker, J. W., Mayne, T. J., & Francis, M. E. (1997). Linguistic predictors of adaptive bereavement. *Journal of Personality and Social Psychology, 72,* 863–871.

Peterson, J. (1995). How are psychologists perceived by the public? *APA Monitor, 31.*

Phillips, D. P. (1977). Motor vehicle fatalities increase just after publicized suicide stories. *Science, 196,* 1464–1465.

Phillips, D. P. (1983). The impact of mass media violence on U.S. homicides. *American Sociological Review, 48,* 560–568.

Phillips, D. P., & King, E. W. (1988). Death takes a holiday: Mortality surrounding major social occasions. *Lancet, 2,* 728–732.

Phillips, D. P., & Smith, D. G. (1990). Postponement of death until symbolically meaningful occasions. *Journal of the American Medical Association, 263,* 1947–1951.

Phillips, D. P., Van Voorhees, C. A., & Ruth, T. E. (1992). The birthdays: Lifeline or deadline? *Psychosomatic Medicine, 54,* 532–542.

Piaget, J. (1965). *The child's conception of number.* New York: Norton.

Pickren, W. E. (2003). An elusive honor: Psychology, behavior, and the Nobel Prize. *American Psychologist, 58,* 721–722.

Pillemer, D. B. (1990). Clarifying the flashbulb memory concept: Comment on McCloskey, Wible, &

Cohen (1988). *Journal of Experimental Psychology: General, 119*, 92–96.

Pingitore, R., Dugoni, B. L., Tindale, R. S., & Spring, B. (1994). Bias against overweight job applicants in a simulated employment interview. *Journal of Applied Psychology, 79*, 909–917.

Pishkin, V., & Shurley, J. T. (1983). Electrophysiological parameters in anxiety and failure: Evaluation of doxepin and hydroxyzine. *Bulletin of the Psychonomic Society, 21*, 21–23.

Pitman, R. K., Kolb, B., Orr, S. P., deJong, J., Yadati, S., & Singh, M. M. (1987). On the utility of ethological data in psychiatric research: The example of facial behavior in schizophrenia. *Ethology and Sociobiology, 8*, 111S–116S.

Plous, S. (1998). Signs of change within the animal rights movement: Results from a follow-up survey of activists. *Journal of Comparative Psychology, 112*, 48–54.

Popper, K. R. (1959). *The logic of scientific discovery.* New York: Basic Books.

Popper, K. R. (1976). *Unended quest.* Glasgow: Fontana/Collins.

Posavac, E. J. (2002). Using *p* values to estimate the probability of a statistically significant replication. *Understanding Statistics, 1*, 101–112.

Posavac, E. J., & Carey, R. G. (2003). *Program evaluation* (6th ed.). Englewood Cliffs, NJ: Prentice-Hall.

Poulton, E. C. (1973). Unwanted range effects from using within-subject experimental designs. *Psychological Bulletin, 80*, 113–121.

Poulton, E. C. (1975). Range effects in experiments on people. *American Journal of Psychology, 88*, 3–32.

Poulton, E. C. (1982). Influential companions. Effects of one strategy on another in the within-subjects designs of cognitive psychology. *Psychological Bulletin, 91*, 673–690.

Poulton, E. C., & Freeman, P. R. (1966). Unwanted asymmetrical transfer effects with balanced experimental designs. *Psychological Bulletin, 66*, 1–8.

Povinelli, D. J., & Bering, J. M. (2002). The mentality of apes revisited. *Current Directions in Psychological Science, 11*, 115–119.

Rachels, J. (1986). *The elements of moral philosophy.* New York: McGraw-Hill.

Rasinski, K. A., Willis, G. B., Baldwin, A. K., Yeh, W., & Lee, L. (1999). Methods of data collection, perceptions of risks and losses, and motivation to give truthful answers to sensitive survey questions. *Applied Cognitive Psychology, 13*, 465–484.

Rauscher, F. H., Shaw, G. L., & Ky, K. N. (1993). Music and spatial task performance. *Nature, 365*, 611.

Richardson, D. R., Pegalis, L., & Britton, B. (1992). A technique for enhancing the value of research participation. *Contemporary Social Psychology, 16*, 11–13.

Riddoch, M. J., & Humphreys, G. W. (1992). The smiling giraffe: An illustration of a visual memory disorder. In R. Campbell (Ed.), *Mental lives: Case studies in cognition* (pp. 161–177). Oxford: Blackwell.

Riley, D. A. (1962). Memory for form. In L. Postman (Ed.), *Psychology in the making* (pp. 402–465). New York: Knopf.

Rimm, D. C., & Masters, J. C. (1979). *Behavior therapy: Techniques and empirical findings* (2nd ed.). New York: Academic Press.

Rind, B., Tromovitch, P., & Bauserman, R. (1998). A meta-analytic examination of assumed properties of child sexual abuse using college samples. *Psychological Bulletin, 124*, 22–53.

Rind, B., Tromovitch, P., & Bauserman, R. (2001). The validity and appropriateness of methods, analyses, and conclusions in Rind et al. (1998): A rebuttal of victimological critique from Ondersma et al. (2001) and Dallam et al. (2001). *Psychological Bulletin, 127*, 734–758.

Robins, R. W., Gosling, S. D., & Craik, K. H. (1999). An empirical analysis of trends in psychology. *American Psychologist, 54*, 117–128.

Rodman, J. L., & Burger, J. M. (1985). The influence of depression on the attribution of responsibility for an accident. *Cognitive Therapy and Research, 9*, 651–657.

Roethlisberger, F. J. (1977). *The elusive phenomena: An autobiographical account of my work in the field of organized behavior at the Harvard Business School.* Cambridge, MA: Division of Research, Graduate School of Business Administration (distributed by Harvard University Press).

Rosenfeld, A. (1981). Animal rights vs. human health. *Science, 81*, 18, 22.

Rosenhan, D. L. (1973). On being sane in insane places. *Science, 179*, 250–258.

Rosenthal, R. (1963). On the social psychology of the psychological experiment: The experimenter's hypothesis as unintended determinant of experimental results. *American Scientist, 51,* 268–283.

Rosenthal, R. (1966). *Experimenter effects in behavioral research.* New York: Appleton-Century-Crofts.

Rosenthal, R. (1976). *Experimenter effects in behavioral research.* (Enlarged ed.). New York: Irvington.

Rosenthal, R. (1990). How are we doing in soft psychology? *American Psychologist, 45,* 775–777.

Rosenthal, R. (1991). *Meta-analytic procedures for social research* (rev. ed.). Newbury Park, CA: Sage.

Rosenthal, R. (1994a). Interpersonal expectancy effects: A 30-year perspective. *Current Directions in Psychological Science, 3,* 176–179.

Rosenthal, R. (1994b). Science and ethics in conducting, analyzing, and reporting psychological research. *Psychological Science, 5,* 127–134.

Rosenthal, R., & Rosnow, R. L. (1991). *Essentials of behavioral research: Methods and data analysis* (2nd ed.). New York: McGraw-Hill.

Rozin, P., Kabnick, K., Pete, E., Fischler, C., & Shields, C. (2003). The ecology of eating: Smaller portion sizes in France than in the United States help explain the French paradox. *Psychological Science, 14,* 450–454.

Rymer, R. (1993). *Genie: A scientific tragedy.* New York: Harper Collins.

Sackeim, H. A., Gur, R. C., & Saucy, M. C. (1978). Emotions are expressed more intensely on the left side of the face. *Science, 202,* 434–436.

Sacks, O. (1985). *The man who mistook his wife for a hat and other clinical tales.* New York: Harper & Row.

Sacks, O. (1995). *An anthropologist on Mars.* New York: Knopf.

Salomon, G. (1987). Basic and applied research in psychology: Reciprocity between two worlds. *International Journal of Psychology, 22,* 441–446.

Satterfield, J. M., & Seligman, M. E. P. (1994). Military aggression and risk predicted by explanatory style. *Psychological Science, 5,* 77–82.

Sax, L. J., Astin, A. W., Lindholm, J. A., Korn, W. S., Saenz, V. B., & Mahoney, K. M. (2003). *The American freshman: National norms for fall 2003.* Los Angeles: Higher Education Research Institute, UCLA.

Schacter, D. L. (1996). *Searching for memory.* New York: Basic Books.

Schlenker, B. R., Phillips, S. T., Boniecki, K. A., & Schlenker, D. R. (1995a). Championship pressures: Choking or triumphing in one's own

territory? *Journal of Personality and Social Psychology, 68,* 632–643.

Schlenker, B. R., Phillips, S. T., Boniecki, K. A., & Schlenker, D. R. (1995b). Where is the home choke? *Journal of Personality and Social Psychology, 68,* 649–652.

Schmidt, F. L. (1996). Statistical significance testing and cumulative knowledge in psychology: Implications for training of researchers. *Psychological Methods, 1,* 115–129.

Schmidt, F. L., & Hunter, J. E. (1997). Eight common but false objections to the discontinuation of significance testing in the analysis of research data. In L. L. Harlow, S. A. Mulaik, & J. H. Steiger (Eds.), *What if there were no significance tests?* (pp. 37–64). Mahwah, NJ: Erlbaum.

Schmidt, W. C. (1997). World-Wide-Web survey research: Benefits, potential problems, and solutions. *Behavior Research Methods, Instruments, & Computers, 29,* 274–279.

Schoeneman, T. J., & Rubanowitz, D. E. (1985). Attributions in the advice columns: Actors and observers, causes and reasons. *Personality and Social Psychology Bulletin, 11,* 315–325.

Schulz, R., & Bazerman, M. (1980). Ceremonial occasions and mortality: A second look. *American Psychologist, 35,* 253–261.

Schuman, H., Presser, S., & Ludwig, J. (1981). Context effects of survey responses to questions about abortion. *Public Opinion Quarterly, 45,* 216–223.

Scoville, W. B., & Milner, B. (1957). Loss of recent memory after bilateral hippocampal lesions. *Journal of Neurology, Neurosurgery, and Psychiatry, 20,* 11–19.

Seale, C. (Ed.). (1999). *The quality of qualitative research.* London: Sage.

Seligman, M. E. P., & Csikszentimihalyi, M. (2000). Positive psychology: An introduction. *American Psychologist, 55,* 5–14.

Shadish, W. R., Cook, T. D., & Campbell, D. T. (2002). *Experimental and quasi-experimental designs for generalized causal inference.* Boston: Houghton Mifflin.

Shapiro, K. J. (1998). *Animal models of human psychology: Critique of science, ethics, and policy.* Seattle, WA: Hogrefe & Huber.

Sharpe, D., Adair, J. G., & Roese, N. J. (1992). Twenty years of deception research: A decline in subjects' trust? *Personality and Social Psychology Bulletin, 18,* 585–590.

Shattuck, R. (1994). *The forbidden experiment: The story of the Wild Boy of Averyon.* New York: Kodansha.

Sieber, J. E., Iannuzzo, R., & Rodriguez, B. (1995). Deception methods in psychology: Have they changed in 23 years? *Ethics & Behavior, 5,* 67–85.

Simon, H. A. (1992). What is an "explanation" of behavior? *Psychological Science, 3,* 150–161.

Simons, D. J., & Levin, D. T. (1998). Failure to detect changes to people during a real world interaction. *Psychonomic Bulletin and Review, 5,* 644–649.

Singer, P. (1990). The significance of animal suffering. *Behavioral and Brain Sciences, 13,* 9–12.

Skinner, B. F. (1966). Operant behavior. In W. K. Honig (Ed.), *Operant behavior: Areas of research and application* (pp. 12–32). New York: Appleton-Century-Crofts.

Skitka, L. J., & Sargis, E. G. (2005). Social psychological research and the Internet: The promise and the perils of a new methodological frontier. In Y. Amichai-Hamburger (Ed.), *The social net: The social psychology of the Internet.* New York: Oxford University Press.

Smith, J. A., Harré, R., & Van Langenhove, L. (1995). Idiography and the case study. In J. A. Smith, R. Harré, & L. Van Langenhove (Eds.), *Rethinking psychology* (pp. 59–69). Thousand Oaks, CA: Sage.

Smith, P. K., & Lewis, K. (1985). Rough-and-tumble play, fighting, and chasing in nursery school children. *Ethology and Sociobiology, 6,* 175–181.

Smith, T. W. (1981). Qualifications to generalized absolutes: "Approval of hitting" questions on the GSS. *Public Opinion Quarterly, 45,* 224–230.

Sokal, M. M. (1992). Origins and early years of the American Psychological Association, 1890–1906. *American Psychologist, 47,* 111–122.

Spitz, R. A. (1965). *The first year of life.* New York: International Universities Press.

Spitzer, R. L. (1976). More on pseudoscience in science and the case for psychiatric diagnosis. *Archives of General Psychiatry, 33,* 459–470.

Stern, S. E., & Faber, J. E. (1997). The lost e-mail technique: Milgram's lost-letter technique in the age of the Internet. *Behavior Research Methods, Instruments, & Computers, 29,* 260–263.

Sternberg, R. J. (1986). A triangular theory of love. *Psychological Review, 93,* 119–135.

Sternberg, R. J. (1997, September). What do students still most need to learn about research in psychology? *APS Observer, 14,* 19.

Sternberg, R. J., & Williams, W. M. (1997). Does the Graduate Record Examination predict meaningful success in the graduate training of psychologists? A case study. *American Psychologist, 52,* 630–641.

Stice, E., & Whitenton, K. (2002). Risk factors for body dissatisfaction in adolescent girls: A longitudinal investigation. *Developmental Psychology, 38,* 669–678.

Strauss, A., & Corbin, J. (1990). *Basics of qualitative research.* Newbury Park, CA: Sage.

Sue, S. (1999). Science, ethnicity and bias. *American Psychologist, 54,* 1070–1077.

Sun, M. (1981). Laetrile brush fire is out, scientists hope. *Science, 212,* 758–759.

Surwit, R. S., & Williams, P. G. (1996). Animal models provide insight into psychosomatic factors in diabetes. *Psychosomatic Medicine, 58,* 582–589.

Susskind, J. E. (2003). Children's perception of gender-based illusory correlations: Enhancing preexisting relationships between gender and behavior. *Sex Roles, 48,* 483–494.

Talarico, J. M., & Rubin, D. C. (2003). Confidence, not consistency, characterizes flashbulb memories. *Psychological Science, 14,* 455–461.

Tassinary, L. G., & Hansen, K. A. (1998). A critical test of the waist-to-hip-ratio hypothesis of female physical attractiveness. *Psychological Science, 9,* 150–155.

Taylor, K. M., & Shepperd, J. A. (1996). Probing suspicion among participants in deception research. *American Psychologist, 51,* 886–887.

Terman, L. M., & Oden, M. A. (1947). *Genetic studies of genius: The gifted child grows up* (Vol. 4). Stanford, CA: Stanford University Press.

Thomas, L. (1992). *The fragile species.* New York: Charles Scribner's Sons.

Thompson, T. L. (1982). Gaze toward and avoidance of the handicapped: A field experiment. *Journal of Nonverbal Behavior, 6,* 188–196.

Tucker, J. S., Friedman, H. S., Schwartz, J. E., Criqui, M. H., Tomlinson-Keasey, C., Wingrad, D. L., & Martin, L. R. (1997). Parental divorce: Effects on individual behavior and longevity. *Journal of Personality and Social Psychology, 73,* 381–391.

Tukey, J. W. (1977). *Exploratory data analysis.* Reading, MA: Addison-Wesley.

Tversky, A., & Kahneman, D. (1974). Judgment under uncertainty: Heuristics and biases. *Science, 185,* 1124–1131.

Ulrich, R. E. (1991). Animal rights, animal wrongs and the question of balance. *Psychological Science, 2,* 197–201.

Ulrich, R. E. (1992). Animal research: A reflective analysis. *Psychological Science, 3,* 384–386.

Underwood, B. J., & Shaughnessy, J. J. (1975). *Experimentation in psychology.* New York: Wiley: Robert E. Krieger, 1983.

U.S. Census Bureau (2000). DP-4. Profile of selected housing characteristics: 2000. Retrieved August 5, 2004, from http://factfinder.census.gov/

Valentiner, D. P., Holahan, C. J., & Moos, R. H. (1994). Social support, appraisal of event controllability, and coping: An integrative model. *Journal of Personality and Social Psychology, 66,* 1094–1102.

van Baaren, R. B., Holland, R. W., Kawakami, K., & van Knippenberg, A. (2004). Mimicry and prosocial behavior. *Psychological Science, 15,* 71–74.

VanBiervliet, A., Spangler, P. F., & Marshall, A. M. (1981). An ecobehavioral examination of a simple strategy for increasing mealtime language in residential facilities. *Journal of Applied Behavior Analysis, 14,* 295–305.

VanderStoep, S. W., & Shaughnessy, J. J. (1997). Taking a course in research methods improves reasoning about real-life events. *Teaching of Psychology, 24,* 122–124.

Watson, J. B. [1914] (1967). *Behavior: An introduction to comparative psychology.* New York: Holt, Rinehart and Winston.

Webb, E. J., Campbell, D. T., Schwartz, R. D., Sechrest, L., & Grove, J. B. (1981). *Non-reactive measures in the social sciences* (2nd ed.). Boston: Houghton-Mifflin.

Weigel, R. H., Loomis, J. W., & Soja, M. J. (1980). Race relations on prime time television. *Journal of Personality and Social Psychology, 39,* 884–893.

Weiner, B. (1975). "On being sane in insane places": A process (attributional) analysis and critique. *Journal of Abnormal Psychology, 84,* 433–441.

Wilkinson, L., & APA the Task Force on Statistical Inference. (1999). Statistical methods in psychology journals. *American Psychologist, 54,* 598–604.

Willems, E. P. (1969). Planning a rationale for naturalistic research. In E. P. Willems & H. L. Raush (Eds.), *Naturalistic viewpoints in psychological research* (pp. 44–71). New York: Holt, Rinehart and Winston.

Wilson, G. T. (1978). On the much discussed nature of the term "behavior therapy." *Behavior Therapy, 9,* 89–98.

Winer, B. J., Brown, D. R., & Michels, K. M. (1991). *Statistical principles in experimental design* (3rd ed.). New York: McGraw-Hill.

Winograd, E., & Neisser, U. (Eds.). (1992). *Affect and accuracy in recall: Studies of "flashbulb memories."* New York: Cambridge University Press.

Yeaton, W. H., & Sechrest, L. (1986). Use and misuse of no-difference findings in eliminating threats to validity. *Evaluation Review, 10,* 836–852.

Zechmeister, E. B., Chronis, A. M., Cull, W. L., D'Anna, C. A., & Healy, N. A. (1995). Growth of a functionally important lexicon. *Journal of Reading Behavior, 27,* 201–212.

Zechmeister, E. B., & Nyberg, S. E. (1982). *Human memory: An introduction to research and theory.* Pacific Grove, CA: Brooks/Cole.

Zechmeister, E. B., & Posavac, E. J. (2003). *Data analysis and interpretation in the behavioral sciences.* Belmont, CA: Wadsworth.

Zechmeister, J. S., & Zechmeister, E. B. (2000). Introductory textbooks and psychology's core concepts. *Teaching of Psychology, 27,* 6–11.

Zechmeister, J. S., Zechmeister, E. B., & Shaughnessy, J. J. (2001). *Essentials of research methods in psychology,* p. 124. New York: McGraw-Hill.

Credits

Chapter 1

Figure 1.1 (top): Royalty-Free/Corbis; 1.1 (bottom): Samuel Ashfield/Getty Images; Box 1.1: Courtesy of Princeton University; Figure 1.2a: Bettman/Corbis; Figure 1.2b: Courtesy of National Library of Medicine; 1.2c: © Bettman/Corbis; Figure 1.3a: Kim Steele/Getty Images; 1.3b: © Will Hart/PhotoEdit; 1.3c: © Spencer Grant/PhotoEdit.

Chapter 2

Figure 2.1 (top & bottom): Courtesy of Thomas A. Sebeok, Distinguished Professor Emeritus, Indiana University, Bloomington; Figure 2.2: © PhotoLink/Getty Images; Figure 2.3: Chris Collins/Corbis; Figure 2.4 (left): © The Museum of Questionable Medical Devices, www.mtn.org/quack; 2.4 (right): Royalty-Free/Corbis; Figure 2.5: © Bill Aron/PhotoEdit; Figure 2.6: From Figure 3, page 453, of R. V. Levine (1990), "The Pace of Life," *American Scientist, 78,* 450–459. Copyright 1990 by Sigma Xi, The Scientific Research Society, Inc. Illustration by Michael Szpir. Used with permission of the publisher and author.

Chapter 3

Extensive quotations from American Psychological Association (2002), "Ethical Principles of Psychologists and Code of Conduct," *American Psychologist, 57,* 1060–1073, Copyright © 2002 by the American Psychological Association (APA). Reprinted by permission of the publisher. Neither the original nor this reproduction can be republished, photocopied, reprinted, or distributed in any form, without prior permission of the APA. Figure 3.1 (top left, bottom left & right): Photos by Eugene B. Zechmeister. Special thanks go to Linda and Hillary Bryant, Candy Bauilat and Peter Berquist for being willing subjects for these photos. Figure 3.1 (top right): Nicola Sutton/Life File/Getty Images; Figure 3.2: © Corbis; Figure 3.3: © Greg Gibson/AP/Wide World; Figure 3.4: Digitalvision; Figure 3.5: Photo of Eugene B. and Jeanne S. Zechmeister by a friendly passerby; Figure 3.6: Copyright © 1965 by Stanley Miligram. From the film *Obedience* distributed by Pennsylvania State Media Sales. Figure 3.7: Royalty-Free/Corbis; Figure 3.8: Photos by Eugene B. Zechmeister (left) and John Shaughnessy (right). We wish to acknowledge the cooperation of the Parmly Institute of Loyola University of Chicago, Bill Shofner, and Rich Bowen for providing experimental settings for some of the photos in this chapter.

Chapter 4

Figure 4.1: © Ken Regan Pictures; Figure 4.2a–d: From D. J. Simons and D. T. Levin, "Failure to Detect Changes to People During a Real-World Interaction" in *Psychonomic Bulletin and Review,* 1998, *5,* 644–648. Reprinted by permission of the Psychonomic Society, Inc.; Figure 4.3: © Farrell Grehan/Corbis; Table 4.2: From J. R. Dickie, and S. C. Gerber (1980), "Training in Social Competence: The Effect on Mothers, Fathers, and Infants," *Child*

Psychological Society and Blackwell Publishing, Oxford, UK. Used with permission of publisher and author; Figure 7.4: © James Kamp Photography; Figure 7.5: © Herb Shitzer/Stock Boston.

Chapter 8

Figure 8.1: Ryan McVay/Getty Images; Figure 8.2 (all): From H. A. Sackeim, R. C. Gur, and M. C. Saucy, in *Science*, 1978, 202, pp. 434–436, Figure 1, page 434. Copyright © 1978 American Association for the Advancement of Science.

Chapter 9

Table 9.1: Adapted from D. G. Bazzini and D. R. Shaffer (1999), "Resisting Temptation Revisited: Devaluation Versus Enhancement of an Attractive Suitor by Exclusive and Nonexclusive Daters," *Personality and Social Psychology Bulletin,* 25, 162–176. Copyright 1999 by Sage Publications, Inc. Adapted with permission of publisher and author; Figure 9.2: Based on data in Table 2, page 913, of R. Pingitore, B. L. Dugoni, R. S. Tindale, and B. Spring (1994), "Bias Against Overweight Job Applicants in a Simulated Employment Interview," *Journal of Applied Psychology,* 79, 909–917. Copyright 1994 by the American Psychological Association. Used with permission of publisher and author; Table 9.3: From J. L. Rodman and J. M. Burger (1985), "The Influence of Depression on the Attribution of Responsibility for an Accident," *Cognitive Therapy and Research,* 9, 651–657. Copyright by Kluwer Academic Publishers. Used with kind permission of Springer Science and Business Media and the authors; Figure 9.6: Royalty-Free/Corbis; Figure 9.7: Courtesy of John Shaughnessy; Figure 9.8 and Table 9.4: From Figure 1, page 341, of M. L. Dittmar, D. B. Berch, and J. S. Warm (1982), "Sustained Visual Attention in Deaf and Hearing Adults," *Bulletin of the Psychonomic Society,* 19, 339–342. Copyright 1982 by The Psychonomic Society, Inc. Adapted by permission of publisher and author.

Chapter 10

Case study illustration from I. Kirsch (1978), "Teaching Clients to be Their Own Therapists: A Case Study Illustration," *Psychotherapy: Theory, Research and Practice,* 15, 302–305. Copyright © 1978 by Division of Psychotherapy (29), American Psychological Association. Used with permission. Figure 10.1: © Bibliotheque Nationale De France. Used with permission; Figure 10.2 (left): Nina Leen/Time Life Pictures/Getty Images; 10.2 (right): © Bettmann/Corbis; Figure 10.3: Adapted from A. E. Kazdin (1998), *Research Design in Clinical Psychology* (3rd ed.). Boston: Allyn & Bacon. Copyright © 1998 by Pearson Education. Used with permission of publisher and author; Figure 10.4: © LWA-Dann Tardif/Corbis; Figure 10.5: Adapted from Figure 1, page 60, of S. V. Horton (1987), "Reduction of Disruptive Mealtime Behavior by Facial Screenings," *Behavior Modification,* 11, 53–64. Copyright 1987 by Sage Publications, Inc. Adapted by permission of publisher and author; Figure 10.6: From Figure 1, page 301, of M. G. Allison and T. Allyon (1980), "Behavioral Coaching in the Development of Skills in Football, Gymnastics, and Tennis," *Journal of Applied Behavioral Analysis,* 13, 297–304. Copyright 1980 by the Experimental Analysis of Behavior, Inc. Reprinted by permission of publisher and author.

Chapter 11

Figure 11.1: © Children's Television Workshop/Hutton Archives/Getty Images; Figure 11.2: Ryan McVay/Getty Images; Figure 11.4: From Figures 5 and 6, page 416, of D. T. Campbell (1969), "Reforms as Experiments," *American Psychologist*, 24, 409–429. Copyright 1969 by the American Psychological Association. Reprinted by permission of publisher and author; Figure 11.5: Adapted from Figure 1, page 287, in G. Gigerenzer (2004), "Dread Risk, September 11, and Fatal Traffic Accidents," *Psychological Science*, 15, 286–287, and data supplied by the author. Copyright © 2004 by American Psychological Society and Blackwell Publishing, Oxford, UK. Used with permission of publisher and author; Figure 11.6: From A. J. McSweeney (1978), "Effects of Response Cost on the Behavior of a Million Persons: Charging for Directory Assistance in Cincinnati," *Journal of Applied Behavior Analysis*, 11, 47–51. Copyright 1978 by the Society for the Experimental Analysis of Behavior, Inc. Reprinted by permission of publisher and author; Figure 11.7: Based on Figure 2, page 444, of G. Salomon (1987), "Basic and Applied Research in Psychology: Reciprocity Between Two Worlds," *International Journal of Psychology*, 22, 441–446. Reprinted by permission of International Union of Psychological Science and Psychology Press (http://www.psypress.co.UK/journals.asp) and author.

Chapter 12

Figure 12.2 (left & right): Photo courtesy of Judy DeLoache, and from Figure 2 of J. S. DeLoache et al., 1998, "Grasping the Nature of Pictures," in *Psychological Science*, 9, 205–210; Figures 12.3 and 12.4: Based on data provided by Judy DeLoache and her colleagues and adapted from Figure 3 of a study by DeLoache et al. (1998), *Psychological Science*, 9, 205–210. Used with permission of the American Psychological Society and Blackwell Publishing, Oxford, UK.

Chapter 13

Table 13.5: From J. L. Rodman and J. M. Burger (1985), "The Influence of Depression on the Attribution of Responsibility for an Accident," *Cognitive Therapy and Research*, 9, 651–657. Copyright by Kluwer Academic Publishers. Used with kind permission of Springer Science and Business Media and author.

Chapter 14

Extensive quotations from *Publication Manual of the American Psychological Association* (5th ed.) Copyright © 2001 by the American Psychological Association. Reprinted with permission. Neither the original nor this reproduction may be republished or distributed in any form or by any means, or stored in a database or retrieval system, without the prior written permission of the publisher.

Appendix

Tables A.2 and A.3: Permission is acknowledged with the tables; Table A.4: Based on Table 2.3.5, pages 36–37, in J. Cohen (1988), *Statistical Power Analysis for the Behavioral Sciences* (2nd ed.). Mahwah, NJ: Erlbaum. Used with permission of the publisher; Table A.5: Based on Tables 8.3.12, 8.3.13, 8.3.14, and 8.3.15, pages 311–318, in J. Cohen (1988). Used with permission of the publisher.

Name Index

Subject Index